THEOLOGY IN A GLOBAL CONTEXT

The Last Two Hundred Years

Hans Schwarz

WILLIAM B. EERDMANS PUBLISHING COMPANY

GRAND RAPIDS, MICHIGAN / CAMBRIDGE, U.K.

© 2005 Wm. B. Eerdmans Publishing Co.
All rights reserved

Wm. B. Eerdmans Publishing Co.
255 Jefferson Ave. S.E., Grand Rapids, Michigan 49503 /
P.O. Box 163, Cambridge CB3 9PU U.K.

Printed in the United States of America

10 09 08 07 06 05   7 6 5 4 3 2 1

ISBN-10: 0-8028-2986-4
ISBN-13: 978-0-8028-2986-3

www.eerdmans.com

Contents

Preface

More than twenty years ago I was asked by the Nineteenth Century Theology Group of the American Academy of Religion to present an essay on Darwinism between Kant and Haeckel. I accepted the invitation and found that group very congenial. Since then I have actively participated in many of its sessions and learned much from my colleagues in this group. I also discovered how influential many figures of the nineteenth century were on the major theological players of the twentieth century and beyond. Moreover, in the nineteenth century there was an astounding international cross-fertilization, especially between Germany, Great Britain, and North America. Therefore, I thought that in the age of the World Wide Web, the story should be told of this kind of interconnectedness between centuries and continents, which in the twenty-first century has become global, extending to Africa, the Americas, Asia, and Australia. Presenting approximately 400 lectures in twenty countries on five continents and guiding some thirty doctoral students from many parts of the world in their research have also sensitized me to the fact that Christian theology has become a worldwide endeavor. What fascinated me most was not so much how one theological position differed from another, but to what extent biography and theology intersected.

To bring two hundred years together in a global context is a formidable venture, and I am sure that almost every reader would like to have this or that facet added to the survey. Yet for the sake of brevity — if 600 pages is brief! — and for the sake of comprehensiveness, many items that were also dear to my own heart had to be omitted. I have endeavored to include at least those persons and movements that made an impact beyond their own denominational and/or geographical boundaries. While the main focus stayed on theology, there were persons, such as Karl Marx and Alfred North Whitehead, and movements, such as the history of religion school, that decidedly impacted theology. While some movements clearly followed after other movements, some went alongside others and some even overlapped others. I have tried to tell the story chronologically. But sometimes I had to jump ahead of the story by several decades and then turn back again. I have attempted to bring together persons and items with the same focus to make the narrative not too disjunctive. In this way I hope the main story is being told. For any glaring omissions or mistakes, I bear sole responsibility.

I want to thank Anna Madsen for help in improving the readability of this text. She also worked on the "For Further Reading" sections. Hildegard Ferme deserves an especially great thanks for putting up with a boss who often puts more in front of her than what one can ordinarily accomplish. Yet she again typed the manuscript with precision and unfailing speed, and also found many mistakes I had made. Together with my graduate research assistant Andrea König, she also compiled the indices; both deserve heartfelt thanks. Then I want to thank my colleagues who helped me with many valuable suggestions: Darrell Jodock (Gustavus Adolphus College), for critically reading the whole manuscript; Adam Seigfried (University of Regensburg) and Otto Weiss (University of Vienna, Austria), for suggestions for telling the story of Roman Catholic theology; D. W. Jesudoss (Gurukul Lutheran Theological College and Research Institute, Chennai, India), for comments on the Indian tradition and on Dalit theology; and Marios Begzos (University of Athens, Greece), for help with rendering the Orthodox story. Also deserving thanks are the staffs of the libraries at the University of Regensburg and at the Lutheran Theological Southern Seminary (Columbia, S.C.) for help beyond the call of duty to make available materials that were often difficult to locate. Finally I want to thank my wife Hildegard for tolerating a husband who all too often escaped to the catacombs of his study to work on this text.

HANS SCHWARZ
Regensburg, 2004

Introduction

A student once told me: "There is nothing more obsolete than yesterday's newspaper." Indeed, the purpose of a newspaper is to tell us whatever is new and not to confront us with dated information. In fact, does it even make sense to consider what occurred in the past if we are virtually unable to assimilate all the information that confronts us every day? Have we not become more and more a now generation that is solely concerned about the latest, in sports, musical entertainment, and science?

No generation before has encountered so many new things every day as do we. This is in large part due to the immense progress and expansion of information technology through the World Wide Web, cable TV, and the immense progress in higher education — more people hold Ph.D.'s now than in all previous centuries combined. At the same time that we are confronted with the immensity of the daily newness, we emphasize, as perhaps never before, where we are from and where we have been. Where we have resided, where we went to primary, secondary, undergraduate, and graduate school, are important references for our lives.

It is exactly this rootedness in the past that makes the confrontation with the present both bearable and meaningful. If we had no past, we would simply drift on the waves of the present. Only the connection between past and future can provide us with an orientation, because it links the present both forward and backward. The present makes sense if there is a future toward which we move, and we can understand the present much better if we consider its past. We realize more and more that even the most wholehearted dedication to the present cannot do away with the fact that we are to a large degree products of the past, of the genetic input of our parents, the education we have received, and the people we have encountered. Therefore, we do well to turn to the past to see from where we have come.

Turning to the roots is all the more important for Christian theology. In contrast, for instance, to Buddhism, the Christian faith is not primarily instruction or teaching, but a historically grounded faith that lives from and retells the story of God's interaction with people and the whole world. Coming from its Jewish context, Christian theology has always been aware of how much it owed the reflection of people of former times, such as Augustine (354-430), Teresa of Ávila (1515-82), or John Calvin (1509-64). Even the Christian creeds and confessions, though occasionally supplemented, hail from centuries long gone and connect us with the Christian tradition.

Turning now to the history of theology, we do not want to cover the last two thousand years, especially not in one volume, but will concentrate on the last two hundred years. The reason for this is a very pragmatic one. Nearly a hundred years ago Albert Schweitzer (1875-1956) published his famous book on the life-of-Jesus research, *The Quest of the Historical Jesus: A Critical Study of Its Progress from Reimarus to Wrede* (1906), in which he covered the previous two hundred years. Schweitzer started with Hermann Samuel Reimarus (1694-1768), a representative of the Enlightenment, betraying the influence of British Deists on him such as John Toland (1670-1722) and Matthew Tindal (1656-1734), while concluding with William Wrede (1859-1906), who with his book *The Messianic Secret* (1901) confronts us with the relatively modern approach to life-of-Jesus research.

To write a history of theology roughly one hundred years after Schweitzer's study and to begin, as he did, with the Enlightenment of the eighteenth century and carry through to the present would hardly make sense. In present-day scholarship one rarely comes across the radical and simplistic arguments of a Reimarus. Simplistic and outrageous claims rather belong to the popular press. Though some people are still haunted by the seeming discrepancy between knowledge and faith, in virtually all areas of knowledge we have become much more tenuous with our assertions than we were barely a century ago. The reason for our cautiousness is not just that our view of reality will always be fragmentary, though it is too easy to claim that the flood of new information is what makes it impossible to assimilate our constantly expanding horizon of knowledge.

Instead there is another important angle to our limitations. Already toward the end of the Enlightenment period, the philosopher Immanuel Kant pointed out with convincing clarity that only within the phenomenal world can we prove anything. We cannot reach beyond this world with reason alone. The theologian Friedrich Schleiermacher then added that we also need intuition. Yet both cautions remained unheeded. Nineteenth-century optimism prevailed, and with it the idea that this world was the only one that really counted. Furthermore, anything shy of reason was seen as an unreliable ally in our mastery of the world. Yet toward the turn of the nineteenth to the twentieth century, our world no longer seemed as simple in its composition as had once been thought. Barely a half-century later, scientific progress, which restricted itself to the material base of life, was seen as threatening this very base. Therefore one searched for other spiritual guidance to make scientific progress more amenable to human life. Kant and Schleiermacher seemed to have been finally vindicated.

Moreover, another restricting or rather formative influence should be noted. While it is too simplistic to claim that there is nothing new under the sun, but rather just new combinations of already existing trends — a claim clearly contradicted by scientific discoveries and technological progress — nobody lives on an island either. Human lives and the achievements and aspirations they embody are always contextual. Therefore we have also attempted, wherever feasible and necessary, to take note of the biographical context of the major voices of theology. Of course, the breadth of the area to cover necessitated an often radical brevity. But we hope we at least shed some light on the context out of which important voices arose.

1 Stemming the Tide of the Enlightenment

Immanuel Kant and Friedrich Schleiermacher are opposites. Kant as a philosopher emphasized reason and knowledge, while the theologian Schleiermacher reintroduced intuition and feeling. As the last leading exponent of the Enlightenment, Kant also defined the limits of reason and thereby opposed any facile rationalism. His main ideas continued to live on in theologians far into the nineteenth and twentieth centuries. The same can be said for Schleiermacher. While influenced by the romantic period, he has continued to fascinate theologians, especially in the hermeneutical discussions of the twentieth century. For instance, the New Testament scholar Ernst Fuchs called hermeneutics the "school of language for faith."[1] At the beginning of the nineteenth century both Kant and Schleiermacher, in their own ways, showed theology new and lasting ways of pursuing its task, and it is no surprise that Karl Barth had portraits of both in the hallway of his home.[2]

Kant wrote in his famous essay "What Is Enlightenment?" (1784): "Enlightenment is man's leaving his self-caused immaturity. Immaturity is the incapacity to use one's intelligence without the guidance of another. Such immaturity is self-caused if it is not caused by lack of intelligence, but by lack of determination and courage to use one's intelligence without being guided by

---

1. Ernst Fuchs, "Hermeneutik?" (1959/60), in Ernst Fuchs, *Glaube und Erfahrung* (Tübingen: J. C. B. Mohr/Siebeck, 1965), 135, where he calls hermeneutics a "Sprachlehre des Glaubens."

2. Cf. Karl Barth, *How I Changed My Mind,* introduction and epilogue by John D. Godsey (Richmond: John Knox, 1966), 11.

1

another. *Sapere Aude!* Have courage to use your own intelligence! is therefore the motto of the enlightenment."[3]

Kant is advocating human freedom in political and religious matters and the dominance of human intellect and reason over any outside force. Humanity should no longer be dependent on someone or something else, and Kant calls such dependence immaturity. We have become mature and are capable of determining our own destiny. This is the optimistic attitude that basically has prevailed throughout modernity. Yet if we are able to forge our own future, what place is there still for faith? Are we then not able to save ourselves? The question where faith comes in if we seemingly have everything under control is an issue that surfaced over and over again throughout the last centuries, and is an issue that was especially important for Kant.

Discerning the Limits of Rational Inquiry: Immanuel Kant

In the preface to the second edition of his *Critique of Pure Reason* (1787), **Immanuel Kant** (1724-1804) stated: "I therefore had to annul *knowledge* in order to make room for *faith*."[4] Kant tried to show in this work what we can know with certainty. That for him faith was not arbitrariness, he made clear when he wrote in his *Critique of Judgment* (1793): "A person is *unbelieving* who denies all validity to the above ideas of reason [i.e., of God and the immortality of the soul] because their reality has no theoretical foundation. Hence, such a person judges dogmatically."[5] For Kant, God and the immortality of the soul are rational ideas, meaning they are neither illogical nor irrational, but most reasonable for us to hold.[6] If dogmatism prevails, however, these *"matters of faith"* are discredited.[7] Kant is very apprehensive of any kind of religious indoctrination. In this way he believes himself a representative of the Enlightenment, since, as he wrote: "I have emphasized the main point of enlightenment, that is of man's re-

3. Immanuel Kant, "What Is Enlightenment?" trans. Carl J. Friedrich, in *The Philosophy of Kant: Immanuel Kant's Moral and Political Writings*, edited with an introduction by Carl J. Friedrich (New York: Random House, Modern Library, 1993), 145.

4. Immanuel Kant, *Critique of Pure Reason*, trans. Werner S. Pluhar, introduction by Patricia Kitcher, unified edition (Indianapolis: Hackett, 1996), 31 (B xxx).

5. Immanuel Kant, *Critique of Judgment* (§91), trans. James C. Meredith, in *The Philosophy of Kant*, 399.

6. Cf. Allen W. Wood, *Kant's Moral Religion* (Ithaca, N.Y.: Cornell University Press, 1970), 17.

7. So Kant, *Critique of Judgment* (§91), 399, where he distinguishes "matters of faith" from "matters of fact," as in mathematical properties (392).

lease from his self-caused immaturity, primarily *in matters of religion.* I have done this because our rulers have no interest in playing the guardian of their subjects in matters of arts and sciences. Furthermore, immaturity in matters of religion is not only most noxious, but also most dishonorable."[8] In his king, Frederick the Great (1712-86), of course, Kant had a very influential mentor. From 1750 to 1753 even Voltaire (1694-1778), the influential representative of French Deism, stayed at Frederick's court, until he got in trouble with his sharp tongue and had to leave.

Kant was born in 1724 in Königsberg, a prosperous city in East Prussia, to Johann Georg Kant, who was of Scottish descent, and Regina Kant nee Reuter, of whom he said in old age: "My mother was a lovely, affectionate, pious and upright woman, and a tender mother who led her children to the fear of God by means of pious instruction and a virtuous example. Often she took me outside of the city, directed my attention to the works of God, spoke with pious rapture of His omnipotence, wisdom and goodness, and impressed on my heart a deep reverence for the Creator of all things."[9]

Together with her husband she was deeply influenced by Lutheran pietism. The piety and moral rectitude of his parents made a deep impression upon young Immanuel. When he was not even twenty-two, both of his parents had died. While he inherited no money from them, they did give him a model of moral propriety. The influence of pietism also was felt at the *Gymnasium,* the Collegium Fridericianum, which Kant attended through the help of his pastor, and to a large extent also at the university.

When Kant entered the University of Königsberg in the fall of 1740, Frederick the Great had ascended to the throne and lifted all religious restraint. The king even promoted French frivolity and skepticism. The contentions between the pietists and the rationalists in Königsberg influenced Kant, who was absorbed in the studies of mathematics and physics at the university, against the established religion. In 1744 he started writing his first book on the problem of kinetic forces, which appeared in 1747, with his uncle paying for the printing. His father died in 1746, and to support himself young Immanuel became a family tutor for nine years, teaching first the children of a Reformed preacher near Königsberg and then those of another family at Arnsdorf, about sixty miles southwest of Königsberg, the farthest he ever journeyed from his native city. Finally he became tutor of Count Kayserling, who lived most of the time in Königsberg. In the count's family he also became acquainted with the etiquette

8. Kant, "What Is Enlightenment?" 152.

9. As quoted by Johann H. W. Stuckenberg, *The Life of Immanuel Kant,* with a preface by Rolf George (New York: University Press of America, 1986 [1882]), 7.

of society, meeting many persons of rank and distinction. These nine years of tutorship not only fostered his excellent conversational powers, they also allowed him to pursue studying his favorite subjects.

In 1755 his *General Natural History and Theory of the Heavens* appeared, in which Kant attempted to account for the origin of the celestial bodies. He suggested that in the beginning matter was dispersed in a nebulous state from which the sun was formed by the attraction of particles. Then the planets and moons originated. This theory is still called the Kant-Laplace theory, since Pierre Laplace (1749-1827) later proposed and more firmly established the same theory. Though the work was dedicated to Frederick the Great, the king never saw a copy of it, since the publisher went bankrupt while the book went to press. After composing another three theses in Latin, Kant became a Privatdozent, i.e., a nonsalaried lecturer, at the University of Königsberg in 1755. He first lectured on mathematics and physics, and then also on logic and metaphysics, which amounted to three or four lectures per day. He even lectured on topics such as physical geography and military fortifications. He failed twice to obtain a professorship at Königsberg, but rejected offers from the universities at Erlangen and Jena. In 1770 Kant finally obtained a professorship of mathematics at his alma mater, which he then exchanged for one of logic and metaphysics.[10] From then on he lectured only twice a day, from seven to nine in the morning, leaving more time for his literary pursuits. In addition, he presented private and public lectures on topics as diverse as physics, rational theology, and physical geography. Kant was well liked as a Privatdozent by the students, and his fame climbed rapidly. In May 1786 Johann Georg Hamann (1730-88) wrote that he went with his son to Kant's lecture room at six o'clock in the morning, one hour before the lecture started, in order to secure a seat.[11]

The result of more than a decade of careful reflection, Kant's *Critique of Pure Reason* appeared in 1781. A second edition in 1787 did not make this important publication more readable, since, following the textbooks of his time, it is highly sophisticated with rigid divisions and subdivisions, precise terms and sentence structure. He deals with the age-old problem of what we can really know and counters the British empiricism of John Locke (1632-1704) and David Hume (1711-76), who claimed that the human spectator is purely receptively passive in viewing the world. According to Kant, the opposite is true. We play an important role in how we view the world. Kant claimed that space and time

---

10. According to Reinhold Bernhard Jachmann, *Immanuel Kant geschildert in Briefen an einen Freund* (Königsberg: Friedrich Nicolovius, 1804), second letter, 14.

11. So Johann Georg Hamann, *Briefwechsel. 1785-1786*, ed. Arthur Henkel (Frankfurt am Main, 1975), 6:380, in a letter of May 4, 1786.

are a priori forms of human perception. The spatial and temporal properties of the objects we perceive do not derive from sense impressions, but derive from our interpretation of these data. This means that we interpret the impressions we receive with our senses in spatial and temporal terms. With this conclusion Kant emphasized the eyes of the beholder.

Then Kant went a step further, claiming that our knowledge is a reflection of both sensory impressions and our own ways of knowing objects. What is given through our senses in space and time of the phenomena is arranged through categories by which we order these objects and provide a framework for our knowledge. In metaphysics, however, the sensory experience is missing and therefore we arrive at contradictory claims. Therefore both sides of the argument appear to be solidly reasonable. The claim of free will versus determinism, a first cause versus no first cause and God or no God, provides equally good reasoning, because epistemological reflections do not lead us from the phenomena to the noumena, the thing itself. This meant for Kant that though the objective reality of a supreme being cannot be proven by speculative use of reason, it also cannot be refuted by it.[12] Kant likened this emphasis on the active role of the observer to the Copernican revolution in astronomy.[13] Indeed, Kant's critique was revolutionary, because he emphasized the significance of the observer, which was much later reaffirmed in modern nuclear theory. Yet in contrast to Kant, 150 years later Albert Einstein (1879-1955) showed that space and time belong to the material and are not instruments for the perception of the observer.

While Kant rejected speculative metaphysics, he was not against religion and morality, as can be seen from his *Critique of Pure Practical Reason* (1788). The ideas of God, freedom, and immortality transcend human sense experience, but they are sensual postulates for modern life. Kant concluded his investigation of practical reason with this admission: "Two things fill the mind with ever new and increasing awe and admiration the more frequently and continuously reflection is occupied with them; the starred heaven above me and the moral law within me. I ought not to seek either outside my field of vision, as though they were either shrouded in obscurity or were visionary. I see them confronting me and link them immediately with the consciousness of my existence."[14] The two realms of reason, the theoretical and the practical, were deeply connected in Kant's own life, drawing all the way back to the influence of

---

12. Kant, *Critique of Pure Reason* (A 641), 616.

13. Kant, *Critique of Pure Reason* (B xvi), 21.

14. Immanuel Kant, *Critique of Pure Practical Reason*, in *The Philosophy of Kant*, 288 (conclusion).

his mother's pietism.[15] Even immortality was brought into the practical sphere because it enables the goal of moral perfection and therefore gives our life its moral meaning.[16] Yet that kind of morality Kant felt was missing in public religion, meaning the church.

His perception of the church, as we see it for instance in *Religion within the Limits of Reason Alone* (1793), was colored in part by his experience with the censors in Berlin. When Frederick William II (1744-97) succeeded Frederick the Great and Johann Christoph Wöllner (1732-1800) became minister of religion in 1788, all teachers of religion were supposed to adhere strictly to the confessions of the church. The first part of Kant's book had appeared in a Berlin monthly in 1792. But when he submitted another installment, the censors refused to permit its publication. When Kant included the censored material in his next book, Wöllner sprang into action again and charged him with distorting and denigrating many of the principal and final doctrines of Christianity. Kant disliked any ultimate religiosity, and for many years "he never attended church, and observed no religious usages whatever. When a new *Rektor* [i.e., president] of the university was inaugurated, the professors marched in procession to the cathedral, to attend religious services; but unless he himself was the *Rektor*, Kant, instead of entering, passed by the church."[17]

In *Religion within the Limits of Reason Alone* Kant considered private prayer, churchgoing, baptism, and communion as a *fetish-faith*, since we use them as means "of making us well-pleasing to God" instead of taking in the realm of religion each step "in a purely moral manner."[18] Important for Kant was the biblical admonition that "we can know men by their fruits."[19] Still, Kant did not advocate any kind of self-redemption, since "the right course is not from grace to virtue, but rather to progress from virtue to pardoning grace."[20] Kant admitted the necessity of grace, yet not as a substitute for our own efforts, but to attain that which is not in our own power.[21] "Man is *evil*,

---

15. Similarly also, Lewis White Beck, *A Commentary on Kant's Critique of Practical Reason* (Chicago: University of Chicago Press, 1960), 282.

16. Cf. Wood, *Kant's Moral Religion*, 178.

17. So Stuckenberg, *Life of Immanuel Kant*, 354.

18. Immanuel Kant, *Religion within the Limits of Reason Alone*, translated with introduction and notes by Theodore M. Greene and Hoyt H. Hudson, 2nd ed. (La Salle, Ill.: Open Court, 1960), 181.

19. Kant, *Religion*, 189.

20. Kant, *Religion*, 190.

21. Cf. Josef Bohatec, *Die Religionsphilosophie Kants in der "Religion innerhalb der Grenzen der bloßen Vernunft" mit besonderer Berücksichtigung ihrer theologisch-dogmatischen Quellen* (Hildesheim: Georg Olms, 1966), who claims (on 531) that Kant rejects the notion of a prevenient grace, a grace necessary to precede human action, but that Kant acknowledges "the

can mean only he is conscious of the moral law but has nevertheless adopted into his maxim the (occasional) deviation therefrom."[22] Our radically evil disposition requires supranatural assistance to overcome it, and since we have a free will, it must be in our power to deserve such aid. To attain perfection there are both freedom and grace.

While Kant was critical of churchly observances, nevertheless he saw the present period as the best in the "entire known history of the church. . . . And this, because, if the seed of the true religious faith, as it is now publicly sown in Christendom, though only by a few, is allowed more and more to grow unhindered, we may look for a continuous approximation to that church, eternally uniting all men, which constitutes the visible representation (the schema) of an invisible kingdom of God on earth."[23] Kant was convinced that the kingdom of God makes progress in its coming. Though it does not come in visible form but is within us, we must labor industriously to set free the pure religion from its present shell. This means dissolution of the ecclesiastical and statutory in place of the pure, moral service of God.

Kant remained true to the tenets of the Enlightenment. He proclaimed a rational faith instead of the historically manifested faith of the Judeo-Christian tradition. His faith could even make sense of prayer, not in terms of a request for bread for another day, but as it "arises in the moral disposition (animated solely by the idea of God)."[24] Subsumed under moral rectitude, many other features of the Christian faith assumed new meaning. What at first may sound as a rejection, becomes at a closer look a transformation. It all serves a moral end, leading to a virtuous life. While Kant succeeded in rescuing the Christian religion and with it God, human freedom, and immortality from becoming empirically untenable, he subsumed everything under the moral imperative. Kant's religion has survived until today. Jesus, or the Teacher of the Gospel, as Kant called him, is still conceived of by many people as the great moral teacher of the Sermon on the Mount.

Religion as the Feeling of Absolute Dependence: Friedrich Schleiermacher

Over against Kant's emphasis on reason, knowledge, and moral rectitude, **Friedrich Daniel Ernst Schleiermacher** (1768-1834) stated that "religion's es-

necessity of a divine assistance" in this writing almost with the same words he did in his lecture on morals (533).

22. Kant, *Religion*, 27.
23. Kant, *Religion*, 122.
24. Kant, *Religion*, 184.

sence is neither thinking nor acting, but intuition and feeling."[25] Schleiermacher, whom Karl Barth called the "church father of the nineteenth (and also the twentieth?!) century," was born in Breslau, Silesia, to the military chaplain Johann Gottlieb Adolph Schleyermacher and his wife Elisabeth Maria Katharina (1736-83).[26] Coming from three generations of Reformed pastors, he had contact with his father mostly through correspondence, while his mother was a loving and supporting force in his life. Yet she died when Friedrich was only fifteen. "From age seventeen Friedrich found support in his uncle Samuel Ernst Timotheus Stubenrauch (1738-1807), his mother's brother and a professor at the University of Halle, who then filled the role of a substitute father."[27] Before that, from age twelve to fourteen, he was at a boarding school in Pless, where he developed an enthusiasm for classical languages. At the same time, he adopted a strange skepticism that convinced him "that all the ancient authors, and with them the whole of ancient history, were suppositious."[28]

When his father became acquainted with the Moravian church, Schleiermacher in 1783 attended the Paedagogium, the Moravian school at Niesky in Upper Lusatia, and two years later the seminary at Barby. Teaching there was free of Enlightenment influence, except for polemics against it. But Schleiermacher made his first contact with the early stirrings of romanticism, reading Christoph Martin Wieland's poems and Johann Wolfgang Goethe's *Werther.* Soon his convictions differed so widely from those adopted by the Moravians that his father allowed him to leave Barby and attend the University of Halle in 1787. There he encountered the critical theologies of Christian Wolff (1679-1754) and Johann Salomo Semler (1725-91) and also the philosophy of Kant. In the summer of 1790, he passed the examination for his licenciate (doctorate) and became tutor in the family of Count Dohna at Schlobbitten in Prussia. There he encountered a warm and congenial atmosphere coupled with a conservative but open and intelligent Christianity that had a lasting impact on him. After a brief stint in 1793 as a member of the seminary for college teachers in Berlin and instructor at an orphanage, he was appointed to a pastorate in Landsberg at the Warthe River in 1794. Finally, in 1796, he became chaplain to the famous Charité hospital in Berlin.

---

25. Friedrich Schleiermacher, *On Religion: Speeches to Its Cultured Despisers,* trans. and ed. Richard Crouter (Cambridge: Cambridge University Press, 1996), 22.

26. Karl Barth, *The Theology of Schleiermacher: Lectures at Göttingen, Winter Semester of 1923/24,* ed. Dietrich Ritschl, trans. Geoffrey W. Bromiley (Edinburgh: T. & T. Clark, 1982), 261.

27. So Robert F. Streetman, "Perspectives on Johann Gottlieb Adolph Schleyermacher," in *Schleiermacher in Context,* ed. Ruth Drucilla Richardson (Lewiston, N.Y.: Edwin Mellen, 1991), 8.

28. *The Life of Schleiermacher as Unfolded in His Autobiography and Letters,* trans. Frederica Rowan (London: Smith, Elder and Co., 1860), 1:4.

The six ensuing years in Berlin were crucial for Schleiermacher, because he became involved in the cultural and learned circles of the city, especially with the Romantic circle headed by Friedrich von Schlegel (1772-1829), who became his close friend. Out of this association ensued in 1799 the publication *On Religion: Speeches to Its Cultured Despisers,* and initially again with Schlegel, he also undertook the translation of Plato's *Dialogues.* In 1802 he became court preacher at Stolpe, and two years later professor at the University of Halle and university preacher. Because of Prussia's defeat by Napoleon I (1769-1821) in the battles at Jena and Auerstedt in 1806, the university was closed. Schleiermacher returned to Berlin, initially without an official appointment, and in 1809 he became professor of the newly constituted university and the first dean of the theological faculty. In the same year he was appointed Reformed preacher of Trinity Church (Dreifaltigkeitskirche). Count Alexander of Dohna, a friend from his earlier Berlin times, was secretary of the interior and consulted Schleiermacher on how to organize the university and especially the theological faculty. A year later Schleiermacher was elected to the Royal Academy of the Sciences at Berlin. This allowed him also to lecture in the philosophical faculty, which he often did, first parallel to Johann Gottlieb Fichte (1762-1814) and then to Hegel. In 1821/22 he published in two volumes his magnum opus, *The Christian Faith.*

Schleiermacher was also active in the church, striving for a union between the Lutherans and the Reformed, working on the new constitution for the Protestant church, and pushing for liturgical renewal. With the latter he got into conflict with the king, since he too had liturgical interests, which were different from those of Schleiermacher. Schleiermacher conducted his last church service on February 2, 1834, celebrated with his family the Eucharist, and died on February 12.

> On the 15th February, 1834, a funeral procession was seen moving through the streets of Berlin, a like of which that capital had rarely before witnessed. The coffin, covered with the black pall and simply decorated with a large copy of the Bible was borne on the shoulders of twelve students of the University, thirty-six of the most robust of whom had volunteered to perform, alternately, this pious service. After these came a train of mourners on foot, extending upwards of a mile in length, and these were followed by one hundred mourning coaches, headed by the equipages of the King and the Crown Prince.[29]

A prince of the church and of theology had died.

29. As related by Rowan in *The Life of Schleiermacher,* 1:ix.

In his youthful work *On Religion,* Schleiermacher, the "father of modern theology,"[30] took on Immanuel Kant, the philosopher of Protestantism. Schleiermacher contended that those who understand religion as right knowledge (metaphysics) or right action (morals) show their ignorance, because religious life arises from our relationship to the universe. While "metaphysics and morals see in the whole universe only humanity as the center of all relatedness," religion "wishes to intuit the universe, wishes devoutly to overhear the universe's own manifestations and actions, longs to be grasped and filled by the universe's immediate influences in childlike passivity."[31] Against the anthropocentrism of Kant, Schleiermacher affirmed that we are part of a larger whole that opens itself to us.

In the first speech Schleiermacher gave an apology for religion, showing the ignorance and misunderstanding of religion by his audience. The second speech focused on the essence of religion, as we mentioned earlier. In the third speech, "On Self-Formation for Religion," he contended that "a person is born with the religious capacity," a notion furthered by his observation of "the longing of young minds for the miraculous and supernatural" (59). Religion must be cultivated in communion between a person and the universe. But religion has also a social element, as he showed in the fourth speech. The more passionately something moves a person, the stronger is the urge to communicate that to others. "The communication of religion must occur in a grander style" than in a quick and easy exchange, "and another type of society, which is especially dedicated to religion, must arise from it" (74). But Schleiermacher's Moravian experience also shows through when he objects to the corrupting influence of the state on the church. Finally he dealt in the fifth speech with the world religions, showing that religion is present in a definite form only because the intuition of the universe is possible only in a definite way. While the individual fragments we encounter in the plurality of the churches are a misunderstanding, the plurality of religions is rooted in the essence of religion. While no one can possess religion completely, since a human being is finite and religion is infinite, each religion must organize itself "in manifestations that are rather different from one another" (97). This means that while denominations need not necessarily differ from each other, the case is different with the plurality of religions.

In his *Speeches* Schleiermacher showed that religion is not just a means for moral improvement or something with which we gain metaphysical knowledge. Religion is essential for human self-realization. In contrast to Schleier-

---

30. So Curtis W. Christian, *Friedrich Schleiermacher* (Waco, Tex.: Word, 1979), 11.

31. Schleiermacher, *On Religion,* 22-23. Page references to this work have been placed in the text.

macher, we must also consider that religion has implications for human conduct and involves cognitive elements. Moreover, Schleiermacher did not distinguish well enough between the universe and God, coming dangerously close to the notion that the universe is God's self. Yet, similar to Kant, he showed that religion is not superstition, and moving beyond Kant, he demonstrated convincingly that it has something to do with feeling and intuition, aspects which to a large extent were missing in Kant's personal life.

The *Speeches* were especially important in the romanticist circle. When Schleiermacher, however, taught at Halle and later at Berlin, he also had to deal with theology proper and not just with religion. His understanding of theology he put forth in his *Brief Outline of Theology as a Field of Study,* first published in 1811 and then in a second edition in 1830. For him, theology was not different from any other learned enterprise. Being related to Christianity, theology has a historical and not a speculative starting point. Similar to law and medicine, it has a practical task to perform. As Schleiermacher wrote: "Christian theology, accordingly, is that assemblage of scientific knowledge and practical instruction without the possession and application of which a united leadership of the Christian Church, that is, a government of the Church in the fullest sense, is not possible."[32] He underscored this practical aspect by calling theology a positive science. According to him, "a positive science is an assemblage of scientific elements which belong together not because they form a constituent part of the organization of the sciences, as though by some necessity arising out of the notion of science itself, but only insofar as they are requisite for carrying out a practical task" (2 [§1]). With this definition Schleiermacher rejected any kind of natural, rational, or speculative theology.

The functional character of theology is explained by theology's relation to Christianity. Therefore Christianity needs to be researched and taught. Unlike in the *Speeches,* it is no longer religion that is important for human self-realization, but now religious communities become necessary elements "for the development of the human spirit" (13 [§22]). To guide those communities one needs to be educated in three areas: philosophical theology, historical theology, and practical theology. Philosophical theology focuses on apologetics and polemics, by comparing what is with what ought to be. Therefore apologetics and polemics are an attempt not to defend Christianity, but to clarify its norms. When Schleiermacher moved to historical theology, he subsumed under this rubric exegetical theology of both the Old and the New Testament, church his-

---

32. Friedrich Schleiermacher, *Brief Outline of Theology as a Field of Study,* translation of the 1811 and 1830 editions, with essays and notes by Terrence N. Tice (Lewiston, N.Y.: Edwin Mellen, 1990), 3 (§5). Page and section references to this work have been placed in the text.

tory, and what he called "historical knowledge of the present condition of Christianity."

Dogmatic theology according to Schleiermacher is "the knowledge of doctrine that now has currency in the evangelical Church," which includes both dogmatics proper and ethics (97 [§195]). Next to dogmatic theology there is church statistics, by which Schleiermacher understood "the knowledge of the existing social condition in all the different parts of the Christian Church" (97 [§195]). The third part is practical theology, which includes church government and service to the congregation. When one reads this *Brief Outline of Theology,* it is clear that theology was taught in a professional school as we see today in the United States, mainly in denominational seminaries. Whether there is a separate branch of philosophical theology was highly debated a century later by neo-Reformation theology. Also, the idea that dogmatics and ethics can be subsumed under historical theology did not win approval. Nevertheless, in some seminaries there are departments of history, theology, and society, indicating a close correlation between them but not the subsumption of one under another. While in the *Brief Outline* Schleiermacher hardly touched the material content of theology, this was different in his *Christian Faith.*

The *Christian Faith,* or, as the German title reads, *The Christian Faith Put Forth Coherently according to the Principles of the Protestant Church,* was the result of Schleiermacher's lectures and may be considered "the classical systematic theological work of Protestant theology in modernity."[33] In the second edition of 1830/31, Schleiermacher made no changes except to put forth his position more clearly. He paved the way for a type of systematic theology that first described and analyzed religion, then proceeded to the specifically Christian religion, and finally took up the Protestant faith. Schleiermacher did not attempt a Thomistic rendition of a Christian doctrine. In an apologetic way he attempted to show the need for Christianity within culture and the general consciousness of truth. Each chapter is summarized with a lead statement, which is similar to what Karl Barth did in his *Church Dogmatics* more than a hundred years later.

In chapter 3 we hear the echo of the *Speeches:* "The piety which forms the basis of all ecclesiastical communions is, considered purely in itself, neither a Knowing nor a Doing, but a modification of Feeling, or of immediate self-consciousness."[34] This feeling is clarified in the following chapter as "the con-

---

33. So Hermann Fischer, "Schleiermacher, Friedrich Daniel Ernst (1768-1834)," in *Theologische Realenzyklopädie,* 30:166.

34. Friedrich Schleiermacher, *The Christian Faith,* ed. H. R. Mackintosh and J. S. Stewart, introduction by Richard R. Niebuhr, English translation from 2nd German edition (New York: Harper and Row Torchbook, 1963), 1:5 (§3). References to this work are placed in the text.

sciousness of being absolutely dependent, or, which is the same thing, of being in relation with God" (1:12 [§4]). This feeling of absolute dependence, meaning the denial of absolute freedom and therefore dependence on God, was for Schleiermacher the highest degree of human self-consciousness. A human person is not a solitary being. In following his ideas expressed in the *Speeches,* Schleiermacher asserted: "The religious self-consciousness, like every essential element in human nature, leads necessarily in its development to fellowship or communion; a communion which, on the one hand, is variable and fluid, and, on the other hand, has definite limits, i.e. is a Church" (1:26 [§6]).

Among the various religions, "Christianity is a monotheistic faith, belonging to the teleological type of religion, and is essentially distinguished from other such faiths by the fact that in it everything is related to the redemption accomplished by Jesus of Nazareth" (1:52 [§11]). Important for the Christian faith is redemption accomplished by Jesus of Nazareth. Schleiermacher made no truth claims here, but remained descriptive: "We entirely renounce all attempt to prove the truth or necessity of Christianity; and we presuppose, on the contrary, that every Christian, before he enters at all upon inquiries of this kind, has already the inward certainty that his religion cannot take any other form than this" (1:60 [§11]). His refusal to demonstrate the truthfulness of the Christian faith was not based on skepticism, but on the conviction that there is already an inward certainty, namely, in the communion with the divine.

Schleiermacher presented a religion of the heart and not an orthodox propositional faith. Therefore he contended: "Christian doctrines are accounts of the Christian religious affections set forth in speech" (1:76 [§15]). The German original renders it even more drastically: "Christian statements of faith are conceptions of the Christian pious states of emotion put forth in speech." The task of dogmatics is to formulate the Christian experience in a thoughtful, reflected manner under the presupposition of Scripture and tradition. Dogmatic theology, Schleiermacher stated, "is the science which systematizes the doctrine prevalent in a Christian Church at a given time" (1:88 [§19]). While he saw that Christianity had not always been divided into different denominations, he conceded for his time that what was suitable for Protestantism could not possibly be suitable for Roman Catholics, and vice versa.

In his exposition of the Christian faith, Schleiermacher paid close attention to the patristic and scholastic sources, but relied most heavily on the Lutheran and Reformed confessions and on Protestant orthodoxy. He treated all the major topics of dogmatics, from creation to consummation, with the centerpiece being the person and work of Christ. But he did not present a traditional dogmatics. The traditional dogmas and confessions were no longer immediately obligatory norms. They were only historically significant expressions of the Christian consciousness of the past. Whether they can still be valid for today is decided by the pious self-consciousness of the individual. Even the reality of God can be acknowledged only through faith.

While Schleiermacher presupposed that God's reality is independent of all religious experience and all human consciousness of faith, nothing should be put forth as doctrine that was not attested by experience. Even atonement was seen in that experiential way, since Jesus has a special place amongst all people not because of his divine nature, but because of his continuous and unbroken God-consciousness, i.e., his complete agreement with the divine will. Salvation means that Jesus draws the faithful person into the power of his own God-consciousness, or, as Schleiermacher put it: "The Redeemer assumes believers into the fellowship of His unclouded blessedness, and this is His reconciling activity" (2:431 [§101]). Since Jesus is no longer immediately present, redemption occurs in the congregation of believers. There the divine work is communicated according to Scripture. Faith ensues as a living communion with Christ. The result is regeneration in the faithful. The new life becomes permanent and indestructible through sanctification. With this kind of interpretation, resurrection, ascension, and the return of Christ are relegated to secondary status.[35] In contrast to Barth's *Church Dogmatics,* Schleiermacher did not begin his exposition with the Trinity, but concluded with it, suggesting that since this doctrine did not receive any fresh treatments when the Protestant church was set up, there must still be a transformation in store for it. Furthermore, it is not an immediate utterance concerning the Christian self-consciousness, but only a combination of several such utterances, meaning it is a concluding reflection of the Christian faith but not its presupposition.

While one might charge that Schleiermacher paid too much attention to religious experience in his reconstruction of the Christian doctrine reacting to Kant's emphasis on knowledge, we notice especially today how important experience and spirituality are for the Christian faith. Schleiermacher rediscovered experience and did away with the idea that religion is just an intellectual pursuit. Furthermore, he showed that theology is not a science for science's sake, but one that allows oneself to act meaningfully and intelligently in the Christian church. Therefore theology and the church belong together, as both Paul Tillich and Barth emphasized more than a century later. What Kant did for reason, Schleiermacher did for the inward person. To both areas theology plays no second fiddle, and as Schleiermacher showed, religion belongs to the self-realization of a human being.

---

35. Schleiermacher, *The Christian Faith,* 703 (§159), where he stated that to the doctrines of the last things he "cannot ascribe the same value as to the doctrines already handled."

For Further Reading

Immanuel Kant (1724-1804)

Guyer, Paul, ed. *The Cambridge Companion to Kant.* Cambridge: Cambridge University Press, 1992.

Kant, Immanuel. *Critique of Pure Reason.* Translated by Werner S. Pluhar. Introduction by Patricia Kitcher. Unified edition. Indianapolis: Hackett, 1996.

————. *The Philosophy of Kant: Immanuel Kant's Moral and Political Writings.* Edited with an introduction by Carl J. Friedrich. New York: Random House, Modern Library, 1993.

————. *Religion within the Limits of Reason Alone.* Translated with introduction and notes by Theodore M. Greene and Hoyt H. Hudson. 2nd ed. La Salle, Ill.: Open Court, 1960.

Kuehn, Manfred. *Kant: A Biography.* New York: Cambridge University Press, 2001.

Rossi, Philip J., and Michael Wreen, eds. *Kant's Philosophy of Religion Reconsidered.* Bloomington: Indiana University Press, 1991.

Friedrich Daniel Ernst Schleiermacher (1768-1834)

Clements, Keith W., ed. *Friedrich Schleiermacher: Pioneer of Modern Theology.* Making of Modern Theology Series. Minneapolis: Fortress, 1991 [1987].

Gerrish, Brian A. *A Prince of the Church: Schleiermacher and the Beginnings of Modern Theology.* Philadelphia: Fortress, 1984.

Schleiermacher, Friedrich. *Brief Outline of Theology as a Field of Study.* Translation of the 1811 and 1830 editions, with essays and notes by Terrence N. Tice. Lewiston, N.Y.: Edwin Mellen, 1990.

————. *The Christian Faith.* Edited by H. R. Mackintosh and J. S. Stewart. Introduction by Richard R. Niebuhr. English translation from the 2nd German edition. New York: Harper and Row Torchbook, 1963.

————. *The Life of Schleiermacher as Unfolded in His Autobiography and Letters.* Translated by Frederica Rowan. London: Smith, Elder and Co., 1860.

————. *On Religion: Speeches to Its Cultured Despisers.* Translated and edited by Richard Crouter. Cambridge: Cambridge University Press, 1996.

Sykes, Stephen. *Friedrich Schleiermacher.* Richmond: John Knox, 1971.

2   Hegel's System and Its Branches

While Kant emphasized the cognitive function of human reason and Schleiermacher pointed to intuition and feeling, **Georg Wilhelm Friedrich Hegel** (1770-1831) attempted to bring the two together in a creative synthesis pushing for a reconciliation between religion and reason. His philosophy of connecting religion and culture had wide appeal in the universities and seminaries in Germany, Great Britain, and the United States in the second half of the nineteenth century. Even in the twentieth century, his seminal ideas decidedly influenced such theologians as Jürgen Moltmann and Wolfhart Pannenberg in their perception of history. Along with Kant and Schleiermacher, Hegel can be seen as the third leading figure at the beginning of the nineteenth century that exerted an abiding influence on theology. Yet with Karl Marx and Friedrich Engels, whose revolutionary spirit also lived from Hegelian ideas, he influenced some of theology's and Christendom's fiercest antagonists.

Hegel's Christian Synthesis of Reason and Revelation

Hegel was born in Stuttgart and studied philosophy and theology from 1788 to 1793 at the Tübingen Stift. This *Stift*, the Protestant seminary attached to the university, had become a fertile training ground for future theologians and philosophers. Therefore it was no surprise that Hegel, together with Friedrich Hölderlin (1770-1843) and Friedrich Wilhelm Joseph Schelling (1775-1854), attended it. Hölderlin became one of the important German poets of the nineteenth century, and Schelling was the philosophical literary mentor for Paul Tillich. The three banded together and discovered their love for the French Revolution of 1789, which they thought would bring in a fresh spirit. They read and discussed the virtue of Greek antiquity, especially the Greek devotion to freedom, but also Kant's writings, for which Hegel never developed much love, since he was "deeply suspicious of claims about 'universal reason.'"[1]

Hegel was afraid that on account of his scholarship he might have to serve in a parish. But this did not come true, and he became a tutor from 1793 to 1800, first in Berne, Switzerland, and then in Frankfurt am Main. In 1801 he went to Jena, where Schelling taught, and wrote a treatise on the difference between the systems of Fichte and Schelling. The same year, he also did his *Habilitation* (second thesis) on the planetary orbits. At Jena Hegel met not only Schelling, but also other German luminaries. After 1776 the secretary of culture, Johann Wolfgang von Goethe (1749-1832), who resided in Weimar, oversaw the affairs of the University of Jena. In 1789 Friedrich Schiller (1759-1805), the famous poet and dramatist, joined the university as *Außerordentlicher Professor* (associate professor), giving his inaugural lecture, "What Does Universal History Mean and to What End Do We Study It?" In 1794 came Johann Gottlieb Fichte, who also joined as an associate professor. He soon drew an immense crowd of students and laid the foundation for the typically modern perception of the university as the gatekeeper for admission to the cultured elite. Then also August Schlegel (1767-1845), a key figure in the romantic movement, came to Jena in 1795, while his brother Friedrich joined him there four years later.

Through Goethe's influence, Hegel obtained an associate professorship at Jena in 1805, and only two years later his *Phenomenology of the Spirit* appeared. By then Napoleon had won the battle against Prussia at Jena (1806), but due to "the fame of its professors" he did not close that university as he had many others.[2] Hegel's associate professorship, however, did not even pay half the minimum income a student needed to live on. Moreover, other funds were quickly drying up. Hegel was soon penniless. When a position as editor of a newspaper was offered to him at Bamberg, he jumped at the chance. Since he did not want to abandon his academic career, he asked for a leave from his Jena professorship. He was also eager to maintain his friendship with Schelling, though this friendship was severely strained when he characterized Schelling's identity phi-

---

1. So Terry Pinkard, *Hegel: A Biography* (Cambridge: Cambridge University Press, 2000), 37, in his comprehensive study.

2. Cf. Pinkard, *Hegel*, 230-33. It is not true that the battle at Jena led to the end of Hegel's professorship as stated by Josef Simon, "Hegel/Hegelianismus," in *Theologische Realenzyklopädie*, 14:530. He abandoned it strictly for financial reasons.

losophy as "the night in which, as we say, all cows are black."[3] But Schelling and Hegel remained on friendly terms, though they no longer discussed philosophy. It is also one of those ironies of history that a few years after Hegel's death, Schelling was called to Berlin with the explicit charge "to expunge the 'dragon's seed' of Hegelian rationalism from the minds of the Prussian youth."[4]

In 1808 a *Gymnasium* in Nürnberg asked Hegel to become its principal, an offer he accepted, though still hoping to return to teaching at a university. Many difficulties at Nürnberg notwithstanding, Hegel succeeded amazingly well in updating education there and even was accepted by the social elite, marrying in 1811 into the famous and wealthy von Tucher family. He did well teaching as a professor of philosophy at the *Gymnasium,* and even became a school supervisor *(Schulreferent)* and built a teachers training college, but he still desired a university position. While inquiring about the possibility at Berlin, he received a call to a professorship in philosophy from Heidelberg University in 1816, which he happily accepted. Only a year later, having settled comfortably at Heidelberg, he received a call to the University of Berlin, where he was greeted with immense interest.

By moving to Prussia Hegel was not moving to the state he had previously despised, since after the wars Napoleon had thrust upon Prussia, a new Prussian state was emerging. The newly founded university at Berlin (1810) was to attract a kind of intellectual leadership that was deemed necessary "for reforming and rebuilding the Prussian state and regaining for Prussia some of the prestige that it had so abruptly lost" through Napoleon's intervention.[5] Since Fichte's death (1814), there had been no systematic philosopher teaching at the university, and therefore Hegel's arrival was greeted with a mixture of optimism, skepticism, anxiety, and expectation. Hegel did not simply come to Berlin to teach there, he came with the conviction that a modern university was the central institution of modern life.

Though Schleiermacher did not especially like Hegel's speculative philosophy, he befriended Hegel and introduced him to one of the prestigious clubs in Berlin. Nevertheless, Hegel's first years at Berlin were not very encouraging, since the political restoration got some of his students in trouble. In the 1820s a quieter period ensued, and Hegel put down his own political views in his *Philosophy of Right* (1821), calling for mediating institutions such as estates and corporations in society. This publication came at a time when the debate about

3. G. W. F. Hegel, *The Phenomenology of Mind,* trans. J. B. Baillie, rev. ed. (London: George Allen and Unwin, 1931), 79.

4. So John Edward Toews, *Hegelianism: The Path toward Dialectical Humanism, 1805-1841* (Cambridge: Cambridge University Press, 1980), 254.

5. So Pinkard, *Hegel,* 425.

national and political unity emerged in German political life. Hegel saw himself as a person of experience who had weathered the storms of the revolution and the Napoleonic wars. Therefore his philosophy could provide the much-needed guidance to bring coherence to German life. Hegel's celebrity and reputation continued to rise.

But suddenly in 1831, after enduring stomach problems for quite a while (perhaps even since 1827), he succumbed to gastrointestinal problems. The doctors diagnosed it as cholera, since such an epidemic was in town at that time.[6] The funeral on November 16, 1831, "turned out to be a massive procession. The wagon carrying Hegel's body was followed by a large crowd of his students and sympathizers from all over the city. Even his opponents were shaken by the news of his sudden and unexpected death. . . . It soon became apparent that Hegel had been to his loyal friends and students more than a philosophy teacher or a valuable colleague; he had come to stand for them as something much more, somebody who had provided them with a new direction in the fractious modern world."[7] Yet what made Hegel so important for theology?

From early on Hegel had been interested in theological topics. While tutoring in Berne and Frankfurt he wrote posthumously published manuscripts entitled *The Positivity of the Christian Religion, The Spirit of Christianity*, and even in 1795 a life of Jesus. While in part I of *The Positivity of the Christian Religion*, written in 1795-96, Hegel still contended that Jesus "was a teacher of purely moral religion," such a Kantian view of the Christian faith was left behind in *The Spirit of Christianity* (ca. 1798-99).[8] He now claimed that the "spirit of Jesus, a spirit raised above morality, is visible, directly attacking laws, in the Sermon on the Mount, which is an attempt, elaborated in numerous examples, to strip the laws of legality, of their legal form."[9] He rightly remarked against Kant: "'Love God above everything and thy neighbor as thyself' was quite wrongly regarded by Kant as a 'command requiring respect for a law which commands love.'"[10] Hegel discerned that love cannot be commanded, "because in love all thought of duties vanishes."

Already in the 1790s Hegel expressed the dialectic between the human and the divine. He followed the thoughts of Martin Luther's famous Christmas hymn when he stated: "The infinite being, filling the immeasurability of space,

6. Cf. Pinkard, *Hegel*, 659, who claims that Hegel showed no symptoms of cholera.

7. So Pinkard, *Hegel*, 660.

8. G. W. F. Hegel, *The Positivity of the Christian Religion*, in *Early Theological Writings*, trans. T. M. Knox, introduction by Richard Kroner (Chicago: University of Chicago Press, 1948), 71.

9. G. W. F. Hegel, *The Spirit of Christianity*, in *Early Theological Writings*, 212.

10. For this and the following quote, see Hegel, *The Spirit of Christianity*, 213.

exists at the same time in a definite space, as it is said, for instance, in the verse: 'He whom all heavens' heaven ne'er contained/Lies now in Mary's womb.'"[11] There is a dialectic of the finite and the infinite and a coincidence of opposites.

In *Phenomenology of the Spirit* (1807) Hegel again dealt with religion in his concluding reflections. Religion for him was "the consciousness of Absolute Being in general."[12] Hegel's anti-Kantian stance became evident again when he wrote that "in the world of the Ethical Order, we met with a type of religion, the religion of the nether world." There we encounter, as Hegel said, the negativity of the Enlightenment. Yet Hegel was not content with a strictly ethical religion as Kant and many other representatives of the Enlightenment provided it. Hegel wanted to move from natural religion (the religion at the level of consciousness) to art (the religion at the level of self-consciousness), and to revealed religion (religion at the level of reason and spirit). The revealed religion, namely, Christianity, was for him the absolute religion. The decisive point is the incarnation. "Here the Divine Being is known as Spirit; this religion is the Divine Being's consciousness concerning itself that it is Spirit. For spirit is knowledge of self in a state of alienation of self: spirit is the Being which is the process of retaining identity with itself in its otherness."[13] This means that the divine being makes itself known as spirit by alienating itself from itself, yet at the same time retaining its identity with itself in that otherness. We are referred back again to the stanza Hegel once quoted from Luther's Christmas hymn. Incarnation made and makes possible God's self-disclosure.

"The Good, the Righteous, the Holy, Creator of Heaven and Earth, etc. — all these are predicates of a subject, universal moments, which have their support on this central point, and only are when consciousness goes back into thought."[14] The Absolute, which often had been considered ahistorical and residing somewhere in the beyond, actualizes itself, according to Hegel, in human consciousness. God, the absolute spirit, comes into consciousness in humanity and realizes itself in humanity. Hegel reflected on Christianity philosophically and concluded that Christianity is the ultimate religion because it conceives of God as triune.

With regard to the place and space of God, Hegel mentioned three forms of the universal spirit. "The first is *outside the world*, spaceless, beyond finitude — God as he is in and for himself. The second form is the *world*, the divine his-

---

11. G. W. F. Hegel, *Fragment of a System*, trans. Richard Kroner, in *Early Theological Writings*, 315. Cf. Martin Luther's hymn "Gelobet seist du, Jesus Christ," stanza 3. The English rendition, "All Praise to You, Eternal Lord," is quite different.

12. See Hegel, *The Phenomenology of Mind*, 685, for this and the following quote.

13. Hegel, *The Phenomenology of Mind*, 758.

14. Hegel, *The Phenomenology of Mind*, 759.

tory as real — God in complete existence. The third is the *inner place,* the community, first of all in the world, but also the community in so far as it simultaneously raises itself to heaven, already having heaven on earth within itself, full of grace — the church in which God is active and present."[15] As a triune God, the spirit is active in the world and in the church, and is the lord of history. It follows that history pursues a reasonable course, since God accomplishes his intentions. History is neither the result of blind fate nor a mere aggregate of accidental events; it is God's history.

Since the absolute spirit is above all and in all, philosophy is not relegated to a corner, but is the science of "the unity of Art and Religion."[16] Whereas in art we see external forms, religion opens us to mental pictures and mediates what is thus opened. Philosophy keeps both together not simply to make a totality, "but even unifies them into the simple spiritual vision, and then in that raises them to self-conscious thought." These quotations from *The Encyclopaedia of the Philosophical Sciences* of 1830 show again what Hegel was striving for: the absolute embraced everything, thereby facilitating a unity, and since it had manifested itself in human consciousness, it provided a much-needed direction for humanity. Since Hegel started with the unproven presupposition that his idealistic interpretation of history is identical with historical reality, objections were soon made and his followers split into a left and a right wing.

The Left-Wing Hegelian Attack on Religion:
David Friedrich Strauss and Bruno Bauer,
Ludwig Feuerbach, and Karl Marx and Friedrich Engels

The left-wing or young Hegelians refuted Hegel's synthesis between idea and reality, and tried to show in their criticism of religion that the origin of religion is wishful thinking and faith in God is a mere projection of human wishes and desires into an artificial beyond. Through this mistaken idea, humanity estranged itself from its ownmost being. Therefore religion ought to be eliminated. This was first suggested by David Friedrich Strauss and Bruno Bauer in theology, and Ludwig Feuerbach in philosophy, and was advocated politically by Karl Marx and Friedrich Engels.

Like Hegel, **David Friedrich Strauss** (1808-74) came from Württemberg.

15. Georg Wilhelm Friedrich Hegel, *The Christian Religion: Lectures on the Philosophy of Religion,* pt. III, *The Revelatory, Consummate, Absolute Religion,* ed. and trans. Peter C. Hodgson (Missoula: Scholars, 1979), 65-66.

16. Hegel, *Philosophy of Mind,* pt. 3 of *The Encyclopaedia of the Philosophical Sciences* (1830), trans. William Wallace, foreword by J. N. Findlay (Oxford: Clarendon, 1971), 302 (§572).

After graduating from the *Gymnasium,* he attended the Tübingen Stift, where he was attracted by the philosophies of Kant and Schelling. He also studied Schleiermacher and Hegel and, after a splendid exam in 1830, served as vicar. Only nine months later he was called as teacher to the Maulbronn Seminary to teach Latin, history, and Hebrew. Again, he stayed only a couple months, and in November of 1831 he moved to Berlin to study with Hegel. In absentia he received his doctorate of philosophy from the University of Tübingen. Only three days before Hegel's death, Strauss had a chance to visit with him and bring him up to date on life in Württemberg and what was going on in Tübingen. The following day he attended Hegel's lectures, but soon thereafter his inspiration was dead.[17] Strauss stayed in Berlin for a while, studied with Hegel's disciples, and also attended some of Schleiermacher's lectures.

The following year Strauss began lecturing in theology at the University of Tübingen and worked on his study of Jesus. In Hegelian fashion (thesis, antithesis, and synthesis) he wanted to divide his work into three parts: a study of the traditional view of Jesus as found in the Evangelists, a critical analysis that would reject the historical record of Jesus, and a speculative reconstruction.[18] When his *Life of Jesus* appeared in two volumes in 1835/36, the first part was missing and the third part was a mere supplement. What he presented was a totally negative critique of the Jesus story as found in the Gospels. In the preface to the second volume, Strauss compared his own endeavor with that of Gotthold Ephraim Lessing (1729-81), who had published the fragments of someone unknown (i.e., actually the life of Jesus by Hermann Samuel Reimarus [1694-1768], the famous Hamburg critic of the Jesus story).[19] Moving away from Hegel, he no longer asserted — as did Hegel — that the union of the human and divine took place in the Jesus of history. To the contrary, he contended that the idea of the unity of the divine and human natures assumes a far greater dimension when we regard the whole race of humanity as its realization. "Humanity is the union of the two natures — God become man, the infinite manifesting itself in the finite, and the finite spirit remembering its infinitude. . . . It is humanity that dies, rises, and ascends to heaven, for from the negation of its phenomenal life there ever proceeds a higher spiritual life."[20]

It is no surprise that there was a huge public outcry over this book.

17. For details about the visit of Strauss, cf. Pinkard, *Hegel,* 657.

18. Cf. for the following William J. Brazill, *The Young Hegelians* (New Haven: Yale University Press, 1970), 106-7.

19. Cf. David Friedrich Strauss, *The Life of Jesus Critically Examined,* edited with an introduction by Peter C. Hodgson, translated from the 4th German edition by George Eliot (Philadelphia: Fortress, 1972), liv.

20. Strauss, *The Life of Jesus,* 780.

Strauss was relieved of ministerial duties, and when he was called to a professorship at the University of Zürich in 1839, there were such strong protests that he was pensioned off.[21] Strauss then moved from place to place and finally became a member of the Württemberg parliament at Stuttgart, advocating a moderate liberalism. But even that stint only lasted one year. For nearly twenty years he published hardly anything in theology, and then came out with his *Life of Jesus for the People* (2 vols., 1864; Eng. trans., 2nd ed., 1879). Nothing new was contained in this popular study of Jesus. While Strauss still considered Jesus a historical figure, he saw in Jesus only a human being who sought to improve humanity. According to Strauss, the Gospels contained many nonhistorical elements and numerous mythical passages since they started with the presupposition that Jesus was the Messiah. Strauss wanted his audience to accept Jesus as a reformer upon whose insights and ideas subsequent generations must build to improve humanity. Strauss was in tune with the sentiment of his time. Darwin's *Origin of Species* had just been published, and the air was filled with ideas of evolutionary betterment. Yet the new book received neither much attention nor the notoriety of his first life of Jesus.

In 1872 Strauss wrote *The Old Faith and the New* (Eng. trans. 1873), which reflected his final position on religion. To clarify his own stand he posed three questions. To "Are we still Christians?" he said, "If we would speak as honest, upright men, we must acknowledge we are no longer Christians."[22] The question whether we are still religious, he contended, can only be answered in the affirmative. Even if we do not believe in God, we must transfer the same piety to the universe that was once given to God. In posing the question: "What is our conception of the universe?" he appealed to Darwin's theory of evolution. In his last question: "What is our rule of life?" he presented the morality of educated middle-class society. With this approach both theology and Hegelian dialectics were finally abandoned in favor of a bourgeois materialism. Two years later in 1874, Strauss died of intestinal problems and by his own wish was buried without a pastor present and without the church bells ringing.[23]

Similar to his mentor Hegel, Strauss was bothered with the correlation of faith, knowledge, and history. Yet apart from asking radical questions, he was unable to provide a satisfying systematic theological answer. But, as Karl Barth stated, "he was probably the best-known and most influential theologian of the

21. Cf. Horton Harris, *David Friedrich Strauss and His Theology* (Cambridge: Cambridge University Press, 1973), 132.

22. David Friedrich Strauss, *The Old Faith and the New,* trans. Mathilde Blind, introduction and notes by G. A. Wells (Amherst, N.Y.: Prometheus, 1997), 107.

23. So Thomas K. Kuhn, "Strauß, David Friedrich," in *Theologische Realenzyklopädie,* 32:242.

nineteenth century, in non-theological and non-church circles."[24] The Darwinistic monist Ernst Haeckel (1834-1919), for instance, called him "the greatest theologian of the 19th century,"[25] while Friedrich Nietzsche (1844-1900) fiercely attacked him as a bourgeois moralist.[26] While theology proper still remained predominantly in conservative hands, the new ideas made public by Strauss's *Life of Jesus* began to spread like a river that had broken through its dikes and began to flood the surrounding countryside. The *Life of Jesus* also started and necessitated a more critical examination of the biblical sources. In this way the issues posed by Strauss gradually became an agenda for theology proper.

Bruno Bauer (1809-82) was born in the old Thuringian city of Eisenberg, then part of the duchy of Saxony-Altenburg. In 1815 his family moved to Charlottenburg where Bauer went to school, and in 1828 he began his theological studies at the University of Berlin. He immediately became an ardent follower of Hegel and developed an increasing antipathy for Schleiermacher. From 1832 to 1834 he worked on his dissertation under Philipp Konrad Marheineke (1780-1846), a right-wing Hegelian. His *Habilitation* (second thesis) followed immediately after his licentiate in 1834. This degree was made possible only through a compromise in the faculty facilitated by Schleiermacher's death.[27] Bauer was now a Privatdozent (private lecturer), though his father had wanted him to become a pastor.

Only two years later Bauer started his own theological journal, the *Journal for Speculative Theology* (*Zeitschrift für spekulative Theologie*, Berlin, 1836-38). All the leading Hegelians contributed to it, with the exception of Strauss, since Bauer had attacked his *Life of Jesus* quite vehemently. Against Strauss, Bauer contended that all the New Testament miracles were necessary, including the virgin birth, to show the coming together of the divine and the human in Jesus. In 1839 even Karl Marx attended Bauer's lectures on Isaiah, and they struck up a friendship. (Bauer visited Marx in London in 1855/56, though by then the two were alienated from each other.) In 1839 Bauer was a conservative right-wing Hegelian convinced that Hegel's philosophy justified the Christian

---

24. Karl Barth, *Protestant Theology in the Nineteenth Century: Its Background and History,* new ed. (Grand Rapids: Eerdmans, 2002), 528.

25. Ernst Haeckel, *The Riddle of the Universe at the Close of the Nineteenth Century,* trans. Joseph McCabe (New York: Harper, 1900), 309.

26. So Friedrich Nietzsche, "David Strauss, the Confessor and the Writer," in *Thoughts out of Season,* vol. 4 of *The Complete Works,* ed. Oscar Frey, trans. Anthony Ludovici (New York: Macmillan, 1926), 68, where he calls Strauss a "Culture-Philistine," meaning an archconservative person.

27. So Joachim Mehlhausen, "Bauer, Bruno," in *Theologische Realenzyklopädie,* 5:314.

dogma because Hegel had permanently united theology and philosophy, demonstrating that faith and knowledge could coexist. All looked good for Bauer. His scholarly work was well received, especially by those theologians who appreciated his attack on Strauss. Bauer had summarily dismissed Strauss's biblical criticism, saying the question whether the Gospel events really happened or not was completely irrelevant, since these stories were philosophical necessities.

The Prussian secretary of education, Freiherr von Stein zum Altenstein (1770-1840), who had arranged Hegel's appointment in 1818 and that of Hegel's successor in 1835, wanted to place Bauer in an important theological position. Since there was no possibility for advancement in Berlin, Altenstein called Bauer to the theological faculty at Bonn. A vacancy suddenly opened up, and Altenstein thought they should also have a representative of Hegelian philosophy in their midst. That high-handed decision infuriated the theological faculty at Bonn since the faculty had not been consulted, and its members did everything to make Bauer's life miserable. As the situation dragged on, unresolved, King Frederick William III (1770-1840) and Altenstein died, and two mighty opponents to Hegelian philosophy, King Frederick William IV (1795-1861) and his secretary of worship and education, Johann Albrecht Friedrich Eichhorn (1776-1856), assumed their positions. To advance his case, Bauer sought to demonstrate his theological scholarship and wrote a study on the Gospel of John in which he showed "that this Gospel was not an historical account at all but an expression of the developed faith of the church."[28]

This 1840 publication facilitated to resolve the matter. Eichhorn was now convinced that Bauer was a threat to orthodox Christianity, since he rejected the Gospel of John as a historical record. Subsequently he tried to remove Bauer from the theological faculty in Bonn. Eichhorn had indeed reason for his suspicion. The following year Bauer published another volume, *Critique of Evangelical History of the Synoptic Gospels (Kritik der evangelischen Geschichte der Synoptiker)*. Similar to what Strauss had done before, he now treated the Gospels as human documents, products of human creativity and consciousness. And similar also to Strauss, he believed in a continual revelation of the immanent spirit within human history. "The gospels were written by men and their content together with their form have gone through a human self-consciousness."[29] Yet in contrast to Strauss, Bauer considered the Gospels not simply the tradition of the community, but creative reflection on real experi-

---

28. So J. C. O'Neill, *The Bible's Authority: A Portrait Gallery of Thinkers from Lessing to Bultmann* (Edinburgh: T. & T. Clark, 1991), 152.

29. Bruno Bauer, *Kritik der evangelischen Geschichte der Synoptiker* (Hildesheim: Georg Olms, 1974 [1841]), 1:xvi.

ences.[30] While Bauer still accepted Jesus' historical existence, the Gospels were artistic creations to present their authors' philosophical viewpoint. "The historical Christ is a person whom religious consciousness has raised into heaven, that is, the man who even then, when he comes down to earth to perform miracles, to teach, and to suffer, is no longer a true person."[31] As for all the young Hegelians, so also for Bauer, humanity had become the subject and God and religion the objects of human self-consciousness. Humanity had alienated its own spirit from itself and worshiped it as transcendent.

How could this change from an orthodox right-wing Hegelian to an outspoken atheistic left-wing Hegelian occur? Bauer's two books on Hegel of 1841/42, *The Trumpet of the Last Judgement against Hegel, the Atheist and Anti-Christ* (Eng. trans. 1989) and *Hegel's Teaching concerning Religion and Art (Hegels Lehre von der Religion und Kunst vom Standpunkt des Glaubens aus beurteilt)*, shed some light on this. According to Bauer, Hegel's true intention was to talk about the inner relationship of the self-consciousness to itself. Hegel had observed that the "I" made a mirror image of itself and in turn worshiped this image as God. Even the grace of God is nothing but the "I" offering its hand to its own image reflected in the mirror of transcendence. It was clear that a theologian, such as Bauer, for whom anything religious was but a projection, was no longer tolerable in a theological faculty. Therefore Eichhorn asked the theological faculties of all the Prussian universities whether Bauer could continue to teach. Their response varied, except for Bonn, where they asked for his teaching license to be withdrawn. The secretary of education then decided the case, and in 1842 Bauer lost his license to teach.

Bauer returned to Berlin and thought the young Hegelians would rally around him and his cause. As nothing of that sort happened, he became ever more polemical, sarcastic, and passionate. His 1843 publication *Christianity Exposed (Das entdeckte Christentum)* was confiscated by the censors before it was published, and only in 1927 could it appear in print. Bauer claimed that religion was the alienation of the human spirit from humanity and could linger on only because humanity was weak, despondent, poor, and unhappy. In the three volumes of *Critique of the Evangelical Gospels and the History of Their Origin* (*Kritik der Evangelien und Geschichte ihres Ursprungs,* Berlin, 1850/51), Bauer finally denied the historical existence of Jesus. The author of the original Gospel was a reflective and creative artist living in the second century. This verdict was similar to one expressed in a later publication, *Christ and the Caesars: The Ori-*

---

30. Cf. Bauer, *Kritik der evangelischen Geschichte der Synoptiker,* 1:71.

31. Bruno Bauer, *Kritik der evangelischen Geschichte der Synoptiker und des Johannes* (Hildesheim: Georg Olms, 1974 [1842]), 3:313-14.

gin of Christianity in Roman Greece (*Christus und die Caesaren. Der Ursprung des Christentums aus dem römischen Griechentum,* Berlin, 1877). There he claimed that Jesus and, with him, Christianity were the creation of a philosophical group in the Roman Empire of the second century. Yet the more Bauer wrote, the less impact he seemed to have. And when he died in 1882, having spent his last years working in the family tobacco shop, his death was hardly noticed by the public. William Montgomery (1871-1930) summed it up well when he said about Bauer: "His was a pure, modest and lofty character."[32] Through his studies of the Gospels he certainly made an impact. While his ideas on Christianity and its origin were mistaken, his influence through Marx and Feuerbach is still felt today.

Like Strauss and Bauer, **Ludwig Feuerbach** (1804-72) started out in theology and ended in philosophy without ever leaving theological concerns by the side. He was born in Landshut, Bavaria, into the large family of a noted lawyer, Anselm Ritter von Feuerbach, who had composed the significant criminal code for the kingdom of Bavaria in 1830. Later he became the presiding judge at the appellate court in Ansbach. Several of Ludwig's brothers also achieved a certain distinction in various fields, such as archaeology, painting, and mathematics. Having attended the *Gymnasium* at Ansbach, Feuerbach began to study theology at Heidelberg University in 1823. He was especially impressed by Karl Daub (1765-1836), who lectured on dogmatics and presented a speculative theology strongly influenced by Hegel. Just a year later, Feuerbach moved to the University of Berlin to attend Hegel's lectures as well as those of Schleiermacher and Marheineke. To the regret of his father, he matriculated in the faculty of philosophy. His scholarship cut off upon the death of King Max I Joseph of Bavaria (1756-1825), Feuerbach in 1826 moved back to Bavaria, to study at Erlangen University because it was cheaper than Berlin. He attended mainly lectures in the natural sciences, and in 1828 earned his doctor of philosophy with the dissertation "Reason: Its Unity, Universality, and Infinity" (*De ratione, una, universali, infinita*). The following year he received his *Venia legendi* (permission to teach).

Feuerbach did not obtain a professorship though, since in 1830 he had anonymously published a little book entitled *Thoughts on Death and Immortality* in which he espoused very liberal thoughts. He verged on collapsing the Hegelian dialectic when he claimed, in pantheistic fashion: "God is life, love, consciousness, Spirit, nature, time, space, everything, in both its unity and its

---

32. This remark, which had been attributed to Albert Schweitzer, is actually from W. Montgomery, as can be seen from *The Quest for the Historical Jesus,* ed. John Bowden, first complete ed. (Minneapolis: Fortress, 2001), 125.

distinction."[33] Then, in disclaiming personal immortality, he wrote: "You exist in God, and therefore with immortality." The work concludes with a long series of epigrams in which he makes a joke out of every contemporary German school of academic theology and of their belief in immortality.[34] Though he published the work anonymously, his authorship was soon recognized and the work's style and content were sufficient to bar him from any permanent university position.

From 1833 to 1838 he published three volumes on the history of modern philosophy, results of his lectures at Erlangen University that gave him the reputation of a historian of philosophy of the Hegelian school. In 1837 he married Berta Löw, who owned a share in a china factory at Bruckberg, not far from Erlangen, and the couple moved to the rustic isolation of the country for more than twenty years. This was also the end of his engagement in university life. Two years later appeared his *Critique of Hegelian Philosophy (Kritik der Hegelschen Philosophie)*, which marked an open break with Hegelian speculative philosophy.

In 1841 he published the work for which he became famous, *The Essence of Christianity*. He started out there to *"objectively"* examine Christianity by employing "the method of *analytic* chemistry."[35] He espoused for the first time his theory of projection.[36] According to Feuerbach, "religion is the dream of the human mind."[37] "Religion is the disuniting of man from himself; he sets God before him as the antithesis of himself. God is not what man is — man is not what God is" (33). But religion, as Feuerbach asserted, also marks the essential difference between humanity and animals. Only humans have a religion, since they can reflect on themselves as individuals (cf. 1). Feuerbach had no desire to abolish religion, but to point out that religion is part of being human and has nothing to do with a transcendent reality. It is a (necessary) projection of the human mind, especially as we consider life after death, through which a person's life experience and its negativity is projected into something positive, a better life after death. "Faith in

---

33. See Ludwig Feuerbach, *Thoughts on Death and Immortality: From the Papers of a Thinker, Along with an Appendix of Theological-Satirical Epigrams, Edited by One of His Friends,* translated with introduction and notes by James A. Massey (Berkeley: University of California Press, 1980), 173, for this and the following quote.

34. So rightly Massey, introduction to Feuerbach, *Thoughts,* xxiii.

35. Ludwig Feuerbach, *Das Wesen des Christentums,* in *Gesammelte Werke,* ed. Werner Schuffenhauer (Berlin: Akademie-Verlag, 1973), 5:6, in his preface to the first edition.

36. So Jörg Salaquarda, "Feuerbach, Ludwig," in *Theologische Realenzyklopädie,* 11:145.

37. Ludwig Feuerbach, *The Essence of Christianity,* trans. George Eliot (Buffalo: Prometheus, 1989), xix, in his preface to the second edition. Page references in the following text are to this work.

the future life is therefore faith in the freedom of subjectivity from the limits of Nature; it is faith in the eternity and infinitude of personality" (184).

Feuerbach did not consider religion part of the infancy state of humanity, as did Sigmund Freud (1856-1939), and he also did not call for the stamping out of this "opium of the people," as we hear from Marx and Engels. Yet the seeds were laid for this development. During the early 1840s, Feuerbach became a leader of the left-wing Hegelians and had an important influence on Marx and Engels, as the latter admitted: "We were all Feuerbachians."[38] It is no surprise therefore that in 1845 Marx sketched out his *Theses on Feuerbach*. What had attracted Marx and Engels and many other progress-minded and revolutionary people to Feuerbach was the exchange of theology for anthropology, the love of God for the love of humanity, and the identification of the divine with humanity. This allowed humanity to progress to new heights. Feuerbach wrote: "The divine being is nothing else than the human being, or, rather, the human nature purified, freed from the limits of the individual man, made objective — i.e., contemplated and revered as another, a distinct being. All the attributes of the divine nature are, therefore, attributes of the human nature" (14). Humanity ought to worship itself and its own works, and the love of God should be turned into the love of humanity. "Love can only be founded on the unity of the species, the unity of intelligence — on the nature of mankind; then only is it well-grounded love, safe in its principle, guaranteed, free, for it is fed by the original source of love, out of which the love of Christ himself arose. The love of Christ was itself a derived love" (266).

In 1848/49 Feuerbach was invited by revolutionary-minded students to give a series of lectures at the Heidelberg City Hall. (In the revolutionary year 1848, the German people, primarily students and intellectuals, clamored for more democracy — this revolution was soon squelched.) These presentations were published as *Lectures on the Essence of Religion* in 1851. While in *The Essence of Christianity* Feuerbach mainly tried to reduce Christianity to its anthropological basis, in these lectures he deals with religion in general. Now the basis for religion is no longer seen in humanity itself, but in nature. In every way humanity is dependent for its existence on nature. "And what man is dependent on, what holds the power of life and death over him and is the source of his joys and fears, is and is called his God."[39] The powers of nature were

---

38. As quoted in Marx W. Wartofsky, *Feuerbach* (Cambridge: Cambridge University Press, 1977), xix, without giving any further reference. Engels wrote of the impact of *The Essence of Christianity:* "Enthusiasm was universal, we were all for the moment followers of Feuerbach." So Friedrich Engels, *Feuerbach: The Roots of the Socialist Philosophy*, translated with introduction by Austin Lewis (Chicago: Charles H. Kerr, 1903), 53.

39. Ludwig Feuerbach, *Lectures on the Essence of Religion*, trans. Ralph Manheim (New

transformed into humanlike beings, i.e., deities. To gain an understanding of religion Feuerbach no longer accounted for it by a single cause, and he proceeded to demonstrate "that religion has human happiness as its *aim*."[40] Abandoning religion contributes to the pursuit and attainment of this happiness. "If we no longer *believe* in a better life, but decide to *achieve* one, not each man by himself but with our united powers, we will *create* a better life, we will at least do away with the most glaring, outrageous, heartbreaking injustices and evils from which man has hitherto suffered. But in order to make such a decision and carry it through, we must replace the love of God by the love of man as the only true religion, the belief in God by the belief in man and his powers."[41]

With this creed in progress and in the perfectibility of humanity, Feuerbach decidedly contributed to the optimistic tone of the nineteenth century that, on the one side, facilitated unprecedented progress and, on the other, caused misery for the less fortunate.

But progress did not come to Feuerbach. In 1860 the china factory went bankrupt, and without that source of income he became financially dependent on friends. He moved to a town near Nürnberg, where he lived until his death. With enthusiasm he read Marx's *Capital* and even joined the German Social Democratic Party.[42] In 1872 he died almost forgotten by the German public, but he was nevertheless buried at St. John's Cemetery in Nürnberg, where notables were laid to rest, among them the famous painter Albrecht Dürer (1471-1528).

Karl Marx (1818-83) was the son of a respected lawyer from Trier who had converted from Judaism to Protestantism. Young Marx started his university education in 1835 at Bonn, studying law. He lasted barely a year there, and on advice from his father he transferred to Berlin. He immersed himself there first in legal studies and then in philosophy, where he found Hegel's thought to be a bridge between the two fields. Marx was attracted to Hegel because that philosopher conceived of and represented the natural, historical, and spiritual aspects of the world as a process of constant transformation and development. His conversion to Hegel was completed by a thorough reading of Hegel's writings. At the same time, Marx increasingly adopted a bohemian lifestyle.[43] In 1839 he decided to start working on a doctoral dissertation to obtain a university posi-

---

York: Harper and Row, 1967), 79. Cf. also Van A. Harvey, *Feuerbach and the Interpretation of Religion* (Cambridge: Cambridge University Press, 1995), 161-62, who points to the change from *The Essence of Christianity* to the *Lectures*.

40. Feuerbach, *Lectures*, 200.

41. Feuerbach, *Lectures*, 284-85.

42. According to Wartofsky, *Feuerbach*, xx.

43. For details cf. David McLellan, *Karl Marx: His Life and Thought* (New York: Harper and Row, 1973), 32-34.

tion as a lecturer in philosophy. The following year he cooperated with Bruno Bauer editing Hegel's *Philosophy of Religion.* Bauer also pushed him to finish his dissertation and join him in Bonn. He duly submitted his thesis in 1841, not at Berlin, however, but at Jena, a university that had a record in the easy production of doctors of philosophy. Indeed, he was granted his degree in absentia.[44] Now he joined Bauer at Bonn and expanded his thesis to obtain a lectureship. Yet these plans evaporated when Bauer was deprived of his teaching post on account of his unorthodox doctrines and Marx had surfaced as a like-minded person. Marx took up the editorship of the *Rheinische Zeitung* but soon moved to Paris because of political problems. There he met Friedrich Engels, with whom he cooperated from then on.

Friedrich Engels (1820-95) was initially trained as a merchant, his father owning a textile factory at Barmen. Serving in the military at Berlin, young Engels took a leave to attend lectures at the university, where he was introduced to Hegelian philosophy. Similar to Marx, he had an interest in literary projects and cooperated with him in the *Rheinische Zeitung.* While in London working for his father's company, he was confronted with the social conditions of the working class and opted for social change. After 1844, when he first met Marx in Paris, there ensued a close cooperation between the two. While Marx hardly ever earned a living and Engels came from a financially well-to-do family, he also was the main contributor to the livelihood of Marx's family. In 1848 they published together the *Communist Manifesto,* advocating the rule of the working class. Soon they realized that their intended revolution was still far in the distance. Nevertheless, they continued to invest their energies for social change. What Marx and Engels wanted to achieve becomes evident from thesis XI in Karl Marx, "Theses on Feuerbach," of 1841: "The philosophers have only *interpreted* the world, in various ways; the point, however, is to change it."[45]

Why did Marx want to go beyond Feuerbach? Again, the answer seems clear: "Feuerbach starts out from the fact of religious self-alienation, the duplication of the world into a religious, imaginary world and a real one. His work consists in the dissolution of the religious world into its secular basis. He overlooks the fact that after this work is completed, the chief thing still remains to be done."[46] Feuerbach was not a revolutionary activist. Yet he knew that once the religious world was dissolved, humanity can turn to its actual task, to improve itself. By contrast, Marx did not want to leave things to their own natural course,

---

44. For details cf. McLellan, *Karl Marx,* 40.

45. Karl Marx, "Theses on Feuerbach," in Karl Marx and Friedrich Engels, *On Religion,* introduction by Reinhold Niebuhr (Chico, Calif.: Scholars, 1982), 72.

46. Marx, in *On Religion,* 70 (thesis IV).

he wanted to speed up history. He witnessed the beginning of the Industrial Revolution and the misery it caused for the working class. Therefore he was impatient, and described the situation with the following words: "The proletariat is beginning to appear in Germany as a result of the rising *industrial* movement. For it is not the *naturally arising* poor but the *artificially impoverished,* not the human masses mechanically oppressed by the gravity of society but the masses resulting from the *drastic dissolution* of society, mainly of the middle estate, that form the proletariat, although, as is easily understood, the naturally arising poor and the Christian-Germanic serfs gradually join its ranks."[47]

But neither Marx nor Engels showed actual solidarity with the proletariat. Marx was habitually overspending and depended on his friend Engels for financial support, whereas Engels lived handsomely from the proceeds of the factory his father owned. Though their approach was largely patronizing, they nevertheless got the workers' movement consolidated and inspired when, at the request of the Central Committee of the Communist League, they wrote the *Manifesto* of the Communist Party. The goal was to unify and inspire the divergent factions within the league by putting forth the principle and aims of the movement. The *Manifesto* starts with the sweeping claim: "The history of all hitherto existing society is the history of class struggles."[48] And it ends with the telling words: The Communists "openly declare that their ends can be attained only by the forcible overthrow of all existing social conditions. Let the ruling classes tremble at a Communistic revolution. The proletarians have nothing to lose but their chains. They have a world to win. WORKING MEN OF ALL COUNTRIES, UNITE!"[49]

This was the beginning of a class struggle that is still not over, as repeated tensions show between workers and employers in virtually all countries. Yet the Communist movement as such ended in great failure. Perhaps Marx and Engels should have not so summarily dismissed religion, even more so because they themselves admitted that early Christianity had notable points of resemblance with the modern working-class movement. While Christianity was originally a movement of oppressed people, they faulted it for refusing to accomplish the social transformation in this world. Instead Christians hoped for salvation from their plight in heaven, in eternal life after death, in the impending "millennium."[50] Thus Marx concluded contemptuously: "The social principles of Christianity preach cowardice, self-contempt, abasement, submission, dejec-

47. Karl Marx, "Contribution to the Critique of Hegel's Philosophy of Right" (1844), in *On Religion,* 57.

48. Karl Marx, *The Communist Manifesto,* ed. Frederic L. Bender (New York: Norton, 1988), 55.

49. Marx, *The Communist Manifesto,* 86.

50. Friedrich Engels, "On the History of Early Christianity," in *On Religion,* 317.

tion."[51] Since the proletariat needs courage, self-esteem, pride, and a sense of independence to attain its goal, it must do away with religion. "The criticism of religion ends with the teaching that *man is the highest essence for man,* hence with the *categoric imperative to overthrow all relations* in which man is a debased, enslaved, abandoned, despicable essence."[52]

Since the religious world is but the reflex of the real world, Marx demanded that we abandon the search "for a superman in the fantastic reality of heaven" where we can find nothing but the reflection of ourselves.[53] Marx therefore claimed that "the abolition of religion as the *illusory* happiness of the people is required for their *real* happiness."[54] As soon as religion as the general theory of this world is abolished — a theory that provides the justification for the exploitation of the working class and the consolation of a better future — we will abandon the fantastic heavenly reality and face our reality on earth.

When we remember the overwhelming otherworldliness of the Negro spirituals, which usually dared to claim only a better beyond and not a better earth, we can understand Marx's claim that "religion is the sigh of the oppressed creature." But we cannot agree with his conclusion that religion "is the *opium* of the people." Religion has certainly been used for this purpose, but since the Judeo-Christian faith is by its very nature a forward-looking and world-transforming faith, this could have never been its main intention. There is undoubtedly also some truth in the claim that religion is a tool of the capitalists to exploit the working class and to sanctify this exploitation with the comfort of a better hereafter. But it is a gross oversimplification to assert that religion is simply an interpretation of present conditions. Religion is just as decisively an anticipation of the "beyond" in earthly form. Engels may have sensed some of this when he conceded that "in the popular risings of the Christian West . . . a new . . . economic order . . . arises and the world progresses," while in the context of other religions, even when the uprisings "are victorious, they allow the old economic conditions to persist untouched. So the old situation remains unchanged and the collision recurs periodically."[55] But both Engels and Marx were influenced by Feuerbach so much that they could not have had any confidence in the function of religion.

51. Karl Marx, "The Communism of the Paper *Rheinischer Beobachter,*" in *On Religion,* 84.

52. Karl Marx, "Contribution to the Critique of Hegel's Philosophy of Right," in *On Religion,* 50.

53. Marx, in *On Religion,* 41.

54. See Marx, in *On Religion,* 42, for this and the following two quotes.

55. Friedrich Engels, "On the History of Early Christianity," in *On Religion,* 317-18, in a footnote.

Marx opted for "a total revolution" in the antagonism between the proletariat and the bourgeoisie.[56] Once the working class is emancipated, "we shall have an association in which the free development of each is the condition for the free development of all."[57] It is not without significance that "free" appears twice in the above sentence. Instead of enslavement and force, Marx envisioned "the realm of freedom" when socialized people, as "associated producers, regulate their interchange with nature rationally, bringing it under their common control, instead of being ruled by it as by some blind power."[58] While the "savage" must wrestle with nature to satisfy his wants and be able to live, modern socialized humanity is "beyond the sphere of material production in the strict meaning of the term." Humanity has passed the point "where labor under the compulsion of necessity and of external utility is required." Then the realm of freedom emerges. This new economic structure of society and the new cultural development thereby determined is eloquently praised by Marx:

> In a higher phase of communist society, after the enslaving subordination of individuals under division of labor, and therewith also the antithesis between mental and physical labor, has vanished, after labor has become not merely a means to live but has become itself the primary necessity of life, after the productive forces have also increased with the all-round development of the individual, and all the springs of the cooperative wealth flow more abundantly — only then can the narrow horizon of the bourgeois right be fully left behind and society inscribe on its banners: from each according to his ability, to each according to his needs.[59]

What does it mean that "labor has become not merely a means to live but has become itself the primary necessity of life"? If necessity still rules supreme, where then is the realm of freedom? Of course, if matter is the base of life, we can get from matter only what we put into it. Though we are now agents of our own fate, fate indeed it is, because as soon as our energies cease just for one moment, whatever we have built will collapse.

To establish here and now the ideal world once envisioned in the beyond,

---

56. Karl Marx, *The Poverty of Philosophy* (1847), in *Karl Marx: The Essential Writings*, edited with an introduction by Frederic L. Bender (New York: Harper Torchbook, 1972), 239.

57. Karl Marx and Friedrich Engels, *The Manifesto of the Communist Party* (1848), in *Karl Marx: The Essential Writings*, 263.

58. For this and the following quotes see Karl Marx, *Capital* (vol. 3), in *Karl Marx: The Essential Writings*, 429-30.

59. Karl Marx, "Critique of the Gotha Program" (1875), in *Karl Marx: The Essential Writings*, 281.

reason is able, according to Marx, to control the material processes of life.[60] Nature is subjected to humanity to serve humanity's needs and desires. The question is not whether nature will yield what Marx envisioned for humanity, but whether humanity can really exercise that reasonable supremacy. Already Marx's notion (that in a fully developed socialism we need no institutions and no legal order, since everyone cooperates freely) has been contradicted by communist reality. Furthermore, the division of labor and the overcoming of the distinction between mental and physical labor is a pipe dream, as Mao's permanent revolution indicated when university professors were sent into fields of agriculture and peasants were supposed to teach.

While Marx developed a vision of paradisiac dimensions, he had forgotten two essentials: when Feuerbach called religion a projection, he claimed that humanity projected on the screen of the beyond that which it could not attain. Humanity then accorded divine attributes to that kind of deification. Yet it was exactly that ideal vision that was merged with humanity in Marx's ideas. Therefore he overestimated humanity and — as the Marxist revolution showed — his utopian vision ended in a catastrophe of apocalyptic dimensions. Furthermore, by disclaiming any beyond, Marx never allowed humanity to relax, since there was no one who could provide for humanity except humanity itself. This means his vision of a realm of freedom turned into a realm of new enslavement.[61]

The Developmental Emphasis of Right-Wing Hegelians: Ferdinand Christian Baur, Alois Emanuel Biedermann

The right-wing Hegelians, who were conservative and decidedly theistic in outlook, did not produce prominent representatives in theology, apart from Philipp Konrad Marheineke (1780-1846). Yet one should note at least the lawyer Eduard Gans (1798-1839), under whom Marx studied in Berlin, and the historian of philosophy Kuno Fischer (1824-1907). There are a few others who deserve mention, though they were theologians in their own right.

Among those who with some justification can be called right-wing Hegelians is the historian and New Testament scholar **Ferdinand Christian Baur** (1792-1860), under whom Strauss studied in Tübingen. Born the son of a pastor near Stuttgart, Baur was the most important church historian of his time. In

---

60. Cf. Guntram Knapp, *Der antimetaphysische Mensch: Darwin — Marx — Freud* (Stuttgart: Ernst Klett, 1973), 139-40.

61. For a good critique of Marx's vision, cf. Walter Bienert, *Der überholte Marx: Seine Religionskritik und Weltanschauung kritisch untersucht*, 3rd ed. (Stuttgart: Evangelisches Verlagswerk, 1975), 261-70.

1809 he entered the *Stift* in Tübingen and left it five years later as the best of his class. Having served briefly as a vicar, he returned to the *Stift* in 1816 as a tutor, and already the following year he was called as a professor for classical languages to the Minor Seminary in Blaubeuren, one of the ecclesial training schools in Württemberg prior to university studies. In 1821 he married the daughter of a Stuttgart court physician. When Ernst Gottlieb Bengel (1769-1826), the premier representative of the old Tübingen school who, with the help of Kantian philosophy, defended the authority of Scripture against rationalism and historical criticism, died, Baur was called in 1827 to a full professorship for historical theology at the University of Tübingen. For thirty-four years he worked as an academic teacher and also preached the early (main) service at the church affiliated with the *Stift*.

Baur is the founder of the new Tübingen school. He followed Schleiermacher in regarding the dogmas as expressions of the Christian consciousness conditioned by their own time, and Hegel in applying a dialectic notion to the development of the dogma. For him, dogma did not develop only after the New Testament documents had been written, but a development can already be discerned in the New Testament writings themselves. Therefore New Testament theology must be considered "the Christian history of dogma as it developed within the New Testament."[62] The Yale historian Jaroslav Pelikan (b. 1923) characterizes Baur with these words: "There was certainly none within Continental Protestantism who ranked as high in both historical scholarship and theological creativity. Indeed, the competence of this phenomenal scholar enabled him to make contributions of far-reaching importance to the study of the New Testament as well as to historical and systematic theology."[63] Yet important as Baur was, he was not uncontested in his work. Emanuel Hirsch (1888-1972), for instance, in his monumental five-volume *History of the More Recent Protestant Theology in Europe,* called him "the greatest and at the same time the most controversial theologian that has been given to German Protestant Christendom after Schleiermacher," and also claimed that he is "the actual author of historical-critical theology."[64] His extreme critics at his own time, however, labeled him a total Hegelian, a pantheist, and even an atheist, judgments that

---

62. Ferdinand Christian Baur, *Vorlesungen über neutestamentliche Theologie,* ed. Ferdinand Friedrich Baur, introduction by Werner Georg Kümmel (1864; new ed. Darmstadt: Wissenschaftliche Buchgesellschaft, 1973), 33.

63. Jaroslav Pelikan, preface to *The Formation of Historical Theology: A Study of Ferdinand Christian Baur,* by Peter C. Hodgson (New York: Harper and Row, 1966), ix.

64. Emanuel Hirsch, *Geschichte der neuern evangelischen Theologie im Zusammenhang mit den allgemeinen Bewegungen des europäischen Denkens* (Münster: Th. Stenderhoff, 1984), 5:518.

carry on till today.[65] As Peter Hodgson (b. 1934) in his insightful doctoral dissertation shows, Baur preferred Hegel to Schleiermacher, but he was not an uncritical Hegelian. While he advocated a panentheistic view of history, his radical historical orientation and his emphasis on Christology allowed him to go beyond the strictures of Hegel.[66]

Baur's indebtedness to Hegel shows especially in his understanding of the history of dogma: "The entire history of dogma is a continual procession of Spirit in never-ending conflict with itself, never able to become truly one with itself; it is a constant binding and loosening, a never-resting work in which Spirit, like Penelope, continually unravels its own web, only to begin again anew."[67] There is a dialectic in the process of history, and at the same time a divinely guided unfolding of the Christian truth. Initially a static understanding of dogma prevailed, according to Baur, and "only the *antithesis* between Catholic truth and heresy was acknowledged."[68] Then evolved the understanding of history as the "eternal uniformity of an unchanging tradition." Only through the Reformation and Protestantism did the possibility "of a purely historical understanding of the dogma" and of its history occur, and therefore the "first historical investigations of the course and alterations of dogma ensued." Baur tried to bring the two things together: a historical investigation as to the origin and course of dogma with a conviction of divine guidance in its unfolding process. But what did Baur actually teach?

He lectured on church history and history of dogma, New Testament studies, and symbolism, i.e., a comparison of different denominations. One of the important works from his early period was *Die christliche Gnosis oder die christliche Religions-Philosophie in ihrer geschichtlichen Entwicklung (The Christian Gnosis or the Christian Philosophy of Religion in Its Historical Development)* of 1835.[69] This work shows that he left both Schelling and Schleiermacher behind and assimilated Hegel, in whom he had found a point of orientation. In 1832 his colleague from the Roman Catholic faculty in Tübingen, Johann Adam Möhler, a representative of the Roman Catholic Tübingen School (see chap. 13), pub-

---

65. Cf. the examples cited by Hodgson, *Formation of Historical Theology*, 2. For a brief and fair treatment cf. also Ernst Barnikol, *Ferdinand Christian Baur als rationalistisch-kirchlicher Theologe* (Berlin: Evangelische Verlagsanstalt, 1970), 5, who emphasizes Baur's devotion to the church and his honest and simple rationalism.

66. Cf. Hodgson, *Formation of Historical Theology*, 136-37.

67. Ferdinand Christian Baur, *On the Writing of Church History*, ed. and trans. Peter C. Hodgson (New York: Oxford University Press, 1968), 300.

68. See Baur, *On the Writing*, 337 and 343, for this and the following quotes.

69. For the following cf. "Baur, Ferdinand Christian," in *Theologische Realenzyklopädie*, 5:354-58.

lished a book with the title *Symbolism: Exposition of the Doctrinal Differences between Catholics and Protestants as Evidenced by Their Symbolical Writings* (Eng. trans. 1997). Möhler contended that the opposing positions between Roman Catholicism and Protestantism could be solved only through a return of Protestantism to the Catholic Church. In 1833 Baur responded with *Der Gegensatz des Katholizismus und Protestantismus nach den Prinzipien und Hauptdogmen der beiden Lehrbegriffe. Mit besonderer Rücksicht auf Herrn Dr. Möhlers Symbolik* (*The Opposing Position of Catholicism and Protestantism according to the Principles and Main Dogmas of Their Doctrinal Concepts: With Special Reference to Dr. Möhler's Symbolics*). In 1836 a second edition of this publication appeared. Baur tried to show that each system has its own version of truth, but taken together they are striving for an idea that can never be fully expressed in either system. Furthermore, he claimed that the Protestant church must distinguish itself from Catholicism, because it is obligated to maintain its protesting position that apart from Scripture no other divine authority can be acknowledged.

Another important facet of Baur's work between 1831 and 1851 was his New Testament studies, in which he demonstrated the difference between Petrine and Pauline Christianity. He also denied that the Pastoral Epistles had Paul as their author. Because of their antignostic tendency, they belong to a later period. He also showed that after the Synoptics and Paul, the Johannine Gospel was a third step in a development of Christianity. Important here are his books *Paul the Apostle of Jesus Christ: His Life and Works, His Epistles and Teachings; A Contribution to a Critical History of Primitive Christianity* (2 vols., 1845; Eng. trans. 1873-75) and *Über die Komposition und den Charakter des Johanneischen Evangeliums* (*Concerning the Composition and the Character of the Johannine Gospel*, 1844). During the same time, his reputation suffered because Strauss's *Life of Jesus* appeared, and Strauss was regarded as his disciple. Therefore the polemic against Strauss was also directed against Baur.

Significant also are his contributions to the history of dogma, in which he treated the historic development of the Christian doctrine of reconciliation (1838), dividing it into a period of predominant objectivity (up to the Reformation), a period of gradual predominant subjectivity (up to Kant), and a final stage (up to Schleiermacher and Hegel). He also wrote works on the doctrine of the Trinity in three volumes, the doctrine of incarnation, and their historical development (1841-43). Finally, in the 1850s he turned to the history of the church, writing on the epochs of ecclesial historiography in *On the Writing of Church History* (1852; Eng. trans. 1968), and with his investigation *Church History of the First Three Centuries* (1853; Eng. trans. 1878). Baur was a prolific writer and thinker, and a century later Rudolf Bultmann and Ernst Käsemann (1906-98) could still declare that they stood on the ground Baur had paved.

Alois Emanuel Biedermann (1819-85) was not as prolific as Baur. Yet Claude Welch (b. 1922) of the Graduate Theological Union in Berkeley calls him "the most prominent dogmatician to emerge from the so-called young Hegelian group" and the main proponent of a "free Christianity" in Switzerland.[70] This means that only in a diminished sense can he be regarded a right-wing Hegelian. Biedermann was born in Bendlikon near Zürich and first studied theology at Basel (1837-39) and then at Berlin (1839-41), with the speculative theologians Wilhelm Vatke (1806-82) and Marheineke. He returned to Basel and took a parish in 1843. Against strong opposition from conservatives, he was appointed associate professor at Zürich (1850) and then in 1860 full professor in dogmatics. His main works are: *Die freie Theologie oder Philosophie und Christentum im Streit und Frieden* (*Free Theology or Philosophy and Christendom in Controversy and Peace*, 1844); *Unsere Jung-Hegelische Weltanschauung oder der sogenannte neueste Pantheismus* (*Our Young-Hegelian Worldview or the So-Called Latest Pantheism*, 1849); *Christliche Dogmatik* (*Christian Dogmatics*, 1869); and *Ausgewählte Vorträge und Aufsätze* (*Selected Lectures and Papers*, 1885).

While Strauss failed at Zürich, Biedermann remained grateful to him for showing that the Christian principle cannot be identified with the Jesus of history. Biedermann was critical of Strauss for never fulfilling the promise of a speculative construction of the Christian faith. But he was willing to accept Strauss's verdict that the divine was incarnate in humanity in general and not in the individual. Biedermann freely acknowledged his indebtedness to Hegel, but he did not follow him blindly. In contrast to Hegel, he did not simply want to identify religion with its characteristic mode of thinking. He also appreciated the contribution of Schleiermacher, whom he called "the great regenerator of modern theology," since Schleiermacher had recognized the specificity of the religious relationship as distinguished from every other spiritual dimension.[71]

According to Biedermann, it was the task of dogmatics to speculatively unfold the religious contents of the dogma in one's own theoretical forms of consciousness, contents that have surfaced through the criticism as a theoretical problem.[72] Biedermann affirmed that the Christian religion has its historical foundation in the person of Jesus, meaning the religious personality of Jesus. In the religious self-consciousness of Jesus the relationship between God and the human ego has entered the history of humanity with a faith-causing power.

---

70. Claude Welch, *Protestant Theology in the Nineteenth Century* (New Haven: Yale University Press, 1972), 1:160.

71. Alois E. Biedermann, *Christliche Dogmatik* (Zürich: Orell, Füssli & Co., 1869), viii.

72. Cf. Biedermann, *Christliche Dogmatik*, 13.

Therewith the religious community of Christendom had been founded. The absolute spirit showed in the finite human ego of Jesus. Thinking about God as absolute spirit makes oblivious the notion of God as person. Yet for the sake of representation, the portrayal of God as personality is both permissible and necessary, though finitude belongs essentially to the concept of personality.[73]

In the religious personality of Jesus and in our faith in it, the Christian principle entered the history of humanity. Church doctrine, Biedermann claimed, personified the Christian principle with the person of the carrier of revelation and described him as a divine-human being. Yet Biedermann preferred to call Jesus the divine humanity, which in us, being children of God, becomes a religious reality in the human spiritual life. "This humanly personal self-consciousness of the absoluteness of spirit is the factual union of the divine and the human essences as the unity of personal spiritual life."[74] In Jesus this union took place for the first time. Therefore he is the wellspring of the effectuality of this principle. The person of Jesus then becomes the example for the efficacy of the principle of salvation. These reflections show that in appropriating the person and work of Christ in his *Dogmatics*, Biedermann is heavily influenced by Schleiermacher. In contrast to Strauss, to whom Biedermann often referred in his *Dogmatics*, Biedermann had more theological skill to integrate and to engage in an open dialogue. He was a "free theologian," always endeavoring to take seriously and appreciate positions different from his own.[75]

Mediation between Faith and Knowledge: Richard Rothe, Julius Müller, and Isaak August Dorner

Next to the more radical left-wing Hegelians, there was a strong stream of Protestant theology in nineteenth-century Germany that was of a mediating type. It was also influenced by both Schleiermacher and Hegel. Its representatives presupposed that a religious consciousness belongs to the essence of humanity, and therefore they rejected the criticism of religion and the resulting atheism of left-wing Hegelians who wanted to dissolve theology into anthropology. These mediating theologians gathered around the journal *Theologische*

---

73. Cf. Biedermann, *Christliche Dogmatik*, 639 (§715-16).

74. Biedermann, *Christliche Dogmatik*, 683 (§798), and see also the translation of portions of Biedermann's *Dogmatics* in *God and Incarnation in Mid-Nineteenth Century German Theology: G. Thomasius, I. A. Dorner, A. E. Biedermann*, ed. and trans. Claude Welch (New York: Oxford University Press, 1965), here 369.

75. So very correctly Rudolf Dellsperger, "Biedermann, Alois Emanuel," in *Theologische Realenzyklopädie*, 6:484.

Studien und Kritiken (*Theological Studies and Criticism*, 1828–1941/42), which appeared in 109 volumes altogether. While its representatives do not form a homogeneous theological school, they exclude both rationalism and purely speculative theology.

Most well-known among them is **Richard Rothe** (1799-1867), who was born in Posen, Silesia, where his father occupied a high position in the Prussian government. In 1809 the family moved to Stettin, and two years later to Breslau in Silesia, where he attended the *Gymnasium* of the Reformed church. Throughout his life he held a tender, childlike faith that he found very early in his life as he recorded in his journal:

> I had found my Lord and Redeemer without the help of any human teacher, and independently of any traditional ascetic method, having been inwardly drawn towards Him, at a very early period, apart from any particular outward influence, under the pressure of a gradually deepening feeling of a personal, as well as a universal human need. But it never occurred to me that there must be anything of a traditional and statutory, or generally of a conventional character, in the Christian doctrine of faith and in the Christian construction of man's life. In short, my Christianity was of a very modern sort; it fearlessly kept itself open on every side, wherever in all God's wide world it might receive influences in the truly human way.[76]

When Rothe started to study theology at the University of Heidelberg in 1817, he was especially impressed with Daub's speculative theology, and also with Hegel. When Hegel moved to Berlin in 1818, Rothe went with him. There he was also fascinated by the church historian Johann A. W. Neander (1789-1850), through whom he also got to know his later friend Friedrich August Tholuck. Through the influence of Neander, who was one of the founders of the revival movement in Prussia, Rothe participated in the prayer circle of Baron Hans Ernst von Kottwitz (1757-1843), who was influenced by Zinzendorf's pietism and in turn was the central figure of the revival movement in Berlin and even beyond. In 1820 Rothe passed his theological exam and entered the Wittenberg preachers seminary (a preachers seminary, or *Predigerseminar*, is a seminary for practical training subsequent to theological education at a university), while Schleiermacher tried to win for him an academic career through the secretary of education, Freiherr von Stein zum Altenstein. But Rothe, after his ordination in 1823, preferred to serve from 1824

---

76. As quoted in John MacPherson's introductory essay in Richard Rothe, *Still Hours*, trans. Jane Stoddart (New York: Funk and Wagnalls, 1872), 12.

on as chaplain of the Prussian embassy at Rome. His proximity to the center of Catholicism changed his Romantic ideas — a number of representatives of the romantic movement converted to Catholicism — as much as it changed his pietism. Gradually he became convinced that the kingdom of God for which Christianity stood could not be realized in an ecclesial configuration nor in a close-knit pietistic community.[77]

In 1828 he assumed a professorship at Wittenberg Seminary, and in 1837 he was called to a professorship at the University of Heidelberg. Simultaneously he became university preacher plus director of the newly founded preachers seminary. While in Heidelberg he became one of the cofounders of *Theological Studies and Criticism*. From 1849 to 1853 he was professor at Bonn for practical theology, and in 1854, on account of the bad health of his wife, he returned to Heidelberg to teach primarily in church history. He was active in the church of Baden and even a delegate to the Badensian first chamber of the parliament.

The eminent American church historian Philip Schaff said of Rothe: "He has evidently learned much from Hegel and Schleiermacher, but his ideas undergo a process of transformation in his brain, and come out as something altogether new and original."[78] Rothe strictly distinguished between philosophical and theological speculation. While the first starts from self-consciousness and proceeds according to the laws of natural reasoning, "the second begins with the consciousness of God in the human soul, rests on religious experience, and finds its objective contents provided ready to its hand in divine revelation." Rothe's "speculation" is informed by Schleiermacher and Hegel (consciousness), pietism (religious experience), and the common Christian heritage. He betrayed his Hegelian influence when he asserted that theological speculation always begins with the idea of God, while on the other hand God is for him the absolutely and immediately certain.

Important are Rothe's *Theologial Ethics* (1845-48), in which he declared that ethics is the theological science of morals as "an integrating part of the system of speculative theology."[79] Schaff regarded *Ethics*, which first appeared in three volumes and in a second edition in five volumes (1867-71), "as the greatest work on speculative divinity which has appeared since Schleiermacher's Dogmatics."[80] It is in some way a complete system of speculative theology, since it deals not only with morals in the widest sense of the word,

---

77. So Falk Wagner, "Rothe, Richard," in *Theologische Realenzyklopädie*, 29:437.

78. So Philip Schaff, *Germany: Its Universities, Theology, and Religion* (Philadelphia: Lindsay and Blakiston, 1857), 363, for this and the following quote.

79. Richard Rothe, *Theologische Ethik*, 2nd ed. (Wittenberg: Hermann Koelling, 1869), 1:3 (§1).

80. Schaff, *Germany*, 361.

but also with the social relations of family, science and art, church and state. Rothe did this under the threefold division of the doctrine of the goods *(Güterlehre)*, the doctrine of virtue *(Tugendlehre)*, and the doctrine of duties *(Pflichtenlehre)*. In his *Dogmatics* (1863), Rothe asserted that by means of an unambiguous supernatural history God enters into the natural history as an active person, and therefore comes so close to humanity that even an eye darkened by sin must perceive God. This outward manifestation of God is complemented by an inner illumination. Considering this kind of reasoning, we must conclude that Rothe was correct when he said: "As a theologian I am a supernaturalistic rationalist."[81]

Yet Rothe is noted for a very different proposition. In his *Ethics* he claimed: "Christendom is *essentially* a political principle and a political power. It builds up the state and carries with it the ability to shape the state and develop it towards its perfection."[82] Since the purpose of the state encompasses the totality of the moral aims, Christendom is essentially intended to become more and more secular by taking off the ecclesial gown it has worn since its entrance into the world and by assuming a common human, meaning a moral, dimension.[83] The decisive point for Christendom was the Reformation, because there it broke through its ecclesial historical period and entered into the political historical one. There in principle it undid the church, but only in principle. Rothe was convinced that Christendom will so penetrate the whole moral life of humanity and all relations of society that there will no longer be room for a separate and distinct religious organization such as the church. This theocracy would include all nations and would, so to speak, be equated with the kingdom of God. Rothe shared the optimism of the nineteenth century, an optimism that in a much more secular way was advocated by Marx and Engels when they dreamed of an egalitarian society. Schaff was certainly right that Rothe, while being "exceedingly popular as a teacher, . . . is too original in his views to form a school in the strict sense of the term."[84]

Julius Müller (1801-78), a friend of Rothe, was born in Silesia (Prussia) as son of a pastor. He began his studies of law at the University of Breslau in 1819, and went the following year to the University of Göttingen, where his older brother taught classics and archaeology. In 1821 there occurred a dramatic change, because, though already in touch with the Silesian revival movement, "for the first time the divine power of the gospel grasped my innermost feeling

---

81. Rothe, *Still Hours,* 323.

82. Cf. Richard Rothe, *Theologische Ethik,* 2nd ed. (Wittenberg: Hermann Koelling, 1871), 5:357 (§1162).

83. Cf. Rothe, *Theologische Ethik,* 5:397 (§1168).

84. Schaff, *Germany,* 360-61.

and I found the blessed peace which Christ alone can give."[85] He studied theology at Breslau (1822/23) and Berlin (1823/24), where he was influenced by Tholuck and the Berlin circle of pietists who gathered around Baron von Kottwitz. He served as pastor from 1825 to 1831 in Silesia, where he rejected the union liturgy, not because he wanted to reject the union but as a reaction against the king's interference with the freedom of the church by imposing this union on the church. In 1831 he moved to Göttingen and was appointed university preacher. There he also did his *Habilitation* with a thesis on Luther's doctrine of predestination and free will (1831). He was appointed associate professor in 1834.

Soon Müller became known beyond Göttingen, and in 1835 he followed a call to the University of Marburg as professor of dogmatics. There he wrote his seminal work, *The Christian Doctrine of Sin*. The first volume appeared in 1839; the second edition, in 1844, was published as a two-volume work. Tholuck managed to have the already well-known professor called to Halle, and in 1841, after declining a call to Tübingen, Müller became counselor to the secretary of church affairs Eichhorn.

Müller is primarily known for his two-volume work on sin, in which he refutes any attempts to "explain" sin: "I have no romantic wish to offer solutions of this great mystery of our being, which will only involve us in further mysteries."[86] In the first part of his treatise, he attempts to establish the emotive power for Christian ethics and comes to the conclusion: "Christian Ethics, accordingly, finds this motive power of progression in the *Divine acts* alone. They are the exciting powers and developing principles in the growing system of Ethics which, like every science imbued with the spirit of Christianity, has to trace out and pursue the ways of God; upon them the introduction of every new duty depends."[87] This biblically founded theocentricity allowed him a certain freedom of being open for new ways while remaining focused through a personal relation to Jesus Christ on the loving obedience to God's will.

Müller made a special effort to make the union between the Reformed and the Lutherans work without attempting to pull one confession over to the other or merge the two into something new. He had a deep sense of the evil of schism in Protestantism and wanted to promote a harmony of the body of Christ. In his book *The Evangelical Union, Its Nature and Divine Right* (*Evangelische Union; ihr Wesen und göttliches Recht*) of 1854, he said: "To unite

---

85. Julius Müller, as cited in Joachim Mehlhausen, "Müller, Julius," in *Theologische Real-enzyklopädie*, 23:394.

86. Julius Müller, *The Christian Doctrine of Sin*, translated from the 5th edition by William Urwick, 2 vols. (Edinburgh: T. & T. Clark, 1868), 2:397.

87. Müller, *Christian Doctrine of Sin*, 1:127.

what is internally divided, is an unprofitable work; but to divide what belongs together, is still more unprofitable."[88] He discussed the doctrinal differences between the Lutherans and Reformed and showed that especially on predestination and the Lord's Supper they represent different aspects of the same truth but do not necessarily contradict each other. He then tried in a formula of consensus to establish the doctrinal basis for the Protestant Church of Prussia, drawing from both the Reformed and the Lutheran symbolic books as far as they agree. Beyond his articles in theological journals and his sermons, he had a lasting impact on the students through his personal piety.

Another representative of the mediating type of theology is **Isaak August Dorner** (1809-84), who was born in Württemberg and was a tutor with Strauss at the Tübingen Stift. He was acquainted with the Scottish Presbyterial constitution, which furthered his interest in ecclesial matters. From 1839 to 1843 he was professor in Kiel, where he established a lasting friendship with Hans Lassen Martensen (1808-84). After that he taught successively in Königsberg, Bonn, Göttingen, and finally Berlin. Dorner went beyond Müller in opting for a German Protestant national church that should be a confederation of churches to ensure the diversity in unity. He also opted for the separation of church and state. But the time was not yet ripe for such ideas. The only suggestions of his put into action were the *Kirchentage,* the first of which took place in 1848 in Eisenach, and the conferences of churches. Theologically Dorner was influenced by Schleiermacher and did not have any contact with the awakening.

The doctrine of justification occupies the center of his theology. But Dorner's christocentric approach does not shy away from employing reason. According to Dorner, we deduce from the concept of God, by means of philosophical logic, one dogmatic proposition after another. The goal of this mediating type of theology was to spell out through scholarly investigation the inner coherence and objective foundation of faith beyond all relative opposing positions. This way one achieves an inner reconciliation, including the reconciliation of faith and reason, to a higher synthesis. This goal is basically Hegelian and precludes a meeting somewhere in the middle or a meandering from one position to the other.

Kierkegaard's Dialectic in Opposition to the System

Søren Aabye Kierkegaard (1813-55), born to a wool merchant and his wife in Copenhagen, Denmark, was certainly not a disciple of Hegel. Yet "the life of

---

88. Müller, as quoted in Schaff, *Germany,* 344.

Søren Kierkegaard may be viewed as a life of growth through conflict."[89] Whether he knew Hegel's writings directly or only through the mediation of others is uncertain.[90] If one is only somewhat familiar with the philosophy of Hegel, however, one "cannot fail to detect innumerable passages which are formulated in strident opposition to the System."[91] In October 1841, Kierkegaard went to Berlin to listen to Schelling, who had just been called there to stamp out Hegel's pantheism. But Schelling could not satisfy him, and so he concentrated on his own work and concluded writing his book *Either/Or,* which was published in 1843.

Kierkegaard had three brothers and three sisters. Yet his mother, his sisters, and two of his brothers died before he reached his twenty-first birthday. Only his older brother Peder Christian (1805-88) and he were left, and both did quite well in school. Punctual fulfillment of their duties and a love for Jesus crucified were primary goals in their education. The strict education and the losses in the family furthered the melancholy that remained throughout Kierkegaard's life. From 1821 to 1830 he went to a private school, since his father had acquired the financial means through which to pay. Kierkegaard then studied theology, aesthetics, and philosophy. The year 1836 was a turning point in his life, since both his philosophy teacher, Paul Martin Møller (1794-1836), and his father died. In addition, he experienced a personal crisis, the reason for which nobody knows with certainty. This crisis seems to have been a further burden on his psyche.

In 1840 Kierkegaard passed his theological exams with distinction and wrote his dissertation on the concept of irony with reference to Socrates. He defended it in 1841. The year before he got engaged to Regine Olsen (1823-1904), but the following year he dissolved this engagement and then went to Berlin. Again it is difficult to find sufficient reason for breaking off the engagement, except that he felt that as a penitent he could not meet the expectations of his bride-to-be. From then on he wrote a flood of discourses and philosophical essays. Apart from *Either/Or,* especially noteworthy are *Repetition* (1843), *Fear and Trembling* (1843), *Philosophical Fragments* (1844), *The Concept of Dread* (1844), *Stages on Life's Way* (1846), *Concluding Unscientific Postscript to Philosophical Fragments* (1846), *The Sickness unto Death* (1849), and *Training in Christianity* (1850). His later life was marked by controversies, and Kierkegaard,

89. So rightly Jerry H. Gill, ed., introduction to *Essays on Kierkegaard* (Minneapolis: Burgess Publishing, 1969), 1.

90. Cf. Henning Schröer, "Kierkegaard, Søren Aabye," in *Theologische Realenzyklopädie,* 18:140, who says it "seems certain that he occupied himself only later (ca. 1836) with original texts of Hegel."

91. So Walter Lowrie, *Kierkegaard* (New York: Harper Torchbook, 1962), 1:244.

who often wrote under pseudonyms, never succeeded in a literary or philosophical breakthrough during his life.

By the end of his life he had become an object of public ridicule and scorn, partly because of a sustained fight he provoked in 1846 with the *Corsar*, a satirical Danish weekly, and partly because of his severe attacks on the Danish state church and its bishop Jakob Peter Mynster (1775-1854), whom he had once appreciated. Kierkegaard's health had suffered from the struggles, and his financial means were almost exhausted. He died on November 11, 1855, a month after he collapsed in the street. At his burial his nephew Henrik Lund protested that Kierkegaard's rejection of official Christianity had been left unmentioned at the funeral.[92]

It would be unfair to Kierkegaard to see him simply as a late bloomer or someone who became famous only after his death. Virtually all modern forms of existential philosophy and theology, including neo-Reformation or dialectical theology of the first half of the twentieth century, are in some way or other dependent on him. Though not accepted, Kierkegaard was an important voice at his own time, speaking to his own context. He raised his voice not only against a Hegelianized Christianity of culture, but also against a state church that had accommodated itself to the world. Kierkegaard saw the Christianity and Protestant theology of his own time as falling away from true New Testament Christianity. In *Training in Christianity* he wrote: "Christendom has done away with Christianity, without being quite aware of it. The consequence is that, if anything is to be done, one must try again to introduce Christianity to Christendom."[93] Christendom had adulterated Christianity, and the official church is the main culprit. He claimed about Bishop Mynster: "In no instance does his preaching bring Christianity up to where it is everywhere in the New Testament, namely, a breach, the very deepest and most incurable breach with this world — any more than did Bishop Mynster's life (as is easily explained by his infinite dread of everything radical) resemble even in the remotest way a breach with this world."[94]

Not accommodation to the present situation is called for, according to Kierkegaard, but rediscovering and continuing the radical otherness of the New Testament. "There is an endless yawning difference between God and man, and hence, in the situation of contemporaneousness, to become a Christian (to be

92. So Schröer, "Kierkegaard," 18:142.

93. Søren Kierkegaard, *Training in Christianity and the Edifying Discourse Which "Accompanied" It*, translated with introduction by Walter Lowrie (Princeton: Princeton University Press, 1952), 39.

94. *Kierkegaard's Attack upon "Christendom"* (1854-55), translated with an introduction by Walter Lowrie (Boston: Beacon Press, 1956), 17.

transformed into likeness with God) proved to be an even greater torment and misery and pain than the greatest human torment, and hence also a crime in the eyes of one's neighbors. And so it will always prove when becoming a Christian in truth comes to mean to become contemporary with Christ."[95]

This otherness of Christianity is seen in that God is totally different from us. Yet we cannot allow a distance between us and Christ. We must become his immediate followers even if such radical discipleship means suffering. The Christian existence to which Kierkegaard called his Danish compatriots is a life in contrast to the life in the world. It is a life of suffering, because it is a life of discipleship with Christ, and it is lived in contemporaneity with Christ, since "Christ's life on earth is not a past event . . . for what true Christians there are in each generation are contemporary with Christ."[96] While Hegel strove for a synthesis between faith and reason and Christ and culture, Kierkegaard opposed that as a compromising of Christ and faith, and instead he opted for an antithesis. The daring decisions of faith and of existence are related to each other and must replace the compromises and half-truths of conventional Christianity. One must become a Christian within Christianity.

Kierkegaard's faith in Christ emphasizes incarnation, namely, the paradox of God coming to us in the lowly figure of a servant. The incognito character of Christ and the nondiscernibility of his Godhead make us wonder how we can even make a decision of faith. Here again we are confronted with a paradox that for human reason is not only improbable, but even absurd. We do not gain access to Jesus Christ through historical research or any other attempts of reason, but only through faith by which we become contemporeal with Jesus Christ and, so to speak, transcend the centuries that separate us from his earthly life. Kierkegaard called for a dialectic existence and for a subjective or existential knowing. Again the emphasis on subjectivity was directed against Hegel and his idea of objective truth. This objective truth is one of relationship, of being related to God, which then provides for a new objectivity. Kierkegaard contended: "Faith is the objective uncertainty with the repulsion of the absurd, held fast in the passion of inwardness, which is the relation of inwardness intensified to its highest."[97] There is always a wager or risk involved, because the difference between God and humanity can never be mediated in a speculative or reasonable way.

Major theologians and philosophers of the second half of the nineteenth century hardly read Kierkegaard's works. Martensen, who had been his teacher

95. Kierkegaard, *Training in Christianity*, 67.
96. Kierkegaard, *Training in Christianity*, 68.
97. Søren Kierkegaard, *Concluding Unscientific Postscript to Philosophical Fragments*, edited and translated with introduction and notes by Howard V. Hong and Edna H. Hong (Princeton: Princeton University Press, 1992), 1:611.

in Copenhagen after 1840, was one of the few exceptions. Upon becoming successor to Bishop Mynster (1854), Martensen was heavily attacked by Kierkegaard, especially on account of his eulogy for the late bishop. Nevertheless, he appreciated Kierkegaard's category of the individual and the significance of a personal decision for faith, but accused him of having little understanding of the church and of congregations that support individuals in their faith. Kierkegaard's significance came only in the twentieth century with Karl Barth and Rudolf Bultmann, who drew on his dialectics of faith, his emphasis on the Christ of faith, and his fight against a Christianity of culture.

Ralph Waldo Emerson: The First Philosopher of the American Spirit and America's Hegel

Ralph Waldo Emerson (1803-82) was no Hegelian by any stretch of imagination. He was "the first philosopher of the American spirit."[98] But he too lived in a historical context from which he could not extricate himself. On the one hand he claimed in an address delivered at Harvard in 1837 that "we have listened too long to the courtly muses of Europe."[99] But on the other hand he conceded: "The scholar is that man who must take up into himself all the ability of the time, all the contributions of the past, all the hopes of the future." And that Emerson, as well as Hegel, certainly did.

Emerson was born in Boston as the son of a pastor of the Second Church. His father died when he was only eight years old, and his mother had to raise the five boys by herself.[100] In 1817 Emerson entered Harvard College and graduated four years later. Then he taught school for four years to help his brother financially so that he could finish school. After that he entered Harvard Divinity School and completed his education in 1829, after which he was ordained as assistant pastor of the Second Church and soon succeeded the pastor in full charge of the parish. In 1832 he announced to his congregation that he would no longer administer the Eucharist because he did not believe that Christ had intended it as a general, regular observance, and then he resigned his position.

98. So Brooks Atkinson, introduction to *The Complete Essays and Other Writings of Ralph Waldo Emerson,* edited with a biographical introduction by Brooks Atkinson (New York: Random House Modern Library, 1950), ix.

99. See Ralph Waldo Emerson, "The American Scholar," in *The Complete Essays,* 62, for this and the following quote.

100. Merlyn E. Satrom, "Emerson, Ralph Waldo," in *Theologische Realenzyklopädie,* 9:558, incorrectly claims that his father was pastor of "First Church Boston" and died when Ralph was six years old.

He went to Italy, partly for health reasons, and then also visited England, where he sought out Coleridge, Wordsworth, and Carlyle, whom he already knew through literature at Harvard. Returning from Italy in good health and good spirits, he settled in Concord in 1835. There he indulged in the love of nature, which heavily influenced his philosophy. He took up his work now as an essayist and lecturer and occasionally supplied the local pulpit. Friendships with people like novelist Nathaniel Hawthorne (1804-64) and naturalist Henry Thoreau (1817-62) were important to him. Especially his address at Harvard entitled "The American Scholar" (1837) made him well known, and was widely circulated. When invited back the following year by the senior class of the Harvard Divinity School, his address aroused so much controversy that the officers of the school publicly disclaimed responsibility for it. It took nearly thirty years before he was invited to speak at Harvard again.

Similar to Kierkegaard, Emerson made a strong distinction between what Jesus intended and what historical Christianity made of it. "Jesus Christ," he contended, "belonged to the true race of prophets. He saw with open eye the mystery of the soul. Drawn by its severe harmony, ravished with its beauty, he lived in it, and had his being there. Alone in all history he estimated the greatness of man. . . . He saw that God incarnates himself in man, and ever more goes forth anew to take possession of his World."[101] Emerson concentrated on the human soul and on the human person. The incarnation, in Straussian ways, is not confined to Jesus, but to the human person in whom God incarnates himself. That, of course, elevates the human person. Emerson could even claim: "If a man is at heart just, then in so far is he God; the safety of God, the immortality of God, the majesty of God do enter into that man with justice" (68-69).

Over against this emphasis on God's oneness with the human soul, historical Christianity corrupted religion and emphasized the ritual and the person of Jesus. Furthermore, the moral law was not explored as the foundation of the established teaching in society, because revelation was considered something long ago given and therefore a thing of the past (cf. 73-75). Yet "it is the office of a true teacher to show us that God is, not was; that He speaketh, not spake" (80). This means that God and Christ are not items of the past, but powers of the present that instill in our souls the sentiment of virtue that alone is God pleasing. Proclaiming the divine nature of humanity and calling for virtue and reverence to be instilled in the souls, Emerson of course struck a fashionable chord in nineteenth-century America, an era in which many people dreamed of unlimited expansion and progress.

---

101. Ralph Waldo Emerson, "An Address," in *The Complete Essays*, 72. Page references to this essay are placed in the text.

His talk at the divinity school had a dual result. On the one hand, he was branded an atheist and no longer welcome in pulpits and on lecture platforms. On the other hand, people appreciated his optimism and his emphasis on the human factor. He was invited to lecture chiefly on spiritual and philosophical subjects all over the country, yet not in churches. In 1847 he was even invited to lecture in England, since he was well-known by then. In 1865 he was invited back to Harvard to speak again, and shortly afterward he was elected a member of the Board of Overseers. In 1870 and 1871 he regularly lectured on philosophy at Harvard. In preparation for his lectures, he read the first three volumes of the *Journal of Speculative Philosophy,* published by the Hegelians in St. Louis.[102]

Emerson is the most prominent representative of New England transcendentalism, meaning an idealistic philosophy espoused by a loosely knit group that intended to infuse a new spirituality into common life. He was also one of the most significant members of the Transcendental Club in Boston. This association shows that Emerson was by no means an atheist or an irreligious person. That could hardly have been the case, because he shared with the romantics their delight in nature. He wrote: "The world proceeds from the same spirit as the body of man. It is a remoter and inferior incarnation of God, a projection of God in the unconscious."[103]

While Feuerbach collapsed the transcendent into the immanent and thereby eliminated it, for Emerson the immanent, be it nature or humanity, became the icon of the transcendent. He believed in the goodness of humanity, because it was God's own incarnation. Emerson cultivated his appreciation of nature, because God was seen as present in it. He espoused progress, because the divine laws to which we have access through our soul guide us to right conduct, which is the way to God. Both Hegel and Emerson shared a common vision of a new age and of a synthesis of the human and the divine. While Hegel had an appreciation for formal religion, Emerson was so set for the future that for him this was a betrayal of God's spirit who speaks to us in the present and does not want us to turn to the past. This kind of faith, unrestrained by ritual and tradition, became both the virtue and the liability of Christianity American-style.

---

102. Cf. Henry A. Pochmann, *New England Transcendentalism and St. Louis Hegelianism: Phases in the History of American Idealism* (New York: Haskell House, 1970), 63.

103. Ralph Waldo Emerson, "Nature" (1836), in *The Complete Essays,* 36.

For Further Reading

Georg Wilhelm Friedrich Hegel (1770-1831)

Beiser, Frederick C., ed. *The Cambridge Companion to Hegel*. Cambridge: Cambridge University Press, 1993.

Hegel, Georg Wilhelm Friedrich. *The Christian Religion: Lectures on the Philosophy of Religion*. Pt. III, *The Revelatory, Consummate, Absolute Religion*. Edited and translated by Peter C. Hodgson. Missoula: Scholars, 1979.

————. *Early Theological Writings*. Translated by T. M. Knox. Introduction by Richard Kroner. Chicago: University of Chicago Press, 1948.

————. *The Phenomenology of Mind*. Translated by J. B. Baillie. Rev. ed. London: George Allen and Unwin, 1931.

————. *Philosophy of Mind*. Pt. 3 of *The Encyclopaedia of the Philosophical Sciences* (1830). Translated by William Wallace. Foreword by J. N. Findlay. Oxford: Clarendon, 1971.

Pinkard, Terry. *Hegel: A Biography*. Cambridge: Cambridge University Press, 2000.

Singer, Peter. *Hegel*. Oxford: Oxford University Press, 1983.

David Friedrich Strauss (1808-74)

Cromwell, Richard S. *David Friedrich Strauss and His Place in Modern Thought*. Fair Lawn, N.J.: R. E. Burdick, 1974.

Harris, Horton. *David Friedrich Strauss and His Theology*. Cambridge: Cambridge University Press, 1973.

Madges, William. *The Core of Christian Faith: D. F. Strauss and His Catholic Critics*. New York: Peter Lang, 1987.

Strauss, David Friedrich. *The Life of Jesus Critically Examined*. Edited with an introduction by Peter C. Hodgson. Translated from the 4th German edition by George Eliot. Philadelphia: Fortress, 1972.

————. *The Old Faith and the New*. Translated by Mathilde Blind. Introduction and notes by G. A. Wells. Amherst, N.Y.: Prometheus, 1997.

Bruno Bauer (1809-82)

O'Neill, John C. *The Bible's Authority: A Portrait Gallery of Thinkers from Lessing to Bultmann*. Edinburgh: T. & T. Clark, 1991.

Ludwig Feuerbach (1804-72)

Engels, Friedrich. *Ludwig Feuerbach and the Outcome of Classical German Philosophy*. New York: International Publishers, 1934.

Feuerbach, Ludwig. *The Essence of Christianity*. Translated by George Eliot. Buffalo: Prometheus, 1989.

————. *Lectures on the Essence of Religion*. Translated by Ralph Manheim. New York: Harper and Row, 1967.

————. *Thoughts on Death and Immortality: From the Papers of a Thinker, Along with an Appendix of Theological-Satirical Epigrams, Edited by One of His Friends.* Translated with introduction and notes by James A. Massey. Berkeley: University of California Press, 1980.

Harvey, Van A. *Feuerbach and the Interpretation of Religion.* Cambridge: Cambridge University Press, 1995.

Wartofsky, Marx. *Feuerbach.* Cambridge: Cambridge University Press, 1982 [1977].

Karl Marx (1818-83)

Berlin, Isaiah. *Karl Marx: His Life and Environment.* Oxford: Oxford University Press, 1981 [1978].

Carver, Terrell, ed. *The Cambridge Companion to Marx.* Cambridge: Cambridge University Press, 1992.

Marx, Karl. *The Communist Manifesto.* Edited by Frederic L. Bender. New York: Norton, 1988.

———. *Karl Marx: The Essential Writings.* Edited with an introduction by Frederic L. Bender. New York: Harper Torchbook, 1972.

McLellan, David. *Marx.* New York: Penguin Books, 1981 [1975].

Friedrich Engels (1820-95)

Carver, Terrell. *Marx and Engels: The Intellectual Relationship.* Bloomington: Indiana University Press, 1983.

Mager, Gustov. *Friedrich Engels, a Biography.* Translated by Gilbert and Helen Highet. London: Chapman & Hall, 1936.

Marx, Karl, and Friedrich Engels. *On Religion.* Introduction by Reinhold Niebuhr. Chico, Calif.: Scholars, 1982 [1964].

Ferdinand Christian Baur (1792-1860)

Baur, Ferdinand Christian. *On the Writing of Church History.* Edited and translated by Peter Hodgson. New York: Oxford University Press, 1968.

Hodgson, Peter. *The Formation of Historical Theology: A Study of Ferdinand Christian Baur.* New York: Harper and Row, 1966.

Kaufmann, Frank. *Foundations of Modern Church History.* New York: Peter Lang, 1992.

Alois Emanuel Biedermann (1819-85)

Vial, Theodore M. "A. E. Biedermann and the Liturgy Debate in Mid-Nineteenth Century Zurich: A Text Case of the Role of a Christian Theologian." Ph.D. diss., University of Chicago Divinity School, 1994.

———. "A. E. Biedermann's Filial Christology in Its Political Context." *Zeitschrift für Neuere Theologiegeschichte* 3, no. 2 (1996): 203-24.

Welch, Claude, ed. and trans. *God and Incarnation in Mid-Nineteenth Century German Theology: G. Thomasius, I. A. Dorner, A. E. Biedermann.* New York: Oxford University Press, 1965.

Richard Rothe (1799-1867)

Barth, Karl. *Protestant Theology in the Nineteenth Century: Its Background and Its History.* New ed. Grand Rapids: Eerdmans, 2002. Pp. 583-92.

Rothe, Richard. *Sermons for the Christian Year.* Translated from the German. Preface by William C. Clark. Edinburgh: T. & T. Clark, 1877.

———. *Still Hours.* Translated by Jane T. Stoddart. Introductory essay by John MacPherson. London: Hodder and Stoughton, 1886.

Julius Müller (1801-78)

Barth, Karl. *Protestant Theology in the Nineteenth Century: Its Background and Its History.* New ed. Grand Rapids: Eerdmans, 2002. Pp. 574-82.

Müller, Julius. *The Christian Doctrine of Sin.* Translated from the 5th edition by William Urwick. 2 vols. Edinburgh: T. & T. Clark, 1868.

Smith, Henry B., ed. *Analysis and Prooftexts of Dr. Julius Müller's System of Theology.* New York: J. M. Sherwood, 1868.

Isaak August Dorner (1809-84)

Dorner, Isaak A. *Divine Immutability: A Critical Reconsideration.* Translated by Robert W. Williams and Claude Welch. Introduction by Robert W. Williams. Minneapolis: Fortress, 1994.

———. *System of Christian Ethics.* Edited by A. Dorner. Translated by C. M. Mead and R. T. Cunningham. Edinburgh: T. & T. Clark, 1887.

Welch, Claude, ed. and trans. *God and Incarnation in Mid-Nineteenth Century German Theology: G. Thomasius, I. A. Dorner, A. E. Biedermann.* New York: Oxford University Press, 1965.

Søren Aabye Kierkegaard (1813-55)

Bukdahl, Jorgen. *Søren Kierkegaard and the Common Man.* Translated by Bruce Kirmsee. Grand Rapids: Eerdmans, 2001 [1961].

Hannay, Alastair, and Gordon Daniel Marino, eds. *The Cambridge Companion to Kierkegaard.* Cambridge: Cambridge University Press, 1998.

Kierkegaard, Søren. *Concluding Unscientific Postscript to Philosophical Fragments.* Edited and translated with introduction and notes by Howard V. Hong and Edna H. Hong. Princeton: Princeton University Press, 1992.

———. *Kierkegaard's Attack upon "Christendom."* 1854-55. Translated with an introduction by Walter Lowrie. Boston: Beacon Press, 1956.

———. *Training in Christianity and the Edifying Discourse Which "Accompanied" It.* Translated with introduction by Walter Lowrie. Princeton: Princeton University Press, 1952.

Marino, Gordon Daniel. *Kierkegaard in the Present Age.* Marquette Studies in Philosophy Series. Milwaukee: Marquette University Press, 2001.

Ralph Waldo Emerson (1803-82)

Andrews, Barry M. *Emerson as Spiritual Guide: A Companion to Selected Essays for Personal Reflections and Group Discussion.* Boston: Skinner House Books, 2003.

Emerson, Ralph Waldo. *The Complete Essays and Other Writings of Ralph Waldo Emerson.* Edited with a biographical introduction by Brooks Atkinson. New York: Random House Modern Library, 1950.

Grossman, Jay. *Reconstituting the American Renaissance: Emerson, Whitman, and the Politics of Representation.* Durham, N.C.: Duke University Press, 2003.

Richardson, Robert. *Emerson: The Mind on Fire; A Biography.* Berkeley: University of California Press, 1995.

3   A New Kind of Orthodoxy

Orthodoxy, both Reformed and Lutheran, emerged through the increasing confessionalization of the Reformation, for which especially Christology and the sacraments became important. Orthodoxy found its end through the predominance of rationalism and the Enlightenment around the middle of the eighteenth century, when the Bible as the unquestioned authority came under historical scrutiny and Aristotelianism gave way to other ways of philosophical thinking. When we speak about a new kind of orthodoxy, this must be heard in part as a reaction against movements of the nineteenth century, such as left-wing Hegelianism and transcendentalism.

A Conciliatory Christocentricity: Horace Bushnell

Horace Bushnell (1802-76) was born in Bantam, Connecticut, a son of a farmer. Though reared in a Christian home, he did not join the church until he was nineteen. In his youth he even joined an "infidel club," at which point his father intervened. From 1823 to 1827 he went to college at Yale. He then taught school for two years before returning to Yale in 1829 as a tutor to first-year students. Simultaneously he attended law school, passing the bar exam in 1831.[1] That same year Yale was the scene of a powerful religious revival, and many students joined the college church or surrounding churches. After some hesitation,

---

1. Cf. for the following Mary Bushnell Cheney, *Life and Letters of Horace Bushnell* (New York: Harper and Brothers, 1880), 53-55.

Bushnell renewed his religious commitment, which marked a turning point in his life. He abandoned his plans to become a lawyer, and the following year entered Yale Divinity School.[2] After graduating, he served the North Church (Congregational) at Hartford, Connecticut, from 1833 to 1859, after which failing health forced him to retire from active ministry.

During his ministry he had a religious experience in 1838. When it was evident that something unusual had happened to him, his wife asked him: "What have you seen?" He replied: "The gospel."[3] He shared this personal discovery of Christ with his public in a sermon entitled "Christ, the Form of the Soul." Already a year earlier he had written a small book, *Discourses on Christian Nurture*, which was republished in 1867 in a revised and expanded version under the title *Christian Nurture*. Following the biblical advice of Ephesians 6:4 ("Bring them up in the nurture and admonition of the Lord"), Bushnell claimed: "THAT CHILD IS TO GROW UP A CHRISTIAN. In other words, the aim, effort, and expectation should be, not, as is commonly assumed, that the child is to grow up in sin, to be converted after he comes to a mature age, but that he is open on the world as one that is spiritually renewed, not remembering the time when he went through a technical experience, but seeming rather to have loved what is good from his earliest years."[4]

While this was the time of the Second Great Awakening, the first being in the eighteenth century, Bushnell's position did not remain uncontested. The conservatives rallied around the Calvinist Bennet Tyler (1783-1858) and thought this emphasis on Christian education was a very dangerous tendency with respect to inborn depravity and the needful regeneration of everyone. Children, too, needed a conversion. Actually, Bushnell was drawn into several controversies that raged in New England during the first half of the nineteenth century. We encountered one earlier with Ralph Waldo Emerson, who led the more progressive party of the Unitarians, also known as the Transcendentalists, and whose emphasis on self-transcendence was rejected by the old-line Unitarians as infidelity to the Christian faith. Another controversy arose around the liberal Calvinist of the Yale Divinity School, Nathaniel W. Taylor (1786-1858), and Tyler.

Taylor interpreted the insight that human beings are by nature sinful to mean that they are not inherently sinful or corrupt. Their nature only constitutes the occasion or reason for sinning, and they will sin only in certain circumstances. Tyler, on the other hand, claimed with Augustine and Luther that

---

2. Cf. H. Shelton Smith, *Horace Bushnell* (New York: Oxford University Press, 1965), 23, in his introduction. This volume, in addition to the helpful biographical setting in the introduction, contains important selections of Bushnell's writings.

3. Cheney, *Life and Letters*, 192.

4. Horace Bushnell, *Discourses on Christian Nurture*, in Smith, *Horace Bushnell*, 379.

human depravity means that humans cannot help but sin, against which Taylor again countered that this would deny human freedom and would make God the author of our sinful nature. The outcome was that Tyler and other conservatives organized a pastoral union and founded the Connecticut Theological Institute, which later became Hartford Seminary, in opposition to the Yale Divinity School. Then there was the old conflict over the control of Harvard College, which the liberals eventually won. The school was once a foundation of the Puritans, but the weight of the sectarians on Harvard's board of overseers became ever more decisive. To counteract the influence of Harvard, the conservatives founded Andover Theological Seminary in 1808 to educate their future ministers, and Harvard became the seedbed of Unitarianism.

Even Bushnell's own parish was divided, though without diminishing his effectiveness, as he recalled on the occasion of twenty years of ministry at North Church.[5] The reason he was accepted by both sides was what he called "Christian comprehensiveness." He presupposed elements of truth and error on both sides of the controversial issues. In his conciliatory stance he claimed to follow the manner and teachings of Christ, who, as he said, "held his equilibrium, flew into no eccentricities, saved what was valuable in what he destroyed, [and] destroyed nothing where it was desirable rather to fulfill than to destroy. . . . It is by this singular comprehensiveness, in the spirit of Christ, that the grandeur of his life and doctrine is most of all conspicuous."[6] Consequently Bushnell did not take sides between Tyler and Taylor. There was something good and something bad in both of them, and the whole truth was held by neither of them. Bushnell's own conception of human nature was then developed in the light of the strength and weakness of their conflicting convictions.

Bushnell was not simply somewhere in the middle. His life was a life of experiences and growth that he divided into four stages:

1. In 1821 "I was led along to initial experience of God, socially and by force of the blind religional instinct in my nature."[7]
2. In 1831 "I was advanced into the clear moral light of Christ and of God, as related to the principle of rectitude."
3. In 1848 "I was set on by the inward personal discovery of Christ, and of God as represented in him."
4. In 1861 "I lay hold of and appropriate the general culminating fact of

---

5. Cf. Cheney, *Life and Letters,* 280.

6. Horace Bushnell, "Christian Comprehensiveness," in Smith, *Horace Bushnell,* 109.

7. See Cheney, *Life and Letters,* 445, in a letter of Horace Bushnell to his wife (Jan. 29, 1861), for this and the following quotes.

God's vicarious character in goodness, and of mine to be accomplished in Christ as a follower."

Bushnell moved from a religious to a christocentric experience of God. Therefore all his works are christocentric, as we can see from the titles *God in Christ* (1849), *Christ in Theology* (1851), and *Nature and the Supernatural* (1858), a work that revolves around Christ as the center and goal of history. The only theological complaint he heard in his congregation was "that I preached Christ too much, which I cannot think is a fault to be repented of; for Christ is all, and beside him there is no gospel to be preached or received."[8]

With his comprehensiveness as a leading motif, it is therefore not surprising that in 1848 he was invited to speak at the three theological centers of New England: at the Yale annual commencement, where he delivered a speech entitled "The Incarnation (A Discourse on the Divinity of Christ)"; at the Harvard Divinity School to the Unitarians about the work of Christ ("A Discourse on the Atonement"); and at Andover Seminary to the Older Rhetorical Society about religious renewal ("A Discourse on Dogma and Spirit; or, The True Reviving of Religion"). Why could he be received by such varied theological audiences? One of the reasons was his understanding of language. While for physical objects and appearances we use words literally, he contended that for intellectual and moral ideas we can use them only figuratively. They are signs of thoughts to be expressed because religious language expresses feeling and subjectivity, the personal experience of the one who speaks. Therefore religious terms cannot be strictly unambiguous, and one cannot prove religious truth by strict definitions. This cautious skepticism was not an attempt to dispose of any claim to religious knowledge, but to point to the truth behind conflicting forms and also to insist on the interiority of religious knowledge, a knowledge of faith in the heart.

We notice here one of the important sources that influenced Bushnell: German romantic idealism as mediated through Samuel Taylor Coleridge (1772-1834), whose *Aids to Reflection* showed him how it was possible to know God intuitively.[9] Bushnell was not only held up as one of the founding figures of the Christian education movement in America, he was also one of the great historical figures in the life of the Christian church in America, a true mediator and a truly christocentric theologian.[10] He had a vision of the catholicity of the church when he said in his 1848 speech at Andover:

8. Cheney, *Life and Letters,* 286.

9. So Smith, *Horace Bushnell,* 27, in his introduction.

10. Cf. the good assessment of William R. Adamson, *Bushnell Rediscovered* (Philadelphia: United Church Press, 1966), 7.

The Spirit of God is a catholic spirit, and there needs to be a grand catholic reviving, a universal movement, penetrating gradually and quickening into the power of the whole church of Christ on earth. Then and then only, in the spiritual momentum of such a day, when the Spirit of God is breathing inspirations into all believing souls, and working graces in them, that are measured, no longer by the dogmas of sect, but by the breadth of his own character — then, I say, feeling the contact, every man, of a universal fellowship, and rising with the flood that is lifting the whole church into freedom and power, it will be seen what possible heights of attainments — hitherto scarcely imagined — what spiritual completeness and fullness of life the gospel and grace of Christ are able to effect, in our sinful race.[11]

Bushnell's vision of more than 150 years ago still has much to commend itself as a vision and an agenda for the "catholic" church of the future.

Protestant Catholicism: The Mercersburg Theology: Philip Schaff and John Nevin

Philip Schaff, "like nobody else in the 19th century was a bridge-builder between German theology and American Christendom."[12] He was born in Chur, Switzerland; was converted as a fifteen-year-old in Korntal, the center of Württemberg pietism; and studied theology from 1837 to 1842 in Tübingen, Halle, and Berlin. In Tübingen he was influenced by the mediating theology of Dorner and the developmental concept of Baur, in Halle by Tholuck and Müller, and in Berlin by the Lutheran confessionalist Hengstenberg, from whom he received his high-church leanings and the communal idea of evangelical catholicity. These are just a few of the influences he soaked up in his formative years. In 1842 he became Privatdozent (private lecturer) at Berlin. Moreover, on his way to America he spent two months in England learning the English language, and also got acquainted with some of the leaders of the Oxford Movement.

In 1844 the small theological seminary at Mercersburg, a village in Pennsylvania, called the twenty-five-year-old to teach in the German language as professor of church history and biblical exegesis. The other faculty member was John Nevin, who conducted his instruction in English.

11. Horace Bushnell, *God in Christ,* ed. Bruce Kuklick (New York: Garland Reprint, 1987 [1849]), 354.

12. So correctly Klaus Penzel, in his informative article, "Schaff, Philip," in *Theologische Realenzyklopädie,* 30:62.

John Williamson Nevin (1803-86) had been born and raised on his father's farm in Pennsylvania's Cumberland Valley, a stronghold of Scotch-Irish Calvinism.[13] At the age of thirty-seven, in 1840, he was called as professor at the seminary in Mercersburg, which was only fifteen to twenty miles from his birthplace. His father had taught him Latin and Greek, and from 1817 to 1821 he attended Union College in Schenectady, New York, after which he spent two years at home. In the fall of 1823 he enrolled at Princeton Theological Seminary, and while Charles Hodge was on a study leave for two years, he took his position. In 1828 he became a licensed minister, and before leaving Princeton, he had already been selected for the chair of biblical literature in the new Western Theological Seminary being established near Pittsburgh. In 1840 he accepted a call to the faculty of Marshall College and Mercersburg Seminary, both located in Mercersburg. Nevin was professor of theology at Mercersburg till 1851, and from 1841 to 1853 also president of Marshall College. Having been instrumental in the relocation of Marshall College and its merger with Franklin College at Lancaster, he served there from 1861 to 1876, initially as professor and then also as college president.

When Schaff came to Mercersburg, he began his collaboration with Nevin, which resulted "in one of the most unique movements in American religious thought of the mid-nineteenth century."[14] Schaff gave his inaugural address in German before the synod in Reading: "The Principle of Protestantism as Related to the Present State of the Church."[15] He enlarged it into a book, and it was translated by Nevin into English and published a year later. Schaff also provided the synopsis of the book in the form of 112 theses. In this presentation he laid out his concept of church history. According to Schaff, the history of the church is an organic development in which each new stage grows out of and fulfills the preceding stage. Since each era is the legitimate bearer of Christian faith and life, we dare not repudiate any stage of church history, for fear that we would cut ourselves off from the stream of organic church life that is essentially relating us to Jesus. Though each stage has its own way of expressing the Christian faith, it also produces its own malformations. In the present stage of Protestantism, according to Schaff, the church has degenerated into an unchurchly subjectivism whereby emotions replace the sacraments, sound teaching, and discipline. Therefore we should look forward to a higher stage of Christianity in which Protestantism and Catholicism are reconciled to form a "Protestant Catholicism."

13. For Nevin's biography see Richard E. Wentz, *John Williamson Nevin: American Theologian* (New York: Oxford University Press, 1997), 3-8.

14. So Wentz, *John Williamson Nevin*, 5.

15. For the following cf. George H. Bricker, *A Brief History of the Mercersburg Movement* (Lancaster, Pa.: Lancaster Theological Seminary, 1982), 15-16.

Concretely Schaff stated: "2. The main question of *our* time is concerning the nature of the Church itself and its relation to the world and to single Christians. 3. The Church is the Body of Jesus Christ. This expresses her communion with her Head, and also the relation of her members to one another."[16] Coming from his German church experience, he concluded: "8. To the Church belong, in a wider sense, all baptized persons, even though they may have fallen back to the world; in the narrower sense, however, such only as believe in Jesus Christ."[17] Against any kind of revival movement, Schaff contended that the church is much more comprehensive than to encompass just the reborn. For him Protestantism is also larger than the post-Reformation era, because "26. Protestantism runs through the entire history of the Church, and will not cease till she is purged completely from all ungodly elements."[18] Against subjective Christianity he rejected the idea that the Reformation consists "in the absolute emancipation of the Christian life subjectively considered from all Church authority, and the exaltation of private judgment to the papal throne."[19]

Schaff had a strong sense of corporate identity. The church is the body of Christ. In current Protestantism he saw "an undervaluation of the sacraments as objective institutions of the Lord . . . [and] a disproportionate esteem for the service of preaching, with a corresponding sacrifice in the case of the liturgy, the standing objective part of divine worship."[20] He charged current Protestantism with a strong measure of subjectivity, overemphasizing the Word at the expense of the sacrament. As a remedy he called for "*Protestant Catholicism,* or genuine historical progress. This holds equally remote from unchurchly subjectivity and all Romanizing churchism, though it acknowledges and seeks to unite in itself the truth which lies at the ground of both these extremes."[21]

Schaff made it clear that he did not opt for a return to Roman Catholicism. But he was against the relativity and subjectivity of a certain brand of Protestantism. Immediately Schaff was accused of Romanizing tendencies and heresy. He defended himself for five hours at the synod meeting at York, Pennsylvania, in 1845 and was exonerated. Yet the controversy now began in the Reformed church, since following the Second Awakening individualistic piety was extolled and anti–Roman Catholic sentiments were militantly expressed both in political and religious circles.

16. Philip Schaff, *Theses for the Time,* in *The Mercersburg Theology,* ed. James Hastings Nichols (New York: Oxford University Press, 1966), 125.

17. Schaff, *Theses for the Time,* 126.

18. Schaff, *Theses for the Time,* 128.

19. Schaff, *Theses for the Time,* 129 (thesis 36).

20. Schaff, *Theses for the Time,* 132 (theses 63 and 64).

21. Schaff, *Theses for the Time,* 134 (theses 83 and 84).

John Nevin took the same stand as did Schaff when, in 1843, he published *The Anxious Bench*. In this work he warned the church against "new measures" revivalism, where the anxious were invited to occupy the front seats so that at the foot of the cross they could convert from their old ways. Over against this "Methodism," as he called it, he emphasized that in the home, "catechetical instruction in particular will be faithfully employed from the beginning." Furthermore, "the correct administration of the word and sacraments forms of course an essential part of the same system. The ordinances of the sanctuary being of divine institution, are regarded as channels of a power higher than themselves."[22] By pointing to catechetical instruction from the very beginning and to Word and sacraments as means of divine grace, Nevin counteracted the individualistic and subjective tendencies of revivalism in a way similar to what Schaff had done earlier. The introduction by John Stahr to the third edition of *The Anxious Bench* is a succinct summary of the impact of this book:

> The publication of "The Anxious Bench" by Dr. Nevin in the spring of 1843, made an epoch in the history of the Reformed Church in this country. Indeed it proved important not only for the Reformed Church, but for the Lutheran church as well, by its direct influence in bringing the Churches of German origin to a consciousness of the precious inheritance which was theirs by birthright, while at the same time it exerted a most salutary influence indirectly upon the English Churches. It served to emphasize the objective or divine side of Christianity, and to curb or rectify the one-sided emotional tendency which, in those days, swept over the country like a destructive tornado, and in many places laid waste God's heritage.[23]

Since this approach was against the grain of majority sentiment, there was a lot of struggle involved. And for a decade the two Mercersburg professors collaborated vigorously in their literary output as well as in their teaching. They also worked on the liturgy toward church renewal, and in 1857 the *Liturgy* or *Order of Christian Worship* was presented to the Eastern Synod of the German Reformed Church. Schaff was the chairman of the liturgical committee and the chief architect of this work. In a revised version, this then became the *Order of Worship* in 1866. This *Order of Worship* had a lasting influence, and when the United Church of Christ was formed in 1957, of which the German Reformed

---

22. John Nevin, *The Anxious Bench,* introduction by John S. Stahr, 3rd ed. (Reading, Pa.: Daniel Miller, 1892), 119-20.

23. Stahr, introduction to *The Anxious Bench,* iii.

Church had been a predecessor body, its influence was felt again in the new hymnal.

Yet all the controversies weighed heavily on Nevin. He considered leaving his denomination, and tried Anglicanism, but found this was no viable option. Roman Catholicism, too, did not provide a way out.[24] So in 1851 he resigned from his professorship at the seminary and joined Franklin and Marshall College at Lancaster. Schaff was then left alone. After a sabbatical (1853-54) in Germany and teaching as visiting professor at Andover (1862-63), he finally left Mercersburg in 1863 to join Union Theological Seminary in New York as professor. In 1870 he joined the Presbyterian Church. During this period the American churches had been almost entirely captured by the debate over slavery and the Civil War (1861-64), and the Mercersburg theology was quickly forgotten.

Yet Schaff carried on in the larger context of Union Seminary, and no other theological scholar of the nineteenth century rivaled his productivity. He visited Europe no fewer than fourteen times to facilitate the exchange between German and American Protestantism. With the help of an interdenominational circle of co-workers, he translated the Bible commentary of Johann Peter Lange (*A Commentary on the Holy Scriptures: Critical, Doctrinal and Homiletical,* 25 vols., 1864-80) and adjusted it to American needs. This was the first comprehensive English Bible commentary in the United States. In the same manner he treated *Hauck's Realenzyclopädie für Protestantische Theologie und Kirche* (1882-84), which became the *New Schaff-Herzog Encyclopedia of Religious Knowledge* (13 vols., 1908-14). He also attempted to revise the English King James Version in collaboration with a committee of British churches. It did not succeed, but was a precursor of the Revised Standard Version. He edited *The Creeds of Christendom* (3 vols., 1877) and also the *Select Library of the Nicene and Post-Nicene Fathers of the Christian Church* (1st ser., 14 vols., 1886-90; 2nd ser. with Henry Wace, 14 vols., 1890-1900). In 1888 he founded the American Society of Church History, and remained its president until his death. Schaff was also one of the founders of the Reformed World Alliance and a leader in the Evangelical Alliance. He was one of the forerunners of the ecumenical movement. Since World War II, even the ideas of his Mercersburg years to recover the joint Christian heritage have found more and more attention as renewed emphasis on liturgy and a common body of hymns indicates in virtually all the more recent hymnals. Though Schaff was an unprecedented bridge builder between German theology and the United States, he is hardly known anymore in Germany.

---

24. For Nevin's deliberations cf. James Hastings Nichols, *Romanticism in American Theology: Nevin and Schaff at Mercersburg* (Chicago: University of Chicago Press, 1961), esp. 193-98.

The Scripture-Based Calvinist Confessionalism of Princeton Theology: Archibald Alexander, Charles Hodge, A. A. Hodge, B. B. Warfield

American theology in the nineteenth century would be incomplete without reference to the mighty voice from Princeton. Princeton theology is represented by four figures: Archibald Alexander, Charles Hodge, Archibald Alexander Hodge, and Benjamin Breckinridge Warfield. They agreed to a remarkable extent on their conception of the theological task, on the view of Scripture, and on the nature of truth. Of course, they were thoroughly Calvinistic in their outlook.

Archibald Alexander (1772-1851) was born in a log house not far from Lexington, Virginia, to Scotch-Irish parents.[25] He was educated privately by a graduate from Princeton College and ordained as a minister in 1790. After four years of private study and evangelistic endeavors, he became a pastor in Virginia, and later in Philadelphia. When in 1808 Andover Seminary was founded in Massachusetts to train the Congregationalists, Alexander gave a sermon as the retiring moderator at the opening of the General Assembly of the Presbyterian Church in the United States. In it he pushed for seminary education among the Presbyterians. He warned against the dangers of a rational Christianity and enthusiasm, since neither of them will submit to the authority of Scripture. Rational Christianity fails because of its pride in reason, and enthusiasm because it imagines that it is under the direction of a superior guide. He called for the "introduction of suitable men into the ministry" and lamented the deficiency "of well-qualified preachers," all leading up to the necessity of establishing a Presbyterian seminary.[26]

In 1812 the General Assembly authorized the establishment of a single seminary and its location at Princeton. Alexander was elected the first professor of the new seminary, and initially had to teach all theological subjects. Along with the other sciences, he conceived of theology as a science, too, the object of which was "to become acquainted with those truths which relate to the being, character, and works of God, and the relations subsisting between him and his creatures."[27]

25. Cf. James W. Alexander, *The Life of Archibald Alexander* (New York: Charles Scribner, 1854), 8, in the detailed biography of his father.

26. "A Sermon Delivered at the Opening of the General Assembly of the Presbyterian Church in the United States. May 1808," as excerpted in the excellent anthology, *The Princeton Theology: 1812-1921; Scripture, Science, and Theological Method from Archibald Alexander to Benjamin Breckinridge Warfield,* ed. Mark A. Noll (Grand Rapids: Baker, 1983), 54.

27. Archibald Alexander, "Nature and Evidence of Truth" (1812), as excerpted in Noll, *The Princeton Theology,* 62.

In his inaugural address of 1812, Alexander enunciated what was to become the program of Princeton theology: "First, to ascertain that the Scriptures contain the truths of GOD: and secondly, to ascertain what these truths are."[28] Scripture, according to Alexander, is the sufficient and authoritative rule of faith and practice. Yet Princeton theology was never known for a literal inspiration of Scripture. Alexander put emphasis on *"the illumination and assistance of the Holy Spirit,"* which enables one "to discern the beauty and real nature of the truths contained in the revelation already made."[29] Here a distinction was made possible between a literal and a figurative or metaphoric interpretation of scriptural passages.

Alexander, and with him the whole Princeton movement, emphasized a Scottish commonsense philosophy. This approach responsibly used the information provided by the senses, and claimed that the real world could actually be grasped and a valid inference made to a purposeful designer. Alexander contended: "A just and impartial consideration of the universe, cannot fail to lead the sincere seeker of truth to the opinion, that there must exist a great first cause, powerful and intelligent, who has made the world for some particular end. . . . Reason, then, clearly indicates that this universe is not God, but is the work of God, and that he must be a being of transcendent perfection."[30] While reason can also be perverted and come to things like atheism, a correct use of reason leads to the recognition of God in nature. This, however, should not ensue in a natural theology, but rather in a theology of nature that serves to glorify God. "The Bible furnishes the full and satisfactory commentary on the book of nature. . . . The universe, which to the atheist is full of darkness and confusion, to the Christian is resplendent with light and glory." By the time Charles Hodge took over the bulk of theological instruction in 1840, Alexander had trained over a thousand theology students.

Charles Hodge (1797-1878) was born of a father of Irish descent and a mother who was a Huguenot. His father, a major in the revolutionary army, died the year after Charles was born and left his widow in rather limited circumstances at their house in Philadelphia.[31] Of his upbringing Hodge said: "Our early training was religious. Our mother was a Christian. She took us regularly to church, and carefully drilled us in the Westminster Catechism" (13). After some schooling in Pennsylvania, she sent him and his brother to the clas-

---

28. Archibald Alexander, "Inaugural Address" (1812), in Noll, *The Princeton Theology,* 75.

29. Archibald Alexander, "Inaugural Address," 85.

30. See Archibald Alexander, "The Bible. A Key to the Phenomenon of the Natural World" (1829), in Noll, *The Princeton Theology,* 95-96, for this and the following quote.

31. Cf. Archibald Alexander Hodge (son), *The Life of Charles Hodge* (New York: Charles Scribner's, 1880), 8. Page references in the following text are to this work.

sical academy in Somerville, New Jersey, in 1810. In 1812 he entered the Princeton Academy and also listened to Alexander's "inaugural address and watch[ed] the ceremony of investiture" (18). In 1815, when revivalism had come to Princeton, Hodge made a public confession of faith in Christ by joining the Presbyterian Church of Princeton. The same year he also graduated from college. He stayed for a year with his mother in Philadelphia and in 1816 entered Princeton Theological Seminary, which by then had two professors yet no public buildings or libraries.

On May 6, 1819, Dr. Alexander suddenly approached Hodge with the question: "How would you like to be a professor in the Seminary?" (65). This was the same year that Hodge graduated from seminary. Naturally the question both flattered him and made him anxious. He had acquired some knowledge in Hebrew and other fields in which he felt not well equipped, and in 1821 the General Assembly passed the resolution to hire him "as a teacher of the original languages of Scripture in the Seminary" and stipulated that he be paid no more than $400 per year (84). The same year he was also ordained. The following year he was called to a professorship of Oriental and biblical literature, and his salary was raised to $1,000 per year.

In 1826 Hodge requested and was granted a leave of absence "for eighteen months or two years for the purpose of visiting Europe and pursuing certain select branches of study, with the peculiar aids which the best institutions in that quarter of the globe can alone furnish" (102).[32] With the approval of the board he left, and John Nevin, who had just graduated, was appointed his substitute. Hodge visited primarily Halle and Berlin. In Halle he struck up a friendship with Tholuck that lasted as long as Tholuck lived. In Berlin he became friends of the brothers Ludwig (1795-1877) and Otto von Gerlach (1801-49) and their pietistic circle. He also met Baron Hans Ernst von Kottwitz (1757-1843), who impressed him as well as the others for whom "confessional differences constituted no barrier to the communion in love and work for the kingdom of God; in the joy and custom of what is common, the idea of a union of believers out of all churches could arise" (150). He also heard Schleiermacher preach in Berlin. He later remarked: "The sermon was peculiar. The words were Biblical, but their whole tenor so general, the ideas so vague and indefinite, that it was impossible for me to understand exactly what he meant" (152).

The impressions Hodge gathered in Halle and Berlin made a lasting impact on him and confirmed him in his own outlook. The Princeton method became narrowly confessionalist, and it was clear that Schleiermacher would have

---

32. From a letter of A. Alexander and Samuel Miller, the other faculty member, to the meeting of the board of directors.

no chance there. In his three-volume *Systematic Theology* (1872-73) Hodge claimed, very much like Alexander, that theology is a science. "The Bible contains the truths which the theologian has to collect, authenticate, arrange, and exhibit in their internal relation to each other."[33] "The Bible is to a theologian what nature is to the man of science. It is his store-house of facts. . . . The duty of the Christian theologian is to ascertain, collect, and combine all the facts which God has revealed concerning himself and our relation to Him."[34] But Hodge did not engage in biblicist proof texting because, as he learned from Augustine and the Reformers, especially Calvin, "the question is not first and mainly, What is true to the understanding, but what is true to the renewed heart?"[35] We must "subject our feeble reason to the mind of God as revealed in his Word, and by his Spirit in our inner life." This implies not just the internal testimony of the Spirit, but also an existential acknowledgment and assent through the guidance of the Spirit.

Throughout his life Hodge was a tireless defender of biblical truth. For that reason he lashed out against Darwinism, since he was convinced that Darwinism would lead to atheism. And he chided Nevin for his approval of Schleiermacher and German idealism and for finding some good in Roman Catholicism.[36] Then he scolded Finney for assuming contested points of doctrine as axioms from which Finney deduced his theological conclusions. He observed that Bushnell did not emphasize strongly enough human depravity. Hodge also established himself as a writer of popular theology and an active commentator on church affairs, yet he was always fair to both sides. As Charles P. Krauth (1823-83), professor of theology at the Lutheran Theological Seminary in Philadelphia, said of Hodge's *Systematic Theology:* "It is a marked feature in Dr. Hodge's book that it does unusual justice to the relative importance of Lutheran theology. . . . But . . . he is also fair. Mistakes he has made, and very important ones; but designed misrepresentations he has never made. Next to having Dr. Hodge on one's side, is the pleasure of having him as an antagonist."[37] Hodge was not just a teacher and a scholar, he also was an institution. "The celebration of the fiftieth year of his professorship in 1872 was without precedent in American academic life. Even the shops in Princeton closed on this day to honor a patriarch, a theologian, and a teacher of more than three thousand ministerial students."[38]

33. Charles Hodge, *Systematic Theology,* 3 vols. (Grand Rapids: Eerdmans, 1981), 1:1.

34. Charles Hodge, *Systematic Theology,* 1:10-11.

35. See Charles Hodge, *Systematic Theology,* 1:16, for this and the following quote.

36. For the following cf. Noll, *The Princeton Theology,* 155-56, 175, 183.

37. A. A. Hodge, *Life of Charles Hodge,* 616.

38. So David F. Wells, in *The Princeton Theology,* ed. David F. Wells (Grand Rapids: Baker,

Archibald Alexander Hodge (1823-86) was the oldest son of Charles Hodge and his wife Sarah. He graduated from Princeton College in 1841 and from the seminary there in 1847. Then he went to India for missionary service but returned after just three years because of ill health.[39] Subsequently he served for fourteen years as a pastor in Maryland, Virginia, and Pennsylvania, and was known for his gift of popular theological exposition. In 1864 he was called as professor of systematic theology to Western Theological Seminary in Allegheny, Pennsylvania. For most of his time there he served concurrently as a pastor of a local congregation. In 1877 he was called to be his father's associate in didactic and polemic theology, and after his father's death he occupied his chair for another seven years.

Among his books are a *Commentary on the Confessional Faith* (1869) and *Popular Lectures on Theological Themes* (1887). His *Outlines of Theology* (1860) was long used as a textbook, and shows his indebtedness to his father while also betraying his own clear analytical and dogmatic thinking. For his last six years, he served as coeditor of the *Presbyterian Review,* a journal specifically designed to hold together the progressive and conservative wings of American Presbyterianism. His fellow editor was the more liberal Charles Briggs (1841-1913), professor of biblical theology at Union Theological Seminary in New York.

Benjamin Breckinridge Warfield (1851-1922) was born near Lexington, Kentucky, his father being a horse and cattle breeder. He was privately educated before entering Princeton College in 1868, from which he graduated in 1871. After a year of traveling in Europe, he became the livestock editor of the *Farmer's Home Journal,* and in 1873, to the surprise of his friends, entered Princeton Theological Seminary with the plan to become a pastor. Upon graduation in 1876, he studied at the University of Leipzig, then served as assistant minister in Baltimore, then in 1879 became professor at Western Theological Seminary at Pittsburgh. In 1887 he was called to be professor of theology at Princeton, to succeed Archibald Hodge.

Warfield wrote an immense number of articles, reviews, and monographs, both of the popular and scholarly type, and was precise, careful, and wide-ranging in his scholarship. He observed that Charles Hodge, his own teacher, was a great teacher of Scripture, but nevertheless showed little interest in exegetical technicalities.[40] In contrast, Warfield covered New Testament criti-

1989), 39. Actually, the number of students was 2,082. The figure of 3,000 students includes those who studied under him as professor of Oriental and biblical literature (so Noll, *The Princeton Theology*, 19).

39. According to Noll, *The Princeton Theology*, 15.

40. According to Noll, *The Princeton Theology*, 15.

cism and interpretation, patristics, and theology, especially of the Reformed type, and also church history. He was a lively teacher, enjoyed controversy, and was influential on generations of students. Thereby he shaped the thought of the Presbyterian church and of other denominations. His most important articles from periodicals and encyclopedias were published in ten volumes, and he wrote books on a range of topics, such as *An Introduction to the Textual Criticism of the New Testament* (1886) and *The Plan of Salvation* (1915). Yet with the rise of Princeton University and the increasing specialization of knowledge, his influence was more confined to theology proper. With his death the great years of Princeton theology came to a conclusion.

God's Love in Christ — the Key to Social Engagement: F. D. Maurice

Frederick Denison Maurice (1805-72), one of the most independent British theologians of the nineteenth century, is the founder of Christian Socialism in England and has been called "the father of modern English theology."[41] He was born the son of a Unitarian pastor in Normanston, Suffolk County, and started his academic training in 1823 at Trinity College, Cambridge. Two years later he changed to Trinity Hall to study law. In 1827 he left the university without an academic degree, because as a Unitarian he could not consent to the confession of the Thirty-nine Articles (1562) of the Church of England, mandatory at the time to obtain an academic degree. Thereupon he moved to London to write for literary journals. Having had a feeling of dissatisfaction with Unitarianism since boyhood, he was rebaptized in 1830 and joined the Church of England.[42] The same year he entered Exeter College at Oxford to study for the ministry. He was ordained in 1834. His first charge was a country curacy in Bobbenhall, Warwickshire, where — now no longer a Unitarian — he wrote *Subscription to No Bondage,* in which he defended the subscription to the Thirty-nine Articles as a requirement at the universities. It is not surprising that this book was praised highly by the members of the Oxford Movement. Yet this praise did not last long.

In 1836 he was called to become chaplain of Guy's Hospital in the Southwark slums of London. There he wrote his theological masterpiece, *The Kingdom of Christ* (1838). It opened with an introductory dialogue with a

41. So C. S. Carpenter, as quoted in W. Merlin Davies, *An Introduction to F. D. Maurice's Theology* (London: SPCK, 1964), ix-x. For more on his social involvement, see chap. 6 below.

42. For a good biographical summary on Frederick Denison Maurice, cf. the introduction by John F. Porter and William J. Wolf in *Toward the Recovery of Unity: The Thought of Frederick Denison Maurice* (New York: Seabury Press, 1964), 5-19.

Quaker, then discussed the principles of the Quakers and the different religious groups that had arisen since the Reformation, such as Lutherans, Calvinists, Zwinglians, Arminians, Unitarians, Anglicans, and Catholics. The reason why there are so many factions, Maurice explained, is "that they set up theories and systems based upon private judgments and individual conceits, when they are professing by some way or other to lead us on to permanent truths which belong to all and are necessary for all; they create new divisions by the very efforts which they make to promote unity; they invent lines and landmarks of their own, but the grand everlasting distinctions which God has established escape them altogether."[43] We notice here Maurice's distaste for theories and systems that are more often humanly induced than divinely inspired.

Soon Maurice was appointed professor of English literature and modern history at King's College in London, and in 1846 he received the chair of divinity in its newly established theological college. Already the year before, the archbishop of Canterbury invited Maurice to give the Warburton Lectures. There he replied to John Henry Newman and his *Essay on the Development of Christian Doctrine* by denying that with Newman's development theory an infallible authority for the contemporary church had been established. For Maurice the historical actuality of Christ and the abiding presence of his spirit in the entire Christian community was more important than any divinely guided development.

While in London, Maurice also impacted Christian Socialism. A group of young men gathered around him for weekly Bible study. As social involvement was highly controversial, Maurice saw the conflict coming up with "unsocial Christians and the unchristian Socialists" and published *Tracts on Christian Socialism*.[44] Yet his cooperation with John M. Ludlow (1821-1912), an English social critic and a representative of the Christian Socialists, and the workers movement soon came to an end. Maurice was not interested in social revolution but in the regeneration of English society by reasserting its foundation in Christ. To that aim in 1855 he founded the Working Men's College in Red Lion's Square in London, an educational institution for the working class. Before that he had already been instrumental in founding Queen's College in London in 1848, first as a school for governesses, but then as a pioneering agency for the higher education of women. Maurice was its principal from 1848 to 1854.

Why was Maurice so concerned about the practical aspects of the Chris-

43. Frederick Denison Maurice, *The Kingdom of Christ or Hints on the Principles, Ordinances, and Constitution of the Catholic Church: In Letters to a Member of the Society of Friends* (London: J. M. Dent, 1907), 1:40.

44. *The Life of Frederick Denison Maurice Chiefly Told in His Own Letters,* 2nd ed. (London: Macmillan, 1884), 2:35.

tian faith? For Maurice the proposition from which all others start is the biblical assertion: "God is light and in him there is no darkness at all" (1 John 1:5). "That demonstration in a Son leads on to the next proposition, that this divine light is not merely hidden inaccessible light; that it has shone out in a Person Who makes us understand what He is by doing human acts and bearing human sorrows. And so we arrive at the third proposition, that the highest end of man's existence is to have fellowship with this Life and Light. And then a fourth . . . that fellowship or communion with each other is implied in this fellowship or communion with God and with His Son."[45] Maurice received his impetus for Christian ethics from the light God has brought into the world through Jesus Christ and that through us should shine into the world.

Not everybody was enthused about Maurice's social involvement. In 1853 he published his *Theological Essays* with a concluding essay entitled "On Eternal Life and Eternal Death." There he criticized the popular equation of eternity with endlessness in reference to future punishment. He wrote: "I am obliged to believe in an abyss of love which is deeper than the abyss of death: I dare not lose faith in that love. I sink into death, eternal death, if I do. I must feel that this love is compassing the universe. More about it I cannot know. But God knows. I leave myself and all to Him."[46] When the conservatives objected to such seeming universalism, the council of King's College decided that these statements "are of dangerous tendency, and calculated to unsettle the minds of the theological students of King's College," and discontinued his tenure.[47] The council had found an easy way to get rid of an incisive yet controversial theological mind.

In 1860 Maurice was appointed to St. Peter's at Vere Street in London, and in 1866 he became Knightbridge Professor of Moral Theology and Moral Philosophy at Cambridge. For Maurice himself it was most important that he was able "to connect Church Reformation with social Reformation — to have all one's thought[s] tested by their application to actual work and by their power of meeting the wants of suffering, discontented, resolute men."[48] Yet it would be wrong to consider him simply a theologian striving for social betterment. In the deepest sense he was a trinitarian, Christ-centered theologian. In this regard he wrote: "All the personal feelings and faith of man are unsafe, unless they rest upon the ground of a universal atonement. Unless each man feels himself to be a member of a body, reconciled and united to God, in Christ, he has no clear

45. F. D. Maurice, *Reconstructing Christian Ethics: Selected Writings,* ed. Ellen K. Wondra (Louisville: Westminster John Knox, 1995), 53.

46. Frederick Denison Maurice, *Theological Essays,* edited and introduction by Edward F. Carpenter (New York: Harper, 1957), 323.

47. *The Life,* 2:191.

48. *The Life,* 2:8, at the occasion of his forty-fourth birthday.

and definite indications of his own relation to Christ: his mind will be continually fluctuating and disturbed. On the other hand, unless this belief of an atonement rests upon the faith of a Trinity, it is unmeaning and baseless."[49] It is not social involvement that saves us, it is not history that saves us, but God in Christ made manifest through the Holy Spirit.

There was an inner consistency to Maurice's theology: God has shown us his love through Jesus Christ. But in the England of the mid–nineteenth century, Maurice witnessed the tremendous contradiction of the height of Great Britain's material wealth and physical expansion and, at the same time, the bitter evils of early ruthless industrialism. This was coupled with an atmosphere of comfortable respectability and pious virtue that we associate with the Victorian age. Maurice noticed the cracks in this Victorian society spiritually, theologically, and ethically, and strove to remedy the situation.[50] He felt compelled to carry to others God's love shown to us, and for that reason dedicated his life to the socially disadvantaged. Small wonder that as a challenger of the status quo, he received more criticism than praise in his lifetime.

The Dutch Struggle with Modernity

From Modernism to Confessionalism

We now move to the Continent, and first look briefly to the Netherlands, where the so-called Groningen School was started by **Herman Muntinghe** (1752-1824), professor and *rector magnificus* of Groningen University (1811-16).[51] This theological movement was an attempt to bridge the gap between the gospel and post-Enlightenment thought. It did so by emphasizing the moral life at the expense of dogma. The doctrines of original sin and atonement were rejected, and God's revelation in Jesus Christ was understood as a means to develop a Christian personality. Important are the person, work, and example of Christ. Christ is subordinated to God, and not human and divine at the same time. In his heavenly and his earthly life, he has only one nature, namely, the divine or spiritual nature, which is possessed by both God and humanity. In Jesus Christ, God has given us his revelation so that we might become more and more like him. This kind of thinking was especially advanced through the student of

49. Maurice, *Reconstructing Christian Ethics*, 6.

50. Cf. Olive J. Brose, *Frederick Denison Maurice: Rebellious Conformist* (Athens: Ohio University Press, 1971), xiv, who points to the societal context of Maurice's work.

51. Cf. for the following Willem Nijenhuis, "Groningen," and Cornelis Augustijn, "Niederlande," both in *Theologische Realenzyklopädie*, 14:265 and 24:488-89, respectively.

Muntinghe, Petrus Hofstede de Groot (1802-86), together with his colleagues Joan Frederick van Oordt (1856-1918) and Lodewijk Louis Gerlach Pareau (1800-1866). Though the Groningen School paved the way for modern theology, in the judgment of many it did not go far enough, neither toward modern tendencies nor toward older Reformed principles, such as the emphasis on God's covenant and predestination.

Johannes Henricus Scholten (1811-85) showed a different way.[52] He first taught at the academy at Franeker. When it was closed in 1843, he taught at Leiden. Influenced by the Swiss mediating theologian Alexander Schweizer (1808-88) and his two-volume *Doctrine of the Evangelical Reformed Church* (*Die Glaubenslehre der evangelisch-reformierten Kirche*, 2 vols., 1844-47), Scholten endeavored to show that the thinking of the Reformers, more specifically of the Reformed confession, found its fulfillment in idealistic thought. The internal witness of the Holy Spirit does not refer to the historical content of the Bible, but to its religious content. This witness is also the highest and purest form of the natural knowledge of God. This means that Scripture is no longer the sole authority. Nevertheless, he staunchly defended Calvinistic determinism in claiming the absolute sovereignty of God over against the world. This sovereignty comes most clearly to the fore in the proclamation of Jesus. It shows that in a long process God has stirred humanity to abandon its animal-like sensuality, meaning sin, and follow the true moral and reasonable nature, i.e., life in God. Thereby humanity attains freedom and humanness. Scholten's highly idealistic thinking impressed many in the Reformed church, since they felt it was a modern and reasonable approach to the gospel, so much so that he can be considered the father of modernism.

There was another attractive proponent of modernism, the lawyer and philosopher **Cornelis Willem Opzoomer** (1821-92), who already at age twenty-five was called to the chair of philosophy at the University of Utrecht. He was less attracted to idealistic speculation than Scholten and emphasized more empiricism. We see that reality is determined materialistically by the laws of nature. Therefore experience and science are atheistic. Yet there is another way of experience and knowledge, namely, by feeling in an aesthetic, ethical, and religious way. Religious feeling points us immediately to the existence of God, as does the observation of the world through our senses. Through this feeling we become aware not only of God's existence, but also of the purposiveness of the

---

52. For the following cf. the extensive treatment of Dutch theology by Hendrikus Berkhof, *Two Hundred Years of Theology: Report of a Personal Journey* (Grand Rapids: Eerdmans, 1989), 97-114, and Hans Schwarz, "European Theology (Modern Period)," in *Encyclopedia of Christianity*, 2:199-200.

world, its infinite development, and the relative and even subjective appearance of sin. Recognizing God as the most perfect spirit cannot be disassociated from the concept of God as perfect wisdom and love. It follows that his kingdom must extend over the whole world so that our existence cannot end with our bodily death. The shadow of Kant's *Critique of Practical Reason* seems to loom behind Opzoomer's thinking. Though Scholten and Opzoomer polemicized each other, the idealism of the one and the realism of the other were in their content not as far apart as they thought. Scholten, in his later works, even adopted some of Opzoomer's empirical emphases.

Next to Scholten and Opzoomer, we must mention the Mennonite **Sytze Hoekstra** (1822-98), professor at the City University of Amsterdam who used Kantian insights for his transcendental a prioristic method. He combined this approach with concepts of developmental psychology to show that in the interpretation of human personality there is room for religion, including the beliefs in sin, penance, grace, and conversion, and also for a personal God and humanity's relation to him. Much of what Hoekstra proposed was later more convincingly developed by Albrecht Ritschl and Wilhelm Herrmann.

Once modernism was on the decline, a mediating alternative developed especially through **Daniel Chantepie de la Saussaye** (1818-74), the father of the famous historian of religion Pierre Daniel Chantepie de la Saussaye (1848-1920), who became a representative of a so-called ethical theology. This term is derived from the emphasis on the ethical character of truth through which Christianity and culture should enter into dialogue. Chantepie stood in direct opposition to Scholten. For him the term "ethical" was not derived from the Greek *ethos,* meaning morals, but meant "mind-set" or "feeling." According to him, God's revelation was the answer to the deepest longing and striving of humanity. Humanity has a feeling of duty and an awareness of the split between what is and what ought to be, a split that does not allow humanity to come to rest. Only Jesus Christ, the mediator between God and humanity, reconciles what is with what ought to be and overcomes this existential anguish. One can discern in his thoughts the influence of both Kant and Schleiermacher. Yet Schleiermacher was too subjectivistic and individualistic for him and Kant too moralistic, so that he would have followed neither of them wholeheartedly. A late exponent of that kind of ethical turn is the phenomenologist of religion Gerardus van der Leeuw (1890-1950), who after World War II served as state secretary for cultic affairs.[53]

---

53. Cf. Åke V. Ström, "Leeuw, Gerhardus van der," in *Theologische Realenzyklopädie,* 20:600-603, who points out his dependence on Nathan Söderblom, and his emphasis on modesty and the service function of theology.

While a mediating type of theology seemed to be the answer to both orthodoxy and modernism, many people did not feel represented by that movement. Therefore the pendulum swung back all the way to a neoconfessional theology whose two important representatives are **Abraham Kuyper** (1837-1920) and **Herman Bavinck** (1854-1921). Kuyper was an enthusiastic student of Scholten at Leiden. He was impressed by Scholten's knowledge of Reformed theology and his intention to bring it on par with the modern times through a new kind of interpretation. Yet as a young pastor he discovered that for the pietistic Calvinistic circles in his church, the Reformed confessions had a very different existential meaning than they had for him and Scholten. So he experienced a spiritual crisis and a rebirth to a renewed appreciation of the Reformed tradition. In this process he tried to reform and reorganize the Reformed church, but his social involvement did not allow him to espouse a repristinating theology that usually eschews such involvement. In 1874 he became a representative of the antirevolutionary party, and from 1880 to 1901 he was professor of dogmatics in the Free University of Amsterdam, which he had founded in 1880. Finally, till 1905 he served as prime minister of the Netherlands. He stood for the ultimate authority of the Bible and a confessional Christianity of "strict Calvinist persuasion (including predestination)."[54] He even attempted to claim the rule of Christ for so-called secular areas, such as school, politics, and science. "No single piece of our mental world is to be hermetically sealed off from the rest, and there is not a square inch in the whole domain of our human existence over which Christ, who is Sovereign of *all,* does not cry: 'Mine!'"[55] This statement from the inaugural address at the Free University in 1880 sums up well Kuyper's theological thrust. Needless to say, his influence was deeply felt in the Dutch immigrant communities of the United States and South Africa.

The other confessional giant was Herman Bavinck, professor of dogmatics and apologetics at the Free University. He came under Kuyper's influence, who tried to wean him away from the ethical theology to which he had been attracted. He finally won Bavinck as his successor at the Free University in 1902, after he had twice declined to leave his professorship in dogmatics at the Theological School of Kampen.[56] Bavinck did not want to return to the sixteenth or

54. B. Steinseifer, "Kuyper, Abraham," in *Evangelisches Lexikon für Theologie und Gemeinde,* 2:1203.

55. Abraham Kuyper, "Sphere Sovereignty," in Abraham Kuyper, *A Centennial Reader,* ed. James D. Bratt (Grand Rapids: Eerdmans, 1998), 488. In this publication Bratt also provides a good introduction to the life and work of Kuyper (1-16).

56. So Henry Zylstra, preface to *Our Reasonable Faith,* by Herman Bavinck, trans. Henry Zylstra (Grand Rapids: Eerdmans, 1956), 6, where he provides a succinct summary of Bavinck's life and work (5-11).

seventeenth century, but was searching for an alternative to modernism and a mediating theology. Similar to Barth, he was not concerned with apologetics, but with theology's most central subject. He therefore wrote a four-volume *Reformed Dogmatics* (1885-1902; Eng. trans. 2003-), which is still considered a treasure chest "of information and insight."[57] As the objective principle of knowledge, Scripture provides an objective revelation through the Holy Spirit. The subjective principle is faith, or rather the testimony of the Holy Spirit, which makes us certain that we are children of God and that Scripture is divine. A one-volume summary of his dogmatics (1909) was translated into English (*Our Reasonable Faith,* 1956) and is still a primer of Reformed doctrine. In Bavinck we discern neo-Thomistic thinking. This means that for him faith is intellectual assent, subjecting oneself to Scripture, rather than dedicating one's life to Christ or to a personal God. Gerrit Cornelis Berkouwer (1903-96) led back to the antischolastic traits in Bavinck's theology, and produced a set of books on dogmatic loci that are all translated into English.

A Biblical Radicalism: Hermann Friedrich Kohlbrügge

A rather solitary but influential figure is **Hermann Friedrich Kohlbrügge** (1803-75), who, Karl Barth complained in his *Protestant Theology in the Nineteenth Century,* "is not even mentioned by name in any of the books on the history of theology known to me."[58] Kohlbrügge was born in Amsterdam and descended on his father's side from a German Lutheran family, although his mother tongue was Dutch. His father owned a soap factory in which he worked in his youth. He attended school in Amsterdam and was well versed in Oriental languages and Greek and Latin literature. He began studying theology in 1823, and at his father's deathbed promised to become a doctor of theology. In 1826 he became auxiliary preacher of the Lutheran congregation in Amsterdam. After only three months he was dismissed, having gotten in trouble with the rationalistic-minded head pastor and the consistory. Kohlbrügge had defended the doctrine of justification and other Christian teachings in a way that they felt was not in tune with the times. After this dismissal he worked on his dissertation for the University of Utrecht, where he obtained his doctorate in 1829, even though the faculty deemed his thesis on Psalm 45 too christocentric. The same year he was married by a judge to a rather wealthy lady, Catharina Luise Engelbert (1808-34),

---

57. So Berkhof, *Two Hundred Years,* 112.

58. Karl Barth, *Protestant Theology in the Nineteenth Century: Its Background and History,* new ed. (Grand Rapids: Eerdmans, 2002), 620.

which made him financially independent. A church wedding was precluded since no pastor wanted to marry a person who stood so much against the theological trends of his time.[59] This estranged him even more from his church, and he turned to the teachings of Calvin, and in 1830 applied to join the Reformed church at Utrecht. However, this congregation requested an endorsement by his own Lutheran congregation, which was rejected.

After the death of his wife, Kohlbrügge went to the area of Wuppertal for health reasons. This region belonged to Prussia and therefore was affected by the union between the Lutherans and the Reformed decreed by King Frederick William III in 1817 to overcome the division of Protestantism. This forced union left many unhappy, and those who wanted to hold on to their Reformed faith sought to win Kohlbrügge as their pastor. Yet this appointment was thwarted by the government, and Kohlbrügge returned to Utrecht, where he taught privately for ten years. By then, King Frederick William IV had ascended to the throne, and in 1847 he allowed the formation of new religious denominations. Immediately the opponents of the union at Elberfeld near Wuppertal formed an independent congregation, the Dutch Reformed Church at Elberfeld, which still exists today. This new congregation was independent of the union and of the state, and called Kohlbrügge as its pastor. He served there until his death.

His congregation stayed in the tradition of the old Reformed church, yet it did not simply return to the old times. Decisive for Kohlbrügge was not repristination, but enfleshing the gospel. Faith was directed toward union with Christ, and therefore repentance, conversion, and sanctification were important. Rebirth is a subjective experience of communion with Christ. Christ's kingdom is already present and God's will occurs in the elect. With this kind of New Testament radicalism, it is clear that Kohlbrügge, together with the presbytery, also checked the purity of life of the members through visitation. If necessary, they took disciplinary actions, even to the extent of expelling those who opposed this style of life.

Barth saw in Kohlbrügge's approach a return to the radicalism of the Reformers, asserting that "the work of Christ and of the Holy Spirit can be detected in man and that Christianity is essentially to be understood from this ascertainable divine working."[60] Barth notices, however, that Kohlbrügge underestimated our still-broken existence as a life in the world but not from it. While he applauded Kohlbrügge's belief that the Bible was "completely and ut-

59. For this and the following cf. the excellent biographical synopsis by Heiner Faulenbach, "Kohlbrügge, Hermann Friedrich," in *Theologische Realenzyklopädie*, 19:356.

60. Barth, *Protestant Theology*, 626-27 and 628, respectively, for this and the following quote.

terly God's work," he saw that this kind of biblicism made him capable of doing violence to the Bible, forgetting that the Bible is God's work in earthen vessels. Yet in the 1930s, when the freedom of the church and of the confession to Jesus Christ was endangered by German National Socialism, Kohlbrügge was rediscovered. At the centennial of his death in 1975, a one-week symposium was conducted at Wuppertal. His influence, though mainly confined to his congregation, was also felt through his printed sermons in Germany, the Netherlands, Great Britain, France, and even America.

Returning to the Biblical Legacy in Germany

In Germany we encounter two different branches of a new kind of orthodoxy that emerged in confrontation with theologians influenced by Schleiermacher and Hegel. One branch was a new confessionalism. The other showed a renewed focus on the Bible as its sole basis of theology, and therefore often turned against both confessionalism and any kind of mediating or liberal theology.

Scripture as the Norm: Johann Tobias Beck

The main proponent of this Bible-focused renewal was **Johann Tobias Beck** (1804-78), who was born in Balingen, Württemberg, as the son of a soap manufacturer. His father was reluctant to agree with his son's desire to become a pastor, but his mother was well versed in the Bible and reflected the earlier Württemberg pietism. At age fourteen he went to the minor seminary in Urach (1818-22), and then he stayed at the *Stift* in Tübingen to study at the theological faculty of the university, "for the most part without even hearing the professors there, much less accepting anything from them."[61] This already indicated a notable trait in him, a strong sense of independence. After his exams in 1827, he received a pastorate in a farming village. When he disagreed with the congregation about his deliveries of wood — pastors at that time were paid partly in goods — he left after only two years and became city pastor and director of the *Gymnasium* at Bad Mergentheim (1829-36).

In 1836 Beck received an associate professorship at the theological faculty in Basel at the recommendation of F. C. Baur. He was called and paid by a pietistic organization, the Society for the Furthering of the Knowledge of Christian Theology and Christian Life. Its members wanted an alternative to the critical

---

61. So according to Barth, *Protestant Theology,* 602.

biblical scholar Wilhelm Leberecht De Wette (1780-1849), who taught at the same faculty. But Beck enjoyed a good relationship with De Wette. While initially Beck was happily received by the pietists, he got in trouble with the lay administration of the Basel Mission Society in 1838 when he preached the mission festival sermon. In his sermon he criticized pious activism, since the kingdom of God does not come with outward signs. Furthermore, he emphasized that one should not be concerned about the souls of other people without applying to oneself the chastising power of the word of God. Finally he implied that the students at the mission seminary were not allowed to exercise their right to a free decision of conscience, something Scripture certainly allows everyone. Beck was not opposed to mission, quite the contrary, but he was against activism both of the pietistic and the confessionalistic type. He also upheld the norm of Scripture above everything else.[62] While in Basel Beck wrote his most important works, such as *Introduction to the System of Christian Doctrine or Propaedeutic Development of the Christian Teachings: An Investigation* (*Einleitung in das System der christlichen Lehre oder propädeutische Entwicklung der christlichen Lehrwissenschaft. Ein Versuch*, 1837); *Fragments of the Christian Doctrine of Morals* (*Bruchstücke aus der christlichen Sittenlehre*, 1839); *The Christian Teachings according to the Biblical Documents: An Investigation* (*Die christliche Lehrwissenschaft nach den biblischen Urkunden. Ein Versuch*, 1842).

In 1843 Beck was called to the chair of dogmatics at Tübingen, again upon the recommendation of Baur, and at the same time was appointed preacher of the early service, meaning the main service, at the *Stift* church. Beck became the main attraction of the theological faculty and one of the most successful theology professors in Germany at the time. Students came in droves from as far away as Scotland and Scandinavia, and of course from neighboring Switzerland. Tübingen became one of the most attractive places to study theology in Germany. Almost all of Beck's lectures and sermons appeared in print. Barth mentions four items that made him so attractive:

1. The unshakable, wrathfully strict *fear of God* and the honesty which was the essence of his being and which expressed itself in a combination of New Testament religion and Old Testament ethics, an incomparable certainty of himself and his subject . . .
2. The supreme independence from both revolutionary and reactionary methods in theology . . .

62. For details of his criticism at the festival, see Geert Sentzke, *Die Theologie Johann Tobias Becks und ihr Einfluß in Finnland*, vol. 1, *Die Theologie Johann Tobias Becks* (Helsinki, 1949), 40, who provides an excellent introduction to Beck and his theology.

3. The marvellous coherence of a pattern of thought in which he himself was both confessor and professor . . .

4. Last and not least . . . the peppery yet enlivening polemic.[63]

For Beck the Bible was the only object of his scholarly pursuit. There is no knowledge of God that goes beyond what we find in Scripture. Therefore ecclesial confessions were secondary for him, because he wanted to deduce the whole system of the Christian faith from Scripture alone. He objected to a confessional theology, arguing that it makes the confessions decide the content of Scripture. Beck was convinced that the Christian doctrine as reflected in the Bible is an "articulated sum of doctrine, a coherent whole of internally correlated teachings, a system."[64] "Our task consists in presenting the Christian doctrine according to Holy Scripture in such a way that we trace it [i.e., the Christian doctrine] in its own principles and basic concepts and then attempt to render this doctrine in its ensuing organism."[65] The duty of a theologian is to show this kind of coherence by unfolding a biblical theology of history.

While again Beck saw God's activity as focused on the whole cosmos, humanity occupies a privileged position in God's plan of creation and salvation. Nevertheless, nature and humanity form a coherent organism. Human sin spoils the whole of creation, and therefore the whole cosmos needs to be redeemed and glorified. Yet Beck's theology is also eschatologically oriented, since the eschaton is the goal of the whole system. But his theology is christocentric too, since "Christ must stand at the pinnacle of the system, and emerge as the foundation of the whole truth which the system represents."[66] God acts in and through the logos, and this logos is not only the creator but also the one that encompasses the creation to the glory of God.

With his heavy emphasis on the Bible, Beck was not a literalist, but noted a difference between the inspiration of the prophet that is confined to composing the prophetic document and the enduring word of truth in the apostles, who can conduct their teaching in full truth.[67] Scripture is a reflection and a mirror of revelation. But it is also the foundational organ of truth. Important for Beck was a developmental view of God's activity in the world. Since God

---

63. Barth, *Protestant Theology*, 603.

64. Johann Tobias Beck, *Christliche Lehrwissenschaft nach den biblischen Urkunden. Ein Versuch*, pt. 1, *Die Logik der christlichen Lehre*, 2nd ed. (Stuttgart: J. F. Steinkopf, 1875), 24.

65. Johann Tobias Beck, *Vorlesungen über christliche Glaubenslehre*, ed. J. Lindenmeyer (Gütersloh: C. Bertelsmann, 1886), 1:125.

66. Beck, *Christliche Lehrwissenschaft*, 30.

67. Cf. Johann Tobias Beck, *Einleitung in das System der christlichen Lehre*, 2nd ed. (Stuttgart: J. F. Steinkopf, 1870), 219 and 286-87.

created the world, God is its interior foundation. The creation is an organism with different levels, so that "the higher levels of life necessitate the lower ones and the latter reach again into the former."[68] This interlocking organism of creation is enlivened through the law of development that is facilitated through the logos and has the logos as its goal. The logos is not only the image of God, but also the original picture and the example of humanity, since humanity and the whole creation have their goal in it. With this kind of organismic thinking, Beck found it difficult to talk about the sinful depravity of humanity. Therefore he emphasized that through the fall the relationship between the Creator and the created is not torn, and Christ can use the positive powers of humanity in his salvific activity and bring them to fulfillment.[69] We notice here that even Beck could not extricate himself from the optimism of the nineteenth century.

With reference to Baptists, he asserted that infant baptism does not correspond with the usage of the apostles. For Beck baptism is a baptism with the spirit that joins the supernatural spirit "with the natural water by connecting human faith with the divine word of grace."[70] Observing apostolic custom and connecting our faith and God's grace, Beck gave no unqualified endorsement to infant baptism. He conceded that one can baptize infants but should not make that custom a law. It is not surprising that Beck maintained a certain distance from the established church, while through his biblically informed teaching he also strengthened that church. While he was too much a solitary figure to create an actual school, thousands of pastors were influenced by him in their dedication to biblical doctrine. Among prominent theologians Beck impacted is Johann Christian Konrad von Hofmann, one of the founders of the Erlangen School. Adolf Schlatter (1852-1938) had actually studied with him, and Beck opened for him an understanding of the New Testament. Martin Kähler (1835-1912) too studied with Beck and was quite impressed with his confidence in the New Testament and his emphasis upon the biblical Christ.

Scripture, Confession, and Experience (the Erlangen School): Adolf von Harless, J. C. K. von Hofmann, Reinhold Frank

Adolf von Harless (1806-79) is the founder of the Erlangen theology and of the *Journal for Protestantism and Church* (*Zeitschrift für Protestantismus und Kirche*,

---

68. Beck, *Christliche Lehrwissenschaft*, 133.

69. Cf. Sentzke, *Die Theologie Johann Tobias Becks*, 144-45.

70. Johann Tobias Beck, *Vorlesungen über die christliche Ethik*, vol. 1, *Die genetische Anlage des christlichen Lebens*, ed. Julius Lindenmeyer (Gütersloh: C. Bertelsmann, 1882), 1:318.

1838-75), the literary organ of the Erlangen theology.[71] He was born in Nürnberg of parents who were politically conservative and had a rationalistic piety. After graduation from school, he studied at Erlangen University, first philology and law from 1823, and then theology. He transferred to the University of Halle (1826-28), where under the influence of August Tholuck, a leading representative of a theology of the awakening, he realized that the biblical witness was an immediate and life-changing truth about oneself. This was the turning point for Harless, and from then on Christian truth was for him no longer a speculative theoretical exercise but an experiential certainty. After his *Habilitation* (second thesis) in 1830, he was appointed associate professor of New Testament exegesis in 1833; in 1836 he became full professor for Christian morals, theological encyclopedia, and methodology at Erlangen, and also the university preacher. In 1845 he accepted a call to the theological faculty in Leipzig for a professorship in dogmatics, ethics, and exegesis, and was appointed only three years later the main court preacher in Dresden. In 1852 King Max II of Bavaria appointed him president of the Protestant Superior Consistory (Protestantisches Oberkonsistorium), a position equivalent to bishop of the Lutheran Church of Bavaria.

In the introduction to his *Commentary on Paul's Letter to the Ephesians* (*Kommentar über den Brief Pauli an die Ephesier, 1834*), Harless emphasized the importance of languages, the necessity of a religious experience in properly exegeting Scripture, and a continuous relationship to Scripture as its disciple. In his *System of Christian Ethics* (1842; Eng. trans. 1887), he started out with Christ's saying: "I am the way, the truth, and the life: no man cometh to the Father but by me" (John 14:6), and continued: "And in this consciousness the cognizance of the Christian is twofold: respecting Christ as the way, and by respecting his own coming as a Christian by that way."[72]

As his biography shows, Harless is more important for the church than for theology, if the two can be separated. For him theology is related to the church, not as Schleiermacher thought as a discipline for church governance, but because theology has its origin in the faith experience within the church. Therefore all true Christian theology must originate from the basis of the Christian ecclesial faith of the community. Theology must attempt to elucidate that faith according to its foundation and essence, and finally lead back to that faith. Both in Saxony and in Bavaria Harless saw as his task to renew Lutheran confessionality by having all pastors subscribe to the Lutheran Confessions, be-

---

71. Cf. Friedrich Wilhelm Winter, *Die Erlanger Theologie und die Lutherforschung im 19. Jahrhundert* (Gütersloh: Gütersloher Verlagshaus, 1995), 12.

72. Gottlieb Christoph Adolf von Harless, *System of Christian Ethics,* translated from the 6th edition by A. W. Morrison, rev. William Findlay (Edinburgh: T. & T. Clark, 1868), 1.

cause he considered the confessions to be the foundation and mark of the respective churches. For the same reason, he campaigned in Bavaria for confessional schools (over against joint Catholic-Lutheran schools in which the Roman Catholics would have had the clear majority). But Harless was no confessional separatist. He was fundamentally convinced of the catholicity of the Lutheran church and the organic confessional development that alone occurred in the Lutheran church, and rejected any kind of ecclesial unions or plans for a German national church.[73]

While Harless started the Erlangen theology, **Johann Christian Konrad von Hofmann** (1810-77) brought it to its height. He was born to parents who were attracted to the German awakening and shaped by the pietism of Bavaria and Swabia. Having attended the Nürnberg *Gymnasium*, Hofmann started to study theology at Erlangen University in 1827. There he came under the influence of the Reformed pastor and later professor of dogmatics and pastoral theology Johann Christian Krafft (1783-1845) and of the professor of mineralogy and history of science Karl Georg von Raumer (1783-1865), who were both advocates of the awakening. From 1829 to 1832 he studied in Berlin and lived in the house of Countess von Bülow, another proponent of pietism. He was especially fascinated by the historian Leopold von Ranke (1795-1886), whereas Schleiermacher and Hegel were not of much use to him. After his exam in 1832, he became professor at the Erlangen *Gymnasium* for history, religion, and Hebrew, and after doing his second thesis *(Habilitation)*, he was appointed associate professor in 1841 at the university. The following year he accepted a call to a full professorship at Rostock in the biblical field.

In 1845 Hofmann became the successor to Harless at Erlangen and taught theological encyclopedia, New Testament, and ethics. Soon he attracted many students and became the most renowned and influential teacher of the whole university. This is attested by his being elected five times vice president of the university *(Prorektor)*, while the president was always the Bavarian king. Having declined a call to the University of Leipzig in 1855, Hofmann was awarded the Order of Merit of the Bavarian crown and personal nobility. Between 1863 and 1869 he also served as a member of the liberal progressive party in the Bavarian diet. His first larger works were devoted to secular history, but already when writing his second thesis he showed a clear concept of his theological slant, from which he never veered.[74]

73. For a good estimate of the contribution of Harless to a sound self-consciousness of Lutheranism, see Martin Hein, "Harless, Gottlieb Christoph Adolf von," in *Theologische Realenzyklopädie*, 14:444-46.

74. So Friedrich Mildenberger, "Hofmann, Johann Christian Konrad v.," in *Theologische*

In his first major work, *Prophecy and Fulfillment in the Old and New Testament* (*Weissagung und Erfüllung im Alten und im Neuen Testament*, pt. I, 1841; pt. II, 1844), he emphasized two aspects that are characteristic of his theology: a coherent organic development and the working of the Holy Spirit in history and nature. He wrote: "Then we have in the self-presentation of Christ in the world at the same time history and prophecy: history, i.e., the continuously progressive shaping of the communion between God and humanity; prophecy, i.e., the ever more definite pointing to the finite shape of the communion between God and humanity. With this prophesying history and with the work of the Spirit through which this history occurs and conceptualizes itself in words, this is what we have to deal with."[75] This means that the word of Christ is initially history and not doctrine.

In his next major work, *The Proof of Scripture: A Theological Investigation* (*Der Schriftbeweis. Ein theologischer Versuch*, 1852-55), he attempted a biblical foundation of Christian doctrine. The starting point for him is "Christianity, the communion of God and humanity, personally mediated by Jesus Christ."[76] He does not want to depict any kind of Christianity but Christ's Christianity, which then, however, will be Christianity "according to the degree to which he [the theologian] is, through Christ, personally united in the ecclesial communion with God." Then he arrived at the often quoted statement: "The acknowledgement and the assertion of Christianity must be first of all self-recognition and one's own assertion by a Christian. . . . Theology is only a truly free science, free in God, when precisely that which makes a Christian to be a Christian, his own independent relationship to God, makes the theologian to be a theologian in scientific self-recognition and one's own assertion: When I the Christian become for me the theologian the essential material of my science."[77] Hofmann excluded both subjectivity and a theoretical description of Christianity by asserting that theological claims must be attested by the theologian's own experience. That experience is not subjectivity, but is derived from being related to God through Christ. Theology is not a theory, according to Hofmann. In the same vein he also claimed that Christianity has an existence independent from

---

Realenzyklopädie, 15:477, in contrast to Karl Gerhard Steck, *Die Idee der Heilsgeschichte. Hofmann — Schlatter — Cullmann* (Zollikon: Evangelischer Verlag, 1959), 23, who claims that Hofmann never produced what he initially intended so that "finally positivism gained the victory over the romantic idealistic heritage."

75. Johann Ch. K. von Hofmann, *Weissagung und Erfüllung im Alten und im Neuen Testament. Ein theologischer Versuch* (Nördlingen: C. H. Beck, 1841), 1:40.

76. See Johann Ch. K. von Hofmann, *Der Schriftbeweis. Ein theologischer Versuch*, 2nd ed. (Nördlingen: C. H. Beck, 1857), 1:8, for this and the following quote.

77. Hofmann, *Der Schriftbeweis*, 10.

the scientific endeavor of the theologian in three respects: through the fact of the rebirth as a Christian, through history and the existence of the church, and through Holy Scripture.[78]

The one point at which Hofmann differed from traditional orthodox views and for which he was attacked, even by his own Erlangen colleagues, was his view of the atonement, where he did not accept that Jesus atoned for us by bearing God's wrath, but rather that God forgave our sins because of the continuous love and fidelity of Jesus to the Father in spite of all the adversity he had to bear under human sinfulness.[79] Hofmann presented a biblically based theology that starts with the theologian believing the subject matter he or she expounds. Yet he did not see the Bible undifferentiatedly, because while the salvation realized in the person of Jesus is evidenced "everywhere in the New Testament . . . in the Old Testament we see a process moving towards this complete salvation, of which the people of Israel, as the national community of the God who sent Jesus, is the witness."[80] There is a big distinction between the Old and the New Testament, but also a continuity.

The emphasis on continuity between the two Testaments, especially in salvation-historical terms, was picked up by many scholars, most prominently in Germany by Gerhard von Rad (1901-71) in his *Old Testament Theology* (1957-60; Eng. trans. 1962-65), by Oscar Cullmann (1902-99) in *Christ and Time: The Primitive Christian Conception of Time and History* (1946; Eng. trans. 1950), and by the American Old Testament scholars John Bright (1911-89) in his *Kingdom of God* (1953) and George Ernest Wright (1909-74) in *God Who Acts: Biblical Theology as Recital* (1952). Hofmann "was the ancestor of them all," known or unknown to them.[81] It is regrettable, however, that "whereas in Germany, Hofmann is counted among the great theologians of the past [nineteenth] century, his name is almost unknown in the English-speaking world, and few of his books are found even in the libraries of the leading theological schools."[82]

Another representative of the Erlangen School who should be mentioned is **Franz Hermann Reinhold Frank** (1827-94), a student of Harless who devel-

---

78. Hofmann, *Der Schriftbeweis*, 23.

79. Johann Ch. K. von Hofmann, *Schutzschriften für eine neue Weise, alte Wahrheit zu lehren* (Nördlingen: C. H. Beck, 1857), 2:105-6, and cf. also Claude Welch, *Protestant Thought in the Nineteenth Century (1799-1870)* (New Haven: Yale University Press, 1972), 1:224-25.

80. Johann Ch. K. von Hofmann, *Interpreting the Bible*, trans. Christian Preus (Minneapolis: Augsburg, 1959), 133.

81. So Roy A. Harrisville and Walter Sundberg, *The Bible in Modern Culture: Theology and Historical-Critical Method from Spinoza to Käsemann* (Grand Rapids: Eerdmans, 1995), 151, who cite these various authors.

82. So rightly Christian Preus in his introduction to Hofmann, *Interpreting the Bible*, xi.

oped the Erlangen theology of experience further and turned it into a system. Characteristic are his two works *System of Christian Certainty* (1870-73; Eng. trans. 1886) and *System of Christian Truth* (*System der christlichen Wahrheit,* 1878-80). Also deserving mention are Gottfried Thomasius (1802-75), professor of dogmatics and university preacher at Erlangen, and Christian E. Luthardt (1823-1902), who taught at Leipzig, and his colleague there, Ludwig Ihmels (1858-1933), who later became bishop of Saxony. Their indebtedness to the theology of experience shows that, at its height, the influence of the Erlangen School extended even to other theological faculties.

For Further Reading

Horace Bushnell (1802-76)

Bushnell, Horace. *God in Christ.* Edited by Bruce Kuklick. New York: Garland Reprint, 1987 [1849].

Cheney, Mary Bushnell. *The Life and Letters of Horace Bushnell.* New York: Harper and Brothers, 1880.

Edwards, Robert. *Of Singular Genius, of Singular Grace: A Biography of Horace Bushnell.* Cleveland: Pilgrim Press, 1992.

Mullin, Robert Bruce. *The Puritan as Yankee: A Life of Horace Bushnell.* Grand Rapids: Eerdmans, 2002.

Smith, H. Shelton. *Horace Bushnell.* New York: Oxford University Press, 1965.

Philip Schaff (1819-93)

Bowden, Henry, ed. *A Century of Church History: The Legacy of Philip Schaff.* Introduction by Jaroslav Pelikan. Carbondale: Southern Illinois University Press, 1988.

Pranger, Gary. *Philip Schaff (1819-1893): Portrait of an Immigrant Theologian.* New York: Peter Lang, 1997.

Schaff, Philip. *Theses for the Time.* In *The Mercersburg Theology,* edited by James Hastings Nichols. New York: Oxford University Press, 1966. Pp. 123-37.

Shriver, George. *Philip Schaff: Christian Scholar and Ecumenical Prophet; Centennial Biography for the Society of American Church History.* Macon, Ga.: Mercer University Press, 1987.

John Williamson Nevin (1803-86)

Appel, Theodore. *The Life and Work of John Williamson Nevin.* Philadelphia: Reformed Church Publishing House, 1889.

Nevin, John. *The Anxious Bench.* Introduction by John S. Stahr. 3rd ed. Reading, Pa.: Daniel Miller, 1892.

Nichols, James Hastings, ed. *The Mercersburg Theology.* New York: Oxford University Press, 1966.

Plummer, Kenneth Moses. "The Theology of John Williamson Nevin in the Mercersburg Period, 1840-1852." Thesis, University of Chicago, 1958.

Wentz, Richard. *John Williamson Nevin: American Theologian.* New York: Oxford University Press, 1997.

Archibald Alexander (1772-1851)

Alexander, James. *The Life of Archibald Alexander, D.D., L.L.D., First Professor in the Theological Seminary, at Princeton, N.J.* Harrisonburg, Va.: Sprinkle Publications, 1991 [1855].

Loetscher, Lefferts. *Facing the Enlightenment and Pietism: Archibald Alexander and the Founding of Princeton Theological Seminary.* Westport, Conn.: Greenwood Press, 1983.

Noll, Mark A., ed. *The Princeton Theology: 1812-1921; Scripture, Science, and Theological Method from Archibald Alexander to Benjamin Breckinridge Warfield.* Grand Rapids: Baker, 2001 [1983].

Charles Hodge (1797-1878)

Hewitt, Glenn. *Regeneration and Morality: A Study of Charles Finney, Charles Hodge, John W. Nevin, and Horace Bushnell.* Chicago Studies in the History of American Religion 7. Chicago: University of Chicago Press, 1986.

Hodge, Archibald Alexander. *The Life of Charles Hodge, 1823-1886.* New York: Arno, 1961 [1880].

Hodge, Charles. *Systematic Theology.* 3 vols. Grand Rapids: Eerdmans, 1981.

Stewart, John W., and James H. Moorhead, eds. *Charles Hodge Revisited: A Critical Appraisal of His Life and Work.* Grand Rapids: Eerdmans, 2002.

Archibald Alexander Hodge (1823-86)

Helseth, Paul Kjoss. "'Right Reason' and the Princeton Mind: The Moral Context." *Journal of Presbyterian History* 77, no. 1 (Spring 1999): 13-28.

Hodge, Archibald Alexander. *Confession of Faith: A Handbook of Christian Doctrine Expounding the Westminster Confession.* London: Banner of Truth Trust, 1958.

Noll, Mark A., ed. *The Princeton Theology: 1812-1921; Scripture, Science, and Theological Method from Archibald Alexander to Benjamin Breckinridge Warfield.* Grand Rapids: Baker, 2001 [1983].

Benjamin Breckinridge Warfield (1851-1922)

Hoffecker, W. *Piety and the Princeton Theologians: Archibald Alexander, Charles Hodge, and Benjamin Warfield.* Grand Rapids: Baker, 1981.

Noll, Mark A., ed. *The Princeton Theology: 1812-1921; Scripture, Science, and Theological Method from Archibald Alexander to Benjamin Breckinridge Warfield.* Grand Rapids: Baker, 2001 [1983].

Van Bemmelen, Peter Maarten. *Issues in Biblical Inspiration: Sanday and Warfield.* Berrien Springs, Mich.: Andrews University, 1988.

Frederick Denison Maurice (1805-72)

Higham, Florence. *F. D. Maurice*. London: SCM, 1947.

Maurice, Frederick Denison. *The Kingdom of Christ or Hints on the Principles, Ordinances, and Constitution of the Catholic Church: In Letters to a Member of the Society of Friends*. London: J. M. Dent, 1907.

———. *Reconstructing Christian Ethics: Selected Writings*. Edited by Ellen K. Wondra. Louisville: Westminster John Knox, 1995.

———. *Theological Essays*. Edited and introduction by Edward F. Carpenter. New York: Harper, 1957.

———, ed. *The Life of Frederick Denison Maurice Chiefly Told in His Own Letters*. 2nd ed. London: Macmillan, 1884.

Ramsey, Michael. *F. D. Maurice and the Conflicts of Modern Theology*. Cambridge: Cambridge University Press, 1951.

Roper, Alexander. *The Theology of F. D. Maurice*. London: SCM, 1948.

Johannes Henricus Scholten (1811-85)

Berkhof, Hendrikus. *Two Hundred Years of Theology: Report of a Personal Journey*. Grand Rapids: Eerdmans, 1989.

Abraham Kuyper (1837-1920)

Bacote, Vincent E. *The Spirit in Public Theology: Appropriating the Legacy of Abraham Kuyper*. Grand Rapids: Baker, 2005.

Kuyper, Abraham. *A Centennial Reader*. Edited by James D. Bratt. Grand Rapids: Eerdmans, 1998.

Herman Bavinck (1854-1921)

Bavinck, Herman. *Our Reasonable Faith*. Translated by Henry Zylstra. Grand Rapids: Eerdmans, 1956.

———. *Reformed Dogmatics*. Translated by John Vriend. Edited by John Boldt. Grand Rapids: Baker, 2003-.

Harinck, George. "'Something That Must Remain, If the Truth Is to Be Sweet and Precious to Us': The Reformed Spirituality of Herman Bavinck." *Calvin Theological Journal* 38 (2003): 248-62.

Hermann Friedrich Kohlbrügge (1803-75)

Barth, Karl. *Protestant Theology in the Nineteenth Century: Its Background and History*. New ed. Grand Rapids, Eerdmans, 2002. Pp. 620-28.

Huenemann, Edward Martin. "Hermann Friedrich Kohlbrügge: Servant of the Word by the Spirit and Grace of God." Th.D. thesis, Princeton Theological Seminary, 1961.

Kohlbrügge, Hermann F. *I Believe in the Holy Spirit*. Translated by E. Buehrer. Green Bay, Wis.: Reliance Publishing, 1950(?).

Johann Tobias Beck (1804-78)

Barth, Karl. *Protestant Theology in the Nineteenth Century: Its Background and History.* New ed. Grand Rapids, Eerdmans, 2002. Pp. 602-10.

Harjunpaa, Toivo. "Beckian Biblicism and Finland: A Study in Historical Perspective." *Lutheran Quarterly* 28 (November 1976): 290-330.

Hauck, Albert. "Beck, Johann Tobias." In *The New Schaff-Herzog Encyclopedia of Religious Knowledge*, 2:20-21. Grand Rapids: Baker, 1949-50.

Adolf von Harless (1806-79)

Harless, Gottlieb Christoph Adolf von. *System of Christian Ethics.* Translated from the 6th edition by A. W. Morrison. Revised by William Findlay. Edinburgh: T. & T. Clark, 1868.

Stähelin, R. "Harless, Gottlieb Christoph Adolf von." In *The New Schaff-Herzog Encyclopedia of Religious Knowledge*, 5:150-51. Grand Rapids: Baker, 1949-50.

Weidner, Revere F. *A System of Christian Ethics: Based on Martensen and Harless.* Philadelphia: G. W. Frederick, 1891.

Johann Christian Konrad von Hofmann (1810-77)

Becker, Matthew L. "Appreciating the Life and Work of Johannes v. Hofmann." *Lutheran Quarterly* 17 (Summer 2003): 177-98.

———. "The Revisionist Christology of Johannes v. Hofmann." *Lutheran Quarterly* 17 (Autumn 2003): 288-328.

Harrisville, Roy A., and Walter Sundberg. *The Bible in Modern Culture: Theology and Historical-Critical Method from Spinoza to Käsemann.* Grand Rapids: Eerdmans, 1995.

Hofmann, Johann Ch. K. von. *Interpreting the Bible.* Translated by Christian Preus. Minneapolis: Augsburg, 1959.

Franz Hermann Reinhold Frank (1827-94)

Frank, Franz Hermann Reinhold. *System of Christian Certainty.* Translated by Maurice J. Evans. Edinburgh: T. & T. Clark, 1886.

Ludolphy, Ingetraut. "Frank, Franz Hermann Reinhold von." In *The Encyclopedia of the Lutheran Church*, edited by Julius Bodensieck, 2:882. Minneapolis: Augsburg, 1965.

Seeberg, Reinhold. "Frank, Franz Hermann Reinhold von." In *The New Schaff-Herzog Encyclopedia of Religious Knowledge*, 4:368-69. Grand Rapids: Baker, 1949-50.

4 Romanticism and the Pietistic Awakening

Romanticism, as a reaction to Enlightenment rationalism, considered the romantic the beautiful without boundary or the beautifully infinite. In the first variety, beauty without boundary, romanticism led to pantheism, as we notice in the British poets John Keats (1795-1821) and Percy Bysshe Shelley (1792-1822) and their appreciation of Roman and Greek antiquity. The other variety, the beautifully infinite, however, proved more interesting for theology. It led back to the classical ideal of the medieval period and its Christian roots, as can be seen in the conversion to Roman Catholicism of representatives of the romantic movement such as Friedrich von Schlegel (1772-1829) and in the development of the art style of the Nazarenes, which to this day influences popular piety in Europe and North America. The pietistic awakening in Germany, in contrast to the Great Awakening in the eighteenth century, was influenced by idealism, romanticism, confessionalism, and neo-Lutheranism, and turned against rationalism and liberalism without being able to overcome them.

Romantic, Confessional Lutheranism:
Claus Harms, Wilhelm Löhe, August Vilmar

The Prussian Union of the Lutheran and Reformed churches proclaimed in 1817 was the result of the endeavors of King Frederick William III (1770-1840) to overcome the inner-Protestant division. It was also advocated by those coming from the Enlightenment who saw in confessionalism a relic of the past. The idea was to leave behind the divisive confessionalism among the Protestants and to form one united church. This enforced union led to emigrations of Prussians to found the Lutheran Church of Australia, and of Saxons to establish what later became the Lutheran Church–Missouri Synod in North America. Opposition against the union from the Lutheran side came from both laity and clergy. The same year the union was proclaimed, pastor **Claus Harms** (1778-1855) from Kiel published anew Martin Luther's Ninety-five Theses and added ninety-five of his own. He rejected rationalism and advocated an ecclesial doctrine guided by Scripture and the Lutheran Confessions as its norm. According to Harms, the Lutheran church is shaped by word and sacrament. It is the actual center of all denominations and is to be preferred to the Roman Catholic and Reformed churches. Harms found wanting theological rationalism, historical critical research, and mediating theology. Though originally Christianity was not primarily doctrine, in the course of its history it had to create doctrine to maintain and defend its peculiarity. In the confessions, the foundation of the church, that doctrine has formulated what is normative for proclamation and theology. The confessions protect against wrong teaching and uncritical adaptation to the respective spirit of the times.

These theses, published at the 300th anniversary of Luther's own theses, intensified the discussions about unionism and made Harms popular far beyond Germany. He received a theological and a philosophical doctorate from the University of Kiel (1834) and was even called to be bishop of St. Petersburg in 1819, a call he declined, as well as in 1843 to become successor to Schleiermacher at Berlin's Trinity Church.[1] He was by no means a narrow confessionalist, but considered Roman Catholics as brothers, though in error. He could even condone intercommunion with nonrationalistic Christians from the Reformed side. He preserved the Lutheran confession for his own Schleswig-Holstein church, now part of the Evangelical Lutheran Church of North Elbia.

While Harms was the main pastor of St. Nicholas in the city of Kiel, **Wilhelm Löhe** (1808-72) was a country parson.[2] Yet he was even more influential for church and theology than was Harms. Johann Konrad Wilhelm Löhe was born to middle-class parents in Fürth near Nürnberg, his father being a merchant. He had a religious outlook already in his boyhood, and confessed: "In our small yard where there was a chopping block, I gathered the children of the rent people who lived in our house, put on a black apron to serve as a gown, stepped onto the chopping block, which served as a pulpit, preached, sang, and prayed. Sometimes my mother would say to my father: 'A minister is lost in that boy if you

---

1. Cf. Lorenz Hein, "Harms, Claus," in *Theologische Realenzyklopädie*, 14:447.

2. For his life and work cf. David C. Ratke, *Confession and Mission, Word and Sacrament: The Ecclesial Theology of Wilhelm Löhe* (St. Louis: Concordia, 2001).

don't let him study.'"[3] At age ten he was sent to a Latin school and, in addition, received private instruction in French, Italian, English, geometry, and drawing, and later also in Greek. His confirmation, together with his first participation in the Lord's Supper, made a deep impression on him. Having graduated from the *Gymnasium* in Nürnberg, he began to study theology at Erlangen University in 1826. He was especially impressed with the Reformed professor Johann Christian Krafft (1784-1845), a representative of the theology of the awakening, with whom he developed a friendship. He spent the summer semester of 1828 at Berlin, where Schleiermacher's style of preaching impressed him. In 1830 he passed his theological exam with distinction and was ordained the following year.

In his vicarage in a small place in Upper Franconia, he received an immense response from the laity, but got in trouble with the authorities when he gathered people for Bible study and prayer in their own homes and in his. Finally he was replaced because of his "pietistic doings," and another candidate "with more moderate theological opinions" was called.[4] All the protests by the congregation, the magistrate, and his friends could not change this decision. In 1834 he was called as administrator to the renowned church of St. Ägidien in Nürnberg. As preacher, religious instructor, and pastor, he made a big impression even on the mayor of the city and the *Rektor* of the *Gymnasium*. He never forced himself on others, and rather had people come to him instead of going after them. Even after a full day's work, he was still ready to have a Bible lesson with a circle of friends. In contrast to his first charge, in Nürnberg he won the support of the authorities.

After his second exam, which he passed again with distinction, Löhe substituted as pastor here and there and hoped for a city pastorate. But instead he was entrusted with the pastorate at Neuendettelsau, at that time, politely speaking, an unattractive village southwest of Nürnberg. Most of the people were so poor they could not even afford shingles on their roofs, but had thatched roofs, and only a few houses were built of bricks. He accepted the charge gladly in 1836, while applying without success for various positions in a city up to 1848. At his first visit he said of Neuendettelsau: "Not even dead would I want to be in that dump."[5] But barely thirty years later, the situation had changed drastically. He pointed out: "Just recently a world map of mission has appeared (Grundemann's World Mission Map of 1862) which can be recommended and on which Neuendettelsau is recorded in the center of Europe."

3. As quoted in Theodor Schober, *Wilhelm Löhe: Witness of the Living Lutheran Church* [Ger. 1959], trans. Bertha Mueller, typescript ed., 5.

4. As quoted by Schober, *Wilhelm Löhe*, 18.

5. See Wilhelm Löhe, "Neuendettelsau" (1864), in *Gesammelte Werke*, ed. Klaus Ganzert (Neuendettelsau: Freimund-Verlag, 1962), 4:403, for this and the following quote.

Just before Löhe had moved to Neuendettelsau, he married one of his former confirmands, Helene Andreae, who was from an industrial family in Frankfurt am Main, and whom he had first met in Nürnberg. She died after they had been married for only six years, and Löhe brought up their four children by himself. He was unable to marry a second time, since his first love remained close to him throughout his life and the sorrow that went with her passing away never subsided.

Löhe revived his congregation. He reintroduced private confession, which had been neglected due to the Enlightenment, and in 1858 alone he administered an estimated 2,250 individual confessions.[6] He concentrated on building up the congregation, leading it to the celebration of the Lord's Supper. He also introduced a new worship setting, *Order for Christian Congregations of the Lutheran Confession* (*Agende für christliche Gemeinde des Lutherischen Bekenntnisses*, 1844), for which he scoured not only the Lutheran tradition, but pre-Reformation, Counter-Reformation, and even Greek and Oriental liturgies. He was active in pastoral theology, and published as a result of his parish work *The Protestant Pastor* (*Der evangelische Geistliche*, 2 vols., 1852-58). He tried to introduce the anointing of the sick, but was prohibited from doing so by the church authorities. Nevertheless, we are told that many sick were healed through his prayers. Therefore, it is not surprising that he had contact with Pastor Johann Christoph Blumhardt (1805-80) in Bad Boll, who had his roots in pietism and who also prayed for the sick.

Since the Roman Catholic king of Bavaria was the actual head of the Lutheran Church in Bavaria, Löhe called "the connection between state and church an unfortunate mismarriage."[7] And about the revolution of 1848 when people were clamoring for more democratic rights, Löhe said: "Now it [i.e., the union of state and church] is dissolving. What God has not bound together, now goes asunder — and now everybody wants to help the church to find a constitution." Löhe too was pressing for a constitution of the church. When initially his pleas brought no response, he even considered becoming independent of the state church. When Adolf von Harless was appointed president of the higher consistory by King Max II (1811-64), Löhe's influence increased. Yet his main impact was through Neuendettelsau.

In 1849 Löhe founded the Society for Home Mission in Accordance with the Lutheran Church (Gesellschaft für Innere Mission im Sinne der Lutherischen Kirche), an attempt to renew the office of the congregational dea-

---

6. Cf. Wolfhart Schlichting, "Löhe," in *Theologische Realenzyklopädie*, 21:411.

7. See Wilhelm Löhe, "Aphorismen über die neutestamentlichen Ämter" (1848/49), in *Gesammelte Werke*, 5/1:320, for this and the following quote.

coness of the early church. His interest in overseas mission ensued on account of Friedrich Konrad Dietrich Wyneken, then pastor in Fort Wayne, Indiana. On a visit to Germany, Wyneken called for help to supply pastors for the rapidly expanding Lutheran church in America due to the mushrooming German immigrant population. Löhe responded to this call and instructed two men, Adam Ernst and Georg Burger, who were ready to be sent to America. Since he did not think they had the necessary qualifications for ministry, he told them their primary task was to be schoolteachers in German schools there. When they arrived in New York, they met Pastor Friedrich Winkler of Newark, New Jersey, who was responding to a call as professor at the Theological Seminary of the Joint Lutheran Synod of Ohio and Adjacent States in Columbus, Ohio. Ernst and Burger followed him, and soon two others were sent.

Wyneken had told Löhe about this seminary, which he thought might become one of the outstanding theological institutions in America if it had assistance in the form of books, students, and even professors from Germany. Löhe agreed to send more men and books. However, in the Ohio Synod there was controversy whether to use the English language or German as the vehicle of instruction in the seminary. Some saw in this move to the English medium a repudiation of the Lutheran heritage. Therefore the men coming from Löhe left and established contact with C. F. W. Walther (1811-87) to join the newly formed German Evangelical Lutheran Synod of Missouri, Ohio, and Other States. At the first regular synodical convention in 1847, the clergy roster listed more pastors coming from Löhe than from the original Missouri group, so that Löhe "deserves recognition as the co-founder of the Missouri Synod."[8] Löhe was asked by the 1847 synodical convention to transfer the title of the Fort Wayne seminary to the Missouri Synod and to continue to support this seminary financially. Löhe had established the seminary in Fort Wayne in 1845 under the presidency of Wilhelm Shiler since it was close to Michigan, where Löhe started a program of establishing German colonies, the most well-known being Frankenmuth, and the last one to be established in 1851, Frankenhilf. The colonies were intended to serve as a base for mission work among the Indians. Besides the colonies, Löhe established also a hospice and a teacher training seminary in nearby Saginaw.

But Löhe got caught in a fight between the Missouri group with Walther and the Lutheran Buffalo Synod with Johann H. A. Grabau (1804-79). Löhe did not give in to Missouri, which stated that Scripture and confession had decided the major questions of the nature of the church and the ministry, but instead

8. James Schaaf, "Löhe and the Missouri Synod," *Concordia Historical Institute Quarterly* 45 (May 1972): 59.

sided with Grabau, who was more lenient at that point. The friendly attitude toward Grabau cost Löhe the friendship with Missouri. It was even suggested that his followers leave the state of Michigan and move to Iowa, where Missouri had no congregations. Since the teachers training seminary at Saginaw that Löhe had established did not belong to Missouri, Löhe's followers took the seminary with them to Iowa and relocated it at Dubuque. Löhe continued to send candidates to that seminary and, "supported by the promise of assistance from Löhe and his missionary-minded friends in Germany, the small group of Lutherans in Iowa was courageous enough to consider forming a synodical organization," the Iowa Synod, in 1854.[9] Therefore, in his doctoral dissertation James Schaaf (1932-96) correctly states: "Without Löhe there would be no Lutheran Church in America as we know it today."[10]

The small village of Neuendettelsau has grown today into a huge church establishment with a hospital, homes for the mentally retarded and for unwed mothers, hospices, shops for making church paraments and communion wafers, a deaconess motherhouse that at its high point supplied three thousand deaconesses for congregations and hospitals throughout Bavaria, a publishing house, a bookstore, numerous primary and secondary schools, a mission institute that has an active exchange with Lutheran churches throughout the world, and a theological seminary. Most of these institutions owe their origin to Wilhelm Löhe, who was a church father not just for his Lutheran Church in Bavaria, but for the whole Lutheran *oikoumene*.

Löhe was not a close-minded confessionalist. In his *Three Books concerning the Church* he stated that the Reformation "is finished in doctrine; it is unfinished in the consequences of doctrine."[11] The Lutheran Formula of Concord was for Löhe the final point in the doctrinal process. Yet this doctrine needs to be applied, and for Löhe this meant one must recognize "all that could be done with it for the salvation of the world and the Church" (160). Lutheran doctrine does not go to the extreme. Instead, it "offers the only possible agreement and union of the extreme contradictions which find expression in the different particular Churches," namely, the Roman Catholic and the Reformed churches (163). Löhe did not want a union of both sides, but a return to that middle ground that for him was the Lutheran position. In that way there is also the possibility of a development, as he showed in his discussions with the Missouri

9. James Schaaf, "Wilhelm Löhe's Relation to the American Church: A Study in the History of Lutheran Mission" (Ph.D. diss., University of Heidelberg, 1961), 175-76.

10. Schaaf, "Wilhelm Löhe's Relation," 3.

11. Wilhelm Löhe, *Three Books concerning the Church: Offered for Friends of the Lutheran Church for Consideration and Discussion,* trans. Edward T. Horn (Reading, Pa.: Pilger Publishing House, 1908), 158. Page references have been placed in the text.

Synod, on the nature of church and ministry. Scripture and confession had not settled everything. Löhe is opposed to "an external union by means of ill-fated disregard of deniable differences." But he hoped and worked "for the union of all souls in one pure teaching" (165). Perhaps this stance of Löhe is also the deeper meaning of the "reconciled diversity" toward which the current ecumenical discussions move.

What Löhe did for the church in Bavaria, **August Friedrich Christian Vilmar** (1800-1868) did for his native state of Hesse. He was born and grew up in a country parsonage at Solz, northeast of Frankfurt am Main, and studied theology at Marburg from 1818 to 1820. Through the encounter with rationalism there he went from faith to unbelief. Yet this move was not long lasting. From 1823 onward he held various teaching positions. During these years he renounced his rationalism, first expressing the idealist notion that the world is the feeling of God, and then through his encounters with the church fathers, especially Tertullian, Irenaeus, and Tholuck's *Guido and Julius,* or *Sin and the Propitiator Exhibited in the True Consecration of the Sceptic* (1823; Eng. trans. 1836), he "arrived at an unwavering faith in Christ, . . . realizing that all he sought was to be found in the Lutheran Church, a process begun by the careful study of the Augsburg Confession and its Apology."[12] Luther's hymn "Dear Christians, one and all, rejoice" (*Lutheran Book of Worship,* no. 229) and article 12 of the Augsburg Confession on repentance expressed most exactly his own thoughts on the deep reality of sin and grace.

After this conversion experience, he was director of the classical high school at Marburg from 1833 to 1850. Then he served for five years as acting superintendent. When the prince elector of Hesse did not approve his election as superintendent in 1855, he was appointed professor of theology at Marburg University.

Vilmar became the most influential professor in the university. His program was set forth in *Theology of Facts against the Theology of Rhetoric* (*Theologie der Tatsachen wider die Theologie der Rhetorik,* 1856), in which he stated that the confessions in their entirety are binding, not just a selection of them, because "half confessions . . . are no confessions at all, since they are crumbling and uncertain confessions."[13] Against the impending union of Lutherans and Calvinists he placed the stronger emphasis on Lutheranism, especially when attempts were made to discard the Augsburg Confession. Similar to

---

12. So J. Haussleiter, "Vilmar, August Friedrich Christian," in *The New Schaff-Herzog Encyclopedia of Religious Knowledge* (Grand Rapids: Baker, 1949-50), 12:190.

13. August F. C. Vilmar, *Die Theologie der Tatsachen wider die Theologie der Rhetorik,* 4th ed. (Gütersloh, 1876; reprint, Darmstadt: Wissenschaftliche Buchgesellschaft, 1968), 79.

Löhe, he advocated the freedom of the church from the state, and was vigorously involved in the conferences of Lutheran pastors in both parts of Hesse, Hesse-Darmstadt in the south and Hesse-Kassel in the north. At Marburg University Vilmar lectured on homiletics, hymnology, and the Reformation. Central to his theological witness was the certainty of the presence of Christ in the church on earth. He even predicted the downfall of the nation as a result of its apostasy from the living God and through the rejection of his law.

The church represented for Vilmar the beginning of a new era, an era of faith. "Clinging firmly to the Lutheran Confessions, and rejecting every false kind of unionism, Vilmar was convinced that the Holy Spirit will lead the church onward . . . to new insights and deeper experiences of the eternal truth (John 16:13)."[14] Therefore he advocated church discipline and obedience, claiming: "Who is not obedient to the church (i.e., who cannot completely absorb the living matter of the church) is not a servant of the church; . . . we also count the *nova obedientia* [new obedience] which results from conversion to be part of obedience."[15] It is understandable that any free inquiry or any Protestant freedom of teaching was for him a dangerous sign of the self-destruction of true theology.

Guarding Lutheran Confessional Identity:
Ernst Wilhelm Hengstenberg

Philip Schaff reported that **Ernst Wilhelm Hengstenberg** (1802-69), professor of Old Testament exegesis in the University of Berlin, "is one of the most unpopular and yet one of the most important and influential men in the kingdom of Prussia. He leads the extreme right wing of the orthodox party in the Established Church, and is the uncompromising opponent of all rationalists and semi-rationalists, all latitudinarians and liberals. He is simply professor, although an editor of a semi-weekly church gazette, and holds no seat" in the church government, "nor does he ever preach."[16] This puts in a nutshell the significance of Hengstenberg, who was born in Westphalia as son of a Reformed pastor; studied classical and Oriental literature, and philosophy at the University of Bonn; did intensive studies in Arabic and got his Ph.D. in 1823. While he attended only a few lectures in theology, he nevertheless wanted to be a theolo-

14. So Friedrich Wilhelm Hopf, "Vilmar, August Friedrich Christian," in *The Encyclopedia of the Lutheran Church*, ed. Julius Bodensieck (Minneapolis: Augsburg, 1965), 3:2442.

15. August F. C. Vilmar, *Die Lehre vom geistlichen Amt* (Marburg: N. G. Elwert, 1870), 124.

16. Philip Schaff, *Germany: Its Universities, Theology, and Religion* (Philadelphia: Lindsay and Blakiston, 1857), 300.

gian. Therefore he declined to specialize further in Arabic studies, went in 1823 for a year as a tutor to Basel, since he could not obtain the scholarship to study at Berlin, and then returned to Berlin, to do first his *Habilitation* in philosophy in 1824, and then his licentiate the following year to start lecturing at the theological faculty in Old Testament exegesis.

Hengstenberg was brought up in a moderate theological rationalism, but Johann August Wilhelm Neander (1789-1850), a church historian and a representative of the awakening, introduced him to the leaders of the awakening in Berlin, such as Baron von Kottwitz and the Gerlach brothers. Having married Therese von Quast (1812-61) in 1829, Hengstenberg was even more at home in that circle. When the conservative ecclesial-theological gazette *Evangelische Kirchenzeitung* was founded, Hengstenberg was asked to be its editor. As such he exerted considerable influence on church politics in Prussia and beyond. Though he had been charged with a Romanizing tendency since he regarded the Roman Catholic Church as an ally in opposition to rationalism and pantheism, he stood on decidedly Protestant ground. Schaff judged correctly his theological slant:

> Although he professes now the distinctive Lutheran tenets, he has unquestionably a striking constitutional resemblance to Calvin. . . . Had he been born and raised in Scotland or New England, he would no doubt be a most rigorous Calvinist. The Calvinist features of his mind and moral character, in connection with his high views on inspiration and the divine authority of the Scriptures, account for the fact that Hengstenberg is better understood and more generally appreciated in England and America, than almost any other German theologian.[17]

Most of Hengstenberg's exegetical works are translated into English. Similar to Calvin, the Old Testament takes on prime importance for him. For instance, he published a four-volume *Christology of the Old Testament, and a Commentary on the Messianic Predictions* (1829-35; Eng. trans. of the 2nd ed. 1861-68), a three-volume *Commentary on the Psalms* (1842-45; Eng. trans. 1845-48), *The Prophecies of the Prophet Ezekiel Elucidated* (2 vols., 1867-68; Eng. trans., 1 vol., 1869), and *History of the Kingdom of God under the Old Testament* (3 vols., 1869-71; Eng. trans., 2 vols., 1871-72), to name just a few of his most important exegetical writings. His main strength and most lasting merit lie in the critical defense and explanation of the Old Testament as an actual revelation of God as contrasted with a rationalistic exegesis.

17. Schaff, *Germany,* 305-6.

Under his leadership the *Kirchenzeitung* first supported the revival of piety and a vital Christianity in Germany, standing solidly on the basis of the Protestant union as established in Prussia. But gradually it assumed an exclusively confessional tone, and by 1848 it had become the organ of the Lutheran part of the Protestant church in Prussia. The Lutheran view of the Lord's Supper was more and more advanced, and with all its privileges the Lutheran confession was guarded within the church of Prussia. This was not so much a turn against the Reformed church as an act done out of fear that both the Reformed and the Lutheran church would be transformed into a more liberal unionistic church. Yet the *Evangelische Kirchenzeitung* was also aggressive against Hengstenberg's own colleagues, for instance against Schleiermacher and his alleged pantheism or against the allegedly unscriptural and anticonfessional theology of the rationalistic theologians Wilhelm Gesenius (1786-1842) and Julius A. L. Wegscheider (1771-1849) in Halle. Since Hengstenberg had great influence in the ministry of education, King Frederick William III even gave orders that only those candidates who adhere to the doctrinal concept of the Protestant church in accordance with the Augsburg Confession should be considered for appointments to theological professorships.[18]

While Hengstenberg certainly contributed to confessional identity and to overcoming the theological reductionism of liberalism, the new challenges of theology and the church as brought about by the rapid industrialization and urbanization escaped his often bitter polemics. He was more a consolidator than somebody pointing to the future.

An Evangelical Passion for Christ and for Students: August Tholuck

Though **Friedrich August Gottreu Tholuck** (1799-1877), like Hengstenberg, had come under the influence of Baron Ernst von Kottwitz, he became a decided supporter of the Protestant union and deplored the confessional and denominational controversies in Germany. Tholuck's studies of seventeenth-century Lutheran theology served as an instruction and warning against any attempt to zealously revive what some considered the best state of the church, i.e., orthodoxy, which had been followed by rationalism.[19]

---

18. Cf. Joachim Mehlhausen, "Hengstenberg, Ernst Wilhelm," in *Theologische Realenzyklopädie*, 15:41, in his careful assessment.

19. Cf. August Tholuck, *Lutherische Theologen Wittenbergs im 17. Jahrhundert* (Hamburg: Friedrich und Andreas Perthes, 1852) and *Das akademische Leben des 17. Jahrhunderts mit*

Tholuck had a very humble upbringing, his father being a small trader in Breslau. The son originally wanted to become a goldsmith, but with the help of some friends he managed to attend the *Gymnasium* of his native city in Silesia and subsequently the University of Berlin. He had an extraordinary gift for languages and intended to become an Orientalist. Already at the *Gymnasium* he had composed a speech in which he glorified Islam as a religion of equal dignity and beauty with Christianity. But as a student in Berlin he was influenced by von Kottwitz and soon found himself in the sphere of the new pietistic awakening. In 1821 he obtained his licentiate in theology and, against Schleiermacher's objections, received the protection of the secretary of education Karl Freiherr vom Stein zu Altenstein, and became Privatdozent in Berlin. Only two years later he was associate professor, and in 1826, through the influence of pietistic circles, he was called to the University of Halle as professor of theology. This call was meant to be a corrective to the rationalistic dogmatician Wegscheider and the equally rationalistic Old Testament scholar Gesenius.[20]

Due to his own personal struggle and his experience of sin and grace, Tholuck published *Guido and Julius, or, Sin and the Propitiator Exhibited in the True Consecration of the Sceptic* (1823). This book, written in just three weeks, influenced many theology students to move "from the barren desert of rationalism to the green meadows and fresh fountains of the gospel of Christ."[21] It became an instant success as the standard tract of a theology of the awakening. While in Berlin Tholuck still devoted himself to Oriental languages and literature and published a volume on Persian Sufism (1821), but in Halle he changed his focus to biblical exegesis to redeem it from the grasp of rationalism, and to introduce again the rich exegetical sources of the church fathers and the Reformers. He also republished in a cheap edition the Latin New Testament commentaries of John Calvin, except for the one on the book of Revelation. Initially Tholuck's position at Halle was exceedingly difficult because he was considered an outsider. Soon, however, rationalism disappeared from the theological faculty and through new appointments the faculty became more and more orthodox and evangelical-minded. For more than two generations Halle was to be the center for the theology of the awakening.

---

besonderer Beziehung auf die protestantisch-theologischen Fakultäten Deutschlands nach handschriftlichen Quellen, 2 vols. (Halle: Eduard Anton, 1853, 1854).

20. Cf. Karl Barth, *Protestant Theology in the Nineteenth Century: Its Background and History,* new ed. (Grand Rapids: Eerdmans, 2002), 496, who however is quite critical of Tholuck, claiming he concerned himself too much with himself instead of with *him,* i.e., Jesus Christ. We doubt that this criticism is fair.

21. So Schaff, *Germany,* 280; a more restrained assessment is rendered by Gunther Wenz, "Tholuck, Friedrich August Gottreu," in *Theologische Realenzyklopädie,* 33:426.

Since Tholuck had no children either by his first wife, who soon after marriage died of tuberculosis, or by his second, his students were his children whom he loved and for whom he cared. He also preached every other week as the university preacher. He was original, suggestive, and eloquent, and possessed a good measure of wit and humor. He was always open to new ideas, yet his heart and piety were Christ centered. With an extraordinary talent for languages, he studied nineteen foreign languages before he was seventeen, and spoke several just like a native. He was also a personal favorite of students and scholars from foreign countries, especially from England, Scotland, and the United States. We remember that he was friends with Charles Hodge as well as with Philip Schaff, who appreciated his conservative and pietistic tenor. In 1873 he was even invited to the United States to attend the General Conference of the Evangelical Alliance, but could not travel because of ill health.[22]

His *Hours of Devotion* (1840; Eng. trans. 1853) gives witness to his evangelical piety with fresh enthusiasm. It had a large influence then and is still used today. A variety of commentaries, such as on Romans, the Gospel of John, Hebrews, and the Psalms, came from his pen and were all translated into English. Thousands of students owe to him their spiritual formation. German theologians as different as Julius Müller, Richard Rothe, Johann Tobias Beck, Albrecht Ritschl, Wilhelm Herrmann, and even Harless studied with him.

Turning People to Christ: Charles Grandison Finney

The German pietistic awakening could produce theologians who were narrowly confessional or broadly Christ centered. American revivalism, however, did not focus on theological formation. Its intent was to address the larger populace and win it for Christ. In this way its outlook was highly optimistic, reflecting the mood of nineteenth-century America. Symptomatic of this attitude is the approach of **Charles Grandison Finney** (1792-1875), "the father of modern revivalism."[23] He was born in Warren, Connecticut, but his family soon moved to Oneida County in upstate New York. There he grew up on a farm in a pioneer community. His schooling was mostly private, except for attendance at the Warren Academy at his birthplace. He intended to study law at Yale, but was persuaded to pursue studies on his own. He studied in New Jersey under a tu-

22. Cf. D. S. Schaff, "Tholuck, Friedrich August Gottreu," in *The New Schaff-Herzog Encyclopedia of Religious Knowledge*, 11:420.

23. So Sydney E. Ahlstrom, *A Religious History of the American People* (New Haven: Yale University Press, 1972), 459.

tor, and in 1818 entered a law office and was later admitted to the bar. Though his upbringing was not very religious, his study of the Bible together with his natural religious sensitivity led to a conversion experience in 1821 wherein "it seemed as if I met the Lord Jesus Christ *face to face.* . . . He said nothing, but looked at me in such a manner as to break me right down at his feet."[24] Finney gave up his law practice immediately and started to convert other people.

Without any formal training in theology Finney was accepted in 1823 as a candidate for the ministry by the Presbyterians and ordained the following year. He conducted revivals along the Erie Canal and in the eastern states using "new measures," such as the "anxious bench" where people needing special exhortation and prayer sat. Against Paul's admonition that women remain silent in the church (1 Cor. 14:34), still adhered to at that time, he encouraged women to pray in public meetings. He made extensive use of "protracted meetings" that continued nightly for a week or more. With direct speech that was very forceful and by including persons in his prayers by name, he had immense success. People burst out in tears and even fainted, yet also lives were transformed and whole towns were brought back to decency. Nevertheless, his method and approach were quite controversial, even opposed by Lyman Beecher (1775-1863) and Asahel Nettleton of his own Presbyterian denomination. Yet the general effect of his revivals was positive, as was also seen by a convention of Presbyterian and Congregational ministers in 1827 in New Lebanon, New York, that approved of his work.

In 1832 he became pastor of the Second Free Presbyterian Church in New York, and four years later he withdrew from the presbytery. His church became Congregational in polity, organizing itself as the Broadway Tabernacle Church with a sanctuary constructed just for Finney. Slavery was a hot topic during this era, but Finney said he did not want to "turn aside to make it [i.e., to talk about slavery] a hobby, or divert the attention of the people from the work of converting souls. Nevertheless in my prayers and preaching I so often alluded to slavery and denounced it, that a considerable excitement came to exist among the people" (362-63). It became very clear where Finney stood, since he refused to give communion to slaveholders and proclaimed that slavery was a sin and demanded immediate abolition of all forms of slavery by the slaveholders, the church, and the government (cf. 362 n. 29).

The issue of slavery had also come up among the students at Lane Seminary, the Presbyterian theological seminary in Cincinnati, since its location bordered on the slave states. When the majority of the students advocated abo-

---

24. *The Memoirs of Charles G. Finney: The Complete Restored Text,* ed. Garth M. Rosell and Richard A. G. Dupuis (Grand Rapids: Zondervan, 1989), 23. Page references in the next few paragraphs are to Finney's memoirs.

litionism, the trustees forbade discussion of the subject. Consequently, most students left the seminary. About a dozen of them came together near Cincinnati, then moved to Oberlin College, in Oberlin, Ohio. In 1835 Finney was invited to establish a theological school there, and a wealthy New York financier, Arthur Tappan, guaranteed him financial support. Finney accepted on the stipulation that he could retain his pastorate in New York and spend six months of the year there. Through a new form of governance, the trustees of Oberlin College also made it possible that Oberlin could "pioneer coeducation and equal educational opportunities for Blacks" (381 n. 108).

Two years later Finney gave up the dual appointment. From 1837 to 1872 he served as pastor of the First Congregational Church in Oberlin; he was also the first professor of theology at the Oberlin School of Theology. From 1851 to 1866 he was also president of the college. He still continued his evangelistic work during a part of each year and even evangelized in Great Britain (1849-50 and 1859-60).

Finney was important for urban evangelism and rising antislavery sentiments. His theological views were a new kind of Calvinism that emphasized the individual's ability to repent and to lead a virtuous life. For Finney "*religion is the work of man*. It is something for man to do. It consists in obeying God. It is man's duty. It is true God induces him to do it. He influences him by His Spirit, because of his great wickedness and reluctance to obey."[25] We notice here the immense emphasis on the human side, on human activity. This is also true in Finney's understanding of the conversion process, since "there are always two agents, God and the sinner, employed and active in every case of genuine conversion. . . . Men are not mere *instruments* in the hands of God. . . . The conversion of a sinner consists in his obeying the truth. It is therefore impossible it should take place without his agency, for it consists in *his* acting right" (8-9). Though God arranges the possibility of conversion and is present through his Holy Spirit, nevertheless it is the sinner who commits himself to God. But where does grace come in?

According to Finney, "grace is favor. The word is often used in the Bible to signify a free gift. The grace of God is the *favor* of God" (471). Grace is still understood as prevenient, yet the subsequent move is on the human side. Therefore Finney emphasized: "Growth in grace is conditioned on increased knowledge of what is involved in *entire consecration* to God. True conversion to God involves the consecration of ourselves and of all that we have to Him, so far as we understand what is implied in this" (473). For Finney sanctification was the consequence of conversion, which again, on account of our decision, was seen

---

25. Charles G. Finney, *Revivals of Religion* (Virginia Beach, Va.: CBN University, 1978), 1. It is interesting that this book was republished in the cited version for the TV evangelist Pat Robertson and the 700 Club. The page references in the following text are to this work.

as a human possibility. Though this kind of emphasis on what a person can do and attain has become very popular not only in evangelical circles but also among the wider public, traditional theology acts vehemently against it, especially since it realizes that human existence, even in its reborn state, is still lived on this earth and therefore is tinged with brokenness. Nevertheless, Finney portrayed accurately the progressive spirit of the nineteenth century and aroused countless people to take seriously the church's message of sin and forgiveness.

A Christocentric Theology of the Heart: Samuel Taylor Coleridge

The poet and theologian **Samuel Taylor Coleridge** (1772-1834) served in England in a similar seminal capacity as did Kant, Schleiermacher, and Hegel in Germany. He was born to a headmaster of a school in Devonshire. His father died when he was only seven, and when he was nine he entered Christ's Hospital, a boarding school in London. In 1791 he went to Cambridge to study at the Jesus College. Two years later, because of debt, he attempted to join the army, intending to go to Pennsylvania — perhaps via Canada — to establish a republican community. He left Cambridge without a degree in 1794 and composed poems. In 1795 he gave lectures in Bristol on politics and religion to earn some money. The following year he went to Somersetshire to cooperate with William Wordsworth (1770-1850), who was to become one of the main proponents of romanticism, and together with him in 1798 composed *Lyrical Ballads*.

Similar to Schleiermacher in his *Speeches*, Coleridge and Wordsworth opposed the kind of negative philosophy "which called the want of imagination Judgment & the never being moved to Rapture Philosophy."[26] Through his father's influence Coleridge had become accustomed to resorting to his imagination, and was not prepared to believe that reality was bounded by what the ear can hear or the eye see and the hand touch. He went beyond the naive empiricism of Hume and conceived of an immaterial or spiritual reality beyond and above the material.[27] Coleridge distinguished imagination, as the living power and incentive of perception, from fantasy, which for him was merely an association of thoughts in allegories and parables.

In 1798 Wordsworth and Coleridge were suspected of being agents of the

---

26. Samuel Taylor Coleridge, *Collected Letters*, ed. Earl Leslie Griggs, 6 vols. (Oxford: Clarendon, 1956), 1:355 (in an autobiographical letter of Oct. 16, 1797).

27. Cf. Robert Shafer, *Christianity and Naturalism: Essays in Criticism,* 2nd ser. (New Haven: Yale University Press, 1926; reprint, Port Washington, N.Y.: Kennikat Press, 1969), 38-39.

French revolutionary regime. Therefore they took off to Germany. One reason for going to Germany was Coleridge's desire to participate in the intellectual movements in that country. He attended lectures at the University of Göttingen, among others by Johann Gottfried Eichhorn (1752-1827), a professor of philosophy and Oriental languages. He was also fascinated by Lessing's daring combinations and wanted to write a biography of him. He also read Kant and wanted to write a systematic metaphysics. The following year he returned to England and again sought the friendship of Wordsworth in the Lake District, the prime region for the romantics.

Soon a period of sickness commenced, which for Coleridge caused dependency on opium. He made heroic attempts to gradually overcome this dependency and the pain that had gotten him into it. By 1816 his health had deteriorated so much that he went to London to stay in the home of a medical doctor. Nevertheless, he remained literarily active and wrote his *Lay Sermons* (1816, 1817), *Aids to Reflection* (1825), and *On the Constitution of Church and State* (1829). In this last major work he pointed out that an industrial society needs stability as much as change. If a people strives too much toward material progress, religion is in danger of becoming hostage to the practical interests and needs of the people. Cut off from learning and imagination, it reduces itself to thoughtless piety. Religion reigns in our thoughts and in the powers akin to thought, because "it is calculated to occupy the whole mind, and employ successively all the faculties of man."[28]

In the eighteenth century religion was largely understood as a mere intellectual assent to a body of metaphysical doctrine, which for some was guaranteed by divine revelation but for others was susceptible of rational proof. This means religion, where it still existed, lacked vitality. Nevertheless, "the public profession of Christianity remained a practically essential badge of respectability throughout the period."[29] Yet for Coleridge religion was something alive that coincides with an external revelation but reverberates in one's heart. He wrote: "Christianity must be *founded* on the testimony of the heart and spirit coinciding with the outward Revelation, not on argument and discourse of reason, metaphysical or logical. . . . So is Christianity based on its own spiritual truths and the receptivity of them in our spirit."[30] This reminds us of

---

28. Samuel Taylor Coleridge, *The Collected Works*, vol. 6, *Lay Sermons*, ed. R. J. White (London: Routledge and Kegan Paul, 1972), 196.

29. So Shafer, *Christianity and Naturalism*, 35.

30. Samuel Taylor Coleridge, *Confessions of an Inquiring Spirit*, 3rd ed. (1853), edited with introduction by H. StJ. Hart (London: Adam and Charles Black, 1956), 104. Yet this text is from Sara Coleridge, his wife, in a "Note on the 'Confessions of an Inquiring Spirit.'" Nevertheless, this is also Coleridge's own conviction.

Schleiermacher's insistence on feeling and intuition, but for Coleridge it is complemented with outward revelation. It should not be confused with the Kantian insistence on the discourse of reason. Therefore Coleridge stated: "A belief, however true and pure, which is held without being spiritually apprehended is but a talent of gold wrapped in a napkin."[31] Intellectual assent is not sufficient, nor is any kind of propositional faith.

He explained: "The truth revealed through Christ has its evidence in itself, and the proof of its divine authority in its fitness to our nature and needs; — the clearness and cogency of this proof being proportionate to the degree of self-knowledge in each individual hearer. Christianity has likewise its historical evidences, and these as strong as is compatible with the nature of history, and with the aims and objects of a religious dispensation."[32] Three items are significant here: the self-evidence of the revelation, the self-awareness of this revelation in the individual human being, and the external historical evidence. Coleridge could even present this in some kind of Hegelian fashion when he showed how God's word comes into our world: "The Eternal Word, Christ from everlasting, is the *Prothesis,* or identity; — the scriptures and the Church are the two poles, or *Thesis* and *Antithesis,* and the Preacher in direct line under the Spirit, but likewise the point of junction of the Written Word and the Church, is the *Synthesis.*"[33] This means that God's word mediated through Christ meets us in Scripture and the church, while the one who proclaims this word, though tied to both Scripture and the church, is directly under Christ through the mediation of the Holy Spirit.

This direct mediation of the divine was important for Coleridge. This can also be seen in his understanding of religious ceremonies. "A man may look at a glass, or through it, or both. That all earthly things be unto thee as glass to see heaven through! Religious ceremonies should be pure glass, not dyed in the gorgeous crimsons and purple blues and greens of the drapery of saints and saintesses."[34] Similar to the function of an icon in Orthodox theology, religious ceremonies are not entities in themselves, but convey what they stand for, a heavenly reality. When Coleridge said baptism "is neither the outward ceremony of Baptism, under any form or circumstance, nor any other ceremony; but such a faith in Christ as tends to produce a conformity to his holy doctrines and example in heart and life," he did not devalue the sacrament.[35] Coleridge

31. Coleridge, *Confessions,* 95 (by Sara Coleridge).

32. Coleridge, *Confessions,* 64.

33. Coleridge, *Confessions,* 35, where he also graphically explains this relationship.

34. Samuel Taylor Coleridge, "Religious Ceremonies," in *The Literary Remains of Samuel Taylor Coleridge,* collected and edited by Henry Nelson Coleridge (London: William Pickering, 1836), 1:340.

35. Samuel Taylor Coleridge, *Aids to Reflection* (XXIV), ed. John Beer, in *The Collected*

rather wanted to point beyond the outward ceremony to what the ceremony stands for.

It follows from his christocentric conception of Christianity that the church is a democracy: there should be "focal points in it, but no superior."[36] This Christocentricity also meant that the church was to be conceived of as universal and not as a particular Anglican, Roman, or Greek church. It thus has its counterpoint not in any particular state, as some kind of national church, but in the world.[37] With his christocentric theology of the heart, Coleridge had an impact on a variety of people: John Henry Newman was influenced by him as well as F. D. Maurice with his Christian Socialism; he also influenced the biblical studies of F. J. A. Hort (1828-92) at Cambridge, and even Horace Bushnell in America.[38] He opened for British theology a much more comprehensive horizon than the empiricism of the day, and endowed theology with a new inspiration.

The Oxford Movement: John Keble, John Henry Newman, and E. B. Pusey

John Locke (1632-1704) rejected the notion of innate ideas and paved the way for empiricism. David Hume (1711-76) claimed that our sense experience, unless it is superstition, stays within space and time and thereby is reduced to the empirical data. With this kind of philosophical mind-set, popularized in many ways, Great Britain took the lead in the Enlightenment movement and set the stage on which theology had to assert itself. Some conservatives picked up the empiricist dogma, for instance, William Paley (1743-1805) in his *Natural Theology, or Evidences of the Existence and Attributes of the Deity Collected from the Appearances of Nature* (1802; 20th ed. 1820) and his *Evidences of Christianity* (1794; 15th ed. 1811). As we can see from the many editions these works went

---

Works, vol. 9 (Princeton: Princeton University Press, 1990), 366, and James D. Boulger, *Coleridge as Religious Thinker* (New Haven: Yale University Press, 1961), 177, who cites this passage. In completely misunderstanding it he states: "Nothing more clearly differentiates him from the growing 'High Church' party of his time, or from certain strains in present-day Anglican orthodoxy, than his insistence that baptism is a ceremonial and not a sacramental rite."

36. Samuel Taylor Coleridge, *Table Talk* (May 12, 1830), ed. Carl Woodring, in *The Collected Works*, vol. 14/1 (Princeton: Princeton University Press, 1990), 133.

37. So J. Robert Barth, *Coleridge and Christian Doctrine* (Cambridge: Harvard University Press, 1969), 165.

38. For the influence on Maurice, cf. Charles Richard Sanders, *Coleridge and the Broad Church Movement* (Durham, N.C.: Duke University Press, 1942), 179-209.

through in a relatively short time, there was a need to confront empiricism on its own turf. Yet, there were others who wanted nothing to do with empiricism, such as the evangelical movement with its leaders John Wesley (1703-91) and George Whitefield (1714-70). We have also seen that Coleridge was very discontented with this approach. With his poetic sensibility and creative use of the imagination, Coleridge contributed to a movement that became something very different from what it was first conceived to be, the so-called Oxford Movement.[39]

Three people are characteristically considered primary contributors to the success and thought of the movement: John Keble, John Henry Newman, and Edward B. Pusey. Generally speaking, the Oxford Movement was more a movement of the heart than of the intellect, concerned more with prayer than with belief. Its members always saw dogma in relation to worship, the numinous, conscience, and moral distress. Similar to the romantic poets and novelists, to the evangelicals and pietistic theologians, the Oxford Movement revolted against the predominance of reason and religious skepticism. "Their leaders wanted to find a place for the poetic or the aesthetic judgment; their hymnody shared in the feelings and in the vocations of the romantic poets; they wished to find a place and value for historical tradition, against the irreverent or sacrilegious hands of critical revolutionaries for whom no antiquity was sacred."[40]

The date for the beginning of the Oxford Movement is July 14, 1833, when **John Keble** (1792-1866) preached an assize sermon in the university church. John Newman wrote of this: "It was published under the title of 'National Apostasy.' I have ever considered and kept the day, as the start of the religious movement of 1833."[41] Of course, there had been events leading up to that. In 1828-29 the British parliament repealed the Corporation and Test Acts and enacted into law the Roman Catholic Relief Bill, which put Protestant dissenters and Roman Catholics on nearly equal footing with the Church of England and Ireland. Four years later the Church Temporalities Bill was introduced to Par-

39. For the influence of Coleridge on the Oxford Movement, cf. Martin Roberts, "Coleridge as a Background to the Oxford Movement," in *Pusey Rediscovered,* ed. Perry Butler (London: SPCK, 1983), who claims that Coleridge had "at least an unconscious influence on the development of the Tractarian tradition" (34). He asserts some influence on Keble and a more implicit one on Newman.

40. So Owen Chadwick in his insightful essay, "The Mind of the Oxford Movement," in Chadwick, *The Spirit of the Oxford Movement: Tractarian Essays* (Cambridge: Cambridge University Press, 1990), 2. Whether "the 'nature-mysticism' of romantic poetry was determinative of their conception of religion," an idea disclaimed by Eugene R. Fairweather, ed., *The Oxford Movement* (New York: Oxford University Press, 1964), 4, remains an open question.

41. John Henry Newman, *Apologia pro Vita Sua,* ed. Ian Ker (London: Penguin Books, 1994), 50.

liament, which should have dissolved ten Protestant bishoprics of the Irish church. This would have meant a considerable reduction of the power of the Irish church in an overwhelmingly Roman Catholic environment. Therefore Keble asked the question in his sermon: "If it be true anywhere, that such enactments are forced on the legislature by public opinion, is APOSTASY too hard a word to describe the temper of that nation?"[42] He was concerned that the very success of the Anglican reformation was threatened by opening the gates to other religious groups.

John Keble was born in Gloucestershire to a clergyman of the Church of England. He attended Corpus Christi College at Oxford, and in 1811 became a fellow of Oriel College, by then the most reputable college at Oxford. He was tutor at Oriel from 1811 to 1823 and was ordained priest in 1816. After pastoring various churches, he held the lectureship in poetry at Oxford from 1831 to 1841. Since he was deeply modest, he anonymously published in 1827 the two volumes of *The Christian Year,* a collection of sacred lyrics that became so immensely popular that by the time the copyright expired in 1873, it had been issued in 140 editions. Given his modesty, it was surprising that he would take up the cause of the Church of England against the government, dissenters, and Roman Catholics.

While the sermon contained basically nothing other high churchmen had not been saying, it brought Newman and Pusey together. In 1838 they began to work on the *Library of the Fathers,* for which Keble translated Irenaeus. This indicated the direction their thinking was going — a return to tradition and a recovery of what had been lost through the centuries. "'Don't be original' was the advice which Keble gave to Newman when he read his sermons and found new ideas."[43] As for many conservatives of his time, the word "tradition" was no longer something negative, but something good that pointed to the traditions received in the church. This also meant a reconsideration of the corporate authority of the church.

Reliance on the Bible only, which had become a Protestant maxim, seemed to mean that everyone could extract from the Bible what he or she wanted without regard for the corporate judgment of the Christian community. Against this trend Keble and Newman emphasized the authority of the sense of the community of the church. It comes therefore as no surprise that in the *Tracts for the Times* that Keble edited with Newman and other Oxford theologians, Keble wrote on the apostolic succession. Beyond that he wrote eight further tracts. While he was the guide and mentor of the Tractarians, as the au-

---

42. John Keble, "National Apostasy," in *The Oxford Movement,* 42.
43. So related by Chadwick, "The Mind," 27.

thors of the *Tracts* were called, Keble was more concerned with his parish than with being an instigator of the new movement. Nevertheless, "little, if anything, was published that he had not seen and approved."[44] He was an eloquent preacher, scriptural and impressive, and had so many friends and admirers that after his death Keble College was established at Oxford.

John Henry Newman (1801-90) was the other main figure, or rather *the* main figure, of the Oxford Movement. Newman was born in London to a Huguenot mother; his father was a banker. At age fifteen Newman was converted to evangelical Calvinism by the influence of one of his schoolteachers. This evangelical Calvinism remained the foundation of his faith. In 1816 he enrolled at Trinity College in Oxford, and two years later he received his B.A. In another two years he had become a fellow of Oriel College, as Keble had, which was the most prestigious scholarship one could obtain at Oxford. In 1825 he was ordained a priest in the Church of England. While at Oxford he gave up his "remaining Calvinism," meaning the doctrine of predestination, and received "the doctrine of Baptismal Regeneration." He also found an appreciation for the "doctrine of Tradition."[45] The doctrine of apostolic succession, however, had no real impact on him at that time.

His friendship with Richard Hurrell Froude (1803-36), another fellow of Oriel College, led him away from considering the Roman Catholic Church "anti-Christian," and "to look with admiration towards the Church of Rome, and in the same degree to dislike the Reformation."[46] When Keble preached his famous sermon in 1833, Newman understood the occasion to be a divine summons to defend the church in the hour of peril. In 1828 he became provost of Oriel College and vicar at the university church St. Mary the Virgin, where he was increasingly renowned for his sermons. They were eventually published in six volumes (*Parochial Sermons*, 1834-42).

As a response to Keble's sermon, Newman said he had "out of my own head begun the Tracts."[47] Initially these were intended as small tracts — his first one was entitled *Thoughts on the Ministerial Commission* — but eventually they became larger publications. We read in these tracts that the church is not just a national institution but a divine society founded by Christ. Its marks are unity, catholicity, apostolicity, and holiness. The faith of the church is preserved through the threefold office of bishop, priest, and deacon, and the apostolic succession through the laying on of hands. In tracts 38 and 41 (1834) and in his

---

44. So Georgina Battiscombe, *John Keble: A Study in Limitations* (London: Constable, 1963), 160.

45. Newman, *Apologia pro Vita Sua*, 29.

46. Newman, *Apologia pro Vita Sua*, 42.

47. Newman, *Apologia pro Vita Sua*, 54.

Lectures on the Prophetical Office of the Church (1837), Newman claimed that the Church of England had maintained a middle way *(via media)* between Roman Catholicism and the Reformation. This meant it was not on the side of the Reformation, but between that and Roman Catholicism. Newman even went a step further in his *Essay on Justification* of 1837, stating that concerning justification, "between Rome and Anglicanism, between high Church and low Church, there was no real intellectual difference on the point."[48]

The Tractarians were unsatisfied with the evangelicals, who emphasized justification by faith alone while not putting emphasis on the sacraments as instruments of grace. The Tractarians shifted the emphasis to sanctification and thought that no Christian theologian "could finally avoid deciding between a Protestantism which preached the reality of grace, yet in fact denied its real presence and power in human life, and a Catholicism which backed up the proclamation of grace with an affirmation of its objective signs and fruits."[49] This was not simply a return to Rome, but an attempt to show that there is indeed something operative in the Christian that he or she owes to divine activity, as Luther had also said when he claimed that faith cannot be without works.

Another issue arose for Newman. In 1841 the Prussian king Frederick William IV, in collaboration with the Anglican primate of Canterbury, appointed an Anglican bishop, who was in apostolic succession, to the seat of Jerusalem. Newman asked himself how the Anglican bishops could reprimand him for moving so close to the Roman Catholic Church, as he believed the Anglican formularies would allow, and also fraternize with Protestant bodies "without any renunciation of the errors or regard to their due reception of baptism and confirmation."[50] He wrote in protest to the bishop of Canterbury, claiming that "Lutheranism and Calvinism are heresies, repugnant to Scripture, springing up three centuries since, and anathematized by East as well as West."[51] Why, he asked, would his church that considered itself to be catholic, connect itself in intercommunion with groups that are strictly sectarian? He wrote: "From the end of 1841, I was on my death-bed, as regards my membership with the Anglican Church."[52]

Newman withdrew more and more from Oxford and devoted himself to the poor members of his congregation and also gathered a small group of disciples in a semimonastic circle for prayer and studies. The same year he also wrote his famous tract 90 *(Remarks on Certain Passages in the Thirty-nine Articles)*. The problem was that by now his via media had collapsed, since it was

---

48. Newman, *Apologia pro Vita Sua*, 80.
49. So Fairweather, *The Oxford Movement*, 11, in his introduction.
50. Newman, *Apologia pro Vita Sua*, 136.
51. Newman, *Apologia pro Vita Sua*, 138.
52. Newman, *Apologia pro Vita Sua*, 141.

founded on three principles: dogma, the sacramental system, and anti-Romanism. He was now prepared to admit that dogma and the sacramental system were more effectively safeguarded by Rome than by Canterbury. Therefore there was really no middle way left. In 1843 he resigned from his pastorate, and on October 9, 1845, he was received into the Roman Catholic Church. The following year he went to Rome to complete his education as priest, and the year after that he was consecrated a priest.

Soon Newman became one of the leading voices of Catholic renewal. He even attempted to establish a Roman Catholic university in Dublin, and in 1864 he wrote his autobiography, *Apologia pro Vita Sua,* through which he explained his own personal journey and therefore regained at least some respect from educated Protestants. In 1877 he published two volumes of pieces from his time as an Anglican, the *Via Media,* in which he described the priestly, prophetic, and kingly office of the church; the role of priesthood and laity in the liturgy; and the responsibility and teaching obligation of the theologians and the institutional authority of pope and Curia. Two years later he was elevated to cardinal. Newman certainly was immensely influential, not only within his own Anglican Church but also in Roman Catholicism. Since his passion for the renewal of the church without relinquishing its tradition was genuine, we are not surprised that at Vatican II "his name and his works have been quoted more extensively than those of any other theologian or historian."[53]

With Newman's departure to Roman Catholicism, the Oxford Movement did not die, though a number of the new school that identified themselves as Catholic went with him. There was still **Edward Bouverie Pusey** (1800-1882), born at Pusey, Berkshire, who also became a fellow of Oriel College in 1823 and got acquainted there with Keble, Newman, and Froude. Pusey went to Germany in 1825, and again the following year, where he became friends with Tholuck and heard lectures from Eichhorn, Schleiermacher, and Neander, studied Syriac and Aramaic with Hengstenberg, and also Arabic. In 1828 he was ordained a priest and endowed with the regius professorship of Hebrew and canon at Christ Church. In his first book, *An Historical Enquiry into the Probable Causes of the Rationalist Character Lately Predominant in the Theology of Germany* (1828), he showed great sympathy for Luther; Johann Gerhard (1582-1637), the most important representative of Lutheran orthodoxy; and German pietism. Theological rationalism, according to him, was caused by neoscholastic Lutheran orthodoxy. Since he was far from being conservative, he, in contrast to

---

53. So Bishop Robert J. Dwyer, "Listening In," *Register* (Denver), Jan. 19, 1964, 1, as quoted by Martin J. Svaglic, introduction to *Apologia pro Vita Sua: Being a History of His Religious Opinions,* by John Henry Newman (Oxford: Oxford University Press, 1990), xiv.

Keble, advocated allowing Roman Catholics and dissenters nearly the same rights as the Church of England.

Three times a week he lectured in Hebrew, and as the principal result of his studies he published *Daniel, the Prophet* (1864), in which he advocated a traditional date and authorship of the book of Daniel and refuted the more recent research of liberal exegesis. His exegetical works and his work with Arabic manuscripts in the Bodleian Library came second to his engagement with the Oxford Movement. Pusey wrote seven of the *Tracts for the Times,* such as number 18 on fasting (1834) and number 81 on the eucharistic sacrifice (1837). He even defended tract 90, which Newman had written concerning the Thirty-nine Articles of the Church of England. Yet when Newman converted to Roman Catholicism, Pusey remained in the Church of England and became the symbolic leader of the Anglo-Catholic movement. Since he was of aristocratic descent, his grandfather being the first viscount of Folkestone, and because he occupied a high academic position and was profoundly erudite, Pusey was not easily swayed. Therefore he became a moderating force in the Oxford Movement. His loyalty to the Church of England was never shaken. At the same time, he was sympathetic toward Luther and Lutheranism, and therefore not as anti-Protestant as were Newman and Froude.

Pusey was the founder and spiritual superintendent of the first Anglican sisterhood. He emphasized individual confession, but warned against the excesses in spiritual disciplines and mortification; he protested against isolationism both from the Roman Catholic Church and also from Protestantism.[54] He acquainted the Church of England with the post-Reformation developments in the Roman Catholic Church in spirituality, including the spiritual exercises of Ignatius of Loyola. Pusey also was a man of prayer who emphasized the validity of the sacramental and ecclesiological vision of the patristic era. He had an affection for the evangelicals because of their shared love for biblical studies. More than anybody else, he was responsible for the consolidation and expansion of the Anglo-Catholic revival initiated by Keble and Newman.[55] After his death, Pusey House was founded with a library and a pastoral center. In 1889, together with other Oxford scholars, its first director Charles Gore (1853-1932) published *Lux Mundi,* a collection of essays in which they attempted to put the Catholic faith in right relationship to the spiritual and moral problems of the present. Another collection, *Essays Catholic and Critical* (ed. Edward Gordon Selwyn, 1926), represented the prevailing mood of Anglican theology at the turn of the nineteenth century.

---

54. Cf. Keith Denison, "Dr. Pusey as Confessor and Spiritual Director," in *Pusey Rediscovered,* 214-27.

55. Cf. Gabriel O'Donnell, "The Spirituality of E. B. Pusey," in *Pusey Rediscovered,* 239.

For Further Reading

Claus Harms (1778-1855)

Carstens, Heinrich C. "Harms, Claus." In *The New Schaff-Herzog Encyclopedia of Religious Knowledge,* 5:155-56. Grand Rapids: Baker, 1949-50.

Ferm, Vergilius. *The Crisis in American Lutheran Theology: A Study of the Issue between American Lutheranism and Old Lutheranism.* Foreword by Luther Allan Weigle. New York: Century Co., 1927. Pp. 118-23 for the ninety-five theses of Claus Harms.

Ludolphy, Ingetraut. "Harms, Claus." In *The Encyclopedia of the Lutheran Church,* edited by Julius Bodensieck, 2:984. Minneapolis: Augsburg, 1965.

Wilhelm Löhe (1808-72)

Heintzen, Erich. *Love Leaves Home: Wilhelm Loehe and the Missouri Synod.* St. Louis: Concordia, 1973.

Löhe, Wilhelm. *Three Books concerning the Church: Offered for Friends of the Lutheran Church for Consideration and Discussion.* Translated by Edward T. Horn. Reading, Pa.: Pilger Publishing House, 1908.

Ratke, David. *Confession and Mission, Word and Sacrament: The Ecclesial Theology of Wilhelm Löhe.* St. Louis: Concordia, 2001.

Stuckwisch, Rich. *Johannes Konrad Wilhelm Löhe: Portrait of a Confessional Lutheran Missiologist.* Fort Wayne: Repristination Press, 1993.

August Friedrich Christian Vilmar (1800-1868)

Haussleiter, Johannes. "Vilmar, August Friedrich Christian." In *The New Schaff-Herzog Encyclopedia of Religious Knowledge,* 12:190-91. Grand Rapids: Baker, 1949-50.

Hopf, Friedrich Wilhelm. "Vilmar, August Friedrich Christian." In *The Encyclopedia of the Lutheran Church,* edited by Julius Bodensieck, 3:2441-42. Minneapolis: Augsburg, 1965.

Kleinig, Vernon P. "Erlangen Theology, August Vilmar, and St. Louis: Influences on Australian Lutheranism." *Lutheran Theological Journal* 28 (May 1994): 28-37.

Ernst Wilhelm Hengstenberg (1802-69)

Hengstenberg, Ernst Wilhelm. *Christology of the Old Testament and a Commentary on the Messianic Predictions.* Translation from 2nd edition by Theod. Meyer. 4 vols. Edinburgh: T. & T. Clark, 1856-58. Reprint of 1847 abridgement, translated by T. K. Arnold, foreword by Walter C. Kaiser, Jr. (Grand Rapids: Kregel, 1970).

Schaff, Philip. *Germany: Its Universities, Theology, and Religion.* Philadelphia: Lindsay and Blakiston, 1857. Pp. 300-319.

Sailhamer, John H. "The Messiah and the Hebrew Bible." *Journal of the Evangelical Theological Society* 44, no. 1 (Mar. 2001): 5-23.

Friedrich August Gottreu Tholuck (1799-1877)

Barth, Karl. *Protestant Theology in the Nineteenth Century: Its Background and History.* New ed. Grand Rapids: Eerdmans, 2002. Pp. 494-504.

Franklin, R. William. "The Impact of Germany on the Anglican Catholic Revival in Nineteenth Century Britain." *Anglican and Episcopal History* 61 (Dec. 1992): 433-48.

Schaff, David S. "Tholuck, Friedrich August Gottreu." In *The New Schaff-Herzog Encyclopedia of Religious Knowledge,* 11:420-21. Grand Rapids: Baker, 1949-50.

Charles Grandison Finney (1792-1875)

Finney, Charles G. *The Autobiography of Charles G. Finney.* Minneapolis: Bethany Fellowship, 1977.

————. *The Memoirs of Charles G. Finney: The Complete Restored Text.* Edited by Garth M. Rosell and Richard A. G. Dupuis. Grand Rapids: Zondervan, 1989.

————. *Revivals of Religion.* Virginia Beach, Va.: CBN University, 1978.

Hambrick-Stowe, Charles E. *Charles G. Finney and the Spirit of American Evangelicalism.* Grand Rapids: Eerdmans, 1996.

Miller, Basil. *Charles G. Finney: He Prayed Down Revivals; Official Biography for the Sesquicentennial Conference, Chicago, 1942.* Minneapolis: Bethany Fellowship, 1942.

Samuel Taylor Coleridge (1772-1834)

Coleridge, Samuel Taylor. *Collected Letters.* Edited by Earl Leslie Griggs. 6 vols. Oxford: Clarendon, 1956-71.

————. *The Collected Works.* Princeton: Princeton University Press, 1971-.

————. *Confessions of an Inquiring Spirit.* 3rd ed. (1853). Edited with introduction by H. StJ. Hart. London: Adam and Charles Black, 1956.

Harding, Anthony. *Coleridge and the Inspired Word.* Kingston, Ont.: McGill-Queens University Press, 1985.

Hedley, Douglas. *Coleridge, Philosophy, and Religion: Aids to Reflection and the Mirror of the Spirit.* Cambridge: Cambridge University Press, 2000.

Niebuhr, Richard. *Streams of Grace: Studies of Jonathan Edwards, Samuel Coleridge, and William James.* Kyoto, Japan: Doshisha University, 1983.

John Keble (1792-1866)

Battiscombe, Georgina. *John Keble: A Study in Limitations.* London: Constable, 1963.

Imberg, Rune. *In Quest of Authority: The "Tracts for the Times" and the Development of the Tractarian Leaders, 1833-1841.* Lund, Sweden: Lund University Press, 1987.

Rowlands, John Henry Lewis. *Church, State, and Society: The Attitudes of John Keble, Richard Hurrell Froude, and John Henry Newman, 1827-1845.* West Sussex: Churchman Publishing, 1989.

John Henry Newman (1801-90)

Jaki, Stanley. *Newman's Challenge*. Grand Rapids: Eerdmans, 2000.

Ker, Ian T. *John Henry Newman: A Biography*. Oxford: Clarendon, 1988.

Newman, John Henry. *Apologia pro Vita Sua*. Edited by Ian Ker. London: Penguin Books, 1994.

Newman Studies Journal (Spring 2004), vol. 1-.

Weatherby, Harold. *Cardinal Newman in His Age: His Place in English Theology and Literature*. Nashville: Vanderbilt University Press, 1973.

Edward Bouverie Pusey (1800-1882)

Butler, Perry, ed. *Pusey Rediscovered*. London: SPCK, 1983.

Forrester, David. *Young Doctor Pusey: A Study of Development*. London: Mowbray, 1989.

Imberg, Rune. *In Quest of Authority: The "Tracts for the Times" and the Development of the Tractarian Leaders, 1833-1841*. Lund, Sweden: Lund University Press, 1987.

C. F. W. Walther (1811-87)

Manteufel, Thomas, and Robert Kolb, eds. *Soli Deo Gloria: Essays on C. F. W. Walther in Memory of August R. Suelflow*. St. Louis: Concordia, 2000.

Suelflow, August R. *Servant of the Word: The Life and Ministry of C. F. W. Walther*. St. Louis: Concordia, 2000.

Walther, C. F. W. *Walther Speaks to the Church: Selected Letters*. Edited by Carl S. Meyer. St. Louis: Concordia, 1973.

5 Cultural Protestantism

The second half of the nineteenth century can be characterized by an optimistic progressive mood that theologically showed itself in a cultural Protestantism, meaning a close connection between Christianity and culture, theology and secular science. This liberal theology disassociated itself from ecclesial dogma and emphasized the relativity of historical insights and the results of research in the history of religion. Especially through Darwin's theory of evolution, many intellectuals believed in the perfectibility of humanity with regard to intellect and moral insight. This mood was not confined to Germany or Europe. It also characterized the American scene, as we will see in the close connections between the representatives of the Social Gospel, such as Henry Churchill King (1858-1934) and Walter Rauschenbusch (1861-1918), and representatives of cultural Protestantism in Germany (cf. chap. 6). There was a missionary zeal in cultural Protestantism to stem the tide of the waning Christian influence on public life and to demonstrate the impact of Christendom on culture. In 1863 the Deutsche Protestantenverein (German Association of Protestants) was founded with the stated goal to renew the Protestant church in the spirit of freedom and in consonance with the development of culture.

The Legacy of Kant and of the
Lutheran Reformation: Albrecht Ritschl

When **Albrecht Ritschl** (1822-89) was born in Berlin, his father had been pastor there since 1810, and a member of the ecclesial governing board of the province of Brandenburg since 1816. When the elder Ritschl was called to become superintendent general of the Church of Pommeria with the actual title "bishop," the family moved to Stettin. Albrecht initially received private schooling there and then attended the *Gymnasium,* from which he graduated in 1839 as the first of his class. There was no doubt in his mind nor in his parents' minds that he would study theology. Young Albrecht first went to Bonn, since a relative of his was professor there in classics. There he read the *Life of Jesus* by Strauss and came into contact with the theology influenced by Hegel. Two years later he moved to Halle for five semesters, and was first attracted by Tholuck, who disappointed him with his lack of scientific rigor. Julius Müller too held no fascination for him. Yet he got deeper into Hegel's philosophy and also into the doctrine of justification, a topic that was to accompany him for many years. Ritschl's acquaintance with the doctrine of justification developed through his contact with the writings of F. C. Baur, who had written a book on this topic. Ritschl then went from Halle to Heidelberg and later to Tübingen, where he was personally fascinated by Baur, and wrote his dissertation on Marcion under him. Ritschl's thesis was accepted at Bonn, where he returned in 1846. There he also obtained his licentiate and became private lecturer (Privatdozent) for New Testament studies in the same year. He did a massive study at Bonn on the origin of the early church (*Die Entstehung der altkatholischen Kirche,* 1850), in which he showed, in the second edition of 1857, his growing independence from Baur.

In 1852 Ritschl became an associate professor at Bonn.[1] Yet before he could be promoted the church administration in Berlin had to make sure he was not a liberal, and therefore he had to vouch for the historical character of the Fourth Gospel. This meant an even greater distancing from the Tübingen School. As associate professor, Ritschl finally had some income of his own and was no longer dependent on financial support from his father. He also gave his first lectures on dogmatics. In a seemingly modernistic way he claimed in these lectures that the only miracle was the appearance of the person of Christ. Subsumed under this miracle were also Jesus' birth, resurrection, and his power over nature, leading again back to a more conservative stance. He also continued his exegetical studies and realized thereby that for Paul justification was a synthetic judgment on account of the work of Christ.[2] While justification is a historic event, reconciliation always occurs in the present. In 1859 Ritschl was called to a full professorship at Bonn. After agreeing to lecture on theological

1. Cf. Rolf Schäfer, "Ritschl, Albrecht/Ritschlsche Schule," in *Theologische Realenzyklopädie,* 29:224.

2. A synthetic judgment is informative by connecting its subject (e.g., humanity) with a further assertion (i.e., the work of Christ). An analytic judgment, however, adds nothing new. It just analyzes the situation of the subject. The distinction actually goes back to Kant.

sciences in accordance with the principles of the Evangelical Lutheran Church, he accepted a call to the University of Göttingen five years later. He stayed there for twenty-five years and declined calls to Berlin, where he was also offered a seat on the governing council of the church, and to Strassburg.

In 1867 he started his most important work, *The Christian Doctrine of Justification and Reconciliation,* the third volume of which appeared in 1874 (Eng. trans., vol. 1, 1872; vol. 3, 1900). Since he never published a dogmatics, Ritschl wrote *Instruction in the Christian Religion* (1875; Eng. trans. 1901). Though intended for use in religious instruction at the *Gymnasium* level, it is actually a very brief dogmatics in ninety paragraphs. Finally he published a *History of Pietism (Geschichte des Pietismus)* in three volumes (1880-86), in which he showed that pietism originated out of pre-Reformation concerns in medieval monasticism. For Ritschl, however, not only the theological content of pietism was important, but also the communal structures and the constitutions that are analogous to what we have in the Reformed and Lutheran church.

Ritschl had an immense influence in theology. About twenty of his students occupied theological professorships, among them Wilhelm Herrmann, Adolf von Harnack, Martin Rade, Johannes Weiss, and even Ernst Troeltsch. Important for his students was that Ritschl showed an appreciation for the history of dogma and for the Lutheran Reformation. He was always praxis-oriented, and he held in high esteem the church of his time and its structure. If there are just two figures in nineteenth-century German theology one should know, they would be Schleiermacher at the beginning of the century and Ritschl toward the end.

His three-volume work *Justification and Reconciliation* shows his indebtedness to Kant, who, according to Ritschl, maintained the obligatory nature of the law that has a moral character stemming from freedom. With this approach Kant marked "not only the defeat of the principles of the Illumination [i.e., the Enlightenment], but also the renewal of the *moral* view of the universe due to the Reformation."[3] This statement shows Ritschl's appreciation of both Kant and the Reformation. Moreover, it indicates the ethical and moral slant of his theology. "Moral" did not mean for Ritschl an advocacy of morality, but in line with Kant, it showed the existential import of duty. This goes hand in hand with his appreciation of Luther's concept of a calling *(Beruf)* as a place in life to which one is called and where one has a moral obligation to the demands arising from that calling.

---

3. Albrecht Ritschl, *A Critical History of the Christian Doctrine of Justification and Reconciliation,* trans. John S. Black (Edinburgh: Edmonston and Douglas, 1872), 390 (which is vol. 1 of *Rechtfertigung und Versöhnung*).

In the second volume of *Justification and Reconciliation,* it is especially interesting how Ritschl treated the wrath of God. He claimed that in the New Testament the wrath of God has an eschatological direction that is prefigured in the prophets with their envisioning of the last judgment. "From there it follows that only the refusal of obedience against the grace of God becomes the occasion for imposing the predestined judging wrath of God; the reverse of this is that those who will be saved are put outside the relationship to that judging wrath through the prevenient election of God."[4] Ritschl concluded that the wrath of God is actually of no concern for Christians, since they are assured that this wrath will not meet them. In keeping with his mentor Schleiermacher, Ritschl evaded therefore the seriousness of the judgment.

Ritschl betrays the influence of both Schleiermacher and Kant when he writes in the third volume: "Christ made the universal moral Kingdom of God His end, and thus He came to know and decide for that kind of redemption which He achieved through the maintenance of fidelity in His calling and of His blessed fellowship with God through suffering unto death."[5] This means that Christ envisioned a universal moral kingdom of God, and by being obedient to God he made redemption possible for us. In line with Kant, Ritschl downplayed the cultic aspect of Christianity and emphasized the ethical, i.e., practical goal: "Since Jesus Himself, however, saw in the Kingdom of God the moral end of the religious fellowship He had to found; since He understood by it not the common exercise of worship, but the organization of humanity through action inspired by love, any conception of Christianity would be imperfect and therefore incorrect which did not include this specifically teleological aspect" (12).

Significant also is Ritschl's introduction of a kingdom of sin, a concept by which he wanted to come to terms with the notion of original sin. There is a sinful federation that does not exclude anyone so that we are all burdened with sin. Ritschl then concluded that from the perspective of a discerning view of guilt, original or hereditary sin can no longer be understood as the primary form of the concept of sin (cf. 341-42). Nevertheless, Ritschl did not feel that he was betraying his Lutheran heritage, in which human depravity is emphasized, but sought to show that his understanding of sin was already to be found in rudimentary form in the Lutheran confessional writings and especially in

4. Albrecht Ritschl, *Die christliche Lehre von der Rechtfertigung und Versöhnung,* vol. 2, *Der biblische Stoff der Lehre,* 4th ed. (Bonn: A. Marcus and E. Weber, 1900), 151.

5. Albrecht Ritschl, *The Christian Doctrine of Justification and Reconciliation: The Positive Development of the Doctrine,* trans. H. R. Mackintosh and A. B. Macaulay (New York: Charles Scribner's, 1900), 10 (which is vol. 3 of *Rechtfertigung und Versöhnung*). Page references to this work are placed in the text.

Melanchthon. He even sought to find support in Paul: "And finally, since Paul neither asserts nor suggests the transmission of sin by generation, he offers no other reason for the universality of sin or for the kingdom of sin than the sinning of all individual men" (348).

Compared with Luther's kingdom of the devil, Ritschl's concept of the kingdom of sin produces an unusually static effect. This is somewhat moderated in that sin is not viewed as an end in itself but as the opposite of universal good. Sin always strives, desires, and acts against God; the kingdom of sin finds its counterpart in the kingdom of God. "This whole web of sinful action and reaction, which presupposes and yet again increases the selfish bias in every man, is entitled 'the world,' which in this aspect of it is not of God, but opposed to Him" (350). We are, so to speak, caught up in a dragnet of evil, which is created and strengthened through us. Yet Ritschl claimed that it is not inevitable that each individual be caught in this sinful web and make his or her own contribution to wickedness and untruthfulness. Through proper education one can escape from it. Moreover, one can act egotistically when one appears to be fighting for the kingdom of God and, for example, for certain goods like family pride, class feeling, patriotism, or loyalty to the confession of the church. Ritschl made it clear, therefore, that the church, as it manifests itself upon this earth, must not be equated with the kingdom of God. The church belongs to the world and must be distinguished from the kingdom of God.

If we wish to do justice to Ritschl, we must consider the context from which he argued. Optimism reigned supreme in the nineteenth century. It is therefore no surprise that Ritschl should claim that "there exists in the child a general, though still indeterminate, impulse towards the good" (337). There is no place here for a doctrine of original sin with which humans are burdened from birth. Humans are capable of improving. At the same time, however, Ritschl remembered Kant's notion of radical evil. Humans do sin. In his corporate understanding of humanity, however, Ritschl emphasizes that humans are not isolated individuals but always live within a context that necessarily influences them. This is made especially clear in his *Instruction in the Christian Religion:*

> The cooperation of many individuals in these forms of sin leads to a reinforcement of the same in common customs and principles, in standing immoralities, and even in evil institutions. So there develops an almost irresistible power of temptation for those who with characters yet undeveloped are so much exposed to evil example that they do not see through the network of enticements to evil. Accordingly, the kingdom of sin, or the (immoral, human) world is reinforced in every new generation. Corporate sin, this opposite of the kingdom of God, rests upon all as a power which at

the very least limits the freedom of the individual with respect to the good. The limitation of the freedom of the individual for the good, by his own sin and by entanglement with the common condition of the world, is, strictly speaking, an absence of the freedom to choose the good. Apart from the kingdom of God, however, this is the common condition of all men.[6]

The recognition and emphasis of the corporate form of sin and evil, clearly expressed in the preceding quotation (Ritschl used sin in the theological sense, whereas evil represented the morally bad), were needed correctives in the nineteenth century. At least some theologians heard this, as is shown by Walter Rauschenbusch and, later, Reinhold Niebuhr in the United States as well as the religious socialists Leonhard Ragaz and Hermann Kutter in Switzerland at the beginning of the twentieth century. They took up Ritschl's terminology and spoke of a kingdom of evil that perverts humans and their institutions.[7] One could thereby no longer push sin and evil on to the individual and seek to convert the individual in order to make possible better living conditions upon the earth. One must therefore concern oneself with the structures of injustice and evil and seek to reform these.

Another concept that had wide-ranging influence came directly from the Reformation, namely, Luther's concept of vocation that Ritschl picked up, saying: "A man's vocation as a citizen denotes that particular department of work in human society, in the regular pursuit of which the individual realizes at once his own self-end and the common ultimate end of society. Every civil vocation is an ethical vocation, and not a means of egoism, in so far as it is pursued under the view that, in society as a whole, and in the individual, the moral law ought to be fulfilled, and the highest conceivable goal for the race attained."[8] Vocation means the location where we find ourselves in society, i.e., the kind of work we do in society, but it also denotes our social standing such as father, mother, child, parishioner, citizen, etc. In all the different places and situations, a person "directs his action toward the end of the kingdom of God in a particular ethical vocation and authenticates his sonship with God and his dominion over the world in the particular conditions of life into which he is placed."[9] Christians help to establish the kingdom of God in whatever they do and thereby express their being children of God. Our activities are not simply an end in themselves or a

6. Albrecht Ritschl, *Instruction in the Christian Religion* (§30), in Albrecht Ritschl, *Three Essays,* translated with an introduction by Philip Hefner (Philadelphia: Fortress, 1972), 233-34.

7. So also David L. Mueller, *An Introduction to the Theology of Albrecht Ritschl* (Philadelphia: Westminster, 1969), 73.

8. Ritschl, *The Christian Doctrine,* 445.

9. Ritschl, *Instruction* (§48), 241.

means of self-gratification, but actually, as Luther said, they are a form of worship, responding to God's call in the situation in which we find ourselves.

With this redirection of the notion of work, away from oneself and toward God, Ritschl elevated any human activity to a dignified action that had God's approval and helped to further the human community. Especially with the latter aim, Ritschl summoned everyone to take a close look as to whether this was still the primary goal. The kingdom of God, however, is for Ritschl not a human attainment. It has a bipolar focus, consisting of the divine initiative and our human response. Through the incarnation, the kingdom breaks into time as realized in Jesus' activity. Jesus, therefore, becomes the example of a morally perfect humanity, and by providing justification he enables us to pursue the kingdom. Jesus founded the church as a religious community, which serves to further the kingdom. The community aims at bringing the kingdom ever more perfectly into this world. Because of human sinfulness, however, the completion of the kingdom has also a future eschatological dimension. Ritschl was too much influenced by the Lutheran Reformation to opt for self-redemption. Just as with Kant, grace alone and faith active in love reigned supreme for Ritschl.

The Legacy of Schleiermacher: Wilhelm Herrmann

The life of **Wilhelm Herrmann** (1846-1922) was uneventful. He was born in the Altmark near Magdeburg as a son of a pastor, and studied theology in Halle from 1866 to 1871. While in Halle he attended lectures by Julius Müller and lived for two and a half years in the home of Tholuck, where he met Ritschl. In Halle he also got acquainted with Martin Kähler. He served in various teaching functions until he became Privatdozent in 1875. A mere four years later he was called to a professorship in systematic theology at the University of Marburg. There he stayed until retirement, declining any other calls. As a teacher he was very influential, and among his students were Karl Barth, Rudolf Bultmann, and John Baillie. His fame spread beyond Germany, and before World War I Marburg was "something like a place of pilgrimage for younger theologians from the British Universities."[10] In 1904 he also traveled to the United States, where he lectured at the University of Chicago.[11] Together with Wilhelm Rade he edited

10. So the translators Nathaniel Micklem and Kenneth A. Saunders of Wilhelm Herrmann, *Systematic Theology (Dogmatik)* (London: George Allen and Unwin, 1927), 7, in their foreword.

11. According to Robert T. Voelkel, *The Shape of the Theological Task* (Philadelphia: Westminster, 1968), 14, who deals in this book extensively with Herrmann.

the journal *Zeitschrift für Theologie und Kirche (Journal of Theology and Church)* from 1907 to 1917, and also contributed frequently to the weekly *Die christliche Welt (The Christian World)*, the editor of which was again Rade.

His thesis for his *Habilitation* (1875), which was his largest work, was entitled "Die Religion im Verhältnis zum Welterkennen und zur Sittlichkeit. Eine Grundlegung der systematischen Theologie" (Religion in Relation to Knowledge of the World and of Morality: A Foundation for Systematic Theology). Yet the work for which he became famous was *The Communion of the Christian with God: Described on the Basis of Luther's Statements* of 1886 (Eng. trans. 1896). This book went through seven editions during Herrmann's lifetime and was similarly successful as his *Ethics (Ethik)*, which first appeared in 1901 and came out in a sixth edition in 1921.

The title of the book, *The Communion of the Christian with God,* reflects Herrmann's own concern of how we can communicate with God and what this means for our daily life. While the title mirrors the deep piety out of which he came, on a deeper level it shows the quandary he and many of his contemporaries faced: the dominant scientific worldview of the late nineteenth century projected a closed causal mechanistic system of the world that allowed no outside interference or heavenly guidance. At the same time, the historical foundation of the Christian faith was ever more called into question. Lessing's ugly, broad ditch between accidental facts of history and what one understood by the necessary truths of reason had become more and more obvious. Especially the left-wing Hegelians had shattered the historical reliability of the biblical documents, and historical relativism was at its height.

How could one still hold on to the Christian faith? Herrmann attempted to provide an answer. He distinguished himself from the representatives of the left wing for whom the person of Jesus had become a problem and who espoused only general ideas on religion. He contended that general ideas "do not transform us. . . . They are rather an expression of what we already are."[12] He also rejected opponents on the right, usually conservative followers of Hegel, who confront us with the sum of doctrine "that is reported or taught about Jesus in the New Testament." For the conservative representatives of the right, the facts become a law to be accepted. But Herrmann cautions that "there is no law there that can make alive" (lxvi).

To escape the dogmatism of both left and right, Herrmann focused on what he knew best from his youth, on personal Christianity. Christians, he

---

12. Wilhelm Herrmann, *The Communion of the Christian with God: Described on the Basis of Luther's Statements,* edited with an introduction by Robert T. Voelkel (Philadelphia: Fortress, 1971), lxvi. Page references to this work have been placed in the text.

wrote, fully agree "to its general meaning. It is a communion of the soul with the living God through the mediation of Christ. Herein is really included all that belongs to the characteristic life of Christendom — revelation and faith, conversion and the comfort of forgiveness, the joy of faith and the service of love, lonely communion with God and life in Christian fellowship. All this is then only truly Christian when it is experienced as communion with the living God through the mediation of Christ" (9). This means that both faith and action for the Christian come through a communion with the living God, and this communion is made possible through Christ. He went even one step further and said: "Our certainty of God may be kindled by many other experiences, but has ultimately its firmest basis in the fact that within the realm of history to which we ourselves belong, we encounter the man Jesus as an undoubted reality" (59-60). This means that our faith does not go back to some kind of historical Jesus but is focused on the present where we encounter Jesus. Our faith is also not founded on other experiences, be it nature or reason. Here we notice Herrmann's emphasis on the personal communion with Christ, not as a construct of the past, but as a present living reality.

Yet how can we encounter Jesus in the present? Tradition does not suffice. Herrmann knew that "a believer cannot base his very existence entirely on what may be given him by other men" (69). He reiterated what Martin Luther had said centuries before him: I cannot build my faith on somebody else's witness or authority. My faith has to be built on my own experience and my own decision. Even in the biblical sources we only have faith statements by the authors of the New Testament writings. Nevertheless, the witness of others is important, because without communion with other Christians the picture of Jesus would not have been preserved in the church, and through that communion that picture shines forth of that inner life that is the heart of the church. Herrmann went on to assert: "He who has found the inner life of Jesus through the mediation of others, in so far as he has really found it, has become free even of that mediation. He is so set free by the significance which the inner life of the man Jesus has for him who has beheld it. . . . The picture of a personality becomes visible to us in this way, and cannot be handed over to us by any communication from others; it must arise within ourselves as the free revelation of the living to the living" (74).

Once we have made that life, which has been communicated to us, part of our own experience, it becomes contemporaneous to us. Herrmann concluded: "Jesus Himself becomes a real power to us when He reveals His inner life to us; a power which we recognize as the best thing our life contains" (74). Through our own experience of Jesus as a living reality, he becomes a power that motivates and shapes our life. In following Jesus we will then want to become obedient to the will of God. But Herrmann cautioned that while for the "righteous enthusiasts round Him . . . precepts relating to the cultus assume greater prominence than commandments dealing with conduct towards other men," Jesus did not allow the claims of the cultus to thrust aside the duty of ministering to the needs of others.[13] If we want to follow Jesus, it is necessary to love our neighbors and our enemies. This love is even stronger than justice. While justice knows exceptions to its rule, love knows none. "The love that Jesus means must be thought of as the highest exercise of will-power, the concentrated force of a mind that knows the object of its will."[14] This love is not just a duty, it is something we experience from Jesus and then allow others to experience.

Who is this Jesus that Herrmann is talking about? (It is interesting that he talks most often about Jesus, not about Christ.) Is there still a difference between Jesus of history and the Jesus we experience, or is the Jesus we experience no longer anchored in history? In other words, has the ground of faith become its content? According to Herrmann, "Jesus is the ground of faith as the one from whom the community of faith arose."[15] The content of faith, however, "varies from Christian to Christian as the impact of the inner life of Jesus, alive in the community, is felt in a variety of historical moments." We are reminded here of Schleiermacher's insistence that we are drawn into Jesus' feeling of absolute dependence. Yet is the distinction between history and community strong enough, or does not the danger loom on the horizon that the community of faith simply produces Jesus as the ground of faith? Martin Kähler's charge that Herrmann's view of Jesus is subjectivistic and portrays a weak idealism, is not far-fetched.[16]

A very similar problem arose when Herrmann considered the christological dogma of Nicea, the Son being "of one being with the Father." He said this "does not mean that the Son is of like nature with the Father. It expresses something much greater, namely, that he is of the same nature as the Father. This means that our faith sees in Jesus Christ no less than in the Father the one personal Spirit who alone is God."[17] While the first two sentences certainly express what is meant by "of one being with the Father," the last sentence points in a different direction, namely, that both Jesus Christ and the Father mirror the one personal Spirit who alone is God. But this is neither the intention of Nicea nor a good rendering of what is meant by the Trinity. Yet Herrmann's position is understandable. He shied away from both ontological and historical state-

---

13. Wilhelm Herrmann, "The Moral Teachings of Jesus" (1904), in Adolf von Harnack and Wilhelm Herrmann, *Essays on the Social Gospel,* trans. G. M. Craik and Maurice A. Canney (New York: Putnam, 1907), 193.

14. Herrmann, "Moral Teachings of Jesus," 197.

15. So Voelkel, introduction to *The Communion,* xl.

16. Cf. Herrmann, *The Communion,* xxxix.

17. Herrmann, *Systematic Theology,* 140.

ments and preferred the level of experience or, as one would say half a century later, of the existential impact. But what do we actually experience, if there is no historical or ontological grounding to our faith? Are we not thrown back upon ourselves? The nineteenth century in Germany seems to close the way it started, with a Schleiermacherian emphasis on feeling. Perhaps this was the only way to escape the theological dogmatism of late orthodoxy and the materialistic dogmatism of the present.

Regaining a Scholarly Foundation, or Cultural Protestantism at Its Height: Adolf von Harnack

"What kind of people are they who live lives in which it is possible to produce a literary legacy of over sixteen hundred titles, while they are full professors at an illustrious university, presidents for lengthy periods of international congresses, general directors of Royal Libraries in their nation's capital and, by an imperial decree, first president of a Royal Society — and all of those positions overlapping with one another?"[18] Thus do we introduce **Adolf von Harnack** (1851-1930), another giant of cultural Protestantism. Son of the Luther scholar Theodosius Harnack (1817-89), he represented a deep piety, immense erudition, a liberal mind-set, and involvement for social betterment. Along with his professorship, he was president of the Evangelisch-Soziale Kongress (1903-12), director general of the Prussian State Library (1905-21), and the first president of the Kaiser-Wilhelm-Gesellschaft (Emperor William Society for the Advancement of the Sciences, 1912-30).

Harnack was born in Dorpat, now Tartu, which was then part of East Prussia and now is part of Estonia. There his father was university preacher at the Lutheran university and professor of church history and homiletics in its theological faculty. Theodosius Harnack accepted a call to Erlangen in 1853. After his first wife died in 1857, he returned with his family to Dorpat in 1866 and taught there again. Thus the Baltic region was to become "home" for young Harnack. As early as 1868 he resented the "Russification" of the Baltic provinces. An almost unbearable pressure was brought "on everything even remotely a product of the German mind; that which related to government and society, German school, and every German Gymnasium."[19]

18. So Martin Rumscheidt, ed., *Adolf von Harnack: Liberal Theology at Its Height* (Minneapolis: Fortress, 1991), 9.

19. Adolf von Harnack in a letter of Apr. 1868, as quoted in Agnes von Zahn-Harnack, *Adolf von Harnack* (Berlin: Hans Bott, 1936), 36.

In 1869 Harnack began to study theology at Dorpat. In 1872 he moved to Leipzig as a thoroughly convinced Lutheran, and in 1873 wrote his dissertation, "Source Criticism and the History of Gnosticism" (Zur Quellenkritik der Geschichte des Gnosticismus). Just a year later he completed his *Habilitation* on a topic related to Gnosticism. Only twenty-three years old, Harnack was Privatdozent, and in his first lecture class on Gnosticism there were already 120 enthusiastic students enrolled.[20] Two years later he was promoted to associate professor, and then he declined a call to a full professorship at the University of Breslau. When he received a call to the University of Giessen in 1878, Leipzig students sent a delegation to the secretary of education of the state of Saxony to have Harnack remain at Leipzig. Nevertheless, at age twenty-eight he became full professor at Giessen. When he arrived the theological faculty had only fifteen students, yet it soon began to flourish under Harnack's impact. In 1886 he wrote the first volume of his seven-volume work *History of Dogma* (Eng. trans. from the 3rd ed. 1958), and the same year he was called to Marburg, at that time part of Prussia.

By this time Harnack had become a thoroughly critical historian. Convinced by his research, he asserted that "the claim of the Church that the dogmas are simply the exposition of the Christian revelation, because deduced from the Holy Scriptures, is not confirmed by historical investigation. On the contrary, it becomes clear that dogmatic Christianity (the dogmas) in its conception and in its construction was *the work of the Hellenic spirit upon the gospel soil*."[21] Two things are important here, namely, Harnack's emphasis on a development from the Bible to the Christian dogmas and even beyond, and also his claim that the dogmas are a product of Hellenism, though on Christian soil. This Hellenization process was for Harnack not necessarily an adulteration of the gospel, but a factor to be taken into consideration in the development of the Christian faith.

Already the following year (1887) Harnack was called to the theological faculty at Berlin for the chair in church history. Yet the church that had to be consulted for the appointment had some problems with his emphasis on the primacy of history and inquired how he understood the New Testament canon, the resurrection of Christ, and baptism as a sacrament. Harnack received the call nonetheless (1888), but the church never asked him to participate in any church exam for the future pastors, contrary to what other professors had been asked to do. Later the church even established a "positive" professorship next to Harnack's, the first occupant of which was to be Adolf Schlatter. But Emperor

---

20. According to Rumscheidt, *Adolf von Harnack,* 12.

21. Adolf von Harnack, *Outlines of the History of Dogma* (1889), as excerpted in Rumscheidt, *Adolf von Harnack,* 110.

William II supported Harnack, and two years later Harnack became a member of the Prussian Academy of the Sciences.[22]

Harnack wrote a three-volume *History of the Academy* (*Geschichte der Königlich-preussischen Akademie der Wissenschaften zu Berlin,* 1900). Another important facet of his work was the founding of the Commission on Church Fathers in 1891, together with a secular historian, Theodor Mommsen (1817-1908), which was supposed to edit and publish in fifty volumes the Greek Christian literature prior to A.D. 325. By 1924 the Texte und Untersuchungen series (Texts and Investigations), edited by Harnack, already comprised forty-five volumes. After World War I he was active in founding the Notgemeinschaft der Deutschen Wissenschaft (Aid Cooperative for German Scientists), today the Deutsche Forschungsgemeinschaft (German Research Foundation). Other important literary ventures were his *History of the Early Christian Literature up to Eusebius* (*Geschichte der altchristlichen Literatur bis Eusebius,* 1893), and *Mission and Expansion of Christianity in the First Three Centuries* (1902; Eng. trans., 2nd ed., 2 vols., 1908). In 1921 he published a comprehensive work on Marcion (*Marcion: The Gospel of the Alien God* [Eng. trans. 1990]), in which he stated that it was regrettable that the early church held on to the Old Testament, but even more regrettable that the Old Testament was retained today. This remark has often been seen as an anti-Semitic slant in Harnack, yet it was not meant that way. As a historian, he wanted to point out the difference between the religion of Judaism and the Christian religion. Since in our days it has become fashionable to designate the Old Testament as the Hebrew Bible, one may wonder whether therewith the Hebrew Bible is not eliminated from the Christian domain as Harnack once wanted. Also, his addresses and essays, mainly of a more popular nature, are collected in the seven-volume *Reden und Aufsätze.*

Harnack had the greatest impact, however, in a book that was not even written by him. It was published from the shorthand notes of a student listener to his public lectures at the university during the winter semester 1899/1900 on "Das Wesen des Christentums" (published in English under the title *What Is Christianity?*). More than six hundred students attended his lectures. By 1927 the book had gone through fourteen printings and was translated into many languages. Rudolf Bultmann called this book "a theological-historical document of the greatest importance."[23] It is significant for two reasons: firstly, in an

22. For an excellent summary of Harnack's life and work, see Friedrich Wilhelm Kantzenbach, "Harnack, Adolf von," in *Theologische Realenzyklopädie,* 14:450-58, here 452, who however mistakenly claimed that Harnack was born in Erlangen.

23. Rudolf Bultmann, introduction to *What Is Christianity?* by Adolf von Harnack, trans. Thomas B. Saunders (Philadelphia: Fortress, 1986), vii. Page references to this work have been placed in the text.

easy-to-understand way Harnack outlined his understanding of the Christian faith, and secondly, as Bultmann pointed out, many people today will advocate a similar view of Christianity unless they belong to traditional pietism or orthodoxy (cf. viii). First, Harnack outlined the main features of Jesus' message; then he related the gospel to certain problems, such as the social issues of his time or christological issues; and in a third part he provided a quick overview of the Christian religion from the apostolic age up to Protestantism. In a similar way, as we noticed with Herrmann, he was a child of his age, of the late nineteenth century, in which the ironclad laws of nature ruled supreme.

Harnack interpreted the order of nature as something that cannot be violated and declared: "Miracles, it is true, do not happen." But then he conceded in the second part of the statement: "But of the marvelous and the inexplicable there is plenty." Harnack explained: "That the earth in its course stood still; that a she-ass spoke; that a storm was quieted by a word, we do not believe, and we shall never again believe; but that the lame walked, the blind saw, and the deaf heard, will not be so summarily dismissed as an illusion" (28). This means that he saw the possibilities that nature allows as much wider than what had been conceded before. This relativistic understanding of a then-ruling worldview was furthered by his historical research, which amply documented the certain statements that, once thought to be absolutely true, at a later stage had to be relativized.

As a historian, however, Harnack thought it important to establish a reliable basis on which to found Christianity. Especially his research concerning the New Testament sources and the development of the New Testament canon proved to be beneficial. It was clear for Harnack that the New Testament Gospels did not provide a biography of Jesus. However, it was just as evident for him that Jesus' historicity could not be doubted, and that the Evangelists *"offer us a plain picture of Jesus' teaching, in regard both to its main features and to its individual application; in the second place they tell us how his life issued in the service of his vocation; and in the third place, they describe for us the impression which he made upon his disciples, and which they transmitted"* (31). In his referring to Jesus' vocation we see the influence of Ritschl. Above all, we notice that Harnack offers a basic, historically grounded trust in the New Testament documents, although, as we have seen, he did not accept everything the New Testament narrated. Also with regard to the coming end of the world and the day of judgment, it was clear for Harnack that Jesus simply did what every preacher who calls people to repentance does: he showed them the imminence of judgment and the day of doom, though not necessarily believing in it (cf. 39-42). Harnack discarded the dramatic eschatological pronouncement of the coming kingdom as the gown of Jesus' message, but not its essence. According to Harnack, three items were essential to Jesus' proclamation:

Firstly, the kingdom of God and its coming;
Secondly, God the Father and the infinite value of the human soul;
Thirdly, the higher righteousness and the commandment of love. (51)

For Harnack, Jesus' message is at the same time great and simple. The kingdom of God, which Jesus announced, is according to Harnack of bipolar structure, which is similar to what we heard from Ritschl. Yet there is a modification. For Harnack it is on the one hand "a purely future event," pointing to the external rule of God. But it is also something inward, "something which is already present and making its entrance at the moment" (52). The first one, the future, external one, which is also related to the kingdom of the devil and its conflict with the kingdom of God, a conflict that at the end of time will climax, "was an idea which Jesus simply shared with his contemporaries" (54). The internal kingdom, however, does not come with any observation but is already here. It was Jesus' own notion of the kingdom. Harnack contended that it is the task of the historian to distinguish between that which is traditional and that which is peculiar, meaning what was Jesus' own view and what he simply accepted being a child of his time. Of course, one could make the same claim with Harnack's own positions, since, as we have seen, Herrmann espoused a similar view of the interior picture of Jesus. It allows one to obtain a position that cannot be assaulted by external evidence. Most important, however, was Jesus' pronouncement of God the Father and the infinite value of the human soul. As Harnack wrote: "In the combination of these ideas — God the Father, Providence, the position of men as God's children, the infinite value of the human soul — the whole Gospel is expressed" (68). Of course, these were typical nineteenth-century tenets of liberal theology. The same goes for Harnack's observation that Jesus cut the connection that existed in his day between ethics and the external forms of religious worship and cultic observance. One cannot send gifts to the temple and at the same time allow neighbors and parents to starve.

But Harnack insisted that "Jesus laid down no social program for the suppression of poverty and distress, if by program we mean a set of definitely prescribed regulations" (97). Harnack reiterated this statement in connection with his involvement with the Protestant Social Congress. Nevertheless, he insisted that the absence of economic precepts in the Gospels does not mean that Christians should not concern themselves with economic issues. Harnack knew that the church from its very beginning had always come to the help of the poor and needy, by arousing the individual conscience, by converting congregations of individuals into communities of active charity and brotherly love, and also by exerting pressure on the world to make the existing order more just. While he insisted that individual Christians "are bound to carry the Gospel into public life and bring it to bear upon current conditions," he noted that since the church still holds a prominent and influential place in society, "it is bound to make use of this position for the advancement of evangelical social ideals, and accordingly to seek the most opportune ways of making its voice heard."[24] Harnack did not pursue an individualistic piety. Appreciating the work of the church, he also saw a redress for current evils through the active involvement of the church as a corporate institution in cooperation with the state.[25] Harnack judged that especially the love commandment elevated Christianity above any religion, even above Buddhism, and spawned an energetic social message that issued from this gospel command.

Yet what kind of gospel did Harnack advocate? It was basically a gospel of the Father and not of the Son. As Harnack contended: *"The Gospel, as Jesus proclaimed it, has to do with the Father only and not with the Son."*[26] Jesus is only the pointer to the Father, he is the way but not the center of the Christian proclamation. The thinking that wants to affirm an ontological unity between Father and Son, Harnack would reply, is the result of Hellenism. It is not part of the Hebrew way of thinking. As a historian Harnack wanted to return to the origins and wellspring of the Christian faith. This indeed he did accomplish. Yet he was less willing to accept the basic dogmatic decisions of the first centuries as being equally grounded in that wellspring. This reduction of the Christian message to its origins did not meet with ecclesiastical approval. But toward the end of his life he was attacked from a very different angle. Young Karl Barth judged that it was totally unnecessary to recover the historical foundation of the Christian faith as Harnack had done.

In 1923 the journal *Die christliche Welt* published an exchange of letters between Harnack and Barth, consisting of three letters by Harnack and two by Barth. In 1906 Barth studied theology at the University of Berlin and "requested and obtained permission to participate as a regular member in Harnack's seminars. He was the youngest student ever to participate in those *colloquia,* an indication that Harnack himself must have been impressed by the student."[27] Indeed, Barth was fascinated by Harnack and his attempt to bring religion and culture into harmony.

---

24. Adolf von Harnack, "The Evangelical Social Mission in the Light of the History of the Church" (1894), in Harnack and Herrmann, *Essays on the Social Gospel,* 80-81.

25. Cf. Harnack, *What Is Christianity?* 98.

26. Harnack, *What Is Christianity?* 144.

27. So H. Martin Rumscheidt, *Revelation and Theology: An Analysis of the Barth-Harnack Correspondence of 1923* (Cambridge: Cambridge University Press, 1972), 4, in this extensive and careful analysis.

In 1908 Barth had gone to Marburg to study with Wilhelm Herrmann, and now Barth was attracted to him and especially to his insistence on the absolute transcendence of God that made it unnecessary to legitimate faith through any external evidence. This stance became very important for Barth. He no longer needed what Harnack had attempted to do, to lay a historic and therefore scientific foundation for the Christian faith. Harnack had heard of this new trend of a generation of younger theologians who showed no respect for historical research. He was afraid this might be another romantic (Schleiermacherian) upsurge, drawing all religious knowledge from the interior side of one's being. Therefore he wrote "Fifteen Questions to the Despisers of Scientific Theology."

In question 2 Harnack asked: "Is the religion of the Bible, or its revelations, so completely a unity and so clear that historical knowledge and critical reflection are not needed for a correct understanding of their meaning?"[28] And in question 6 he continued: "If God and the world (life in God and life in the world) are complete opposites, how does education in godliness, that is, in goodness, become possible? How is education possible without historical knowledge and the highest valuation of morality?"[29] Barth — by then professor of Reformed theology at the University of Göttingen — responded with "Fifteen Answers to Professor Adolf von Harnack." He conceded that historical knowledge and critical reflection are aids that can be helpful, irrelevant, or obstructive to the understanding of the Bible. The actual understanding of the Bible is however attained "by virtue of *that* Spirit which is identical with the content of the Bible and that by *faith*."[30]

Similar to the way Schleiermacher had responded to Kant, Barth now claimed against Harnack that neither historical knowledge nor critical reflection opens the Bible, but only that spirit, meaning the spirit of God that is identical with what the Bible mediates. Concerning the question about education in godliness, which Harnack equated with goodness, Barth answered with the biblical quotation: "No one can come to me unless the Father who sent me draws him and will raise him up at the last day."

Harnack responded to Barth's reply and again made very clear the difference between Barth and him. For Barth the task of theology is identical with the task of preaching, while for him the task of theology is equal to the task of science in general. Harnack ventured a prediction: If "your way of doing this

28. Adolf von Harnack, "Fifteen Questions to the Despisers of Scientific Theology," as excerpted in Rumscheidt, *Revelation and Theology*, 29.

29. Harnack, "Fifteen Questions," 30.

30. Karl Barth, "Fifteen Answers to Professor Adolf von Harnack," as excerpted in Rumscheidt, *Revelation and Theology*, 32.

comes to prevail, it will not be taught any more; it will rather be given over into the hands of devotional preachers who freely create their own understanding of the Bible and who set up their own dominion."[31] Scientific theology had run its course. It had regained the respectability of the colleagues in other faculties of the universities. It had also regained the respectability of the educated people. This is how Harnack and others succeeded. But even with his most sincere attempts in the Evangelisch-Soziale Kongress, Harnack could not win back the masses. While his fears concerning Barth and the kind of theology he would promulgate did not materialize, it was now up to another generation with a different approach to try their way to advance the gospel.

Cultural Protestantism and Beyond: Martin Rade

Martin Rade (1857-1940) was born of a Lutheran pastor in the Oberlausitz, Silesia. From 1875 to 1880 he studied theology at Leipzig University, where his teacher was Harnack. In 1881 he received his licentiate under Harnack's guidance with a thesis on the beginning of the Roman primacy. Then he took a parish. In 1883, the 400th anniversary of Luther's birth, Rade started to write a Luther biography that was published in three volumes. With friends from Harnack's seminar, in 1886 he founded what was to become in 1888 *Die christliche Welt (The Christian World)*, one of the most important weekly papers of German Protestantism. Since Rade was interested in social issues and their relevancy for the Protestant church, he took an active part in the Evangelisch-Soziale Kongress. At the turn of the century, he did his *Habilitation* in systematic theology at the University of Marburg; in 1904 he was appointed associate professor; and in 1921 full professor. Together with Wilhelm Herrmann, from 1907 onward he edited the *Journal for Theology and the Church (Zeitschrift für Theologie und Kirche)*, and became active in various political parties and associations. At the beginning of World War I, national conservative circles accused him of betraying his country since he believed that the beginning of the war signaled the "bankruptcy of Christianity," since Christians should not wage war against each other.[32] To the contrary, the Christian faith should tie together people of different nationalities.

Karl Barth had helped Rade with editing *Die christliche Welt*, but when

31. Adolf von Harnack, "Open Letter to Professor Karl Barth," as excerpted in Rumscheidt, *Revelation and Theology*, 39.

32. Cf. Christian Schwöbel, *Martin Rade. Das Verhältnis von Geschichte, Religion und Moral als Grundproblem seiner Theologie* (Gütersloh: Gerd Mohn, 1980), 182.

Barth perceived that the journal supported the worldly, sinful necessity of this war, he turned away from this kind of cultural Protestantism. Yet Rade rejected any nationalistic war ideology. He was, however, convinced that even this war could not have been waged without God being present and active in it.[33] It was the 400th anniversary of the Reformation in 1917, at which Rade called for rediscovering faith in justification as a new orientation for church and theology. This call decidedly rekindled interest in the theology of Luther. In 1932 he handed over the editorship of *Die christliche Welt* to his successor, Hermann Mulert (1879-1950), and the following year he was dismissed from civil service as a professor when he labeled National Socialist ideology as a crazy racist fanaticism. The rise of this Nazi ideology notwithstanding, Rade continued his work on behalf of the Jewish population in Germany.

Similar to Harnack, Rade understood theology as a historical science founded in a historical way in the gospel as the origin for life and faith of Christianity. With Harnack and Ritschl he was christocentric in his orientation and directed toward the needs of the local congregation and its social ethics. Editing *Die christliche Welt* for many years, Rade wanted to confront its audience with the opportunities of the Christian faith in the social, political, and cultural challenges of his day. For him, God could not be seen without the world and the world not without God, reiterating a statement of Schleiermacher.[34] This means that Schleiermacher's emphasis on the correlation between God and the world was still remembered far into the twentieth century.

But before we journey into that century, we should note how theology responded to the big challenges of the nineteenth century: (1) the Industrial Revolution and the social problems that came with it; (2) the scientific and technological advancements and the materialistic reductionist worldview they facilitated; and (3) the discoveries in archaeology and ethnology and the challenge they created for the Christian faith. It is to these issues that we now turn.

For Further Reading

Albrecht Ritschl (1822-89)

Hefner, Philip. *Faith and the Vitalities of History: A Theological History Based on the Work of Albrecht Ritschl.* New York: Harper and Row, 1966.
Jodock, Darrell, ed. *Ritschl in Retrospect: History, Community, and Science.* Minneapolis: Fortress, 1995.

---

33. Cf. Schwöbel, *Martin Rade,* 181, in his discerning study of how Barth misunderstood Rade during these years.
34. So Martin Rade, *Glaubenslehre* (Gotha: Leopold Klotz, 1926), 1:40.

Richmond, James. *Ritschl, a Reappraisal: A Study in Systematic Theology.* London: Collins, 1978.

Ritschl, Albrecht. *The Christian Doctrine of Justification and Reconciliation: The Positive Development of the Doctrine.* Translated by H. R. Mackintosh and A. B. Macaulay. New York: Charles Scribner's, 1900.

———. *A Critical History of the Christian Doctrine of Justification and Reconciliation.* Translated by John S. Black. Edinburgh: Edmonston and Douglas, 1872.

———. *Three Essays.* Translated with an introduction by Philip Hefner. Philadelphia: Fortress, 1972.

Wilhelm Herrmann (1846-1922)

Harnack, Adolf von, and Wilhelm Herrmann. *Essays on the Social Gospel.* Translated by G. M. Craik and Maurice A. Canney. New York: Putnam, 1907.

Herrmann, Wilhelm. *The Communion of the Christian with God: Described on the Basis of Luther's Statements.* Edited with an introduction by Robert T. Voelkel. Philadelphia: Fortress, 1971.

———. *Systematic Theology. (Dogmatik).* London: George Allen and Unwin, 1927.

Sockness, Brent. *Against False Apologetics: Wilhelm Herrmann and Ernst Troeltsch in Conflict.* Tübingen: Mohr Siebeck, 1998.

Voelkel, Robert T. *The Shape of the Theological Task.* Philadelphia: Westminster, 1968.

Adolf von Harnack (1851-1930)

Glick, Garland Wayne. *The Reality of Christianity: A Study of Adolf von Harnack as Historian and Theologian.* New York: Harper and Row, 1967.

Harnack, Adolf von. *What Is Christianity?* Translated by Thomas B. Saunders. Philadelphia: Fortress, 1986.

Pauck, Wilhelm. *Harnack and Troeltsch: Two Historical Theologians.* New York: Oxford University Press, 1968.

Rumscheidt, H. Martin. *Revelation and Theology: An Analysis of the Barth-Harnack Correspondence of 1923.* Cambridge: Cambridge University Press, 1972.

Martin Rade (1857-1940)

Clayton, John. "Martin Rade — 50 Years After." *King's Theological Review* 13 (Autumn 1990): 45-49.

Ludolphy, Ingetraut. "Rade, Martin." In *The Encyclopedia of the Lutheran Church*, edited by Julius Bodensieck, 3:2001. Minneapolis: Augsburg, 1965.

Smith, Rennie. "Half a Century of German Liberalism." *Modern Churchman* 44 (1954): 38-44.

6 The Challenge of the Industrial Revolution

The rapid industrialization in the second half of the nineteenth century brought immense wealth to a few, but misery and poverty to the great masses, as is graphically portrayed by the British novelist Charles Dickens (1812-70) in his *Christmas Carol* (1843). The blatant economic disparity provided a challenge on both sides of the Atlantic. This challenge was picked up by both Roman Catholics and Protestants. In Roman Catholicism — in French social Catholicism or with Adolph Kolping (1813-65) in Germany, for instance — it spawned no independent theological movement but worked within the organizational structures of the church. However, the situation was different in Protestantism.

In America, these concerns were addressed by various groups. There was on the one hand a social Christianity of a decidedly conservative persuasion that sought to deal with the social problems on an individualistic scale. Important movements from this angle were the Salvation Army, which spread from England to North America, and the rescue missions. However, another tendency opted for a new social order. Many theologians associated with this persuasion came from the new or liberal theology that — in contrast to the older Unitarian or transcendentalist theology — was evangelical and christocentric. In 1883 Theodore Munger (1830-1910), a Congregational pastor in New England, expressed in *Freedom of Faith* this new theology as "a somewhat larger and broader use of the reason than has been accorded to theology" in the past. He wanted to "replace an excessive individuality by a truer view of the solidarity of the race."[1]

---

1. Munger, in Ronald C. White, Jr., and C. Howard Hopkins, *The Social Gospel: Religion and Reform in Changing America* (Philadelphia: Temple University Press, 1976), 31.

This new theology did not reject any specific doctrines, but rather wanted to work within the existing church.

Most American churches at this time were largely conservative, middle-class, and had at the most a paternalistic attitude toward the poor. For example, the terrible railway strike of 1877, when a 10 percent wage cut was instituted on the majority of the railroads east of the Mississippi; or the labor troubles of 1886, the same year as the Haymarket Square Riot in Chicago; or a series of strikes in the early 1890s, when for instance the Pullman Company cut wages by 25 percent — even these did not cause Protestant leaders and their churches to reconsider their social views in relation to faith.[2] Here the representatives of the Social Gospel made a difference in a society that was alarmed about labor unrest and in a quandary as to whether it could continue its advocacy of the status quo. Like everyone else, the Social Gospel representatives were concerned with the search for a better society. Yet instead of insisting on the all-sufficiency of individual regeneration as a solution for social problems, they looked for concrete measures of improvement in society.

The Social Gospel Movement in America: Washington Gladden, Richard Ely, Walter Rauschenbusch

Washington Gladden (1836-1918), a friend of Theodore Munger and probably the most influential of the Social Gospel theologians, is indicative of the change that theology took. He was born to a New England schoolteacher-farmer. His labor being needed on the farm, Gladden had only the winter term for school education. This prepared him for identification with the working class. While he was brought up a pious Presbyterian, he did not have an emotional experience of God's favor, then considered necessary for salvation.[3] Through the influence of an evangelist, he joined the Congregational church in his youth and resolved to enter the ministry. He entered Williams College in 1856 and graduated there three years later, taught public school in Owego, Massachusetts, and was finally called to a pastorate in Brooklyn, New York. Then he received another call to a small village north of New York City. While there he attended lectures at Union Theological Seminary, where he got acquainted with the writings of Horace Bushnell, whose friend he later became.

2. For details cf. Henry F. May, *Protestant Churches and Industrial America* (New York: Harper, 1949), 91-111.

3. Cf. Robert T. Handy, ed., *The Social Gospel in America, 1870-1920: Gladden — Ely — Rauschenbusch* (New York: Oxford University Press, 1966), 19, in his introduction to Gladden.

When he was called in 1866 to North Adams, Massachusetts, he got a firsthand experience of the struggle between labor and capital in the form of a disagreement about wages in a shoe factory. The conflict led to a lockout and the employment of Chinese workers from the West Coast. He had a similar experience in 1875 in Springfield, Massachusetts, when he encountered numerous unemployed people, the casualties of a long industrial depression. There he began a series of lectures on labor questions, later published as *Working People and Their Employers* (Boston, 1876), the first of a growing number of books on the Social Gospel. While Gladden denounced all forms of radicalism and socialism, he suggested for the future a more cooperative form of society that might someday replace the wage system: "The transition from the wages system to the system of cooperation is likely to be made through the introduction of what are called industrial partnerships: By which the work people in a manufacturing establishment are given an interest in the business; and, in addition to their wages, a stipulated portion of the profits is divided among them at the close of every year, in proportion to the amount of their earnings."[4] Gladden advocated profit sharing and also a shareholder interest for the workers.

In 1882 Gladden accepted a call to the First Congregational Church in Columbus, Ohio, where he stayed for the rest of his life. There he became one of the most influential pastors of his time in America. He preached twice every Sunday and gave many addresses and several important series of lectures; he was twice the Beecher Lecturer at Yale, for example. Although Gladden had written half a dozen books before coming to Columbus, while there he added more than thirty to that list. Many of these volumes were compilations of sermons or lectures. His speech was simple and his illustrations were drawn from experience. He preached exactly what the moderately progressive Protestants of his day were willing to accept.

Gladden did not confine himself to labor issues. For instance, he gave a series of lectures to the students at Ohio State University on evolution in which he stated: "At any rate, there is room here, even under the theory of Darwinism as expounded by its ablest defenders, for the work of a creative intelligence."[5] Gladden was not afraid of new insights; to the contrary, he had an interest in modern science and also in a historical approach to the Bible. Yet his most important contribution is as a central figure of the Christian social movement. He

4. Washington Gladden, *Working People and Their Employers* (Boston: Lockwood, Brooks & Co., 1876), in Handy, *Social Gospel in America*, 48.

5. Washington Gladden, *Burning Questions of The Life That Now Is and of That Which Is to Come,* 3rd ed. (New York: Century Co., 1892), 23.

was continuously called upon to represent the Social Gospel in the discussions of the major church organizations. When there was another bitter railroad strike in 1886, he was asked to address the issue, both for employers and for employees. The address, "Is It Peace or War?" became a chapter in *Applied Christianity: Moral Aspects of Social Questions* (Boston, 1894), one of his best-known books. In this address he stated: "If war is the order of the day, we must grant to labor belligerent rights."[6] While Gladden was certainly not for war, he was outraged that a 300 percent rise in the value of manufactured goods produced in America from 1860 to 1880 had not been equally divided. Therefore he urged the consideration of workers.

Theologically speaking, he envisioned "the complete christianization of all life," which he equated with the kingdom of heaven.[7] "Every department of human life — the families, the schools, amusements, art, business, politics, industry, national policies, international relations — will be governed by the Christian law and controlled by Christian influences." This also meant that denominational strife and exclusivity were not tolerable. But he noticed that there are "local churches which are, essentially, religious clubs . . . which . . . admit only those whose opinions and tendencies are similar to their own."[8] If congregations and denominations act like this, Gladden noted, they are a serious obstruction to the growth of the kingdom.

Gladden was not just a liberal visionary, he was also a man of social integrity. In 1904 he was elected moderator of the National Council of the Congregational Churches. When the American Board of Commissioners for Foreign Missions announced that they had received a gift of $100,000 from John D. Rockefeller of the Standard Oil Company, Gladden strongly protested against accepting this "tainted money," because this would discredit the church in the eyes of right-minded people.[9]

Washington Gladden was an effective interpreter of liberal and social Christianity at a critical period in American life. However, while he saw the social ills and pointed them out, an awareness of the intrinsic corruption of humanity was missing in his view. He was too much part of the progressive mood of his time. He was convinced that "God is our Father and that we are his children. He is not only the Former of our bodies, he is the Father of our spirits. If anything is clear it is that children must be of the same nature as their father. Everything that is essentially human is included in the nature of God; every-

6. Washington Gladden, "Is It Peace or War?" (1886), in Handy, *Social Gospel in America*, 61.

7. Washington Gladden, "The Church and the Kingdom" (1894), in Handy, *Social Gospel in America*, 104, for this and the following quote.

8. Gladden, "Church and the Kingdom," 111-12.

9. Cf. Handy, *Social Gospel in America*, 119, in his introduction.

thing that is essentially divine is found in the nature of man."[10] This means that Gladden was convinced of the essential divinity and goodness of humanity. Therefore he could appeal to the social consciousness and work for the betterment of humanity. This he did at a crucial time in the life of church and society in America.

Richard Theodore Ely (1854-1943), though not a theologian, had probably the strongest influence on the economic thinking of pastors and the general religious public of all the representatives of the Social Gospel. By working on the farm of his father, a civil engineer and a schoolteacher, his upbringing was similar to Gladden's. He was born in Ripley, New York, went to Dartmouth College in 1872 and then to Columbia College, where he received free tuition and lived in the home of an uncle in New York. He graduated in 1876 and won a fellowship that allowed him to take graduate studies in Germany. He first went to the University of Halle to study philosophy, but soon changed to economics and political science, which he studied there and at the University of Heidelberg. There he earned a Ph.D. summa cum laude under the guidance of Karl Knies (1821-98), one of the founders of the historical school of economic thought. He returned to America in 1880, and the following year began to teach at Johns Hopkins University in the department of political economy.

Soon Ely was known as a prolific and effective writer. In 1884 he published *The Past and the Present of Political Economy,* in which he attacked the classical individualistic laissez-faire version of economics in favor of a historical approach. In his 1886 *Labor Movement in America,* he first came out in favor of the Social Gospel: "An ethical demand of the present age is a clear perception of the duties of property, intelligence, and social position. It must be recognized that extreme individualism is immoral. . . . The absolute ideal was given two thousand years ago by Christ, who established the most perfect system of ethics the world has ever known."[11] According to Ely, Christian ethics should influence the entire labor movement. Therefore, the workers have to become acquainted with the ethical precepts of Jesus. This means a turn from the study of social problems to the teachings of Jesus, in order to discover that they contain just what is needed at the present time. These ethics Ely saw expressed in the double command of loving God and loving one's neighbor.[12] When people live seven days a week by the Golden Rule, they realize that they cannot serve God and

10. Washington Gladden, *Present Day Theology,* 3rd ed. (Columbus, Ohio, 1913), as excerpted in Handy, *Social Gospel in America,* 163.

11. Richard Th. Ely, *The Labor Movement in America,* new rev. ed. (New York: Macmillan, 1905), 311-13.

12. Cf. Richard Th. Ely, *Social Aspects of Christianity, and Other Essays* (New York, 1889), as excerpted in Handy, *Social Gospel in America,* 184-85.

mammon, they cannot pray to God on Sunday and then devour the widows' houses on Monday. For Ely the function of social science was to teach how Jesus' second command, to love the neighbor, might be fulfilled. To that end he expended his energy.

In 1885 Ely was instrumental in founding the American Economic Association, for which he served as first secretary from 1885 to 1892 and president from 1899 to 1901. Many of the leading proponents of the Social Gospel were charter members. This association worked for the development of legislative policy to improve economic conditions and to resolve the conflict of labor and capital. His *Outlines of Economics* (New York, 1893) went through six editions and sold over a million copies. Again, he advocated a return to Christ's teaching and to "the doctrine of brotherhood," i.e., that we should act toward each other as brothers and sisters, as a powerful economic factor. In 1892 he became professor of political economy and director of the School of Economics, Political Science, and History at the University of Wisconsin at Madison. He remained there for more than thirty-five years and became Wisconsin's most widely known faculty member. Yet not everybody was pleased with Ely. In 1894, in a public attack, he was accused of believing in strikes and boycotts and holding socialist and anarchist views. An investigating committee was formed at the university. Calling attention to his published works, Ely could deny the charges, and his accuser, a member of the board, was censured in turn. "Ely emerged from the ordeal more popular than ever."[13]

In the late 1890s, Ely devoted himself more to professional affairs and ceased promoting the Social Gospel. He was disturbed by the disunity among Protestants, and turned his attention to the state as that divine institution where people of all religious persuasions cooperated. While he was not satisfied with the influence of the churches, since their members were not leading the life expected of them, he nevertheless insisted: "There is one law, and only one, taught by the Christian religion and on its manward side; that is, the law of love, which finds expression in the social law of service. Christianity and ethical science agreed perfectly. Social welfare is the test of right conduct."[14] Again he saw Christian ethics, as enunciated by Jesus, as an important influence on society. Ely's impact has been long lasting. Even Walter Rauschenbusch, to whom we turn next, learned from him. (Parenthetically it should be mentioned that because he was unable to accept the doctrine of predestination, Ely converted from the Presbyterian to the Episcopal Church.)

13. Handy, *Social Gospel in America*, 182, where one also finds details of the affair.
14. Richard Th. Ely, *The Social Law of Service* (New York, 1896), as excerpted in Handy, *Social Gospel in America*, 224.

Walter Rauschenbusch (1861-1918) was born in Rochester, New York. His father was a German Lutheran missionary who subsequently turned Baptist and became a professor in the German department of Rochester Theological Seminary. Walter was therefore brought up in a pietistic German Baptist environment. As an eighteen-year-old he went back to Germany and graduated from the *Gymnasium* in Gütersloh in 1883. He also studied briefly at the University of Berlin. When he returned to the United States, he was allowed to simultaneously complete his senior year at the University of Rochester and begin his theological studies at Rochester Theological Seminary.

After graduating from seminary in 1885, he held his first pastorate at the Second German Baptist Church in New York City, which was located at the edge of the depressed area known as "Hell's Kitchen." There he was directly confronted with all the pressing social problems of the times: unemployment, poverty, wretched housing conditions, malnutrition, ignorance, and crime. He found some insight to the problems in the book *Progress and Poverty* by U.S. economist and land reformer Henry George (1839-97). This best seller caught the spirit of discontent as America was emerging from the great depression of 1873-78. It was translated into many languages and sold over two million copies. George pointed out that the main cause for poverty was the immense land speculations. Huge tracts of land in outlying areas were bought cheaply and then, as the cities expanded, sold for immense profits. Therefore George advocated that land be made common property and advocated cooperation between the classes: *"We are made for co-operation,"* he said, referring to a saying of the Roman emperor Marcus Aurelius.[15]

Rauschenbusch got interested in social analysis and reform, and with two other Baptist pastors founded a society to foster the members' spirituality, evangelism, and Christian social reform. Though initially he just wanted to save souls, he realized that this makes little sense if the stomach of the hearer is empty. He took a leave from his pastorate in 1891 and went to England to study social movements, and later to Germany to do New Testament studies. After these experiences his theology became more liberal, but also more romantic and idealistic. About his experiences in Germany he wrote: "So Christ's conception of the Kingdom of God came to me as a new revelation. . . . When the Kingdom of God dominated our landscape, the perspective of life shifted into a new alignment. I felt a new security in my social impulses."[16] We can easily see here the in-

---

15. Henry George, *Progress and Poverty: An Inquiry in the Cause of Industrial Depressions and of Increase in Want with Increase in Wealth — the Remedy* (1880; London: Kegan Paul, Trench, Trübner, 1908), 234. For Rauschenbusch's indebtedness to George, see Walter Rauschenbusch, *Christianizing the Social Order* (New York: Macmillan, 1912), 394.

16. Rauschenbusch, *Christianizing the Social Order*, 93.

fluences of Schleiermacher, Ritschl, and Harnack. In typical nineteenth-century American fashion, Rauschenbusch also believed in progress and human betterment. He wrote: "The swiftness of evolution in our own country proves the immense latent perfectibility in human nature."[17] But he was not a utopian, since he knew the paradox that "we shall never have a perfect social life, yet we must seek it with faith. We shall never abolish suffering. There will always be death and the empty chair and heart."[18] To what extent, however, he really had a sense of the depth of human depravity remains to be seen.

In 1893, with other younger Baptist ministers, Rauschenbusch formed the Brotherhood of the Kingdom, a group that met annually for more than two decades and became increasingly interdenominational, involving many of the nation's leaders in the social Christian movement. Many of his ideas were first presented at gatherings of the Brotherhood. Rochester Theological Seminary called him back in 1897 as a teacher in its German department, and in 1902 he finally became professor of church history on the regular faculty. Contrary to his own fears, his book *Christianity and the Social Crisis* (1907) was extremely well received and went through half a dozen editions in two years. As would an American president almost a century later, he called for "a new social order."[19] Rauschenbusch opened his book by delineating the social message of the Hebrew prophets, then focused on the social aims of Jesus and the social impetus of early Christianity. Finally he came to the present crisis as a result of the Industrial Revolution, and then lined out the stake of the church in the social movement and what the church ought to do. "The spiritual force of Christianity should be turned against the materialism and mammonism of our industrial and social order."[20]

His last important work, *A Theology for the Social Gospel*, was written in 1917 as a result of the Taylor Lectures at Yale University. While already in *Christianizing the Social Order* he stated: "Sin is a social force,"[21] he devoted six out of nineteen chapters in his new book to the issue of sin. The work also contains a chapter on the kingdom of evil. Though Rauschenbusch was never entirely satisfied with Ritschl because Ritschl supposedly gave too little attention to social analysis, this publication is clearly influenced by Ritschl.[22] Rauschen-

---

17. Walter Rauschenbusch, *Christianity and the Social Crisis*, foreword by Douglas E. Ottati (1907; Louisville: Westminster John Knox, 1991), 422.

18. Rauschenbusch, *Christianity,* 420.

19. Rauschenbusch, *Christianity,* 420.

20. Rauschenbusch, *Christianity,* 369.

21. Rauschenbusch, *Christianizing the Social Order,* 116.

22. Cf. Walter Rauschenbusch, *A Theology for the Social Gospel* (1917; New York: Macmillan, 1922), 138-39 n. 1, for his discussion of Ritschl. Parenthetical page numbers in the following text refer to this work.

busch distinguished between three forms of sin: sensuousness, selfishness, and godlessness, and he pointed out that sin as an assault against God always has implications for our behavior in this world. For Rauschenbusch "sin is essentially selfishness," and this "definition is more in harmony with the social gospel than with any individualistic type of religion. The sinful mind, then, is the unsocial and anti-social mind" (50). In contrast to many of his contemporaries, he did not discard the notion of original sin, yet he emphasized that this kind of sin "is transmitted along the lines of social tradition. . . . That sin is lodged in social customs and institutions and is absorbed by the individual from his social group" (60). From this notion it is only a short step to the kingdom of evil, since "the life of humanity is infinitely interwoven, always renewing itself, yet always perpetuating what has been. The evils of one generation are caused by the wrongs of the generation that preceded, and it will in turn condition the sufferings and temptations of those who come after" (79).

Central for Rauschenbusch is the kingdom of God, which "is itself the social gospel" (131). The kingdom is not a transcendent idea, but offers a teleological dimension: "The social gospel tries to see the progress of the Kingdom of God in the flow of history; not only in the doings of the Church, but in the clash of economic forces and social classes" (146). Important is how the divine life of Christ gets control of human society. Individual piety is rejected in favor of a more communal approach. In one's own piety one must discover the real personality of Jesus, who set into motion a great historical process. "It is by virtue of his personality that he became the initiator of the Kingdom" (151). Like other Social Gospel theologians, Rauschenbusch contended that "Jesus was not a pessimist. Since God was love, this world was to him fundamentally good. He realized not only evil, but the Kingdom of Evil; but he launched the Kingdom of God against it, and staked his life on its triumph. His faith in God and in the Kingdom of God constituted him a religious optimist" (156).

Even with Rauschenbusch's cognition of the kingdom of evil, human sinfulness and the evils of his world were only a transitory phenomenon. God in Christ would triumph over it all, not just in the life beyond, but already here and now. If we were to look at other representatives of the Social Gospel movement, such as Henry Churchill King (1858-1934), Francis Greenwood Peabody (1847-1936), or Shailer Mathews (1863-1941), we would obtain a similar picture. The kingdom is a concrete reality and is to be progressively realized, since we are sons and daughters of God who will care for his children and will see to it that things will come out all right. This kind of optimism gave the representatives of the Social Gospel movement the confidence to engage in social change together with the churches out of which they came. To some extent they did effect a change. As the pervasiveness of sinfulness even in today's society shows, such change cannot be accomplished once and for all, but it is a never-ending agenda.

The English Response to Social Problems

Reaching Out to the Poor — the Evangelical Solution

At the beginning of the nineteenth century, it was primarily the evangelicals who reached out to the poorer working classes. For instance, evangelical Nonconformity, i.e., free churches, looked after the material welfare and security of its members through its chapel communities.[23] As a result of the wars with Napoleon, the national debt had nearly quadrupled since 1793. During the postwar depression after 1816, soup kitchens were opened by the Baptists in the Black Country, i.e., the coal-mining areas, and clothing was provided for those of their members worst affected. Wesleyan and other Methodist bodies provided similar help. In the early stages of industrialization the parochial system of the established church broke down, since new industrial settlements seldom coincided exactly with the preindustrial settlement patterns. Therefore the demand for Nonconformity was in many cases simply a response to the massive failure in the supply of parochial services.

The evangelical engagement with the working class can be seen in two ways. For instance, in 1804 the *Evangelical Magazine* offered its readers the advice: "Religion promotes industry, industry gains respect, respect gains recommendation, recommendation gains business, business gains wealth; and thus religion itself naturally leads to prosperity."[24] Such advice can be seen as a typical and yet bad example of the Protestant work ethic. At the same time, one can find just as many cautions against worldly preoccupation with moneymaking and against involving oneself too much in worldly business. The prevailing sentiment was still to foster religion among the working class, since this led to stability and prosperity for the constitutional government. Without religion and the corresponding Christian virtues, it was believed prisons would be filled with desperate offenders, and streets with juvenile ignorance, wretchedness, and plundering rapacity. Richard Yates (1769-1834), chaplain to the Chelsea Hospital and one of the most influential clerical propagandists of his genera-

---

23. Cf. for the following Alan D. Gilbert, *Religion and Society in Industrial England: Church, Chapel, and Social Change, 1740-1914* (London: Longman, 1976), 91 and 114.

24. Quoted in E. R. Norman, *Church and Society in England, 1770-1970* (Oxford: Clarendon, 1976), 33.

tion, called for tending to the working population and its spiritual needs in his book *The Church in Danger* (1815).[25] For Yates, the solution to these ills lay in an act of Parliament to furnish public money for the building of new churches in populous districts, providing for the easy subdivision of parishes and the stipends and accommodation of the clergy to serve them. By 1830, 134 new churches had been built and 50 more were under construction.

Most influential churchmen still thought the prevailing poverty could easily be eradicated by changes in education and moral standards of the poor. Bishop Charles James Blomfield (1786-1857) of London, the chairman of the Royal Commission on the Poor Laws, was convinced in 1833 that public relief only encouraged indigence and that the real solution to social distress lay in the provision of popular education and Christian worship. If people were just induced to exercise foresight, this would render relief unnecessary.[26] This means that in the first decades of the nineteenth century the church advocated the education of the poorer classes and the building of churches in populous districts as a means of bringing the masses within the realm of Christian truth and morality. The church simply picked up the prevailing mood of the educated class and political economy and responded to it with corresponding action.

By 1851, the year of the religious census, the Church of England had built 2,529 new churches since the start of the century.[27] That the church struck a popular sentiment with this policy is shown by the fact that two-thirds of the money had been contributed through voluntary offerings, and the rest through parliamentary funds made available to the Church Building Commissioners. But the new churches were usually more than half empty, and those who did attend them were more likely from the lower middle class than from the working class. The facts revealed by the census of 1851 helped the church to face the reality that the preparation for social betterment through the creation of a worshiping society did not work. The Roman Catholics and Protestant dissenting churches fared no better with the working classes.

The works of Charles Dickens may serve as an example that society at large did not have any better ideas of how to introduce social change. Dickens came from a family of the lower middle class, and like his contemporaries, was convinced that literary works should be instruments of social reform. This became evident in his novel *Oliver Twist* (1837-38).[28] In *Hard Times* (1854) he also shows that his solution to the problems created by industrialization was to opt

25. Cf. Norman, *Church and Society,* 52-53.
26. According to Norman, *Church and Society,* 65.
27. Cf. for the following Norman, *Church and Society,* 124-25.
28. Cf. Samuel C. Chew, in *A Literary History of England,* ed. Albert C. Baugh (London: Routledge and Kegan Paul, 1948), 1347.

for a benevolent attitude toward the poor. He saw no need to change the system of society, since he believed in the fundamental goodness of human nature. Therefore the reform of individuals would be an easy matter. The church shared this sentiment and used the parishes for most of its social work during the Victorian age. The clergy was charged with visiting the sick, caring for orphans, widows, and the destitute. With the expansion of popular education, most parsons also had schools to supervise.[29] The working class neither expected nor wanted pastors to touch on political issues, since they belonged to different social classes that rarely shared anything with each other. There was no solidarity with the poor, just philanthropy.

But the clergy neither shied away from involvement with the poor nor were ignorant of their lot. Their expert opinion in many fields of inquiry concerning social conditions was sought out many times by the Royal Commission and Select Committees. It was not unusual for a priest to run in one parish a choir school, an orphanage, an infant nursery, a youth club, a Sunday breakfast for destitute boys, and a soup kitchen. Parish priests also often acted as the local organizers of the large national philanthropic bodies, centralized in London. Between 1850 and 1860 alone, 144 new societies for social or moral improvement were founded.[30] Nevertheless, by the end of the century it was generally realized that remedial measures through Christian philanthropy alone were lamentably inadequate for effectively dealing with the despair and misery of the poor.

Christian Socialism Phase 1: John M. F. Ludlow, F. D. Maurice, and Charles Kingsley

There was still another movement that focused on social issues — Christian Socialism. It had a short-lived first period from 1848 to 1854, and a longer one from 1877 onward. The first period, and to a large extent the second, is connected with three names, John Malcolm Forbes Ludlow, F. D. Maurice, and Charles Kingsley.

John Malcolm Forbes Ludlow (1821-1911), born in India, his father serving in the East India Company, was educated in France, where he got to know some of the socialist pioneers, among them the works of the social theorist Henri de Saint-Simon (1760-1825), who expounded a "new Christianity" primarily concerned with the plight of the poor. Ludlow was a lawyer by profession, and in the spring of 1848, while visiting Paris, he wrote Maurice a letter in

29. Cf. Norman, *Church and Society*, 127.
30. According to Norman, *Church and Society*, 131.

which he expressed his conviction that socialism "must be Christianized or it would shake Christianity to its foundation."[31] **Charles Kingsley** (1819-75), born in Devonshire and educated at King's College in London and Magdalene College in Cambridge, spent most of his life at the curacy of Eversley Hants, and from 1860 to 1869 was also regius professor of modern history at Cambridge. He was keenly interested in the movement for a social reform.

When Ludlow returned from Paris, he and **F. D. Maurice** (1805-72) decided to issue a weekly periodical called *Politics for the People,* for which they would be joint editors. Under political matters they included not only government actions, but also the rate of wages, the interest people got for their money, the books people read, the love they had for their wives and children, and the blessings they asked from God. Yet after only three months, *Politics for the People* suspended publication. Nevertheless, the periodical had brought to Maurice a group of serious young men who set up a free evening school for men and boys. A few months later Maurice began a series of weekly meetings devoted to Bible readings.[32]

When Ludlow went again to Paris in 1849, he was so impressed with the brotherly spirit and the material prosperity of the societies for productive cooperation that he urged the formation of such societies in England. At the same time, he started a series, called Tracts on Christian Socialism, and a year later a weekly paper called the *Christian Socialist.* Maurice wrote to Ludlow: "'Tracts on Christian Socialism' is, it seems to me, the only title which will define our object, and will commit us at once to the conflict we must engage in sooner or later with the unsocial Christians and the unChristian socialists."[33] His intention was "to Christianize Socialism," since Christian Socialism was for him Christianity active in love. Therefore "Christianity was the only foundation of socialism, and a true socialism was the necessary result of a sound Christianity."[34]

The first tract on Christian Socialism, which Maurice himself wrote, was entitled *A Dialogue between Somebody (a person of respectability) and Nobody (the writer).* In that pamphlet of 1850, Maurice wanted to make clear the real meaning and objects of the Christian Socialists. He wrote: "A watchword of the

31. *The Life and Letters of Frederick Denison Maurice Chiefly Told in His Own Letters,* 2 vols. (London: Macmillan, 1884), 1:458.

32. For the following cf. Arthur V. Woodworth, *Christian Socialism in England* (London: Swan Sonnenschein, 1903), 10-14. For the whole period cf. the detailed account of Torben Christensen, *Origin and History of Christian Socialism, 1848-1854* (Aarhus: Universitetsforlaget, 1962).

33. See *Life and Letters,* 2:35-36, for this quote and the next.

34. So Olive J. Brose, *Frederick Denison Maurice: Rebellious Conformist* (Athens: Ohio University Press, 1971), 186.

socialist is CO-OPERATION; the watchword of the Anti-Socialist is COMPE-TITION. Any one who recognizes the principle of cooperation as a stronger and truer principle than that of competition, has a right to the honor or the disgrace of being called a Socialist."[35] He did not want to proclaim a new social order, but to understand God's method, which he believed was harmony and not confrontation. Kingsley chimed in with the same motto, comparing competition with cannibalism.

In 1850 the Christian Socialists advanced funds for the first association of working tailors to be formed, with the intention that it should employ the Christian principles of cooperation, joint work, and shared profits. Twelve associations were founded altogether, but they were all of trades that did not use machinery, such as tailors, shoemakers, piano makers, etc.[36] Yet the society for promoting Working Men's Associations that was supposed to help these cooperatives to get started and work, came to an end in 1854 with an empty treasury. Maurice and Kingsley felt that the associations were a failure because the men involved were not fit for them. They could not work in a brotherly spirit. The different associations fought with each other and some of them could never really pay their way. Though the Christian Socialists failed in taking production into their own hands, at least the notion of a cooperative movement and the principle of brotherliness were ideals that exercised a helpful influence. Maurice, as we have seen, was not a revolutionary; to the contrary. He wrote: "Christian Socialism is in my mind the assertion of God's order. Every attempt, however small and feeble, to bring it forth I honour and desire to assist."[37] With the failure of the productive cooperative associations, the first chapter of Christian Socialism was closed in England.

Christian Socialism Phase 2: Stewart Headlam and William Temple

The Christian Socialist revival of the 1870s received its inspiration to a large extent from the midcentury pioneers, such as Maurice, Kingsley, and Ludlow.[38] According to Maurice, the kingdom must encompass the whole of God's creation, and therefore humanity cannot develop contrary to that.

Stewart Headlam (1847-1924) was born near Liverpool. His father and

---

35. As reprinted in F. D. Maurice, *Reconstructing Christian Ethics: Selected Writings,* ed. Ellen K. Wondra (Louisville: Westminster John Knox, 1995), 196-97.

36. Cf. for the following Woodworth, *Christian Socialism in England,* 27-32.

37. *Life and Letters,* 2:44.

38. Cf. Peter d'Alroy Jones, *The Christian Socialist Revival, 1877-1914: Religion, Class, and Social Conscience in Late-Victorian England* (Princeton: Princeton University Press, 1968), 9-10.

grandfather were both underwriters. Therefore Headlam had some private means at his disposal. He was brought up in a strictly evangelical environment, then went to Eton from 1860 to 1865, and to Trinity College in Cambridge from 1865 to 1869. There he met Maurice, and his "insistence on the Fatherhood of God and the Brotherhood of Humanity through the Eternal Sonship of Christ came as an immense liberating experience to Headlam."[39] After various assignments he came to Bethnal Green (London), and there at St. Matthew's he held study evenings for teachers and other people, and out of these local study groups the Guild of St. Matthew emerged in 1877, originally having been a parish guild. Soon it became known as the red-hot center of Christian Socialism. It was by no means just social thought or activity that the members of the Guild of St. Matthew wanted to propagate. They pledged themselves to communicate on all great festivals and also to be present at Holy Communion on Sundays and saints' days, and to promote the study of social and political questions in light of the incarnation.

The guild, however, advocated socioeconomic reform and became increasingly radical in its demands. Headlam had also become friends with Henry George, and his book *Progress and Poverty* influenced him.[40] Three items were especially important for the guild: reform and extension of public secular education, church reform, and the single tax. George had advocated this latter tax, which was defined as a confiscatory taxation of the increment of land values, to avoid land speculation.[41] The guild started with 40 members and grew to over 300 by 1895, then fell to 200 by 1906. Many Anglican priests were among the membership, and even some bishops.

The Christian Social Union grew out of the Oxford academic environment and was, to some extent, a child of the guild. In 1879 a tiny precursor of the Christian Social Union was founded. It was called PESEK, an acronym for politics, economics, socialism, ethics, and Christianity, and held private meetings at Oxford. In 1889 *Lux Mundi. A Series of Studies in the Religion of the Incarnation,* edited by Charles Gore, was published. As Gore explained in the preface, this volume had been written by servants "of the Catholic Creed and Church aiming only at interpreting the faith we have received."[42] This learned volume proved to be a huge success, and within one year reached its tenth edi-

---

39. Kenneth Leech, "Stewart Headlam, 1847-1924, and the Guild of St. Matthew," in *For Christ and the People: Studies of Four Socialist Priests and Prophets of the Church of England between 1870 and 1930*, ed. Maurice B. Reckitt (London: SPCK, 1968), 61.

40. So Jones, *The Christian Socialist Revival*, 103.

41. Cf. Jones, *The Christian Socialist Revival*, 117.

42. Charles Gore, ed., *Lux Mundi. A Series of Studies in the Religion of the Incarnation*, 12th ed. (London: John Murray, 1891), viii.

tion. It did not just include doctrine, but Christian ethics, and therefore the Holy Party, as this group of Anglican priests called itself, set up the social discussion group of PESEK and also conducted economic lectures.

In 1889 the Christian Socialist Union was established by Gore and Henry Scott Holland (1847-1918), canon at St. Paul's Cathedral in London, with three aims in mind:

1. To claim for the Christian law the ultimate authority to rule social practice.
2. To study in common how to apply the moral truths and principles of Christianity to the social and economic difficulties of the present time.
3. To present Christ in practical life as the living Master and King, the enemy of wrong and selfishness, the power of righteousness and love.[43]

Subsequently other unions sprang up, such as the Socialist Quaker Society (1898), the Catholic Socialist Society (1906), the Friends' Social Union (1904), and the Wesleyan Methodist Social Union (1905). The New Testament scholar and, later, bishop of Durham (1890) B. F. Westcott (1825-1901) served as the first president of the Christian Social Union. His sermons of 1886, "Social Aspects of Christianity" and "Christian Aspects of Life," show how much he owed to Maurice.

The Christian Social Union was organized primarily to study and publicize social and economic problems, but not to act as a pressure group in one way or another. In this way it was different from the Guild of St. Matthew. Yet by publicizing the right things, it could also exert considerable pressure. One sees its potential, for instance, when in 1893 the Oxford Christian Social Union drew up a list of twenty local firms that had adopted acceptable trade union wage rates, and publicly encouraged its members to buy only from such firms.[44] As another example, one notes that in 1898/99 a London deputation of the union heavily influenced legislation concerning working conditions in factories. What made the Christian Social Union so important was that many of its members were bishops, college heads, and other dignitaries, and that its membership was counted in the thousands.

Venturing into the twentieth century, we must mention **William Temple** (1881-1944), who "is believed by many to have been the greatest Archbishop of Canterbury of the century."[45] Temple was born in Exeter where his father, Fred-

---

43. So Jones, *The Christian Socialist Revival,* 177.

44. Jones, *The Christian Socialist Revival,* 183.

45. So Trevor Beeson, *Rebels and Reformers: Christian Renewal in the Twentieth Century* (London: SCM, 1999), 77, in his brief biographical description of Temple.

erick Temple (1821-1902), served as bishop (1872), then became bishop of London (1885) and finally archbishop of Canterbury (1896). William went to Balliol College at Oxford and was then appointed fellow and lecturer in philosophy at Queen's College (Oxford). In 1906, when he wanted to be ordained, he was turned down because of his hesitations over the virgin birth and the physical resurrection of Jesus. Two years later, his doubts now resolved, he was ordained in Canterbury Cathedral. After serving in various capacities, he became bishop of Manchester in 1920, the same year he assumed editorship of the *Pilgrim,* a quarterly "Review of Christian Politics and Religion," in which he wrote: "A religion which offers no solution to world-problems, fails to satisfy."[46]

The year before he became bishop, the idea was conceived to have a large-scale conference on Christianity and the social order known as the Conference on Christian Politics, Economics, and Citizenship (COPEC). In twelve committees every facet of social life was addressed, since, as Temple had declared, the Christian faith gave the vision and the power necessary for solving social problems, and not merely for regenerating the individual. At that time Temple had also introduced four social principles that he and many others had used: freedom, or respect for the person; fellowship; the duty to serve; and the power to sacrifice. When the conference opened in April 1924 at Birmingham, 1,500 delegates attended, 80 from outside the British Isles, 6 from European countries, plus China and Japan. Messages were read from the king, the prime minister, and two ex–prime ministers, among others.[47] Almost all denominations were represented, except the Roman Catholics, who withdrew a few weeks before the conference. The principles of the Christian faith were used to expose deficiencies of the current system, and to pass on suitable recommendations. While there was very little criticism and a remarkable unanimity, the conference was much better in stating the problems than in suggesting solutions, because of the complexity of the issues.[48]

COPEC provided a systematic and coherent statement of the social involvement of the church and the individual, and disseminated its findings to the parish level, at least among the clergy. Subsequently Temple was regarded as one of the most prominent social teachers of the Church of England. COPEC's findings were also publicized at the Stockholm Life and Work conference of 1925. Yet there was little continuing work at home, and therefore COPEC folded quickly. This was also due to the general strike and the miner strike of 1926.

46. According to Alan M. Suggate, *William Temple and Christian Social Ethics Today* (Edinburgh: T. & T. Clark, 1987), 32.

47. Cf. Frederic A. Iremonger, *William Temple, Archbishop of Canterbury: His Life and Letters,* abridged ed. (London: Oxford University Press, 1963), 154.

48. Cf. Suggate, *William Temple,* 35.

Moreover, in 1929 Temple became archbishop of York and was thus more and more involved in the ecumenical movement, such as being appointed chairman of the continuation committee of the Lausanne Faith and Order conference (1927) and chairman of the Edinburgh Faith and Order conference (1937). Thereby he also became increasingly concerned with the unity of the church. Finally, he occupied the see of Canterbury, though only for two years (1942-44). Yet his interest in social issues had not waned. In 1942 his *Christianity and Social Order* appeared in paperback and sold 150,000 copies in a few months.[49] There he was much more cautious than he had been before in pointing to a definite course of action.

Temple stated that the church's impact upon society at large should be twofold, to "announce Christian principles and to point out where the existing social order at any time is in conflict with them."[50] But it is up to Christian citizens in their civic capacity to reshape the existing order into a closer conformity with these principles. When the church is asked what one should do, the response should be: I cannot tell you what is the remedy, but I can tell you what is wrong and what should be the case instead. It is then up to the individuals, the experts, and other concerned parties to find a course of action. But the church should not sketch out a perfect social order, since such an order cannot be found or established in this world, where sin reigns. There is an order, however, that would work best in this world, and this is to be discovered by those who have sufficient data and power to carry it through. Temple was neither an idealist nor a starry-eyed visionary, but a realist, deeply convinced of the perversity of sin and of the complexity of the issues. These issues needed experts to seek solutions and not the church to dispense its "wisdom." On earth we are concerned with how people are and not with how they ought to be, and therefore the task is to lead them nearer to what they ought to be, although this will also involve failure and disaster.

Temple saw a tension between humanity made in the image of God and our animal nature. Nevertheless, we are children of God and capable of communion with God, from whom we receive our dignity and value. From that postulate, that "Man is a child of God and is destined for a life of eternal fellowship with Him," follow three principles of the Christian social order: freedom, fellowship, and service.[51] For Temple social ethics is not divorced from his compassion for the well-being of the whole person, including his or her eternal des-

---

49. According to Beeson, *Rebels and Reformers,* 77.

50. William Temple, *Christianity and Social Order,* foreword by Edward Heath, introduction by Ronald H. Preston (London: SPCK, 1976 [1942]), 58.

51. Temple, *Christianity and Social Order,* 77.

tiny. Its starting point therefore is not anthropology, but theology, because it starts from the commission given to the church to carry out the purpose of God and to participate "in the great work, the fulfillment of God's purpose in the world and beyond it."[52]

William and Catherine Booth and the Salvation Army

Because of its unrestrained evangelical zeal, the Salvation Army is often wrongly considered an American phenomenon. Yet the founder of the Salvation Army, **William Booth** (1829-1912), was British, born in Nottingham as the son of an unsuccessful builder. William served as an apprentice to a pawnbroker because his father thought this profession might enrich him. The contact with human misery in the pawnbroking business aroused in Booth a lifelong passion directed against poverty and the wretchedness in which many nineteenth-century English people lived.

While attending a service in a Wesleyan chapel, Booth experienced a religious conversion (1844), and two years later, influenced by the American evangelist James Caughey, he began to preach. A year later he became a Methodist "local preacher," retaining his love for the Methodist church. As he could not find any work in Nottingham, he moved to London, where he was employed by a pawnbroker. He continued with his lay preaching, but since this did not give him enough to do, he began to hold open-air meetings. Naturally this caused friction with his pastor, and he became part of the Methodist New Connexion (1854-62) and was ordained in 1858. Though successful as a regular pastor, he resigned in 1862 to dedicate himself to itinerant evangelism, conducting evangelical campaigns in various parts of the country.

In 1865 Booth was invited by the East London Special Services Committee to conduct a tent mission for the working class in Whitechapel (London). Two years later this work evolved into the East London Christian Mission, and only three years after that he acquired a permanent facility, the People's Mission Hall in Whitechapel. That same year, the first preaching station outside East London was started in Croydon, and the organization was renamed the Christian Mission. During the 1870s his work expanded through middle and north England, concentrating on the poorest of the people the church could not reach because of its alignment with the establishment. In 1878 the organization was renamed the Salvation Army, and the members started to use martial language and military titles and uniforms. Booth himself, who had been

---

52. Temple, *Christianity and Social Order*, 37.

superintendent general of the Christian Mission, now became general of the new army.[53]

But the Salvation Army's pursuit of spreading the gospel met resistance. The soldiers also suffered violent persecution from ignorant and often alcohol-imbibing roughnecks, and even some magistrates prosecuted his followers because the military image and the open-air evangelism were too unconventional. Many denominations regarded the Salvation Army initially with distrust. "In one year alone — 1882 — 669 Salvation Army soldiers were knocked down or brutally assaulted. Sixty buildings were virtually wrecked by the mob."[54] But disorder and distrust gradually abated, and Booth even received friendly overtures from the Church of England. By the end of the century Booth's work became recognized. Oxford University bestowed on him an honorary doctorate, and he was officially invited in 1902 to the coronation of King Edward VII, and also opened a session of the United States Senate with prayer.

His followers carried his work to the United States in 1879, and to Australia a year later. By 1890 the Salvation Army was established in most European countries and also in India, South Africa, and South America. The same year, Booth published an influential book, *In Darkest England and the Way Out*, picking up on the story of British explorer Sir Henry Stanley (1841-1904) in which he talked about "Darkest Africa."[55] Booth's book contained proposals for relieving poverty and fighting vice; establishing homes for the homeless; founding training centers for those who wanted to emigrate to overseas countries; creating rescue homes for women and girls who were endangered by prostitution and alcoholism, as well as homes for released prisoners; providing legal aid for the poor and practical help for alcoholics. Many of these ideas were put into action.

It is not without significance that due to the role of Booth's wife, **Catherine Booth** (1829-90), the "mother of the army," women have played an important role in the Salvation Army. By 1878 almost half the officers in the army were women. Catherine, whose father was a carriage builder and occasional Methodist lay preacher, was a convinced believer in a woman's right to preach the gospel. She began to preach in her husband's church in 1860, and between 1880 and 1884 she conducted successful meetings in various halls in the

53. For details cf. David Bennett, *William Booth* (Minneapolis: Bethany House, 1986), 46-49 ("The Salvation Army Is Born").

54. Richard Collier, *The General Next to God: The Story of William Booth and the Salvation Army* (Glasgow: William Collins, 1977), 94, who provides many examples of the resistance of the mob to the Salvation Army.

55. General Booth, *In Darkest England and the Way Out* (London: Funk and Wagnalls, 1890), 9.

West End of London. She also wrote *Female Ministry* (1859) and participated in 1885 in a campaign to secure the passing of the Criminal Law Amendment Act, designed to protect young girls. Even the writer George Bernard Shaw (1856-1950) helped in the campaign.[56] While their oldest son, William Bramwell Booth (1856-1929), became the second general of the Salvation Army, their younger daughter Evangeline Cordy Booth (1865-1950) went to Canada in 1896 and in 1904 took over the command of the Salvation Army in the United States, where she remained until 1934 when she was elected general of the whole Salvation Army enterprise.

The Salvation Army represents orthodox evangelical Protestantism, believing in the Bible as the inspired word of God, the Trinity and the human and divine natures of Jesus Christ, the total corruption of humanity through the fall, salvation through faith in Christ, and his substitutionary suffering. The members of the Salvation Army believe in personal sanctification, and avoid smoking and imbibing alcoholic beverages. Since 1882 they have also refrained from the sacraments of baptism and the Lord's Supper, because they consider them divisive factors among Christians.

While the organization suffered heavily in the twentieth century, its work brought to naught in the Soviet Union and hampered severely in World War II in Germany and Japan, the Salvation Army has resumed its work in former Communist territories and now maintains thousands of social havens, such as hospitals, homes for the homeless, and schools, while freely cooperating with other churches to help those who are poor and destitute.

The German Response to Social Problems

When we turn to Germany, we notice that the challenge of the Industrial Revolution was first picked up on the Protestant side by the pioneers of the home mission. This movement had already a long tradition in August Hermann Francke (1663-1727), who was a pastor near Halle and after 1698 professor of theology at the newly founded University of Halle. He founded the Francke Institutions, the first great colony of mercy, with an orphanage, residential high school and secondary school, and a refuge for single women and widows, among many other enterprises.

56. Cf. Bennett, *William Booth,* 119-20.

The Legacy of Pietism — Christian Home Mission: Johann Friedrich Oberlin, Theodor and Friederike Fliedner, Friedrich von Bodelschwingh, Johann Hinrich Wichern

The pietistic concern for the poor and helpless was carried on by **Johann Friedrich Oberlin** (1740-1826), who was born in Strasbourg. There he studied theology, and then became pastor in Steintal, Alsace. While his theology was more of an Enlightenment type, through his mother he got in contact with pietism. Oberlin tried to approach the people in a comprehensive way, as one sees in his numerous activities, e.g., the establishment of preschool and kindergarten, the introduction of obligatory schooling for boys and girls, courses for adults, and the offer of medical help and education in ecologically sound agriculture.[57] He believed in the goodness of humanity and in its freedom that is the result of its connection with the divine. The human body too was to be cared for and not neglected, since the goal of the material world is the spiritual world into which souls are received after death. Underlying these thoughts was a theosophical worldview that seemed to grasp the origin and dealing of humanity and the world through immediate contact with God or the divine.

Oberlin's pedagogical and diaconal work influenced Theodor Fliedner and Johann Hinrich Wichern. Even a college in the United States was established in 1832 bearing his name, Oberlin College in Ohio, which at that time already admitted women and blacks.

Other pioneers were **Theodor Fliedner** (1800-1864) and his wife **Friederike** (1800-1842). Theodor, the son of a pastor, was born not far from Frankfurt and studied theology in Giessen and Göttingen and, similar to Oberlin, was influenced by rationalism. In 1822 he came as pastor into the impoverished congregation of Kaiserswerth near Düsseldorf, which was a product of the Prussian Union. He journeyed to Holland (1823) and England (1824) to raise funds for his congregation, because it was economically near collapse and about to dissolve. Influenced by the Dutch awakening movement, he returned from these journeys with a renewed biblical theology.

When Fliedner saw the misery in the Dutch and English prisons, as well as in Düsseldorf, he founded the Rhenish-Westphalian Prison Society (1826) in which high-ranking representatives of the government and of Protestant and Roman Catholic churches participated. This provided strong impulses for a reform of the prison system. In 1833 Fliedner started counseling prisoners in Kaiserswerth and also caring for female ex-prisoners. Three years later he

---

57. For a brief biography see Eberhard Zwink, "Oberlin, Johann Friedrich," in *Theologische Realenzyklopädie*, 24:720-23.

founded the first deaconess hospital to train Protestant nurses. He and his wife became renewers of the office of deaconess in the church according to Protestant understanding. These deaconesses cared for the sick, the poor, children, and also prisoners. Within twenty years he and his wife trained 228 deaconesses.[58] They also opened a nursery, an orphanage for girls, a teacher training school for women, etc. Deaconesses also served in many other hospitals and educational institutions. They went as far as Pittsburgh, Pennsylvania, Jerusalem, and Constantinople.

Even before Friederike married Theodor, she worked in a children's rescue mission. And in 1836 she became the first head of the deaconess motherhouse. In this context we should also remember Wilhelm Löhe, who, independently of Fliedner, opened a deaconess motherhouse to alleviate the plight of unmarried women, for whom at that time there was no opportunity for outside employment. To elevate the deaconess to the level of the married women, they received a hat when they made their vows to become a deaconess, similar to the hat worn by married women.

Another important figure is **Friedrich von Bodelschwingh** the Elder (1831-1910), who was born of an upper-class family and grew up in Berlin as a playmate of Emperor Frederick III (1831-88), who ruled for only ninety-nine days before he died of cancer.[59] Touched by a mission sermon, von Bodelschwingh desired to study theology and attended successively the universities of Basel, Erlangen, and Berlin, but he named especially Wilhelm Löhe and Johann Christoph Blumhardt his theological teachers. From 1858 to 1864 he pastored the German congregation in Paris and cared there also for maidservants, collectors of rags, and city cleaners. After serving a congregation in Germany and being military chaplain in the wars of 1866 between Prussia and Austria and 1870/71 between France and Germany, he assumed in 1872 the leadership of the institution for epileptics and the Westphalian deaconess motherhouse Sarepta in Bethel near Bielefeld that had been founded there five years prior. From these humble beginnings he built a city of mercy.

Von Bodelschwingh asserted that the sick were also created in the image of God. He encouraged healthy and sick people to live together, and also to come together to do whatever work they were able to do. In 1877 he founded the deaconess motherhouse Nazareth, and soon he cared not only for epileptics but also for the mentally sick and retarded, and for the homeless. He also built a set-

---

58. For a brief biography see Johannes Degen, "Fliedner, Friederike und Theodor," in *Theologische Realenzyklopädie*, 11:214-15.

59. For biographical details see Gerhard Ruhbach, "Bodelschwingh, Friedrich von, Vater und Sohn," in *Theologische Realenzyklopädie*, 6:744-47.

tlement for workers. Though he rejected the idea of a Christian state, he became a member of the Prussian Diet in 1903 and was in continuous contact with the different political parties, asking for help for his mission. To combat the liberal theology that was prevalent at most theological faculties, he planned to found a seminary at Bethel, which was approved by the government in 1905. His work was continued by Friedrich von Bodelschwingh the Younger (1877-1946), and the whole enterprise today has an annual budget exceeding $500 million, and is indeed a city of mercy in the widest, most comprehensive sense of the word.[60]

Yet the one who is the actual founder of "home mission" is **Johann Hinrich Wichern** (1808-81), who used that term at least from 1836 on.[61] He was born in Hamburg, and after graduating from the *Gymnasium* he studied at Göttingen and Berlin. In Berlin he became acquainted with the circle around Baron Ernst von Kottwitz, a physician and a member of the awakening movement who advocated prison reform. Upon his return to Hamburg, he engaged in Sunday school work, meaning academic schools on Sunday for those who had to work during the week. This provided him with good insight into the desolate condition of the poor. He obtained a small house with a garden and field, the so-called Rauhe Haus near Hamburg, where together with his mother and sister he took in twelve homeless boys. In contrast to German idealism that believed in the original goodness of humanity, Wichern took seriously the reality of sin and God's pardoning grace. This insight was the foundation for his educational work. Important for him was the renewal of the family as the cell of the human community.

Through the wars of liberation from French domination in the first decades of the century and through the rapid industrialization and urbanization, many families were uprooted and destroyed. As a consequence, many children were orphaned or left homeless. To strengthen the family and to integrate those unfortunate children into surrogate families to give them a sense of belonging and security, was critical for Wichern. "Home mission is not one manifestation of life outside or next to the church, nor does it [home mission] want to be the church itself now or in the future, as some had feared, but it wants to disclose one side of the life of the church, namely the life of the spirit of faithful love which seeks the lost, forlorn, and neglected masses until it finds

---

60. Cf. *The City of Mercy: The Story of Bethel,* compiled and translated from German sources by Margaret Bradfield (Bethel, Germany: Verlagsanstalt, 1964).

61. For Johann Hinrich Wichern see Martin Gerhardt, *Johann Hinrich Wichern. Ein Lebensbild,* 3 vols. (Hamburg: Agentur des Rauhen Hauses, 1927-31), here 1:261, to this point. Cf. also Erich Freudenstein, *The Home Mission of the Evangelical Church in Germany: Facts and Features,* trans. Friedrich Köhler (Bielefeld-Bethel: Deutscher-Heimat-Verlag, 1949).

them."[62] For Wichern home mission was a significant manifestation of a vital church as it seeks to express its faith and translate it into action.

In 1844 Wichern founded the deacon institution of the Rauhe Haus and thereby became the renewer of the male deaconate. The deacons served not only by educating homeless and endangered youth, but also by caring for ex-convicts, by working as missionaries in the cities and as housefathers for hostels, and by doing congregational work. After the March 1848 revolution, Wichern founded the Central Committee of the Home Mission of the German Protestant Church (1849). The same year he also published his manifesto of the Home Mission: *The Home Mission of the German Protestant Church: A Memorial to the German Nation (Die innere Mission der deutschen evangelischen Kirche, eine Denkschrift an die deutsche Nation)*. Through this Central Committee he also furthered the idea that the various Protestant churches, regionally constituted, actually belonged together. One after another joined the Central Committee. When he started his work at the Rauhe Haus in 1833, he declared at the constituting convention of the supporters: "This rescue institution intends to become a refuge and to grant an education to street children, both male and female, up to confirmation, and provide that substitute for the place of paternal care as much as possible."[63]

Most important was Wichern's impromptu speech at the Wittenberg Church Assembly *(Kirchentag)* in 1848, where he made a passionate plea for home mission in front of more than 500 leaders of various Protestant churches in Germany. He said:

> Home mission has absolutely nothing to do with politics and if it does not function in that way, then the church will go bankrupt with the state. Though it is not its task to judge different forms of government or to decide between political parties, it is its task that citizens are filled with the Christian spirit, regardless under which form of government, and this must be one of its most serious concerns from this day onward. . . . My friends, one thing is necessary, that the Protestant Church in its totality recognizes: "The work of the home mission is mine!" that it [the Church] puts a big seal on the sum total of this work: *love belongs to me as much as faith. The saving love must become its great tool, whereby she proves the facticity of faith.*[64]

---

62. Johann Hinrich Wichern, *Die innere Mission der deutschen evangelischen Kirche. Eine Denkschrift an die deutsche Nation*, 5th ed. (Hamburg: Agentur des Rauhen Hauses, 1914), 4.

63. According to Gerhardt, *Johann Hinrich Wichern*, 1:136.

64. According to Gerhardt, *Johann Hinrich Wichern*, 2:109-10.

Home mission is above and beyond politics. But it sees its task as serving the state in imbuing the citizen with a Christian spirit. It was decisive for Wichern that the church does not confine itself to the proclamation of faith, but that it also makes that faith active in love. When he designed the bylaws for the Central Committee, he made it clear that its work was to be conducted in the faith and service of the Protestant church, and that it resulted from the German Evangelical Federation of Churches, as first announced in 1848 at Wittenberg. In the memorial to the German nation on Home Mission, he spelled out what he understood by home mission: "As home mission, we do not understand this or that singular work, but the total work of love which is born out of faith in Christ through which it wants to renew inwardly and outwardly those masses of Christendom which have fallen prey to the power and dominion of the manifold external and internal perditions which come directly or indirectly from sin and which, as it would be necessary for the Christian renewal, are not reached by the respective Christian offices."[65] Home mission is not a particular work, but is the total work of faith active in love, and it strives for renewal, not just inner renewal, but also external renewal. It works on something that so far has not been achieved by the church.

Home mission is not primarily directed to the baptized and to members of one's own denomination. "It does not enter the controversy among the denominations."[66] Moreover, it does not focus only on churched people, because "it does not ask whom it serves, but already has served before it asks according to the example of the great Samaritan." Home mission is not the missionary arm of the church to win people over from other denominations and to add people to one's own fold. It is an expression of selfless love, extending help regardless of denominational affiliation. Here it sees its work in analogy to that of the state. The state summons all of its citizens to help combat material poverty in all its origins, consequences, and forms. In a similar way, it combats its own internal poverty, "namely those manifestations of a mass deprivation with regard to morals and Christianity among the people."[67]

All church members have not just the right but the duty to engage in home mission, whether they be pastors, housefathers and housemothers, employers, schoolteachers, businessmen, etc. "This activity is the realization of the *common priesthood* (that lay principle) in which the church completes itself from itself and this in Christ who manifests himself in individuals as the saving Lord."[68]

---

65. Wichern, *Die innere Mission*, 2.
66. For this and the following quote, see Wichern, *Die innere Mission*, 4-5.
67. Wichern, *Die innere Mission*, 6.
68. Wichern, *Die innere Mission*, 7.

While Wichern summons the support of the government, his primary focus is on individuals in their respective places to translate the common priesthood of all believers into their everyday activities. Yet to go beyond the individual level, Wichern sought and obtained government support.

In 1852 King Frederick William IV granted the deacons of the Rauhe Haus the privilege of becoming overseers in the Prussian prison service. The following year Wichern was appointed to the ministry of interior as adviser for the prison service, in which capacity he visited prisons throughout Prussia, investigated their conditions and suggested means of correcting existing defects, especially with regard to rehabilitation of ex-convicts. While in Berlin, Wichern founded the Protestant Johannesstift in 1858, where he pursued work similar to that of the Rauhe Haus near Hamburg. His leading motif was taken from Paul's admonition of "faith active in love." Since the Prussian kings were influenced by both a Calvinistic spirit and the awakening and had adopted as their own motto "I serve," appeals for cooperation with the government in ameliorating the plight of the poor and destitute did not fall on deaf ears. We see this also with the more political involvement of people such as Naumann and Stoecker, to whom we now turn.

Christian Sociopolitical Involvement and the Evangelisch-Soziale Kongress: Friedrich Naumann and Adolf Stoecker

Home mission was just the first step for the social involvement of the church. The second step belonged to the sociopolitical involvement of two important figures, Friedrich Naumann and Adolf Stoecker. The Evangelisch-Soziale Kongress (ESK) (Protestant Social Congress) provided the forum in which their concerns were brought to a wider audience.

Friedrich Naumann (1860-1919) was born near Leipzig and studied theology there and at Erlangen. He was influenced by the Erlangen Lutheran dogmatician Reinhold Frank, who emphasized the necessity of social activity in the pastorate. Upon his final exams, Naumann worked under Hinrich Wichern at the Rauhe Haus in Hamburg, and then became pastor in Saxony while he advocated the founding of Protestant workers associations. In 1890 he was called to Frankfurt am Main to become the pastor of the Protestant Association for Home Mission. There he intensified his interest in politics and became active in Protestant workers associations. He also involved himself in the ESK, which had its first meeting at Berlin in 1890, an association in which theologians, historians, and sociologists came together, among them the church historian Adolf von Harnack and the sociologist Max Weber.

The members of the ESK wanted to develop a Christian social alternative to the demands of the Social Democrats, who were decidedly antichurch. In 1894 Naumann founded a journal, *Die Hilfe (Help)*. Its subtitle, *The Help of God. Self-Help, Government Help, and Brotherly Help,* indicates a certain program. Yet he got into a controversy with Stoecker, who was more conservative and objected to his attempt to fuse social engagement with nationalism. After this Naumann left the ESK and founded the National Social Association (Nationalsozialer Verein). As chairman, he wanted to realize the connection between a national, but not nationalistic, direction and a Christian social orientation. At first he appreciated the flexibility of his contemporary, Emperor Wilhelm II, but then was very disappointed at his romantic and nationalistic tendencies. Naumann had a liking for supranational cooperation that went beyond narrow nationalistic interests.

Gradually Naumann left the home mission and moved to Berlin to participate in the elections for the national diet in 1898 and 1903. Since he was able to obtain very few votes from the Social Democrats for his National Social Association, he dissolved that association and, with most of its members, joined the Association of Free Thinkers (Freisinnigen Vereinigung). A visit to Palestine confirmed in him the idea that Jesus could not have been a popular person who addressed the elementary needs of the people. Therefore, Naumann contended, our own involvement in social issues cannot be grounded in the example of Jesus' own life.

Naumann realized that home mission with its emphasis on individual groups and their needs could not solve the impoverishment of the masses caused by industrialization and the emergence of a large proletariat. Therefore he looked for a social program through which governmental activity could be channeled and the needy themselves could activate their own organizations. For him "the future of home mission is the future of socialism."[69] In strict demarcation from the antichurch Social Democrats, he wanted to renew society independent of its governmental form but through governmental help, so that the witness of Holy Scripture and especially the Gospels could be made useful. As a Lutheran he was convinced of the two kingdoms, and did not want to found his social programs on a Christian basis, but wanted to enflesh a Christian existence confronted with the issues of his time. In that regard he was also instrumental in helping to draw up the Weimar Constitution of the German Reich after World War I and advocating the basic rights in the social and economic obligations of the state over the traditional individual rights of the per-

---

69. Friedrich Naumann, *Werke,* ed. Walter Uhsadel (Cologne: Westdeutscher Verlag, 1964), 1:104.

son of liberty and pursuit of happiness. It is noteworthy that Theodor Heuss, the first president of the Federal Republic of (West) Germany, was called by Naumann to be his personal aide when he was a twenty-one-year-old student.[70]

Adolf Stoecker (1835-1909), influenced by an orthodox pietistic piety, was born of commoners in Halberstadt near Magdeburg. After several pastorates he was called in 1874 to become the fourth court preacher of the Prussian king at the cathedral (Dom) in Berlin.[71] Already before this call he had an interest in home mission and evangelization, something he continued within the Berlin home mission. At Berlin he realized that this center of modern industrialism and capitalism was, through bourgeoisie liberalism and proletarian socialism, going to turn into a post-Christian culture. His idea was to re-Christianize the societal and political life on the basis of a Christian understanding of faith and order. Toward that goal he preached and spoke against an enlightened liberalism, atheistic materialism, and democracy and socialism. He also saw culture endangered through the enlightened Jewry he encountered in Berlin.

In 1878 Stoecker founded the Christian Socialist Workers' Party (Christlich-Soziale Arbeiterpartei) to fight the Social Democrats. They represented for him just an offspring of the international Jewry that wanted to obtain power over the world. Social Democrats, capitalists, and independently working artists and writers were for Stoecker agents of religious and moral decay of the German nation.[72] The considerably large and influential Jewish population of Berlin was similarly classified. This simplistic approach to societal problems verged on demagoguery. At the same time, however, he was progressive in developing a German social policy. In the Protestant church he was the leader of socially conservative Protestantism against a liberal capitalistic theory. He advocated trade unions, reduction of the workweek, and protection for the workers. During the big strikes he was on the side of the justified demands of the workers. Together with Harnack, he founded the ESK, through which many proposals were offered that were enacted in legislation. After many controversies with the social liberal Protestantism that was represented in the ESK, Stoecker became one of the founders of the Free Ecclesial Social Conference

---

70. Theodor Heuss, "Friedrich Naumann und sein Vermächtnis an unsere Zeit," in Alex Hans Nuber, D. Friedrich Naumann. Katalog der Gedächtnisausstellung in Heilbronn anläßlich seines 100. Geburtstages am 25. März 1960 (Heilbronn: Städt. Archiv, 1962), 20, who very appreciatingly remembers Naumann's contribution to his country and to the people.

71. For a discerning assessment of Stoecker, cf. Günter Brakelmann, Martin Greschat, and Werner Jochmann, Protestantismus und Politik. Werk und Wirkung Adolf Stoeckers (Hamburg: Hans Christians, 1982), esp. in the introduction by Jochmann (7-17).

72. Cf. Günter Brakelmann, "Stoecker, Adolf," in Theologische Realenzyklopädie, 32:194-95, for a concise and accurate portrayal of Stoecker.

(Freie kirchlich-soziale Konferenz [FSK]) in 1897. Nevertheless, he was not working against the established churches but had contacts with Christian workers unions and the confessional women's movement. Through his anti-Semitism he could be of use as a forerunner of Adolf Hitler by later National Socialism. Yet for many within Protestantism he was one of the advocates for solving the social issues through a social and societal reform of the government against the excessive capitalism and a collective class socialism. He was incisive as well as divisive, helpful as well as misleading.

According to its 1891 bylaws, the ESK had as its goal "to research the social state of our nation without prejudice, to compare [it] with the yardstick of the moral and religious demands of the gospel, and to make these demands more useful and effective for the economic life of today than has been done up to now."[73] The double goal of a predominantly theoretical investigation and its evaluation on the basis of a Protestant Christian ethics was maintained from the inception of the ESK to its end in 1945.

The main public activity of the ESK was the annual meeting. It was spread over several days and held in a major city, especially in industrial regions where there was a majority of Protestants. At its height, fifteen hundred people attended, and at its low point slightly more than two hundred were present. The actual membership reached its height in 1914 with close to two thousand members. Along with annual meetings there were membership meetings and open evenings with theoretical or practical topics being presented predominantly by scientists, but also by politicians, representatives of interest groups, pastors, etc. While the ESK did not want to be associated with any party or group in the church, its main outlook was nevertheless determined by its main representatives, be they conservatives of the Christian socialist persuasion or nationalistic liberals. There were also regional associations of the ESK that worked with other organizations.

The ESK was founded when announcements by both the church and the emperor pointed to the urgent social problems and asked people to participate in their solution. The idea was to win back for church and state the blue-collar workers who had come under Social Democrat influence. Yet especially through the influence of Harnack, who presided over the ESK from 1902 to 1912, the ESK moved away from being predominantly directed against the Social Democrats and rather provided a platform for free discussion of sociopolitical and social ethical issues. Regardless of internal differences, the congress was unanimous that the existing situation was not the only societal order justified

---

73. As quoted in Klaus Erich Pollmann, "Evangelisch-sozialer Kongreß" (ESK), in *Theologische Realenzyklopädie*, 10:645.

by the gospel. In addition, the church should not appear to be a tool of a state divided by classes but should contribute to overcoming class consciousness.

There was also polemic against this open approach, even to the point of the church in Prussia reversing its stand and advising its pastors to concentrate on caring for souls. The emperor too talked contemptuously about the "Christian social nonsense." Stoecker and the more conservative part then left the ESK and formed the FSK, which was more interested in the social work of the church and preferred social measures over theoretical discussions. The ESK had no problems with their departure, and even cooperated with the FSK. Under the influence of Max Weber and Friedrich Naumann, the ESK questioned whether a societal reform showed much promise if it were based on the Christian message. According to Ernst Troeltsch's social teachings, it was then emphasized that state, economy, and technology have their own inherent laws, and therefore social issues were ultimately understood as issues of one's conscience. After World War I, the religious socialists wanted to engage themselves in the ESK and had, at least in the discussions of the annual congresses, a significant say. Together with the representatives of neo-Reformation theology, they criticized the liaison of church and state and the myopic vision that resulted from that cooperation, over against capitalistic and nationalistic ideas. During the Third Reich the ESK made some verbal concessions to National Socialism, but nevertheless was very much muted. Therefore it was discontinued after World War II. The ESK certainly provided a platform not only to discuss social issues, but also to bring diverse people together. In so doing it counteracted the danger of societal fragmentation. Its legislative influence, however, was more confined to the persuasiveness of its prominent members than to the congress in general.

The Swiss Religious Socialists:
Hermann Kutter and Leonhard Ragaz

Religious socialism is a movement of the twentieth century and is connected with Hermann Kutter and Leonhard Ragaz. The term "religious socialism" was used by the two to demark their own position against other socially engaged groupings.[74] Central to religious socialism was the realization of the kingdom of God that is not of this world but for this world. Ragaz stated: "We look to-

---

74. As Ragaz wrote, "the name 'religious social movement' is, as often with such names, accidental and therefore superficial since it is derived from the fact that they initially invited people to 'religious and social conferences.'" So Leonhard Ragaz, *Mein Weg* (Zürich: Diana, 1952), 1:240.

ward the becoming new *[Neuwerden]* of our world both in a religious and social respect, a world tortured, burdened, and threatened by decay, yet a world also blessed with a big promise as we steadfastly believe, and we invite to us all of those who want to pursue with us this way."[75] Yet there were others such as Paul Tillich who called themselves religious socialists without following Ragaz and Kutter.[76]

Hermann Kutter (1863-1931) was born in Berne, Switzerland, son of an engineer and a pastor's daughter. Having passed his theological exams, he was called to a small rural congregation in 1887.[77] Important for him was his visit in Bad Boll (1889) with Christoph Blumhardt (1842-1919), who continued there the legacy of his father, Johann Christoph Blumhardt (1805-80). The younger Blumhardt emphasized a new kind of congregational activity, the trademark of which was healing, confessional tolerance, and social responsibility. (In nearby Möttlingen his father cared for a twenty-year-old woman in a pastoral way who, according to the consulted doctor, was obsessed by demons. From a biblical perspective Blumhardt tried to exorcise these powers of darkness and was successful. Subsequently many members of his congregation flooded his office to confess their sins and to have absolution pronounced to them. Many of them were also freed from diseases.) When Kutter returned from Bad Boll, his pastoral activity no longer subjectively focused on the believing person but was centered in God.

Soon Kutter was interested in the workers movement. When he was called as pastor to the Neumünster in Zürich, the church the Reformer Zwingli had pastored, he encountered both bourgeoisie and proletarian members in the city and in his congregation. In 1903 he wrote *They Must; or, God and the Social Democracy: A Frank Word to Christian Men and Women* (Eng. trans. 1908), a publication in which he sees the presence of the living God in Jesus Christ in the proletarian masses. After that he cooperated with Ragaz toward a religious socialism, a term that both of them coined in 1906. Later there was also a personal relationship with Karl Barth and his friend and fellow pastor Eduard Thurneysen, since they also had socialist leanings. Yet the ties loosened when Kutter noticed that Barth's eschatology was missing the essentially eschatological urgency in the sense of Blumhardt. Barth's eschatology was perceived as too static with regard to the realization of the kingdom of God.

75. Leonhard Ragaz, "Zu meinem Austritt aus der sozialdemokratischen Partei" (1936), in *Leonhard Ragaz. Religiöser Sozialist, Pazifist, Theologe und Pädagoge,* ed. Leonhard-Ragaz-Institut (Darmstadt: Lingbach, 1986), 103.

76. Cf. the chapter "Religious Socialist," in Wilhelm and Marion Pauck, *Paul Tillich: His Life and Thought,* vol. 1, *Life* (New York: Harper and Row, 1976), 67-75.

77. Cf. for details of his life the biography written by his son Hermann Kutter, Jr., *Hermann Kutters Lebenswerk* (Zürich: EVZ, 1965).

Leonhard Ragaz (1868-1945) was born in a mountain village in Graubünden, Switzerland, his father being a small tenant farmer. The community in which he grew up shared many things; forests, mountains, and meadows were used in a communal way. This communal idea was influential for Ragaz. He studied theology from 1886 to 1890 in Basel, Jena, Berlin, and again in Basel, and was influenced by the Zürich systematician Biedermann. Soon he worked on behalf of the poor, and his fight against alcoholism also led him to social engagement. After earlier pastorates, he was called to the *Münster* (cathedral) in Basel in 1902. There he encountered the social question as the question of God, since he realized that behind the demands of the Social Democrats must be the living God. In 1908 he was called as professor of systematic and practical theology at the University of Zürich. In 1921 he resigned to live with the workers, a step he interpreted as following Christ.

Ragaz wanted to engage in educational work for the workers, but had little success. He was also a strict pacifist as World War I broke out in 1914. In World War II he helped the fugitives that came to Switzerland. As Ragaz had stated, the Swiss religious socialists wanted to uncover the societal political goals of socialism, and in contrast to the Protestant Social Congress, they thus took a positive attitude toward socialism. Social Democracy is the judgment of God over the ecclesial bourgeoisie society, because God brings his kingdom forward through this atheistic party. For Kutter this meant that the task of Christians and of the church is neither to convert Social Democracy nor to actively work in it, but rather to accept God's judgment and wait for his further activity. Ragaz, by contrast, was more action oriented and sought a synthesis between Christianity and socialism.

Kutter, too, learned from Christoph Blumhardt that in socialism there was already a hope manifested for the realization of the kingdom of God on earth. Yet the church had become reactionary and only talked about sin and judgment. Therefore he claimed that the Social Democrats had become the tools of the living God and proclaimers of the divine truth. Both the Social Democrats and the gospel announce new conditions, and "God's promises are being fulfilled in the Social Democrats."[78] This amounted to a decided defense of the Social Democrats and a passionate plea for the church to take this movement seriously in a positive way. In analogy to the Protestant Social Congress, a Religious Social Congress (Religiös-Soziale Konferenz) was formed as a platform for discussion. This congress conceived the social movement of its day as a means to realize the kingdom of God. Its publication was *New Ways. Leaflets for*

---

78. Hermann Kutter, *Sie müssen! Ein offenes Wort an die christliche Gesellschaft* (Jena: Eugen Diederichs, 1910), 204.

Religious Work (Neue Wege. Blätter für religiöse Arbeit). In the first edition, under the title "Concerning the Religious Situation of the Present," Ragaz wrote: "Christian and socialist must seek each other again and again; regardless how many unsatisfying relationships they have established with each other, they will not come to rest until they have found a genuine and enduring relationship."[79]

For Ragaz the neutrality of the new movement waned, and in 1913 he became a member of the socialist party, while Kutter never joined the party.[80] Ragaz was highly idealistic, because for him this move did not mean joining a political party, its program or its dogmas. He considered it a movement that cared only for the class of the uprooted, the disinherited, and the politically, religiously, and morally disenfranchised. Socialism was for him "fundamentally an *idealistic* movement."[81] Without most people realizing it, socialism is God's insurrection against the world estranged from him. God's people have been despised and oppressed. This Ragaz saw especially in the Peasants' War (1524/25). In Ragaz's view, Martin Luther and the establishment turned against the legitimate claims of the peasants, namely, the exploited people, and therefore disenfranchised them. Ragaz, however, discovered a remedy in Marxism. "The religion of Marxism is old and has an old name; it is *messianism*, which means faith in a kingdom of righteousness on earth, which shall be imparted to the oppressed and disenfranchised. This faith which first loomed high in the prophets of Israel, was taken over by Christianity, but to a large extent forgotten, and which nevertheless over and over again erupted as a radiant stream from the depths and has entered the scene in modern socialism, especially in its Marxist gown, as a world-changing power."[82]

While Ragaz agreed with the idealistic and messianic aspirations of Marxism, he rejected its naturalistic and materialistic gown of the second half of the nineteenth century. Contrary to Marxism, for Ragaz the spiritual was not simply secondary. The principle of socialism is an ethical demand for the sanctity of humanity, its community, and the moral faith of a community that is aware of human worth. Ragaz wanted to give Marxism a human face. He pointed to the foundational principles of all socialism, the sanctity of humanity, all humans being children of God, the infinite value of the human soul, a universal brotherhood, equality before God, and a mutual relationship and re-

79. Leonhard Ragaz, "Zur religiösen Situation der Gegenwart," *Neue Wege* 1 (Nov. 1906): 12.

80. Cf. the informative contribution by Daniela Dunkel, "Religiöser Sozialismus," in *Theologische Realenzyklopädie*, 28:507.

81. Leonhard Ragaz, *Von Christus zu Marx — Von Marx zu Christus* (Wernigerode am Harz: Harder, 1929), 13.

82. Ragaz, *Von Christus zu Marx*, 63.

sponsibility among the people.[83] With these claims we have returned to liberal theology, as we have seen well pronounced in Harnack. In this optimistic vein Ragaz contended: "Christianity and Socialism in this largest and most comprehensive sense, will be the two powers, who shape the future."[84]

It is not surprising that Ragaz did not find many followers in Germany for his religious socialism. It was a visionary picture that, at least in its Marxist form, collapsed under the impact of historic reality. Political socialism in Germany, however, abandoned more and more its Marxist basis, and gradually became a centrist movement pulling together both workers and employers. The Protestant churches, too, became again a home for the workers' movement, as the blue collars became less and less soiled, when the standard of the whole of society advanced. Yet Kutter and Ragaz rightly pointed to the necessity of the church to be inclusive and not exclusive, as its own master had taught the church.

From Reaction to Discernment: The Role of Roman Catholicism

Through its protest against King Louis XVI (1754-93), the French clergy were instrumental in June of 1788 in the calling together of the Estates General, which included the clergy, the nobility, and the third estate, the bourgeoisie, to consider alleviating the taxation on the people. Since the French Revolution became more and more radical, and also turned against church and clergy, Roman Catholicism became often reactionary in its opposition toward social issues, as we see, for instance, in the fate of Lamennais (cf. chap. 13). However, the Roman Catholic Church could not close its eyes to pressing social issues, as we note especially in the papal encyclicals.

The Papal Encyclicals

In the wake of the French Revolution, the Roman Catholic Church lost most of its landholdings in France. Similarly in Germany through the collapse of the so-called Holy Roman Empire, both ecclesial landholdings and many monasteries were turned over to secular powers. In Italy, too, the papal estates were severely curtailed and even threatened with total abolition. It is no surprise, therefore, that in the Syllabus of Errors Pope Pius IX (b. 1792, 1846-78) in 1864

83. Cf. Ragaz, *Von Christus zu Marx*, 192.
84. Ragaz, *Von Christus zu Marx*, 202.

condemned any liberal and socialist ideas.[85] Nevertheless, the Syllabus stated that the decrees of the Apostolic See should not be seen as a hindrance to "true progress of science" (n. 12). The ministry of the church and the Roman pontiff also did not want to be seen as excluded "from every charge and dominion over temporal affairs" (n. 27). To that extent it is not true that "the doctrine of the Catholic Church is hostile to the well-being and to interests of society" (n. 40). However, the tone of the Syllabus was defensive and was seen so by many people.

It was only in the encyclical of Pope Leo XIII (b. 1810, 1878-1903), *Rerum Novarum (The Condition of Labor)* of 1891, that the church officially interacted in a positive way with the social problems of industrialization. There the pope stated: "Every man has by nature the right to possess property as his own."[86] Against the socialists who contended that individual possessions should become the common property of all and against the impoverishment of the masses through unrestrained capitalism, *Rerum Novarum* stated that private possessions are justified by natural law. Yet the encyclical distinguished "that it is one thing to have a right to the possession of money, and another to have a right to use money as one pleases."[87] With reference to Luke 11:41, almsgiving was encouraged as it promotes Christian charity. Again with a view toward nature, the encyclical stated that "the preservation of life is the bounden duty of each and all, and to fail therein is a crime. It follows that each one has a right to procure what is required to live."[88] While this encyclical still condemned socialism and liberalism as materialistic, it showed that workers have a right to appropriate remuneration, even advocating labor unions.[89] In short, it asserted that there is a duty issuing from work and also from the amassed capital. Its main purpose was to give an injunction against the brutal exploitation of the poor workers and their misuse as simply instruments for advancing one's own profit.

For the fortieth anniversary of *Rerum Novarum*, Pope Pius XI (b. 1857, 1922-39) published the encyclical *Quadragesimo Anno (After Forty Years)* of 1931. While Pius often referred to *Rerum Novarum* and quoted it frequently, he distinguished between "the social and public aspect of ownership" with which he

---

85. The quotes follow the translation in Anne Fremantle, ed., *The Papal Encyclicals in Their Historical Context* (New York: Putnam, 1956), 145-47.

86. *Rerum Novarum*, as translated in David J. O'Brien and Thomas A. Shannon, eds., *Catholic Social Thought: The Documentary Heritage* (Maryknoll, N.Y.: Orbis, 1992), 16 (Denzinger #3265).

87. *Rerum Novarum* 22.

88. *Rerum Novarum* 31.

89. Cf. *Rerum Novarum* 33.

agreed, and a "collectivism" on the one side and an "individualism" on the other that he rejected.[90] While the hierarchically constructed social order he advanced was too much in line with traditional thinking to be fruitful, the "principle of 'subsidiarity'" was much more far-reaching.[91] This idea was first advanced here, and means that decisions should not be made centrally, but in a decentralized way by those "members of the social body" most immediately affected by them (n. 203).[92] He picked up here the notion of communal "associations" that furthered the ordering of society and promulgating of justice among the people.

For the seventieth anniversary of *Rerum Novarum*, just before the beginning of the Second Vatican Council, Pope John XXIII (b. 1881, 1958-63) issued his encyclical *Mater et Magistra (Christianity and Social Progress)* of 1961 in which he summed up the teachings of his predecessors, Leo XIII, Pius XI, and Pius XII. He addressed the issues of establishing norms for fair trade, worldwide injustice, underdeveloped countries, and the difficult plight of farm workers.[93] Here we have for the first time an inkling that the church would engage in what was later called liberation theology.

How important *Rerum Novarum* has been for the Roman Catholic Church can be seen in that Pope Paul VI (b. 1897, 1963-78) also commemorated it with his own encyclical, *Octogesima Adveniens (A Call to Action on the Eightieth Anniversary, 1971)*, where he took up new social problems. Most important for the social involvement of the papacy, however, has been Pope John Paul II (b. 1920, 1978-2005), who himself had been a professor of social ethics prior to his election as pope. In his encyclical of 1981, *Laborem Exercens (On Human Work)*, he showed the significance of work for the dignity of human beings. He also pointed out the importance of workers having a share in the industrial enterprise. In *Sollicitudo Rei Socialis (On Social Concern)* of 1987, he condemned excessive consumption and the striving for power. Similar to Walter Rauschenbusch almost a century earlier, he mentioned "structures of sin," a term he "applied to the situation of the contemporary world."[94]

In the centennial encyclical *Centesimus Annus (On the Hundredth Anniversary)* of 1991, the pope considered the peaceful collapse of the Marxist system in Eastern Europe and pointed to the dangers that capitalism might cause in former Marxist countries. The pope called for a new society based on truth

90. *Quadragesimo Anno* 192, as translated in *Catholic Social Thought*, 52 (Denzinger #3726).

91. *Quadragesimo Anno* 60 (Denzinger #3738).

92. Brian Hebblethwaite, in his instructional article "Sozialethik," in *Theologische Realenzyklopädie*, 31:502, notes that the notion of subsidiarity was first promulgated here. He noted that it even made it into the 1991 Maastricht Treaty of the European Community.

93. Cf. *Mater et Magistra*, as translated in *Catholic Social Thought*, 108-13.

94. *Sollicitudo Rei Socialis* (§37), in *Catholic Social Thought*, 419-20.

and justice. He also criticized the Western socialist notion of a welfare state and opted for subsidiarity that brings back to society human warmth and communal feelings. Neither excessive individualism nor governmental monopoly in social issues is to be recommended.

These various encyclicals of the papal office read like a commentary on society and its problems, a commentary that becomes more and more discerning and also points to solutions in the future rather than simply attempting to turn back to the past. Yet the main argumentation is still very much based on natural law and not so much on the primacy of biblical injunctions.

Addressing the Plight of the People: Wilhelm Emmanuel Freiherr von Ketteler, Adolph Kolping, Jacques Maritain, John Courtney Murray

The papal encyclicals were not issued in splendid isolation. Pope Leo XIII, for instance, consigned a matter he wanted to address "to a trusted author in papal Rome with some oral instructions. Then the pope would have it revised and rewritten until it corresponded to his intentions."[95] This means these encyclicals were also indicative of what was going on in the church by both reacting to it and providing needed direction. Yet those further away from the papal office, by necessity, were closer to the people and their immediate needs, and therefore often more immediately involved in ameliorating the plight of the people.

Symptomatic of those was the so-called worker bishop of Mainz, Germany, **Wilhelm Emmanuel von Ketteler** (1811-77). Ketteler was from old Westphalian nobility. He was born in Münster and first worked as a civil servant. Having briefly studied theology in Munich (1841-43), he was consecrated a priest in 1844. After two pastoral assignments, he was elected to the Frankfurt National Assembly in 1848 and soon discovered that social issues were most pressing. In an Advent sermon on Romans 13:11 in the Mainz cathedral entitled "The Big Social Issues of the Present" (Die großen sozialen Fragen der Gegenwart), he claimed: "If we want to understand our times we must attempt to fathom the social issues. Who comprehends them understands the present, to him who does not comprehend them, the present and the future is an enigma."[96] He was consecrated bishop of Mainz in 1850, and soon gave new life to this neglected diocese.

---

95. So Paul Misner, in his instructive investigation *Social Catholicism in Europe: From the Onset of Industrialization to the First World War* (London: Darton, Longman and Todd, 1991), 214.

96. Wilhelm Emmanuel Freiherr von Ketteler, "Zweite Predigt am ersten Adventssonntage, den 3. Dec 1848," in *Sämtliche Werke und Briefe*, ed. Erwin Iserloh (Mainz: V. Hase & Koehler, 1977-85), pt. I, 1:35.

He reopened the seminary for educating priests and founded the congregation of the Sisters of Divine Providence, who worked in schools and cared for the sick and the poor, who were primarily the factory workers.

In 1864 Ketteler published *The Issue of the Workers and Christianity (Die Arbeiterfrage und das Christentum)*, in which he largely adopted the analyses and critique of the plight of the working class of Ferdinand Lasalle (1825-64), one of the main promulgators of the Socialist Party as the political organ of organized labor. Ketteler stated in the opening pages: "The so-called issue of the workers is in its essence an issue of *feeding the workers*. . . . In its scope it touches by far the largest portion of all people."[97] It was not sufficient for Ketteler to call on the workers to help themselves, as liberals thought. Instead, he insisted that to escape their misery they must become co-owners of the facilities where things are produced, because then they can also participate in the earnings. In contrast to Lasalle, Ketteler did not want government to force justice on the factory owners, but he opted for a change of attitude. It is a Christian duty to love the neighbor, because "only *Jesus Christ,* the Son of the living God, can help the working class even in the future. If faith in him and his spirit permeates the world, then the issue of the working class is solved."[98]

Ketteler demanded just wages and did not even shy away from strikes as a legitimate means to obtain them, knowing well that at his time strikes were still shunned in Germany. He also demanded child labor to be outlawed and that mothers and young girls be spared from factory work. He did not want to work against capitalism, but with it in order to shape a new society and just world. Since there was no indication "that the modern industrial system would be replaced by a better and different one in the near future, one should soften the bad consequences of the present system and search for appropriate remedies."[99] Moreover, one should see to it that the "workers are allowed, as far as possible, to participate in that which is good in the system and its blessings."[100]

Ketteler fought not only for the rights of the workers, but also for the rights of the church, meaning the independence of the Roman Catholic Church against interference by the government. He appreciated the Prussian Constitution as an example of how the relationship between church and state ought to be regulated. When that constitution was not adopted for the new German Empire of 1871 under the chancellor Otto von Bismarck (1815-98), he abdicated his

97. Wilhelm Emmanuel Freiherr von Ketteler, *Die Arbeiterfrage und das Christentum,* in *Sämtliche Werke,* pt. I, 1:372.

98. Ketteler, *Die Arbeiterfrage und das Christentum,* pt. II, 1:461.

99. Wilhelm Emmanuel Freiherr von Ketteler, "Fürsorge der Kirche für die Fabrikarbeiter" (1869), in *Sämtliche Werke,* pt. I, 2:433.

100. Ketteler, "Fürsorge der Kirche für die Fabrikarbeiter," pt. I, 2:438.

seat in the Federal Diet in 1872. Ketteler also fought for freedom in the church. Though he was convinced of the truthfulness of papal infallibility and also taught it in his diocese without problems for him or the faithful, he very much rejected it as a dogma.[101] The problem for him was that one "cannot comprehensively deal with papal authority without at the same time dealing with episcopal authority."[102] Here he anticipated the deliberations of the Second Vatican Council, where the authority of the church was seen more inclusively to include the bishops, the priests, and even to some extent the laity.

Another practically oriented priest was **Adolph Kolping** (1813-65), who was born near Cologne as a son of a shepherd and peasant. After attending the village school, the thirteen-year-old Kolping started to learn shoemaking and became a journeyman in that trade. As a twenty-three-year-old, he prepared in self-study to be admitted to the *Gymnasium* in Cologne intending to become a priest. In 1841 he began to study theology in Munich. There he became a friend of Döllinger (cf. chap. 13) and also met Wilhelm von Ketteler, with whom he discussed the distressed situation of the journeymen.[103] The following year he moved to Bonn, and three years later he was consecrated a priest.

In his first parish in Elberfeld he became acquainted with an association of journeymen in which they and other young workers gathered for lectures and companionship. Remembering his own problems as an apprentice and journeyman and perceiving in his parish the social problems of journeymen and the industrial proletariat, he wanted to get involved with those who, through the dissolution of the guilds, became part of the mass proletariat. In 1848 he became a member of the cathedral chapter of Cologne and became instrumental there in establishing an association for journeymen *(Gesellenverein)*. Central to his efforts was to create a pleasant environment for these young people and provide an opportunity for economic betterment. He also inspired other priests to do the same and to become spiritual presiders of those associations. In many other cities similar associations were founded as well as dormitories for young workers. Kolping also tried to win the support of both the church and the faithful for this enterprise.

By the time he died there were 24,600 members in 418 associations. By contrast the General German Workers' Association had just 5,000 members.[104]

101. Cf. Wilhelm Emmanuel Freiherr von Ketteler, "Konzilsrede über den Primat des Papstes vom 23. Mai 1870," in *Sämtliche Werke*, pt. I, 3:605.

102. Ketteler, "Konzilsrede über den Primat des Papstes vom 23. Mai 1870," pt. I, 3:593.

103. Cf. Misner, *Social Catholicism in Europe*, 97, for more details on Kolping's development.

104. For the statistics and other helpful information, cf. Victor Conzemius, "Kolping, Adolph," in *Theologische Realenzyklopädie*, 19:377-78.

While Kolping did not press for structural reform, he nevertheless sensitized the Roman Catholic Church to the problems of the working class and to the need for a commensurate social program. Still today the Kolping Society (Kolpingwerk) has 260,000 members in 2,600 associations in Germany alone. As was true at the time of Kolping, it is still critical to provide a family-like setting for workers, especially for those young people who are socially disadvantaged and have little chance to be educated for a job and for gainful employment.

Much more theoretical in its approach, but not removed from social reality, is the work of **Oswald von Nell-Breuning** (1890-1991), who was born in Trier as son of a well-to-do farmer. Having briefly studied mathematics and natural sciences in Munich and Berlin (1908-10), he began to study theology at Innsbruck, joined the Jesuit Order in 1911, and after military service during World War I and teaching at a Jesuit *Gymnasium,* was consecrated priest in 1921. He obtained his doctorate and became professor of moral theology, canon law, and social sciences at the Jesuit school in Frankfurt, St. Georgen. He was also instrumental in shaping the papal encyclical *Quadragesimo Anno* (1931).

The main foci of his work were developing and promulgating Roman Catholic social teachings and overcoming the estrangement of the working class from that church. He realized the unfair treatment the workers had received from the church, and that even the justified concerns of Karl Marx had been rejected. He collaborated on many documents promulgated by the church, was influential in governmental offices, and was a well-respected teacher and public speaker. He interpreted the official social teachings of the church in such a way that he related them to concrete social problems. Coming from the classical natural law tradition of neoscholasticism, he considered the well-being of the person and of the community and subsidiarity important.

Another significant social ethicist was the French Thomist philosopher **Jacques Maritain** (1882-1973). Brought up in a liberal Protestant home, Maritain started at the Sorbonne in Paris, where he was attracted by teachers who claimed that the natural sciences alone could provide all the answers to human life. There, however, he met a Russian Jewish student, Raïssa Oumansoff (1883-1960), who also shared his quest for truth. Soon disillusioned with the scientism of the Sorbonne, the two began to attend lectures by Henri Bergson and realized their need for "the absolute." They married in 1904 and two years later converted to Catholicism. Maritain studied biology at Heidelberg (1906-8) and Thomism at Paris (cf. also chap. 13 for more on Maritain). While he was the author of many books, important for us are *True Humanism* (1938; *Humanisme intégral,* 1936), *Christianity and Democracy* (1944; *Christianisme et démocratie,* 1943), and *La Philosophie Morale: Examen historique et* *critique des grands systèmes* (1960; Eng. trans. *Moral Philosophy: An Historical and Critical Survey of the Great Systems,* 1964).[105]

Though a layperson, his writings on political ethics had enormous influence on the foundation of the Christian Democratic parties in Europe after World War II. This is especially true for Italy.[106] Maritain advocated a new Christianity in which autonomous institutions permeated by the Christian spirit motivate all people of good will toward common work for the realization of interpersonal values in a true democracy. He also was a personal friend of Pope Paul VI. While in the United States he developed a sympathy for the American form of democratic capitalism. He was convinced that due to God's providence Christianity could transform human society. To the extent that humans are creatures, they need to learn responsibility and submission to political order, but to the extent that they are "redeemed" by Christ they "must continually seek to transform and elevate that order."[107] In his Aristotelian Thomism Maritain emphasized the importance of the individual as well as of the Christian community for society.

The public character of the work of **John Courtney Murray** (1904-67) can be gleaned from his being on the cover of *Time* (Dec. 12, 1960). He was a Jesuit who obtained his Ph.D. with a study on Matthias Scheeben at the Pontifical Gregorian University in Rome, and after 1937 served as professor of dogmatics at Woodstock College. Murray was influenced by Maritain in accepting the principle of religious freedom. "Of Murray's 166 published works and manuscripts, 68 deal with the problem of civil religious freedom."[108] He was also actively involved in the proceedings of Vatican II, especially in the council's declaration *Dignitas Humanae Personae (The Dignity of the Human Person),* which clearly endorsed civil religious freedom and thereby reversed the Roman Catholic opposition to religious freedom. For Murray there can be no Roman Catholic country, because the church has primarily a spiritual role. Yet the church is also indirectly involved in society through the participation of the Christian in societal life. Therefore a modern democratic constitution is the most appropriate context for applying the principles of Roman Catholic social teachings to change society. His approach can be seen best in his 1960 publication *We Hold*

---

105. For a bibliography of Jacques and Raïssa Maritain, cf. Donald Gallagher and Idella Gallagher, *The Achievements of Jacques and Raïssa Maritain: A Bibliography, 1906-1961* (Garden City, N.Y.: Doubleday, 1962), with a total of 7,423 entries.

106. For the following cf. Hebblethwaite, "Sozialethik," 505.

107. So William J. Nottingham, *Christian Faith and Action: An Introduction to the Life and Thought of Jacques Maritain* (St. Louis: Bethany, 1968), 82.

108. According to J. Leon Hooper, ed., in his introduction to John Courtney Murray, *Religious Liberty: Catholic Struggles with Pluralism* (Louisville: Westminster John Knox, 1993), 27.

These Truths: Catholic Reflections on the American Proposition, where he concludes with an appeal to a modified natural law:

> If there is a law immanent in man — a dynamic, constructive force for rationality in human affairs, that works itself out, because it is a natural law, in spite of contravention by passion and evil and all the corruptions of power — one may with sober reason believe in, and hope for, a future of rational progress. And this belief and hope is strengthened when one considers that this dynamic order of reason in man, that clamors for expression with all the imperiousness of law, has its origin and sanction in an external order of reason whose fulfillment is the object of God's majestic will.[109]

We have noticed that from its position that initially opposed a rapidly changing political and industrial society, Roman Catholic theology now feels confident enough to permeate society through its own members, while still attempting to shape society according to its own Christian social principles. This constructive and dynamic approach is certainly not very different from that which Protestants advocate, too.

FOR FURTHER READING

Washington Gladden (1836-1918)

Gladden, Washington. *Burning Questions of The Life That Now Is and of That Which Is to Come.* 3rd ed. New York: Century Co., 1892.
———. *Recollections.* Boston: Houghton Mifflin, 1909.
Handy, Robert T., ed. *The Social Gospel in America, 1870-1920: Gladden — Ely — Rauschenbusch.* New York: Oxford University Press, 1966.
Knudten, Richard. *Systematic Thought of Washington Gladden.* New York: Humanities Press, 1968.

Richard Theodore Ely (1854-1943)

Ely, Richard Th. *The Labor Movement in America.* New rev. ed. New York: Macmillan, 1905.
———. *Social Aspects of Christianity, and Other Essays.* New York: T. Y. Crowell, 1889.
Everett, John Rutherford. *Religion in Economics.* New York: King's Crown Press, 1946.
Handy, Robert T., ed. *The Social Gospel in America, 1870-1920: Gladden — Ely — Rauschenbusch.* New York: Oxford University Press, 1966.

---

109. John Courtney Murray, *We Hold These Truths: Catholic Reflections on the American Proposition* (New York: Sheed and Ward, 1960), 335-36.

Walter Rauschenbusch (1861-1918)

Evans, Christopher H. *The Kingdom Is Always but Coming: A Life of Walter Rauschenbusch.* Grand Rapids: Eerdmans, 2004.

Handy, Robert T., ed. *The Social Gospel in America, 1870-1920: Gladden — Ely — Rauschenbusch.* New York: Oxford University Press, 1966.

Minus, Paul. *Walter Rauschenbusch: American Reformer.* New York: Macmillan, 1988.

Rauschenbusch, Walter. *Christianity and the Social Crisis.* Foreword by Douglas E. Ottati. 1907. Louisville: Westminster John Knox, 1991.

———. *Christianizing the Social Order.* New York: Macmillan, 1912.

———. *A Theology for the Social Gospel.* 1917. New York: Macmillan, 1922.

Smucker, Donovan E. *The Origins of Walter Rauschenbusch's Social Ethics.* Montreal: McGill-Queen's University Press, 1994.

John Malcolm Forbes Ludlow (1821-1911)

Massanari, Ronald L. "Christian Socialism of J. M. Ludlow." *Theology* 77 (Apr. 1974): 193-202.

Mastermann, Neville C. "Christian Socialists of 1848-54." *Theology* 73 (Jan. 1970): 15-23.

———. *John Malcolm Ludlow: The Builder of Christian Socialism.* Cambridge: Cambridge University Press, 1963.

F. D. Maurice (1805-72)

Maurice, Frederick, ed. *The Life and Letters of Frederick Denison Maurice Chiefly Told in His Own Letters.* 2 vols. London: Macmillan, 1884.

See also chapter 3.

Charles Kingsley (1819-75)

Engner, G. *Apologia pro Charles Kingsley.* London: Sheed and Ward, 1969.

Martin, Robert. *Dust of Combat: A Life of Charles Kingsley.* New York: Norton, 1960.

Pope-Hennessy, Una. *Canon Charles Kingsley: A Biography.* Millwood, N.Y.: Kraus Reprint Co., 1973.

Stewart Headlam (1847-1924)

Bettany, Frederick G. *Stewart Headlam: A Biography.* London: J. Murray, 1926.

Norman, Edward R. "Stewart Headlam and the Christian Socialists." *History Today* 37 (Apr. 1987): 27-32.

Reckitt, Maurice B., ed. *For Christ and the People: Studies of Four Socialist Priests and Prophets of the Church of England between 1870 and 1930.* London: SPCK, 1968.

William Temple (1881-1944)

Iremonger, Frederic. *William Temple, Archbishop of Canterbury: His Life and Letters.* London: Oxford University Press, 1948.

Kent, John. *William Temple: Church, State, and Society in Britain, 1880-1950.* Cambridge: Cambridge University Press, 1992.

Lowry, Charles. *William Temple, an Archbishop for All Seasons.* Washington, D.C.: University Press of America, 1982.

Temple, William. *Christianity and Social Order.* Foreword by Edward Heath. Introduction by Ronald H. Preston. London: SPCK, 1976 [1942].

William Booth (1829-1912)

Booth, General. *In Darkest England and the Way Out.* London: Funk and Wagnalls, 1890.

Johann Friedrich Oberlin (1740-1826)

Beard, Augustus Field. *The Story of John Frederic Oberlin.* New York: Christian Rural Fellowship, 1946.

Dawson, Marshall. *Oberlin, a Protestant Saint.* Chicago: Willett, Clark and Co., 1934.

Kurtz, John. *John Frederick Oberlin.* Boulder, Colo.: Westview Press, 1976.

Theodor Fliedner (1800-1864) and Friederike Fliedner (1800-1842)

Gallison, Marie. *The Ministry of Women: One Hundred Years of Women's Work at Kaiserswerth, 1836-1936.* London: Lutterworth, 1936.

Weiser, Frederick S. "The Origins of Lutheran Deaconesses in America." *Lutheran Quarterly,* n.s., 13 (Winter 1999): 423-34.

Wentz, Abdel. *Fliedner the Faithful.* Philadelphia: Board of Publication of the United Lutheran Church in America, 1936.

Friedrich von Bodelschwingh the Elder (1831-1910)

Bradfield, Margaret. *The Good Samaritan: The Life and Work of Friedrich von Bodelschwingh.* London: Marshall, Morgan and Scott, 1960.

The City of Mercy: The Story of Bethel. Compiled and translated by Margaret Bradfield from German sources. Bethel, Germany: Verlagsanstalt, 1964.

Ludolphy, Ingetraut. "Bodelschwingh, Father and Son." In *The Encyclopedia of the Lutheran Church,* edited by Julius Bodensieck, 1:314-15. Minneapolis: Augsburg, 1965).

Johann Hinrich Wichern (1808-81)

Christianson, Gerald. "J. H. Wichern and the Rise of the Lutheran Social Institution." *Lutheran Quarterly* 19 (Nov. 1967): 357-70.

Ludolphy, Ingetraut. "Wichern, Johann Hinrich." In *The Encyclopedia of the Lutheran Church,* edited by Julius Bodensieck, 3:2476-77. Minneapolis: Augsburg, 1965.

Massanari, Ronald L. "Christian Socialism in Nineteenth Century Germany: A Case Study in a Shift in Anthropological Perspective." *Union Seminary Quarterly Review* 29 (Fall 1973): 17-25.

Friedrich Naumann (1860-1919)

Groh, John E. "Friedrich Naumann: From Christian Socialist to Social Darwinist." *Journal of Church and State* 17 (Winter 1975): 25-46.

Moses, John A. "Justifying War as the Will of God: German Theology on the Eve of the First World War." *Colloquium* 31 (May 1999): 3-20.

Adolf Stoecker (1835-1909)

Fout, John C. "Adolf Stoecker's Rationale for Anti-Semitism." *Journal of Church and State* 17 (Winter 1975): 47-61.

Massanari, Ronald L. "Christian Socialism: Adolf Stoecker's Formulation of a Christian Perspective for Social Change." *Lutheran Quarterly* 22 (May 1970): 185-98.

———. "Christian Socialism in Nineteenth Century Germany: A Case Study in a Shift in Anthropological Perspective." *Union Seminary Quarterly Review* 29 (Fall 1973): 17-25.

Hermann Kutter (1863-1931)

Kutter, Hermann. *Social Democracy: Does It Mean Darkness or Light?* A summary of the works of Hermann Kutter with a preface by Richard Heath. Letchworth: Garden City Press, 1910.

———. *They Must; or, God and the Social Democracy: A Frank Word to Christian Men and Women.* American editor Rufus W. Weeks. Chicago: Co-operative Printing Co., 1908.

Leonhard Ragaz (1868-1945)

Bock, Paul. "Leonhard Ragaz." *Reformed Journal* 37 (Jan. 1987): 7-8.

Pasztor, Janos D. "Leonhard Ragaz: Pioneer Social Theologian." *Union Theological Seminary Review* 29 (Fall 1973): 27-33.

Ragaz, Leonhard. *Signs of the Kingdom: A Ragaz Reader.* Edited and translated by Paul Bock. Foreword by M. Douglas Meeks. Grand Rapids: Eerdmans, 1984.

Wilhelm Emmanuel von Ketteler (1811-77)

Dorgan, Dermot. "A Charter for Workers: The Context and Content of the Encyclical *Rerum Novarum.*" *Lutheran Theological Journal* 25 (Aug. 1991): 91-100.

Lenhart, L. "Ketteler, Wilhelm Emmanuel von." In *New Catholic Encyclopedia,* 2nd ed., 8:160-61.

Adolph Kolping (1813-65)

Fischer, H. "Kolping, Adolf, Bl." In *New Catholic Encyclopedia,* 2nd ed., 8:230-31.

Krewitt, H. A. "Kolping Society, Catholic." In *New Catholic Encyclopedia,* 2nd ed., 8:231.

Misner, Paul. *Social Catholicism in Europe: From the Onset of Industrialization to the First World War.* New York: Crossroad, 1991.

Neitzel, Sarah C. "Priests and Proletarians: The Catholic *Gesellenverein*, 1847-65." *Fides et Historia* 16, no. 1 (Fall-Winter 1983): 35-44.

Jacques Maritain (1882-1973)

Gallagher, Donald, and Idella Gallagher. *The Achievements of Jacques and Raïssa Maritain: A Bibliography, 1906-1961.* Garden City, N.Y.: Doubleday, 1962.
See also chapter 13.

John Courtney Murray (1904-67)

Fremantle, Anne, ed. *The Papal Encyclicals in Their Historical Context.* New York: Putnam, 1956.
Hughson, Thomas. *The Believer as Citizen: John Courtney Murray in a New Context.* New York: Paulist, 1993.
McElroy, Robert. *The Search for an American Public Theology: The Contribution of John Courtney Murray.* New York: Paulist, 1989.
Murray, John Courtney. *Religious Liberty: Catholic Struggles with Pluralism.* Louisville: Westminster John Knox, 1993.
————. *We Hold These Truths: Catholic Reflections on the American Proposition.* New York: Sheed and Ward, 1961.
O'Brien, David J., and Thomas A. Shannon, eds. *Catholic Social Thought: The Documentary Heritage.* Maryknoll, N.Y.: Orbis, 1992.
Pelotte, Donald. *John Courtney Murray: Theologian in Conflict.* New York: Paulist, 1976.

7 Stemming the Tide of Scientific Materialism

The nineteenth century was an age of rapid industrialization, with manual labor trying to compete with machines and the masses coming to the cities to look for employment. Furthermore, millions of people emigrated to the "New World" and became easy prey for ruthless employers. As we have noted, this provided a challenge for both church and theology. Industrialization was possible because of the pursuit of progress and the increasing mechanization of the production process. This provided the mind-set for a mechanical materialistic thinking and the theory of evolution. Again these developments challenged both church and theology. The British Anglican theologian William Paley (1743-1805) taught in his *Natural Theology* (1802): "Amongst the invisible things of nature, there must be an intelligent mind, concerned in its production, order, and support."[1] Things do not happen by themselves, and they always occur in orderly form. This arrangement, expressed in laws, "presupposes an agent; for it is only the mode according to which an agent proceeds: it implies a power, for it is the order according to which the power acts. Without this agent, without this power, which are both distinct from itself, the 'law' does nothing; is nothing."[2] God is the presupposed agent behind all processes.

Yet when the French mathematician and astronomer Pierre Laplace (1749-1827) had finished his monumental five-volume work *Mécanique céleste*

---

1. William Paley, *Natural Theology; or, Evidences of the Existence and Attributes of the Deity Collected from the Appearances of Nature* (Westmead, Farnborough, England: Gregg International, 1970 [1802]), 579.
2. Paley, *Natural Theology*, 447.

(*Celestial Mechanics*, 1799-1825), he replied to Napoleon's inquiry as to where the proper place for God was in the system: "Sire, I do not need this hypothesis." God was no longer seen as necessary within a scientific worldview. The world made sense without any reference to God. Not even the hypothesis of a creator seemed necessary. In 1842 the German physicist H. Robert Mayer (1814-78) formulated the first law of thermodynamics (or the law of the conservation of energy), which states that within an isolated system the amount of energy neither increases nor decreases. This law made it possible to endow the world with the attribute of eternity. Thus the first creation and the God hypothesis of a first creator seemed obsolete. It is no surprise therefore that Andrew Dickson White (1832-1918), the founder and first president of Cornell University, entitled his two-volume inquiry into the relationship between theology and science *A History of the Warfare of Science with Theology in Christendom* (New York, 1896). But White oversimplified the matter. First of all, the lines were not that clear, since scientists and theologians were on both sides of the issue. Some of them felt that science posed a threat to faith, while others claimed the opposite. Secondly, the discussions went very differently if we compare the scene only in America, Germany, and Great Britain.

Especially some French thinkers presented a reductionistic view of humanity. In his book *Man a Machine* (1748; Eng. trans. 1912), the French physician and philosopher Julien Offroy de la Mettrie (1709-51) presented a naturalistic view of humanity and explained spiritual processes through physiological causes. The soul, for instance, originates from the organization of the body, and the higher development of the reasonable human soul is due to the larger and more intricate development of the brain. According to la Mettrie, this thoroughgoing naturalism leads to atheism. Already in 1745 in his *Natural History of the Soul* (Eng. trans. of extracts 1912), he rejected metaphysical dualism and explained the spiritual faculties through a motorlike power that resides in matter. The French naturalist Jean-Baptiste Lamarck (1744-1829) continued this line of thought, though his materialism was neither aggressive nor antireligious. In his *Zoological Philosophy* (1809; Eng. trans. 1914) Lamarck proposed a complete theory of evolution and showed how biology could explain everything about animals. He described the physical causes of life that are entirely mechanical and explain in both animals and humans sensitivity, perception, memory, and intelligence.[3] Though his ideas remained vague, he still held on to an idea of creation that did not prevent him from believing that everything in nature was

3. For Lamarck cf. Jacques Roger, "The Mechanistic Conception of Life," in *God and Nature: Historical Essays on the Encounter between Christianity and Science*, ed. David C. Lindberg and Ronald L. Numbers (Berkeley: University of California Press, 1986), 290-91.

the result of natural processes. In mid-nineteenth-century Germany, physiologists such as Emil Du Bois-Reymond (1818-96) and Hermann von Helmholtz (1821-94) reduced life to physicochemical processes.

The Materialistic Mood in Germany: Ludwig Büchner, Carl Vogt, Jacob Moleschott, and Ludwig Feuerbach

Most influential in advocating this materialistic and ultimately monistic worldview were Ludwig Büchner, Carl Vogt, and Jacob Moleschott, who also advanced evolutionary thought.[4] Büchner's *Force and Matter* indicates in its title the two main components of materialistic monism, force and matter.[5] In the second part of the nineteenth century, this book was the most widely read popular philosophical German book. By 1904 it was in its twenty-first edition and translated into all major languages.[6]

Ludwig Büchner (1824-99), a physician in Darmstadt, rejected the notion of a life force in the world, and while conceding that the details of the origin of the first organic matter are still unknown, he claimed that "by her own power — whether in one fashion or another — she [nature] brought forth the first materials and forms of life; by her own power she caused these to develop further and further."[7] He observed that there is always a certain relationship between the environmental conditions and the existence of certain forms of organic life.[8] Earlier forms disappear and new ones emerge as the external conditions change. When the earth was still a primordial fireball, it was without organic life or even hostile to organic life.

Büchner assumed that occasionally there still may be spontaneous generation of life today, since it must be regarded as "a logical postulate or as a necessary demand of human reason and science" (138). But he knew from fossil findings that lower forms of life are usually earlier and that from them the ascent to

4. Cf. for the following Hans Schwarz, "Darwinism between Kant and Haeckel," *Journal of the American Academy of Religion* 48 (1980): 585-602.

5. Ludwig Büchner, *Kraft und Stoff. Empirisch-naturphilosophische Studien,* 6th ed. (Frankfurt am Main: Meidinger, 1859; Eng. trans. 1870).

6. Emanuel Hirsch, *Geschichte der neueren evangelischen Theologie im Zusammenhang mit den allgemeinen Bewegungen des europäischen Denkens,* 3rd ed. (Gütersloh: Gerd Mohn, 1964), 5:585-86.

7. Ludwig Büchner, *Force and Matter or Principles of the Natural Order of the Universe: With a System of Morality Based Thereon; A Popular Exposition,* translated from the 15th edition (New York: Truth Seeker, 1950), 144.

8. Cf. for the following Büchner, *Force and Matter,* 145-47. The parenthetical references in the following text are to Büchner's *Force and Matter.*

further development occurred (cf. 171). When he said the marked resemblance of different species in their embryonic development can be explained by a common history of origin, he anticipated what the zoologist Ernst Haeckel later called the fundamental biogenetic law. Any notion of a development from design was abandoned when Büchner stated: "Nature accomplishes many alleged objects in a clumsy, roundabout fashion, while it cannot be denied that if it had only been a question of attaining these objects, the result might have been obtained in a very much easier and simpler way" (189). But Büchner replaced the idea of a goal-directing force outside nature with an even stronger force within nature, namely, the natural laws. The laws, according to which nature is active, "are immutable" (75). An inflexible, unrelenting necessity governs the universe. Since humanity is a product of nature according to its bodily and spiritual existence, all its doings "similarly obey that inexorable regularity which rules throughout all existence and which admits of no exception" (77).[9] If nature is that determinative, we are not surprised to hear that "the universe with its properties, conditions, or movements, which we name force, must have existed and will exist to all eternity" (8). Büchner concluded: "To-day the indestructibility or permanence of matter is a scientific fact firmly established and no longer to be denied" (19).

It is not surprising that there is hardly a place for God in Büchner's system. If God is held to be eternal, we are told, this is only a different expression for the eternity of the world.[10] Büchner especially rejected the purposiveness of nature and thereby disclaimed the idea of a creative God. In analogy to Kant, he argued that the notion of a purpose is introduced by reflective reason, but it cannot be deduced from nature.[11] For instance, a deer does not have long legs to run fast, but it can run fast because it has long legs. As soon as Darwin's thesis of nondirectional "mutations" became known, it was eagerly picked up to substantiate these claims. The world was no longer the best possible world, but a world of turmoil and imperfections. Yet in advocating "atheism or philosophical monism," Büchner did not fall back on fate. Since the motifs of our ethos are no longer dependent on an otherworldly God, this monism of nature leads to "freedom, reason, progress, recognition of man and of true humanity — with *one word* — it leads to *humanism*."[12]

---

9. Some of Büchner's deterministic conclusions are not without humor for us today. For instance, he surmised that perhaps the "rapid and gigantic growth of the American commonwealth, is in some way connected with the excessive dryness of the air" (369).

10. Ludwig Büchner, *Der Gottesbegriff und dessen Bedeutung in der Gegenwart* (Leipzig: Theodor Thomas, 1874), 18.

11. Büchner, *Der Gottesbegriff*, 25-26.

12. Büchner, *Der Gottesbegriff*, 46.

While the monistic understanding of the world, advocated by Büchner, proved to be especially attractive to common people, others remembered that one could not do away that easily with the Kantian distinction between the world as phenomenon and the world as "thing-in-itself."[13] Had not the pessimistic philosopher Arthur Schopenhauer (1788-1860), who felt himself the true disciple of Kant, claimed that "materialism is the philosophy of the subject that forgets to take account of itself"?[14] Can there really be an object without a subject and therefore ultimate objectivity? In his classic *History of Materialism and Criticism of Its Present Importance* (1866; Engl. trans. 1877), the Neo-Kantian philosopher Friedrich Albert Lange (1828-75) conceded that materialism was a scientific method of investigation.[15] But he rejected the metaphysical implications of materialism since he affirmed that we have to restrict our assertions to the world of the phenomena while the thing-in-itself is withdrawn from sense experience.

As **Carl Vogt** (1817-95), *Köhlerglaube und Wissenschaft. Eine Streitschrift gegen Hofrat Rudolph Wagner in Göttingen* (*Backwoods Faith and Science. A Pamphlet against Counsellor Rudolf Wagner at Göttingen,* 1854), proved, it was difficult to argue with the representatives of materialistic monism. While Büchner attacked the chemist Justus von Liebig (1803-73) quite frequently in *Force and Matter,* since Liebig denied materialistic conclusions from science, Vogt, professor of zoology in Giessen and later in Geneva, now attacked the Göttingen professor of medicine Rudolph Wagner (1805-64). This debate climaxed in a literary exchange in the *Augsburger Allgemeine Zeitung (Augsburg General Newspaper)* in 1852, and around the year 1854-55 led to the so-called materialism controversy, a significant event in the intellectual and religious history of Germany. In 1854, at the Thirty-first Convention of Natural Scientists in Göttingen, this controversy reached its peak when the ecclesiastically conservative Wagner postulated the descent of all humans from one single couple that at the same time resembled the ideal portrayed by the Indo-European race. Though Wagner thought spiritual impressions and activities are correlated to the brain and the nerves, he attempted to show that this cannot preclude the existence of a special substance called "soul" that cannot be weighed and is invisible. Therefore the existence of individual immortal souls cannot be excluded. His lecture entitled "Concerning the Creation of Humanity and the Substance

13. Julius Frauenstädt, *Der Materialismus. Seine Wahrheit und sein Irrtum. Eine Erwiderung auf Dr. Louis Büchners "Kraft und Stoff"* (Leipzig: F. A. Brockhaus, 1856), 4.

14. Cf. Arthur Schopenhauer, *The World as Will and Idea* (London: Routledge and Kegan Paul, 1957), 2:176.

15. Friedrich Albert Lange, *The History of Materialism and Criticism of Its Present Importance,* introduction by Bertrand Russell (London: Routledge, 2000 [1865]), 3:358-65.

of the Soul" was followed in the same year (Göttingen: Wigand, 1854) by another publication, *Knowledge and Faith with Special Relationship to the Future of Souls (Über Wissen und Glauben mit besonderer Beziehung zut Zukunft der Seelen)*. Vogt responded to these papers in 1854 with a publication entitled *Köhlerglaube und Wissenschaft (Backwoods Faith and Science)*, which has been reprinted many times since.

In juxtaposing *Köhlerglaube* (backwoods faith) and *Wissenschaft* (science), Vogt indicated how unwilling he was to take the other side seriously. He claimed that the fossils found in excavations demonstrate that humanity is not the last species that appeared on earth. Many of its contemporaries gave way to other species. Scientific investigation also showed that the different races of humanity could not possibly stem from one couple. Vogt arrived at the conclusion that *"the teachings of Scripture about Adam and Noah and the twofold origin of mankind, each time from one couple, are, scientifically speaking, untenable fairy tales."*[16] Science also proved for Vogt that human existence is a transitory one, after which no other life will follow.[17] Again monistic materialism is seen as a kind of liberation. Since our short stay on earth will not be terminated by some kind of "sinister vengeance," we can live as equals and enjoy the pleasures of life.[18]

When we now turn briefly to **Jacob Moleschott** (1822-93) and his book *Der Kreislauf des Lebens* (1852, *The Circulation of Life*), we notice that he radicalized most of the issues introduced by Büchner and Vogt. We are not surprised that Büchner confessed that Moleschott had stimulated him to write *Force and Matter*. The cause-and-effect sequence was so dominating for Moleschott that it did not tolerate any kind of ultimate dependence once suggested by Schleiermacher. "Research, therefore, excludes revelation."[19] The omnipotence

16. Carl Vogt, *Köhlerglaube und Wissenschaft. Eine Streitschrift gegen Hofrat Rudolph Wagner in Göttingen,* 4th ed. (Giessen: J. Ricker, 1856), 83.

17. Vogt, *Köhlerglaube und Wissenschaft,* 122.

18. The remark about living as equals indicates the socialist tendency in Vogt, a tendency we can observe in Büchner too, when he rejected authoritative faith, monarchism, and the rule of the priests (*Der Gottesbegriff,* 45). Moleschott (*Der Kreislauf des Lebens. Physiologische Antworten auf Liebigs Chemische Briefe,* 2nd ed. [Mainz: Victor von Zabern, 1855], 480) became even more explicit about the connection between science, which for him meant materialism, and socialism, when he said: "The natural scientists are the most active workers of the social issue. . . . Its solution lies in the hand of the natural scientist, the hand which is guided with certainty by sense experience."

19. Though the fifth edition of Moleschott's work was published after Darwin became known in Germany, we continue to quote from it. While in its first editions the work was part of the debate on materialism directed against Liebig, the fifth edition was expanded into a two-volume work and carried forth the materialistic monistic standpoint most forcefully, especially

of the creator of the world stands in irreconcilable opposition to the laws of nature. Revelation and knowledge are related to each other like fiction to truth; the one guesses whereas the other researches. Truth can be gained only from nature and its course. The essence of a thing is the sum of its properties, and the essence of all properties is force. But force is not a divine agent, not an essence of things separated from its material foundation; it is the inexorable property of matter indwelling since eternity. For both Moleschott and Büchner, force and matter were identical. There was just one substance that is immortal — matter. The unchangeability of matter was the foundation for the eternal cycle of nature, of origin and decay (1:35).

Moleschott found the immortality of matter affirmed by Julius Robert Mayer's law of the conservation of energy, which states that in a closed system the amount of energy remains constant (2:608-9). Moleschott was right when he observed that by changing from one form of energy to another no energy is lost. We might even agree with him when he claims that energy is as indestructible as matter. Yet we wonder why he completely ignored the law of entropy or the nonconvertibility of energy that physicist Rudolf Emanuel Clausius (1822-88) had introduced in 1851. Thus Moleschott could claim that "in the universe the amount of force remains always the same. . . . The sum total of energy and the living force in the universe remains always the same" (2:609). Mass is part of the eternal process.

While Büchner was still uncertain, it was clear for Moleschott in 1887 that the first organism was formed through spontaneous generation (cf. 2:593). Moleschott was certain that even if we were never able experimentally to reproduce spontaneous generation, the assertion that life on earth had sprung up from inanimate matter would not be affected. Humanity is part of the evolutionary process, having ascended via the primeval cell, the monkeys, and the anthropoid apes. Since the whole evolutionary process started with inorganic matter and evolved toward humanity, humanity is understood in strictly materialistic terms. "There is no thought without phosphorus, without grease, and without water" was Moleschott's verdict (2:599). "Speech, style, attempts and conclusions, good actions and crimes, courage and hesitation and treason, they are all natural phenomena, and, as much as the revolutions of the globe they stand as necessary consequences in a direct relationship to indispensable causes" (2:606). Humans are the sum total of parents, space and time, air and

---

in its summary conclusion at the end of volume 2. Since it does not deal explicitly with Darwin's theories, we feel it permissible to use this later edition. *Der Kreislauf des Lebens,* vol. 1, 5th ed. (Giessen: Emil Roth, 1875), 7; vol. 2 (Giessen: Emil Roth, 1887). Parenthetical references in the following text are to *Der Kreislauf des Lebens,* 5th ed., with the volume number preceding the page location.

weather, food and dress. Since there are so many influences on humanity, it is a constantly developing natural product (2:608).

Suddenly, however, Moleschott broke out of the consistent determinism he had set up. Though all of our knowledge stems from our senses, and though the history of human education is the developmental history of our senses, Moleschott now declared that "man is the measure of all things for man" (2:583). Since we are always becoming, we can always strive for betterment. And indeed, he confessed, "the moral and spiritual activity of mankind is constantly developing" (2:613). In his appeal to humanity to realize the new opportunities of monistic materialism, Moleschott implicitly went beyond a strictly monistic view and distinguished between ego and world. This relationship between the own self and matter is precisely the issue that, in spite of their fervent assertions, pre-Darwinian materialistic monists did not seem to have resolved when they proposed their coherent view of the world.[20]

Though we do not want to classify **Ludwig Feuerbach** as a materialist monist, we must at least parenthetically mention him here again. While Feuerbach was concerned more with a philosophy of religion than with a philosophy of nature, his thoughts were deeply influenced by evolutionary thinking. In his treatise *The Essence of Religion* (1846; Eng. trans. 1873) he postulated: "The feeling of dependence in man is the source of religion."[21] God is the highest or most powerful being and can achieve what humans cannot do. He is the eternal being. God is also the First Cause and serves as a hypothesis to solve the problem of the origin of nature, or rather of organic life. It is the power of God that sustains us. But, Feuerbach wondered, "We are placed right in the midst of Nature, and should our beginning, our origin lie outside of Nature? We live within Nature, with Nature, by Nature, and should we still not be from her? What a contradiction!"[22] Indeed, Feuerbach concluded, the fundamental concept of God as distinguished from humanity is none other than nature.

Contrary to his mentor Hegel, he asserted that the deduction of the world from God, or of nature from the spirit, is only a logical game. Religion, therefore, has as its presupposition a dichotomy or contradiction between willing and ability, desire and accomplishment, idea and reality. The traditional understanding of faith in God is the anthropomorphic phenomenon of faith in nature. But Feuerbach wanted this faith to be faith in the human being as a being in and of nature. In attempting to dissolve God into nature, he did not want to

20. Theobald Ziegler, *Die geistigen und sozialen Strömungen des neunzehnten Jahrhunderts,* 2nd ed. (Berlin: Georg Bondi, 1901), 350.

21. Ludwig Feuerbach, *The Essence of Religion,* trans. Alexander Loos (London: Progressive Publishing, 1890), 7.

22. Feuerbach, *The Essence of Religion,* 21.

advocate a divinization of nature. On the contrary, he argued, "the power of Nature is not unlimited like the power of God, i.e., the power of human imagination; she cannot do everything at will at all times and under all circumstances — her productiveness and effects on the contrary are dependent on conditions."[23] This postulate provided for him the starting point for his evolutionary ideas. Geology had proved that the earth underwent a series of developments until it arrived at its present state. The origin and development of organic life are intimately tied to the evolution of the earth. But the earth did not first provide the conditions for the origin of life or of the human species as some kind of Garden of Eden in which life or the human species originated.

Feuerbach contended that as soon as conditions on the earth were such that life or humanity could originate, they originated. Therefore, the argument that since life is not spontaneously generated today it could not have originated from inanimate matter, was wrong. Nowadays environmental conditions are different, and the earth is in a state of stability. Yet this did not imply for Feuerbach that today the evolutionary thrust has been lost. Feuerbach's claim of dissolving God into nature was proposing an evolutionary progression. If humanity is no longer for nature, nature can be for humanity; it can attain self-determination, dignity, and power. (Remembering, however, that in a preface to Jacob Moleschott's *Lehre der Nahrungsmittel: Für das Volk* [1850] Feuerbach wrote that "man is what he eats," we doubt whether he had succeeded in determining any better the relationship between ego and world than the monistic materialists.)

The Challenge of Monistic Darwinism in Germany: David Friedrich Strauss, Ernst Haeckel, Christoph Luthardt, and Otto Zöckler

The stage was amazingly well prepared for Darwin's evolutionary ideas. The main arguments in favor of a comprehensive evolutionary worldview did not even come from biology. It was rather geology, partly in connection with biological research, partly by itself, that paved the way for evolutionary theories.[24] Geology opened the way for understanding the immense eons necessary for biological change; and by providing a variety of fossils, it also allowed for understanding the actual changes that were involved.

23. Feuerbach, *The Essence of Religion*, 22.

24. Otto Zöckler, *Geschichte der Beziehungen zwischen Theologie und Naturwissenschaft, mit besonderer Berücksichtigung der Schöpfungsgeschichte*, vol. 2, *Von Newton und Leibniz bis zur Gegenwart* (Gütersloh: C. Bertelsmann, 1879), 581-82.

An interesting pre-Darwinian theory is advanced by Heinrich Friedrich Link, *Die Urwelt und das Altertum erläutert durch die Naturkunde* (1821, *The Primeval World and Antiquity Explained by Natural Science*), who assumed forty years before Darwin that the ape could be considered the historical link between animals and humans.[25] He claimed that the Negroes were the primal form of the human race and the whites were a degeneration of the Negroes. Like the ardent follower of Darwin, Ernst Haeckel, he was looking for the cradle of humanity not in Asia or Africa but on a lost continent between India and East Africa. Other evolutionary theories were proposed by Dr. Vollmer in his *Natur- und Sittengemälde der Tropenländer* (1828, *Depicting Nature and Morals in Tropical Countries*), in which he postulated the gradual development of the living species, including humanity, from formless matter. One should also mention the work of Karl Ernst von Baer, *Über die Entwicklungsgeschichte der Tiere; Beobachtung und Reflexion* (vol. 1, 1828, *Concerning the Developmental History of Animals; Observation and Reflection*), who discovered what Haeckel later called the fundamental biogenetic law. Baer observed that during their embryonic development higher animals recapitulate the lower stages of life. Yet this recapitulation is not an exact repetition, only a similar one.

The mention of these few naturalists should preclude Darwin's theories taking anyone by surprise. The Greifswald theologian Otto Zöckler (1833-1906) even pointed out that each year after the middle of the 1840s, several scientific monographs or textbooks in different fields anticipated the Darwinian theories.[26] The stage was so well prepared that as soon as Darwin's main concepts became known, many of his German followers immediately surpassed him in the consequences they reached from evolutionary thought. In their exuberance they even committed gross scientific exaggerations and distortions. Vogt, for instance, claimed that an important link between humans and apes was the microcephalics or those born with abnormally small brains. They are examples of a pathologically abnormal formation leading back to the anthropoid apes as our predecessors. Under heavy attacks, however, Vogt had to withdraw his theory in 1872, admitting that he had never anatomically investigated a microcephalic brain. While there were also some moderate approaches to Darwin, the most forceful and lasting influence of Darwinian ideas in Germany, picking up the pre-Darwinian monistic tendencies, came from David Friedrich Strauss and Ernst Haeckel.

At first glance it may seem inappropriate to begin our review of monistic tendencies in German Darwinism with **David Friedrich Strauss** (1808-74). As

---

25. Zöckler, *Von Newton und Leibniz*, 604-5.
26. Zöckler, *Von Newton und Leibniz*, 613.

we have seen, he was an advocate of Hegelian philosophy and not so much of Darwinian thought. In *Die christliche Glaubenslehre in ihrer geschichtlichen Entwicklung und im Kampfe mit der modernen Wissenschaft dargestellt* (vol. 1, 1840, *The Christian Doctrine Depicted in Its Historical Development and in Its Struggle with Modern Science*),[27] he indeed portrayed strict Hegelian methodology, dividing each section into thesis, antithesis, and synthesis (616). He affirmed with Hegel that the Absolute is essentially result; it is only in the end that the whole of reality emerges (643). Evolutionary or progressive thinking is therefore the very center of his understanding of the relationship between God and creation. Strauss is convinced that all organic beings evolved in successive layers from inanimate matter (681-82). Only gradually did our planet obtain its present form. There was a creative force in our planet that sustained the created and mediated the sustenance of higher forms of life through procreation. The human origin, of course, was part of the natural process (685-86). But Strauss assured his audience that neither the polygenetic origin of humanity nor the naturalness of its origin would impair the notion of the unity of humanity and the notion of God the Creator. While not yet aware of an actual evolutionary process in the strict sense, he was convinced of a natural progression of nature.

When we turn to *The Old Faith & the New* (1871; Eng. trans. of the 6th ed., 1873), which Strauss published one year after Darwin's *Descent of Man*, we cannot but realize the amazing impact the Darwinian theory had on him. Gone now is the possibility of reconciling the progression of nature with the belief in a Creator. We are told that the only choice is between belief in the divine creative hand and belief in Darwin's theory. "Natural Science," Strauss declared, "has long endeavored to substitute the evolutionary theory in place of the conception of creation, so alien to her spirit; but it was Charles Darwin who made the first truly scientific attempt to deal seriously with this conception, and to trace it throughout the organic world."[28] Of course, he admitted that Darwin was not the first to suggest this theory. Most other proponents of this theory, however, had too many parts missing in it to introduce it as a convincing and comprehensive theory. While Strauss conceded that Darwin pointed toward more possible solutions than he actually provided, he was convinced that Darwin had introduced the evolutionary process so persuasively that "a happier coming race will finally cast out miracles" from creation (1:205). Thus Strauss

---

27. The parenthetical page numbers in this paragraph are from Strauss, *Die christliche Glaubenslehre in ihrer geschichtlichen Entwicklung und im Kampfe mit der modernen Wissenschaft dargestellt*, vol. 1. (Darmstadt: Wissenschaftliche Buchgesellschaft, 1973 [1840]).

28. David Friedrich Strauss, *The Old Faith & the New*, 2 vols. in 1, with introduction and notes by G. A. Wells (Amherst, N.Y.: Prometheus, 1997), 1:202 (for the following references page numbers are given in the text).

proclaimed Darwin "one of the greatest benefactors of the human race" (1:205). For the progressive natural science of today, an intelligent architect of the organism, or even a purposiveness of nature that one could understand as the work of an intelligent creator, was no longer tenable (cf. 2:23-25). Even human instincts were gradually acquired through natural selection. This showed, for Strauss, the amazing gap between the old worldview and the new one.

Strauss did not hold the details of Darwin's theory to be surprising. He argued, for instance, that "Darwin's 'struggle for existence' is nothing else but the expansion of that into a law of Nature, which we have long since recognized as a law of one social and industrial life . . . competition" (1:216-17). Of course, Strauss realized that some people might find humanity's descent from apes offensive (cf. 2:4). But he questioned whether it would be so much better to be created in the image of God and then be thrown out of paradise, and still today not have regained the status we once had. For some people, he said, even a failure from a good family is more respectable than someone who, through his or her own efforts, has made it in life. According to the evolutionary theory, humanity did not start high to fall so far immediately afterward. On the contrary, it started low, to move slowly but "to ever greater heights" (2:39). Humanity is part of the ascending movement of life (cf. 2:55). In it nature reflects itself, Strauss declared in accordance with his mentor Hegel. Though humans are still natural beings, they sublimated the higher goal implanted in them. Humanity should understand and dominate nature, not as a tyrant but as humans. While these assertions about the human "destiny" may be interpreted as resembling teleological thought, it was evident for Strauss that the evolutionary theory is in opposition to any "dualistic" Christian understanding of the world. This theory endeavors to explain the whole of phenomena from one single, monistic principle. Compared with Christianity, both materialism and idealism may "be regarded as Monism" (2:19). Their common enemy is dualism, "which pervaded the conception of the world throughout the Christian era" (2:19). While idealism attempts to explain the world from above, materialism attempts to explain it from below, and ultimately one leads to the other. We are not wrong to conclude that Darwin's theory of the development of the species through natural selection brought for Strauss the solution to the great enigmas of the world.

In **Ernst Haeckel** (1834-1919), professor of zoology at the University of Jena, we are dealing with the person who in regard to evolutionary thought had perhaps the deepest impact on German Protestantism. Different from Büchner, Vogt, and Moleschott, he was a scholar in his own right who made his own significant contributions to the theory of evolution. His popular books, the two-volume *History of Creation* (1868; Eng. trans. 1906) and *The Riddle of the Universe* (1899; Eng. trans. 1900), were best sellers on the German market and were translated into many languages. About his *History of Creation* Charles Darwin remarked in his *Descent of Man:* "If this work had appeared before my essay had been written, I should probably never have completed it. Almost all the conclusions at which I have arrived I find confirmed by this naturalist, whose knowledge on many points is much fuller than mine."[29] Most of Haeckel's thoughts, however, can be traced back to earlier thinkers, such as Giordano Bruno (1548-1600), Baruch Spinoza (1632-77), Gottfried Wilhelm Leibniz (1646-1716), Feuerbach, and others. Haeckel's monistic worldview is nothing new, but under the impact of the theory of a uniform evolution, it gains in precision and persuasion.

Already in his two-volume work *The History of Creation,* Haeckel ended on a highly optimistic note. He found that the mind of the whole human race has gone through a process of slow, gradual, and historical development. "We are proud," he claimed, "of having so immensely outstripped our lower animal ancestors, and derive from it the consoling assurance that in the future also, mankind, as a whole, will follow the glorious career of progressive development, and attain a still higher degree of mental perfection."[30] Especially the application of evolutionary thought to practical human life, as begun by the British philosopher and popularizer of Darwin's ideas, Herbert Spencer opens up "a new road towards moral perfection."[31] Shaping politics, morals, and the principles of justice in accordance with natural laws, and this means with the laws of evolution, will provide *"an existence worthy of man,* which has been talked of for thousands of years."[32] The strong religious overtones in his scientific and philosophic work are most clearly expressed when he concludes: "The simple religion of Nature, which grows from a true knowledge of Her, and of Her inexhaustible store of revelations, will in the future ennoble and perfect the development of mankind far beyond that degree which can possibly be attained under the influence of multifarious religions of the churches of the various nations, — religions resting on a blind belief in the vague secrets and mythical revelations of a sacerdotal caste."[33]

The religious overtones of his worldview can be seen throughout his

---

29. Charles Darwin, *The Descent of Man,* in *The Works of Charles Darwin,* ed. Paul H. Barrett and R. B. Freeman (London: William Pickering, 1989), 21:5 [original pagination: 3/4]. Darwin also mentioned approvingly the evolutionary thought of Büchner and Vogt.

30. Ernst Haeckel, *The History of Creation: On the Development of the Earth and Its Inhabitants by the Action of Natural Causes,* trans. E. R. Lankester, 2 vols. (New York: D. Appleton, 1876), 2:367.

31. Haeckel, *The History of Creation,* 2:367.

32. Haeckel, *The History of Creation,* 2:368.

33. Haeckel, *The History of Creation,* 2:369.

widely publicized lecture *Monism as Connecting Religion and Science: The Confession of Faith of a Man of Science* (1893; Eng. trans. 1894). Haeckel claimed as an "article of faith" the fundamental unity of organic and inorganic nature and thereby rejected the distinctions between natural science and humanities.[34] While most older religions and philosophical systems are dualistic, distinguishing between God and world, creator and creation, spirit and matter, Haeckel advocated a uniform understanding of all nature. Reminiscent of Feuerbach's position, he contended that in dualistic systems the most fundamental thought is an anthropomorphism. This means humanity devises an anthropomorphous concept of God that is "separated by a great gulf from the rest of nature" (14). Yet in referring both to Robert Mayer's law of the conservation of energy and to Lavoisier's law of the conservation of matter, and claiming that these two laws merge into the laws of the conservation of substance, Haeckel advocated a monistic worldview. The world is made up of "the inert heavy mass as material of creation" and "the mobile cosmic ether as creating divinity" (25). Thus with the ether theory, which at that time was still upheld as the means of the propagation of electromagnetic waves, no God as creator was necessary. God is not to be placed over against the material world as an external being, but must be placed as a "divine power" or "moving spirit" with the cosmos itself (15).

The evolutionary theory shows that in the cosmos everything is in flux. Paleontology, comparative anatomy, and ontogeny show us how life developed step by step, and how the cosmos emerged from a chaotic primeval state to the present world order. Haeckel conceded that one could label this worldview materialism, but he felt the term "monism" was more appropriate. He did not consider his worldview atheistic in the strict sense, though it was a-theistic, because it did not want to reduce God to "a gaseous vertebrate" as did those who hold on to "God as a 'spirit' in human form" (115). Therefore, Haeckel concluded his "monistic Confession of Faith with the words: 'May God, the Spirit of the Good, the Beautiful, and the True, be with us!'" (89).

Small wonder that Haeckel sought support from Bruno and Spinoza, claiming that "of the various systems of pantheism, which for long have given expression more or less clearly to the monistic conception of God, the most perfect is certainly that of Spinoza" (79). Haeckel was so certain of the persuasiveness of his monistic system that he contended that if Kant had developed his philosophy now with all our scientific knowledge at hand, his "system of

---

34. Ernst Haeckel, *Monism as Connecting Religion and Science: The Confession of Faith of a Man of Science*, trans. J. Gilchrist (London: Adam and Charles Black, 1894), 93. Page references to this work are supplied in the text.

critical philosophy would have turned out quite otherwise from what it was, and purely monistic" (102 n. 8).[35]

In his most influential book, *The Riddle of the Universe,* Haeckel's earlier unbridled optimism has been toned down. He confessed at the outset that he is "wholly a child of the nineteenth century" and that his "own command of the various branches of science is uneven and defective."[36] But he did not desist from presenting a monistic worldview, a view of a universe that is infinite and eternal. There is a universal movement of substance in space, we hear, that "takes the form of an eternal cycle or of a periodic process of evolution" (243). The eternal drama of periodic decay and rebirth of cosmic bodies does not stop short of our own solar system. Unlike the monistic pre-Darwinian materialists, Haeckel did not shy away from discussing the entropy or nonconvertibility of energy to strengthen his point of the eternal movement of the universe. While in any finite system "every attempt to make such a *perpetuum mobile* must necessarily fail . . . the case is different, however, when we turn to the world at large, the boundless universe that is in eternal movement" (246). Since the universe is infinite, the law of entropy does not affect it; there is no beginning and no end to the universe. Again Haeckel praised Spinoza's monistic system, so closely resembling his own (290).

As once before expressed in *Monism as Connecting Religion and Science,* Haeckel had a twofold objective: (1) "to give expression to the rational view of the world which is being forced upon us with such logical rigor by the modern advancements in our knowledge of nature as a unity," and (2) to make monism into a connecting link "between religion and science, and thus contribute to the adjustment of the antithesis so needlessly maintained between these, the two highest spheres in which the mind of man can exercise itself."[37] It is interesting that in so doing he also spoke out against Christian ethics, since it is "a very ideal precept, but as useless in practice as it is unnatural" (353). On principle it attacks and despises egotism and exaggerates the love of one's neighbor at the expense of self-love. We are reminded here of Friedrich Nietzsche (1844-1900), who went even further on this point, labeling Christian ethics the morals of slaves, which he contrasted with the morals of a master race *(Herren-*

35. It should be mentioned parenthetically at least that Haeckel praised Strauss greatly, because he "had already clearly perceived that the soul-activities of man, and therefore also his consciousness, as functions of the central nervous system, all spring from a common source, and, from a monistic point of view, come under the same category [i.e., monism]" (Haeckel, *Monism,* 46).

36. Ernst Haeckel, *The Riddle of the Universe at the Close of the Nineteenth Century,* trans. J. McCabe (New York: Harper, 1900), ix. Page references to this work are supplied in the text.

37. Haeckel, *Monism,* vi-vii, and cf. Haeckel, *Riddle of the Universe,* 332.

Moral).[38] Yet the greatest surprise awaits us at the conclusion of *Riddle* when Haeckel confessed that "only one comprehensive riddle of the universe now remains — the problem of substance" (380). Then he conceded: "We grant at once that the innermost character of nature is just as little understood by us as it was by Anaximander and Empedocles twenty-four hundred years ago, by Spinoza and Newton two hundred years ago, and by Kant and Goethe one hundred years ago. We must even grant that this essence of substance becomes more mysterious and enigmatic the deeper we penetrate into the knowledge of its attributes, matter and energy, and the more thoroughly we study its countless phenomenal forms and their evolutions" (380).

But Haeckel did not want to end in resignation just because he did not discern the "thing-in-itself" that lies behind the knowable phenomena. Instead he asked us to rejoice in the immense progress that has actually been made by the monistic philosophy of nature. The monism of the cosmos "proclaims the absolute dominion of 'the great eternal iron laws' throughout the universe" (381). Instead of being devoted to the ideals of God, freedom, and immortality, we can engage in the cult of the true, the good, and the beautiful, "which is the heart of our new monistic religion" (382). Haeckel concluded that he hoped that in the twentieth century the great antithesis between theism and pantheism, vitalism and mechanism can be resolved "by the construction of a system of pure monism" (383).

The Riddle of the Universe stands at the close of the nineteenth century and is indicative of the general outlook of nineteenth-century Protestant thought in Germany. With the church historian Friedrich Loofs (1858-1928), one could attack the accuracy of some of the scientific arguments that Haeckel used. One can also argue that his monistic worldview is nothing new, that it is common to most philosophers in their endeavor to provide a comprehensive worldview.[39] With the physicist and politician Rudolf Virchow (1821-1902), *The Freedom of Science in the Modern State,* one could also caution that all our knowledge is only partial.[40] Virchow suggested that we confine our hypotheses

---

38. Friedrich Nietzsche, *Jenseits von Gut und Böse* (260), in *Nietzsches Werke in zwei Bänden,* ed. Gerhard Stenzel (Salzburg: Bergland, n.d.), 2:803. J. B. Müller, "Herrenmoral," in *Historisches Wörterbuch des Philosophie,* ed. Joachim Ritter and Karlfried Gründer, 3:1078, states that Nietzsche with his theory of morals of a master race is "one of the leading representatives of Social Darwinism."

39. Oliver Lodge, *Life and Matter: A Criticism of Professor Haeckel's "Riddle of the Universe"* (New York: Putnam, 1907), 7, 9.

40. Rudolf Virchow, *Die Freiheit der Wissenschaft im modernen Staat. Rede* (Berlin: Wiegandt, Hempel & Parey, 1877; Eng. trans. 1878), 13. Page numbers to this work are placed in the text.

to the fields for which they were designed and not expand them to universal principles (18-20). Against a universal theory of descent Virchow claimed that nobody had observed a spontaneous generation of life and that every progress in prehistoric anthropology has only widened the gap between human ancestors and other vertebrates (29). Therefore, Virchow concluded: *"We cannot teach, we cannot label it as an achievement of science that man is descended from apes or from any other animal"* (31).[41] Against these objections we must note that Haeckel did not claim originality for his ideas, nor that he had all the answers, nor that his system was without flaws. As we have seen with the earlier materialistic monists, even without the detailed theory of descent Haeckel would perhaps not have wanted to abandon his thoroughgoing monism.

How did theology respond to that challenge? Two examples may suffice. The first, Lutheran theologian **Christoph Ernst Luthardt** (1823-1902), professor of systematic theology and New Testament exegesis at Leipzig, beginning in 1856 emphasized in his *Die christliche Glaubenslehre gemeinverständlich dargestellt (Exposition of the Christian Faith)* that the Bible is not a book about scientific research nor the scientific knowledge of nature, but a book of religion that has to do with humanity's relationship to God and with the relationships between people on earth.[42] Referring to the materialism debate that arose in 1852, Luthardt distinguished between a psychological materialism that denies the existence of the soul and a later cosmological materialism "which denies the existence of the absolute Spirit and reduces everything existing to matter only."[43] Luthardt attributed this kind of materialistic thinking to pantheism, because it explained being from the idea. The absolute idea is everything, it reproduces being and permeates it. The Spirit then posits matter. Luthardt rejected this Hegelian dialectic. He noted that if all life is the movement of matter

41. It should be noted here that, similar to Zöckler, Virchow discerned a close and dangerous relationship between the theory of descent and socialism (12). For further details on the dispute between Haeckel and Virchow, especially on the relationship between socialism and the theory of descent, cf. the excellent book by Ernst Benz, *Evolution and Christian Hope: Man's Concept of the Future, from the Early Fathers to Teilhard de Chardin*, trans. H. G. Frank (Garden City, N.Y.: Doubleday, Anchor Book, 1968), 96-98. The idea of an upward-slanting continuing evolutionary process provided the main stimulus for socialist reform claims. We should also remember that both Karl Marx and Friedrich Engels were familiar with the works of Darwin and felt they established the basis for their theory in natural history (Benz, 83-85).

42. Cf. Christoph Ernst Luthardt, *Die christliche Glaubenslehre gemeinverständlich dargestellt,* 2nd ed. (Leipzig: Dörffling & Franke, 1906 [1898]), 212.

43. Christoph Ernst Luthardt, *Die modernen Weltanschauungen und ihre praktischen Konsequenzen: Vorträge über Fragen der Gegenwart aus Kirche, Schule, Staat und Gesellschaft im Winter 1880 zu Leipzig gehalten* (Leipzig: Dörffling & Franke, 1880), 167, in his lecture "Der Materialismus und seine Konsequenzen."

and all development is the development of matter, then there is no higher Spirit possible that sets a goal and an aim for the developmental process. This means that theology would be obsolete, and all that would be left is a causality with its cause-and-effect sequence.

This kind of pantheism actually becomes a monism and a materialistic pantheism. The diversity of the world is nothing but the progressive development of the world's actual foundations and beginnings. Darwinism fits well into this kind of thought pattern. Yet Luthardt asked how progress and development are possible if the effect cannot contain more than is contained in its cause. The world cannot be its own creator. If one dissociates God from the material realm, there is no spiritual world possible, not even a humanity. Luthardt concluded: "The result of the development is either pessimism or Christendom."[44] Either the world makes no sense whatsoever and one must despair, or one assumes some kind of spiritual meaning or beliefs. Materialism too is a faith; it is not a fact.

The Lutheran theologian **Otto Zöckler** (1833-1906), from 1886 till his death professor of historical and exegetical theology at the University of Greifswald, Germany, was less confrontational than Luthardt. He attempted to demonstrate that the principles of good science and good theology do not necessarily conflict. In his article on Zöckler, Victor Schultze rightly claimed that his scholarship "was rated very high as was his authority as a theologian in the realm of natural science."[45] Zöckler, who taught in Greifswald most of his life, had indeed an astounding command of scientific knowledge, especially in its historic dimension.

In his two-volume *Geschichte der Beziehungen zwischen Theologie und Naturwissenschaft mit besonderer Rücksicht auf Schöpfungsgeschichte (The History of the Relationship between Theology and the Natural Sciences with Special Attention to the Creation Narrative)*, he showed his immense erudition in the history of science and his critical awareness. For instance, while he knew that Darwin rejected a Christian teleological worldview, he realized that Darwin "does not regard the sequence of the main events in the life of nature and humanity as 'the result of blind accident.'"[46] Zöckler concluded that Darwin's teachings do not contain anything that would necessitate the abandonment of the Christian theistic notion of creation.[47] While Zöckler rejected Darwinism as a pathological disease that eventually will run its course, he was convinced

44. Luthardt, *Die modernen Weltanschauungen*, 185.
45. Victor Schultze, "Zöckler, Otto," in *The New Schaff-Herzog Encyclopedia of Religious Knowledge* (Grand Rapids: Baker, 1949-50), 12:520.
46. Otto Zöckler, *Geschichte der Beziehungen*, 642-43.
47. Zöckler, *Geschichte der Beziehungen*, 719.

that, true to the Pauline saying that "all things are yours" (1 Cor. 3:21), the theological doctrines of creation and providence and the understanding of humanity's original state can gain new insights from the findings of Darwin.[48] Zöckler introduced the concept of a theory of concordance through which the findings of evolutionary speculation, insofar as they are scientifically proven, complement the assertions of theology.

The hypothesis of concordance or of harmonizing is also employed in his lectures, *Die Urgeschichte der Erde und des Menschen (The Primal History of the Earth and Humanity)*. He claimed that the contempt with which some scientists treat the first chapters of the Bible can only be the result of misinformation about the biblical Christian worldview as it pertains to the creation of the universe.[49] The eternal and infinitely grand perception contained in these stories has room for all the scientific details through which sober empirical research will enrich our understanding of how creation has occurred and still does occur. Even concerning the six days of creation, there is a concordance between the record of geology and the book of Genesis.[50] This mutually complementing avenue had already been pursued by the French naturalist Georges Cuvier at the beginning of the nineteenth century, and according to Zöckler there seemed to appear "an ever stronger consensus of all scientists in this area even in Germany which will soon lead to a complete victory over any contrary perspective."[51]

Zöckler's optimism was based on his historical research. He realized that the claim made by the "modern fanatics of unbelief" that natural science sooner or later will do away with religion and with the Christian faith was simply not true.[52] There is no correlation between a comprehensive scientific education and religious unbelief. In each epoch there have been conservative and decidedly irreligious scientists, but most have pursued a middle course. He was convinced that the future does not belong to materialism but to a true empiricism that collects and analyzes the experiences available within the realm of the visible. *"True scientists will time and again be able to read from the two texts placed alongside each other, from the Book of Nature and from the Book of Revelation. They will over and over again return to the religion of Kepler and Galilei, of Haller and Euler, and of Cuvier and Agassiz."*[53] Of course, Zöckler conceded that

---

48. Zöckler, *Geschichte der Beziehungen*, 798-800.

49. Otto Zöckler, *Die Urgeschichte der Erde und des Menschen: Vorträge gehalten zu Hamburg im März 1868* (Gütersloh: C. Bertelsmann, 1868), 1-2.

50. Cf. Zöckler, *Urgeschichte*, 42.

51. Zöckler, *Urgeschichte*, 48-49.

52. Otto Zöckler, *Gottes Zeugen im Reich der Natur: Biographien und Bekenntnisse grosser Naturforscher aus alter und neuer Zeit*, 2nd ed. (Gütersloh: C. Bertelsmann, 1906), 482.

53. Zöckler, *Gottes Zeugen*, 485.

in the future some will become so radical as to deny the existence of everything that is not visible and tangible. But the true representatives of science will overcome these destructive forces.

True witnesses to God in the realm of nature will never die out as long as nature remains, because it is God's. Therefore human witness to the divine truth and the grandeur contained in it will never be wanting. That nature witnesses to God is especially emphasized in Zöckler's earlier publication, *Theologia naturalis (Natural Theology)*. According to the maxim *credo ut intelligam* (I believe in order to understand), he wanted to "explain, complete, and confirm the immediate revelation of God through the mediated one which is given in nature."[54] The book of nature will illustrate the book of the Bible, while the latter will explain the former. According to Zöckler, such a positive theology of nature will expand and illustrate the organic development of dogmatics. How nature and the Bible come together can be seen especially well in the metaphors and parables of the Old and New Testaments.[55] The biblical symbols relating nature as well as the Bible's picturesque language exemplify the illustrative character of nature for God's revelation. Theological insight and scientific research do not go in separate or opposite ways but complement and in some respects even correct each other. Revelation and God's action do not occur in a realm removed from the natural world but in the midst of nature. Nature is fundamentally the arena and medium of God's action. Otto Zöckler impresses with both his historical and scientific erudition and the ease with which scientific knowledge, for him, complements theological insights. He might have been overly optimistic in asserting the complementarity of the two, but at least he saw a vigorous engagement with the sciences indispensable for theological assertions. With this approach he differed from most of his contemporaries.

If we reviewed other significant theologians of the latter part of the nineteenth century, such as Albrecht Ritschl and Wilhelm Herrmann, or even Adolf von Harnack, we would notice that the apologetic endeavor of Otto Zöckler was an exception. For most theologians the world hardly came into focus. God touches only the interior side of humanity. This retreat from the external and tangible was facilitated by the Kantian distinction between the phenomenal and the noumenal and also by Schleiermacher's claim that religion concerns itself primarily with feeling and intuition. Beyond that, the materialistic claim

54. Otto Zöckler, *Theologia naturalis: Entwurf einer systematischen Naturtheologie vom offenbarungsgläubigen Standpunkte aus,* vol. 1, *Die Prolegomena und die specielle Theologie enthaltend* (Frankfurt am Main and Erlangen: Heyder & Zimmer, 1860), 6. Volume 2 never appeared. This may perhaps serve as an indication that his project was more difficult than he had initially envisioned.

55. Zöckler, *Die Prolegomena,* 200-201.

that everything existing can be reduced to matter and is subjected to an all-embracing cause-and-effect system left, in the eyes of most theologians, no other choice than to escape to something beyond the created order. With this retreat from the world, theology assumed increasingly a ghetto mentality.

The British Controversy over Darwin

The situation was different in Great Britain than in Germany because the predominant philosophical mind-set in Germany was idealist, while in Britain it was empirical. This was also the level on which theology worked. For instance, the Baptist Andrew Fuller (1754-1815), a popular author and pastor, claimed about the Scriptures: "Though they give us no system of astronomy, yet they urge us to study the works of God, and to teach us to adore him upon every discovery."[56] Through nature we can discover how God works. It was only those groups influenced by romanticism that had deep-seated antiscientific convictions, as we noticed with Coleridge in his antipathy to Paley and as we also saw with the Tractarians. Some even attempted to reconcile development with God's creative activity, such as the Scottish evangelical amateur geologist Hugh Miller (1802-56), who edited a journal of the Free Church and wrote: "God might as certainly have *originated* the species by a law of development, as he *maintains* it by a law of development; the existence of a First Great Cause is as perfectly compatible with the one scheme as with the other."[57] This means that various means were employed to come to terms with developmental theories as they became more and more popular in the nineteenth century.[58]

There was another facet, however, that made a rapprochement between theology and science very difficult. Biblical scholarship, especially as it pertained to the discussion of creation versus evolution, was badly missing in Great Britain. In the German theological faculties, by contrast, especially at Göttingen, Berlin, and Halle, there existed a freedom of scholarship almost unknown in British institutions. The Old Testament could be studied critically and professionally without regard for the practical needs of the ministry. By the

56. Andrew Fuller, *The Gospel Its Own Witness; or, The Holy Nature and Divine Harmony of the Christian Religion Contrasted with the Immorality and Absurdity of Deism*, in *The Complete Works of the Rev. Andrew Fuller*, ed. Andrew G. Fuller (London: Henry G. Bohn, 1848), 41.

57. Hugh Miller, *Foot-prints of the Creator; or, The Asterolepsis of Stromness*, with memoir by Louis Agassiz (Edinburgh: Adam and Charles Black, 1861), 12.

58. Cf. David N. Livingstone, D. G. Hart, and Mark A. Noll, eds., *Evangelicals and Science in Historical Perspective* (New York: Oxford University Press, 1999), who show the various strategies employed by the evangelicals to come to terms with evolution.

early decades of the nineteenth century, "the Old Testament was being studied in Germany with a critical intensity and professionalism matched only by that of the sciences in Britain and America."[59] We remember here, for instance, Coleridge and Pusey, who had both been introduced to Old Testament studies at Göttingen. When some of these insights were introduced in Great Britain, many were ill prepared for it and condemned such heresies outright.

One of the books that aroused a storm was *Essays and Reviews* (1860), written by theologians who employed higher criticism. "The book went through thirteen editions in five years, called forth in reply more than four hundred books, pamphlets, and articles, and caused Anglo-Catholics and Evangelicals at Oxford jointly to sponsor a declaration reaffirming the inspiration and authority of the Bible."[60] Under the leadership of E. B. Pusey, this so-called Oxford Declaration on Inspiration and Eternal Punishment was prepared on February 24, 1864, and sent to every clergy of the established church in England, Wales, and Ireland with the plea to sign it without delay. The authors of the *Essays* claimed to *"interpret the Scripture like any other book."*[61] This meant that one has to ascertain first the literal use, namely, "the meaning which it had to the mind of the prophet or evangelist who first uttered or wrote, to the hearers or readers who first received it." This also meant for the authors that if one wanted to maintain the value of the Bible as a book of religious instruction, one should not try every possibility "to prove it scientifically exact at the expense of every sound principle of interpretation, and in defiance of common sense, but by the frank recognition of the erroneous use of nature which it contains."[62] While the Bible is still God's word, it is that in human form, and that human form is not beyond reproach.

With this approach the authority of the Bible was by no means abandoned, as shown in a sermon delivered at Oxford University by Frederick Temple (1821-1902), the later archbishop of Canterbury and father of William Temple. He was one of the collaborators of this volume and stated in the sermon: The student of science

> if he be a religious man, he believes that both books, the book of Nature and the book of Revelation, come alike from God, and that he has no more right to refuse to accept what he finds in the one than what he finds in the

---

59. So James R. Moore, "Geologists and Interpreters of Genesis in the Nineteenth Century," in *God and Nature*, 332.

60. Moore, "Geologists," 341.

61. For this and the following quote, see Benjamin Jowett, "On the Interpretation of Scripture," in *Essays and Reviews,* edited with an introduction by Frederic H. Hedge (Boston: Walker, Wise, and Co., 1862), 416 and 417 respectively.

62. Charles W. Goodwin, "The Mosaic Cosmogony," in *Essays and Reviews,* 238.

other. The two books are indeed on totally different subjects; the one may be called a treatise on physics and mathematics; the other, a treatise on theology and morals. But they are both by the same Author; and the difference in their importance is derived from the difference in their matter, not from any difference in their authority. Whenever, therefore, there is a collision between them, the dispute becomes simply a question of evidence.[63]

This kind of separation between the two books, of nature and of the Bible, while maintaining the common author, God, in the charged atmosphere that surrounded Darwin's *Origin of Species,* amounted for many to a capitulation of theology. If nature no longer witnesses to design, then natural theology has lost its cause. This was dangerous, since in the *Origin of Species* (1859) Darwin advanced four major points: (1) there are random variations among species; (2) populations increase at a geometrical rate, and as a result, there is a severe struggle for life at one time or another; (3) since there are variations useful to organic beings, individuals with useful variations "will have the best chance of being preserved in the struggle for life"; and (4) individuals with useful variations will pass on the beneficial traits to the next generation and "will tend to produce offspring similarly characterized."[64] Darwin's *Origin of Species* was met with both eagerness and outrage. "The small first edition of 1,250 copies sold the day of publication, and a second edition of 3,000 copies soon afterwards."[65]

The watchword for controversy was "random variations," because with this concept the argument from design was eliminated. Even the British geologist Charles Lyell (1797-1875) pleaded with Darwin to introduce just a little divine direction into his system of natural selection.[66] One either had to stay with religion, then there was design, or with Darwin, which excluded design. Samuel Wilberforce (1805-73), bishop of Oxford, who also warned his clergy against the *Essays and Reviews,* launched a theological offensive against Darwin in an article condemning Darwinism for contradicting the Bible.[67] On June 30, 1860, in

63. Frederick Temple, "The Present Relations of Science to Religion" (1860), in *Essays and Reviews,* 494.

64. Charles Darwin, *On the Origin of Species,* in *The Works of Charles Darwin,* 15:92 [126/28].

65. According to Charles Darwin, *Autobiography,* in *The Works of Charles Darwin,* 29:146 [122/24].

66. According to William Irwin, *Apes, Angels, and Victorians: The Story of Darwin, Huxley, and Evolution* (New York: Time, 1963), 144-45.

67. Cf. for the following David C. Lindberg and Ronald L. Numbers, "Beyond War and Peace: A Reappraisal between Christianity and Science," in *American Church History: A Reader,* ed. Henry Warner Bowden and P. C. Kemeny (Nashville: Abingdon, 1998), 224.

an address at Oxford before the British Association for the Advancement of Science, Wilberforce postulated the exaggerated claim that Darwin had said "Humanity is descended from monkeys," a claim Darwin never made.[68] To this charge the zoologist Thomas H. Huxley (1825-95) retorted that he would rather be a descendant of a humble monkey than of a man who is misrepresenting those who search for truth. While this debate was played up more and more as time went on, this meeting only showed the basic difference in perception. If there was evolution and a basic cohesion among all living beings, the creation account could no longer be true. This is what the good bishop found reprehensible, and many others agreed with him.

When in 1871 Darwin also included humanity in his theory of evolution (*The Descent of Man and Selection in Relation to Sex*) and attempted to show that all human characteristics can be explained through gradual modifications of humanlike ancestors through a process of natural selection, the tide had changed and the reception was much less hostile. One important reason for this can be seen in Frederic W. Farrar's Bampton Lectures of 1886 on the history of interpretation. Born in India, Farrar (1831-1903) became a distinguished author and was made dean of Canterbury in 1895. In going through the history of exegesis from the rabbinic times to the nineteenth century, Farrar shows the danger of stagnation, "which poisons the atmosphere of Theology when Progress is violently arrested, and Freedom authoritatively suppressed."[69] Theology cannot stand in the way of progress, and it can also not impose an authority on fields over which it has no claim. Presenting these lectures three years after Darwin's death, he said with specific reference to Darwin: "A scientific observer, second perhaps to none since the days of Newton, after having been treated all his life long as an enemy to religion, was laid, but three years ago, in his honored grave in Westminster Abbey. His theories, which have been scores of times denounced from this very pulpit, are now not only accepted by the great majority of scientific men throughout the world, but have been admitted by many leading theologians to be in no sense irreconcilable with sacred truths."[70] Less than a generation after *The Origin of Species*, Darwin was no longer seen as the enemy of faith and religion felt no longer threatened by someone it once considered its archenemy.

---

68. Cf. Irwin, *Apes, Angels, and Victorians*, 6.

69. Frederic W. Farrar, *History of Interpretation. Eight Lectures Preached before the University of Oxford in the Year MDCCCLXXXV* (New York: E. P. Dutton, 1886), xv.

70. Farrar, *History of Interpretation*, 426.

Darwinism, American Style

No Conflict between Science and Religion

When we turn to America and look at the Princeton theologians, we notice that the scientific discovery of nature could provide no threat or challenge to their faith. To the contrary, everything discovered in nature could only strengthen their faith. Archibald Alexander stated: "The Bible furnishes the full and satisfactory commentary on the book of nature. With the Bible in our hands, the heavens shine with redoubled lustre. The universe, which to the atheist is full of darkness and confusion, to the Christian is resplendent with light and glory. The first sentence in the Bible contains more to satisfy the inquisitive mind than all the volumes of human speculation."[71] There is a difference between a Christian and a non-Christian looking at nature. The Bible is not a literal proof text for what we ought to find in nature, nor is the universe necessarily leading to God as in natural theology. Similar to what Johannes Kepler (1571-1630) held, nature only underscores for the Christian what he or she already knows about God; it declares the beauty of God's creation. The Bible attests to that by saying that God indeed created the whole universe.

Even the creation account in Genesis 1 posed no problem for the Christian mind. Though general chronology had it that the earth existed only for a few thousand years, one could also interpret the word "day" to mean a geological period of indefinite duration. Therefore **Charles Hodge** (1797-1878) asserted confidently:

> As the Bible is of God, it is certain that there can be no conflict between the teachings of the Scriptures and the facts of science. It is not with facts, but with theories, believers have to contend. Many such theories have, from time to time, been presented, apparently or really inconsistent with the Bible. But these theories have either proved to be false, or to harmonize with the Word of God, properly interpreted. The Church has been forced more than once to alter her interpretation of the Bible to accommodate the discoveries of science. But this has been done without doing any violence to the Scriptures or in any degree impairing their authority.[72]

---

71. Archibald Alexander, "The Bible. A Key to the Phenomena of the Natural World" (1829), in *The Princeton Theology: 1812-1921; Scripture, Science, and Theological Method from Archibald Alexander to Benjamin Breckinridge Warfield,* ed. Mark A. Noll (Grand Rapids: Baker, 1983), 96.

72. Charles Hodge, *Systematic Theology* (Grand Rapids: Eerdmans, 1952), 1:573.

Hodge maintained that the Bible is God's word and therefore cannot conflict with the facts of science, since science deals with God's creation. Yet he conceded that scientific theories have been advanced that were inconsistent with the Bible and therefore had to be discarded sooner or later. He also admitted that the interpretation of the Bible had to be changed more than once to accommodate new scientific insights. For Hodge this did not undercut biblical authority, because whatever was factual on one side had to agree with what was factual on the other side, and vice versa. There was a unity of truth that could require a reinterpretation of Scripture. By and large this was also the reaction of the American public. There was nothing to be afraid of in science, since science meant progress, and that was certainly beneficial and could not be against God's will. Even Darwin's *Origin of Species* could not change this widespread sentiment. Moreover, evolution was not seen so much in biological terms, but in social and economic terms, interpreted in the evolutionary framework of the British philosopher Herbert Spencer.

Evolutionary Theory in a Theistic Gown

Asa Gray, the Theistic Interpreter of Darwin

In March 1860 **Asa Gray** (1810-88),[73] who began his tenure as professor of natural history at Harvard in 1842, published a long and careful review of *The Origin of Species* in the *American Journal of Science and Arts*.[74] Gray, a member of the First Church in Cambridge (Congregational), freely admitted that not everyone would agree with Darwin's ideas. He mentioned, for instance, James Dwight Dana (1813-95), the editor of the *American Journal of Science* and professor of natural history at Yale, who he was sure would not accept Darwin's doctrines (11). He also cited the outstanding Swiss-born American naturalist Louis Agassiz (1807-73), professor of zoology at Harvard beginning in 1848, who connected the phenomenon of origin and distribution of the species directly to the divine will and therefore was not able to accept Darwin's proposal of a "natural" origin and distribution of the species. Although Gray judged Agassiz "to be theistic to excess," he suggested that there "need be no ground of difference here between Darwin and Agassiz" (14). Gray showed that teleolo-

---

73. Cf. for the following Hans Schwarz, "The Significance of Evolutionary Thought for American Protestant Theology," *Zygon* 16 (1981): 262-79.

74. Reprinted in Asa Gray, *Darwiniana: Essays and Reviews Pertaining to Darwinism* (New York: D. Appleton, 1876), 9-61. Page references to this work are placed in the text.

gists such as Agassiz were quite selective. They referred only particular facts to special design but left an overwhelming array of the widest facts inexplicable. This meant that, taking the picture of nature as a whole into consideration, one could only say that it was so because it had so pleased the Creator to construct each plant and animal. Now Darwin proposed a theory that showed how each plant and animal was created, and therefore we could trust that "all was done wisely, in the largest sense designedly, and by an intelligent first cause" (53).

Gray admitted that Darwin's doctrine of "natural" selection could also be denounced as atheistic. Yet he cautioned that such statements should not be made on scientific grounds. Gray reminded us that Newtonian physics was already compatible with an atheistic universe. But he was convinced that "it is far easier to vindicate a theistic character for the derivative theory" (54). In conclusion Gray asserted again that Darwin's book is not a metaphysical treatise: "The work is a scientific one, rigidly restricted to its direct object; and by its science it must stand or fall" (56). Although the first edition of Darwin's book had left the matter unresolved, Gray suggested that Darwin probably had not intended to deny any creative intervention in nature. On the contrary, the idea of natural selection implied so many manifoldly repeated independent acts of creation that the whole process was considered "more mysterious than ever." Before his review went to press, Gray saw the second edition of Darwin's book and noticed "with pleasure the insertion of an additional motto on the reverse of the title page, directly claiming the theistic view which we have vindicated for the doctrine" (61).

In his perceptive review two points gained special emphasis. (1) Darwin's theory of evolution was not a denial of religion but a scientific theory substantiated on scientific grounds and therefore to be refuted only on those grounds. (2) Darwin's theory did not diminish God's creative activity. If interpreted theistically, it even enhanced our understanding of the magnitude of divine creation.

In a series of articles that followed his review, Gray said Darwin's theory of descent, or any other such theory, should not yet be accepted as true and perhaps might never become truth. He insisted, however, that the same care should guide any nonacceptance of such a theory, that is, the claim that there are no secondary causes that account for the existence of the manifoldness of plants and animals. With these assertions Gray did not want to flee into aloof neutrality, but he wanted to make sure scientific truth must rest on unambiguous proofs. This stage he claimed had not yet been attained with an evolutionary theory. But he was certain that the theory of descent would become more and more probable, and if it were ever established, it would be so "on a solid theistic ground" (175).

Gray was convinced that natural science raised no formidable difficulties to Christian theism.[75] But we should not settle for a system of interpreting nature "which may be adjusted to theism, nor even one which finds its most reasonable interpretation in theism, but one which theism only can account for."[76] The latter, he assured, had been found in Darwinism. Of course, he conceded immediately that the opposite hypothesis is possible, namely, that there is no overall design in nature. Yet "the negative hypothesis gives no mental or ethical satisfaction whatever. Like the theory of immediate creation of forms, it explains nothing."[77]

Gray was evidently walking a tightrope here. He did not want to say that Darwin's theory offered a compelling belief in a personal divine being. But he also wanted to assure any possible doubters of Darwin's theory that a theistic interpretation was the only satisfying one. Since the ethical and mental satisfaction with this kind of interpretation evidently does not come from external (natural) evidence, or from authority of Scripture (supernatural evidence), it must rest with the individual. Thus Gray's theistic interpretation of Darwin's theory is a personal predilection though reinforced by the overwhelming consent of other scholars. However, it is not anchored in the necessity of nature or of the human individual (cf. Immanuel Kant) but rests on persuasion. Therefore it is a vulnerable argument if personal preferences change.

John Fiske, the Interpreter of Spencer

John Fiske (1842-1901), a popular lecturer, writer, and assistant librarian at Harvard (1872-79), was an ardent defender of evolutionary thought. As a junior at Harvard he already had the reputation of being a well-equipped Darwinian, and he was reprimanded by Harvard president Cornelius C. Felton (1807-62) for reading the positivist philosopher Auguste Comte (1798-1857) in church.[78] Less than ten years later when Fiske was asked to give a series of lectures entitled "The Positive Philosophy" (1869-70) at the school — a change of presidency and educational goals having taken place in the meantime — it was clear that he had left Comte behind to adopt Spencer as his philosophical mentor. The lectures eventually evolved into a two-volume work, *Outlines of Cosmic Philosophy Based on the Doctrine of Evolution, with Criticisms on the Positive Philosophy*

---

75. Cf. Asa Gray, *Natural Science and Religion: Two Lectures Delivered to The Theological School of Yale College* (New York: Scribner's, 1880), 65.

76. Gray, *Natural Science and Religion*, 91.

77. Gray, *Natural Science and Religion*, 91.

78. For details cf. H. Burnell Pannill, *The Religious Faith of John Fiske* (Durham, N.C.: Duke University Press, 1957), 12.

(1875). He even made a special trip to England to converse with Spencer, Darwin, Huxley, and others before publishing the work.

As with Gray's relationship to Darwin, Fiske was not a blind follower of Spencer. Herbert Spencer (1820-1903), an English philosopher and avid follower and popularizer of Darwin's theory of evolution, developed a cosmic theory of an all-embracing evolutionary process and advanced his thesis of the "survival of the fittest."[79] Spencer claimed that an unknown and unknowable absolute power is continuously at work in the material world and brings forth diversity, coherence, integration, specialization, and individuation. For a young and expanding country such as the United States, it was a matter of course that the biological theory of Darwin became an appendix to the social, economic, and philosophical theory of progress as advanced by Spencer.

While Spencer attempted to provide an interpretation of the cosmos from a purely scientific point of view, relegating all implications of evolution for understanding God to a secondary place, Fiske wanted to show the religious side of the cosmic philosophy as well as the scientific one.[80] In arriving at a cosmic theism that left the anthropomorphic theism behind, he wedded theism much more closely with scientific data than Gray dared do. Fiske declared: "The existence of God — the supreme truth asserted alike by Christianity and by inferior historic religions — is asserted with the equal emphasis by that Cosmic Philosophy which seeks its data in science alone."[81] He gave this assurance: "Though science must destroy mythology, it can never destroy religion; and to the astronomer of the future, as well as to the Psalmist of old, the heavens will declare the glory of God."[82] Fiske's God, however, bears little resemblance to the God encountered in Psalms. This is illustrated by Fiske's statement: "There exists a POWER, to which no limit in time or space is conceivable, of which all phenomena, as presented in consciousness, are manifestations, but which we can know only through these manifestations."[83]

We are not surprised that such disembodied theism would not pass unchallenged by theologians.[84] But it is much more significant that both Spencer

---

79. Cf. Herbert Spencer, *First Principles* (New York: De Witt Revolving Fund, 1958 [1862]), where he forcefully sets forth his notion of evolution.

80. Cf. Pannill, *Religious Faith*, 22-23, esp. n. 68.

81. John Fiske, *Outlines of Cosmic Philosophy Based on the Doctrine of Evolution, with Criticisms on the Positive Philosophy*, 2 vols. (Boston: James R. Osgood, 1875), 2:415.

82. Fiske, *Outlines*, 2:416.

83. Fiske, *Outlines*, 2:415.

84. Cf. the extensive review article by B. P. Bowne, "The Cosmic Philosophy," *Methodist Quarterly Review* 58 (Oct. 1876): 678, where Bowne doubts "if the new doctrine will much advance the interest of either religion or science."

and Darwin, though pleased with Fiske's work, avoided any comments about the religious implications that Fiske had drawn. Darwin, for instance, told him, "I think that I understand nearly the whole — perhaps less clearly about Cosmic Theism and Causation than other parts," and then proceeded to emphasize that he, Darwin, was mainly an inductive and empirical thinker and therefore Spencer's deductions impressed him although they could not convince him.[85]

Like Gray, Fiske did not introduce to the American audience Spencer's philosophy or Darwin's theories but his own theistic interpretation of their work. This was, for instance, totally different from the materialistic interpretation of Darwin's theory by the agnostic Ernst Haeckel when he introduced it to the German audience. Fiske's deep concern and interest come to the fore especially well in a speech at the farewell dinner given to Spencer in New York on November 9, 1882, at the conclusion of his visit to the United States.

In the speech, entitled "Evolution and Religion," Fiske showed that Spencer's services to religion had been no less than those to science.[86] The reason for this was that the doctrine of evolution asserted "that there exists a Power to which no limit in time or space is conceivable, and that all the phenomena of the universe," material and spiritual alike, "are manifestations of this infinite and eternal Power."[87] This power, Fiske claimed, forms the basis of all religions. Yet the doctrine of evolution also has an ethical side. As Spencer had shown, moral beliefs and moral sentiments are products of evolution. Therefore, contrary to anybody today who would question the binding value of morals, Fiske affirmed: "When you say of a moral belief or a moral sentiment that it is a product of evolution, you imply that it is something which the universe through untold ages has been laboring to bring forth, and you ascribe to it a value proportionate to the enormous effort that it has cost to produce it."[88] Fiske shows that the theory of evolution has an intrinsic ethical dimension since right living is intimately connected with the whole doctrine of the development of life on earth. That is to say, what is right tends to enhance the fullness of life and what is wrong tends to diminish it.

---

85. Charles Darwin, "Letter to John Fiske, December 8, 1874," in *The Life and Letters of Charles Darwin, Including an Autobiographical Chapter,* ed. Francis Darwin (New York: D. Appleton, 1896), 2:371.

86. John Fiske, *Excursions of an Evolutionist* (Boston: Houghton, Mifflin & Co., 1884), 294-305. For details of Spencer's enthusiastic reception in the United States, see *Herbert Spencer on the Americans and the Americans on Herbert Spencer,* comp. Edward L. Youmans (1883; reprint, New York: Arno Press, 1973).

87. Fiske, *Excursions of an Evolutionist,* 301.

88. Fiske, *Excursions of an Evolutionist,* 303.

Agassiz and Le Conte, a Cautious Reaction

Louis Agassiz was so deeply influenced by his teacher, the French naturalist Georges L. Cuvier (1769-1832), that he opposed the theory of evolution until his death in 1873.[89] While Agassiz admitted minor modifications within the species, he argued that the animals first called into existence were followed by a succession of creations until the time "when, as the crowning act of the Creator, man was placed on the earth as the head of creation."[90]

It is significant that Agassiz did not oppose evolutionary theory on ideological grounds. He conceded that living beings could be the products or results of laws established by the Almighty or the work of the Creator directly.[91] But he insisted that one must decide on the basis of scientific facts between these two possibilities, the former held by the evolutionists and the latter by himself. According to Agassiz, scientific investigation showed that there had been interruptions in the sequence of living species. The first set of animals had gone on multiplying up to a certain period or level "and then disappeared to make room for another set of animals, and so in their turn each set of newcomers had vanished to give place to others."[92] Since these successions did not occur by one generation making room for another but were promulgated by great disturbances in the natural course of events and extensive changes in the prevailing conditions of the earth, and since there was no indication that the animal world had grown from small and simple beings to its present diversity, Agassiz sided with catastrophism. Huge catastrophes wiped out whole animal populations, which then were replaced by new ones.

His rejection of Darwinism did not occur on theological or religious grounds. He was convinced that divine Providence was compatible with Darwinism. But he repudiated Darwin's theory for strictly scientific reasons. His student **Joseph Le Conte** (1823-1901) attempted to update Agassiz by showing that Agassiz had actually laid the groundwork for the success of the evolutionary theory when he demonstrated the geological successions of different forms of animals and the embryonic recapitulation of these successions.[93]

---

89. For details cf. the informed study by Richard Hofstadter, *Social Darwinism in American Thought*, rev. ed. (New York: George Braziller, 1969), 17-18.

90. Louis Agassiz, *The Structure of Animal Life: Six Lectures* (New York: Charles Scribner, 1866), 6.

91. Cf. Agassiz, *The Structure*, 91.

92. Agassiz, *The Structure*, 91.

93. Joseph Le Conte, *Evolution: Its Nature, Its Evidences, and Its Relation to Religious Thought*, 2nd ed. (New York: Appleton, 1892), 44. Surprisingly Le Conte also claimed that Agassiz rejected evolution since it conflicted with his religious convictions. That his rejection of

While Agassiz was unwilling to accept Darwin's theory, Le Conte was less hesitant. Contrary to Fiske's flamboyant advocacy of evolutionism, Le Conte proceeded more cautiously. He distinguished between organic evolution and human evolution. The former, he taught, arises slowly according to the principle of natural selection (cf. 96-97). Since our spiritual nature would forbid a ruthless struggle for human survival, our only hope for human evolution would be in accord with the Lamarckian idea "that useful changes, determined by education in each generation, are to some extent inherited and accumulated in the race" (98).

For Le Conte the kingdom of God is not something soon to be attained in the evolutionary process, as Fiske made us believe. Evil, we hear, will not soon be eliminated; but it "has its roots in the necessary law of evolution. It is a necessary condition of all progress, and pre-eminently so of moral progress" (373). Evil allows us a choice, and it makes us go forward to acquire virtue. When we hear, however, that "virtue is the *goal of humanity;* virtue cannot be given, it must be *self-acquired*," we wonder whether these deliberations do not imply a similarly self-redemptive moralism as Fiske advocated (372). When we notice further that Le Conte understood God's sovereignty to work strictly within the limits of the laws of nature, we need not be surprised that initially theologians were rather hesitant to accept any evolutionary model of the world, fearing that it would endanger the truth of the Christian faith.[94] But within the learned community evolutionary ideas had become more and more acceptable.

In the early 1860s the *Atlantic Monthly* published expositions by Gray on the Darwinian theory, and it also allowed Agassiz to present the opposite view. Much more on the side of Darwin and Spencer were *Appleton's Journal,* founded in 1867, and the successful *Popular Science Monthly,* started in 1872, which brought the evolutionary theory to more than ten thousand subscribers.[95] Soon college students' interest in English science (i.e., Spencer, Darwin, and Huxley) had replaced that in English literature, and in 1872 an editorial in the *Atlantic Monthly* claimed that natural selection had "quite won the day in Germany and England, and very nearly won it in America."[96] But how did the

---

Darwin's theory was based on religious grounds seems to be a misunderstanding, as I have shown above. The page numbers in the following text refer to Le Conte's *Evolution.*

94. Joseph Le Conte, *Religion and Science: A Series of Sunday School Lectures on the Relation of Natural and Revealed Religion, or the Truths Revealed in Nature and Scripture* (London: Bickers & Son, 1874), 301, where he wrote: "God himself works in Nature only within the limits of law. He cannot do otherwise (I speak it with reverence), He cannot violate law, because law is the expression of his will, and his will is the law of reason."

95. According to Hofstadter, *Social Darwinism,* 22.

96. As quoted in Hofstadter, *Social Darwinism,* 23.

religious community respond to the new evolutionary theories of Spencer and Darwin?

From Fear to Embrace: Protestant Theology and Evolutionary Thought

If we consult Andrew D. White's *History of the Warfare of Science with Theology in Christendom* (1896), we get an impression of "myriad attacks on the Darwinian theory by Protestants and Catholics."[97] Richard Hofstadter conveyed the same idea when he wrote: "The last citadels to be stormed were the churches."[98] Frank Hugh Foster, in his meritorious book *The Modern Movement in American Theology: Sketches in the History of American Protestant Thought from the Civil War to the World War* (1939), was much closer to the truth when he suggested: "In strict accordance with its own principles, the appearance of evolution on the theological stage and the perception of its importance for the philosophy of religion was a very gradual affair."[99] Indeed, there was no Gray among the theologians who immediately introduced Darwin and his theories to them.

Theological periodical literature of the 1860s and 1870s does not offer many outright rejections of evolutionary thought in general. Yet many articles implied that the Darwinian theory of natural selection was founded on a shaky basis. The main argument did not come from theology. Theologians did not conduct a battle between the biblical truth and the knowledge of science. But they developed their opinions by listening to respectable scientists of their time and from their own scientific knowledge. They quite often conceded that if the Darwinian theory should be proven correct, it would not pose any threat to the Christian faith since it could be interpreted theistically.

The Fears of Charles Hodge

The most significant and influential attack on evolutionary thought came from Charles Hodge, who published his three-volume *Systematic Theology* in 1871. In 1874 he issued *What Is Darwinism?* in which he sought to demolish the Darwinian heresy. According to Hodge, Darwin's "grand conclusion is 'man (body, soul

97. Andrew D. White, *A History of the Warfare of Science with Theology in Christendom*, 2 vols. (New York: D. Appleton & Co., 1896), 1:78.

98. Hofstadter, *Social Darwinism*, 24.

99. Frank Hugh Foster, *The Modern Movement in American Theology: Sketches in the History of American Protestant Thought from the Civil War to the World War* (New York: Revell, 1939), 38.

and spirit) is descended from a hairy quadruped, furnished with a tail and pointed ears, probably arboreal in its habits, and an inhabitant of the Old World.'"[100] Yet Darwin did not say anything about the human soul, contrary to what Hodge implied. Darwin also would have rejected Hodge's suggestion: "In using the expression Natural Selection, Mr. Darwin intends to exclude design, or final causes" (41).

Though enjoying a certain degree of overkill in his argument, Hodge did not want to be unfair to Darwin. He conceded that Darwin explicitly and repeatedly admitted the existence of a creator. But then he chided him for not saying anything about the nature of the creator or of his relation to the world (27). With reference to complicated organs of plants and animals, Hodge asked: "Why doesn't he say, they are the product of the divine intelligence? If God made them, it makes no difference, so far as the question of design is concerned, how He made them: whether at once or by a process of evolution. But instead of referring to the purpose of God, he laboriously endeavors to prove that they may be accounted for without any design or purpose whatever" (58).

Like Agassiz, Hodge admitted that God could have made the living beings at once or gradually through the process of evolution. But unlike Agassiz, he did not fault Darwin for advocating evolution. What he rejected was the notion that evolution was explained in natural terms instead of supernatural ones. By explaining the evolutionary process in natural terms and by natural causes, Hodge implied that Darwin had effectively banished God from the world. It is important to note that Hodge distinguished here between "Darwinism," meaning the explanation of the development of the world without reference to God, and "evolution," the evolvement of the world through God's design (104). He realized that one could affirm evolution without admitting Darwinism.

The reason for Hodge's uneasiness with Darwinism is evident. "God, says Darwin, created the unintelligent living cell . . . after that first step all else follows by natural law, without purpose and without design."[101] To remove design from nature is therefore the dethronement of God the creator. Thus Hodge reached this verdict: "The conclusion of the whole matter is, that the denial of design in nature is virtually the denial of God. Mr. Darwin's theory does deny all design in nature; therefore his theory is virtually atheistic; his theory, not he himself. He believes in a Creator."[102] Hodge's evaluation of Darwin culminated in the paradox: "A man, it seems, may believe in God, and yet teach atheism."[103]

100. Charles Hodge, *What Is Darwinism?* (New York: Scribner, Armstrong & Co., 1874), 39-40. Page numbers in the following text refer to this work.
101. Charles Hodge, *Systematic Theology,* 3 vols. (New York: Charles Scribner, 1871), 2:15.
102. Hodge, *Systematic Theology* (1871), 2:173. Cf. Hodge, *What Is Darwinism?* 148.
103. Hodge, *Systematic Theology* (1871), 2:19.

If it really proved true, as Darwin had declared, that random variations were the cause of evolutionary change, then this had nothing to do with design. At the most, God played dice with his creation. We should remember that even Albert Einstein (1879-1955), who certainly was not theologically as conservative as Hodge, rejected spontaneity in nature and therefore had grave reservations about the Copenhagen interpretation of quantum mechanics. There must be a plan discernible in nature even for those who are not theists. If there were only random variations, then we could hardly speak of a creator who had designed the universe and everything that was within it.[104] Here Hodge's son and successor was wiser when A. A. Hodge no longer looked primarily at the random variations, but put more emphasis on the general course that evolution took and saw there "a providential unfolding of a general plan."[105] This meant for him that even the Darwinian theory, if one considered the overall concept, could be considered in theistic terms.

Yet it was not simply as defender of the argument of design that made Charles Hodge react so vehemently against Darwinism. When we see the authors he referred to in *What Is Darwinism?* then we get a further clue. He mentioned the British naturalist Russel Wallace (1823-1913), who together with Darwin proposed the theory of the origin of species by natural selection. Then he refers to Huxley, Büchner, Vogt, Haeckel, and Strauss. For instance, he quoted Haeckel as saying that Darwin's theory of evolution led inevitably to atheism and materialism.[106] Since Hodge was familiar with the Continental discussion about Darwin and the antireligious propaganda by people such as Vogt, Büchner, Haeckel, and Strauss, he was afraid that the same might happen in the United States.

But his fears were unfounded for two reasons. (1) The evolutionary ideas that came to America were not so much those of Darwin as those of Spencer. Darwin never visited the United States as Spencer had done. (On his 1882 visit, Spencer was celebrated and treated like royalty.) (2) Neither Darwin's nor Spencer's theories were simply received in the United States without adaptation. As Hodge perceptively noted, Darwin's most fervent advocate in America, Asa Gray, though an avowed evolutionist, was not a Darwinian. He interpreted Darwin's theory theistically.[107] The same happened with Spencer's philosophy

---

104. Cf. David N. Livingstone, *Darwin's Forgotten Defenders: The Encounter between Evangelical Theology and Evolutionary Thought* (Grand Rapids: Eerdmans, 1987), 102, who states that while Hodge followed "the Scottish tradition in placing very definite limits on his adoption of natural theology, he remained convinced that the teleological argument was sufficient to establish the existence of God as an intelligent voluntary agent."

105. So Livingstone, *Darwin's Forgotten Defenders*, 114.

106. Hodge, *What Is Darwinism?* 95.

107. Hodge, *What Is Darwinism?* 174-75.

through the writings of Fiske. The United States was founded by people who had a religious vision, and the materialists and atheists there had no chance of turning evolutionary theory into an instrument that would advance their cause.

There was still another reason for the theistic reception of evolutionary thought in the United States. Most institutions of higher learning that would provide the platform for an intellectual exchange concerning evolution were church operated, or at least in some way affiliated with the church. In England and especially on the Continent, however, they were mostly state owned and thus provided a more liberal intellectual environment unrestrained by ecclesiastical guidance.

In May 1874 Gray published an extensive review of *What Is Darwinism?* declaring that one should not blame a naturalist for leaving the problems of purpose and design to the philosopher and theologian.[108] Purpose on the whole, Gray asserted, was not denied but implied by Darwin. Gray was right when he surmised that Hodge's treatise "will not contribute much to the reconcilement of science and religion."[109] As a result of Hodge's pamphlet many people who had never read a line of Darwin became convinced that Darwin was the great enemy of the Christian faith. But by now the great opponent of evolution, Agassiz, had died (1873). In the 1874 edition of his *Manual of Geology,* James D. Dana, professor of natural history and geology at Yale and the leading figure among American geologists, endorsed the concept of natural selection, and George F. Wright (1838-1921) of Andover helped Gray publish his *Darwiniana* (1876).

From Hesitancy to Enthusiasm: J. William Dawson, James McCosh, Henry Ward Beecher, and Lyman Abbott

That even conservatives had become amenable to evolution can be seen in the geologist **J. William Dawson** (1820-99), president of McGill University and president of both the American and the British Association for the Advancement of Science. He had once supported Hodge, and in 1890 stated in his book *Modern Ideas of Evolution as Related to Revelation and Science* that the current Darwinian and neo-Lamarckian forms of evolution "fall certainly short of what even the agnostic may desiderate as religion."[110] Yet he observed: "Creation was not an instantaneous process, but extended through periods of vast duration.

---

108. *Nation,* May 28, 1974, reprinted in Gray, *Darwiniana,* 266-82.

109. Gray, *Darwiniana,* 279.

110. J. William Dawson, *Modern Ideas of Evolution as Related to Revelation and Science* (New York: Fleming H. Revell, 1890), 226.

In every stage we may rest assured that God, like a wise builder, used every previous course as support for the next; that He built each succeeding story of the wonderful edifice on that previously prepared for it; and that His plan developed itself as His work proceeded."[111] Evolution was not objectionable as long as it was not Darwinian, that is, proceeding with blind force and blind chance, or Lamarckian, proceeding from the impact of the environment.

Even before Dawson, **James McCosh** (1811-94), a philosopher-theologian and president of Princeton College, had accepted evolutionary thought in Hodge's own backyard. McCosh was critical of Darwin's theory, especially of his attempt to attribute the whole evolutionary process to natural selection. He also doubted that humanity should be as closely associated with the animal kingdom as Darwin had claimed. But then he confessed: "There are clear indications, in the geological ages, of the progression from the inanimate up to the animate and from the lower animate to the higher. The mind, ever impelled to seek for causes, asks how all this is produced. The answer, if an answer can be had, is to be given by science, and not by religion; which simply insists that we trace all things up to God, whether acting by immediate or by mediate agency."[112]

Here a leading figure of American Presbyterianism declared his acceptance of the Darwinian theory. Yet he was not simply going with the times. As McCosh acknowledged, it had become known "that Darwin was a most careful observer, that there was great truth in the theory, and that there was nothing atheistic in it if properly understood."[113] But McCosh was also compelled by an evident pastoral concern:

> I have all along had a sensitive apprehension that the undiscriminating denunciation of evolution from so many pulpits, periodicals, and seminaries might drive some of our thoughtful young men to infidelity, as they clearly saw development everywhere in nature, and were at the same time told by their advisers that they could not believe in evolution and yet be Christians. I am gratified beyond measure to find that I am thanked by my pupils, some of whom have reached the highest position as naturalists, because in showing them evolution in the works of God, I showed them that this was not inconsistent with religion, and thus enabled them to follow science and yet retain their faith in the Bible.[114]

111. Dawson, *Modern Ideas*, 230.

112. James McCosh, *Christianity and Positivism: A Series of Lectures to the Times on Natural Theology and Apologetics* (New York: Robert Carter, 1871), 63.

113. James McCosh, *The Religious Aspect of Evolution* (New York: Charles Scribner, 1890), vii.

114. McCosh, *The Religious Aspect*, ix-x.

When George Wright's review article argued that Darwinism was the Calvinistic interpretation of nature since it was antisentimental, realistic, and to some extent fatalistic, this was a sign that evolutionary thought had become respectable.[115]

This became even more obvious when the most prominent preacher of that time, **Henry Ward Beecher** (1813-87), finally came out in favor of evolution. In *Evolution and Religion* Beecher declared that "the theory of evolution is the *working* theory of every department of physical science all over the world."[116] He claimed that it was taught in all schools of higher education and the children were receiving it, since it was fundamental to astronomy, botany, and chemistry, to name just a few academic subjects. But Beecher insisted that evolution was "substantially held by men of profound Christian faith," and although theology would have to reconstruct its system, evolution would "take nothing away from the grounds of true religion."[117]

The reason for Beecher's confidence regarding evolution was his belief in two kinds of revelation: "God's thought in the evolution of matter" (nature) and "God's thought in the evolution of mind" (reason and religion).[118] Our task is to unite and to harmonize them, and then we will notice that the interpretation of evolution "will obliterate the distinction between natural and revealed religion, both of which are the testimony of God."[119] Beecher was convinced that there could be no disharmony between the God who was active in nature and the God disclosing himself in Scripture. But he even went one step further, a step that eventually caused protest from the conservative side, asserting that God disclosed himself as much in nature as in religion. Thus natural religion was revealed religion.

Under Beecher's influence **Lyman Abbott** (1835-1922), Beecher's successor at Plymouth Church (Congregational), joined the ranks of theistic evolutionists and contributed much through his sermons and journalistic efforts to the idea that Darwinism was acceptable to Protestant thought.[120] In his *Reminiscences* (1915) Abbott confessed that he studied Spencer in 1866

---

115. Wright, "Recent Works Bearing on the Relation of Science to Religion. No. V: Some Analogies between Calvinism and Darwinism," *Bibliotheca Sacra* 37 (1880): 76.

116. Henry Ward Beecher, *Evolution and Religion* (New York: Fords, Howard & Hulbert, 1885), as reprinted in part in Gail Kennedy, ed., *Evolution and Religion: The Conflict between Science and Theology in Modern America* (Boston: D. C. Heath, 1967), 18.

117. Beecher, *Evolution and Religion*, 19.

118. Beecher, *Evolution and Religion*, 15.

119. Beecher, *Evolution and Religion*, 20.

120. Ira V. Brown, in his interesting study, *Lyman Abbott, Christian Evolutionist: A Study in Religious Liberalism* (Cambridge: Harvard University Press, 1953), 141.

but not Darwin or Huxley, since he was not much interested in science.[121] In *The Theology of an Evolutionist* (1897), however, he called himself "a radical evolutionist" or "a theistic evolutionist."[122] We are immediately assured that he reverently and heartily accepts "the axiom of theology that a personal God is the foundation of all life" but that he also believes that "God has but one way of doing things; that His way may be described in one word as the way of growth, or development, or evolution, terms which are substantially synonymous."[123]

While Abbott noticed that all biologists were evolutionists, he also observed that not all were Darwinians, that is, not all regarded the struggle for existence and survival of the fittest as adequate statements of the process of evolution.[124] He understood evolution as the history of a process, and not an explanation adduced by giving causes. Therefore he accepted Fiske's aphorism: "Evolution is God's way of doing things."[125]

By the 1890s evolution had become a universal system and was also applied to the Bible. Here of course, the big problem was how to reconcile the story of the fall with the descent, or rather ascent, of humanity. Abbott discovered that, apart from Genesis 3, the story of the fall played no role in the Old Testament. Even in the New Testament there is no mention of it, except when Paul talks of the struggle between flesh and spirit. Abbott found that Paul's description of this struggle was effectively interpreted by "the evolutionary doctrine that man is gradually emerging from an animal nature into a spiritual manhood."[126] Abbott understood Paul to say that sin "enters every human life, and the individual 'falls' when the animal nature predominates over the spiritual."[127] Incarnation is then interpreted as the perfect dwelling of God in a perfect human being. For Abbott, Christ lived and suffered "not to relieve men from future torment, but to purify and perfect them in God's likeness by uniting them with God."[128] Since Christ did not appease God's wrath, he simply laid down his life in love that others might receive life.

As was Beecher, Abbott was convinced that God, dwelling in the world, spoke through all its phenomena. Suddenly evolution not only had become ac-

---

121. Lyman Abbott, *Reminiscences* (Boston: Houghton Mifflin, 1915), 285.
122. Lyman Abbott, *The Theology of an Evolutionist* (Boston: Houghton Mifflin, 1897), 9.
123. Abbott, *Theology of an Evolutionist,* 9.
124. Abbott, *Theology of an Evolutionist,* 6-7, 19.
125. Abbott, *Reminiscences,* 460, and many other places.
126. Abbott, *Reminiscences,* 459.
127. Abbott, *Theology of an Evolutionist,* 186.
128. Abbott, *Theology of an Evolutionist,* 190.

ceptable to Christian faith but also had become the tool with which to interpret the Christian faith and religion in general.[129]

Discerning the Mixed Blessing of Darwinism: William Graham Sumner, William James, and the Scopes Trial

With relative ease Darwinism became accepted in America in a thoroughly theistic fashion. This was different from the bitter struggle over Darwin between the freethinkers and conservatives in Germany that carried well into the twentieth century. But actually it was not Darwin and his theory of natural selection that became accepted, but Spencer and his cosmic theory of an all-encompassing evolutionary process and of the survival of the fittest. For a young and expanding country like the United States, it was only fitting that the biological theory of Darwin became an appendix to the social, economic, and philosophical theory of Spencer.

The social Darwinism, or rather Spencerianism, of **William Graham Sumner** (1840-1910), professor of political and social science at Yale, and of the industrialists John D. Rockefeller (1839-1937) and Andrew Carnegie (1835-1919), is still active today when those on welfare are classified as lazy; or when, regardless of calls for hidden or overt government support, free enterprise is advocated as the best economic system; or when competition is believed to supply us indefinitely with oil and natural gas. According to its own principles, this kind of Darwinism will have to modify itself through pressure either from outside or from within; or if it does not change, it will be modified through the collapse of the socioeconomic system. But this Darwinism, widely advocated by the so-called political conservatives, did not make much stir in theology. It has therefore been widely neglected by theologians since theology, being usually exercised by members of the socioeconomic establishment or the "fittest," benefits from it.

There is also a liberal Darwinism, which is perhaps even causally related to the first kind. This optimistic evolutionism considers development and evolution as God's way of doing things. As the philosopher **William James** (1842-1910) perceptively noted, "the idea of a universal evolution lends itself to a doctrine of general meliorism and progress which fits the religious needs of the healthy-minded so well."[130]

---

129. Cf. Washington Gladden, *Who Wrote the Bible? A Book for the People* (Boston: Houghton Mifflin, 1891), in which he attempted to demonstrate that the Bible had a "natural history" as well as a supernatural one.

130. William James, *The Varieties of Religious Experience: A Study in Human Nature* (New

It is interesting that James, who first studied and then taught together with Fiske at Harvard, discovered the shortcomings of this new optimistic religion of nature, in which form Darwinism was introduced by Fiske, Beecher, and Abbott. James criticized it for its attempt to explain evil away instead of seeing it as an intrinsic part of existence. He correctly stated: "The method of averting one's attention from evil, and living simply in the light of the good is splendid as long as it will work."[131] And it did work as long as America was expanding and was still unaware of its boundaries and limitations. But with World War I and the Great Depression, things appeared in a different light.

Then many people discovered, as James did in 1902, that Christianity was not synonymous with the gospel of the essential goodness of humanity and of eternal Darwinian (better: Spencerian) progress. They remembered that Christianity was essentially a religion of deliverance, that we were called to die before we could be born again into real life.[132] People felt betrayed by the unjustified evolutionary optimism, and some demanded that evolutionary theories be outlawed altogether.

The course of events might have been considerably different if evolutionary thought had not made its strongest impact on the American mind through Spencer and his interpreter Fiske, who declared that evolution was God's way of doing things. If it would have been through Darwin and his interpreter Gray, who confessed himself to be "a Darwinian, philosophically a convinced theist, and religiously an acceptor of the 'creed commonly called the Nicene,' as the exponent of the Christian faith," both social Darwinism and the conservative backlash might have been avoided.[133]

The End of the Gilded Age. We must remember how Darwin was received in America if we want to assess properly the lasting impact of his ideas. Darwin's evolutionary theory was introduced in America in a decidedly theistic framework. This initially mitigated against the possible clash with the tenets of the Christian faith concerning creation and providence. The vast majority of American Protestant theologians initially saw nothing in Darwin's theory that was irreconcilable with the Christian faith, provided the theory was scientifically acceptable and was clad in a theistic framework that maintained a personal God who created and sustained the world. In the wake of the expansion

---

York: Collier Books, 1961), 88. Cf. also Edward A. White's penetrating study, *Science and Religion in American Thought: The Impact of Naturalism* (Stanford, Calif.: Stanford University Press, 1952), 4-8, where White emphasizes the influence of William James and Reinhold Niebuhr in the rediscovery of the true significance of the Christian faith against optimistic evolutionism.

131. James, *Varieties*, 140.

132. Cf. James, *Varieties*, 141.

133. Gray, preface to *Darwiniana*, vi.

of the new American continent, Darwin's theory was seen as part of Spencer's comprehensive evolutionary theory, which also included socioeconomic aspects. After its initial overwhelming success, this idealistic and speculative system clashed with the reality of radical evil and injustice exhibited in history and society. Failing to distinguish between Spencer and Darwin, more conservative theological minds began to react against evolutionary theory in general; and some wanted to ban it from the earth altogether.

The Social Gospel movement at the turn of the century still accepted evolutionary categories in its attempt to address the social injustices that accompanied the phenomenal expansion of America by emphasizing the social dimension of sin. This is evident in remarks by Walter Rauschenbusch, who wrote: "Jesus was not a pessimist. Since God was love, this world was to him fundamentally good. He realized not only evil but the Kingdom of Evil; but he launched the Kingdom of God against it, and staked his life on its triumph. His faith in God and in the Kingdom of God constituted him a religious optimist."[134] For Rauschenbusch, Jesus took his illustrations from organic life to express the idea of the gradual growth of the kingdom. He was shaking off catastrophic ideas and substituting developmental ideas.[135] The evolutionary, forward-reaching, and upward-moving process was central to the ideas of social betterment espoused by the Social Gospel. Yet Rauschenbusch also recognized that World War I "has deeply affected the religious assurance of our own time, and will lessen it still more when the excitement is over and the aftermath of innocent suffering becomes clear."[136] Although the progressive drive was deeply entrenched in the American spirit, there were ominous signs that affairs might not continue as usual. World War I had been a relatively short episode for America, since America entered it only at the tail end. But the many thousands of European immigrants pouring into America as a result of the war showed that the victory gained left many problems unsolved.

The Conservative Backlash. In America, conservative movements picked up significant momentum in the first decades of the twentieth century. For instance, the temperance movement of the nineteenth century, interrupted by the internal strife of the Civil War, gained amazing popularity and finally led to prohibition starting in January 1920. This was celebrated by evangelicals as a major victory against social evils such as poverty and the corruption of morals. A few years earlier the publication of a series of small volumes of essays entitled

---

134. Walter Rauschenbusch, *A Theology for the Social Gospel* (1917; reprint, New York: Abingdon, 1945), 156.

135. Rauschenbusch, *A Theology,* 220.

136. Rauschenbusch, *A Theology,* 181.

The Fundamentals (1910-15) had meant another breakthrough for the conservative cause. Against the ever-growing influence of continental European theologians such as Albrecht Ritschl, Martin Rade, and Adolf von Harnack, an influential group of British, American, and Canadian writers presented the conservative stand. In this somewhat uneven series, conservative but scholarly contributions were mingled with dispensationalist articles. These contained extensive reference to evolution and included one contribution with the characteristic title "The Decadence of Darwinism." Publication of *The Fundamentals* was financed by two wealthy laypeople, and eventually three million copies were distributed to pastors, evangelists, missionaries, theology students, and active laypeople throughout the English-speaking world. The five fundamentals testified to in these volumes were the inerrancy of the Bible, the virgin birth, the atonement, the resurrection, and the second coming of Christ. While *The Fundamentals* could not stop the liberal trend by rallying the conservative forces, it widened the gulf between the two.

The fundamentalists' determination to stamp out, wherever possible, teachings that appeared to contradict Scripture was sooner or later prone to lead to a clash with the theory of evolution. This clash was even more likely since not everyone was preoccupied with progress. Large numbers of people outside metropolitan centers and places of learning were virtually unaffected in their beliefs and habits by the intellectual and cultural climate of the day. They lived in essentially the same way, in the same world, and with the same beliefs as their pioneer ancestors had. Their conservative mood needed only to be rallied around a common cause, and they could form a respectable force in society.

One such rallying point proved to be the teaching of evolution in public schools. Between 1920 and 1930 some thirty-seven antievolution bills were introduced in twenty state legislatures and passed in several states such as Tennessee, Mississippi, and Arkansas. For instance, in Tennessee, fundamentalist groups had become powerful enough to pressure the state legislature in 1925 to adopt legislation making it unlawful to "teach any theory that denies the story of divine creation of man as taught in the Bible."[137]

The antievolution issue came to a climax when, in the summer of the same year, the high school teacher John Scopes of Dayton, Tennessee, was put on trial for violating the recently passed statute prohibiting the teaching of evolution in tax-supported schools. The trial gained lasting fame since two prominent people took sides in it. On the side of the law was William Jennings Bryan (1860-1925), three-time presidential hopeful and ardent champion of the fun-

---

137. According to Clifton E. Olmstead, *History of Religion in the United States* (Englewood Cliffs, N.J.: Prentice-Hall, 1960), 549.

damentalist cause; and on the side of the accused, Clarence Darrow (1857-1938), famous criminal lawyer and militant agnostic who ridiculed biblical literalism sharply. The trial aroused not merely national but international interest, and was accompanied by an immense amount of publicity. Although Scopes's conviction in the lower court was overturned by the Supreme Court of Tennessee on grounds that the fine had been improperly imposed, the effect of the publicity on the general public was to discredit fundamentalism. As time passed, fewer and fewer thoughtful people took seriously the categoric rejection of evolution by fundamentalists; and this extreme stance has virtually passed from the American scene.[138]

There is still a vocal minority of people today, usually called creationists, who advocate the teaching of the first chapters of Genesis as an alternative to the teaching of evolution in public schools. The very fact that they advocate creation as an alternative to evolution indicates that they assume the biblical creation stories and the theory of evolution actually cover the same ground. This means that they have not really discerned the difference between the scientific or physical level of reality and the spiritual or metaphysical one. (How difficult it has been for the Roman Catholic Church to accept an evolutionary concept of life can be seen with Pierre Teilhard de Chardin [cf. chap. 13], whose lifework of achieving a synthesis between Christian faith and the theory of an all-embracing evolution was vindicated only at the Second Vatican Council.)

For Further Reading

Ludwig Büchner (1824-99)

Büchner, Ludwig. *Force and Matter: Empirico-philosophical Studies, Intelligibly Rendered.* From the 10th German edition. London: Trübner, 1870.
———. *Man in the Past, Present and Future. A Popular Account of the Results of Recent Scientific Research as Regards to the Origin, Position and Prospects of the Human Race.* Translated by W. S. Dallas. London: Asher, 1872.
Janet, Paul. *The Materialism of the Present Day. A Critique of Dr. Büchner's System.* Translated by Gustave Masson. London: Williams and Norgate, 1867.

Ludwig Feuerbach

See chapter 2.

David Friedrich Strauss

See chapter 2.

138. There are occasional backlashes, however. In August 1999 a Kansas school board decided to eliminate evolution entirely from the curriculum. But these are clear exceptions.

Ernst Haeckel (1834-1919)

Bölsche, Wilhelm. *Haeckel, His Life and Work*. Translated by Joseph McCabe. London: T. F. Unwin, 1906.

Gasman, Daniel. *The Scientific Origins of National Socialism: Social Darwinism in Ernst Haeckel and the German Monist League*. New York: American Elsevier Publishing, 1971.

Haeckel, Ernst. *The History of Creation: On the Development of the Earth and Its Inhabitants by the Action of Natural Causes*. Translated by E. R. Lankester. 2 vols. New York: D. Appleton, 1876.

————. *Monism as Connecting Religion and Science: The Confession of Faith of a Man of Science*. Translated by J. Gilchrist. London: Adam and Charles Black, 1894.

————. *The Riddle of the Universe at the Close of the Nineteenth Century*. Translated by J. McCabe. New York: Harper, 1900.

Moore, James R., ed. *History, Humanity, and Evolution: Essays for John C. Greene*. New York: Cambridge University Press, 1989.

Christoph Ernst Luthardt (1823-1902)

Luthardt, Christoph Ernst. *Apologetic Lectures on the Moral Truths of Christianity*. Translated by Sophia Taylor. Edinburgh: T. & T. Clark, 1876.

————. *Apologetic Lectures on the Saving Truth of Christianity. Delivered in Leipsic in the Winter of 1866*. Translated from the 3rd German edition by Sophia Taylor. Edinburgh: T. & T. Clark, 1872.

Weidner, Revere Franklin. *An Introduction of Dogmatic Theology Based on Luthardt*. New York: Fleming H. Revell, 1895.

Otto Zöckler (1833-1906)

Schultze, Victor. "Zöckler, Otto." In *The New Schaff-Herzog Encyclopedia of Religious Knowledge*, 12:520. Grand Rapids: Baker, 1949-50.

Charles Darwin (1809-82)

Hodge, Jonathan, and Gregory Radick, eds. *The Cambridge Companion to Darwin*. Cambridge: Cambridge University Press, 2003.

Hunter, Cornelius. *Darwin's God: Evolution and the Problem of Evil*. Grand Rapids: Baker, 2001.

Ong, Walter. *Darwin's Vision and Christian Perspectives*. New York: Macmillan, 1960.

Asa Gray (1810-88)

Fry, George. *Congregationalists and Evolution: Asa Gray and Louis Agassiz*. Lanham, Md.: University Press of America, 1989.

Gray, Asa. *Darwiniana: Essays and Reviews Pertaining to Darwinism*. New York: D. Appleton, 1878.

————. *Natural Science and Religion: Two Lectures Delivered to The Theological School of Yale College*. New York: Scribner's, 1880.

————. *Scientific Papers of Asa Gray*. Selected by Charles Sprague Sargent. 2 vols. New York: Kraus, 1969 [1889].

John Fiske (1842-1901)

Clark, John. *The Life and Letters of John Fiske*. Boston: Houghton Mifflin, 1917.
Fiske, John. *A Century of Science and Other Essays*. Boston: Houghton Mifflin, 1899.
————. *Excursions of an Evolutionist*. Boston: Houghton Mifflin, 1884.
————. *Outlines of Cosmic Philosophy Based on the Doctrine of Evolution, with Criticisms on the Positive Philosophy*. 2 vols. Boston: James R. Osgood, 1875.
Pannill, H. Burnell. *The Religious Faith of John Fiske*. Durham, N.C.: Duke University Press, 1957.

Louis Agassiz (1807-73)

Agassiz, Louis. *The Structure of Animal Life: Six Lectures*. New York: Charles Scribner, 1866.
Clark, David W. "Agassiz: Chrysostom of Science." *Methodist Review* 106 (Nov. 1923): 899-903.
Croce, Paul J. "Probabilistic Darwinism: Louis Agassiz vs Asa Gray on Science, Religion, and Certainty." *Journal of Religious History* 22 (Fall 1998): 35-58.
Fry, George. *Congregationalists and Evolution: Asa Gray and Louis Agassiz*. Lanham, Md.: University Press of America, 1989.

Joseph Le Conte (1823-1901)

Le Conte, Joseph. *Evolution: Its Nature, Its Evidences, and Its Relation to Religious Thought*. 2nd ed. New York: D. Appleton, 1892.
————. *Religion and Science: A Series of Sunday School Lectures on the Relation of Natural and Revealed Religion, or the Truths Revealed in Nature and Scripture*. London: Bickers & Son, 1874.

Charles Hodge (1797-1878)

Hodge, Charles. *What Is Darwinism?* New York: Scribner, Armstrong & Co., 1874.
Livingstone, David N. *Darwin's Forgotten Defenders: The Encounter between Evangelical Theology and Evolutionary Thought*. Grand Rapids: Eerdmans, 1987.
See also chapter 3.

J. William Dawson (1820-99)

Dawson, John William. *Eden Lost and Won: Studies of the Early History and Final Destiny of Man as Taught in Nature and Revelation*. New York: F. H. Revell, 1896.
————. *Facts and Fancies in Modern Science*. Philadelphia: American Baptist Publication Society, 1882.
————. *Modern Ideas of Evolution as Related to Revelation and Science*. New York: Fleming H. Revell, 1890.
O'Brien, Charles. *Sir William Dawson: A Life in Science and Religion*. Philadelphia: American Philosophical Society, 1971.

James McCosh (1811-94)

Hoeveler, J. David. *James McCosh and the Scottish Intellectual Tradition: From Glasgow to Princeton.* Princeton: Princeton University Press, 1981.

McCosh, James. *Christianity and Positivism: A Series of Lectures to the Times on Natural Theology and Apologetics.* Des Moines: LBS Archival Products, 1990 [1871].

———. *The Life of James McCosh; a Record Chiefly Autobiographical.* New York: Scribner, 1896.

———. *The Religious Aspect of Evolution.* New York: Charles Scribner, 1890.

Henry Ward Beecher (1813-87)

Abbott, Lymon. *Henry Ward Beecher: A Sketch of His Career.* Hartford: American Publishing Company, 1887.

Beecher, William Constantine. *A Biography of Rev. Henry Ward Beecher.* New York: C. L. Webster & Company, 1888.

Clark, Clifford. *Henry Ward Beecher: Spokesman for a Middle-Class America.* Urbana: University of Illinois Press, 1978.

Kennedy, Gail, ed. *Evolution and Religion: The Conflict between Science and Theology in Modern America.* Boston: D. C. Heath, 1967.

Lyman Abbott (1835-1922)

Abbott, Lyman. *Reminiscences.* Boston: Houghton Mifflin, 1915.

———. *The Theology of an Evolutionist.* Boston: Houghton Mifflin, 1897.

Brown, Ira. *Lyman Abbott, Christian Evolutionist: A Study in Religious Liberalism.* Cambridge: Harvard University Press, 1953.

William Graham Sumner (1840-1910)

Healy, Mary Edward. *Society and Social Change in the Writings of St. Thomas, Ward, Sumner, and Cooley.* Westport, Conn.: Greenwood, 1972 [1948].

Sumner, William Graham. *Social Darwinism: Selected Essays.* Introduction by Stow Persons. Englewood Cliffs, N.J.: Prentice-Hall, 1963.

Sumner, William Graham, et al. *The Science of Society.* New Haven: Yale University Press, 1927.

William James (1842-1910)

Gale, Richard. *The Divided Self of William James.* Cambridge: Cambridge University Press, 1999.

James, William. *The Varieties of Religious Experience: A Study in Human Nature.* New York: Collier Books, 1961.

Myers, Gerald. *William James: His Life and Thought.* New Haven: Yale University Press, 1986.

Perry, Ralph Barton. *The Thought and Character of William James.* 2 vols. Boston: Little, Brown, 1935.

8 The Challenge of Religion

The romantic movement of the nineteenth century led to a renewed interest in religion in general, as can be seen in Schleiermacher's *Speeches* and also in the rediscovery of the treasures of antiquity. Both sometimes went together, as we notice in representatives of romanticism such as Coleridge in Great Britain and the brothers August Wilhelm von Schlegel (1767-1845) and Karl Wilhelm Friedrich von Schlegel (1772-1829) in Germany. We remember that Friedrich even prodded Schleiermacher to write his *Speeches,* and also suggested they do a joint translation into German of Plato's *Dialogues,* something Schleiermacher then did on his own. Yet sometimes the appreciation of religion and that of antiquity turned against each other, especially when one religion was extolled above all others regarding claims of superiority and priority. This can best be seen in the so-called Babel-Bible Controversy in Germany. Here the usually unquestioned claim of the Christian religion to be the only or at least primary avenue of salvation was severely challenged on grounds of chronological and cultural inferiority. The context of the world's religions, whether those of antiquity or of the contemporary age, challenged theologians to reevaluate and assert their claims within the context of other religions. Furthermore, such contextualization has led to a discovery of common concepts and concerns and also to a more nuanced theological reflection. This concern even extends into the present, as we will see with John Hick and Paul Knitter, among others (cf. chap. 15).

The Babel-Bible Controversy: Friedrich Delitzsch

Friedrich Delitzsch (1850-1922), son of the conservative Old Testament professor Franz Julius Delitzsch (1813-90), taught at Leipzig and Breslau, and in 1899 followed a call to Berlin as professor of Assyriology. There he presented in 1902 a public lecture entitled "Babel und Bibel" (Babel and Bible). This presentation was published the same year, and in 1903 and 1905 supplemented by two further publications. These papers caused an immense controversy. Up to that point the faith of ancient Israel was considered an ancient religion supported by equally ancient documents. Delitzsch, however, flatly rejected this position: "Now that the pyramids have opened their depths and the Assyrian palaces their portals, the people of Israel, with its literature, appears as the youngest member only of a venerable and hoary group of nations."[1] The point of contention was not one of historical analogies between the Israelite faith and the Babylonian religion, since analogies can always be enlightening, but the conclusions that Delitzsch drew from them. Since Babylonia's culture is much older than Israel's, he contended that everything that is religiously, morally, and culturally significant in the Old Testament must stem from that older religion. He went so far as to reject the claim that the ethical monotheism of Israel was superior to Babylonia, making the claim that the kings of Judah and Israel were ineradicably polytheistic.[2] Even to talk about a high ethical level in Israel in the preexilic period is unwarranted. While Delitzsch admitted that the Assyro-Babylonians were cruel and barbarous, "so was the conquest of Canaan by the Hebrew tribes accompanied by a torrent of innocent blood." Since the God of Israel appears in Deuteronomy immensely cruel and the exclusively national monotheism of Israel is quite narrow, one can hardly regard the Hebrew Scriptures as inspired. Nevertheless, Delitzsch conceded that the early Hebrew Scriptures will "always maintain their great importance, especially as a unique monument of the great religio-historical process which continues even into our own times."[3]

Delitzsch discarded the notion of revelation and instead talked about a historical process of which we are to be proud. He exhorted listeners to "search the ancient Babylonian world and see the leading spirits of Babylon endeavoring with earnest zeal, even with fear and trembling to seek God and the truth."[4]

---

1. Friedrich Delitzsch, *Babel and Bible: Three Lectures on the Significance of Assyriological Research for Religion Embodying the Most Important Criticisms and the Author's Replies,* trans. from the German (Chicago: Open Court, 1906), 3 (first lecture).

2. Cf. Delitzsch, *Babel and Bible,* 106, for this and the following quote (second lecture).

3. Delitzsch, *Babel and Bible,* 113.

4. Delitzsch, *Babel and Bible,* 237, for this and the following quote (third lecture).

We are on a spiritual journey which, however, will not continue forever. Delitzsch assured his readers: "The human spirit [may] expand as it will, it will never advance beyond the sublimity and the moral elevation of Christianity as it glistens and gleams in the Gospels."

It is not surprising that many objected to Delitzsch's ideas, since a special revelation was denied the Judeo-Christian religion. If revelation is denied, a religion ceases to exist too, as Rudolf Kittel (1853-1929) rightly objected.[5] Kittel himself was a representative of the history of religion school, and professor of Old Testament in Breslau and later in Leipzig, and editor of the *Biblia Hebraica* (1906), the Hebrew text of the Old Testament. He researched especially the relationship between the Egyptian mystery cults and the Old Testament. This means that research into the ancient Near Eastern documents needed not result in the conclusions Delitzsch had advanced. Even the German emperor William II (1859-1941) entered the debate, writing in a letter: "I can only urgently advise him [Delitzsch] to proceed cautiously, step by step, and at any rate to ventilate his thesis only in theological books and in the circle of his colleagues. Spare us, the laymen, and, above all, the Oriental Society, from hearing of them."[6]

The History of Religion School: Ernst Troeltsch and Rudolf Otto

Generally, however, the history of religion school, which had its center at Göttingen, refrained from such simplified conclusions as drawn by Delitzsch. This was also due to the positive influence of Adolf von Harnack and his research in the development of dogma and the impact of Hellenism on Christianity. Other representatives exhibited a similarly well balanced stance. Gustav Dalman (1855-1941), professor of Old Testament at Leipzig, for instance, investigated the Judaic background of the life of Jesus. Count Wolf Wilhelm von Baudissin (1847-1926), successively professor of Old Testament at Strassburg, Marburg, and Berlin, researched the Phoenician context, and Adolf Deissmann (1866-1937), professor of New Testament at Heidelberg and later in Berlin, pointed out Jesus' Hellenistic context. We already mentioned Kittel, who established a critical text for the Hebrew Old Testament.

The systematician among the history of religion school was **Ernst**

---

5. Rudolf Kittel, *Der Babel-Bibel-Streit und die Offenbarungsfrage. Ein Verzicht auf Verständigung* (Leipzig: A. Deichert, 1903), 9.

6. Emperor William II, "Letter of February 15, 1903," as reprinted in Delitzsch, *Babel and Bible*, 120-21.

Troeltsch (1865-1923), who was born in Augsburg as son of a physician. He was brought up in an open atmosphere with a conscientious Christian tradition.[7] After some deliberation he began to study theology, which fascinated him primarily from a scholarly angle, at Erlangen University in 1884. There he got acquainted with Wilhelm Bousset (1865-1920), later a cofounder of the history of religion school, with whom he enjoyed a lifelong friendship. After just one year Troeltsch left for Berlin and Bousset went to Leipzig. The following year Troeltsch went to Göttingen, where Ritschl fascinated him. He asked Bousset to join him, and Bousset consented. Troeltsch appreciated Ritschl's historical seriousness and his endeavor to demonstrate the uniqueness of religious experience in contrast to all other forms of knowledge. Troeltsch wrote there a piece on the apologetics of the Christian religion, for which he received a faculty prize.

In 1888 Troeltsch returned to Erlangen to prepare for his final exams. Since he was one of the best students of his class, he was asked to do his vicarage at Munich. The following year he was granted a two-year leave of absence from his church position to continue his studies at Göttingen. His thesis for his licenciate was "Reason and Revelation in Johann Gerhard and Melanchthon." The faculty considered it such a significant work that they also accepted it as a thesis for his *Habilitation.* In 1891, having passed his exams summa cum laude, he defended this thesis in a public disputation. The same year he passed his second church exam in Bavaria before the Church Board. They were impressed with his knowledge, but contended that his thoughts on Christianity jeopardized whether he could serve in a congregation as a teacher of the church and abide by the confessions of the Lutheran church. Their concerns were for naught, for Troeltsch's academic career advanced quickly, and he never became a pastor. Starting in the summer of 1891, he served as Privatdozent in Göttingen, and the following year he was called as associate professor to Bonn. By 1894 he was already full professor at the University of Heidelberg. Now he could start his academic career, because his position was secure.

Troeltsch was only twenty-nine when he came to Heidelberg and looked rather youthful, and his students were surprised to see such a young professor. But his lectures surprised them too. He was much more interested in religion than in Christianity itself, though he still had to lecture on dogmatics for four to five hours a week.[8] Important for Troeltsch was that in 1897 Max Weber

---

7. For a comprehensive biography see Hans-Georg Drescher, *Ernst Troeltsch: His Life and Work,* trans. John Bowden (Minneapolis: Fortress, 1993), here 5.

8. These lectures are translated in English as Ernst Troeltsch, *The Christian Faith,* based on lectures delivered at the University of Heidelberg in 1912 and 1913, foreword by Marta Troeltsch, ed. Gertrud von le Fort, trans. Garrett E. Paul (Minneapolis: Fortress, 1991).

(1864-1920) joined the university in Heidelberg, coming from Freiburg. Troeltsch, who was about his age, befriended him. Through his involvement in the Evangelisch-Soziale Kongress, Troeltsch became quite interested in political issues, which was Weber's field of expertise. In the following years their friendship deepened and they even moved into the same big old house, with the Weber family occupying the lower floor and Troeltsch the upper. Troeltsch confessed that the daily contacts with Weber were very stimulating, and he owed to him a great part of his knowledge and ability.[9] In 1905 the Webers and Troeltsch even journeyed together to the United States to attend the Scientific World Congress, which had been organized in connection with the World's Fair at St. Louis. During World War I, due to some unfortunate circumstances and Weber's temper, their friendship came to an end, and later on only professional contacts were resumed.

In 1908 Troeltsch was supposed to be called to the theological faculty in Berlin and soon after to the philosophical faculty. Yet both calls came to naught, because in each faculty there was too much opposition to Troeltsch. For the theologians Troeltsch was too philosophical, and for the philosophers he was too theological. Six years later he finally received a call to the philosophical faculty at Berlin, to a professorship that was just what he had desired. The council of the city of Heidelberg gave a public farewell party for him, an event that was advertised in the local newspaper. This indicates the kind of esteem the city held for Troeltsch. Troeltsch gave his inaugural lecture at Berlin in the auditorium maximum, the largest lecture hall of the university, on the topic "Philosophy of Culture and Ethics." As in Heidelberg, Troeltsch had little contact with colleagues, except with Harnack, whom he appreciated because of his scholarly achievements. In 1923 Troeltsch was invited to lecture at the British universities in London, Oxford, and Edinburgh, as well as at the London Society for the Study of Religion. This journey was to have shown the British a kind of Germany that was "concerned for balance and compromise."[10] But then Troeltsch suddenly died of lung and heart problems. Harnack delivered the funeral address, calling Troeltsch "*the* German philosopher of history of our time."[11] Indeed, history was *the* topic for Troeltsch.

In his 1898 essay "Historical and Dogmatic Method in Theology," Troeltsch stated the agenda of historicism: "The historical method itself, by its use of criticism, analogy, and correlation, produces with irresistible necessity a

9. Cf. Wilhelm Pauck, *Harnack and Troeltsch: Two Historical Theologians* (New York: Oxford University Press, 1968), 70.

10. So Drescher, *Ernst Troeltsch*, 315.

11. Adolf von Harnack, "Ernst Troeltsch: A Funeral Address Delivered on 3 February 1923," in *Harnack and Troeltsch*, 122.

web of mutually interacting activities of the human spirit, which are never in-dependent and absolute but always interrelated and therefore understandable only within the context of the most comprehensive whole."[12] Historical criti-cism treats its sources critically, it looks for analogies and then tries to correlate analogous, antecedent, and subsequent movements and ideas. This means that not one idea or movement is totally independent and absolute. The same, how-ever, must also be said for the results of historical research, since they too are placed in an ever increasing horizon.

Troeltsch was not satisfied with historicizing, psychologizing, and relativizing everything connected with religion, which thereby disclaimed reli-gion's validity. He rightly saw that "this very process cuts off our access to all that is normative and objective, and therefore leads to an increasing yearning for the absolute — precisely for religion."[13] Religion for him is not to be explained away because "religion is a constitutive part of historical existence."[14] Since religions are part of our historical existence, they also change with us and with history. He showed how religion has changed with regard to one particular aspect in *The So-cial Teaching of the Christian Churches*. This massive two-volume research pro-ject, published in 1911 (Eng. trans. 1931), covers from early Christianity up to the end of the eighteenth century.[15] On a smaller scale Troeltsch did a similar inves-tigation: *The Significance of Protestantism for the Rise of the Modern World* (1906). There he showed that the Protestant Reformation in some cases main-tained and "even re-enforced the opposing influences drawn from the Late-Medieval view of life" instead of furthering the rise of the modern world.[16] While doing away with the hindrances of the Catholic system, the Reformation gave "an impulse towards progress. But even within the Protestant domain the new world did not come into being without much conflict and opposition."

Troeltsch not only described religious movements. He also asked what they amount to and what ultimately motivates them in a religious sense. Thereby he did not adhere to the positivistic theory according to which "one

12. Ernst Troeltsch, "Historical and Dogmatic Method in Theology" (1898), in Ernst Troeltsch, *Religion in History: Essays*, trans. James Luther Adams and Walter F. Bense, introduc-tion by James Luther Adams (Minneapolis: Fortress, 1991), 15.

13. Ernst Troeltsch, "On the Question of the Religious A Priori" (1909), in *Religion in His-tory*, 34.

14. Ernst Troeltsch, "Christianity and the History of Religion" (1897), in *Religion in His-tory*, 77.

15. Ernst Troeltsch, *The Social Teaching of the Christian Churches*, trans. Olive Wyon, foreword by James Luther Adams, 2 vols. (Louisville: Westminster John Knox, 1992).

16. Cf. Ernst Troeltsch, *Protestantism and Progress: The Significance of Protestantism for the Rise of the Modern World*, Eng. trans. 1912 (Philadelphia: Fortress, 1986), 87-88, for this and the following quote.

knows to begin with what religion is and what it can only be: namely, an intellectual error of the primitive mentality which has managed to survive so long because of its great importance for social cohesion and its connection with the human need for happiness."[17] On the other hand, he does not want to agree with an idealistic interpretation of religion that sees in religion "a qualitatively individual and creative power of spiritual life."[18] He wants to adopt a position between these various theories that are represented by Kant and Hegel and their followers on the one hand, and Auguste Comte and his school on the other. Troeltsch offered the results of these deliberations in his book *The Absoluteness of Christianity and the History of Religions* (1901), where he asserted: "Christianity must be understood not only as the culmination point, but also as the convergence point of all the developmental tendencies that can be discerned in religion. It may therefore be designated, in contrast to other religions, as the focal synthesis of all religious tendencies and the disclosure of what is in principle a new way of life. . . . Christianity is the culmination point not despite, but in terms of its particularity and distinctive features, and on this basis the goal of religion undergoes decisively new determinations."[19]

Troeltsch was historian enough to know that history does not stand still, and therefore "it cannot be proved with absolute certainty that Christianity will always remain the final culmination point, that it will never be surpassed." Troeltsch also concedes that in every living religion there is a power at work that provides genuine deliverance from guilt, grief, and earthly life.[20] Troeltsch checks his universalistic ideas by pointing out that Christianity is unlikely to be surpassed as the way of attaining deliverance from the human predicament and loving fellowship with God.

When Troeltsch wrote his first lecture for his intended visit to Great Britain, he entitled it "The Place of Christianity among the World Religions." He wanted to indicate how his thoughts had developed since his 1901 publication *The Absoluteness of Christianity*.[21] Now Troeltsch went a decisive step further

17. Ernst Troeltsch, "Religion and the Science of Religion" (1906), trans. Michael Pye, in Ernst Troeltsch, *Writings on Theology and Religion*, trans. and ed. Robert Morgan and Michael Pye (London: Duckworth, 1977), 85.

18. Troeltsch, "Religion," 86.

19. Cf. Ernst Troeltsch, *The Absoluteness of Christianity and the History of Religions*, introduction by James Luther Adams, trans. David Reid (Richmond: John Knox, 1971), 114-15, for this and the following quote.

20. Troeltsch, *The Absoluteness*, 126.

21. Ernst Troeltsch, "The Place of Christianity among the World Religions" (1923), in Ernst Troeltsch, *Christian Thought: Its History and Application*, edited with an introduction by Baron F. Von Hügel (Westport, Conn.: Hyperion, 1979 [1923]), 4.

and pulled together his analysis of religion and culture and recognized that a religion always depends upon the intellectual, social, and national conditions that provide the context within which it exists. This means for Christianity that although it was once a Jewish sect, it "has become the religion of all Europe."[22] Now Christianity stands or falls with European civilization because it has entirely lost its Oriental character and become Westernized and Hellenized. "Our European conceptions of personality and its eternal, divine right, and of progress towards a kingdom of the spirit and of God, our enormous capacity for expansion and for the interconnection of spiritual and temporal, our whole social order, our science, our art — all these rest, whether we know it or not, whether we like it or not, upon the basis of this deorientalized Christianity."

With this assertion Troeltsch recognized Christianity as the seminal ground for the Western way of life. Therefore it is not surprising that he stated: "The only religion we can endure is Christianity, for Christianity has grown up with us and has become a part of our very being." He continued: "Christianity could not be the religion of such a highly developed racial group if it did not possess a mighty spiritual power and truth; in short, if it were not, in some degree, a manifestation of that Divine Life itself."[23] Religion experienced in this way can then obtain a criterion of validity, but, as he said, only for us in the West. For other racial groups that live under entirely different cultural conditions, the divine life may express itself in a very different way.

Troeltsch no longer claimed the absolute superiority of Christianity he had twenty years earlier. He only stated a unity of religion as to its common goal and its common ground, saying: "As all religion has thus a common goal in the Unknown, the Future, perchance in the Beyond, so too it has a common ground in the Divine Spirit ever pressing the finite mind onward towards further light and fuller consciousness, a Spirit Which indwells the finite spirit, and Whose ultimate union with it is the purpose of the whole many-sided process."[24] When Troeltsch affirmed here both a common goal and a common ground for religion, one may wonder whether the idealistic conception of religion that he rejected so vehemently had not gained again the upper hand.

Rudolf Otto (1869-1937), whom Troeltsch would have liked as his successor at Heidelberg when he moved to Berlin, was the son of a malt-factory owner. The wealth of his parents allowed him some degree of financial independence and means to travel. Otto was born in Peine, northern Germany, and from 1880 on his family lived in Hildesheim, where he went to school. Upon graduation from

---

22. Cf. Troeltsch, "Place of Christianity," 24-25, for this and the following two quotes.
23. Troeltsch, "Place of Christianity," 26.
24. Troeltsch, "Place of Christianity," 32.

school in 1888, he began to study theology at Erlangen and two years later continued his studies at Göttingen. He passed his first theological exam in 1891, and upon further education at the preachers seminary, he did his second exam in 1895. While tutor at the Theological Stift at Göttingen, he finished his thesis on the concept of the Holy Spirit in Luther. In 1898 and the following year he was Privatdozent of systematic theology at Göttingen. In 1901 Otto wrote a little book on the life and actions of Jesus according to a historical-critical viewpoint. Here he interpreted Jesus as a teacher of morality, similar to what Kant had done. Consequently, when a university position opened at Breslau, the church did not approve of Otto being called because he was considered too liberal.

Yet in 1904 Otto both became associate professor at Göttingen and published his book *Naturalism and Religion*. In it he contrasted a naturalistic interpretation of the world with a religious one, and then attempted to vindicate "against the counter-claims of naturalism, the validity and freedom of the religious outlook."[25] Otto dealt here extensively with Darwinism and the mechanistic worldview. But rather than simply juxtaposing the two, he asked whether the religious understanding of the world does not gain something from the notions of evolution and development as examples "of the way in which physical processes are constantly subject to a peculiar guidance, which certainly cannot be explained from themselves or in terms of mechanism, organization, and the like."[26] He claimed that the strange, mysterious, and marvelous in nature intimate something of God and points to something outside of and beyond itself. "Religion demands no more than this. It does not insist upon finding a solution for all the riddles of theoretical world-lore."[27] According to Otto, there is an openness for religion that naturalism cannot suffocate.

With his next book, *The Philosophy of Religion Based on Kant and Fries* (1909), Otto delved more into what would concern him from then on, namely, how religion and the Christian faith should be correlated. He conceived of modern theology as a science of religion and Christian theology as a science of the Christian religion. In contrast to the mainly descriptive approach of Troeltsch, Otto went one step further: "The Science of Religion is not a description of religions. . . . The Science of Religion searches for the validity of religion and for religion that is valid."[28] To accomplish the search for the validity of religion and for the religion that is valid, one must conceive of and present the real

25. Rudolf Otto, *Naturalism and Religion*, trans. J. Arthur and Margaret R. Thomson, edited with an introduction by W. D. Morrison, 2nd ed. (London: Williams and Norgate, 1913), 1.
26. Otto, *Naturalism and Religion*, 276.
27. Otto, *Naturalism and Religion*, 361.
28. Rudolf Otto, *The Philosophy of Religion Based on Kant and Fries*, trans. E. B. Dicker, foreword by W. Tudor Jones (London: Williams and Norgate, 1931), 222.

nature and spirit of Christianity both in the form of doctrine, which is critically assessed, and in its practice. The focal point "for all science of religion, and especially for the Christian branch of that science, is Religious Experience, a thing that is not interpreted by mythology and archaeology."[29] The important thing, Otto contended, is not a theoretical assessment, but the practical experience. This is true for the Christian religion as well as for any other.

To discover that experience of religion, Otto traveled widely, to the Middle East (Egypt and Palestine), to Russia, India, and East Asia, including Japan, China, and Siberia. Through a grant, he had money to obtain religious objects, and he established at Marburg in 1927 a collection of objects pertaining to the history of religion. During one of these journeys he presumably contracted malaria, which made life miserable for him ever after.[30] In 1915 he accepted a call to the University of Breslau, and two years later he became successor to Wilhelm Herrmann at Marburg. At that time also his book *The Idea of the Holy* appeared. Within a short time this publication made him internationally famous. In it he represented "an original and creative synthesis of theology and the history of religions."[31]

In *The Idea of the Holy* Otto asked about the origin of religion in terms of the religious experience. He arrived at the *noumenous*, a category that is grounded a priori in the nonrational but discloses itself in the rational. There are two sides to the *noumenous*, the *mysterium tremendum* disclosing awfulness, overpowering might, and urgency. In this way the *noumenous* is the holy other. But there is also a fascinating aspect to the *noumenous*. Otto exemplified the *noumenous* with examples from the Old and New Testament and also from Luther, especially from *The Bondage of the Will* (1525). Otto contended that while not everyone has an a priori cognition of the holy, everyone is capable of having it. One must have a special endowment to produce it. On the level of the prophet, this cognition then becomes reality through the power of divination. Otto concluded his book by saying: "We can look, beyond the prophet, to one in whom is found the Spirit in all its plenitude, and who at the same time in his person and in his performance is become most completely the object of divination, in whom Holiness is recognized apparent. Such a one is more than Prophet. He is the Son."[32] Searching through the basic structures of religion, Otto arrived unashamedly at Jesus Christ, the manifestation of the holy.

---

29. Otto, *The Philosophy of Religion*, 227.

30. So Carl Heinz Ratschow, "Otto, Rudolf," in *Theologische Realenzyklopädie*, 25:559.

31. Melissa Raphael, *Rudolf Otto and the Concept of Holiness* (Oxford: Clarendon, 1997), 15.

32. Rudolf Otto, *The Idea of the Holy: An Inquiry into the Non-rational Factor in the Idea of the Divine and Its Relation to the Rational*, trans. John W. Harvey (New York: Oxford University Press, 1939), 182.

This procedure is typical in all of Otto's writings. For instance, in his 1928 Haskell Lectures in Oberlin, Ohio, *Mysticism East and West: A Comparative Analysis of the Nature of Mysticism,* he first compared the mysticism of Meister Eckhart with the great mysticism of India, but then he said: "The task of comparative religion is not completed by the demonstration of similarities, its finer work then begins."[33] One must then also show the differences. This discernment is demonstrated with the actual world affirmation of Meister Eckhart. He sees the world not only as a painful and miserable place to flee from and deny, but "when it is found again in God, [it is] a place of joy and of joyous spontaneous action in all good works."[34] In his 1930 book *India's Religion of Grace and Christianity Compared and Contrasted,* Otto proceeded in a similar way and showed that in the bhakti religion, which looks at first glance so akin to Christianity, there is no "expiating grace," since there is no "expiator," no Golgotha, and no cross.[35]

In his last major work, *The Kingdom of God and the Son of Man: A Study in the History of Religion* (1934), Otto pointed out that Jesus was a charismatic person and "an eschatological redeemer."[36] Yet the church has lost this "charisma." When people make the charisma and "the inbringing kingdom belonging to it trivial by allegories, [this] does not show that this church is now on a higher level, but is a sign of its decay." In contrast to Troeltsch, Otto was fascinated by religion in the service of the Christian faith and not merely out of academic curiosity. He saw the challenges that the world religions posed for Christianity and tried to meet them by analyzing and comparing them. At the same time, he knew that not only denominations but also different religions should cooperate to work for world peace, to further social justice, and stem the demonic forces of group egotism. To that end he was promoting an "interreligious league."[37] This idea was picked up much later by the World Parliament of Religions and Hans Küng's project of a global ethos.

---

33. Rudolf Otto, *Mysticism East and West: A Comparative Analysis of the Nature of Mysticism,* trans. Bertha L. Bracey and Richenda C. Payne (New York: Macmillan, 1932), 165.

34. Otto, *Mysticism East and West,* 211.

35. Rudolf Otto, *India's Religion of Grace and Christianity Compared and Contrasted,* trans. Frank Hugh Foster (New York: Macmillan, 1930), 108.

36. Cf. Rudolf Otto, *The Kingdom of God and the Son of Man: A Study in the History of Religion,* translated from the revised German edition by Floyd V. Filson and Bertram Lee-Woolf, new and rev. ed. (London: Lutterworth, 1951), 375-76, for this and the following quote.

37. Cf. Rudolf Otto, "An Inter-Religious League," in Rudolf Otto, *Religious Essays: A Supplement to "The Idea of the Holy,"* trans. Brian Lunn (London: Oxford University Press, 1931), 150-56.

The Critique and Reassessment of Positive Religion:
Auguste Comte, James G. Frazer, and William James

When we consider the work of Comte and Frazer, we obtain some understanding of the materialistic concept of religion to which Otto was reacting. **Auguste Comte** (1798-1857) was born into a Roman Catholic royalist family in Montpellier, France. He studied a few years at the polytechnical school there, and in 1817 became secretary to the French social reformer Claude Henri Saint-Simon (1760-1825). After Comte left Saint-Simon, he gave private lessons in mathematics and then courses on positive philosophy and astronomy. Beginning in 1832, he served as assistant headmaster of the Ecole Polytechnique, but he did not obtain a chair at the Collège de France, something he badly desired. While lacking an official teaching position, he had some private means that helped him survive.[38]

From his private lectures resulted his *Cours de philosophie positive* (6 vols., 1830-42; Eng. trans., *The Positive Philosophy of Auguste Comte*, 2 vols., London, 1853), through which he became the founder of positivism. With his thesis of the three stages in the history of humanity, Comte showed which course religion should take. (1) The first stage is the theological or fictitious phase in which humanity conceives of the events in nature as dependent upon the will of higher personal forces. These forces are first thought to be embodied in objects of nature (period of fetishism), then in God's rule over larger areas of nature (polytheism), and finally in one God who is thought to rule the whole world (monotheism). The human mind directs itself thereby mainly to the inner nature of being and to the first and final causes of the phenomena humanity observes. (2) In the second phase of human development, the metaphysical or abstract period, humans replace the anthropomorphism of the first period by more abstract forces, such as powers, inner natures, or souls. (3) It is not until the third, scientific or positive, phase that humanity recognizes its limitations by giving up the search for the origin and hidden causes of the universe, and for the knowledge of final causes of phenomena. By a well-combined use of reasoning and observation, humanity endeavors to discover the actual laws of phenomena.

Comte did not want to do away with religion, because he saw "the need of a spiritual power."[39] But he was convinced that "Monotheism in Western Europe is now as obsolete and as injurious as Polytheism was fifteen centuries ago.

---

38. For a brief description of his life and thoughts, cf. Frank E. Manuel, *The Prophets of Paris* (Cambridge: Harvard University Press, 1962), 249-96.

39. Auguste Comte, *A General View of Positivism*, trans. J. H. Bridges, official centenary ed. (New York: Robert Speller, 1957), 84. The page references in the following text are to this work.

The discipline in which its moral value principally consisted has long since decayed" (442). Monotheism supplies no field for the imagination, and it never sincerely promoted the pursuits of practical life. However, there is another religion that replaces monotheism. "Positivism becomes, in the true sense of the word, a Religion; the only religion which is real and complete; destined therefore to replace all imperfect and provisional systems resting on the primitive basis of theology" (365). In this new religion love is the principle, order the basis, and progress the end (cf. 55). For positivism humanity is the "only true Great Being," and "the highest progress of man and of society consists in gradual increase of our mastery over all our defects, especially the defects of our moral nature" (365, 362). Reason will be brought to its right use in helping humanity toward self-perfection. "Positive religion brings before us in a definite shape the noblest of human problems, the permanent preponderance of Social feeling over Self-love" (441). In this system the goddess of reason which had been decreed at the height of the French Revolution is received into positivism, now a philosophic and religious system. Comte reiterates here the creed of the nineteenth century, faith in humanity and in human progress, a faith that claimed it could dispense with transcendent forces.

James G. Frazer (1854-1941) was born in Glasgow as the son of a successful pharmacist, his parents being devout members of the conservative Free Church of Scotland. In 1869 Frazer entered the University of Glasgow. The school inspired his love of classics, introduced him to the mechanistic worldview, and relieved him of the religious faith of his childhood. After taking a degree at Glasgow, he entered Trinity College at Cambridge in 1874 for a second baccalaureate and obtained a fellowship at Trinity in 1879 that was finally granted for life. He was knighted in 1914, became a fellow of the Royal Society in 1920, and was awarded the Order of Merit in 1925.

Frazer's first writings in anthropology were the articles on "taboo" and "totem" in the ninth edition of *Encyclopaedia Britannica*. In 1900 *The Golden Bough* was published in two volumes, and soon thereafter in an enlarged edition in three volumes. The third edition came out in 1911-15 in twelve volumes. *The Golden Bough* is his best-known work. Here Frazer treated the beliefs of the ancient Greeks and Romans from a philosophical, evolutionary point of view, as if they were primitives. This also allowed him to introduce many other rites from other "primitive" societies. Though he never mentioned the name of Jesus, it was clear that Christianity, too, shares this imperfect and therefore irrational understanding of the universe with these pagan rites.[40]

---

40. Cf. Robert Ackerman, "Frazer, James G.," in *The Encyclopedia of Religion*, ed. Mircea Eliade, 5:416, where he makes extensive reference to *The Golden Bough*.

In *The Golden Bough* Frazer established his thesis concerning religion, which he reiterated in many other places, that there is "the movement of the higher thought, so far as we can trace it, . . . from magic through religion to science."[41] In magic humanity depends on itself to meet the difficulties and dangers of daily life. It believes in a certain established order of nature on which it can count and which it can also manipulate. As this fails, religion sets in which explains the natural phenomena as being regulated by the will, the passion, or the caprice of spiritual beings that are like humans though vastly superior to them. As this proves unsatisfactory too, finally scientific reasoning sets in. Frazer concluded: "In the last analysis magic, religion, and science are nothing but theories of thought; and as science has supplanted its predecessors, so it may hereafter be itself superseded by some more perfect hypothesis."[42]

In other publications Frazer was less hesitant to draw parallels to the Christian religion. For instance, in *Man, God, and Immortality: Thoughts on Human Progress* (1927) he arrived at a very appropriate definition of religion: "By religion, then, I understand a propitiation or conciliation of powers superior to man which are believed to direct and control the course of nature and of human life. Thus defined, religion consists of two elements, a theoretical and a practical, namely, a belief in powers higher than man and an attempt to propitiate or please them."[43] These powers from whom conciliation is sought are understood as personal agents. Next to these natural phenomena that are personified, one also worships the dead since one believes that "the dead retain their consciousness and personality" and "that they can powerfully influence the fortunes of the living."[44] Then Frazer contended that the birth of Christ is superseded by the nativity of the sun, and that the Phrygian god Attis coincides with Christ and resembles in his destiny the definite resurrection of Christ. He concluded that "taken altogether, the coincidences of the Christian with the heathen festivals are too close and too numerous to be accidental."[45] This meant for Frazer that Christianity did not just replace the religions of Greece and Rome, but that the major tenets of the Christian faith were developed to facilitate such replacement.

Frazer distinguished three kinds of gods: the first kind humanity infers from observing the surrounding nature; then come human gods humanity rec-

---

41. James George Frazer, *The Golden Bough: A Study in Magic and Religion,* abridged ed. (New York: Macmillan, 1979), 824.

42. Frazer, *The Golden Bough,* 825-26.

43. James George Frazer, *Man, God, and Immortality: Thoughts on Human Progress,* rev. ed. (London: Macmillan, 1927), 297.

44. Cf. Frazer, *Man, God, and Immortality,* 302.

45. Frazer, *Man, God, and Immortality,* 334.

ognizes by virtue of certain extraordinary mental manifestations in itself or in others; and finally there are "the deified spirits of dead men. To judge by the accounts we possess not only of savage and barbarous tribes but of some highly civilized peoples, the worship of the human dead has been one of the commonest and most influential forms of natural religion, perhaps indeed the commonest and most influential of all."[46] Again, in this threefold distinction of the gods the reference to Christianity — a worship of a dead Jesus — is implicit rather than explicit. Yet Frazer left no doubt that religion is a thing of the past, and therefore he as an anthropologist could classify and compare the various religious features. Humanity had progressed from the magic via the religious to the scientific sphere. As Frazer admitted, that may not even be the final stage of development. Again, evolutionary concepts rule supreme. As Otto has shown, however, it is not sufficient simply to note analogies but one must also discern the subtle differences between various religious phenomena. Not everything that looks alike is alike.

In his philosophy **William James** (1842-1910) also embodied the struggle between science and religion. But unlike European critics of religion, he did not want to abandon religion or supplant it by reason. Since the new world of North America was originally settled by religious visionaries who believed in God and their own doing, religion and human reason needed to not be on a collision course.

James's paternal grandfather had emigrated from Ireland and, by judicious investment in the Erie Canal, amassed a fortune and made adequate provision for the welfare of his descendants. Therefore the next two generations of the James family could engage in whatever pursuits they wished without too much concern for money.[47] His father started at Princeton Theological Seminary and was a literary friend of Emerson. William was born in New York City and attended several schools both in America and in Europe, thereby attaining fluency in French and German. His brother Henry (1843-1916) was a noted novelist who wrote twenty novels, among many other items. In 1861 William entered the Lawrence Scientific School at Harvard, and in 1864 the Harvard Medical School. There he got acquainted with Louis Agassiz. In 1869 he received his M.D. from Harvard, and in 1873 became an instructor in anatomy and physiology there. Two years later he taught the first courses in psychology ever offered in America. His two volumes of *Principles of Psychology,* published in 1890, were

46. James George Frazer, *The Belief in Immortality and the Worship of the Dead,* Gifford Lectures, 1911-1912 (London: Macmillan, 1913), 1:23f.

47. For a brief biography and a good introduction to the thought of William James, see Edward C. Moore, *American Pragmatism: Peirce, James, and Dewey* (New York: Columbia University Press, 1961), 107-80, here 107.

for a long time the standard work on that subject. In 1879 he began teaching philosophy, and in the following year he became assistant professor of philosophy. In 1901/2 he gave the Gifford Lectures at Edinburgh, which were published in 1902 as *The Varieties of Religious Experience.*

Ever since James became interested very early in science, particularly in physiology and psychology, the question that bothered him was whether a human being was just a machine as science seemed to suggest, or whether humans had a free will, as he preferred to believe. When he was asked why he lectured to college audiences on religion, he said he would not necessarily do that at other places, "but academic audiences, fed already on science, have a very different need."[48] Their native capacity for faith is paralyzed "by the notion, carefully instilled, that there is something called scientific evidence by waiting upon which they shall escape all danger of shipwreck in regard to truth. But there is really no scientific or other method by which men can steer safely between the opposite dangers of believing too little or of believing too much." In contrast to that scientific skepticism concerning religion, James contended: *"Anything short of God is not rational, anything more than God is not possible."*[49] For James faith was not obtained by sacrificing the intellect, but through careful reflection on the world.

In addressing whether there is a God, James took recourse to pragmatism.[50] In so doing he did not introduce a new proof for the existence of God, but tried to prove "that we have a right to believe that God exists and to act as though religion were true."[51] The reason for this is twofold: Since we cannot decide the truth of religion on intellectual grounds but nevertheless must decide it, we have a right to decide it on emotional grounds, and if we prefer to believe then we have a right to do so. And secondly, "since religion might be such that it cannot become true unless we believe it, we have a right to believe it, and to act accordingly."

In his Gifford Lectures, a series established to present lectures in the defense of "natural religion," James devoted himself to a defense of religion. He established that religious life includes the following beliefs:

1. That the visible world is part of the more spiritual universe from which it draws its chief significance.
2. That union or harmonious relation with that higher universe is our true end.
3. That prayer or inner communion with the spirit thereof — the spirit

---

48. William James, *The Will to Believe and Other Essays in Popular Philosophy and Human Immortality* (New York: Dover, 1956), x-xi.

49. James, *The Will to Believe,* 116.

50. So Moore, *American Pragmatism,* 116-17.

51. Moore, *American Pragmatism,* 129, for this and the following quote.

"God" or "law" — is a process wherein work is really done, and spiritual energy flows in and produces effects, psychological or material, within the phenomenal world.[52]

Yet in the light of other sciences and of general philosophy, the science of religion cannot decide whether such beliefs can be considered true. Most likely the conclusion is that such beliefs are an anachronism, belonging to a past age.

In that situation James referred to the world of our experience, since it consists of an objective and a subjective part. While the objective part is "the sum total of whatsoever at any given time we may be thinking of, the subjective part is the inner 'state' in which the thinking comes to pass."[53] This inner state James claimed "is our very experience itself; its reality and that of our experience are one." This means that reality and our experience go together even to the point that the internal belief produces the external object. While usually an internal belief follows the discovery of an external object, there can also be an exception to that wherein "the external object can only follow on the internal belief."[54] This was exactly the point of contention between James and the scientific proponents of materialism. They had no internal belief, and therefore the missing external object corroborated their internal disbelief.

James concluded: "Whatever it may be on its *farther* side, the 'more' with which in religious experience we feel ourselves connected is on its *hither* side the subconscious continuation of our conscious life. . . . The theologian's contention that the religious man is moved by an external power is vindicated, for it is one of the peculiarities of invasions from the subconscious region to take on objective appearances, and to suggest to the Subject an external control."[55] This religious power is not something we control, because whatever we experience from that side is opened to us as a gift. For Christians this supreme reality is God. As James stated: "We and God have business with each other; and in opening ourselves to his influence our deepest destiny is fulfilled. The universe, at those parts of it which our personal being constitutes, takes a turn generally for the worse or for the better in proportion as each one of us fulfills or evades God's demands. As far as this goes I probably have you with me, for I only translate into schematic language what I may call the instinctive belief of mankind: God is real since he produces real effects."[56]

52. William James, *The Varieties of Religious Experience: A Study in Human Nature,* introduction by Arthur Darby Nock (Glasgow: William Collins Fountain Book, 1977), 464.

53. James, *Varieties of Religious Experience,* 476-77, for this and the following quote.

54. So Moore, *American Pragmatism,* 129.

55. James, *Varieties of Religious Experience,* 487-88.

56. James, *Varieties of Religious Experience,* 491.

Appealing to the instinctive beliefs of humanity, as James did, can become dangerous once these beliefs change and the claim is made that God no longer produces any real effects. This is at least what more than half a century later the God-is-dead theologians claimed. While James employed reason, he nevertheless wanted to get away from irrationalistic access to religion, with regard to both its defenders and those who reject it. Instead he appealed to the inner side of humanity. The reason for this was that, as he contended, "reality would always be a mystery to human understanding."[57] Yet for James God and humanity are part of the same universe. God is not absolutely infinite and, furthermore, we are called into cooperation with God.[58] Our efforts do count. This final emphasis on the human factor was especially important in a growing and expanding country such as the United States.

Christianity among the World's Religions: Nathan Söderblom and Einar Billing

When we move back again to the European continent, we see that especially in Scandinavia research in the history of religion is pursued with amazing rigor. This is due primarily to **Nathan Söderblom** (1866-1931), who was also one of the pioneers of the ecumenical movement. He was born to a pastor's family shaped by pietism in the Swedish province of Hälsingland. He studied theology and languages at Uppsala University (1883/84). In 1890 he participated in the first international Christian youth meeting in Northfield, Massachusetts, and in 1891 in the YMCA meeting in Amsterdam. He was ordained in 1893 and served as a hospital chaplain; from 1894 to 1901 as chaplain for sailors in Calais, France; and then as pastor of the Swedish embassy in Paris. At the same time, he studied at the Protestant theological faculty of the Sorbonne in Paris and received his doctorate in 1901 with a thesis on comparative eschatology. He was then called to the University of Uppsala to occupy the chair for theological encyclopedia and introductory science and served at the same time as pastor at Trinity Church. In 1912 he was asked to occupy as visiting professor the newly established chair for history of religion at Leipzig. To the consternation of the conservatives, in 1914 the government named Söderblom archbishop of Uppsala. Söderblom was active in the precursor movements to the World Council of Churches. For instance, he was instrumental in preparing for and

57. So Gerald E. Myers, *William James: His Life and Thought* (New Haven: Yale University Press, 1986), 447.

58. For further details cf. Moore, *American Pragmatism*, 133-34.

conducting the first Universal Conference for Life and Work in Stockholm (1925). He also worked in the movement for Faith and Order and attended the first world conference in Lausanne, Switzerland, in 1927. In 1930 he received the Nobel Peace Prize. The following year he presented the first part of his Gifford Lectures. On his deathbed the same year, he still determined what their title should be: "'There is a living God,' he said, 'I can prove it by the history of religions.'"[59] With this assertion we are in the center of his research on religion, because according to Söderblom all religions participate in the process of divine self-revelation that finds its culmination in Christ.

While Söderblom's work covers many areas, in ecumenical relations, peace — especially reconciliation between the nations after World War I — and Christian mission, most interesting for us here is his understanding of religion. In his Gifford Lectures he presented a review of the different types of religion, including primitive religion, religion as method (Yoga), as psychology (Jainism and Hinayana), as devotion (bhakti), as revelation in history, and the religion of incarnation. In humanity there are two movements, a search for the divine and a positioning of it, without humanity being able to comprehend and explain God (cf. 284). In the Mosaic religion, Söderblom discerned an intolerance against other gods and, as the most striking feature in distinction from other higher religions, the *activity of God* in history (303). He sees the Christian church, in spite of its divisions, united in its understanding of "the *uniqueness of Christ,* as a historic person and revealer of God, and the *supernatural character of the divine revelation* through the prophets and through Christ" (319). With Christ revelation has not stopped, because of the self-communication of God's creating power and saving will in nature and history and in moral life. In the latter it leads to "the individual's regeneration and forming of character" (352). This means that God continues to be at work in nature and in the course of history, as well as in the individual life toward salvation.

In an earlier essay, "The Religion of Revelation" (1903), Söderblom traced the development of religion even more persuasively by distinguishing between nature religion and culture religion on the one hand, and prophetic religion on the other. While the first type is earlier and perhaps more primitive, it is nevertheless religion, too, and as Söderblom asserted, "a revelation of God is present wherever a real religion is found. Where God is known, it may be even imperfectly and through a destroying medium, there he has in some degree allowed

---

59. According to Ingve Brilioth, biographical introduction to *The Living God: Basic Forms of Personal Religion,* by Nathan Söderblom, Gifford Lectures, 1931 (Boston: Beacon Press, 1962), xxviii. The page numbers in the next paragraph refer to this work.

himself to become known, yes, made himself known."[60] This means that we cannot distinguish between the Christian religion of God's self-disclosure and the other religions that are simply our own doing, contrary to what Karl Barth later claimed. For Söderblom genuine religion is genuine religion, wherever it may occur. When talking about nature religion and culture religion, Söderblom made it clear that "*no religion is a product of culture,* all religion depends on a revelation" (42).

Of course, a religion always develops in a certain context, and this means it is not without the given cultural conditions. Even polytheism, as a step forward in religion, issues from a certain cultural context. Söderblom claimed that one can trace clearly the development from polytheism to monarchic supremacy, meaning the rule of one God in a pantheon, and from there to pantheism, idealism, acosmism or religious agnosticism, as we see, for instance, in Lao-tse. If a higher intellectual and moral culture were attained, such as in pantheism and in idealism, the folk religion was still being practiced by venerating personal divine beings. But not everything, according to Söderblom, is development.

Söderblom asserted here with regard to the Israelite religion: "The religion of the prophets is not a stage in the development of religion, but a phenomenon by itself. Attempts to make it the product of the development of national religion, fascinating as they may be, are contrary to the actual records of the history of religions" (55). Nevertheless, there is external cultural continuity, Söderblom admitted, because the prophets did not come into history detached from that which preceded them. This means there is historical and psychological continuity.

When we come to Zoroaster and Moses, and the prophets, we encounter a revealed religion.

> The faith of this revealed religion is directed to *the one, living, spiritual God, who is active in history and there revealed.* The conception of the unity of God and of his living personality in reality at once excludes the experiences and thoughts of the divine found outside the prophetical religion. Even though other religions may have a conception of God as living and active, comforting and helping, warning and punishing, in other words, a conception of God that is filled with religious content, still the deity is not monotheistically conceived in religions outside of the prophetic religion. (63-64)

---

60. Nathan Söderblom, *The Nature of Revelation,* edited with an introduction by Edgar M. Carlson, trans. Frederic E. Pamp (Philadelphia: Fortress, 1966), 41 (the first part of this book contains "The Religion of Revelation"). The page numbers in the following text refer to this work.

There are two religions that fall into that category of revealed religion, namely, Zoroastrianism and the Israelite religion. Yet the former is disqualified because of its own narrow limitations and the fact that it was never fully carried out. Zoroastrianism, as Söderblom saw it, is too limited in its historical impact and restricted to Zoroaster alone. In the revealed religion God is active in history. There God is not merely active in nature and the social order, as in nature religion. Moreover, God is revealed in the consciousness of the prophet as the living God. As we can see in the Old Testament documents, Yahweh became the God of Moses and then also the one who redeemed Israel from Egypt. Therefore Söderblom concluded: "History is the true workshop of God. So also is nature in its way."

In nature religion nature and spirit are seen in opposition. For instance, in India nature is regarded as a deceptive illusion, and in Greece as something impure and evil. The prophetic religions break through this barrier. Then the world is open for all kinds of positive pursuits both in ethical life and in culture. While Söderblom portrayed a positive understanding of religion, something he learned from Schleiermacher, he emphasized at the same time the uniqueness of the Judeo-Christian tradition and its culmination in Jesus Christ.

Another theologian who only in his early phase showed a decided interest in the history of religion, but who was quite influential in determining the course of Swedish theology by training the future representatives of the Lundensian School, was **Einar Billing** (1871-1939). He did his *Habilitation* in 1900 at Uppsala and became there in 1908 professor of dogmatics and moral theology. After 1920 he served as bishop at Västerås. In his largest work, *The Ethical Thoughts of Early Christendom* (*De etiska tankarna i urchristendomen*, Uppsala, 1907), he compared the understanding of history in Greek philosophy with the prophets of Israel. In seeing the concept of the election of Israel and of the individual through Jesus' death and resurrection as derivatives of one and the same history of election, Billing pointed to the significance of motif research. Such a line of inquiry is for Scandinavian theology quite important. Yet Billing's most important influence was as bishop when he opted to make the Church of Sweden an open people's church, allowing people to leave it and found their own denominational communities, instead of having to belong to it regardless of their actual affiliation.

Motif Research and Beyond: The Lundensian School; Anders Nygren, Gustaf Aulén, Gustaf Wingren, and Knud E. Løgstrup

When the time of Billing and Söderblom had passed, the theological faculty at Lund assumed leadership in Sweden. There developed the Lundensian theology under Anders Nygren, professor (1924-48) and bishop in Lund (1948-58), and the first president of the Lutheran World Federation (1947-52); Gustaf Aulén; Ragnar Bring (1895-1990), professor at Åbo (1930) and from 1934 to 1962 successor to Aulén in Lund. Bring is well known for his research on the "dualism" in Luther's theology and on the relationship between law and gospel.

Anders Nygren (1890-1978) is the founder of Lundensian theology, and internationally its most influential representative. He started his theological proposal in *Religious A Priori* (*Religiöst apriori*, 1922) and concluded it in *Meaning and Method* (1972), whose subtitle explains what he endeavored to do, namely, to lay out "prolegomena to a scientific philosophy of religion and a scientific theology." According to Nygren, "philosophy is analysis of meaning and its method is the logical analysis of presuppositions."[61] Without these presuppositions there is no meaning, but the presuppositions refer to the context, because without context there is also no meaning. Therefore the analysis of meaning must proceed in two steps: (1) analysis that leads to the context of meaning and (2) analysis of the motif context, which is significant for the meaning of a statement. The significance for systematic theology becomes evident when he describes its task as "to understand and elucidate the Christian faith in its uniqueness, its distinctively Christian character, . . . its precise meaning and content, showing what is specifically Christian about it that makes it different from everything else" (371).

While the execution of this task may sound very simple as long as we deal only with a single expression of the Christian faith, it is much more difficult when we consider the totality of "the Christian faith." Yet Nygren pointed to a solution: "At this point motif research comes in, and its significance for systematic theology consists precisely in the fact that it provides an objective way of determining the uniqueness of the Christian faith. Instead of motif research we could in this connection speak just as well of typological research or structural research" (372). The task is not yet accomplished when we have elucidated the Christian motifs, but Nygren urged theologians to penetrate further to the fundamental motif of Christianity. What is the motif, he asked, that impinges on

---

61. Anders Nygren, *Meaning and Method: Prolegomena to a Scientific Philosophy of Religion and a Scientific Theology*, trans. Philip S. Watson (Philadelphia: Fortress, 1972), 227. The page numbers in the following text refer to this work.

every aspect of the Christian relationship to God and determines the structure of that relationship? His answer is love. Since God is love *(agape)*, "the fundamental Christian motif is *the Agape motif*" (374).

In Judaism, which is Christianity's own prehistory, we encounter the *nomos* motif, since fellowship with God is bound to the presupposition of the law in Judaism. In the Hellenistic environment of early Christianity, we encounter the *eros* motif, meaning the longing for the divine life with its fullness of riches and the attempt to reach up to the divine. The *agape,* however, signifies the condescension in self-giving divine love through which fellowship is established between God and humanity.

In another significant publication, *Agape and Eros: A Study of the Christian Idea of Love* (2 vols., 1930-37; Eng. trans. 1932-39), Nygren exemplified what he later substantiated through a theoretical framework. In that investigation he traced the relationship between the Hellenistic *eros* motif and the Christian *agape* motif from the New Testament up to the Lutheran Reformation. Perusing the New Testament account, he showed that salvation comes from God and leads to God, the way of *agape.* In *eros,* however, the heavenward desire is a means to an end, essentially not to seek God, but one's own highest good, which is then identified with God. Nygren pointed to Augustine, who, on one hand, influenced by Neoplatonic philosophy, portrays the ascent of the soul in most glowing colors, but on the other hand, "like no other since Paul, he can exalt and praise Divine grace, which in absolute sovereignty, moved by its own love and mercy alone, elects and saves."[62] According to Nygren, Augustine finds in *caritas* a synthesis of humanity's heavenward movement and God's downward movement. Martin Luther seeks to destroy the Augustinian interpretation of Christian love, which for Luther contains more Hellenistic *eros* love than Christian *agape* love, and points out once again that "God is Agape. That is why He has come to us in His Son. Only at the cross do we find God, but there we really find Him. *'Theologia crucis'* is the only true theology."[63]

Nygren showed that with this kind of motif research one can trace differences in the use of the same concept not only within one religious tradition (Christianity) but also in different religious traditions (Christianity and Hellenism). In executing his research Nygren pointed out the specific Christian understanding of love that is different from that of Hellenism. Moreover, he also demonstrated, contrary to widespread opinion, that Luther and Augustine held different understandings of this central Christian motif.

---

62. Anders Nygren, *Agape and Eros,* trans. Philip S. Watson (Philadelphia: Westminster, 1953), 560.

63. Nygren, *Agape and Eros,* 740.

At the early age of twenty-seven, **Gustaf Aulén** (1879-1977) was called to the University of Uppsala to teach theological prolegomena. Four years later he moved into systematic theology, and in 1913 he became professor of dogmatics at the University of Lund. There he served till 1933, when he became bishop. During the nine years (1924-33) when both Nygren and Aulén taught at Lund, the specific Lundensian theology was born, with Nygren being the main proponent while Aulén was initially still impacted by his Uppsala heritage. After retiring from his ecclesial position in 1952, Aulén was again actively involved in academic theology. While a student of Nygren, Aulén did not pursue the combination of philosophy and motif research, though we see some of the influence of Nygren's thinking in the way he contrasted the historic epochs of Christianity. His theological production was voluminous and his books were translated into ten different languages. Especially his influential 1930 book, *Christus Victor* (Eng. trans. 1931), saw more than twenty editions.

In *Christus Victor* Aulén contrasted the classic type of atonement that he found in the Greek and Latin Fathers and then again in Martin Luther, and the Latin type most prominently advocated by Anselm of Canterbury and also by Albrecht Ritschl and again in post-Reformation Lutheran orthodoxy, with a third type he discerned in the Enlightenment and in liberal Protestant theology. There "the Atonement is no longer regarded as in any true sense carried out by God. Rather, the Reconciliation is the result of some process that takes place in man, such as conversion and amendment."[64] In the classic type, God reconciled the world with himself. This means God is reconciled only "because He Himself reconciles the world with Himself and Himself with the world."[65] This classic type is basically dualistic in outlook, because of "the Divine warfare against the evil that holds mankind in bondage, and the triumph of Christ." For the Latin type, a legal theory of satisfaction is presented by Anselm, whereby "God is the object of Christ's atoning work."[66] While this objective type of the doctrine, also represented by Ritschl, rejected the subjective theory represented by Schleiermacher, both sought to verify their position through Scripture. In *Christus Victor* Aulén wanted to point out unmistakably that atonement is from beginning to end God's own work. Therefore only the classic type is in agreement with the Christian proclamation that God so loved the world that God gave his only Son.

In another book, *Eucharist and Sacrifice* (1956; Eng. trans. 1958), Aulén again applied this lead motif of God reconciling the world with himself

---

64. Gustaf Aulén, *Christus Victor: An Historical Study of the Three Main Types of the Idea of the Atonement*, trans. A. G. Herbert (London: SPCK, 1970), 146.

65. See Aulén, *Christus Victor*, 146, for this and the following quote.

66. Aulén, *Christus Victor*, 2.

through Christ. Medieval theology, according to Aulén, associated the sacrifice of Christ exclusively with Christ's death on the cross. This allowed them to see, in the eucharistic sacrament, this sacrifice as a repetition of Christ's sacrifice on Golgotha.[67] The Reformers rejected this notion by clinging in their Lutheran persuasion to the real presence of Christ in the Lord's Supper. Anglican theologians, by contrast, emphasized the sacrifice, saying it was not finished at death since Christ as the Great High Priest continually offers it on the heavenly altar. The church being somehow identified with Christ does something similar to Christ in the Lord's Supper.

Aulén agreed that Holy Communion is inseparably connected with the sacrifice of Christ. But sacrifice did not just occur on the cross. It started already with Christ's incarnation and continued throughout his earthly sojourn. The Christ who is present in the Lord's Supper is the living Lord, and he is none other than the crucified. "The possibility of his presence depends on the fact that he is the ascended Lord who sits on the right hand of the Father, and that he is therefore independent of the limitations of space and time."[68] The sacrifice completed with his death and made eternally valid is actualized anew when Christ comes to us in Holy Communion. If sacrifice and presence were separated, the presence could only be a spiritual one with bread and wine as the symbols of the sacrifice that was fulfilled in his death. If sacrifice and real presence, however, are identified, bread and wine are "changed" into and identified with the sacrifice of Christ's body and blood. "But in reality the real presence ceases then to be the presence of the living Lord, and is reduced to an impersonal presence. As a consequence the way is opened for the conception that the sacrifice is something which we, the church, control and administer."[69]

Aulén showed here that if we identify sacrifice and real presence, the lead motif of God in Christ reconciling the world with himself is being put in jeopardy and the Lord's Supper becomes our contribution to Christ's salvific sacrifice. In a later publication (1965) Aulén no longer went through the history of dogma, but concerned himself primarily with the modern authors and Nobel laureates Pär Lagerkvist and Harry Martinson to illustrate present problems with the image of God.[70] Altogether Aulén contributed more than any other theologian in the past century to the formation of a Swedish systematic theology in its own right.

67. Cf. Gustaf Aulén, *Eucharist and Sacrifice,* trans. Eric H. Wahlstrom (Philadelphia: Muhlenberg, 1958), 186.

68. Aulén, *Eucharist and Sacrifice,* 203.

69. Aulén, *Eucharist and Sacrifice,* 203-4.

70. Cf. Gustaf Aulén, *The Drama and the Symbols: A Book on Images of God and the Problems They Raise,* trans. Sydney Linton (London: SPCK, 1970).

Gustaf Wingren (b. 1910) grew up in a small manufacturing town that had never brought forth a theologian, and in a family from which no one ever attended university. He tells of his youth: "All the culture and civilization I came across in my surroundings seemed to be a flight from reality, escapism."[71] When he began his theological studies in 1929, neo-Reformation theology stood at its height with the emphasis on a discontinuity between Christian faith and human life in general. In reaction to this, he wrote his licentiate thesis on Irenaeus and Marcion with the subtitle "Studies in the Area of Creation" (1939). This subject matter, creation, law, and salvation, he took up again in book form as *Creation and Law* (1958; Eng. trans. 1961). In a different way he wrote in 1942 *Luther on Vocation* (Eng. trans. 1957). At that time he was called to be associate professor at Lund.

Wingren sees a distinct and fundamental connection between Irenaeus's idea of restoration and Luther's idea of vocation. Yet he noticed that there had been a reluctance to talk about creation, since such discourse might introduce a Catholic theory of "natural law," which has often been used to conserve and defend existing economic and social conditions. Another reason for shying away from creation was the misapplication of orders of creation to the program of National Socialism in Germany.[72] In his book *Creation and Law*, Wingren avoids both dangers and shows that the gospel cannot function without an understanding of creation because "there is a unity between man's pre-history and the Gospel, and when man accepts the Gospel he always accepts this pre-history. Or, to put it in a different way, the assent of faith to the second article is dependent on assent to the first article."[73]

This belonging together of creation and the gospel with the new creation is reiterated in a more recent publication, *Creation and Gospel*, which is largely autobiographical. There he writes: "The core of the Gospel is the resurrection of Christ, and this core is Creation, new and victorious Creation that overcomes destruction and death. Creation and Gospel do not tend in different directions. . . . Instead they support one another. Indeed, they are one."[74] Reacting against the neglect of creation especially during this past century by Barth and Bultmann, Wingren showed that this is an important topic that anchors the Christian message in the world and at the same time makes the gospel of redemption more concrete.

71. Gustaf Wingren, *The Flight from Creation* (Minneapolis: Augsburg, 1971), 14.

72. Cf. Wingren, *The Flight from Creation*, 25.

73. Gustaf Wingren, *Creation and Law*, trans. Ross Mackenzie (Philadelphia: Muhlenberg, 1961), 120.

74. Gustaf Wingren, *Creation and Gospel: The New Situation in European Theology*, introduction and bibliography by Henry Vander Goot (New York: Edwin Mellen, 1979), 158-59.

With this unashamed emphasis on the gospel in today's world Wingren contrasts another development in Swedish systematic theology that picks up on the so-called Uppsala philosophy, an analytic and antimetaphysical philosophy, the most important representative of which was Axel Hägerstrøm (1868-1939) and which was influenced by British analytic philosophy and formal logic. Here the question of truth in religion was put forth again, a search for presuppositions that can be examined and arguments that have logical consistency. In pursuing this quest, more and more theologians are convinced that there are good reasons to ascribe meaning and truth to foundational religious sentences, though that truth can be neither empirically nor logically established. This means that theologians started to contradict the empiricism and positivism of analytic philosophy without abandoning the demand for conceptual and logical clarity. Theology's effort was no longer to determine in an argumentative way what is comprised by Christian dogmatics, but to show the different possibilities and thereby to indicate the complexity of knowledge about humanity and the universe. Some of the theologians active in this area are Hampus Lyttkens (b. 1916), a philosopher of religion at Lund; Axel Gyllenkrok (1910-2002) from Uppsala; and Urban Forell (b. 1930), a systematic theologian from Copenhagen. Finnish systematic theology has developed similarly to that in Sweden. This has been furthered by the theological faculty in Åbo, where theology is taught in Swedish. One could mention here the Finnish Luther scholar Lennart Pinomaa (1901-96), and in the philosophy of religion, Simo Knuuttila (b. 1946).

Since Wingren cooperated very closely with Knud Løgstrup, we should also pay at least passing attention to this significant Danish philosopher of religion.[75] **Knud E. Løgstrup** (1905-81) was born in Copenhagen and studied theology there. He continued his studies of theology and philosophy in France, Austria, and especially Germany, where he was influenced by Martin Heidegger and Rudolf Bultmann. From 1943 to 1975 he was professor of ethics and philosophy of religion at the University of Aarhus.

According to Løgstrup, human life is created and therefore has an ethical content that can be determined through phenomenological analysis. In his 1956 book, *The Ethical Demand,* which appeared in 1991 in a thirteenth edition, he attempted to show the attitude toward the other person in a purely nonreligious way, something contained in the religious proclamation of Jesus. The reason for being able to do this, Løgstrup contended, is that "Jesus' proclamation contains no directions, no rules, no morality, no casuistry. It contains nothing which relieves us of responsibility by solving in advance the conflicts

75. Cf. Henry Vander Goot, introduction to *Creation and Gospel,* xxix.

into which the demand places us."[76] Jesus does not give us an ethic that would relieve our responsibility to use our imagination and insight in ordering our lives. Therefore Christians must make their decisions "on exactly the same basis as those upon which anyone else decides" (111). We must use our reason, insight, and considerations in clarifying the questions of life for ourselves and then appeal to other persons' reason, insight, and considerations to do the same. Resorting to natural law would work only among people who are in some way or other related to each other, but would not function with strangers (cf. 142-43).

To further his argument for a common basis of ethical consideration, Løgstrup claimed that in human existence there is a root relationship of trust between persons. Out of this evolves the element of mutual obligation of caring for the other without ever being "in a position to demand something in return for what we do" (123). This ethical demand occurs again in Jesus' summons to love our neighbor (cf. 143-44). This means that the love of neighbor is an inseparable part of life itself given with the notion of creation. The ethical demand is then a universal that can be discussed both in theology and philosophy. We notice here again the emphasis on making the Christian ethical deliberation understandable in the wider context of human life and thereby establishing a basis for dialogue with the world.

Other Danish theologians, well known beyond Denmark, include Niels Hansensøe (1895-1978), professor in Copenhagen after 1934, who pursued a more Barthian trend, and Regin Prenter (1907-90), after 1945 professor in Aarhus. Prenter presented a more classical line, especially with his well-known dogmatics *Creation and Redemption* (Eng. trans. 1967). As a Danish theologian, he did not rely exclusively on German exegetical insights, but also gleaned results from the British discussion.

FOR FURTHER READING

Friedrich Delitzsch (1850-1922)

Delitzsch, Friedrich. *Babel and Bible: Three Lectures on the Significance of Assyriological Research for Religion Embodying the Most Important Criticisms and the Author's Replies.* Translated from the German. Chicago: Open Court, 1906.
Kohler, Kaufmann. *Assyriology and the Bible.* Baltimore: Lord Baltimore Press, 1903.

---

76. Knud E. Løgstrup, *The Ethical Demand,* trans. Theodor I. Jensen et al., introduction by Alasdair MacIntyre and Hans Fink (Notre Dame: University of Notre Dame Press, 1997), 108-9. The page numbers in the following text refer to this work.

Ernst Troeltsch (1865-1923)

Drescher, Hans-Georg. *Ernst Troeltsch: His Life and Work.* Translated by John Bowden. Minneapolis: Fortress, 1993 [1992].

Riest, Benjamin. *Toward a Theology of Involvement: The Thought of Ernst Troeltsch.* Philadelphia: Westminster, 1966.

Troeltsch, Ernst. *The Absoluteness of Christianity and the History of Religions.* Introduction by James Luther Adams. Translated by David Reid. Richmond: John Knox, 1971.

————. *The Christian Faith.* Based on lectures delivered at the University of Heidelberg in 1912 and 1913. Foreword by Marta Troeltsch. Edited by Gertrud von le Fort. Translated by Garrett E. Paul. Minneapolis: Fortress, 1991.

————. *Christian Thought: Its History and Application.* Edited with an introduction by Baron F. Von Hügel. Westport, Conn.: Hyperion, 1979 [1923].

————. *Protestantism and Progress: The Significance of Protestantism for the Rise of the Modern World.* English translation 1912. Philadelphia: Fortress, 1986.

————. *Religion in History: Essays.* Translated by James Luther Adams and Walter F. Bense. Introduction by James Luther Adams. Minneapolis: Fortress, 1991.

————. *The Social Teaching of the Christian Churches.* Translated by Olive Wyon. Foreword by James Luther Adams. 2 vols. Louisville: Westminster John Knox, 1992.

————. *Writings on Theology and Religion.* Translated and edited by Robert Morgan and Michael Pye. London: Duckworth, 1977.

Yasukata, Toshimasa. *Ernst Troeltsch: Systematic Theologian of Radical Historicality.* Atlanta: Scholars, 1986.

Rudolf Otto (1869-1937)

Almond, Philip. *Rudolf Otto: An Introduction to His Philosophical Theology.* Chapel Hill: University of North Carolina Press, 1984.

Davidson, Robert. *Rudolf Otto's Interpretation of Religion.* Princeton: Princeton University Press, 1947.

Otto, Rudolf. *Autobiographical and Social Essays.* Berlin: Mouton de Gruyter, 1996.

————. *The Idea of the Holy: An Inquiry into the Non-rational Factor in the Idea of the Divine and Its Relation to the Rational.* Translated by John W. Harvey. New York: Oxford University Press, 1939.

————. *India's Religion of Grace and Christianity Compared and Contrasted.* Translated by Frank Hugh Foster. New York: Macmillan, 1930.

————. *The Kingdom of God and the Son of Man: A Study in the History of Religion.* Translated from the revised German edition by Floyd V. Filson and Bertram Lee-Woolf. New and rev. ed. London: Lutterworth, 1951.

————. *Mysticism East and West: A Comparative Analysis of the Nature of Mysticism.* Translated by Bertha L. Bracey and Richenda C. Payne. New York: Macmillan, 1932.

————. *Naturalism and Religion.* Translated by J. Arthur and Margaret R. Thomson.

Edited with an introduction by W. D. Morrison. 2nd ed. London: Williams and Norgate, 1913.

———. *The Philosophy of Religion Based on Kant and Fries.* Translated by E. B. Dicker. Foreword by W. Tudor Jones. London: Williams and Norgate, 1931.

———. *Religious Essays: A Supplement to "The Idea of the Holy."* Translated by Brian Lunn. London: Oxford University Press, 1931.

Raphael, Melissa. *Rudolf Otto and the Concept of Holiness.* Oxford: Clarendon, 1997.

Auguste Comte (1798-1857)

Caird, Edward. *The Social Philosophy and Religion of Comte.* New York: Kraus Reprint, 1968 [1885].

Comte, Auguste. *A General View of Positivism.* Translated by J. H. Bridges. Official centenary edition. New York: Robert Speller, 1957.

Manuel, Frank E. *The Prophets of Paris.* Cambridge: Harvard University Press, 1962.

Simon, Walter Michael. *European Positivism in the Nineteenth Century: An Essay in Intellectual History.* Ithaca, N.Y.: Cornell University Press, 1963.

Wernick, Andrew. *Auguste Comte and the Religion of Humanity: The Post-Theistic Program of French Social Theory.* Cambridge: Cambridge University Press, 2002.

James G. Frazer (1854-1941)

Ackerman, Robert. *J. G. Frazer: His Life and Work.* Cambridge: Cambridge University Press, 1987.

Downie, Robert A. *Frazer and the Golden Bough.* London: Gollancz, 1970.

Frazer, James George. *The Belief in Immortality and the Worship of the Dead.* Gifford Lectures, 1911-1912. London: Macmillan, 1913.

———. *The Golden Bough: A Study in Magic and Religion.* Abridged ed. New York: Macmillan, 1979.

———. *Man, God, and Immortality: Thoughts on Human Progress.* Rev. ed. London: Macmillan, 1927.

Malinowski, Bronislaw. *A Scientific Theory of Culture, and Other Essays.* Preface by Huntington Cairns. Chapel Hill: University of North Carolina Press, 1944.

William James (1842-1910)

James, William. *The Varieties of Religious Experience: A Study in Human Nature.* Introduction by Arthur Darby Nock. Glasgow: William Collins Fountain Book, 1977.

———. *The Will to Believe and Other Essays in Popular Philosophy and Human Immortality.* New York: Dover, 1956.

Moore, Edward C. *American Pragmatism: Peirce, James, and Dewey.* New York: Columbia University Press, 1961.

Myers, Gerald E. *William James: His Life and Thought.* New Haven: Yale University Press, 1986.

See also chapter 7.

Nathan Söderblom (1866-1931)

Curtis, Charles. *Söderblom: Ecumenical Pioneer.* Minneapolis: Augsburg, 1967.
Katz, Peter. *Nathan Söderblom: A Prophet of Christian Unity.* London: J. Clarke, 1946.
Söderblom, Nathan. *The Nature of Revelation.* Edited with an introduction by Edgar M. Carlson. Translated by Frederic E. Pamp. Philadelphia: Fortress, 1966.
Sundkler, Bengt. *Nathan Söderblom: His Life and Work.* Lund: Gleerup, 1968.

Einar Billing (1871-1939)

Billing, Einar. *Our Calling.* Translated by Conrad Bergendoff. Rock Island, Ill.: Augustana Press, 1955.
Wingren, Gustaf. *An Exodus Theology: Einar Billing and the Development of Swedish Theology.* Philadelphia: Fortress, 1969.
―――. "The Theology of Einar Billing." *Lutheran Quarterly* 2 (1950/51): 396-413; 3:60-69.

Anders Nygren (1890-1978)

Hall, Thor. *Anders Nygren.* Peabody, Mass.: Hendrickson, 1991 [1978].
Johnson, William Alexander. *On Religion: A Study of Theological Method in Schleiermacher and Nygren.* Leiden: Brill, 1964.
Nygren, Anders. *Agape and Eros.* Translated by Philip S. Watson. Philadelphia: Westminster, 1953.
―――. *Meaning and Method: Prolegomena to a Scientific Philosophy of Religion and a Scientific Theology.* Translated by Philip S. Watson. Philadelphia: Fortress, 1972.
Wingren, Gustaf. *Theology in Conflict: Nygren, Barth, Bultmann.* Translated by Eric H. Wahlstrom. Philadelphia: Muhlenberg, 1958.

Gustav Aulén (1879-1977)

Anderlonis, Joseph J. *The Soteriology of Gustav Aulén: The Origins, Development, and Relevancy of the Christus Victor Atonement View.* Rome: Pontificia Universitas Gregoriana, 1988.
Aulén, Gustaf. *Christus Victor: An Historical Study of the Three Main Types of the Idea of the Atonement.* Translated by A. G. Herbert. Foreword by Jaroslav Pelikan. New York: Macmillan, 1969.
―――. *The Drama and the Symbols: A Book on Images of God and the Problems They Raise.* Translated by Sydney Linton. London: SPCK, 1970.
―――. *Eucharist and Sacrifice.* Translated by Eric H. Wahlstrom. Philadelphia: Muhlenberg, 1958.

Ragnar Bring (1895-1990)

Bring, Ragnar. *How God Speaks to Us: The Dynamics of the Living Word.* Philadelphia: Muhlenberg, 1962.
Hall, Thor. *A Framework for Faith: Lundensian Theological Methodology in the Thought of Ragnar Bring.* Leiden: Brill, 1970.

Gustaf Wingren (b. 1910)

Preece, Gordon R. *The Viability of the Vocation Tradition in Trinitarian, Credal, and Reformed Perspective: The Threefold Call.* Lewiston, N.Y.: Edwin Mellen, 1998.

Wingren, Gustaf. *Creation and Gospel: The New Situation in European Theology.* Introduction and bibliography by Henry Vander Goot. New York: Edwin Mellen, 1979.

————. *Creation and Law.* Translated by Ross Mackenzie. Philadelphia: Muhlenberg, 1961.

————. *The Flight from Creation.* Minneapolis: Augsburg, 1971.

Knud E. Løgstrup (1905-81)

Løgstrup, Knud E. *The Ethical Demand.* Translated by Theodor I. Jensen et al. Introduction by Alasdair MacIntyre and Hans Fink. Notre Dame: University of Notre Dame Press, 1997.

————. *Metaphysics.* Translated with an introduction by Russell L. Dees. 2 vols. Milwaukee: Marquette University Press, 1995.

9 The Battle for Jesus

The nineteenth century marks the high point of the search for the life of Jesus. Various factors contributed to this search. (1) A greater awareness of the different sources contained within the New Testament, as attested by the research of F. C. Baur and his school, for instance. (2) The considerable background material for the biblical texts adduced through the efforts of the school of religion with scholars such as Bousset, Deissmann, and others. (3) The emergence of romanticism with its interest in antiquity at the beginning of the century. Consequently the classical culture of Italy and Greece was rediscovered. Beyond that, travels to the Holy Land became popular due to the beginnings of archaeology, and with them a natural curiosity emerged about the "founder" of the Christian religion.

The Life of Jesus Research and Its Initial Impasse:
Johannes Weiss and Albert Schweitzer

Friedrich Schleiermacher was the first theologian to lecture publicly on the life of Jesus.[1] Books on the life of Jesus had been published before, but the topic had not yet become a distinct part of academic studies. Schleiermacher attempted to perceive Jesus in the context of his time and in his own right. He was convinced that we can have a firm faith only if we ascertain its grounding. "If

---

1. So Jack Verheyden, introduction to *The Life of Jesus,* by Friedrich Schleiermacher, trans. Jack Verheyden (Philadelphia: Fortress, 1975), xi.

the person of Christ is not to be retained, then Christianity as such must be given up and only what is true for itself about it must remain."[2] With this caution in mind, and knowing he could not present a detailed biography, Schleiermacher attempted to sketch out Jesus' life and ministry.

In *The Positivity of the Christian Religion* (1795-96), Georg Friedrich Wilhelm Hegel attempted to answer how the religion of Jesus was transformed into the positive Christian religion practiced by the Christians.[3] He presented Jesus as the teacher of a primarily moral religion. While Schleiermacher and Hegel did not doubt the historicity of Jesus as a person, David Friedrich Strauss and Bruno Bauer did. Strauss initially still considered Jesus a historical human being. But Bauer even disclaimed the historicity of Jesus. In contrast to the skeptics Strauss and Bauer, the French Orientalist Ernest Renan (1823-92) presented a novel-like depiction of the life of Jesus. Renan was from 1884 to his death administrator of the Collège de France. In 1863 while in Palestine he wrote *The Life of Jesus* (Eng. trans. 1927). Jesus was for him a gentle Galilean whom John the Baptist had transformed into a religious revolutionary and a sinister prophet. As Albert Schweitzer had shown in his magisterial study *The Quest of the Historical Jesus: A Critical Study of Its Progress from Reimarus to Wrede* (1906), one could find just as many interpretations of Jesus in the nineteenth century as interpreters.

By the second half of the nineteenth century, confidence in historical sources had been reestablished. In *The Christian Doctrine of Justification and Reconciliation*, Albrecht Ritschl, for instance, entitled a section "The Doctrine of Christ's Person and Life-Work." Here he stated: "Beyond all doubt Jesus was conscious of a new and hitherto unknown relation to God, and said so to His disciples; and His aim was to bring His disciples into the same attitude toward the world as His own and to the same estimate of themselves that under these conditions He might enlist them in the world-wide mission of the Kingdom of God, which He knew to be not only His own business, but theirs."[4] The aim of Jesus' life was the union of people in the kingdom of God. They should expend their energies to further the establishment of the kingdom. We also remember that according to Adolf von Harnack the kingdom of God and its coming was one of the main points of Jesus' message. As a historian, Harnack labored hard

2. Schleiermacher, *The Life of Jesus,* 22.

3. For a good treatment of the different phases in Hegel's understanding of the Christian faith, see Bernard M. G. Reardon, *Hegel's Philosophy of Religion* (New York: Barnes and Noble, 1977).

4. Albrecht Ritschl, *The Christian Doctrine of Justification and Reconciliation: The Positive Development of the Doctrine,* trans. H. R. Mackintosh and A. B. Macaulay (New York: Charles Scribner's, 1900), 386.

to establish the historical reliability of the New Testament documents. While he recognized the central role of the theme of the kingdom of God in Jesus' teaching and ministry, he did not develop a sense of eschatological realism. He spiritualized the kingdom notion, which is "a still and mighty power in the hearts of men," while the coming kingdom "was an idea which Jesus simply shared with his contemporaries."[5] To avoid the error of discarding the external coming kingdom, Harnack should have paid attention to Johannes Weiss, Ritschl's former student and son-in-law.

Johannes Weiss (1863-1914) was professor of New Testament in Göttingen when he published *Jesus' Proclamation of the Kingdom of God* in 1892. Rejecting Ritschl's understanding of the kingdom of God as an ethical ideal and, we might say, also in contrast to the spiritualization of the kingdom notion by Harnack, Weiss contended: "This interpretation of the Kingdom of God as an innerworldly ethical ideal is a vestige of the Kantian idea and does not hold up before a more precise historical examination."[6] For Weiss the kingdom is totally otherworldly. Its realization is up to God alone and does not rely on human action. Weiss denied that Jesus thought of a this-worldly development of the kingdom. When Jesus talked about a kingdom that has already commenced, he was expressing a prophetic, future-directed view. Generally, however, Jesus thought of the realization of the kingdom as still outstanding. "The disciples were to pray for the coming of the Kingdom, but men could do nothing to establish it."[7] The coming of the kingdom is totally God's action, and it will come as something utterly different from what we experience now in this world.

Nevertheless, having established the otherworldly notion of the kingdom, Weiss's own conclusion was not significantly different from that of Harnack: "The real difference between our modern Protestant world-view and that of primitive Christianity is, therefore, that we do not share the eschatological attitude, namely, that the shape of this world will pass away."[8] While pointing out that Jesus' proclamation focused on an actual eschatological transformation of this world, Weiss could not agree with such a prospect. He was still too much a child of the nineteenth century and its materialistic worldview.

In 1901 **Albert Schweitzer** (1875-1965), the famous Bach interpreter, medical doctor in tropical Africa, and New Testament scholar, published a book with

5. Adolf von Harnack, *What Is Christianity?* trans. Thomas B. Saunders (Philadelphia: Fortress, 1986), 54.

6. Johannes Weiss, *Jesus' Proclamation of the Kingdom of God* (1892), translated and edited with an introduction by Richard Hyde Hiers and David Larrimore Holland (London: SCM, 1971), 133.

7. Weiss, *Jesus' Proclamation,* 129.

8. Weiss, *Jesus' Proclamation,* 135.

the title *The Mystery of the Kingdom of God: The Secret of Jesus' Messiahship and Passion,* in which he attempted to portray a life of Jesus. This booklet contained enough dynamite to shatter many cherished thoughts of conservatives and liberals alike. His entire approach was somewhat unorthodox. He began not at the beginning of Jesus' life but in the middle. Schweitzer asked, similarly to Strauss: Did Jesus regard himself as the Messiah? If so, why did he not act like the Messiah as commonly understood at this time, e.g., by bringing about the messianic conditions of prosperity and peace? If Jesus did not think he was the Messiah, how did he come to be regarded as the Messiah?[9] The point was that Jesus either really understood himself to be the Messiah or this title was first ascribed to him by the early church. Unlike Strauss, Schweitzer did not opt for a literary solution. Like Harnack, he was convinced that Jesus knew himself to be the Messiah. But unlike both Strauss and Harnack, Schweitzer took eschatology to be the key to understanding Jesus. The secret of Jesus' identity was disclosed to Jesus at his baptism — he was the one God has chosen to be the Messiah.

Jesus' task was to suffer and labor for the kingdom of God as the "unrecognised and hidden Messiah."[10] According to Schweitzer, he was an eschatological — even apocalyptic — figure like John the Baptist. They shared a similar message: repent and attain righteousness, because the kingdom of God is close at hand. Unlike John, Jesus performed miracles. But Jesus' life and activity was a disappointment. His preaching did not yield much success despite his best efforts, and the coming of the kingdom was delayed. One of the signs of the coming kingdom was the discovery that John the Baptist was Elijah reincarnate. The final disappointment was the beheading of John. With that and the realization that the kingdom was not immediately at hand, Jesus knew he too had to suffer death. Thus he turned with his disciples to Jerusalem and claimed to be the Messiah. The Jewish authorities, who had always been suspicious of him, accused him of blasphemy and put him to death. He died, but nothing happened. This portrayal of Jesus' life was the first significant attempt to explain Jesus' mission as founded on an idea that had proved to be wrong. Nonetheless, Schweitzer saw heroic qualities in Jesus and stated that his intent was *"to depict the figure of Jesus in its overwhelming heroic greatness and to impress it upon the modern age and upon the modern theology."*[11]

A different reception greeted Schweitzer's 1906 book, *The Quest of the Historical Jesus: A Critical Study of Its Progress from Reimarus to Wrede.* It was

9. Cf. Albert Schweitzer, *The Mystery of the Kingdom of God: The Secret of Jesus' Messiahship and Passion,* translated with an introduction by Walter Lowrie (New York: Schocken, 1964), 4.

10. Schweitzer, *Mystery of the Kingdom,* 254.

11. Schweitzer, *Mystery of the Kingdom,* 274.

the first massive and conscientious attempt to assess the value of the numerous investigations into the life of Jesus. Each generation (rationalism, liberalism, modern theology, etc.), Schweitzer argued, tore down the picture of Jesus erected in the preceding generation and started to build its own without realizing that this new edifice mirrored its own aspirations and desires more than the Jesus who had actually walked on this earth. Though these biographies reflected utmost sincerity, they were without value for our faith. "The abiding and eternal in Jesus is absolutely independent of historical knowledge and can only be understood by contact with His spirit which is still at work in the world. . . . Jesus as a concrete historical personality remains a stranger to our time."[12] Schweitzer did not give up in despair, since it is Jesus' spirit that is important; but this spirit is accessible only if we conceive of Jesus as an eschatological figure. Therefore the two people mentioned in Schweitzer's title, Hermann Samuel Reimarus and William Wrede, circumscribe his program. Reimarus (1694-1768) provided an eschatological picture of Jesus, though he disclaimed its historical truthfulness. Wrede (1859-1906) showed that a noneschatological view of Jesus was untenable. Schweitzer again proposed the alternative already advanced in *The Mystery of the Kingdom of God:* "There is, on the one hand, the eschatological solution, which at one stroke raises the Markian account as it stands, with all its disconnectedness and inconsistencies, into genuine history; and there is, on the other hand, the literary solution, which regards the incongruous dogmatic element as interpolated by the earlier Evangelist into the tradition and therefore strikes out the Messianic claim altogether from the historical life of Jesus. *Tertium non datur.*"[13] Once again Schweitzer took a clear stand for a thoroughgoing eschatological interpretation of Jesus. He declared that Jesus' ethics were interim ethics aimed at the preparation for the kingdom of God, but since the kingdom had not come when Jesus expected it, our ethics cannot be derived from Jesus' ethics. Jesus' demand of world denial and perfection of personality is still valid for us, although it is in contrast to our ethics of reason. We need more persons like Jesus. His enthusiasm and heroism are important for us, because they were derived from Jesus' faith in this kingdom, which was only strengthened by his encounter with obstacles.

In the knowledge that He is the coming Son of Man [Jesus] lays hold of the wheel of the world to set it moving on that last revolution which is to bring

---

12. Albert Schweitzer, *The Quest of the Historical Jesus: A Critical Study of Its Progress from Reimarus to Wrede,* trans. W. Montgomery, 3rd ed. (London: A. & C. Black, 1954 [1910]), 399.
    13. Schweitzer, *Quest,* 335.

all ordinary history to a close. It refuses to turn, and He throws Himself upon it. Then it does turn; and crushes Him. Instead of bringing in the eschatological conditions, He has destroyed them. The wheel rolls onward, and the mangled body of the one immeasurable great Man, who was strong enough to think of Himself as the spiritual ruler of mankind and to bend history to His purpose, is still hanging upon it. That is His victory and His reign.[14]

It is relatively unimportant for Schweitzer that Jesus was actually deceived in his eschatological expectations. All-decisive was Jesus' attitude toward both history and the obstacles he had to overcome in accomplishing his goal.

The Quest of the Historical Jesus caused an immense uproar. Liberal Protestantism could tolerate Schweitzer's portrayal of Jesus as a deceived religious fanatic but not the idea that his ethics were mere interim ethics. Regardless of how critical Protestant liberalism had been toward the Jesus of the New Testament, it cherished his ethical ideals. Now Schweitzer had declared quite rightly that it was impossible to separate Jesus' ethics from his eschatological proclamation. The attempt of liberal theology to eliminate the eschatological dimension of Jesus' proclamation and to confine itself to the "timeless" validity of his ethical teachings could no longer be founded in the historical Jesus. Conservative scholars also reacted, arguing that Schweitzer fell into the very trap he had pointed out as futile, namely, the attempt to write a life of Jesus. They argued that the true historical Jesus could not be found strictly by historical investigation but only through faith. Yet in England, Schweitzer found acclaim. F. C. Burkitt (1864-1935), a leading New Testament scholar, immediately translated *The Quest* and attached a preface to it. William Sanday (1843-1920), another prominent figure in British New Testament scholarship, initially praised Schweitzer's books but later realized the radical attitude behind them and quickly changed his mind.

Schweitzer's study marked several breakthroughs in the life of Jesus research. Schweitzer not only recognized the eschatological dimension of Jesus and his ministry, but also realized that this dimension was central to Jesus and his proclamation. Therefore it could not be disassociated from him. Yet Schweitzer claimed that with regard to this central tenet, Jesus was mistaken. He had hoped for something that did not occur. Schweitzer's second break-

---

14. Schweitzer, *Quest,* 368-69. In a posthumously published manuscript, *The Kingdom of God and Primitive Christianity* (1950/51), edited with an introduction by Ulrich Neuenschwander, trans. L. A. Garrard (New York: Seabury Press, 1968), 123, Schweitzer continued this same line, saying that Jesus eventually concluded that through his death the kingdom of God would be ushered in. Schweitzer consistently maintained that Jesus was a "heroic failure."

through was showing with convincing clarity that the New Testament sources do not allow us to ascertain a life of Jesus. Furthermore, all reconstructions of the supposedly "original" Jesus were projections of the one researching Jesus.

His claim that Jesus was mistaken notwithstanding, and having recognized the problematic nature of writing a life of Jesus, Schweitzer was not discouraged. He maintained that "Jesus means something to our world because a mighty spiritual force streams forth from Him and flows through our time also. This fact can neither be shaken nor confirmed by historical discovery. It is the solid foundation of Christianity."[15] Jesus is no longer a historical reality for us. But his spirit is still alive and active among us. Schweitzer therefore concluded his investigation: "He comes to us as One unknown, without a name, as of old, by the lake-side, He came to those men who knew Him not. He speaks to us the same word: 'Follow thou me!' and sets us to the tasks which He has to fulfill for our time."[16] In unparalleled fashion Schweitzer himself followed the call.

Having been born of liberal Protestant parents in a parsonage in Alsace, which was then part of Germany, Schweitzer started to study theology and philosophy at the University of Strasbourg in 1893 and then continued his studies briefly in Paris and Berlin. He also spent several weeks each spring and often in autumn in Paris taking organ lessons from Charles-Marie Widor (1844-1937), the founder of the new French organ school. In 1896 he vowed that from his thirtieth year of life on he would "dedicate himself to the immediate human service."[17] In 1899 he finished his doctoral thesis on Kant's philosophy of religion, and a year later he was ordained and took a vicarage in Strasbourg, which he maintained until 1912. He declined to do his *Habilitation* in philosophy, since he did not want to give up his preaching office. Yet in 1900 he did his licentiate in theology with a thesis on the Lord's Supper ("The Problem of the Lord's Supper according to the Scholarly Research of the 19th Century and the Historical Accounts" [Eng. trans. 1982]). Already the following year he did his *Habilitation,* which became the aforementioned *Mystery of the Kingdom of God.* The next year he started teaching as Privatdozent for New Testament at the theological faculty at Strasbourg. In 1905 he began his medical studies and did his dissertation on the psychiatric evaluation of Jesus. Schweitzer then wanted to join the Mission Society in Paris to work in Africa. Yet that organization was distrustful of his liberal theology.

In 1912 he gave up his professorship at Strasbourg and married Helene

---

15. Schweitzer, *Quest,* 397.

16. Schweitzer, *Quest,* 401.

17. As quoted in the informative article by Erich Gräßer, "Schweitzer, Albert," in *Theologische Realenzyklopädie,* 30:676.

Bresslau (1879-1957), a nurse. He studied tropical medicine for a year in Paris, and in 1913 went with his wife to Lambaréné, in what is today Gabon. There he built his own hospital with his own means. He financed his engagement in Africa with organ recitals and lecture tours in Europe. Although his work was interrupted by World War I (1914-18), Schweitzer returned to Africa in 1924. He stayed there altogether for more than thirty years. Along with being a professional theologian and a medical doctor, he was an expert on Johann Sebastian Bach (1685-1750) and his organ work. In 1905 he published a treatise on Bach, which still sets the standard today. In eight volumes he also published a critical practical edition of Bach's entire organ works. Schweitzer declined calls to professorships in the theological faculties of Zürich and Leipzig, and many honors were bestowed on him during his long life. In a Festschrift for his eightieth birthday, such diverse people as Rudolf Bultmann, Pablo Casals, Martin Buber, and Albert Einstein contributed essays.

In his heart Schweitzer was a theologian. For him the Christian religion was not a merely spiritual religion, but as he had stated in the conclusion of his *Quest,* it meant for him to follow the call of his Master. That was the reason why he went to central Africa. And when in the wake of World War I he was not allowed to continue his work there, he picked up again his vicarage in Strasbourg. As he wrote in a sermon of 1902: "Not by meditation and reflection does one grasp the great secret which hovers over the world and human life. The higher realization flowers only in work and action. For this highest realization there is no difference between the wise and the simple. The simple, if they act, are given insights kept from the wise."[18]

But for what should one work and in which direction should one act? Schweitzer started with the observation that there is a will-to-live that can be observed in everything around us, in humans as well as in animals and in nature. Therefore, Schweitzer claimed, we must start "from the most immediate and comprehensive fact of consciousness, which says: 'I am life which wills to live, in the midst of life which wills to live.'"[19] Day by day we experience this in ourselves and around us. Schweitzer concluded: "Ethics consist, therefore, in my experiencing the compulsion to show to all will-to-live the same reverence as I do to my own. There we have given us that basic principle of the moral which is a necessity of thought. It is good to maintain and to encourage life; it is bad to destroy life or to obstruct it." Life affirmation and living in the world go

---

18. Albert Schweitzer, *Reverence for Life,* foreword by Elton Trueblood, trans. Reginald H. Fuller (New York: Harper and Row, 1969), 25, in a sermon on Luke 10:17-21.

19. Albert Schweitzer, *Civilization and Ethics,* trans. C. T. Campion, rev. Lilian M. R. Russell, 3rd ed. (London: Adam and Charles Black, 1949), 242, for this and the following quote.

together. From there evolves Schweitzer's maxim of reverence for life. Of course, as a medical doctor Schweitzer realized that he could not encourage every life and had to make decisions in favor of one form and therefore against another form of life. Since every kind of life is sacred, however, this maxim of reverence for life should make us think twice if we naturally accord this reverence to human life only. The importance of this maxim, which basically is an extension of the Golden Rule, can be seen with the philosopher Hans Jonas (1903-93) and his call for an ethics of responsibility.[20] Similar to Schweitzer, he exhibits a strong humanitarian concern. For Schweitzer the humanitarian attitude embodied in the reverence for life had global significance, because according to him humanity can either "realize the kingdom of God or perish."[21]

Escaping from the Strictures of Historical Research: Martin Kähler and Rudolf Bultmann

Martin Kähler (1835-1912), in a different way from Schweitzer, wanted to get away from relying on the historical Jesus to found a Christian theology. Kähler was born as son of a pastor near Königsberg in eastern Prussia. Initially he wanted to study law, but due to ill health transferred to the theological faculty. In Heidelberg he studied with Richard Rothe, and in Tübingen with Johann Tobias Beck. In Heidelberg Julius Müller and August Tholuck were influential for him. He did his dissertation under Tholuck on the biblical notion of conscience, and was appointed Privatdozent at Halle in 1860. Four years later he was called to Bonn as associate professor, and three years after that he returned to Halle as associate professor. When in 1879 he was promoted to full professor of systematic theology and New Testament, the number of his students increased significantly. Soon he was known all over the country and attracted many students. Tholuck had inspired Kähler not only to appreciate pietism, but also to care for his students.

Kähler was a prolific writer. *Die Wissenschaft der christlichen Lehre, von dem evangelischen Grundartikel aus im Abriß dargestellt (The Science of the Christian Doctrine Explained from the Foundational Protestant Article)* of 1883, an early book by him, is a precisely written and carefully argued piece of theological reflection. In the first part on Christian apologetics, justification becomes the principle and the context for unfolding the whole Christian doc-

---

20. Hans Jonas, *The Imperative of Responsibility: In Search for an Ethics for the Technological Age* (Chicago: University of Chicago Press, 1984).

21. Albert Schweitzer, *Gesammelte Werke in fünf Bänden* (Munich: C. H. Beck, n.d.), 5:373.

trine. The second part deals with Protestant dogmatics, again from the point of justification, and the third part is devoted to theological ethics as the result of justification by faith. With this emphasis on justification, it is not surprising that he requested that on his tombstone be inscribed: "The *articulus stantis et cadentis ecclesiae*, the evangelical article on justification which had formed the center of his theological system as well as of his faith and life."[22] This inscription shows that most important for him was the existential awareness of being accepted by God on account of Jesus' salvific activity as reflected in the biblical documents and not on account of a fragmentary biography that New Testament scholars could ascertain.

This ties in well with what Kähler is most well known for, a small book that evolved from a series of lectures to pastors, entitled *The So-called Historical Jesus and the Historic, Biblical Christ*, of 1892. For him the search for the historical Jesus goes in the wrong direction. Just like Schweitzer, he claimed that we do not have any sources to write a life of Jesus that a historian will accept as reliable and adequate. The reason for this is simply that the New Testament was not written for this purpose. Therefore Kähler wanted to criticize and reject the wrong aspects of this approach and establish the validity of an alternative. Now he came to his all-decisive question: "*Why* do we seek to know the figure of Jesus?" and his answer was: "I rather think it is because we believe him when he says, 'He who has seen me has seen the Father' (John 14:9), because we see in him the revelation of the invisible God" (58).

Kähler contended that the reason for our interest in the historical Jesus is neither to establish a historically reliable basis for Christology nor to disperse the distrust that since Reimarus was brought forth repeatedly that the New Testament sources are tendentious. The reason is that we want to show that Jesus is more than a human person, that he gives us access to God. Therefore Kähler continued: "Now if the Word became flesh in Jesus, which is the revelation, the flesh or the Word?" (58). And the answer he would have liked, of course, is that the Word is more important than its earthly embodiment. Therefore he stated: "How he was like us is self-evident" (59). This means it is a matter of fact that Jesus was a human being. Therefore this fact is of no great interest to us. The reason why we want to establish contact with the Jesus of the Gospels is to learn more about the one who is at the right hand of God and through whom God revealed himself. Yet this Jesus we cannot know through historical research.

---

22. So Carl Braaten, introduction to *The So-called Historical Jesus and the Historic, Biblical Christ*, by Martin Kähler, translated and edited with an introduction by Carl E. Braaten, foreword by Paul Tillich (Philadelphia: Fortress, 1964), 7. Page numbers in the immediately following text are from Kähler's book.

Kähler contended that there must be another way to reach the historic Christ, apart from these inconclusive scientific reconstructions. He arrived at a solution by analogy, saying that any truly historic figure who made an impact on history lives through his or her work. But what, he asked, "is the decisive influence that Jesus had upon posterity? According to the Bible and to church history it consisted in nothing else but the faith of his disciples, their conviction that in Jesus they had found the conqueror of guilt, sin, temptation, and death. From this one influence all others emanate" (63). This was summed up in the affirmation that Jesus is Lord. Therefore "the risen Lord is not the historical Jesus *behind* the Gospels, but the Christ of the apostolic preaching, of the *whole* New Testament." This Christ of the apostolic preaching, or as Kähler called him, the historic Christ of the Bible, is then actually identical with the *viva vox evangelii*, the living word of the gospel. Kähler then summed it up: "*This real Christ is the Christ who is preached.* The Christ who is preached, however, is precisely the Christ of faith" (65-66). The Christ who has exercised an influence in history is not the historical Jesus of New Testament research, but he is the Christ who is proclaimed and who, through this proclamation, has reached the ends of the world.

Kähler cautioned, however, that not everything that is proclaimed is Christ. Often the fantasy of the preacher intervenes, and therefore Kähler called for sobriety and restraint. The preacher ought merely to present to the hearers the old, often-heard stories of the biblical Christ. It is important for Kähler that "the most learned theologian . . . comes no nearer to the living Savior than the simple Christian" (73). Faith is not engendered by knowledge about the historical Jesus, but by the encounter with the biblical Christ. Faith is not identical with knowledge. It is a trust relying on the one who is encountered. Kähler contended: "We put our trust in the Bible as the Word of our God for the sake of its Christ" (75). The living word of the Christ issues forth from the Bible and thereby authenticates itself. We notice here a thoroughly Lutheran approach to the proclamation of Christ and the sources on which this proclamation is nourished. Christ is seen as the living word of the gospel. This Christocentricity in no way deters from appreciating the Old Testament, because the New Testament and its portrayal of Jesus cannot be understood without the Old. Kähler does not need any kind of inspiration of the biblical sources or a dogmatic authority because "*Christ himself is the originator of the biblical picture of the Christ*" (87). Kähler is convinced: "The Bible itself can awaken faith in revelation even when it is read divested of all authority, for it places before us the fact of revelation just as clearly — and just as unclearly — as Jesus, the prophets, and his apostles once did" (144). While the church values these documents, since from them comes our knowledge of Christ as it is preached in the church,

Kähler is not concerned that they are not historical documents in the strict sense of the term. They give us access to Christ who initiates faith, and thereby they are authenticated.

With this kind of approach Kähler influenced countless pastors and encouraged them in their service of the word. Moreover, he had an impact on many theologians who later taught in theological faculties. While escaping both biblicism and dogmatism, he pointed to "the necessity to make the certainty of faith independent of the unavoidable incertitudes of historical research."[23] In this way faith again won space to breathe without anxiously looking for historical support. His work and that of Schweitzer also hailed the end of the traditional lives of Jesus.

Then came **Rudolf Bultmann** (1884-1976), one of the most prominent and influential New Testament theologians of the twentieth century. As we will see, Bultmann was not just a New Testament scholar, because for him *"essentially theology and exegesis or systematic and historical theology coincide"*[24] (cf. chap. 10). He was born in a parsonage near Oldenburg and studied theology in Tübingen, Berlin, and Marburg. In 1910 he earned his doctorate in theology at Marburg, and there two years later he also did his *Habilitation*. In 1916 he was appointed associate professor at Breslau, and in 1920 he was called as a professor of New Testament studies at Giessen. The following year he received a call to Marburg, where he stayed until his death. "The pietistic heritage of his grandfather and a Lutheran biblicism of his father shaped the spiritual atmosphere of his parents' home. The study of theology added the influence of 'liberal' theology and of the 'history of religion.'"[25]

Like Kähler, Bultmann claimed that he was not interested in "Christ after the flesh," nor in the personality of Jesus, nor even in his teaching. He flatly stated in an article on Christology: "I often have the impression that my conservative New Testament colleagues feel very uncomfortable. . . . I calmly let the fire burn, for I see that what is consumed is only the fanciful portraits of Life-of-Jesus theology, and that means nothing other than 'Christ after the flesh himself.' . . . But the 'Christ after the flesh' is no concern of ours. How things looked in the heart of Jesus I do not know and do not want to know."[26]

---

23. So Tillich, foreword to *The So-called Historical Jesus*, xii, who was an appreciative student of Kähler, as he himself claimed.

24. Rudolf Bultmann, "Das Problem einer theologischen Exegese des NT," in *Anfänge der dialektischen Theologie*, ed. J. Moltmann (Munich: Chr. Kaiser, 1967), 2:68.

25. So Walter Schmithals in his extensive and appreciative biographical sketch, "Bultmann, Rudolf," in *Theologische Realenzyklopädie*, 7:387-96, here 388.

26. Rudolf Bultmann, "On the Question of Christology," in *Faith and Understanding*, ed. Robert W. Funk, trans. Louise Pettibone Smith (New York: Harper, 1969), 132.

In his 1926 book on Jesus, Bultmann even wrote: "By the tradition Jesus is named as bearer of the message. . . . Should it prove otherwise, that does not change in any way what is said in the record."[27] Here lies the big difference between Kähler and Bultmann. While the former showed no interest in the Christ after the flesh either, his tacit assumption was that the Christ after the flesh, of course, is the one who encounters us through the biblical record and is none other than the present Lord whom we meet in his preached word. For Bultmann such assumed continuity was no longer necessary. He not only distinguished between the Christ after the flesh and the Christ after the spirit, but he separated the two and concentrated exclusively on the latter. Neither is the personality of Jesus decisive — we know precious little about him. Nor is the timeless value of his teaching significant — by looking for that we remove him from the context of history. Important only is "what he *purposed,* and hence to what in his purpose as a part of history makes a present demand on us."[28]

Bultmann did not intend to look at history objectively, but rather to be drawn into a personal encounter with history. With this existential interpretation of the New Testament message, Bultmann did not need to distinguish between what can be reliably traced to the historical Jesus and what was later added and should be discarded. The entire New Testament could again be appreciated as leading us to an encounter with the kerygmatic Christ, the Christ who became alive in the Christian proclamation. The cut-and-paste system of the life-of-Jesus theology was now a thing of the past.

Bultmann employed existential analysis, which he had learned through his friendship with Martin Heidegger at Marburg. In turn, he reduced the whole biblical Christ to the that-ness of the Christ event, that there had been a historical person who claimed in one way or another to be the Christ. The reason why he had no interest in Jesus and his message is stated clearly in his *Theology of the New Testament:* "*The message of Jesus* is a presupposition for the theology of the New Testament rather than a part of theology itself. . . . Christian faith did not exist until there was a Christian kerygma."[29] This means that Jesus does not belong to New Testament theology, but forms its premise. Jesus was also not the first Christian, since the Christian faith rests on the proclamation of Jesus Christ crucified and risen, something that could only occur after his death.

Bultmann's disinterest in the historical Jesus did not deter him from deal-

27. Rudolf Bultmann, *Jesus and the Word,* trans. Louise Pettibone Smith and Erminie Huntress Lantero (New York: Charles Scribner's, 1958), 14.

28. Bultmann, *Jesus and the Word,* 8.

29. Rudolf Bultmann, *Theology of the New Testament,* trans. Kendrick Grobel, 2 vols. (New York: Charles Scribner's, 1954), 1:3.

ing with "the message of Jesus" in the first chapter of his *Theology of the New Testament,* and also from analyzing the Synoptic material. While Karl Ludwig Schmidt (1891-1956) wrote *Der Rahmen der Geschichte Jesu (The Framework of the Story of Jesus)* in 1919, the same year that Martin Dibelius (1883-1947) published *From Tradition to Gospel* (Eng. trans. 1965), Bultmann introduced two years later (1921) *The History of the Synoptic Tradition.* Bultmann endeavored to uncover the history of the individual units of the tradition, beginning with its origin, its subsequent stages of transformation, and its literal fixation in the Gospels. By reconstructing the origin and history of the individual entities through inter-Synoptic comparison, he claimed that one can detect the relatively strict rules of growth and change, and even illuminate some facets of the preliterary tradition.[30] Underlying the attempt to decipher and trace certain literary forms was the conviction that the literature emerging from the Christian communities spoke to a certain situation out of which it originated. This respective *Sitz im Leben* (life setting) was thought to be indicative of distinct literary forms.

But Bultmann did not want to deal solely with the Christian community. He also wanted to determine the historical reliability of the New Testament sayings and stories about Jesus: Do they lead back to Jesus or not? In his impressive analysis of the Synoptic material, Bultmann unambiguously associated precious little with the Jesus of history. He saw quickly that he was confirming the conviction of Kähler that, under the scrutiny of modern critical historical research, the biblical sources are not historical documents. Bultmann's main concern was not to elucidate what the followers of Jesus remembered about their leader, contrary to what many scholars had naively proposed to do in the nineteenth century. Instead, he sought to discern the faith conviction of the community of the resurrected Lord. This community believed in Jesus as the crucified and resurrected one, and believing in him they proclaimed him in literary forms that exemplified his significance for salvation and for the life of the community. It is no wonder that the growth of the material, now being attributed to the community, needed no longer to be seen as an aberration from the simple faith of Jesus, contrary to what liberal theology had claimed. It was rightly seen as the consequent development of this faith in their Lord. Yet the perception shifted when Bultmann wrote his 1941 article "New Testament and Mythology." Schubert Ogden (b. 1928) claimed it was "perhaps the single most discussed and controversial theological writing of the century."[31]

---

30. Cf. Rudolf Bultmann, *The History of the Synoptic Tradition,* trans. John Marsh, rev. ed. (New York: Harper, 1968), 5.

31. Schubert M. Ogden, preface to *New Testament and Mythology and Other Basic Writings,* by Rudolf Bultmann, selected, edited, and translated by Schubert M. Ogden (Philadelphia: Fortress, 1984), vii.

In "New Testament and Mythology" Bultmann did two things. (1) He claimed that many of the events related in the New Testament are no longer tenable for us today. (2) He insisted that we cannot save ourselves. We are saved only through God's action in the cross of Christ. This second point was hardly heard, however, because the first one caused such an uproar. Regarding the first point, Bultmann claimed that there is a radical discontinuity between our view of the world and that of the time of Jesus. What was credible then is no longer credible today. He wrote: "We cannot use electric lights and radios and, in the event of illness, avail ourselves of modern medical and clinical means and at the same time believe in the spirit and wonder world of the New Testament."[32] Either we live in the first century or we live in the present century, but we cannot live in both. "Thus, the stories of Christ's descent and ascent are finished, and so is the expectation of the Son of man's coming on the clouds of heaven and of the faithful's being caught up to meet him in the air (1 Thess 4:15ff.). Also finished by knowledge of the forces and laws of nature is faith in spirits and demons. . . . The wonders of the New Testament are also finished as wonders." Moreover, all these things are expressed in a mythical worldview. That is to say, the myth presents "a reality which lies beyond the reality that can be objectified, observed, and controlled, and which is of decisive significance for human existence."[33] Even "mythical eschatology is finished basically by the simple fact that Christ's parousia did not take place immediately as the New Testament expected it to, but that world history continues and — as every competent judge is convinced — will continue."[34] Under the same verdict falls even the doctrine of substitutionary atonement as an event through which a power to live is released that is appropriated through the sacraments.

Contrary to what had been so fashionable in the nineteenth century, Bultmann did not pick and choose what we can still accept and what is no longer tenable. He called both theologians and preachers to honestly let their audience know that we live in a world different from that of the first century A.D. He had no intention of giving up the Christian faith. But he contended: "The real point of myth is not to give an objective world picture; what is expressed in it, rather, is how we humans understand ourselves in our world. Thus, myth does not want to be interpreted in cosmological terms, but in anthropological terms — or, better, in existentialist terms" (9). Bultmann claimed it was not his idea to

---

32. See Rudolf Bultmann, "New Testament and Mythology," in *New Testament and Mythology and Other Basic Writings*, 4, for this and the following quote.

33. Rudolf Bultmann, "On the Problem of Demythologizing" (1961), in *New Testament and Mythology and Other Basic Writings*, 160.

34. Rudolf Bultmann, "New Testament and Mythology," 5. Page numbers in the following text refer to this essay.

advocate an existentialist interpretation of the New Testament. Since much of the New Testament is mythological, and since the myth contained therein urges toward an existentialist understanding, he had no other option than to comply. While the New Testament depicts human beings as being cosmically determined by the powers of evil or by God, they are, on the other hand, summoned to decide to whom they want to give allegiance and whom they want to follow. In asking how we want to understand ourselves and summoning us to understand ourselves authentically, i.e., not relying on the past, which meant for Bultmann on history, but being open for the future in following God's call, Bultmann's existential interpretation of the New Testament message even has a pietistic tinge.

Now to the second part of Bultmann's proposal: If, as Bultmann asserted, "faith as obedient surrender to God and as inner freedom from the world is possible only as faith in Christ," then "the decisive question is whether this claim is a mythological remainder that must be eliminated or demythologized by critical interpretation. It is the question whether the Christian understanding of being can be realized without Christ" (21). This alternative, namely, whether we can save ourselves or whether we still need Christ, did not just result from pursuing the issue of demythologization. It had already been introduced by philosophy. Bultmann reminded readers that "Martin Heidegger's existentialist analysis of human existence seems to be only a profane philosophical presentation of the New Testament view of who we are: [We are] beings existing historically in care for ourselves on the basis of anxiety, ever in the moment of decision between the past and the future, . . . or . . . we will attain our authenticity by surrendering all securities and being unreservedly free for the future" (23). This portrayal of inauthentic existence that we are focused on ourselves and therefore lose ourselves to the world, or alternatively, that we are free for the future (provided by God) and thereby exist authentically, can indeed be understood as a variation of the alternative the New Testament poses to us.

While the New Testament says, according to Bultmann, that without the saving act of God we cannot make the transition from inauthentic to authentic existence, philosophy claims that once both possibilities are pointed out to us, we can make on our own the transition from one to the other. Bultmann would even concede that this is possible, as can be seen with Paul, who summons us to authentic existence. Yet Paul's summons presupposes that we have already allowed God's liberating act to take place in our existence. Otherwise, we are in bondage to sin and cannot free ourselves. Yet would such saving act of God not also come under the verdict of mythology? Bultmann denied this, because in salvation "the cross of Christ is not a mythical event but a historical occurrence that has its origin in the historical event of the crucifixion of Jesus of Nazareth"

(35). Whatever is mythological talk about this, seeks to express nothing else but the significance of this historical event. But what about the resurrection? Here Bultmann asserted that "cross and resurrection are a unity in that together they are the one 'cosmic' event through which the world is judged and the possibility of genuine life is created" (37). One cannot separate the resurrection as an authenticating miracle from the cross, because the resurrection cannot be established as an objective fact.

When we talk about "God's decisive eschatological act," as did Bultmann, do we not again use mythological language? Bultmann would say that this is the risk one must take, but it is no longer mythology in the old sense, "so that it would have now become obsolete with the passing away of the mythical world picture" (41). The reason for this is that this act is not a miraculous, supernatural occurrence, but rather a historical occurrence in space and time, namely, that Jesus died on the cross. Bultmann ultimately points to a paradox: in a historical occurrence of a person dying on the cross God has decisively acted for all of human history. One might question whether this assertion is credible. But here Bultmann would again summon us to faith. For him it is exactly this *skandalon* that in the earthly form something trans-earthly has occurred.

With this kind of reasoning Bultmann accomplished two things. (1) It was possible again to preach without any sacrifice of the intellect on all the New Testament texts, whether allegedly mythological or not, since they could now be interpreted in an existential way. From the perspective of an existential interpretation, no longer were any of the New Testament narratives incredible or outdated. This existential interpretation also provided a unified hermeneutical approach to the New Testament. It could be understood as a summons for an existential decision for or against God. Yet in continuously calling for a decision, the New Testament proclamation was in danger of becoming monotonous. But (2) by separating the New Testament message completely from its historical anchor, from the person and proclamation of Jesus of Nazareth, the issue of continuity or discontinuity between this proclamation and Jesus of Nazareth became obliterated. Having no historical anchor but the cross of Jesus, the proclamation could also have evolved as one big myth.

The New Quest (James M. Robinson) and the Continued Quest

James M. Robinson (b. 1924), who taught most of his career at the Claremont School of Theology, pointed exactly to the issue of historical continuity when he claimed that the concern of the kerygma for the historicity of Jesus necessitates a new quest. "For how can the indispensable historicity of Jesus be affirmed, while at the same time maintaining the irrelevance of what a historical encounter with him would mean, once this has become a real possibility due to the rise of modern historiography? Such a position cannot fail to lead to the conclusion that the Jesus of the *kerygma* could equally well be only a myth, for one has in fact declared the meaning of his historical person irrelevant."[35] Of course, a new quest, Robinson assured, cannot verify the truth of the kerygma that this person actually lived out of transcendence and makes transcendence available to us in our historical existence. But "it can test whether this kerygmatic understanding of Jesus' existence corresponds to the understanding of existence implicit in Jesus' history, as encountered through modern historiography."[36] This means the new quest does not provide a new effort in the life of Jesus, but more modestly asks whether what Jesus portrayed in his person and action corresponds to what then was and still is proclaimed through the kerygma.

Even before Robinson had issued the call for a new quest, there had been scholars who had never given up the quest for the historical Jesus. We can geographically divide them into a German group that was rather small, a Scandinavian group, and an Anglo-Saxon group.

The Continued Quest in Germany: Joachim Jeremias and Ethelbert Stauffer

Most prominent among the Germans were Joachim Jeremias and Ethelbert Stauffer. **Joachim Jeremias** (1900-1982) was in a unique position, since he had lived in his youth in Palestine (1910-15) when his father was pastor in Jerusalem, and had become intimately familiar with Palestinian customs and the Hebrew and Aramaic spoken in Jesus' time. He confronted the neglect of the historical Jesus with the claim that "at no time had there been in early Christendom a kerygma without a didache."[37] Missionary preaching *(kerygma)* had always been supplemented with instruction *(didache)* of the congregation. This means that the kerygma points beyond itself to the history through which it was engendered.

In dealing with the sources, Jeremias wanted to go beyond the criterion of dissimilarity, a method by which one discerns the oldest tradition by eliminating everything that can be traced back to Jewish or Hellenistic parallels.[38] Jeremias

35. James M. Robinson, *A New Quest of the Historical Jesus* (London: SCM, 1959), 88.
36. James Robinson, *A New Quest*, 94.
37. Joachim Jeremias, *Das Problem des historischen Jesus* (Stuttgart: Calwer, 1960), 15.
38. See for the following Joachim Jeremias, *New Testament Theology: The Proclamation of Jesus,* trans. John Bowden (New York: Charles Scribner's, 1971), 2.

cautioned that this principle relies too much on the assumption of originality. Were this principle applied in every instance that Jesus used available material, all of this material would be eliminated. We would arrive at a dangerous reduction of what can be attributed to Jesus. Jeremias himself preferred linguistic and stylistic criteria, asking where we find sayings that sound as if Jesus could have said them. He pointed to Aramaisms in the Gospels, the avoidance of God's name, antithetical (Semitic) parallelisms, and so on. With this method he wanted to penetrate to the *ipsissima vox* (the very voice) of Jesus' original sayings. Yet he, too, did not entirely abandon the criterion of dissimilarity, claiming that Jesus' parables were unique and belonged to "the bedrock of the tradition about him."[39] According to Jeremias, the same is true with Jesus' mention of the *basileia tou theou* (kingdom of God), which has no parallel among his contemporaries, the affirmative "Amen" at the beginning of a saying, and the *abba* (colloquial, "father") in addressing God. Especially by pointing to the Aramaic language noticeable behind the Gospel text of the Greek New Testament, Jeremias could unearth a treasure of sayings that he attributed to Jesus.

While Jeremias focused on the text of the New Testament, **Ethelbert Stauffer** (1902-79) concentrated on its context. He was convinced that, with the help of still-neglected sources, we can discern which materials in the New Testament tradition reliably portray a Jesus who actually walked on this earth. The first category of sources is indirect sources, such as contemporary testimonies to the conditions, events, and persons who in some way or other were connected to the history of Jesus.[40] For instance, unearthing the then valid Jewish and Roman legal provisions can explain and/or correct many details about Jesus' trial as reported in the Gospels. The second category is those sources found in Jewish antiquity that allude to Jesus or even mention him explicitly. Though they are often of a polemical nature, they provide valuable contrasting material over against the accounts in the Synoptics. For instance, when in his anti-Christian polemics the Platonist philosopher Celsus from Alexandria, Egypt, told around A.D. 178 of a Roman soldier who impregnated Mary, we might have another witness to the fact that Joseph was not the biological father of Jesus. Finally, there is a third group of texts that provide valuable insights: the literature of late Jewish apocalypticism. This body of literature, including the Qumran writings, shows that Jesus was intimately familiar with apocalyptic thought forms, an insight that may help us better understand major facets of his proclamation. Altogether these materials will not allow us to write a biogra-

---

39. Jeremias, *New Testament Theology*, 30.

40. See for the following Ethelbert Stauffer, *Jesus and His Story*, trans. Dorothea M. Barton (London: SCM, 1960), 8-12.

phy of Jesus analogous to the nineteenth-century tradition, but they do give us clues for the history of Jesus. When one reads Stauffer's treatise on Jesus, one wonders, however, his many new insights notwithstanding, whether he is not sometimes inclined to return to a romantic biographical narrative that overextends the limits of his material.[41]

The Continued Quest in Scandinavia: Harald Riesenfeld and Birger Gerhardsson

Harald Riesenfeld and Birger Gerhardsson are the most prominent Scandinavian scholars active in the quest for the historical Jesus. The Swedish New Testament scholar **Harald Riesenfeld** (b. 1913) was born in Freiburg im Breisgau, Germany, but received his theological training at Uppsala, Sweden, and also taught there from 1953 to his retirement in 1979. At the Congress on the Four Gospels held in London in 1957, he presented a paper entitled "The Gospel Tradition and Its Beginnings" in which he attacked head-on the form-critical approach and proposed a noteworthy alternative. Against the claim made by form critics that the Synoptic material was composed in the earliest Christian community, he countered that "the very existence of such an anonymous creative generation in primitive Christianity presupposes . . . a truly miraculous and incredible factor in the history of the Gospel tradition."[42] And he went on to assert that "mission preaching was not the *Sitz im Leben* of the Gospel tradition" (13). Riesenfeld attempted to show that the Gospel tradition belongs to a category of its own, and therefore has its own *Sitz im Leben*. This *Sitz im Leben* was neither mission preaching nor communal instruction. However, mission preaching pointed and led to the Gospel tradition. Riesenfeld found it significant that "the original New Testament designation for the Gospel tradition was not *euangelion* — this word stands for missionary appeal — but *logos, rhema,* and then *logos theou* — all terms which correspond with the names current in Judaism for Holy Scripture" (22). The words and deeds of Jesus were considered holy, as in the Old Testament, and the tradition of this precious material was entrusted to special persons. Riesenfeld regarded Jesus as a teacher or rabbi. "It is evident that Jesus did not preach indiscriminately nor continually, but that he imposed certain limitations on his preaching as he did in the case of his mir-

---

41. James Robinson, *A New Quest,* 14, calls him, not unjustifiably, "an extremist who clearly went too far."

42. Harald Riesenfeld, *The Gospel Tradition and Its Beginnings,* 2nd ed. (London: A. R. Mowbray, 1961), 9. Page numbers in the following text refer to this work.

acles. And what was essential to his message he taught his disciples, that is, he made them learn it by heart" (26). One cannot discount that Jesus reckoned with the recital of the Gospel tradition in the epoch between his death and his parousia. Furthermore, if he regarded himself in some way or other as the Messiah, we need not be surprised that "Jesus was conscious of himself as the bearer of revelation, as the bringer of the new law and as a teacher" (28-29). That is, once one considers Jesus in the context of the Old Testament and of Judaism, one can easily explain many facets of the origin of the Gospel tradition.

The bold strokes with which Riesenfeld sketched the origin of the Gospel tradition were drawn out in detail by **Birger Gerhardsson** (b. 1926), especially in his book *Memory and Manuscript: Oral Tradition and Written Transmission in Rabbinic Judaism and Early Christianity*. Gerhardsson, who taught at the University of Lund (1965-92), picked up on Bultmann's comment: "It can hardly be doubted that Jesus did teach as a Rabbi, gather disciples and engage in disputations."[43] Investigating the traditioning process in rabbinic Judaism, he concluded: "It is not possible historically to understand the origin of early Christian tradition by beginning with the *preaching* of the primitive Church. Such procedure is both unhistorical and theologically dubious."[44] Though Jesus taught through word and deed, his ministry not only fulfilled a pedagogical function. Instead the emerging church also saw his whole life as a teaching mission. Gerhardsson claimed that with Jesus we must distinguish between text and interpretation, just as we would with Jewish and Hellenistic teachers. "If he taught, he must have required his disciples to memorize."[45] He suggested that the exposition of the parables' interpretation may have been derived from Jesus' own interpretive exposition of the parables. Gerhardsson stated that, against the background of the Jewish milieu, the early Christian apostles were compelled to present their message as an eyewitness account of that which they had seen and heard, which then was supported by scriptural quotations. Thus in the early Christian kerygma both eyewitness accounts and Scripture were present.

Gerhardsson's main criticism of the form-critical approach was that it is not sufficiently historical. It does not convincingly show how the Gospel tradition could have originated, given the Jewish milieu of Palestine and elsewhere at the time of the New Testament. In turn, he claimed that in the light of the ancient Jewish method of teaching, it seems entirely reasonable that Jesus presented sayings two or more times in an effort to impress them upon the minds

43. Bultmann, *History*, 50; cf. Birger Gerhardsson, *Memory and Manuscript: Oral Tradition and Written Transmission in Rabbinic Judaism and Early Christianity* (Lund: C. W. K. Gleerup, 1961), 12.

44. Gerhardsson, *Memory and Manuscript*, 324.

45. Gerhardsson, *Memory and Manuscript*, 328.

of his hearers. "If Jesus created *meshalim* [parables] during his public ministry, it is reasonable to assume that his disciples preserved these texts right from the beginning. They must have fixed them in their memories, pondered them, and discussed them. Otherwise, they were not his disciples."[46] Gerhardsson's contextual approach, which has affinities to Stauffer's position, has certain merits and can provide insights into one aspect of Jesus' life and mission, since Jesus was a rabbi and teacher.

The Continued Quest in Great Britain and the USA: Charles H. Dodd, Thomas W. Manson, Vincent Taylor, Norman Perrin, and Raymond E. Brown

The Anglo-Saxon approach, which was not as unified as the Scandinavian, proceeded along various lines and is represented by scholars such as C. H. Dodd, T. W. Manson, and Vincent Taylor in Great Britain, and Norman Perrin and Raymond Brown in the USA. For **Charles H. Dodd** (1884-1973), who taught New Testament successively at Oxford (1914-30), Manchester (1930-35), and Cambridge (1935-49), the Gospels were indeed religious documents that bore witness to the faith of the church. But in contrast to form criticism, he asserted that they are historical documents and that their authors had an interest in historical facts. Consequently, "the attempt to make a sharp division between fact and interpretation and set them over against one another is misguided."[47] He also saw this reflected in historical scholarship, since for the serious historian, as opposed to the mere chronicler, "the interest and meaning which an event bore for those who felt its impact is a part of the event."[48] This sentiment is widely accepted in secular historiography. Since in the New Testament the facts are communicated with the intention of bringing out as forcibly as possible the meaning the authors believed to be their true meaning, there is no strict biography of Jesus available. Yet we obtain a lively picture "of the *kind* of thing that Jesus did, the *kind* of attitude which his actions revealed, the *kind* of relations in which he stood with various types of people he encountered, and the causes of friction between him and the religious leaders."[49] This means we do not obtain a photograph of Jesus but rather a reliable painting.

In his research Dodd concerned himself extensively with John, the Fourth

46. Birger Gerhardsson, *The Origins of the Gospel Traditions* (Philadelphia: Fortress, 1979), 72.

47. Charles H. Dodd, *The Founder of Christianity* (London: Macmillan, 1970), 27.

48. Dodd, *The Founder of Christianity*, 27-28.

49. Dodd, *The Founder of Christianity*, 36.

Gospel, showing that it was not nearly as nonhistorical and theological as many German scholars had claimed. In a way similar to that of the Synoptics, it reflected an Aramaic background (the language Jesus spoke) and provided valuable additions and corrections to the Synoptics. "It transmitted a credible account of an early ministry of Jesus . . . [and] preserved a considerable body of topographical information, indicating at least certain steps in the itinerary of Jesus and some of the scenes of his work."[50] The late bishop John A. T. Robinson (1919-83), a student of Dodd, was similarly convinced that John gives us "a much more detailed topographical and chronological framework" of Jesus' ministry than the Synoptics.[51] He also stated that "it is surely evident that the early Christians had an interest in the historical story for its own sake,"[52] a claim we also heard from Riesenfeld.

Thomas W. Manson (1893-1958) succeeded Dodd as professor of New Testament at Oxford in 1932 and then again at the University of Manchester in 1935. Manson claimed in a 1943 lecture, in opposition to the form critics, that Mark contained not just patchwork accounts but respectable historical material on the life and ministry of Jesus.[53] Much earlier he proposed four motifs to compile a record of Jesus' teachings in the New Testament material. First, there was the pastoral work of the churches, that is, to find out from the acts and words of Jesus what his will and his spirit were for the lives of the people. Second, there was the personal interest of the disciples in their Master, "who pondered His sayings in their hearts, not with an eye to the future needs of the Church, but simply because they had known the author of them and loved Him."[54] Third, such teaching had apologetic value in the Gentile world, where, especially for the better educated, missionary preaching alone did not suffice but had to be supplemented by the sayings and deeds of Jesus to demonstrate the value of the new religion. And fourth, the Palestine community needed to defend itself against Jewish misrepresentation. One had to refer to Jesus to show that this interpretation of the law uncovered its actual intention. The teachings of Jesus were also important as propaganda among Jewish scholars who might show some sympathy toward Christianity.

50. Charles H. Dodd, *Historical Tradition in the Fourth Gospel* (Cambridge: University Press, 1963), 429.

51. See John A. T. Robinson's remarkable book, *Can We Trust the New Testament?* (Grand Rapids: Eerdmans, 1977), 116.

52. John Robinson, *Can We Trust?* 115.

53. See Thomas W. Manson, "The Life of Jesus: A Study of the Available Materials" (1943), in *Studies in the Gospels and Epistles,* ed. Matthew Black (Manchester: Manchester University Press, 1962), 26.

54. Thomas W. Manson, *The Sayings of Jesus* (London: SCM, 1971 [1937]), 10.

Manson was convinced that the tradition concerning Jesus' teaching rested on a broader basis than we commonly imagine. Thus "the Church's task in meeting the problems which arose in its own life and in its relations with Jewish authorities was not of creating words of Jesus applicable to these situations, but rather that of selecting what was relevant from the available mass of reminiscences."[55] This, of course, was a clear refutation of the form critics, who saw the creativity not so much with Jesus as with the early Christian community. Trying to decide between Manson and the form critics is perhaps futile, since the truth is most likely somewhere in the middle. Yet there cannot be much doubt that the original body of tradition contained much more material than what is included in the four Gospels, since the Gospels preserved a rather deliberate selection (cf. John 20:30-31).

Vincent Taylor (1887-1968), in *The Life and Ministry of Jesus* (1954), picked up on the distinction between the Jesus of history and the Christ of faith, claiming that "we cannot see the Jesus of history if we close our eyes to the Christ of faith; we do not see the Christ of faith except in the light of the Jesus of history."[56] In other words, we must consider both the inferences drawn from the sources and to what extent they cohere with the religious and theological aspects of his person. We simply cannot proclaim Christ unless we know of Jesus. Yet in dealing with Jesus, the dangers of distortion are as great as the problems of understatement. Modern and critical study of the Gospel tradition has shown that it is trustworthy "provided we do not make impossible demands upon it."[57] We will not be able to know the last detail about Jesus with ultimate accuracy, and many items will remain unsolved, but "within their limitations, the Gospels, while always subject to literary and historical criticism, are a reliable guide to the study of the mind and purpose of Jesus and to the turning points of his ministry in Galilee and Jerusalem." Moreover, "the Fourth Gospel, along with the interpretative element in it, supplies independent tradition of great value to the historian."[58]

Norman Perrin (1920-76), professor of New Testament studies at the University of Chicago Divinity School where he taught until his death in 1976, was a student of T. W. Manson at Manchester University. But he did his doctorate with Joachim Jeremias at Göttingen (*The Kingdom of God in the Teaching of Jesus* [Philadelphia: Westminster, 1963]), and also spent a year at the Kirchliche Hochschule in Berlin. Perrin was convinced that "the early Church absolutely

---

55. Manson, *The Sayings of Jesus*, 13.
56. Vincent Taylor, *The Life and Ministry of Jesus* (London: Macmillan, 1961), 36.
57. Taylor, *Life and Ministry*, 33.
58. Taylor, *Life and Ministry*, 27.

and completely identified the risen Lord of her experience with the earthly Jesus of Nazareth and created for her purposes, which she conceived to be his, the literary form of the gospel, in which words and deeds ascribed in her consciousness to both the earthly Jesus and the risen Lord were set down in terms of the former."[59] This admission at once betrays a conservative bent toward the relationship between the message of the Gospels and the historical Jesus contained in them.

Nevertheless, Perrin found it immensely difficult to penetrate to the earthly Jesus, since "there is no single pericope anywhere in the gospels, the present purpose of which is to preserve the historical reminiscence of the earthly Jesus."[60] Yet by employing the criteria of dissimilarity, meaning that something is different from ancient Judaism and the early church; of coherence, meaning that it shows a coherence with the material established as authentic by means of the criterion of dissimilarity; and multiple attestation, that it is attested in all, or most, of the sources that can be discerned behind the Synoptic Gospels, he arrived at a considerable body of authentic materials regarding the notion of the kingdom of God, the ethical teaching of Jesus, and his emphasis on the present as the anticipation of the future.

Why would Perrin have been concerned about the historical Jesus if the early church was not? He gave three reasons. (1) Historical knowledge of Jesus "is significant to faith in that it can contribute to the formation of the faith-image. In a tradition which 'believes in Jesus,' historical knowledge can be a source for the necessary content of faith."[61] For instance, if somebody would doubt that Jesus was indeed resurrected from the dead, we could show that "the more we study the tradition with regard to the appearances the firmer the rock begins to appear on which they are based."[62] This might help that person overcome the doubts regarding the resurrection. (2) Today we face a variety of Christian proclamations, all of which claim to be Christian. Here the historical knowledge of Jesus as we possess it will help us "to test the validity of the claim of any given form of the Church's proclamation to be *Christian* proclamation."[63] (3) Since the early church identified itself so much with the earthly ministry of Jesus, we may also "apply historical knowledge of the teaching of Jesus directly to the situation of the believer" in our age.[64] This means that it was

59. Norman Perrin, *Rediscovering the Teaching of Jesus* (London: SCM, 1967), 15.

60. Perrin, *Rediscovering*, 16.

61. Perrin, *Rediscovering*, 244.

62. Norman Perrin, *The Resurrection Narratives: A New Approach* (London: SCM, 1977), 83.

63. Perrin, *Rediscovering*, 247-48.

64. Perrin, *Rediscovering*, 248.

not just historical curiosity that led Perrin back to the historical Jesus, but some very practical necessities of our own peculiar situation.

Raymond E. Brown (1928-98) was born in New York City and educated at the Catholic University of America in Washington, D.C., and at St. Mary's Seminary in Baltimore, where he received a doctorate in theology in 1955. That he earned a Ph.D. from Johns Hopkins in 1958 is especially interesting for a Roman Catholic scholar, since it was only Vatican II (1962-65) that approved in principle a critical exegesis of the New Testament.[65] Brown, an internationally renowned scholar who served and advised on many ecumenical committees, was an ordained priest and a member of the Society of St. Sulpice. Having taught as professor of sacred Scripture at St. Mary's Seminary in Baltimore from 1959 to 1971, he was appointed professor of biblical studies at Union Theological Seminary in New York. Brown wrote many volumes on the New Testament.

On the historical Jesus, Brown published the massive volume *The Birth of the Messiah* (1977), in which he concluded: "We have no real knowledge that any or all of the infancy material came from a tradition for which there was a corroborating witness."[66] We have only the Markan and Lukan accounts, and they are independent of each other and do not really support each other. Therefore "a close analysis of the infancy narratives makes it unlikely that either account is completely historical" (36). But Brown was no historical skeptic, and therefore he found it probable that Jesus was of Davidic descent (cf. 511). With regard to the virgin birth, however, he left the issue open, but also ruled out the likelihood of illegitimacy. With regard to Jesus' birthplace, he questioned Bethlehem, but found positive evidence for Nazareth as Jesus' hometown (cf. 527 and 541, and 515). Yet he assured us that we are in a better position with the main body of the Gospel material, since there is "a claim to be anchored in the reminiscences of those who accompanied Jesus from shortly after his baptism until his death (see Acts 1:22) and to whom he appeared after his resurrection (Acts 10:41; 1 Cor 15:3)" (32).

Brown cautioned that one should not be obsessed with historical issues, because such obsession betrays a distortion. The life and teaching of Jesus were not reported simply for the sole purpose of being remembered, but the gospel

---

65. Cf. Raymond E. Brown, *Jesus, God, and Man: Modern Biblical Reflections* (Milwaukee: Bruce, 1967), 43. While Pope Pius XII in an encyclical of 1943, *Divino Afflante Spiritu,* approved a critical use of the original text of the Bible, such freedom was tenuous, as the same pope showed in his 1950 encyclical *Humani Generis,* which was much more restrictive in its approach to Scripture.

66. Raymond E. Brown, *The Birth of the Messiah: A Commentary on the Infancy Narratives in Matthew and Luke* (Garden City, N.Y.: Doubleday, 1977), 33. Page references in the following text are to this work.

is actually proclamation intended to induce faith in the hearer.[67] This is also made clear in another massive two-volume investigation, *The Death of the Messiah*, of 1993. Nevertheless, Brown remained convinced that we can move back from the Gospel narratives to Jesus himself and that ultimately "there were eyewitnesses and earwitnesses who were in a position to know the broad lines of Jesus' passion. . . . It is inconceivable that they showed no concern about what happened to Jesus after the arrest."[68] When the passion narrative was told mainly with reference to the Psalms and the prophets, meaning to Scripture, this does not mitigate against such historical knowledge, because, Brown contended, one wanted to show that Jesus' death was part of God's plan.

In discerning what is historical, Brown employed a strategy similar to that of Perrin. He used the criteria of multiple attestation, coherence, and embarrassment, meaning that if something reported about Jesus was embarrassing to the early church, the church most likely did not invent that, plus the criterion of discontinuity or dissimilarity. With the last criterion Brown had some problems, because it "is inapplicable to a very high percentage of material that might well be historical. Since Jesus was a Jew of the first third of the 1st cent., it is inconceivable that much of his language and symbolism would not have had parallels in the Judaism of that time."[69] While the Gospels certainly are not unanimous in their account, there is a remarkable agreement that after he was arrested Jesus was subjected to a Jewish legal inquiry involving the priesthood of the temple, and was then handed over to Pilate. The four Gospels also agree that a Sanhedrin was involved in Jesus' death. Even with regard to Jesus' resurrection, Brown was confident that the Gospel narratives "that have been built around the discovery of the empty tomb" deserve preference "to the poorly supported hypothesis that the place of Jesus' burial was unknown."[70] We see that scholars from various parts of the world have moved away from the extreme skepticism of Bultmann and the neglect of history. At the same time, they agree with him that the main intent of the New Testament is not to provide history, but to give basis for proclamation.

---

67. Cf. Raymond Brown, *The Death of the Messiah: From Gethsemane to the Grave: A Commentary on the Passion Narratives in the Four Gospels* (New York: Doubleday, 1993), 1:24, where he cites approvingly the 1964 "Instruction on the Historical Truth of the Gospels" of the Roman Pontifical Biblical Commission.

68. Brown, *Death of the Messiah*, 1:14.

69. Brown, *Death of the Messiah*, 1:19.

70. Raymond E. Brown, *The Virginal Conception and Bodily Resurrection of Jesus* (London: Geoffrey Chapman, 1973), 126.

A Third Quest for the Historical Jesus

Toward the end of the twentieth century there arose "a third quest of the historical Jesus," with a resurgence of books on the historical Jesus, some of which were the result of added media attention and lacked solid scholarship.[71] The lively debate on whether the Qumran manuscripts should remain entrusted to the editors to whom they had originally been assigned or be handed over to scholars who would publish them in a relatively short time span led to rumors that the reason the Dead Sea Scrolls had not yet been published was that their publication would undermine the Christian faith.[72] A German translation was published by Robert H. Eisenman and Michael O. Wise, *The Dead Sea Scrolls Uncovered: The First Complete Translation and Interpretation of 50 Key Documents Withheld for Over 35 Years.* Together with the translation of Michael Baigent and Richard Leigh, *The Dead Sea Scrolls Deception,* they quickly became best sellers for Bertelsmann, the largest book club in Europe.[73] Immediately there was a rejoinder by the New Testament scholars Otto Betz (1917-2005) and Rainer Riesner (b. 1950), *Jesus, Qumran, and the Vatican: Clarifications.*[74] Betz had taught at Chicago Theological Seminary from 1962 to 1967 and subsequently at Tübingen, and Riesner, who had both received his doctorate (1980) and done his *Habilitation* (1990) at Tübingen, is now professor at the University of Dortmund (since 1998). They refuted the charge that the Vatican had anything significant to do with the delay of the scholarly publications of the Qumran manuscripts. They also attacked the claim that Jesus must be seen in direct line with the Qumran community.

The other noteworthy event indicative of a renewed interest in the historical Jesus is the Jesus Seminar. It was founded in 1985 by Robert Funk (b. 1926), with John D. Crossan (b. 1934) as cochair. Funk, who had taught religious stud-

---

71. The term "third quest" was used by Marcus J. Borg, *Jesus in Contemporary Scholarship* (Valley Forge, Pa.: Trinity, 1994), ix.

72. For the following see James H. Charlesworth, ed., *Jesus and the Dead Sea Scrolls* (New York: Doubleday, 1992), 4, who refers to the theses by R. H. Eisenman and the more outlandish claims by Barbara Thiering, *Jesus and the Riddle of the Dead Sea Scrolls: Unlocking the Secrets of His Life Story* (San Francisco: Harper, 1992), that Jesus "was born at Qumran and did not die on the cross but spent the remainder of his life in an Essene monastery."

73. Robert H. Eisenman and Michael O. Wise, *The Dead Sea Scrolls Uncovered: The First Complete Translation and Interpretation of 50 Key Documents Withheld for Over 35 Years* (Rockport, Mass.: Element, 1992); Michael Baigent and Richard Leigh, *The Dead Sea Scrolls Deception* (London: Cape, 1991).

74. Otto Betz and Rainer Riesner, *Jesus, Qumran und der Vatikan: Klarstellungen,* rev. ed. (Freiburg: Herder, 1993); Eng. trans. *Jesus, Qumran, and the Vatican: Clarifications,* trans. John Bowden (New York: Crossroad, 1994).

ies at the University of Montana since 1969, was concerned that scholars make their research readily available to the general public. Therefore the seminar made frequent use of the media through press releases and news conferences. The purpose of the seminar was "to evaluate historicity of every utterance and every deed attributed to Jesus in Christian sources from the first three centuries."[75] Consensus was reached by voting members dropping red, pink, gray, or black beads into boxes to indicate a higher or lower degree of historical probability for a particular saying or act of Jesus. Of the two hundred members that have participated at least once, thirty to forty usually attend each semiannual meeting.[76]

The first phase of the seminar focused on the authentic words of Jesus, and its results were published in 1993. Then commenced the second phase, regarding the authentic actions of Jesus, completed in 1997.[77] Along with the Synoptics, they also included in their considerations the Gnostic *Gospel of Thomas*. Participation in the seminar is open to any biblical scholar with a Ph.D. or its equivalent. Yet, "as of 1995 its membership contained no active members of the NT faculties of Harvard, Yale, Union (NYC), Princeton (Seminary), Duke, Emory, Vanderbilt, the University of Chicago; or of the major European faculties."[78] The Jesus who emerged from the seminar did not claim to be the incarnate Son of God who came to the earth to save us from sin. He did not think of himself as the suffering servant of Isaiah 53, and the seminar also added "its collective voice against the apocalyptic portrait of the historical Jesus."[79] The new Jesus who emerged there was a "wisdom teacher."

This means that, at the end of the century, the battle for Jesus negated exactly that result with which the century started, that Jesus' message was thoroughly apocalyptic. Now Jesus is at the most a teacher of subversive wisdom. Of course, not everybody agrees with this portrayal, and therefore the claims of the third wave are highly controversial.[80] While at the beginning of the century most of the scholars taught at theological faculties in Germany or were at least

---

75. Robert J. Miller, *The Jesus Seminar and Its Critics* (Santa Rosa, Calif.: Polebridge, 1999), 15.

76. According to Miller, *The Jesus Seminar*, 19.

77. Robert W. Funk, Roy W. Hoover, and the Jesus Seminar, *The Five Gospels: The Search for the Authentic Words of Jesus* (San Francisco: HarperSanFrancisco, 1993); Robert W. Funk and the Jesus Seminar, *The Acts of Jesus: The Search for the Authentic Deeds of Jesus* (San Francisco: HarperSanFrancisco, 1998).

78. According to Raymond E. Brown, *An Introduction to the New Testament* (New York: Doubleday, 1997), 820 n. 8.

79. Miller, *The Jesus Seminar*, 24.

80. As one dissenting voice among others, see Ben Witherington III, *The Christology of Jesus* (Minneapolis: Fortress, 1990).

influenced by German scholarship, these scholars of the third wave hail mainly from North America, and many teach in religious studies departments within secular academia. This secular environment yields corresponding results: (1) The old consensus that Jesus was an eschatological prophet who proclaimed the imminent end of the world has disappeared. (2) There is a new understanding of Jesus as a teacher, especially a teacher of subversive wisdom. (3) Studies of the social world of Jesus have become central. Nevertheless, the historical Jesus still holds fascination and is still regarded essential for the Christian faith. A neglect of Christianity's historical basis could at the most be temporary.

For Further Reading

Johannes Weiss (1863-1914)

Misner, Paul. "The Historical Jesus: Two Views of His Significance for Twentieth Century Christianity." In *Critical History and Biblical Faith: New Testament Perspectives,* edited by Thomas J. Ryan, 177-207. Villanova, Pa.: Villanova University Press, 1979.

Weiss, Johannes. *Jesus' Proclamation of the Kingdom of God* (1892). Translated and edited with an introduction by Richard Hyde Hiers and David Larrimore Holland. London: SCM, 1971.

Albert Schweitzer (1875-1965)

Anderson, Erica. *The Schweitzer Album: A Portrait in Words and Pictures.* New York: Harper and Row, 1965.

Marshall, George, and David Poling. *Schweitzer: A Biography.* Baltimore: Johns Hopkins University Press, 2000.

Mozley, Edward N. *The Theology of Albert Schweitzer for Christian Inquirers.* Epilogue by Albert Schweitzer. London: A. & C. Black, 1950.

Schweitzer, Albert. *Civilization and Ethics.* Translated by C. T. Campion. Revised by Lilian M. R. Russell. 3rd ed. London: Adam and Charles Black, 1949.

———. *The Mystery of the Kingdom of God: The Secret of Jesus' Messiahship and Passion.* Translated with an introduction by Walter Lowrie. New York: Schocken, 1964.

———. *Out of My Life and Thought: An Autobiography.* Translated by Antje Bultmann Lemke. Foreword by Jimmy Carter. Preface by Rhena Schweitzer Miller and Antje Bultmann Lemke. Baltimore: Johns Hopkins University Press, 1998.

———. *The Quest of the Historical Jesus: A Critical Study of Its Progress from Reimarus to Wrede.* Edited by John Bowden. First complete edition. Minneapolis: Fortress, 2001.

———. *Reverence for Life.* Foreword by Elton Trueblood. Translated by Reginald H. Fuller. New York: Harper and Row, 1969.

Martin Kähler (1835-1912)

Henant, Barry W. "Is the 'Historical Jesus' a Christological Construct?" In *Whose Historical Jesus?* edited by William E. Arnal and Michel Desjardins, 241-68. Waterloo, Ont.: Wilfrid Laurier University Press, 1997.

Kähler, Martin. *The So-called Historical Jesus and the Historic, Biblical Christ.* Translated and edited with an introduction by Carl E. Braaten. Foreword by Paul Tillich. Philadelphia: Fortress, 1964.

Rudolf Bultmann (1884-1976)

Bultmann, Rudolf. *The History of the Synoptic Tradition.* Translated by John Marsh. Rev. ed. New York: Harper, 1968.

———. *Jesus and the Word.* Translated by Louise Pettibone Smith and Erminie Huntress Lantero. New York: Charles Scribner's, 1958.

———. *New Testament and Mythology and Other Basic Writings.* Selected, edited, and translated by Schubert M. Ogden. Philadelphia: Fortress, 1984.

———. *Theology of the New Testament.* Translated by Kendrick Grobel. 2 vols. New York: Charles Scribner's, 1954.

Fergusson, David. *Bultmann.* Outstanding Christian Thinkers Series. Collegeville, Minn.: Liturgical Press, 1992.

Johnson, Roger, ed. *Rudolf Bultmann: Interpreting Faith for the Modern Era.* Minneapolis: Fortress, 1991.

Schmithals, Walther. *An Introduction to the Theology of Rudolf Bultmann.* Translated by John Bowden. London: SCM, 1968.

James M. Robinson (b. 1924)

Asgeirsson, Jon Ma., Kristin de Troyer, and Marvin W. Meyer, eds. *From Quest to Q.* Leuven: Leuven University Press, 2000.

Goehring, James E., ed. *Gospel Origins and Christian Beginnings: In Honor of James M. Robinson.* Sonoma, Calif.: Polebridge, 1990.

Goehring, James E., Charles W. Hedrick, Jack T. Sanders; with Hans Dieter Betz, eds. *Gnosticism and the Early Christian World: In Honor of James M. Robinson.* Sonoma, Calif.: Polebridge, 1990.

Robinson, James M. *A New Quest of the Historical Jesus.* London: SCM, 1959.

Joachim Jeremias (1900-1982)

Jeremias, Joachim. *New Testament Theology: The Proclamation of Jesus.* Translated by John Bowden. New York: Charles Scribner's, 1971.

Mattison, Robin D. "God/Father: Tradition and Interpretation." *Reformed Review* 42 (Spring 1989): 189-206.

Oldenhage, Tania. *Parables for Our Time: Rereading New Testament Scholarship after the Holocaust.* New York: Oxford University Press, 2002.

Vander Broek, Lyle D. "Jeremias, Joachim (1900-1979)." In *Historical Handbook of Ma-*

jor Biblical Interpreters, edited by Donald K. McKim, 495-500. Downers Grove, Ill.: InterVarsity, 1998.

Ethelbert Stauffer (1902-79)

Achtemeier, Paul J. "The Historical Jesus: A Dilemma." *Theology and Life* (Lancaster) 4 (May 1961): 107-19.

Barrett, Charles Kingsley. "Recent Biblical Theologies." *Expository Times* 72 (Summer 1961): 356-60.

Harrisville, Roy A. "Resurrection and Historical Method." *Dialog* 1 (Spring 1962): 30-37.

Stauffer, Ethelbert. *Jesus and His Story.* Translated by Dorothea M. Barton. London: SCM, 1960.

Harald Riesenfeld (b. 1913)

Bauckham, Richard J. "The Lord's Day." In *From Sabbath to Lord's Day,* edited by D. Carson, 220-50. Grand Rapids: Zondervan, 1982.

Davies, William D. "Reflections on a Scandinavian Approach to 'the Gospel Tradition.'" In *Neotestamentica et Patristica:* Eine Freundesgabe Herrn Professor Dr. Oscar Cullmann überreicht, 14-34. Leiden: Brill, 1962.

Riesenfeld, Harald. *The Gospel Tradition and Its Beginnings.* 2nd ed. London: A. R. Mowbray, 1961.

Birger Gerhardsson (b. 1926)

Fitzmyer, Joseph A. "Memory and Manuscript: The Origins and Transmission of the Gospel Tradition." *Theological Studies* 23 (Summer 1962): 442-57.

Gerhardsson, Birger. *Memory and Manuscript: Oral Tradition and Written Transmission in Rabbinic Judaism and Early Christianity.* Lund: C. W. K. Gleerup, 1961.

———. *The Origins of the Gospel Traditions.* Philadelphia: Fortress, 1979.

Neusner, Jacob. "Gerhardsson's *Memory and Manuscript* Revisited: Introduction to a New Edition." In *Approaches to Ancient Judaism,* n.s., vol. 12, edited by Jacob Neusner, 171-90. Atlanta: Scholars, 1998.

Widengren, Geo. "Tradition and Literature in Early Judaism and in the Early Church." *Numen* 10 (July 1963): 42-83.

Charles H. Dodd (1884-1973)

Davies, William D. *The Background of the New Testament and Its Eschatology.* Cambridge: Cambridge University Press, 1956.

Dillistone, Frederick W. *C. H. Dodd, Interpreter of the New Testament.* Grand Rapids: Eerdmans, 1977.

Dodd, Charles H. *The Founder of Christianity.* London: Macmillan, 1970.

———. *Historical Tradition in the Fourth Gospel.* Cambridge: University Press, 1963.

Sullivan, Clayton. *Rethinking Realized Eschatology.* Macon, Ga.: Mercer University Press, 1988.

Thomas W. Manson (1893-1958)

Black, Matthew. "Thomas Walter Manson." *Expository Times* 75 (April 1964): 208-11.

———, ed. *Studies in the Gospels and Epistles.* Manchester: Manchester University Press, 1962.

Higgins, A. J. B. *New Testament Essays: Studies in Memory of Thomas Walter Manson, 1893-1958.* Manchester: Manchester University Press, 1959.

Hooker, Morna D. "New Testament Scholarship: Its Significance and Abiding Worth." *Bulletin of the John Rylands University Library of Manchester* 63, no. 2 (Spring 1981): 419-36.

Manson, Thomas W. *The Sayings of Jesus.* London: SCM, 1971 [1937].

Vincent Taylor (1887-1968)

Balchin, Frank. "The Person and Work of Christ." *South East Asia Journal of Theology* 1, no. 2 (1959): 65-67.

Nineham, Dennis E. "Eyewitness Testimony and Gospel Tradition." *Journal of Theological Studies* 9 (1958): 13-25, 243-52; 11 (1960): 253-64.

Smith, Morton. "Comment on Taylor's Commentary on Mark." *Harvard Theological Review* 48, no. 1 (1955): 21-64.

Taylor, Vincent. *The Life and Ministry of Jesus.* London: Macmillan, 1961.

Norman Perrin (1920-76)

Betz, Hans Dieter, ed. *Christology and a Modern Pilgrimage: A Discussion with Norman Perrin.* Missoula, Mont.: Society of Biblical Literature and the Scholars Press, 1974.

Fuller, Reginald H. "The Resurrection Narratives in Recent Study." In *Critical History and Biblical Faith: New Testament Perspectives,* edited by Thomas Ryan, 91-107. Villanova, Pa.: Villanova University Press, 1979.

Mercer, Calvin. *Norman Perrin's Interpretation of the New Testament: From "Exegetical Method" to "Hermeneutical Process."* Macon, Ga.: Mercer University Press, 1986.

Perrin, Norman. *Rediscovering the Teaching of Jesus.* London: SCM, 1967.

———. *The Resurrection Narratives: A New Approach.* London: SCM, 1977.

Raymond E. Brown (1928-98)

Brown, Raymond E. *The Birth of the Messiah: A Commentary on the Infancy Narratives in Matthew and Luke.* Garden City, N.Y.: Doubleday, 1977.

———. *The Death of the Messiah: From Gethsemane to the Grave; A Commentary on the Passion Narratives in the Four Gospels.* New York: Doubleday, 1993.

———. *Jesus, God, and Man: Modern Biblical Reflections.* Milwaukee: Bruce, 1967.

———. *The Virginal Conception and Bodily Resurrection of Jesus.* London: Geoffrey Chapman, 1973.

Kelly, George A. *The New Biblical Theorists: Raymond E. Brown and Beyond.* Ann Arbor: Servant, 1983.

Larsson, Tord. *God in the Fourth Gospel: A Hermeneutical Study of the History of Interpretations*. Stockholm: Almquist & Wiksell International, 2001.

Robinson, Robert Bruce. *Roman Catholic Exegesis since "Divino Afflante Spiritu": Hermeneutical Implications*. Atlanta: Scholars, 1988.

10 Neo-Reformation Theology

World War I (1914-18) severely shattered the optimism prevalent in the nineteenth century. Theological liberalism and cultural Protestantism had lost their attraction. The decisive reorientation came through Karl Barth, who in the second edition of his *Letter to the Romans* (1922) actualized the biblical message and decisively refuted earlier theological trends. Swiss and German theologians collaborated in the project of a theology of the word of God, also labeled neo-Reformation theology. In addition to Barth in this movement were Emil Brunner, Friedrich Gogarten, Rudolf Bultmann, Georg Merz, and Barth's lifelong friend Eduard Thurneysen (1888-1974). As the avenue for their publications they founded and edited the journal *Zwischen den Zeiten* (*Between the Times,* 1922-33). The title indicates their assessment of the situation in which they found themselves.

Returning to Theology's Own Task: Karl Barth

Karl Barth (1886-1968) was initially anything but a neo-Reformation theologian. He was born in Basel, and while his grandfather was one of the first students of Johann Tobias Beck, his father was one of the last. When Barth was born, his father had just begun to teach at the preachers school founded in opposition to the liberal university faculty. Barth's mother also came from a Reformed parsonage. Three years after his birth, the family moved to Berne, his father having accepted a call to the theological faculty to become successor to the conservative Swiss Reformed theologian Adolf Schlatter (1852-1938), who followed a call to Greifswald in 1888 to a professorship in New Testament and dogmatics. Karl Barth began his theological studies in Berne in 1904, having decided already as a confirmand to become a theologian. He wanted to continue his studies at Marburg, yet through the influence of his father he went to Berlin (1906), where he was especially attracted by Adolf von Harnack. He also studied Schleiermacher, who supplemented his earlier interest in Kant. In 1907 he went to Tübingen, because his father wanted him to study with Schlatter, who had moved there in 1898. In 1908 Barth finally went to Marburg, where Wilhelm Herrmann became his actual teacher. Having passed his exams the same year and done a short vicarage, he returned again to Marburg to work as a helper to Martin Rade publishing *Die christliche Welt.*

In 1911 Barth became pastor in Safenwil, Switzerland, where he was confronted with the social plight of the workers, which made him turn both theoretically and practically to social issues. This went so far that in 1915 he became a member of the Social Democratic Party. In Safenwil he also developed a friendship with Eduard Thurneysen that lasted through their whole lives. When Barth saw that his former teachers such as Herrmann and Rade advocated World War I, he turned away from liberal theology, and also from identifying the kingdom of God with the social movement. Instead he discovered the expectation of the kingdom of God as a divine activity as enunciated by Johann Christoph Blumhardt (1805-80) and his son Christoph Blumhardt (1842-1919) in Bad Boll. As Barth confessed: "Once I was a religious socialist. I discarded it because I believed I saw that religious socialism failed to take as serious and profound a view of man's misery and of the help for him, as do the Holy Scriptures."[1]

The weekly preaching schedule confronted Barth with Scripture too, and above all with the question how God is known and how we can communicate God. He characterized the problem as follows: "*As ministers we ought to speak of God. We are human, however, and so cannot speak of God. We ought therefore to recognize both our obligation and our inability and by that very recognition give God the glory.* This is our perplexity. The rest of our task fades into insignificance in comparison."[2] In a nutshell the three italicized sentences above contain the program of neo-Reformation theology, namely, the rediscovery of the theology of the word of God as the prime focus and content of both the Christian proclamation and theology. Our task is not to talk about morality and culture, about religion, worship, and the possible existence of other worlds, because people already concern themselves about these issues. But "they want to learn more about

1. Karl Barth, *God in Action,* translated with an introduction by Elmer G. Homrighausen (Manhasset, N.Y.: Round Table, 1963), 125.

2. Karl Barth, "The Word of God and the Task of the Ministry" (1922), in Karl Barth, *The Word of God and the Word of Man,* trans. Douglas Horton (New York: Harper Torchbook, 1957), 186. The page references in the next few paragraphs of the text are to this essay.

what is on the farther edge of living — *God.* . . . Man as man cries for God. He cries not for *a* truth, but for the *truth;* not for *something* good, but for *the* good; not for answers but for the answer" (189-90). Therefore we should not settle for anything penultimate, but strive for the ultimate. Only from the ultimate can we address the human need because humans need salvation and not solutions.

The same focus that is important for the pastor is also mandated for the theologian at the university. "As a science like other sciences theology has *no* right to its place; for it becomes then a wholly unnecessary duplication of disciplines belonging to the other faculties. Only when a *theological* faculty undertakes to say or at least points out the need for saying, what the others . . . dare not say, or dare not say out loud, . . . only then is there a *reason* for it" (193-94). This means that a theological faculty should not become a faculty for the study of religion and talk about religious insights, but it must be a faculty of theology, speaking of God and of eternity in time. Barth turns against Schleiermacher's emphasis on religion, saying "that one can *not* speak of God simply by speaking of man in a loud voice" (196). Instead Barth turns to Kierkegaard, Luther, Calvin, the apostle Paul, and Jeremiah, saying that they realized that humanity is made to serve God and not the other way round. Both from the pulpit and in the classroom must we enunciate God. Yet how can we speak of God, since we are human?

Barth cautioned that we certainly cannot speak of God in a dogmatic way. We also cannot do it introspectively, because then we end up in mysticism. Instead there is a third way, "that of *dialectic.* It is the way of Paul and the Reformers, and intrinsically is by far the best" (206). This does not mean that the truth is somewhere in the middle, but that in dialectic fashion we find the yes in the no and the no in the yes. This is similar to the realization that one is unjust and then awakening to the fact that as such one is justified, or that in this human person (Jesus) we indeed encounter God. Yet how, Barth asked, can we give witness of God? Here he left the dialectic and said there is "the possibility that God *himself* speaks when he is spoken of," whereby the living truth attests to itself (211).

This emphasis on the word of God also showed up in Barth's commentary on Paul's epistle to the Romans, which was published in 1919 in Munich with the help of his friend Georg Merz (1892-1959). Yet after Barth got deeper into Paul's letter and also discovered Kierkegaard, he realized that he had to say things even more pointedly, and so rewrote his whole commentary. The New Testament scholar Karl Ludwig Schmidt and Harnack thought Barth's commentary was heretical, and even Bultmann dismissed it as "enthusiastic revivalism."[3] Neverthe-

---

3. As quoted by Eberhard Busch, *Karl Barth: His Life from Letters and Autobiographical Texts,* trans. John Bowden (Philadelphia: Fortress, 1976), 113, who was the last of Barth's assistants and wrote this excellent biography.

less, before the second edition of the commentary was published in 1922, Barth received a call to the University of Göttingen as honorary but salaried professor for a newly established professorship of Reformed theology. In 1922 he also received an honorary doctorate from the University of Münster, thus giving him also an academic degree.

What was so extraordinary about this commentary that it facilitated a call to a theological professorship? Already in the first two sentences Barth made clear what he wanted to accomplish: "Paul, as a child of his age, addressed his contemporaries. It is, however, far more important that, as Prophet and Apostle of the Kingdom of God, he veritably speaks to all men of every age. . . . If we rightly understand ourselves, our problems are the problems of Paul; and if we be enlightened by the brightness of his answers, those answers must be ours."[4] This means that Barth wanted to bridge the ugly broad ditch of history not by turning Paul's letter into a timeless truth, but by making Paul contemporaneous with us and us with him. Of course, this amounted to an outright attack on a historical investigation of the Scriptures as had been carried on by Harnack, Troeltsch, and others. While Barth conceded that the historical-critical method of biblical investigation "has its rightful place," he unashamedly claimed that if he had to choose between that method and the doctrine of inspiration, he would "without hesitation adopt the latter." Barth was by no means a biblicist. But he contended that a historical-critical investigation adds to our knowledge only because it is a "preparation of the intelligence" while the doctrine of inspiration "is concerned with the labor of apprehending," meaning the incorporation into our existence of what is contained in the text. Barth was not concerned with the neutral investigation of what is stated in the text, or what happened back in history. He wanted to make Paul and his letter alive for us today.

When one reads the commentary, one gets the impression that Barth actually wrote a new letter to the Romans instead of expounding in neutrality from a historical distance what Paul had said in the first century A.D. This approach amounted to a radical break with the theological sentiment prevalent at that time. Barth too realized this, and thought his commentary would not sell. Therefore he closed his introduction like this: "Should I be mistaken in this hope of a new, questioning investigation of the Biblical Message, well, this book must — wait. The Epistle to the Romans waits also."[5] But Barth was mistaken. While opinions were split, the commentary sold and was read.

---

4. For this and the following quotes see Karl Barth, "Preface to the First Edition" of *The Epistle to the Romans,* translated from the 6th ed. by Edwyn C. Hoskyns (London: Oxford University Press, 1968 [1933]), 1.

5. Barth, *Epistle to the Romans,* 2.

In the preface to the second edition, he once more made clear his stand when he noted that biblical commentaries that apply historical criticism only interpret the text, a procedure he said amounts to no commentary at all, "but merely the first step towards a commentary."[6] Once the text has been reconstructed, then the actual work begins: "the Word ought to be exposed in the words."[7] Therefore Barth preferred the exegesis of von Hofmann, Beck, and Schlatter because the important point is to break down the distinction between yesterday and today and to make the critical historian critically aware of his own approach.

Barth said his method was the same as Kierkegaard's, namely, to emphasize "the 'infinite qualitative distinction' between time and eternity" and to discover that God is in heaven and we are on earth (10). This means that Paul "knows of God what most of us do not know; and his Epistles enable us to know what he knew" (11). The exciting point for Barth was that in Paul's letter this infinite qualitative difference had been overcome and therefore God meets us in this letter. By the time the second edition of the commentary had appeared, this new way of doing theology was already more acceptable. Even Bultmann was now on Barth's side, though he complained that Barth was too conservative. Schlatter, however, in a friendly way rejected the commentary.

When we take a glance at the commentary, we notice Barth's dialectic bent from beginning to end. For instance, he stated that in Jesus Christ

> two worlds meet and go apart, two planes intersect, the one known and the other unknown. . . . As Christ, Jesus is the plane which lies beyond our comprehension. The plane which is known to us, He intersects vertically, from above. Within history, Jesus as the Christ can be understood only as Problem or Myth. As the Christ, He brings the world of the Father. But we who stand in this concrete world know nothing, and are incapable of knowing anything, of that other world. The Resurrection from the dead is, however, the transformation: The establishing or *declaration* of that point from above, and the corresponding discerning of it from below. The Resurrection is the revelation: the disclosing of Jesus as the Christ, the appearing of God, and the apprehending of God in Jesus. (29-30, on Rom. 1:4-7)

There is no point of contact between our world and God, so that we would have some kind of notion of God on which to build. Any historical in-

---

6. Karl Barth, "Preface to the Second Edition" of *Epistle to the Romans*, 6.

7. Barth, *Epistle to the Romans*, 8. From here on, page references to the commentary are in the text.

vestigation of Jesus as the Christ can only get us into a blind alley. Neither proofs of the existence of God nor proofs of Jesus' divinity are possible. Yet there is another way to make contact, God's way, meaning establishing or declaring through the resurrection what God is all about. Once this is declared, we can discern the significance of the resurrection. Barth's approach to the Christian message and to theology was totally theocentric, and in that, totally christocentric.

Barth could even write an introductory essay to Feuerbach's *Essence of Christianity,* since he agreed with Feuerbach that religion is just a human projection. Barth insisted that "the power of God can be detected neither in the world of nature nor in the souls of men. It must not be confounded with any high, exalted force, known or knowable" (36, on Rom. 1:16). When God appears among us, he can be "received and understood by us, only as contradiction" (38, on Rom. 1:16). God is entirely different from who we are and what we encounter in this world. While Christians, however, know about a dialectic between this world and God, the unbeliever does not accept this and therefore, though encountering God, "does not penetrate to the truth of God that is hidden from him" (43, on Rom. 1:18).

Barth summed up his main point once more: "The gospel is not a religious message to inform mankind of their divinity or to tell them how they may become divine. The gospel proclaims a God utterly distinct from men. Salvation comes to them from Him, because they are, as men, incapable of knowing Him, and because they have no right to claim anything from Him" (28, on Rom. 1:1-2). Since there is only one way God comes to us, namely, through Jesus Christ, Barth rejected religion as the wrong way and the wrong attitude. "Religion is unbelief."[8] It is the one great concern of godless humanity. The divine reality offered and manifested to us in revelation is replaced in religion "by a concept of God arbitrarily and willfully evolved by man. . . . It is the attempted replacement of the divine work by a human manufacture" (302-3). In religion humanity does the talking instead of letting God talk to us. We reach out and venture to grasp God instead of letting God act on our behalf. Because religion is this reaching and grasping for God, it is opposed to revelation and is "the concentrated expression of human unbelief" (302-3). While revelation is God's self-offering and self-manifestation through which he wants to reconcile us to himself, humanity tries through religion to come to terms with its own life, to justify and sanctify itself. Yet God rejects this self-redemptive attitude of humanity.

---

8. Karl Barth, *Church Dogmatics,* vol. 1, *The Doctrine of the Word of God,* trans. G. T. Thomson and Harold Knight (New York: Charles Scribner's, 1956), I/2:299-300. The page numbers placed in the text refer to this volume of the *Church Dogmatics.*

According to Barth, the real challenge to religion is revelation, since there the whole religious process is reversed. God comes to us, and in contrast to religion we no longer try to come to terms with God on our own. Since Christian faith has its foundation in God's self-disclosure, "the Christian religion is the true religion" (326). Revelation is a strictly Christian phenomenon, because "the Christian religion is the predicate to the subject of the name of Jesus Christ," and through the name Jesus Christ it becomes the true religion (347). The adjective "Christian" thereby can never express "a grasping at some possession of our own. It can only be reaching out for the divine possession included in this name" (349). In other words, the name of Jesus is the one thing that "is really decisive for the distinction of truth and error" among religions (343). The name of Jesus Christ does not stand for our own accomplishment, as do the divine projections in the world religions. It stands for God's own doing. "Christ is not the king chosen by us; on the contrary, we are the people chosen by him."[9] This relationship between the name Jesus Christ and the Christian "religion" is not to be reversed. With this approach Barth sought to reestablish Christianity's uniqueness and render pointless the attacks on Christianity by the secular sciences, since they attacked the wrong target. The Christian faith is not one religion among others. It is the religion established by God's activity and inaccessible to any human endeavor.

In 1922 the journal *Zwischen den Zeiten (Between the Times)* was founded and Friedrich Gogarten wrote the first contribution, "Zwischen den Zeiten," to indicate the direction of the journal. The crisis that was felt after the disaster of World War I, with the disappearance of the monarchies in central Europe, the disappearance of the Austrian-Hungarian Empire, a redrawing of the national borders, and widespread social unrest, plus the instability of the Weimar Republic in Germany, had taken hold of the general population and was ventilated through neo-Reformation theology. Dialectic theology understood this situation as a symptom and expression of the divine crises pronounced over humanity against all attempts of human self-redemption. The main advocates of *Between the Times* and of dialectic theology came from vastly different backgrounds and were joined together in a common concern for refounding the theological enterprise. When the menace of National Socialism emerged, their response was varied, and this led to the dissolution of *Zwischen den Zeiten* in 1933.

Barth too went his own way. In 1925 he accepted a call as professor of dogmatics and New Testament theology at Münster, where he started on *Die christliche Dogmatik im Entwurf (Christian Dogmatics, 1927)*, of which he wrote only the first volume, namely, on the Word of God. When he accepted a call to

9. So Otto Weber, *Karl Barth's Church Dogmatics*, trans. Arthur C. Cochrane (Philadelphia: Westminster, 1953), 54.

Bonn in 1930, he began a new project, the *Church Dogmatics,* a monumental exposition of the Christian doctrine, which occupied him for the rest of his life.

Barth lasted only four years in Bonn, because he refused to pledge an unconditional oath of allegiance to Hitler, a requirement for every civil servant. Barth was dismissed and when he appealed, he was sent into retirement the following year. But retirement did not last long for Barth, because the same year (1935) he was called back to his alma mater, the University of Basel, where he taught until 1967. From there, his own safe haven, he encouraged the Christians of Europe to politically resist German National Socialism.

Already in 1934, in the famous Barmen Declaration, which very much showed Barth's authorship, he rejected Nazi ideology. Thesis 1 declared: "Jesus Christ, as he is being attested for us in Holy Scripture, is the one Word of God which we have to hear and which we have to trust and obey in life and in death. We reject the false doctrine that the church could and should acknowledge as a source of its proclamation, beyond and besides this one Word of God, yet other events and powers, figures and truths, as God's revelation."[10] No natural revelation is possible whether in state, ideology, or historical events, because God's self-disclosure occurs only in the one word of God, in Holy Scripture. The Nazi movement and its rise to power can have no theological sanction, but must come under the critique of Scripture. This means that the theocentricity and Christocentricity that Barth proclaimed is not only an event for church and theology, but pertains to the whole of history and the whole world. Already in 1933 Barth had published a brochure entitled *Theological Existence To-day! (A Plea for Theological Freedom);* within a year 37,000 copies had been printed, one of which was sent to Hitler. In it Barth rejected the program of the National Socialists to form a National Protestant Church with Reichsbischof Ludwig Müller (1883-1945), a Hitler appointee, at its helm, and the National Socialist sympathizers of the "German Christians" showing the way to that new church. He wrote: "We stand in the great peril of having a State-Church (Caesaro-Papal) like that of the Age of Charlemagne, and again of the eighteenth century. If this happens, then it will outwardly and automatically be all over with liberty of preaching and of theology. For then a different Gospel from that of 'The Gospel in the *Third Reich*' will simply have been suppressed by machinery. Then the Churches will be famished and infected. The liability is therefore laid upon us: we are responsible for the Church and have to ward off this peril."[11]

10. Thesis 1 of the "Barmen Theological Declaration," in Rolf Ahlers, *The Barmen Theological Declaration of 1934: The Archeology of a Confessional Text* (Lewiston, N.Y.: Edwin Mellen, 1986), 40.

11. Karl Barth, *Theological Existence To-day! (A Plea for Theological Freedom),* translated with a foreword by R. Birch Hoyle (London: Hodder and Stoughton, 1933), 71-72.

Barth perceptively realized the danger that was threatening the church, namely, that it was becoming an instrument for Nazi ideology and thereby suffocated a clear proclamation of the actual word of God. But enough resistance arose within the church that at least some of this was averted.

Barth continued to be actively involved in the affairs of the day. He also showed an amazing ecumenical openness toward Roman Catholicism, especially during the Second Vatican Council. But his main task remained his *Church Dogmatics*, which in the end, though far from finished, comprised 9,185 tightly printed pages. The *Church Dogmatics* is divided into five parts: *The Doctrine of the Word of God, The Doctrine of God, The Doctrine of Creation, The Doctrine of Reconciliation*, and *The Doctrine of Redemption*. Only the first three parts are finished, while the fourth part is nearly complete. When the last fragment of volume IV, part IV was finished (1967), Barth retired — at age seventy-six! Since the text of the *Church Dogmatics* formed the text of his academic lectures and then became the material for his seminars in German, English, and French, this impetus was now missing and Barth drew his project to a close. It may be surprising that he never thought of ethics as a special field of investigation. They are subsumed under the concept of the command of God from the viewpoint of order in *The Doctrine of Creation*. From the viewpoint of the law, they were supposed to be treated again in *The Doctrine of Reconciliation*, and finally from the viewpoint of promise at the end of *The Doctrine of Redemption*.

While for Barth dogmatics is a theological discipline, "theology is a function of the Church."[12] It follows that there is no theological dogmatics or Christian dogmatics, but a dogmatics of the church evolving from and also furthering the proclamation of the church. That proclamation is nurtured by the word of God as revealed in Christ through the triune God. In contrast to Schleiermacher, for whom the doctrine of the Trinity was a postscript, for Barth it is the presupposition pointing to the Christian triune God.

In remarkable consistency Barth carried through his dialectic approach. We read in part III on creation: "There is free scope for natural science beyond what theology describes as the work of the Creator. And theology can move freely where science which really is science, and not secretly a pagan *Gnosis* or religion, has its appointed limit."[13] There can be no controversy between science rightly understood and theology properly conceived of, since the first one talks about nature and the second one about creation. Science can neither help

---

12. Karl Barth, *Church Dogmatics*, vol. 1, *The Doctrine of the Word of God (Prolegomena to Church Dogmatics)*, trans. G. T. Thomson (Edinburgh: T. & T. Clark, 1936), I/1:1.

13. Karl Barth, *Church Dogmatics*, vol. 3, *The Doctrine of Creation*, trans. J. W. Edwards, O. Bussey, and Harold Knight (Edinburgh: T. & T. Clark, 1958), III/1:x.

nor threaten theology. Too, without looking beyond its borders and forgetting its own task, theology has nothing to do with science.

Nevertheless, Barth broke through the strict dialectic between God and humanity. While he still rejected any kind of *analogia entis,* meaning analogy in essence between the human and the divine, he conceded an *analogia relationis,* an analogy of relationship. To this he wrote: "If man is ordained to be God's partner in this covenant, and if his nature is a likeness corresponding to this or-dination, necessarily it corresponds in this respect to the nature of God Him-self. God has created him in this correspondence, as a reflection of Himself. Man is the image of God."[14] With this statement Barth not only maintained that humanity is created in the image of God, but he conceded that humanity is also a reflection of God and thereby one ought to be able to draw inferences from humanity to God. This meant even he could not maintain the strict sepa-ration between God and the world.

Another point where Barth surprised many was in his last fragmentary volume. In 1948 he had written *The Teaching of the Church regarding Baptism,* and there he vehemently rejected the notion of infant baptism. Now he distin-guished baptism with water from baptism with the Holy Spirit, and wrote that "the meaning of baptism is the conversion which is to be achieved by a man in concert with the Christian community, and by the community in concert with this man. It is their conversion to God, namely to the God who acts and is re-vealed in Jesus Christ through the Holy Spirit. It is thus the first step of the Christian life."[15] Baptism is an act of obedience, conversion, and renouncing the old ways. One wonders, when one reads these deliberations, what happened to the primacy of God's word and of God's activity. Is this not surrendered to looking first at what humanity does and can do? Perhaps Barth could not leave Schleiermacher behind, as he had intended. Nevertheless, his work, even with some inconsistencies, or perhaps rather because of them, influenced a whole generation. It was only in the sixth decade of the twentieth century that in Ger-many new theological voices were heard. Yet in America and in Great Britain, with few exceptions, Karl Barth was never received as the great dialectician. Natural theology was too strongly imbedded in the Anglo-Saxon tradition. Here Barth was much more the evangelical neo-Reformation theologian and

14. Karl Barth, *Church Dogmatics,* vol. 3, *The Doctrine of Creation,* trans. G. W. Bromiley, Harold Knight, J. K. S. Reid, and R. H. Fuller (Edinburgh: T. & T. Clark, 1960), III/2:323; cf. also III/2:220.

15. Karl Barth, *Church Dogmatics,* vol. 4, *The Doctrine of Reconciliation,* pt. 4, *The Chris-tian Life (Fragment): Baptism as the Foundation of the Christian Life,* trans. G. W. Bromiley (Ed-inburgh: T. & T. Clark, 1969), 152.

also the one who fearlessly stood up against the perversities of German National Socialism. Yet what about Barth's collaborators?

Controversial Collaborators: Rudolf Bultmann, Friedrich Gogarten, and Emil Brunner

Rudolf Bultmann was actually the least likely advocate of dialectic theology, since he was the only one who was not a systematician. In 1924 he wrote still very much in the vein of that movement: "The subject of theology is *God,* and the chief charge to be brought against liberal theology is that it has dealt not with God but with man. God represents the radical negation and sublimation of man."[16] This was the charge that Barth also leveled against liberal theology and nineteenth-century theology in general. Similar to Barth, Bultmann was receptive to the existential message of Kierkegaard, as one can see especially well in his book *Jesus* (1926). Yet Bultmann adopted more and more the existential interpretation of Martin Heidegger. Then he also came out with his essay on demythologization, to which Barth wrote in 1952 a sharp rejoinder, *Rudolf Bultmann: An Attempt to Understand Him (Rudolf Bultmann. Ein Versuch ihn zu verstehen).* He claimed that Bultmann wanted to interpret the Christian faith on an anthropological basis through his existential interpretation. Bultmann's call for demythologization also meant for Barth a return to issues that had already been debated in the nineteenth century. But by the mid–twentieth century Bultmann had long left the dialectic method to which he was primarily attracted because he, too, opposed nineteenth-century liberalism.

Friedrich Gogarten (1887-1967) was much closer to Barth, as he was a pastor and also a systematician. There are also some affinities in their intellectual histories. Gogarten was born as a son of a watchmaker in Dortmund, Westphalia, and his father died the year he was born. After graduating from the *Gymnasium* in 1907, Gogarten went to the University of Munich to study art history, German literature, and psychology. However, a pastor from his hometown was instrumental in bringing him to theology, and the same year he moved to Jena to study theology, a field he initially did not dare to pick up. In 1909 he studied for two semesters at Berlin, but was especially disappointed with dogmatics, since it was so abstract and had nothing to do with the reality he encountered in urban Berlin. Then he moved to Heidelberg and found in

---

16. Rudolf Bultmann, "Liberal Theology and the Latest Theological Movement" (1924), in Rudolf Bultmann, *Faith and Understanding,* vol. 1, edited and introduction by Robert W. Funk, trans. Louise Pettibone Smith (New York: Harper and Row, 1969), 29.

Ernst Troeltsch the teacher who directed him to history. He passed his first and second theological exams in 1911 and 1912 respectively, and then went to Zürich for further study. There he became acquainted with Ragaz and Kutter. What really interested him, however, was Fichte's idealism, about which he wrote his doctoral thesis. Since the thesis was published in connection with Fichte's centennial in 1914, Gogarten could no longer submit it to the theological faculty at Heidelberg as he had intended. It did not matter that much to him, since he had decided to become a pastor.

Things changed, however, when he was invited by the friends of the journal *Die christliche Welt* to present a main lecture at Eisenach at their symposium in 1920. This lecture was also announced in *Die christliche Welt,* and therefore Gogarten's name became known throughout Germany. Gogarten did not intend to speak about the demise of the Western world and its rejuvenation, because at that time he was very pessimistic on the human possibilities. He claimed instead that when everything human disappears and human activity ceases, then God's activity actually starts. He echoed Luther's insight that God always creates out of nothingness without any human precondition.[17] Similar to Barth, Gogarten experienced the crisis after World War I as God's judgment on this world because God judges humanity and all its creations in a radical way. There is an absolute distance between God and humanity because God is the radically other, the absolute question for us that we cannot answer but that has to be answered.

Barth and Gogarten had met the year before (1919) at Tambach, Thuringia. The religious socialists had invited Barth to present a lecture for which he chose the title "The Christian's Place in Society."[18] In that lecture Barth made clear that neither Christ nor the kingdom of God is synonymous with any human actions, contrary to what the religious socialists had hoped he would say. But he agreed with them that the kingdom of God is a protest against the prevailing order of things because it is utterly different from what we do or are able to do. He claimed: "Our ideals being impossible and our goals unattainable, . . . God alone can save the world."[19] This was exactly the direction in which Gogarten had been thinking too.

In 1922 Barth and Gogarten agreed to publish the journal *Zwischen den Zeiten.* The religion of modernity started for Gogarten with the autonomy of

17. Cf. Hermann Götz Göckeritz, "Friedrich Gogarten," in *Profile des Luthertums. Biographien zum 20. Jahrhundert,* ed. Wolf-Dieter Hauschild (Gütersloh: Gütersloher Verlagshaus, 1998), 215-58, in his carefully researched and very readable biography, here 225-26.

18. Cf. Göckeritz, "Friedrich Gogarten," 228.

19. Karl Barth, "The Christian's Place in Society" (1919), in *The Word of God and the Word of Man,* 281.

modern humanity. This resulted in the opposition between the self-determined autonomous human being and the creature created by God. When the latter recognizes its guilt, salvation is imparted and the creature becomes human and no longer wants to stand in God's place.[20]

In 1927 Gogarten could finally do his *Habilitation* at Jena and became Privatdozent there while still fulfilling his duties in a pastorate. In 1931 he received a call to a professorship in systematic theology at the University of Breslau. In 1933 he gave there a main lecture entitled "Secularized Theology and the Doctrine of the State." For the first time he focused on secularization as a theological concept, a concept that became more and more important to him. Secularization occurs, according to Gogarten, "under the immense impetus of an important historical idea, namely the *autonomy of humanity* . . . which originated out of Christianity."[21] The creature that is responsible to its creator becomes a creative being that exists by itself. This means that the state comes to stand in the place of the divine sovereign. The foundational order of creator and the created is reversed, and state and the people obtain an ultimacy that does not pertain to them. The situation can be remedied only if the state and the people again "are recognized as worldly entities and . . . the demand of humanity finds its limits in the immediate demand" of the eternal power.[22]

It was evident that the National Socialists did not really like this kind of lecture. Nevertheless, Gogarten was sympathetic to the German Christians, because he thought that by working with them he could help those powers to gain the upper hand that related state and church in such a way that both the proclamation of the church and the needs of the state were being met. To that effect, he even joined the German Christians, but left them again before he even received a membership card, since he saw the unacceptable direction to which they were turning. When Barth got notice of these naive politico-theological inclinations of Gogarten, he immediately severed his ties with him. Gogarten very much regretted Barth's decision, since this also meant the end of *Zwischen den Zeiten*. In 1935 Gogarten had been asked to replace Barth in Bonn, something he very hesitatingly did. In the same year, however, Gogarten obtained a professorship in systematic theology at Göttingen, and at the same time was appointed university preacher there.

Finally Gogarten found a different perception of modern secularity by distinguishing between secularity and secularism. He got his cues from Paul,

20. Cf. Göckeritz, "Friedrich Gogarten," 237.

21. Friedrich Gogarten, "Säkularisierte Theologie in der Staatslehre (1933)," in Friedrich Gogarten, *Gehören und Verantworten. Ausgewählte Aufsätze*, ed. Hermann G. Göckeritz in cooperation with Marianne Bultmann (Tübingen: Siebeck/Mohr, 1988), 128.

22. Gogarten, "Säkularisierte Theologie in der Staatslehre," 140.

who wrote: "So you are no longer a slave, but a child, and if a child then also an heir, through God" (Gal. 4:7). This meant for Gogarten that Christians are not from the world, but are "responsible for the world in order that it remain God's creation."[23] Humans have a filial responsibility toward God and are no longer in servitude to the world. Being children of God, we are free from the world and free for the world. Yet in this freedom we are responsible toward God for our actions. We receive the world as a heritage from God, and the way we manage this heritage shows our understanding of being children of God. The twofold freedom as child and heir is safeguarded by faith. This means that the law is no longer binding for us. Once humanity thought a work-righteous attitude toward God was sufficient to fulfill the requirements of being children of God, and that the obedience to certain rules would mean being in compliance as heirs of the world. The gospel, however, changed this demanding and accusing character of the law into responsible freedom. "Modern man is no longer responsible to the world and its power as the classical man and, in a modified way, even the medieval man was. Instead he has become the one who is responsible *for* this world."[24] The law as a sum of demands, valid once and for all, has been reduced to our responsibility for the world and for its being and remaining a world. This is a responsibility that has continued to be perceived and achieved anew.

Gogarten recognized that the filial freedom that asks us to assume independent, rational responsibility through our actions, offers a great temptation to act strictly on our own behalf instead of on God's behalf. To safeguard against this new form of secularism, he introduced the term "subjectivism." He wrote: "In modern subjectivism, then, this independence [toward the world and its law] has received a completely different meaning. Subjectivism is not a matter of clearheaded, methodical, scientific research. It is, rather, a world view . . . which claims to be valid for everything there is."[25] While in the Christian faith we understand ourselves as being created, in modern subjectivism humanity elevates itself to the source of meaning for all existence. It has forgotten the twofold responsibility and becomes the measure of all things. Secularism that stands for this kind of autonomy then goes in either of two directions: it may attempt to answer the quest for wholeness and assume the form of an ideology, or it declares such a quest utterly useless and expresses itself in nihilism.[26]

---

23. Friedrich Gogarten, *Despair and Hope for Our Time,* trans. Thomas Wieser (Philadelphia: Pilgrim Press, 1970), 29.

24. Friedrich Gogarten, *The Reality of Faith: The Problem of Subjectivism in Theology,* trans. C. Michalson et al. (Philadelphia: Westminster, 1959), 168.

25. Gogarten, *The Reality of Faith,* 156.

26. Cf. Gogarten, *Despair and Hope,* 108-9.

Since both humanity and the world receive their true meaning from being related to God, their wholeness is lost when humanity separates itself from God. In this secularistic autonomous drive humanity could then opt for one of two possibilities: either base the concept of wholeness on its own ideas and arrive at an ideology that would soon be countered by other ideologies, or renounce the quest for wholeness as meaningless. In the latter case, one confines oneself to the visible world and arrives at a nihilistic worldview that is closed for any ultimate questions. Gogarten claimed that subjectivism and secularism originated from a wrong understanding of faith. Faith was not understood as justifying and thereby liberating, but as a restricting force.[27] Therefore, in an attempt to rid humanity of these stifling tendencies, modern subjectivism asserted its absolute autonomy. We notice that Gogarten moved away from the strict dialectic of the beginning of neo-Reformation theology and opted more for a Lutheran dialectic between law and gospel. Thereby he gained a more appreciative understanding of the world. Yet Gogarten did not lose the emphasis on the primacy of the word and of God's action over any human activity.

Like Barth, **Emil Brunner** (1889-1966) was Swiss, born in Winterthur to decidedly Christian parents who had been drawn into the religious socialist movement through Christoph Blumhardt, Kutter, and Ragaz. It did not take much deliberation for Brunner to pick up the study of theology, first at the University of Zürich, where again Ragaz and also Kutter were influential for him. For one semester (1911) he went to the University of Berlin, where Harnack made an impact on him. Brunner did his doctorate in Zürich on "The Symbolic Element in Religious Knowledge," showing interest in the phenomenology of Edmund Husserl (1859-1938). Just before World War I he went to England to teach for a year in a high school, and there got acquainted with William Temple and the Christian Labor Movement. But then came World War I. "With this event my faith in progress was shattered and my Religious Socialism began to look suspiciously like a beautiful illusion. But my Christian faith itself was not thereby shaken. I came to see that the catastrophe resulting from those conditions in Europe which had led to this collapse was a divine judgment upon the godlessness of the Christian peoples."[28]

Through the catastrophe of World War I, the foundations and aims of religious socialism were due for a thorough reappraisal by Brunner. Yet first he worked as a vicar in Kutter's congregation and then, after the war, in 1919, he was invited to spend one year as a fellow at Union Theological Seminary in New

27. Cf. Gogarten, *The Reality of Faith*, 157.
28. Emil Brunner, "Intellectual Autobiography," in *The Theology of Emil Brunner*, ed. Charles W. Kegley (New York: Macmillan, 1962), 7.

York. Before that he had gotten hold of Barth's *Epistle to the Romans* and found it a forceful confirmation of his own thoughts. Upon his return from the USA, he worked on his inaugural thesis, "Experience, Knowledge, and Faith" (1921). Afterward he wrote *Mysticism and the Word* (*Die Mystik und das Wort*, 1924), in which he critically assessed Schleiermacher and insisted that we adhere to either the Christian faith or the modern understanding of religion, because next to the biblical God there can be no other.[29] Upon publishing these works he was appointed to the chair of systematic and practical theology at the University of Zürich, which he occupied from 1924 until his retirement in 1955.

While he joined the circle of contributors to *Zwischen den Zeiten*, he confessed that "from the very beginning I had taken a position independent of that of Karl Barth, which in the course of the ensuing years was to receive a more pronounced character."[30] This was indeed true. When he was invited to the United States in 1928 to deliver a series of lectures, his mind was still on the crisis of the war and its effects. Of course, they were much more felt on the Continent, where big social, political, and economic postwar changes were taking place, than in America, a country where economic prosperity and political security did not yet create a climate of crisis. Oswald Spengler's (1880-1936) *The Decline of the West* (2 vols., 1918-22) was on the mind of virtually everyone in Europe, as well as whether he was right when he claimed that we are witnessing the disappearance of Western civilization. Yet Brunner was also aware that in America not everything was well, especially concerning theology and the profusely and indiscriminately used label "religious." He said: "A God who is identical with the depth of the world or the soul is not really God. He is neither the sovereign of the world nor of man."[31] Over against the God of religious introspection and contemplation Brunner posited the word of God that was made flesh and is present to us as and in a person. Yet to encounter that word, faith is needed since "the Christ according to the Spirit who must be discerned in the Christ according to the flesh, the eternal Son of God who must be seen by faith as a mystery of the man Jesus, is the incarnate Word of God."[32] In Jesus God became a human being in contrast to what we encounter in all other affirmations of divine apparitions in the field of the world religions. This one-and-for-all-ness is decisive. That Christocentricity Brunner never abandoned throughout his life.

On the lecture circuit in Europe and the USA, involved in numerous con-

---

29. Cf. Emil Brunner, *Die Mystik und das Wort. Der Gegensatz zwischen moderner Religionsauffassung und christlichem Glauben dargestellt an der Theologie Schleiermachers* (Tübingen: J. C. B. Mohr, 1924), 391.

30. Brunner, "Intellectual Autobiography," 9.

31. Emil Brunner, *The Theology of Crisis* (New York: Charles Scribner's, 1929), 29-30.

32. Brunner, *The Theology of Crisis*, 35.

ferences of what was to become the World Council of Churches, and above all, influenced by the Jewish philosopher of religion Martin Buber (1878-1965) and his emphasis on relational structures, Brunner was not satisfied with the dichotomy between world and God. In 1934 appeared his *Nature and Grace*. In this slim publication Brunner argued that "wherever God does anything, he leaves the imprint of his nature upon what he does. Therefore the creation of the world is at the same time a revelation, a self-communication of God."[33] This is true for humanity as God's creation as well as for nature in general. Brunner mused that when we consider the human conscience, the only reason why we can sin is that we have some idea of the law as God's will. Of course, such revelation through universal knowledge is not a source of salvation. If we do not know anything about these divine ordinances, or that they are from God, we cannot really be human and sinners. Since we do know something, we are not fully out of touch with God and there is a point of contact between us and God. Brunner also insisted that a human being has a capacity for words as a presupposition for hearing "the Word of God. But the Word of God itself creates man's ability to believe the Word of God, i.e., the ability to hear it in *such a way* as is only possible in faith."[34]

Since Brunner used in this connection the term "natural theology," it came as no surprise that Barth reacted immediately and strongly with a pamphlet using the shortest book title possible: *No!* Barth contended that there can be no natural theology whatsoever and no point of contact. "In my experience the best way of dealing with 'unbelievers' and modern youth is not to try to bring out their 'capacity for revelation,' but to treat them quietly, simply (remembering that Christ has died and risen also for them), as if their rejection of 'Christianity' was not to be taken seriously."[35] This means there is no point of contact necessary between the message and its receiver, because the word of God establishes its own point of contact. Humanity and God, nature and God, are totally separated unless God graciously establishes his line of communication. But the line of communication between Brunner and Barth was severed, and only toward the end of their lives was the personal hurt overcome that ensued from Barth rejecting Brunner's overtures to continue their friendship.

In his 1927 edition of *The Mediator*, Brunner refers to Barth as "my friend" and declares in the vein of dialectic theology: "'God alone matters': This is the one question which concerns humanity supremely. For it is this which gives

33. Emil Brunner, *Nature and Grace*, in *Natural Theology*, comprising "Nature and Grace" by Professor Dr. Emil Brunner and the reply "No!" by Dr. Karl Barth, trans. Peter Fraenkel, introduction by John Baillie (London: Geoffrey Bles, 1946), 25.

34. Brunner, *Nature and Grace*, 32.

35. Karl Barth, *No! Answer to Emil Brunner*, in *Natural Theology*, 127.

meaning and significance to all other questions. . . . The question of God — in the form of decision — is the question of Christ."[36] Though there is much religiosity in today's culture, Brunner nevertheless contended that this religiosity is not sufficient. What matters alone is Christ. But he also insisted: "It is impossible to believe in a Christian way in the unique revelation, in the Mediator, without believing also in a universal revelation of God in creation, in history, and especially in the human conscience. . . . The recognition of the indirect *(gebrochen)* general revelation is the presupposition of the Christian religion of revelation, with its unique character."[37] In outlining his Christology, Brunner was convinced that he needed a point of contact to comprehend what God's self-disclosure in Jesus Christ meant in contradistinction to all other religious manifestations.

In 1935 appeared Brunner's book *Man in Revolt,* in which he described humanity as a citizen of two worlds. Through God's gift humanity has a share in the life of God. It is so created that it "can perceive God's eternal Word, and can answer it as the reason which perceives, and as a self-determining will. . . . Through this participation in the divine life and in spiritual existence man, for his part, stands 'over against' the world, as its master — in accordance with the divine appointment."[38] This means humanity is not created like all other creatures. But it cannot reach to God on its own. Only in rationalism and idealism it commits the error and behaves as if it were an autonomous rational being and could determine its own life. Humanity has been created to be God's representative on earth, and therefore it has an antenna for God, whether it makes use of it or perverts it.

In an appendix to *The Mediator* Brunner again reacted to Barth's sharp criticism of this approach and insisted that a human being can indeed know the law. Yet this is exactly what Barth had ruled out. For Barth it is only and just because of the gospel that we have an understanding of what the law even means. Brunner's approach has often been called an eristic theology, an apologetic approach that attacks the sinfully warped intellect and pushes thinking to the point at which humanity does not know anything anymore on its own. Consequently theology can show humanity which direction it should take to solve its helplessness and hopelessness. Brunner never forgot, however, that the foremost task of theology is to develop an understanding of humanity as a Christian anthropology from the perspective of God's self-disclosure in Jesus Christ. This agenda he also carried through in his three-volume *Dogmatics* (1946-60)

36. Emil Brunner, *The Mediator: A Study of the Central Doctrine of the Christian Faith,* trans. Olive Wyon (Philadelphia: Westminster, 1947), 15 and 13, in his preface to the German edition.

37. Brunner, *The Mediator,* 32.

38. Emil Brunner, *Man in Revolt: A Christian Anthropology,* trans. Olive Wyon (Philadelphia: Westminster, 1947), 109.

under the subtitles *The Christian Doctrine of God, The Christian Doctrine of Creation and Redemption,* and *The Christian Doctrine of the Church, Faith, and the Consummation.*

An interesting publication is Brunner's 1938 book *Wahrheit als Begegnung,* which appeared first in English as *The Divine-Human Encounter* (1943) and then in a second edition and enlarged as *Truth as Encounter* in 1964. His point is that according to the Christian understanding truth is not a fixed deposit, but occurs in the encounter with God through God's self-disclosure. According to Greek thought, which provides for us the basis for philosophy and science, truth was understood as something objective that was open for discovery and definition. The relation between God and humanity is not developed in the Bible in terms of a doctrine, but rather as an event. Therefore "men are also considered as those who are not something in and for themselves, but only as those who from the first are placed in a specific relation to God and then also place themselves in such a relation: either positive or negative, obedient or disobedient, true or false."[39] With this kind of approach that portrays the influence of Martin Buber, Brunner sought to overcome the notion of truth as something objective that often leads to controversy or to outright rejection.

The engaging style of Brunner's writings and speeches made him very popular, and he received numerous invitations in Europe, America, and Asia. Shortly before the outbreak of World War II, he was even offered "a combined professorship at the university and the theological seminary in Princeton."[40] But he declined out of his love and responsibility for his home country and for his own church. Another invitation after World War II to teach for two years (1953-55) at the New International Christian University in Tokyo he happily accepted. In Japan, Brunner discovered how important it was to establish a point of contact between our life and God. Since Barth's influence on the European continent was so overwhelming, however, Brunner's more dialogical approach was more appreciated on the British Isles and above all in Asia and America.

From Continuation to Reversal: Dietrich Bonhoeffer, John A. T. Robinson, and the Death-of-God Theologians

Dietrich Bonhoeffer (1906-45) belongs to the second generation of neo-Reformation theology. His father was professor of psychiatry and neurology

---

39. Emil Brunner, *Truth as Encounter,* trans. David Cairns (Philadelphia: Westminster, 1964), 88.

40. Brunner, "Intellectual Autobiography," 20.

and his mother was a niece of the church historian Karl von Hase (1800-1890). She was a schoolteacher who gave her children their first private school instruction. The spirit of his parents' home was that of educated Christians of liberal persuasion. As we can see by the books for which Bonhoeffer asked when he was imprisoned by the National Socialists, the standard of an all-round educational level persisted with him throughout his short life.

Already at age fourteen he decided to study theology. Three years later, in 1923, he began his studies at Tübingen, and the following year he continued them in Berlin. At the early age of twenty-one he did his licentiate (doctorate) with a study entitled *Sanctorum Communio: A Dogmatic Inquiry into the Sociology of the Church.* He wanted to bring together a sociological study of the church with a theology of revelation that he had learned from Barth. He came up with the understanding of Christ existing as community. He wrote: "The church is established in reality in and through Christ — not in such a way that we can think of the church without Christ himself, but he himself 'is' the church. He does not represent it, for only what is not present can be represented."[41] This work won him high praise. Even Barth wrote in his *Church Dogmatics:* "I openly confess that I have misgivings whether I can even maintain the high level reached by Bonhoeffer, saying no less in my own words and context, in saying it no less forcefully, than did this young man so many years ago."[42] In 1928 Bonhoeffer passed his first theological exam and then went to Barcelona, to work there as vicar in a congregation.

After his second exam he did his *Habilitation* in 1930 in systematic theology, which became *Act and Being: Transcendental Philosophy and Ontology in Systematic Theology.* Picking up the philosophical discussion as engendered by Heidegger's *Being and Time,* Bonhoeffer again focused on the church and therewith on Christ. He wrote: "There is a genuine future only through Christ and the reality, created anew by Christ, of the neighbor and creation. Estranged from Christ, the world is enclosed in the I, which is to say, already, the past. In it, life is reflection."[43] This means that the I can never really extend itself to the future, it is captured by the past and therewith by the world. Yet Christian revela-

---

41. Dietrich Bonhoeffer, *Sanctorum Communio: A Dogmatic Inquiry into the Sociology of the Church,* trans. R. Gregor Smith et al. (London: Collins, 1963), 115. Bonhoeffer's life and work has been especially carefully researched thanks to his friend Eberhard Bethge, *Dietrich Bonhoeffer: Theologian — Christian Contemporary,* trans. Eric Mosbacher et al. (London: Collins, 1970), xxiv, 867.

42. Karl Barth, *Church Dogmatics,* vol. 4, *The Doctrine of Reconciliation,* pt. 2, trans. G. W. Bromiley (Edinburgh: T. & T. Clark, 1958), 641.

43. Dietrich Bonhoeffer, *Act and Being: Transcendental Philosophy and Ontology in Systematic Theology,* trans. H. Martin Rumscheidt, in *Works* (Minneapolis: Fortress, 1996), 2:157.

tion is open to the future, "because it is, in the qualified once-and-for-all occurrence of the cross and resurrection of Christ, always something 'of the future.' It must, in other words, be thought in the church, for the church is the present Christ, 'Christ existing as community.'"[44] The phrase "Christ existing as community" is picked up from *Sanctorum Communio*.

The same year he did his *Habilitation* (1930), Harnack died, and at the memorial service he spoke as the representative of Harnack's former pupils. Too young to be ordained, he received a scholarship to study for a year at Union Seminary in New York, and the following year visited with Barth in Bonn. Now he began lecturing as Privatdozent at the University of Berlin and also served as student chaplain at the Technical University there, plus being engaged with ecumenical youth work, especially for world peace. When the National Socialists came into power in 1933, he uncompromisingly opposed them, especially their advocacy of the supremacy of the Aryan race. In 1934 he took up a pastorate in London, serving a German congregation for one year. In 1935 he was appointed director of studies at the preachers seminary *(Predigerseminar)* of the Confessing Church at Finkenwalde, Pomerania, where those opposed to Hitler's interference with the church continued their studies. When the seminary's existence was terminated in 1937 by the police, he supervised future pastors in their first calls. He introduced them to daily prayers and the life of Anglican monastic tradition through which they obtained a new style of life. His seminars soon became the spiritual center in Pomerania.

In 1936 the National Socialist regime withdrew his license to teach, and in 1938 he was even expelled from Berlin. Within another two years he was no longer allowed to publish or to speak in public. In 1939 he traveled again to England and the USA. However, he did not stay there out of the felt obligation to be with his people either to suffer through the destruction of civilization if the National Socialists won or, if Hitler's regime was defeated, to help in the reconstruction process so that Christian civilization could continue to live. He worked for the resistance movement, and in 1943 was imprisoned as a suspected member of that movement. During the last days of the war (April 9, 1945), he was put to death by hanging.

Since Bonhoeffer was just thirty-nine years old when he died and barely twenty-seven when his academic work was violently cut off, we do not have a complete oeuvre in front of us. Nevertheless, the deliberate sacrifice of his life has made his writings immensely popular. By 1974 his *Letters and Papers from Prison* had been translated into thirteen languages, and because of his open-ended work — his theology was still very much in the making when he died —

---

44. Bonhoeffer, *Act and Being*, 2:111.

he has been claimed for various movements. Especially his *Letters and Papers from Prison* and the notion of "the world come of age" found there attracted many "followers" who proclaimed that religion is on the way out. Even the death-of-God movement of the 1970s claimed that it followed the way Bonhoeffer had shown.

To assess Bonhoeffer's contribution, one must first consider that he was influenced by Barth in his understanding of religion. Even in his *Letters and Papers from Prison* he could still use the term "religion" indiscriminately to denote "Christian faith" and he could say that "'Christianity' has always been a form — perhaps the true form — of 'religion.'" At the same time, he also warned of the consequences if it were discovered that the religious a priori on which Christian preaching and theology have rested for nineteen hundred years did not exist at all, that it was "a historically conditioned and transient form of human self-expression."[45] With this last remark, Bonhoeffer understands religion in a much narrower sense than does Barth, namely, as the garment of Christianity and as a point of contact for the Christian proclamation.

Observing his fellow prison inmates, he realized that the God of religion is invoked for help when human knowledge ends or when human resources fail. According to Bonhoeffer, it is pointless to relegate God to a realm beyond our cognitive faculties. The transcendence of God must rather be affirmed in such a way that "God is beyond in the midst of our life."[46] Similarly, in our effort to rescue God from irrelevancy and resort to the so-called ultimate questions of death and guilt, it is futile claiming that only God can answer them. Bonhoeffer affirmed that the world has come of age and someday these "ultimate" questions can be answered without God. Even Barth's positivism of revelation, as Bonhoeffer calls his unmitigated affirmation of the word of God, can be of no help at this point. We must get used to the fact that we have to live in the world *etsi deus non daretur* (as if God were not), and in recognizing this, we must live before God. "Our coming of age leads us to a true recognition of our situation before God. God would have us know that we must live as men who manage our lives without him. The God who is with us is the God who forsakes us (Mk 15:34). The God who lets us live in the world without the working hypothesis of God is the God before whom we stand continually. Before God and with God we live without God."[47] God lets himself be pushed out of the world. The Bible directs us to God's powerlessness and suffering because only the suffering God

---

45. Dietrich Bonhoeffer, *Letters and Papers from Prison*, ed. Eberhard Bethge, trans. Reginald Fuller, revised and enlarged ed. (New York: Macmillan, 1967), 139-40.

46. Bonhoeffer, *Letters*, 142.

47. Bonhoeffer, *Letters*, 188.

who came to us in the humility of Jesus of Nazareth can help us. Thus the starting point for our secular interpretation of the gospel, Bonhoeffer surmised, will probably be the weakness of God.

Here we touch the center of Bonhoeffer's nonreligious interpretation, the humanity of Christ. He emphasized the humanity of Christ already in his lectures on Christology when he stated, for instance, that "even as the Risen One, he [Christ] does not break through his incognito."[48] This christocentric nonreligious interpretation of the gospel with its emphasis on the humility of Christ, enunciated but never carried out in detail, proved attractive for laypeople and theologians.

Before we briefly deal with those who claimed Bonhoeffer on their side, we should mention two more books from his pen that made an impact on the spiritual and devotional life of many people, *The Cost of Discipleship* and *Life Together*. Both publications grew out of his involvement at Finkenwalde where he educated future pastors. In *The Cost of Discipleship* (1937) he attempted to fathom the concept of faith in all its implications. At the beginning he cautioned against cheap grace because this would mean "the justification of sin without the justification of the sinner."[49] If one is justified, this entails leading a new life and not continuing to live as if nothing had happened. Looking at the Sermon on the Mount, he concluded that Jesus "does not mean that it is to be discussed as an ideal, He means really putting it into practice."[50] According to Bonhoeffer, justification leads to sanctification. Again he emphasizes the community aspect of the Christian life: "No one can become a new man except by entering the Church, and becoming a member of the Body of Christ. It is impossible to become a new man as a solitary individual. The New Man means more than the individual believer after he has been justified and sanctified, it means the Church, the Body of Christ, in fact it means Christ Himself."[51] Bonhoeffer had a passion for the church, and to that extent he was also involved in the ecumenical movement, showing his friends in England that many like him were fighting the takeover of the church by the so-called German Christians.

---

48. Dietrich Bonhoeffer, *Christ the Center,* trans. John Bowden, introduction by Edwin H. Robertson (New York: Harper, 1966), 117. He states that only at the point of the parousia will Christ have ceased to be the lowly one. Cf. also Rainer Mayer, *Christuswirklichkeit. Grundlagen, Entwicklung und Konsequenzen der Theologie Dietrich Bonhoeffers,* 2nd ed. (Stuttgart: Calwer Verlag, 1980 [1969]).

49. Dietrich Bonhoeffer, *The Cost of Discipleship,* trans. Reginald Fuller, preface by Reinhold Niebuhr (1937; New York: Macmillan, 1957), 37.

50. Bonhoeffer, *The Cost of Discipleship,* 168.

51. Bonhoeffer, *The Cost of Discipleship,* 186.

In *Life Together* (1938) Bonhoeffer elucidated that the Christian community means community through Christ and in Christ. He delineated the daily schedule in the community from morning prayers to table fellowship, work in the world, prayer, etc. Yet he cautioned that "a Christian community is not a spiritual sanatorium."[52] People should not seek the community for wrong reasons, because then they will be disappointed. Being alone is also necessary for silence and meditation. One can also be together and not really be in communion, if there is no confession and forgiveness. Bonhoeffer concluded his book by pointing to the Lord's Supper, because here "the community has reached its goal. Here joy in Christ and his community is complete. The life of Christians together under the Word has reached its perfection in the sacrament."[53] It is important to remember this christocentric communal and sacramental approach to the Christian faith to keep in proper perspective Bonhoeffer's remarks about the powerlessness of God, remarks he made during his last year of life in the gestapo prison cell.

In the 1960s it was especially **John A. T. Robinson** (1919-83), a New Testament scholar and once bishop of Woolwich, who brought Bonhoeffer's ideas to the attention of a worldwide public in his best seller *Honest to God* (1963). Because he was educated in the English tradition, it is not surprising that Robinson first of all attacked a supernatural or theistic notion of God, in which God is seen as the supreme being whose existence can be proved. Then he combined Bonhoeffer with Paul Tillich and claimed that God is not to be thought of as transcendent, but as the ultimate depth of our being, as the creative ground and the reason for our whole existence. He still asserted God as personal. It is in personal relationships that we find the ultimate reason of our existence better than anywhere else. "A view of the world which affirms this reality and significance in personal categories is *ipso facto* making an affirmation about the *ultimacy* of personal relationships: it is saying that *God,* the final truth and reality 'deep down things,' *is* love."[54] In moving past Bonhoeffer's claim that God is in the midst of us beyond, Robinson regarded God no longer as being apart from the world, but he "locates" God within our world. This opened the possibility of turning God into a "worldly" phenomenon, something the death-of-God theologians of the 1960s pursued further.

William Hamilton (b. 1924), Thomas J. J. Altizer (b. 1927), Richard Rubenstein (b. 1924), and Harvey Cox (b. 1929) banded together in the mid-

---

52. Dietrich Bonhoeffer, *Life Together,* translated with an introduction by John W. Doberstein (New York: Harper, 1954), 76.

53. Bonhoeffer, *Life Together,* 122.

54. John A. T. Robinson, *Honest to God* (Philadelphia: Westminster, 1963), 49.

1960s as the so-called **death-of-God theologians.** Their assertion that God had died even made it to the cover of *Time* magazine (April 8, 1966). Claiming to follow Bonhoeffer by stating that the traditional sovereign and omnipotent God is difficult to perceive or to meet, Hamilton called for a drastic alternative: "In place of this God, the impotent God, suffering with men seems to be emerging."[55] This impotence is substantiated in both non-Christians and Christians by a growing sentiment that God has withdrawn, that he is absent and even somehow dead. God seems to have withdrawn from the world, but he is still experienced as a pressure and a wounding from which we would want to be free. If we turn to Jesus the Lord, our experience is not much different. Still "the God of the time of the death of God and the God coming in Jesus the Lord are somehow both with us."[56] This means that the experience of Jesus is no longer a liberating and freeing, it is as baffling and bewildering as that of God.

Following Hamilton, Altizer proposed "a consistent kenotic Christology."[57] He rejected Barth's proposal that a fully kenotic Christ is the result of God's omnipotence, through which God assumes the form of weakness to triumph in it. Altizer abandoned the dialectic, and for him the descent of God into human flesh is final and irrevocable. Therefore the death of God becomes an event in history. "We must realize that the death of God is an historical event, that God has died in our cosmos, in our history, in our *Existenz.* While there is no immediate necessity in assuming that the God who has died is the God of 'faith,' there is also no escaping of the inevitable consequence that the dead God is not the God of idolatry, or false piety, or 'religion,' but rather the God of the historic Christian Church and beyond the Church, of Christendom at large."[58]

Altizer contended that God has actually died in Christ's own death, since God moved into this world and became one with it in Christ. "The death of God in Christ is an inevitable consequence of the movement of God into the world, of Spirit into flesh."[59] Yet, like Strauss a century earlier, Altizer did not want to confine the identification of the divine spirit with the human spirit just to one singular person, Jesus, but claimed: "The forward movement of the Incarnate Word is from God to Jesus, and the Word continues its kenotic move-

55. William Hamilton, *The New Essence of Christianity* (New York: Association, 1966), 54.

56. Hamilton, *New Essence of Christianity,* 95.

57. Thomas J. J. Altizer, *The Gospel of Christian Atheism* (Philadelphia: Westminster, 1966), 11.

58. Thomas J. J. Altizer, "America and the Future of Theology," in Thomas J. J. Altizer and William Hamilton, *Radical Theology and the Death of God* (Indianapolis: Bobbs-Merrill, 1966), 11-12.

59. Altizer, *Gospel of Christian Atheism,* 110.

ment and direction by moving from the historical Jesus to the universal body of humanity, thereby undergoing an epiphany in every human hand and face."[60] We have now gone full circle. As the divine ceases as the one that is the totally other, the divine emerges again in the human person. But Altizer abandoned the radical dialectic of Kierkegaard and even the dialectic of Hegel, whose heir he thought himself. The dialectic is no longer pursued to the final synthesis of thesis and antithesis. Instead Altizer stops with the negation of the thesis and places the human antithesis in place of God. This elevation of humanity seems to be the prominent feature of theology in the last two centuries with which neo-Reformation theology vigorously wrestled by providing a respite, albeit only a temporary one.

For Further Reading

Karl Barth (1886-1968)

Barth, Karl. *Church Dogmatics.* Translated by G. W. Bromiley et al. Vols. I-IV. Edinburgh: T. & T. Clark, 1936-69.

———. *The Epistle to the Romans.* Translated from the 6th edition by Edwyn C. Hoskyns. London: Oxford University Press, 1968 [1933].

———. *God in Action.* Translated with an introduction by Elmer G. Homrighausen. Manhasset, N.Y.: Round Table, 1963.

———. *Theological Existence To-day! (A Plea for Theological Freedom).* Translated with a foreword by R. Birch Hoyle. London: Hodder and Stoughton, 1933.

———. *The Word of God and the Word of Man.* Translated by Douglas Horton. New York: Harper Torchbook, 1957.

Busch, Eberhard. *Karl Barth: His Life from Letters and Autobiographical Texts.* Translated by John Bowden. Philadelphia: Fortress, 1976.

Dorrien, Gary. *The Barthian Revolt in Modern Theology: Theology without Weapons.* Louisville: John Knox, 2000.

Hunsinger, George. *Disruptive Grace: Studies in the Theology of Karl Barth.* Grand Rapids: Eerdmans, 2001.

Webster, John, ed. *The Cambridge Companion to Karl Barth.* Cambridge: Cambridge University Press, 2000.

Rudolf Bultmann (1884-1976)

Bultmann, Rudolf. *Faith and Understanding.* Vol. 1. Edited and introduction by Robert W. Funk. Translation by Louise Pettibone Smith. New York: Harper and Row, 1969.

See also chapter 9.

60. Altizer, *Gospel of Christian Atheism,* 83.

Friedrich Gogarten (1887-1967)

Beschnidt, Dietlind G. "The Anthropology of Freedom: A Study in Friedrich Gogarten and Karl Barth." Th.D. thesis, Southwestern Baptist Theological Seminary, 1996.

Gogarten, Friedrich. *Despair and Hope for Our Time.* Translated by Thomas Wieser. Philadelphia: Pilgrim Press, 1970.

————. *The Reality of Faith: The Problem of Subjectivism in Theology.* Translated by C. Michalson et al. Philadelphia: Westminster, 1959.

Haynes, Stephen R. "Between the Times: German Theology and the Weimar Zeitgeist." *Soundings* 74 (Spring/Summer 1991): 9-44.

Shiner, Larry E. *The Secularization of History: An Introduction to the Theology of Friedrich Gogarten.* Nashville: Abingdon, 1966.

Emil Brunner (1889-1966)

Brunner, Emil. *Man in Revolt: A Christian Anthropology.* Translated by Olive Wyon. Philadelphia: Westminster, 1947.

————. *The Mediator: A Study of the Central Doctrine of the Christian Faith.* Translated by Olive Wyon. Philadelphia: Westminster, 1947.

————. *The Theology of Crisis.* New York: Charles Scribner's, 1929.

————. *Truth as Encounter.* Translated by David Cairns. Philadelphia: Westminster, 1964.

Jewett, Paul K. *Emil Brunner: An Introduction to the Man and His Thought.* InterVarsity Press Series in Contemporary Christian Thought. Chicago: InterVarsity, 1961.

Kegley, Charles, ed. *The Theology of Emil Brunner.* New York: Macmillan, 1962.

Lovin, Robin. *Christian Faith and Public Choices: The Social Ethics of Barth, Brunner, and Bonhoeffer.* Philadelphia: Fortress, 1984.

Natural Theology. Comprising "Nature and Grace" by Professor Dr. Emil Brunner and the reply "No!" by Dr. Karl Barth. Translated by Peter Fraenkel. Introduction by John Baillie. London: Geoffrey Bles, 1946.

Dietrich Bonhoeffer (1906-45)

Bethge, Eberhard. *Dietrich Bonhoeffer: A Biography.* Minneapolis: Fortress, 2000.

Bonhoeffer, Dietrich. *Act and Being: Transcendental Philosophy and Ontology in Systematic Theology.* Translated by H. Martin Rumscheidt. In *Works.* Minneapolis: Fortress, 1996.

————. *Christ the Center.* Translated by John Bowden. Introduction by Edwin H. Robertson. New York: Harper, 1966.

————. *The Cost of Discipleship.* Translated by Reginald Fuller. Preface by Reinhold Niebuhr. 1937. New York: Macmillan, 1957.

————. *Letters and Papers from Prison.* Edited by Eberhard Bethge. Translated by Reginald Fuller. Revised and enlarged edition. New York: Macmillan, 1967.

————. *Life Together.* Translated with an introduction by John W. Doberstein. New York: Harper, 1954.

————. *Sanctorum Communio: A Dogmatic Inquiry into the Sociology of the Church.* Translated by R. Gregor Smith et al. London: Collins, 1963.

————. *Witness to Jesus Christ.* Edited by John de Gruchy. Minneapolis: Fortress, 1991. 2000.

Raum, Elizabeth. *Dietrich Bonhoeffer: Called by God; A Biography.* New York: Continuum, 2002.

John A. T. Robinson (1919-83)

Edwards, David. *The "Honest to God" Debate: Some Reactions to the Book "Honest to God."* Philadelphia: Westminster, 1963.

Hamilton, William. *The New Essence of Christianity.* New York: Association, 1966.

James, Eric. *A Life of Bishop John A. T. Robinson: Scholar, Pastor, Prophet.* Grand Rapids: Eerdmans, 1987.

McBrien, Richard. *The Church in the Thought of Bishop John Robinson.* Philadelphia: Westminster, 1966.

Robinson, John A. T. *Honest to God.* Philadelphia: Westminster, 1963.

Thomas J. J. Altizer (b. 1927)

Altizer, Thomas J. J., and William Hamilton. *Radical Theology and the Death of God.* Indianapolis: Bobbs-Merrill, 1966.

Cobb, John B. *The Theology of Altizer: Critique and Response.* Philadelphia: Westminster, 1970.

Ogletree, Thomas W. *The Death of God Controversy.* Nashville: Abingdon, 1966.

11 Relating God and the World in North America

Neo-Reformation theology was certainly the dominating voice after World War I. This can be substantiated by the almost immediate translation of the main writings of its main proponents into the English medium. While the international attention to Karl Barth made him the most prominent Protestant theologian during the first half of the twentieth century, not everybody who made the pilgrimage to his lectures and seminars actually followed in his footsteps. And many of those who did in other countries made their own particular adaptations. Especially in North America, Barth was held in high esteem. He was celebrated as the one who clearly spoke out against the Nazi dictatorship, and many also appreciated and followed his neoorthodox outlook. His emphasis on the triumph of God's grace also made him attractive especially for theologians of the Reformed tradition. But the dialectic between God and the world and between human words and the word of God was rarely followed. North America did not experience the same cultural crisis as did western Europe after World War I. Moreover, the legacy of natural theology going all the way back to Thomas Jefferson (1743-1826) and his rational Christianity did not allow for a dichotomy between God and the world. Some interesting developments of its own therefore took place in the "New World," such as empirical theology or, more recently, process theology. But Barth's insights were not lost either, as one sees especially well with the Niebuhr brothers, one advocating a more neoorthodox approach whereas the other advocated social involvement.

Empirical Theology: The Chicago School

One of the remarkable movements in the United States of America was empirical theology under the lead of the so-called Chicago School. Empiricism is commonly defined as the method of inquiry that presumes to find knowledge and its verification by appealing to experience. Given this kind of definition, we could classify Schleiermacher's quest for religion in this category, as well as Rudolf Otto with his concern for the holy, and certainly William James in his quest for the independence of the religious factor. As Bernard Meland, one of the representatives of the Chicago School, wrote: "The empirical method of theological study in the Divinity school became explicit in the rise of the early Chicago school under Shailer Mathews and Shirley Jackson Case, sometimes referred to as the socio-historical school of theology."[1]

The empirical effort of the early Chicago School was also influenced by the pragmatism of John Dewey (1859-1952), who taught in the department of philosophy at the University of Chicago at that time. Dewey was born in Burlington, Vermont. He attended the University of Vermont and was one of eighteen graduates of the class of 1879. After teaching high school, he took up graduate studies in philosophy and received his doctorate at Johns Hopkins with a dissertation on the psychology of Kant. Having taught at the University of Michigan and the University of Minnesota, he was appointed in 1894 as chairman of the department of philosophy, psychology, and education at the University of Chicago. In 1904 he left Chicago for Columbia, after increasing friction with the university administration concerning his laboratory school where he tested and developed his psychological and pedagogical hypotheses. While in Chicago he also became acquainted with the enormous social and economic problems brought about by urbanization, rapid technological advance, and the influx of immigrants. The key notion in Dewey's philosophy is experience, as he wrote: "All philosophies employ empirical subject-matter, even the most transcendental; there is nothing else for them to go by. But in ignoring the kind of empirical situation to which their themes pertain, and in failing to supply directions for empirical pointing and searching they become non-empirical."[2] If one moves away from the empirical, one's truth claims become private. Since most of life consists of experiences that are not primarily reflective, it is wrong to concern oneself predominantly with epistemological issues. Rather the context of nonreflective experience ought to be appreciated. Grad-

---

1. Bernard Meland, "The Empirical Traditions in Theology at Chicago," in *The Future of Empirical Theology*, ed. Bernard E. Meland (Chicago: University of Chicago Press, 1969), 14-15.
2. John Dewey, *Experience and Nature* (Chicago: Open Court, 1925), 38.

ually we move here to a naturalism that appreciated the experimental method as practiced by the sciences.

The Sociohistorical Emphasis of Shailer Mathews and Shirley Jackson Case

Shailer Mathews (1863-1941) was born in Portland, Maine, of Baptist parents. When his father's wholesale business went bankrupt, young Mathews had to drop out of high school for a time to work in his father's office. Upon graduation from Colby College in Waterville, Maine, he went to a Baptist seminary, Newton Theological Institution, in Newton, Massachusetts, and graduated from there in 1887. He was not committed to the ministry, but wanted to teach and obtained a position at Colby College, as associate professor of rhetoric. In 1889 he became professor of history and political economy there. The following year he was granted a year's leave to study at the University of Berlin, where he stayed till 1892. He engaged there mainly in historical studies under Leopold von Ranke (1795-1886), the chief exponent of an objectivistic approach to writing history. Moreover, Adolf Wagner (1835-1917) became a mentor for him in economics. Wagner endeavored to apply ethical principles to economic affairs. Upon his return to Colby, Mathews also came under the influence of Richard T. Ely with regard to the social conception of economic problems. In 1894 he was invited to become associate professor of New Testament history and interpretation at the University of Chicago Divinity School. Because of his lack of training he hesitatingly accepted this call. He remained in this position until 1906, when he became professor of historical and comparative theology. From 1908 to his retirement in 1933 he served as dean at the Divinity School and so helped to shape the development of the Chicago School of Theology.

From his earlier training Mathews maintained a sociohistorical approach to theology and understood Christianity as a religious movement subject to social forces. Through a series of articles on Christian sociology written for the *American Journal of Sociology* that were published in book form as *The Social Teaching of Jesus* (1897), he decidedly influenced the Social Gospel movement. Economics and politics were important and recurring themes in that book. According to Mathews, Jesus "was neither socialist nor individualist. . . . He calls the poor man to sacrifice as well as the rich man. He was the Son of Man, not the son of a class of men."[3] The kingdom was neither a merely political king-

3. Shailer Mathews, *The Social Teaching of Jesus: An Essay in Christian Sociology* (New York: Macmillan, 1910 [1897]), 156-57.

dom, nor a theocratic state, nor a subjective state of the individual, nor exclusively eschatological. The kingdom was a concrete reality and not an idea. Furthermore, "this reality was not to be left as an unattainable ideal, but was to be progressively realized, perhaps evolved."[4] Indeed, the theme of an evolutionary progression of the kingdom is prominent in Mathews's interpretation of the historical Jesus. The evolutionary progression of the kingdom of God was an ideal by which humanity related to God as sons and daughters and therefore to each other as sisters and brothers.[5] This relationship of humanity with God and with one another is the propelling force of social amelioration and will usher in the kingdom. But the kingdom will not be brought about by our own efforts. At one point, we do not know when, the growth of the kingdom will be supplemented by a divine cataclysm. Then the new social order will triumph and offenders of this order will be isolated. "Individual and institutional life will no longer testify to the reign of even an enlightened selfishness. The world will, by virtue of man's endeavor and God's regenerating power, have been transformed into the kingdom."[6] The kingdom is the result of our cooperation with God as his sons and daughters and as brothers and sisters among ourselves.

Mathews revised and expanded the themes of *The Social Teaching of Jesus* in *Jesus on Social Institutions* (1928), using the frame of the "revolutionary spirit" that he developed as a consequence of his research on the French Revolution. He discerned the revolutionary expectations of Jesus' time and the general mood of instability. Jesus is portrayed as an agitator. But Jesus was not an agitator primarily of social change or one who discussed morals in general. He was an agitator with the messianic-revolutionary point of view who had "adopted what might be called the revolutionary technique, and, like John, formed his group *(ecclesia)* of sympathizers."[7] His teaching was intended for the active soul and is carried on by the church. True disciples of Jesus are "those who possess something of the revolutionary attitude."[8] Yet a revolutionary spirit does not imply violence, bloodshed, and war. On the contrary, it is the realization "that God is love and that brotherliness rather than coercion is the true basis for human relations."[9] The revolutionary spirit recognizes the truth of Jesus' teaching that "goodwill is a practicable basis upon which to build hu-

---

4. Mathews, *Social Teaching of Jesus*, 53.

5. The famous slogan of the Social Gospel movement is "the fatherhood of God and the brotherhood of man." So Mathews, *Social Teaching of Jesus*, 62 and cf. 54.

6. Mathews, *Social Teaching of Jesus*, 228-29.

7. Shailer Mathews, *Jesus on Social Institutions*, edited with an introduction by Kenneth Cauthen (Philadelphia: Fortress, 1971), 40.

8. Mathews, *Jesus on Social Institutions*, 134.

9. Mathews, *Jesus on Social Institutions*, 39.

man society."[10] In his presentation of Jesus' mission, Mathews was as optimistic and positive as was Walter Rauschenbusch. Though objecting to the social problems of their time, they were optimistic about solutions.[11]

After World War I Mathews realized that the time of the social gospel, founded on an optimistic assessment of humanity, was passed and its message should now be implemented in direct efforts at social organization and action. For that purpose he had already written *The Church and the Changing Order* (1908), in which he summoned the church to social leadership and its members to the speedy support of "the amelioration and the transformation of social conditions."[12] While Christians should engage in the struggle for social betterment, he was no optimist when he wrote: "It is better to fight against the indifference of culture and the materialism of a commercial age at the risk of winning a reputation for quixotic enthusiasm and commercial obtuseness than to permit the evangelical light that is within us to become darkness."[13]

In his many ecumenical involvements — he was president of the Federal Council of the Churches of Christ in America (1912-16) and an active participant in many international ecumenical gatherings — Mathews realized that Christianity was more a religious social movement than a body of truth. He confessed: "One comes to feel that in religion one is dealing with highly complicated social situations and histories. The history of doctrine becomes the history of people who make doctrines."[14] In applying a sociohistorical method he sought to appeal to the various groups of the Christian community regardless of denominational or creedal differences. This can be seen in many of his writings. For instance, in *The Spiritual Interpretation of History* (Cambridge: Harvard University Press, 1916) he tried to trace the historical processes to discover in what direction human society had moved. Through historical and social analysis Mathews wanted to determine whether there was within this process a spiritual quality that could justify a functional theology and the belief in religion as a legitimate element of social life.

Mathews endeavored to be descriptive (and empirical) since he was con-

---

10. Mathews, *Jesus on Social Institutions*, 154.

11. Cf. William D. Lindsey, *Shailer Mathews's Lives of Jesus: The Search for a Theological Foundation for the Social Gospel* (Albany: State University of New York Press, 1997), who provides a critical but positive evaluation and points to the connections with later liberation theology and political theology.

12. Shailer Mathews, *The Church and the Changing Order* (New York: Macmillan, 1908), 242.

13. Mathews, *The Church*, 254.

14. Shailer Mathews, "Theology as Group Belief," in *Contemporary American Theology: Theological Autobiographies*, ed. Vergilius Ferm (New York: Round Table, 1933), 2:171.

vinced that faith shows itself in certain forms of behavior. In the preface to *The Growth of the Idea of God* (1931), he stated: "To my mind the development of the idea of God is more important than its origin. It is its own answer to the charge that religion is superstition. Religious thought and practices are as necessary as economic, political, or scientific."[15] From the outset he was convinced that "in Christianity, as in no other religion, there has been a unique development of monotheism. . . . The growth of such a supreme religious conception has been due to no single set of forces. It is the coefficient of a still continuing social evolution with ever new social mind-sets."[16] Then he traced the idea of God from primitive religion, to the Israelite religion, to the monotheism in the Roman Empire, and finally to Christianity. Having followed this developmental history, he could ascertain that

> the history of the growth of the idea of God is that of a personal concept of the personally responsive activity in a cosmic environment from which humanity has come and upon which it is dependent. Though the content of the word God may be subject to social permutation, the personal organic relationship of men with environing activities as established by the use of some coordinating personal pattern, is as real as man's relationship with things of sense. The conception of God is no more illusion than the scientist's conception of the electron. Both are subject to experimental validation.[17]

Since humanity relates to a God, this God must be true, because the relationship between humanity and God can be traced through history. This was Mathews's actual proof of the matter. Presupposed, of course, is that there actually is a God. Yet that premise was left unexamined. While Shailer Mathews's remains found their rest in the crypt of the First Unitarian Church near the University of Chicago, he remained a Baptist at heart. Regardless of all the sociohistorical empiricism through which he wanted to circumvent theological doctrines, he could state: "I trust God not as a formula, but as I would trust a person. But in the formula by which I justify such a faith I find inspiration and a basis for courage to do what I can to serve my day and generation. For it is another way of saying that I believe that Jesus Christ has shown me the way to the Father."[18]

Shirley Jackson Case (1872-1947) was born in Hatfield Point, New Brunswick, Canada, as son of a farmer and carriage builder. His parents belonged to

---

15. Shailer Mathews, *The Growth of the Idea of God* (New York: Macmillan, 1931), vii.
16. Mathews, *The Growth*, 23-24.
17. Mathews, *The Growth*, 233-34.
18. Mathews, "Theology as Group Belief," 191.

the Free Baptist Church, a rather liberal group. After going through college and earning a master's degree in 1896 in classical studies and mathematics, he assumed teaching positions in mathematics and then in Greek. He entered Yale University Divinity School in 1901 to specialize in biblical languages and to earn a bachelor's degree (1904) — the B.D. conferred at this time now corresponds to the M.Div. degree — and a Ph.D. (1906). Upon graduation he received an appointment as professor of history and philosophy of religion at Bates College. Two years later he was appointed assistant professor of New Testament interpretation at the University of Chicago Divinity School, and in 1913 was promoted to associate professor, in 1915 to full professor, in 1917 to professor of early church history, and in 1923 to chairman of the church history department. From 1933 to 1938, when he retired, he served as dean of the Divinity School, succeeding Shailer Mathews. In 1924 he was elected president of the American Society of Church History, and with that the journal *Church History* began its regular publication. In 1927 he also became editor of the *Journal of Religion.*

Case's main contribution was in the area of historical scholarship both in New Testament studies and in history of early Christianity. He also employed the so-called sociohistorical method, which we notice at once in the preface of his book *The Social Origins of Christianity* (1923): "This book seeks to illuminate the oft-told story of Christianity's rise by a new reading of the history in the light of contemporary social experience. Attention is fixed especially to the environments, attitudes, and activities in real life of those persons and groups who, from generation to generation, constituted the membership of the new movement."[19] His concern was for the total environment in which the historic event, the rise of Christianity, occurred. Here the economic, political, social, psychological, philosophical, and geographical dimensions all contribute to our understanding of a certain historical development. There are three items to which an empirical historian has to attend. (1) The search for facts: "The empirical historian's first loyalty is to his available sources of information."[20] (2) The discovery of causes: "To determine just what happened is only preliminary to the task of discovering the causes that induce the event. Since history is the product of social evolution . . . one endeavors to amplify historical knowledge by examining the causal nexus in which every event has its necessary setting" (66). (3) The problem of progress: "In this empirical pursuit the standard for

19. Shirley Jackson Case, *The Social Origins of Christianity* (New York: Cooper Square, 1975 [1923]), v. For a good introduction and evaluation of Case, cf. William J. Hynes, *Shirley Jackson Case and the Chicago School: The Socio-Historical Method* (Atlanta: Scholars, 1981), where he also mentions Troeltsch as a possible influence on Case (99-101).

20. Shirley Jackson Case, *The Christian Philosophy of History* (Chicago: University of Chicago Press, 1943), 57. Page numbers in the following text refer to this work.

measuring progress is the value which each successive generation attaches to its accomplishments over those of its predecessors" (80). This means there is no necessity for progress, but progress is measured in the eye of the beholder.

But what is the actual reason for historical investigation? It is not simply to tell how and why things have happened. Since history is the long record of human activity, we receive a new sense of our responsibility "for creating a better society. Man makes his own world of culture; civilization is the product of his ideals and activities" (89). With this rigorous historical approach, one is reminded very much of Ernst Troeltsch. Even revelation comes under this verdict of the sociohistorical method. "Revelation is always mediated through human persons who entertain their religious convictions with so much assurance that their words seem to them, or to their successors, to be the very utterance of the Deity" (169-70). What then does history have to do with religion? Summing up his *Christian Philosophy of History,* Case wrote: "Religious living is a creative process in the growth of human persons, consciously striving to subject their material existence to their moral and spiritual ideals. These ideals develop with enlarging experience as this is acquired from history and from current life. Religion, like every other phase of human culture, is a process of evolutionary growth" (186-87).

This sociohistorical interpretation of humanity working out its own religion could be sustained only in an environment that was genuinely religious; otherwise the verdict of Feuerbach would have struck such theological reflection in labeling it a human product. Yet Case has no notion of dispensing with God. To the contrary, in the preface of *Christian Philosophy of History* he assured us: "God is discovered working within history, where he willed that men should learn to be the efficient instruments of the divine energy. Upon their shoulders has been placed the responsibility for learning and pursuing God's designs for bringing his kingdom to realization on earth" (vi). These words were written just two years before Dresden was turned into a burning inferno in which tens of thousands of people died and Hiroshima and Nagasaki encountered a similar fate. Case exhibited the optimistic mind-set of America, and certainly did not have in mind the sociohistorical context of human sinfulness.

The Theocentric Phase and the Transition to Process Thought: Henry Nelson Wieman, Bernard Meland, Bernard Loomer, and Daniel D. Williams

With **Henry Nelson Wieman** (1884-1975) we come to the next phase of empirical theology. Though Wieman's father was a Presbyterian minister, religion was not that important. Henry Nelson was born in Rich Hill, Missouri, and only during his last year at Park College did he decide to devote his life to the philosophy of religion. Upon his theological studies at San Francisco Theological Seminary and a year (1910-11) in Jena and Heidelberg, he obtained his Ph.D. in 1917 from Harvard Divinity School. Upon returning to the United States from Germany, he served for two and a half years in the ministry, because he could not get the position he wanted in teaching. Then he served for ten years as professor of philosophy at Occidental College in Los Angeles, until he was called to become professor of philosophy of religion at the University of Chicago Divinity School, where he stayed till his retirement in 1947. After retirement he continued to teach philosophy at the University of Oregon and later on at the University of Houston. But his actual interest was in the study of religion.

Wieman's main interest was "to promote a theocentric religion as over against the prevalent anthropocentric. The first requirement of a theocentric religion is that we make the actuality of God himself, and not our ideas about God, the object of our love and devotion. The second requirement is another side of the same thing. It is that we do not allow our wishes and needs to shape our idea of God, but shall shape it solely in the light of objective evidence."[21] In contrast to the sociohistorical investigation, the starting point was now the actuality of God and not the human situation. The approach again was "scientific," namely, through a combination of observation and reason. We check the constructs of reason by observation and then the observation is guided by the constructs of reason, so that gradually one obtains a notion of the objective reality. Wieman's main concern was to escape subjectivism and to make contact with the sacred reality. Though he conceded that one must use ideas, these ideas are turned into tools through the method of observation and reason.

We can observe this method at work in his examination of whether God is a personality. He contended that a personality can exist only in society, since a personality is generated by interaction between individuals. Yet God cannot derive his personality from human society, otherwise he would be no different from the way we are. "Since personality can not exist apart from a society, and since the society which generates and sustains God cannot be human society, he must belong to some society of angels."[22] Since, however, we have no evidence that there exists a society of angels, it would have to be a different society, perhaps in the Godhead itself, namely, the Trinity. But since that interaction would take place in God himself, God would not be a personality but a kind of

21. Henry Nelson Wieman, "Theocentric Religion," in *Contemporary American Theology: Theological Autobiographies*, ed. Vergilius Ferm (New York: Round Table, 1932), 1:346.
22. Wieman, "Theocentric Religion," 1:350.

interaction between individuals, an interaction that sustains and promotes all the values of personality. This means that whatever God is, God is not a personality but more than that.

In *Religious Experience and Scientific Method* (1926), Wieman developed his "scientific" approach to religion to reach a more objective sense of reality. As he stated in his preface: "The chief purpose of this book is to show that religious experience is experience of an object, however undefined, which is as truly external to the individual as is any tree or stone he may experience."[23] Yet in "Intellectual Autobiography" (1963), Wieman focuses his analysis on the human level: "In human life, in the actual processes of human existence, must be found a saving and transforming power which religious inquiry seeks and which faith must apprehend."[24] While he did not advocate a humanistic attitude through which humanity can transform itself, he wanted to discover empirically "what operates in the form of 'grace.'"[25] He adopted from the philosopher Alfred North Whitehead the term "creativity" and stated: "Man in existence is the religious problem, not the cosmos and not eternal being, except as these enter into man's existence. Furthermore, since all existence is process, the religious problem is man and the processes which create and destroy, save and pervert, liberate and bind."[26] In turning to this human side, he could understand religion as a ruling commitment that is believed to be essential for all human living and under which control a life is lived. It is important that such a ruling commitment enables us to deal effectively with the problem we encounter in human history. The decisive question in today's world is then to what extent this ruling commitment "creates and sustains love and justice, beauty and truth, courage and human power or control."[27] This ruling commitment is not given to some kind of "cosmic consciousness," but is a "creative interchange" that "can provide the greatest possible diversity together with mutual support of these diversified activities."[28] Wieman rejected Whitehead's notion that the cosmos is God's body or that God would guide and support human striving. We must deepen our mutually sustaining activities through creative inter-

---

23. Henry Nelson Wieman, *Religious Experience and Scientific Method* (Westport, Conn.: Greenwood, 1970 [1926]), 5.

24. Henry Nelson Wieman, "Intellectual Autobiography," in *The Empirical Theology of Henry Nelson Wieman*, ed. Robert W. Bretall (New York: Macmillan, 1963), 4.

25. Wieman, "Intellectual Autobiography," 5.

26. Wieman, "Intellectual Autobiography," 10.

27. Henry Nelson Wieman, *Religious Inquiry: Some Explorations* (Boston: Beacon Press, 1968), 44.

28. Wieman, *Religious Inquiry*, 217.

change. The creative transformation of which Wieman spoke, however, is not engendered by God but by humanity.[29]

Bernard Meland (1899-1993), a student of Wieman and an ordained Presbyterian minister, was professor of constructive theology at the University of Chicago Divinity School and editor of the *Journal of Religion*. He discovered the limits of a strictly empirical approach, and in an appreciative way tried to find an avenue to exercise the reflective act in a disciplined manner, in probing or even pondering the witness of faith. Because if one appeals only to "a scientifically tested or rationally defensible notion, presumably distilled from experience, . . . theological words such as love, revelation, or forgiveness, having been given an ontological or instrumental meaning, are then taken to be meaningful simply as words, simply as linguistic realities."[30] This means that ontology is reduced to linguistic semantic, and therefore the life is really taken out of the religious experience. Yet Meland contested that perhaps we have no alternative to what Schleiermacher advanced in the *Speeches*, the experiential base of religion given by the individual human being. Meland therefore opted for a "more of experience," similar to what William James had advocated. This more of experience exceeds conceptualization, and therefore "our conceptualizations provided us but with a margin of intelligibility."[31] This means that we must go beyond that which we actually conceptualize. Of course, Meland knew that since the rise of natural science educated people have become supersensitive to anything "beyond" because of their aversion to supernaturalism. Yet this *much more* "is what religious thinking must clarify more adequately than it has done thus far."[32]

Meland attempted to spell out this more of experience in his writings. For instance, in a 1947 publication, *The Seeds of Redemption*, he pointed out that redemption is showing itself through a repentant mood that has taken hold of people here and there. There is a renewed bent toward community, of making democracy work in villages and in groups within cities, meaning the manifestations in general life. Then he continued: "More deep-going than any of these manifestations is the awakening in religion itself to an empirical understanding of the processes of grace and redemption that proceed from the creative work

29. Contrary to Creighton Peden, "A Scientific Based Christianity," in Henry Nelson Wieman, *Science Serving Faith*, ed. Creighton Peden and Charles Willig (Atlanta: Scholars, 1987), xv, who makes Wieman sound decidedly theistic.

30. Bernard Meland, "Can Empirical Theology Learn Anything from Phenomenology?" in *The Future of Empirical Theology*, ed. Bernard Meland (Chicago: University of Chicago Press, 1969), 293.

31. Meland, "Can Empirical Theology?" 297.

32. Bernard Meland, *Seeds of Redemption* (New York: Macmillan, 1947), 35.

of God."[33] While in an ultimate sense redemption is a working beyond our efforts, it occurs in our own affairs when this repentant mood takes hold of the human spirit. For Meland the divine activity and its manifestation in human actions go together. The former is no longer bracketed as in a stringent empirical theology. Meland therefore also arrived at a more explicit Christology: "Christ as our life in God is inseparable from our life as individual men and women and from our life in the community of men. What it offers to each of these facets of our human experience is a new dimension of freedom in grace, enabling us to transcend our self-imposed limits expressive of our own internal freedom, and opening up resources beyond these given capacities."[34] Meland even shows a new appreciation of the church in understanding it as "the body of Christ, the living organon, purposively bodying forth and proclaiming the witness to the good news that is redemptive with a degree of vocation and commitment that cannot be found in the culture at large."[35] Yet with Meland we have arrived at a new stage, because Paul Tillich's presence was being felt by then, and also Karl Barth's shadow reached across the Atlantic.

When we briefly look at **Bernard M. Loomer** (1912-85), we notice both continuity and difference. He took his Ph.D. under Wieman and was dean at the University of Chicago Divinity School and also professor of philosophy of religion. Yet he was influenced by process thinking and sought a demarcation from neo-Reformation theology. He claimed that "a naturalistic version of Christology is needed."[36] Loomer contended that a christological figure is both logically and ontologically impossible if humanity and God are essentially discontinuous in nature, if God is wholly other. A christological figure, according to Loomer, has a bridge function, being revelatory for both God and humanity, meaning that this figure reveals in relation to the other and in the context of the other. The same goes for redemption. It is an activity of both God and humanity in relation to and in the context of the other. If Christ were truly human, then he must be understood in terms of categories descriptive of all human being. This means that he not only gave something to others, but also received something from them. Loomer then concluded: "Christ's relation to his fellows and theirs to him were constitutive of his very being."[37] Loomer rejected a kenotic theory of incarnation, saying that since God chose to become related,

33. Meland, *Seeds of Redemption*, ix.

34. Bernard Meland, *The Realities of Faith: The Revolution in Cultural Forms* (New York: Oxford University Press, 1962), 307.

35. Meland, *The Realities of Faith*, 314.

36. Bernard Loomer, "Empirical Theology within Process Thought," in *The Future of Empirical Theology*, 161.

37. Loomer, "Empirical Theology," 163.

this refers "to God's fulfillment of himself through the redemption of his crea-tures."[38] The interaction between God and humanity is one of mutual enrich-ment and fulfillment. With this kind of thinking we are deep into process thought. This is no surprise because Loomer had already treated this topic in his doctoral dissertation: "The Theological Significance of the Method of Em-pirical Analysis in the Philosophy of A. N. Whitehead" (1942).

Loomer did not have to go far to come up with his dissertation topic. Charles Hartshorne had been teaching simultaneously at the department of philosophy and at the Divinity School of the University of Chicago for more than a quarter-century (1928-55). Then there was also **Daniel D. Williams** (1910-73), who used Whitehead's vision of reality for a perspective within which theo-logical reflection could be fruitfully pursued. Williams was convinced that both theology and philosophy need each other in the common search for truth that lies beyond any particular achievement of either mode of inquiry. Yet he saw untenable the proposition that God is a cause outside the world, since this would render impossible any rational experiential knowledge of God. To rem-edy the situation, God must be a "reality which is involved in the structure and becoming of everything that is, and which is necessary to give coherence, relat-edness, and an ultimate valuation to each occasion of experience."[39] God does not stand apart from the world, but is participating in all becoming and pro-vides new possibilities within the world. Yet Williams shied away from an or-ganismic understanding of God and the world, because that would easily lead to monism. He preferred a social concept because a social relationship includes the logic of an ever enlarging experience that embraces past, present, and fu-ture. This goes for the present events in the world as well as for its ultimate per-fection, since perfection is not to be understood as a static completeness, but it includes "the continual search for new good beyond present actuality. The ad-venture of life is involved in the meaning of fulfillment."[40]

Williams realized already the one problem of process thought, that such a doctrine of perfection does not do justice to the problem of evil. Nevertheless, he was convinced that process thought allows theology to understand God's ac-tivity in a dynamic way as being involved in both history and nature. Philo-sophical study can, for him, illumine the life of faith and fortify as well as en-large the scope of theological inquiry. This he saw possible with the adoption of process thought. This could also give him hope for the future. But he cautioned

38. Loomer, "Empirical Theology," 164.
39. Daniel D. Williams, "A Philosophical Outlook" (1970), in Williams, *Essays in Process Theology,* ed. Perry LeFevre (Chicago: Exploration Press, 1985), 10.
40. Williams, "A Philosophical Outlook," 17-18.

that "any enduring hope must be based, not upon man alone, but upon the fact that God is present in human history, and is there creatively and redemptively at work. To try to establish the City of Man on anything other than faith in God is to build on quicksand."[41] Now we should finally turn to process thought itself, which has its originator in Alfred North Whitehead.

Process Thought

Laying the Philosophical Groundwork: Alfred North Whitehead and Charles Hartshorne

Alfred North Whitehead (1861-1947) was born in Kent, England, a son of an Anglican priest and his wife, who was the daughter of a prosperous military tailor. Whitehead was first taught at home and then sent to one of the prestigious public schools. He was outstanding in mathematical studies and rugby, and in 1880 entered Trinity College in Cambridge, to which he won a scholarship. In 1884 he obtained his bachelor's degree and was also elected a fellow of Trinity, with his dissertation being on Clerk Maxwell's theory of electricity and magnetism. He was appointed assistant lecturer in mathematics, then senior lecturer in 1903, and got his doctorate in science in 1905. He came under the influence of Cardinal Newman and read many theological books, but as a result gave up organized religion and never belonged to any church. In 1903 he was elected to the Royal Society, owing to the first volume of his *Treatise on Universal Algebra* (1898). Together with Bertrand Russell (1872-1970), who had been one of his students, he wrote the *Principia Mathematica* (published 1910-13). He then wrote three more books on the foundation of natural science.

In 1924, at age sixty-three, Whitehead was offered a five-year appointment in the department of philosophy at Harvard. The move appealed to both him and his wife. Since he had never dealt with metaphysics, he felt this was a good chance, and he expounded his ideas in the course of eight lectures that he published in 1925 under the title *Science and the Modern World*. The lectures were an instant success. The following year he gave another series of lectures, which were published as *Religion in the Making*. In these lectures he argued that religion needs a metaphysics and he wanted to make his own contribution to that. This was then worked out in what were initially the Gifford Lectures at the University of Edinburgh in 1928 and published in an expanded version in 1930 un-

---

41. Daniel D. Williams, *God's Grace and Man's Hope* (New York: Harper and Brothers, 1949), 11.

der the title *Process and Reality,* his most significant writing on metaphysics. Needless to say, Harvard revised the terms of his appointment and he did not have to retire until 1937. Whitehead was well liked by the students and took a strong interest in their work. He also lectured on many campuses throughout the United States. When he died, his body was cremated and there was no funeral, but a memorial service was held at Harvard. "Whitehead's widow, as he had asked, destroyed his unpublished manuscripts and his correspondence."[42]

Whitehead's thinking in *Process and Reality* is organismic and process oriented. He is dissatisfied with both the Aristotelian notion that God is the first unmoved mover and the "Christian" notion that God is the "eminently real." According to Whitehead, in the Western tradition both notions were fused into the idea that God is the "aboriginal, eminently real, transcendent creator, at whose fiat the world came into being, and whose imposed will it obeys."[43] Thus God was understood as a primordial tyrant fashioned in the image of the Egyptian, Persian, and Roman imperial rulers. Even the "brief Galilean vision of humility" of Jesus of Nazareth did not change this, because John lost out to Paul. "If the modern world is to find God," Whitehead claimed, "it must find him through love and not through fear, with the help of John and not of Paul."[44] Assistance in this endeavor can be found in Jesus, or as Whitehead called him, the Galilean origin of Christianity. Jesus has shown that "love neither rules, nor is it unmoved; also it is a little oblivious as to morals. It does not look to the future; for it finds its own reward in the immediate present."[45]

To attain the notion of a loving God and not of a tyrant God, Whitehead suggested that we limit the possibilities of God. He attempted this limitation by attributing to God a primordial and a subsequent nature. In his primordial nature God is "the unlimited conceptual realization of the absolute wealth of potentiality."[46] This did not mean for Whitehead that God is prior to all creation, but that he is with all creation. Apart from God there would be no actual world, since nothing could be actualized, and apart from the actual world with its cre-

---

42. So Victor Lowe, in his informative biography, "Whitehead, Alfred North," in *Dictionary of American Biography,* supp. 4, 1946-1950 (New York: Charles Scribner's, 1974), 878-84, here 884.

43. Alfred North Whitehead, *Process and Reality: An Essay in Cosmology* (New York: Macmillan, 1960), 519.

44. Alfred North Whitehead, *Religion in the Making* (New York: Macmillan, 1926), 76. The notion of a "primordial tyrant" against which most process thinkers are fighting is certainly a distortion of the compassionate and loving God portrayed in the Bible and was never advanced by any serious theologian except when clearly marked as caricature.

45. Whitehead, *Process and Reality,* 520-21.

46. Whitehead, *Process and Reality,* 521.

ativity, there would be no rational explanation of the ideal vision that constitutes God.[47] Thus God needs the world as its arena of actualization and the
world needs God as the granter of these actualizations. This interdependence
becomes even more evident in God's consequent nature. Since all things are interrelated, Whitehead assumed that the world reacts to God. Thus God "shares
with every new creation its actual world."[48] While in God's primordial nature
all groundwork for the possible world is given, God in his consequent nature
provides through a kind of feedback the weaning of his physical feelings from
his primordial concepts. Therefore Whitehead described the nature of God's
subsequent involvement in the world as "the perpetual vision of the road which
leads to deeper realities."[49] Since the subsequent nature is always moving on
and integrates the actualities of the world into the primordial whole that is unlimited conceptual reality, God provides the binding element in the world. He
confronts what is actual in the world with what is possible for it, and at the
same time provides the means of merging the actual with the possible.

God and the world are the instrument of novelty for each other. But God
and the world move conversely to each other in respect to their processes. God,
as primordially one, acquires in the interchange with the world through his consequent nature the multiplicity of actual occasions and absorbs them into his
own primordial integrative unity. The world, however, as primordially many, acquires in the interchange with God through his subsequent nature an integrative
unity, which as a novel occurrence is absorbed into the multiplicity of its primordial nature. God and world are coaxing each other along, God being completed by the finite and the finite being completed through confrontation with
the eternal. Whitehead summed up his thoughts: "What is done in the world is
transformed into a reality in heaven, and the reality in heaven passes back into
the world. By reason of this reciprocal relation, the love in the world passes into
the love in heaven, and floods back again into the world. In this sense, God is the
great companion — the fellow-sufferer who understands."[50]

Many questions have been raised against Whitehead's dipolar notion of
God. For instance, the idea of creation out of nothingness is naively discarded,

---

47. Cf. Whitehead, *Religion in the Making*, 157.

48. Whitehead, *Process and Reality*, 523.

49. Whitehead, *Religion in the Making*, 158.

50. Whitehead, *Process and Reality*, 532. With this last statement Whitehead does by no
means consider God as a projection of a father image. God is rather for him the ground of all reality, including that of our finite being. This is substantiated when he says at another occasion:
God can be conceived "as the supreme ground for limitation; it stands in His very nature to divide the Good from the Evil, and to establish Reason 'within her dominions supreme.'" So Alfred North Whitehead, *Science and the Modern World* (New York: Macmillan, 1960 [1925]), 258.

and it is too easily assumed that evil will simply be destroyed instead of being punished. Yet contrasted with a perfect though unmoved first principle, Whitehead's notion of a compassionate and understanding God certainly looks attractive.[51] Also, the insistence on God's involvement in the continuous creative process[52] finds open ears in those who claim that Christianity has forgotten the necessity for creative social change. But can one so easily circumvent Kant's *Critique of Pure Reason* and introduce in highly speculative fashion a new interpretation of Plato's concept of a world soul?[53] Also, the shadow of Spinoza's philosophy of identity seems to loom behind this approach, which could easily lead to an identification of God with nature's own creative principles.

Charles Hartshorne (1897-2000) was born in western Pennsylvania, his father being an Episcopal priest and his mother also coming from an Episcopal manse. He attended Haverford College (1915-17) and then served in the army as a hospital orderly for another two years. He resumed his academic studies at Harvard University, obtaining a B.A. degree (1921), an M.A. degree (1922), and in 1923 his Ph.D. with a dissertation on the unity of being. Then he spent two years in Europe, primarily at the University of Freiburg, studying with the phenomenologist Edmund Husserl, and at Marburg with Martin Heidegger. From 1925 to 1928 he was a research fellow at Harvard, also serving as assistant to Whitehead for one semester. Then he received a call to the University of Chicago in 1928, first teaching in the department of philosophy and from 1943 to 1955 also simultaneously in the Federated Theological Faculty of the Divinity School. This allowed him to touch on more explicitly religious topics. Then he taught at Emory University (1955-62), and finally at the University of Texas at Austin. He also held many visiting professorships both in the United States and in Europe as well as in Asia and Australia. Hartshorne was a prolific writer, and as he stated many times, at least from his perspective, "my teaching was found less impressive than my writing."[54] His most important books, as far as they pertain to theology, are, among others, *Man's Vi-*

51. Daniel D. Williams, "Reality, Monarchy, and Metaphysics: Whitehead's Critique of the Theological Tradition," in *The Relevance of Whitehead: Philosophical Essays in Commemoration of the Centenary of the Birth of Alfred North Whitehead*, ed. Ivor Leclerc (London: George Allen and Unwin, 1961), 372, is right when he states that it is a great gain for Christian theology to be able to conceive of God in a coherent, intelligible metaphysical structure as a fellow sufferer who understands instead of depicting him as an unfeeling and unmoved monarch.

52. Norman Pittenger emphasizes this point in his concise and illuminative introduction, *Alfred North Whitehead* (Richmond: John Knox, 1969), xiv.

53. Whitehead's Platonism, especially in *Process and Reality*, is very well analyzed by Edward Pols, *Whitehead's Metaphysics: A Critical Examination of "Process and Reality"* (Carbondale: Southern Illinois University Press, 1967), esp. 159-61.

54. Charles Hartshorne, "Some Causes of My Intellectual Growth," in *The Philosophy of Charles Hartshorne*, ed. Lewis Edwin Hahn (La Salle, Ill.: Open Court, 1991), 33.

sion *of God and the Logic of Theism* (1941), *The Divine Relativity: A Social Conception of God* (1948), and *A Natural Theology for Our Time* (1967).

Similar to his onetime mentor Whitehead, Hartshorne disclaimed a theology that advances "that Deity must be the transcendental snob, or the transcendental tyrant, either ignoring the creatures or else reducing them to his mere puppets." God must rather be conceived of as "the unsurpassable interacting, loving, presiding genius and companion of all existence."[55] Hartshorne finds such a God logically possible if we assume a middle way between the two prevalent types of theism. The first type of theism advances a purely rational approach to God. God is understood as being in all respects absolutely perfect or unsurpassable, and he is considered to be in no way and in no respect surpassable or perfectible. Hartshorne sees this position represented in Thomism and in most of European theology prior to 1880. The other type of theism, or the third type as Hartshorne calls it, offers a juxtaposition to the first type. It is a purely empirical approach and asserts that "there is no being in *any* respect absolutely perfect; all beings are in all respects surpassable by something conceivable, perhaps by others or perhaps by themselves in another state." Hartshorne saw this position advanced by some forms of pantheism and of atheism. Between these two types Hartshorne discovered the possibility of a mediating type of theism or, as he called it, of a second type of theism. According to this theism, "there is no being in all respects absolutely perfect; but there is a being in some respect or respects thus perfect, and in some respect or respects not so, in some respects surpassable, whether by self or other being left open. Thus it is not excluded that the being may be relatively perfect in all the respects in which it is not absolutely perfect."[56]

This second type of theism asserts a God who is partly finite and partly infinite, in some parts perfect and in other parts perfectible. It is clearly distinguished from the first type, which asserts an absolute tyrant God, and from the third type, which advances a merely finite God. Hartshorne was aware that such notion of God as he introduced with his second type of theism could by no means be "the entire actual God whom we confront in worship," since it would still be an impersonal it and not a personal thou.[57] Yet Hartshorne was convinced that the essence of his human concept of a second-type theism could

---

55. Charles Hartshorne, *A Natural Theology for Our Time* (La Salle, Ill.: Open Court, 1967), 137.

56. Charles Hartshorne, *Man's Vision of God and the Logic of Theism* (Chicago: Willett, Clark & Co., 1941), 11-12.

57. Charles Hartshorne, *The Logic of Perfection and Other Essays in Neo-Classical Metaphysics* (La Salle, Ill.: Open Court, 1962), 4. While Hartshorne wants to push the possibilities of human reason as far as possible, he is still aware that God cannot be defined, i.e., limited, by human concepts.

very well qualify God and no one else. Similar to Whitehead, Hartshorne understood God as both finite and infinite, eternal and temporal, necessary and contingent. Yet this did not mean a partly human God, because Hartshorne affirmed that God cannot be surpassed even in his perfectible traits by anyone or anything else. "'God' is the name for the one who is unsurpassable by any conceivable being other than himself."[58] The twofold nature of God can also be compared with two poles in God, an abstract pole, which is the logical necessity that some events be actualized, and a concrete pole, fully contingent upon what happens in the universe.[59] Because of his dipolar nature, of being both necessary and contingent, neither metaphysics alone nor all the special sciences taken by themselves can arrive at an adequate notion of God. The former would confine itself to God's necessary nature, while the special sciences would focus only on his contingent aspect. But God is "the integrated sum of existence."[60] He is "alive" and changing together with the changes of history, whose possibilities he provides. Whenever novel events occur, they change the reality of God out of which they act by adding to his reality. God and the universe are seen as interdependent and involved in significant interaction. The purpose of our life can then be understood as contributing to the concrete whole, "a contribution made meaningful, because it really affects ultimate reality."[61]

In his attempt to provide an integrative vision, Hartshorne even ventured to merge Jesus' assertion that God is love with Spinoza's pantheism. He claimed that we no longer have to choose between Spinoza and Jesus, because we should conceive of nature not only as God, as did Spinoza, but as God of love. If we really love humanity, we cannot be indifferent to nature upon which all our practical power depends.[62] Hartshorne then concluded: "The ultimate ideal of knowledge and of action remains this: to deal with the world as the body of a God of love, whose generosity of interest is equal to all contrasts, however gigantic, between mind and mind, and to whom all individuals are numbered, each with its own life history and each with its own qualitative — enjoying and suffering, more or less elaborately remembering and anticipating, sensing and spontaneously reacting — natures."[63]

58. Hartshorne, *A Natural Theology*, 128.

59. Ralph E. James, *The Concrete God: A New Beginning for Theology — the Thought of Charles Hartshorne* (Indianapolis: Bobbs-Merrill, 1967), 125.

60. Hartshorne, *Man's Vision*, 72.

61. James, *The Concrete God*, 126. James is right when he emphasizes that Hartshorne strives for and is convinced of an ultimate theological-ontological harmony (175-77).

62. Charles Hartshorne, *Beyond Humanism: Essays in the Philosophy of Nature* (Lincoln: University of Nebraska Press, Bison Books, 1968 [1937]), 7.

63. Hartshorne, *Beyond Humanism*, 315-16.

Though this notion of God cannot deny its Christian resemblance, Hartshorne maintained that it is found on strictly logical ground. Yet on closer examination it is more an idealistic vision colored by rational, Neoplatonic, mystic, and even existential shades.[64] Hartshorne himself, however, claimed that he disregarded all intuitive notions, and arrived at his understanding of God on strictly logical grounds. While Hartshorne was still a philosopher who ventured into theology, the main task now was to make this type of philosophy fruitful for theology proper. This was tackled vigorously by John Cobb and his Center for Process Studies at Claremont, California.

Unfolding Process Theology: John B. Cobb, Jr., and David Ray Griffin

John B. Cobb, Jr. (b. 1925), was born of missionary parents in Kobe, Japan, where he lived until 1940 when the Americans were encouraged to leave. Then he stayed with his grandmother in Georgia, finished high school and attended junior college. In 1944 he joined the United States Army and, on advice of his army friends, enrolled later at the University of Chicago in an interdepartmental program (1947). This proved to be a shattering experience for his pietistic faith and his deep prayer life. As he looked for some affirmative religious study, he enrolled after a year at the University of Chicago Divinity School. There Charles Hartshorne became a major intellectual influence upon him. David Griffin narrates: "Cobb says, 'It was through his teaching that I was once again able to take the idea of God seriously.' Hartshorne introduced him to the thought of Whitehead, and a Hartshornean Whiteheadianism has cohabited with philosophic relativism in Cobb's mind ever since."[65] Cobb wrote then his dissertation, "The Independence of Christian Faith from Speculative Belief," wherein he dealt with Wieman, Schleiermacher, and Tillich. Before finishing his doctoral studies, he returned to Georgia to take care of the family so that his

---

64. Cf. Hartshorne's dedication of his book *A Natural Theology for Our Time*, in which he mentions in one breath, among others, Fausto Sozzini, Gustav Fechner, Nikolai Berdyaev, and Alfred North Whitehead. When Howard L. Parsons, "Religious Naturalism and the Philosophy of Charles Hartshorne," in *Process and Divinity: Philosophical Essays Presented to Charles Hartshorne*, ed. William L. Reede and Eugene Freeman (La Salle, Ill.: Open Court, 1964), 533-60, classifies Hartshorne's philosophy of religion as a new naturalism, he seems to have captured Hartshorne's intentions very precisely.

65. David Ray Griffin, in his very enlightening biography, "John B. Cobb, Jr.: A Theological Biography," in *Theology and the University: Essays in Honor of John B. Cobb, Jr.*, ed. David Ray Griffin and Joseph C. Hough, Jr. (Albany: State University of New York Press, 1991), 225-42, here 228.

mother could resume her missionary work in Japan. Upon obtaining his Ph.D. from Chicago in 1952, he taught at the Emory School of Theology, and five years later he was invited to teach systematic theology at the School of Theology at Claremont, California. Griffin says in the conclusion of his biography: "Cobb has developed a warm, forgiving, encouraging, concerned, generous spirit which reflects well upon his new God. These characteristics, his originality and clarity of thought, his self-deprecating sense of humor, and his continued sense of responsibility to his institutions, his fellow creatures, and his God make him beloved by his colleagues and students alike."[66] Indeed, after a long struggle — with the help of process thought and perhaps also of his earlier pietistic upbringing — he found his way back to the new and yet old God.

In his *Living Options in Protestant Theology: A Survey of Methods* (1962), Cobb made a plea for Christian natural theology that was further developed in *A Christian Natural Theology: Based on the Thought of Alfred North Whitehead* (1965). Though Cobb knew that according to Barth and Bultmann theology should avoid any natural theology, he wondered whether in our time an exclusive revelational theology is still the option of many.[67] Breaking with the neo-Reformation concern of an exclusive Christomonism, he advocated a "Christian natural theology" as the starting point for theology. Here, similar to the New Testament, faith is not seen in radical discontinuity with our usual world experience. Though taking the task of constructing a natural theology with utmost seriousness, Cobb did not feel that he would have to employ a rationality unaffected by Christian commitments.[68] The reason for this assumption is that one is unable to formulate even a Christology without employing a conceptuality that requires clarification in natural theology. When faith proceeds directly to christological formulations, there are always assumptions made, for instance, about the nature of language, and about the reality of history and of nature, that are not directly validated by faith but are simply taken for granted. To make Christian faith survive and to restore it to health, we must justify the horizon in which prominent theological terms, such as "God" or "Jesus Christ," can have their appropriate reference. This is most urgent, since the cosmological horizons that once gave meaning to the existence of medieval and early modern humanity are no longer applicable.

Cobb claimed that unfortunately natural theology had been identified

---

66. Griffin, "John B. Cobb, Jr.," 240.

67. John B. Cobb, Jr., *Living Options in Protestant Theology: A Survey of Methods* (Philadelphia: Westminster, 1962), 320-21.

68. Cf. for the following John B. Cobb, Jr., *A Christian Natural Theology: Based on the Thought of Alfred North Whitehead* (Philadelphia: Westminster, 1965), 11-15. Page numbers in the text refer to this work.

with philosophic doctrines that rendered God impassible, immutable, and hence unaffected by and uninvolved in the affairs of human history. Yet he saw the God depicted in the Old and New Testament and in the liturgy of the church being deeply involved with his creation, even with its suffering (260). All along there have been serious tensions between philosophy and Christian theology. Again the philosophy of Whitehead provided for Cobb a way to escape this tension. He suggested that "Whitehead's work is obviously already Christianized in a way Greek philosophy could not have been. Hence, it proves, I am convinced, more amenable to Christian use" (268). Cobb even called it Christian, since it is deeply affected in its starting point by the Christian vision of reality. In adopting Whiteheadian philosophy instead of developing our own philosophical framework, he claimed we would stand in succession with the great theologians of the past such as Augustine and Thomas Aquinas. They did not create their own Christian philosophy either. Their great contribution to philosophy lies in their adaptation and development of the philosophical material they adopted. This did not mean they had to abandon their theological concern, because it was precisely out of their consciously Christian convictions that they made their philosophical contribution. Cobb proposed that, similarly, it is our task to examine the intrinsic excellence of any thought structure we intend to adopt and adapt, since theology is not to be distinguished from philosophy by a lesser concern for rigor of thought. Further, we should consider whether such thought structure is congenial enough to Christian faith to be transformed into Christian natural theology. "A Christian theologian should select for his natural theology a philosophy that shares his fundamental premises, his fundamental vision of reality. That philosophy is his Christian natural theology, or rather that portion of that philosophy is his natural theology which deals most relevantly with the questions of theology" (266).

Cobb did not want everyone to be tied to the same particular philosophy, because he knew that every argument begins with premises and the final premises themselves cannot be proved. Thus the quest for total consensus is an illusion. Though no thought system is final and though there is no human attainment of final truth, we do not end up in a kind of hopeless relativism. There are always approximations of truth that are more adequate and others that are less adequate. When theologians appeal for the justification of their statements to the general experience of humanity, they are engaged in Christian natural theology and must justify the degree of approximation to the truth attained in their statements. Without pretending that they are privileged to apprehend the reality as a whole, they can and must believe that in their witness also, somehow the truth is served. But the Christian theologian "must also witness directly to what is peculiar to his own community and to that revelation of truth by which it is constituted." At this point he or she is engaged in Christian theology proper, (1) in interpreting the biblical text with the assumption that the truth for humanity's existence is to be found in the text, (2) in reflecting on the confessions of the community as a believing participant who confesses the redemptive and revelatory power of the key events in the history of the respective community, and (3) in a dogmatic function of making claims of truth that are relevant to all people whether or not they are within the community (277-79).

Cobb is convinced that Whiteheadian categories will prove useful both for the formulation of a natural theology and for engaging theology proper. According to Cobb, Whitehead's philosophy favors the Judeo-Christian concern for persons and interpersonal relations, its monotheism, and its belief that there is meaning in the historical process. He also finds that Whitehead's philosophy has many points of contact with Eastern religions, especially with Buddhism (282). Yet Cobb does not think we can solve our problems of religious diversity simply by adding together the beliefs of all faiths. Though conceding that each faith apprehends the truth, he affirms that our final needs may ultimately be met only in one vision of reality. We can only agree with Cobb when he concludes his *Christian Natural Theology* with the assertion that "what the Christian dare not claim for himself or for his church, he may yet claim for Jesus Christ, namely, that there the universal answer is to be found" (284). In a later writing, however, Cobb admitted that the claim of finality as found in the Christian faith is problematical for him and that he has arrived at more relativistic conclusions.[69] Debating the advantages of a Buddhist view of reality, he is still convinced "that our scientific knowledge of the world can best be fitted with our human self-awareness and with the witness of aesthetic and religious experience in a comprehensive synthesis that points to the reality of God."[70] He confessed that his own beliefs allow for and suggest spiritual existence, and he could not hold these beliefs if he did not find in them great persuasive power. Thus the present advantage of Buddhism at the level of beliefs may only be temporary.

It is one of the peculiarities of Cobb that he did not confine himself to a philosophical theology, but branched out to wherever he thought theology was needed, be it in the interreligious dialogue, not just with Buddhism but also with Judaism; in the concern for the earth, as his involvement with ecological issues shows (*Is It Too Late? A Theology of Ecology,* 1972); in his dealing with economic problems (*The Earth's Challenge to Economism: A Theological Critique of*

69. John B. Cobb, Jr., *The Structure of Christian Existence* (Philadelphia: Westminster, 1967), 137.

70. Cobb, *Structure of Christian Existence,* 149.

the *Worldbank,* 1999); or in his concern for feminist issues (*Postmodernism and Public Policy,* 2002) and even for the position of evangelicals (*Searching for an Adequate God: A Dialog between Process and Free Will Theists,* 2000).

Most interesting is his Christology. In *Christ in a Pluralistic Age* (1975) he claimed "that for us Christ is the Way that excludes no Ways."[71] Cobb brings together the notion of the logos and of Christ in claiming that "'Christ' is therefore a name for the Logos. No statement can be made about Christ that is not true of the Logos. But 'Christ' does not simply designate the Logos as God as the principle of order and novelty. It refers to the Logos *as* incarnate, hence *as* the process of creative transformation in and of the world" (76). While in the classical Greek understanding, the logos stood for the world order, through Christ the logos for Cobb has become immanent or incarnate in the world of living things and especially of human beings. Since God as logos is present in the world, he is present and felt in all events. This divine immanence is the creative transformation of the world urging on to maximum incorporative elements from the past in a new synthesis. "To what extent the new aim is successful, to that extent there is creative transformation. This creative transformation is Christ" (76).

According to Cobb, Christ as the power of creative transformation can be discerned in Jesus. This does not mean that Jesus is immediately named the Christ, because it leaves open "the possibility that Jesus is to be seen alongside hundreds of other creative transformers who have fashioned our history" (107). If Jesus is in a more significant sense the Christ, he must have advanced creative transformation more than these others. While the structure of existence is far from what Jesus had in view, his words do indeed contribute to creative transformation in the hearer. One can see "that they are the occasion for the realization of Christ within the hearer" (110). For those who did not hear him, so the conclusion would go, Jesus is not the Christ. Since Christ is at work throughout the world, the eventual goals must be similar. Cobb shows this in trying to wed together the Buddhist notion of a postpersonal existence and the Christian goal that goes beyond a fully developed personal individualization. "That Christianity and Buddhism could each be so transformed by their internalization of each other as to move toward a future unity is an image of hope in a time of fragmentation" (220).

Cobb even went beyond that in trying to wed together Paolo Soleri's vision for the city of God, Whitehead's understanding of the kingdom of heaven, and Pannenberg's affirmation of the biblical doctrine of the resurrection. All

---

71. John B. Cobb, Jr., *Christ in a Pluralistic Age* (Philadelphia: Westminster, 1975), 22. Page numbers in the text refer to this work.

these images of hope point toward a transcendence of separating individuality in a full community with other people and with all things. "In this community the tensions between self and Christ decline, and in a final consummation they would disappear. This is the movement of incarnation" (258). Christ is the way that excludes no other ways, since he is intrinsic to all ways. John Cobb is an integrative thinker who has a passion for those who are left out and therefore a concern for a theological and social integration.

David Ray Griffin (b. 1939), professor of philosophy of religion and theology at the School of Theology at Claremont and Claremont Graduate School, was until his retirement in 2004 the executive director of the Center for Process Studies that he and Cobb established in 1973 with the support of both aforementioned institutions. Similar to Cobb, he wrote *A Process Christology* (1973) in which he considered Jesus as "God's supreme act."[72] In Jesus' message of word and deed, a deep vision of reality is expressed that contains a view of God's character and purpose. He had not only a special insight into the nature of things, but his special activity was based on the impulses given to him by God. *"The aims given to Jesus and actualized by him during his active ministry were such that the basic vision of reality contained in his message of word and deed was the supreme expression of God's eternal character and purpose"* (218). Since Jesus as the Christ is God's supreme act of self-expression, it is appropriate to receive him "as God's decisive revelation" (221). If Jesus' life provides the decisive revelation of God, then we should find here the supreme exemplification of the mode of God's activity in relation to the world. Indeed, Griffin is convinced "that God supremely expressed his character and purpose, and concomitantly his mode of activity, in the event of Jesus' ministry" (227). This Johannine notion that "who sees me, sees the Father" is expressive of the sufficiency of God's self-disclosure in Jesus the Christ, yet it is not an expression of Jesus' exclusivity.

Griffin also dealt with one of the touchy issues of process thought, the problem of evil, in *God, Power, and Evil: A Process Theodicee* (1976). If God is not the absolute power but only the relative one, as process thought claims, how can God control or eliminate evil? But Griffin contended that the actual problem is not so much with God, but with our inadequate understanding of God as either controlling or being able to control every detail of the events of our world. If God, however, is seen as persuasive and not controlling, God cannot be held accountable for the evil in the world. Evidently the claim he made in this book was not satisfying even for Griffin, because in *Evil Revisited: Responses and Reconsiderations* (1991) he wrote: "I have argued that process theism can

---

72. David R. Griffin, *A Process Christology* (Philadelphia: Westminster, 1973), 216. Page numbers in the text refer to this work.

provide us with a satisfactory solution to the problem of evil. I have suggested that the gap between such a solution and the position I presented in *God, Power, and Evil* can be bridged by reformulating some of the ideas more carefully, by filling in some omitted presuppositions, and by making some revisions, especially with regard to ultimate meaning and hope."[73] Yet Griffin is not just pursuing the issue of process thought. He also wants to engage in a constructive dialogue with contemporary forms of theological reflection, such as deconstructionism, liberation theology, and the movement of postmodernity.[74]

Process Theology with an Existential Tinge: Schubert Ogden

Finally we should mention **Schubert M. Ogden** (b. 1928), who like Cobb is a Methodist minister and who also was one of Hartshorne's students in Chicago. He graduated in 1950 from Ohio Wesleyan University with a bachelor's degree and received his B.D. and Ph.D. from the University of Chicago in 1954 and 1958 respectively. He also spent some time at Marburg, which showed in his leaning toward the existential interpretation of the New Testament according to Bultmann. For three years he was university professor of theology at the University of Chicago (1969-72), and from 1956 to 1969, and again from 1972 to 1993, he taught at Southern Methodist University, from where he retired. In his *Christ without Myth: A Study Based on the Theology of Rudolf Bultmann* (1961), he stated that the "New Testament sense of the claim 'only in Jesus Christ' is not that God is only to be found in Jesus and nowhere else, but that the only God that is to be found anywhere — *though he is to be found everywhere* — is the God who is made known in the word that Jesus speaks and is."[75] Ogden not only suggested that God can be found everywhere, but that it is possible and even necessary to affirm the realization of authentic existence apart from Christ. Though Christian faith or authentic existence is always "a possibility in fact," the decisive manifestation of divine love that enables such existence occurs in the event of Jesus of Nazareth. In him all other manifestations of this divine love are corrected and fulfilled. Ogden is convinced that this is also the stance of the New Testament. Paul, for instance, in his letter to the Romans did not present God's original self-disclosure as something different from his final

73. David Ray Griffin, *Evil Revisited: Responses and Reconsiderations* (Albany: State University of New York Press, 1991), 212-13.

74. Cf. David Ray Griffin et al., *Varieties of Postmodern Theology* (Albany: State University of New York Press, 1989).

75. Schubert M. Ogden, *Christ without Myth: A Study Based on the Theology of Rudolf Bultmann* (New York: Harper, 1961), 144.

self-disclosure in Jesus of Nazareth. The content of these two forms of manifestation is strictly the same. Even the church affirmed that "the word addressed to men *everywhere*, in all events of their lives, is none other than the word spoken in Jesus and in the preaching and sacraments of the church."[76]

Though Ogden emphasized the natural element in Christian faith, he still maintained the decisiveness of the historical manifestation of the essential God-man relationship in Jesus. Ogden found that Jesus is not an accidental occasion through which some timeless and impersonal truth can be appropriated by the intellect. Rather "the eternal Existence or Thou in whom all truth is grounded is himself personally present" in him.[77] This eternal Existence or Thou provides for us the objective ground of our ineradicable confidence in the final worth of our existence.[78] Belief in God, Ogden concluded, is unavoidable, reflectively as well as existentially, because even modern secular man, with his characteristic affirmation of life in the world in its proper autonomy and significance, has at least implicitly discovered the reality of God. Ogden therefore opted for a secular faith, and like Gogarten, accepts secularity as the true consequence of Christian faith.

He argued that in affirming the significance and autonomy of our life in the world, we presuppose two things. First, the ground of our life's significance exists absolutely, relative to no cause or condition whatsoever. Otherwise the significance of our life could not be truly ultimate and the object of unshaken confidence. Secondly, to endow our life with autonomy, the ground of our life's significance must be a supremely relative reality. Ogden concluded that God as this ground of our life's significance cannot act like an impenetrable wall, but God must enjoy real internal relations to all our actions and so be affected by them in God's own being. This would mean that the conception of God, more or less clearly implied in a secular affirmation of the ultimate significance and autonomy of our life, "is intrinsically two-sided or dipolar. It conceives God as at once supremely relative and supremely absolute, thereby explicating both essential elements in a secular faith in the ultimate worth of our life" (48-50). Traditional supernaturalism and theism, however, conceived God as monopolar. In contrast to the biblical understanding of God, it became more and more difficult to assert God's absoluteness and at the same time God's meaningful relationship to anything beyond himself. Thereby Scripture's most characteristic designations of God became completely emptied of meaning. This showed for

---

76. So Ogden, *Christ without Myth*, 153-56, esp. 156.

77. Ogden, *Christ without Myth*, 163.

78. Cf. for the following Schubert M. Ogden, *The Reality of God and Other Essays* (New York: Harper, 1966), 37-45. The page numbers in the text from here to the end of this section are to Ogden's *Reality of God*.

Ogden that both traditional supernaturalism and theism have in the long run prevented an adequate expression of biblical and secular faith in God. At this crucial point he saw the chance and necessity for process philosophy, because it provides a conceptuality that "enables us to conceive the reality of God that we may respect all that is legitimate in modern secularity, while also fully respecting the distinctive claims of Christian faith itself" (56-57).

By understanding God as an infinite personal existence or creative becoming, according to Ogden process philosophy enables us to assert God's independence of the actual world without saying that God is wholly external to it. On the other hand, it also allows us to affirm God's inclusion in the actual world without denying that the world in its actuality is completely contingent and radically dependent upon God as its sole necessary ground. God is no longer merely the barren absolute that by definition can be really related to nothing. Instead God is truly related to everything in immediate sympathetic participation. Ogden was convinced that the conception of such a "temporal" God could even maintain the truth of the claim that God created everything out of nothingness. Ogden was right when he proposed that the heart of the doctrine of *creatio ex nihilo* is the belief that God alone is the necessary ground of whatever exists or of whatever is possible, and not the conviction that God once existed in lonely isolation (62-67). Not without justification did Ogden claim that the new theism developed from process philosophy is able to provide a fully developed conceptuality that is understandable in the present situation and is also appropriate to the essential claims of the scriptural witness. It shows a God whose love is pure and unbounded and whose relation to God's creatures and theirs to God is direct and immediate (177). Ogden saw this love uniquely coming to expression in Jesus Christ.

Ogden recognized that the human word of promise and demand addressed to us in Jesus Christ is infinitely more than merely a human word and it has the divine power and authority to claim our ultimate allegiance. It thereby brings our lives to their authentic fulfillment. No other promise and demand have this same divine significance. Of course, Ogden realized that such affirmation cannot be an affirmation with one's mind or one's lips, but must be asserted as a free, personal decision with one's whole heart, with the whole weight of one's existence. In other words, a purely natural theology does not suffice. There must always be a decision of faith (203-5).

Similar to Cobb, Schubert Ogden also betrays a wide range of interests, from the Christian-Buddhist dialogue, in which he participates, to the American Academy of Religion, of which he was president in 1977. More than with Cobb, the New Testament bears for him special significance because it makes manifest what is already disclosed in human existence. For Ogden, Christianity is the true and authentic expression of what it means to be a human being. This again shows that he was influenced not only by Whitehead, but much more so by Bultmann.

Theology and Culture

While process theology is presently one of the most influential theological movements in North American religious studies departments and heavily influences discussions there, it has hardly made an impact on the Continent. There classical positions still enjoy a solid majority. But these classical positions are not neglected in the United States either, and were prominently represented there in the twentieth century, especially with Paul Tillich and the Niebuhr brothers. While for process theology it was especially philosophy that provided the main avenue to relate God to the world, for Tillich and the Niebuhr brothers, though in various ways, the various manifestations of culture served as the connecting medium.

Correlating Culture and the Christian Message: Paul Tillich and Langdon Gilkey

Paul Tillich (1886-1965) spans two continents and two cultures in his career, namely, those of Europe and America. He was born in Starzeddel, a small industrial town in the province of Brandenburg near the Silesian border. His father, a Lutheran pastor in the Prussian church, moved after four years to Schönfliess, and in 1900 to Berlin. In the small town of Schönfliess where Tillich spent his youth, he got in touch with nature, which furthered a romanticism that stayed with him throughout his life. Important was also his early discovery of Friedrich Schelling (1775-1854) and his philosophy of nature. He also came across Rudolf Otto's idea of the holy, which also resonated with young Tillich.

After graduation from a *Gymnasium* in Berlin, he studied theology in Berlin, Tübingen, and finally Halle. In 1909 he passed his first theological exam, and in 1910 he obtained his doctorate in philosophy from the University of Breslau with the thesis *The Conception of the History of Religions in Schelling's Positive Philosophy: Its Presuppositions and Principles* (*Die religionsgeschichtliche Konstruktion in Schellings positiver Philosophie, ihre Voraussetzungen und Prinzipien* [Breslau: H. Fleischmann, 1910]). The next year he obtained his licentiate of theology at the University of Halle with another thesis on Schelling: *Mysticism and Guilt-Consciousness in Schelling's Philosophical*

Development (Eng. trans. 1974). Then he did his *Habilitation* at Halle: *The Concept of the Supernatural, Its Dialectic Meaning and the Principle of Identity, in the Supra-naturalistic Theology prior to Schleiermacher* (*Der Begriff des Übernatürlichen, sein dialektischer Charakter und das Prinzip der Identität, dargestellt an der supra-naturalistischen Theologie vor Schleiermacher* [Königsberg: H. Madrasch, 1915]), which allowed him to become Privatdozent. Everything seemed to be set for an academic career. But then World War I erupted and he joined the German army as a chaplain. While still in the army, he transferred his credentials to the University of Berlin to become Privatdozent there. His inaugural lecture in 1919 was "The Existence of God in the Psychology of Religion." Philosophically he had been well prepared before he ever started at the university, since he had read a good amount of Kant, Fichte, Schleiermacher, Hegel, and Schelling. Though he always had been interested in philosophy, at heart he was a theologian.

The war shattered many illusions for Tillich. First, he discovered that there was no unity in the German nation, but a very strong class consciousness. Since shortly before the war, he had been assistant pastor in the workers district of Berlin. He had become aware of the problems of the workers firsthand and sympathized with their cause. Therefore, after the 1918 revolution he was active in the religious socialist movement and in sympathy with the social side of the revolution, but was against the Marxists and their terrorist scheme. In 1924 he was appointed associate professor of theology at the University of Marburg, and he soon realized that the cultural problems were excluded by neoorthodox theology. Tillich therefore tried to find a new way, which eventually resulted in his *Systematic Theology*.[79] His assessment of the contemporary setting also was put into print as *The Religious Situation* (1926; Eng. trans. 1932). The same year he was called as professor of philosophy and religious studies at the Dresden Institute of Technology, and from 1927 to 1929 he served simultaneously as adjunct professor of systematic theology at the University of Leipzig. In 1929 he was called as professor of philosophy to the University of Frankfurt. The same year he received that call, he joined the Social Democratic Party, and in 1932 he published *The Socialist Decision* (Eng. trans. 1977). Therefore, it came as no surprise that the National Socialists suspended him from his professorship as soon as they got into power in 1933. Yet thanks to Reinhold Niebuhr, he had already been asked to come to Union Theological Seminary in New York. He arrived there in November of the same year as a visiting professor. Soon he became an associate, and finally a full professor of philosophy of religion and systematic

---

79. Cf. Paul Tillich, "Autobiographical Reflections," in *The Theology of Paul Tillich*, ed. Charles W. Kegley (New York: Pilgrim Press, 1982), 14.

theology. Soon he was elected to the Philosophy Club, an East Coast association then meeting at Columbia University whose roster had included William James and John Dewey, among others. Its monthly meetings he almost never missed. He was also elected to the American Theological Society, also primarily located on the East Coast, which introduced him to the prominent academic theologians of his generation.[80]

Coming to America changed Tillich's life and theology. From life as a solitary academic individual, he was now incorporated into a living community with daily chapel services and a continuous stream of visitors from various countries. Having moved from a secular university to a theological institution, he no longer maintained his relationship with artists, poets, and writers as he had in postwar Germany. But he continued his interest in culture in general, and his contact with the depth-psychology movement. In Germany he had touched theology in his lectures only on the periphery, conducting his courses mainly on philosophical topics such as the development of philosophy or the philosophy of religion, or the religious interpretation of history, or religion and the city. But now he had to tackle actual theological topics. In 1936 his first English publication appeared, *On the Boundary: An Autobiographical Sketch*. The reaction to this book, however, was muted. It was not just a confession about himself that he was living on the boundary between the old and the new country, but he wanted to show that a boundary existence is typical of us living in this world as an existence in transition, still moving toward something new. Four years before he reached mandatory retirement age in 1955, the first volume of his *Systematic Theology* appeared. He was at the height of his fame.

But the year before he retired from Union, Tillich accepted an invitation to become university professor at Harvard. University professors were "five or six distinguished productive scholars representing interdisciplinary areas to Harvard at the same time. Such scholars were free to teach as much or as little as they wished and were reappointed from year to year, depending on their state of health, until they reached the mandatory retirement age of seventy-five."[81] Just before that he declined an invitation to return to Germany to become professor at Marburg University. Nearly every weekend he traveled to nearby or distant destinations to lecture to ever increasing audiences. Yet when it was time to retire in 1962 from Harvard, Jerald Brauer, then dean of the Divinity School of the University of Chicago, invited him to become the first Nuveen Professor of Theology, a professorship that had been set up by the directors of a

80. Cf. Wilhelm Pauck and Marion Pauck, *Paul Tillich: His Life and Thought* (New York: Harper and Row, 1976), 1:313 n. 98.

81. Pauck and Pauck, *Paul Tillich*, 1:247.

banking firm. There he continued his teaching career until he died in 1965 after a brief illness.

Since the German edition of his work comprises fourteen volumes and eight supplementary volumes, there are many facets of his theology on which one could dwell. Yet since he worked most of his academic life on his *Systematic Theology*, this provides the key to his thinking. There are five parts to his three-volume *Systematic Theology*: (1) "Reason and Revelation," (2) "Being and God," (3) "Existence and the Christ," (4) "Life in the Spirit," (5) "History and the Kingdom of God." Significantly, his "Christology," contained in volume 2, is rather short. If one subtracts from this volume what he had written on sin and evil, then for the actual Christology there remain hardly eighty pages. In his introduction to "Christology," Tillich asserted: "There is no logically necessary or deductive step from . . . God to the Christ."[82] That there is a Christ, meaning that God assumed humanity, or, to stay within Tillichian terminology, that essence lived under the condition of existence, is totally nonrational and paradoxical.

One would assume that Tillich is constructing a Christology from below when he claims: "Jesus as the Christ is both a historical fact and a subject of believing reception" (*ST* 2:98). That is, a Christian theology is completely undercut if the historical fact or the believing reception is completely ignored. But then Tillich went into the research for the historical Jesus and its failure, and assured us that not the historical argument but participation, meaning the immediacy of the self-consciousness of the believer, warrants the reality of the event upon which Christianity is based (*ST* 2:114). Analogous to Kähler's claim that the historical Christ of the Bible is significant, we can say that the "Biblical historical Christ is normative for Tillich" and not the historical Jesus.[83] This does not mean that Tillich constructed a biblical Christology, but that the biblical imagery became informative for his Christology.

Humanity, according to Tillich, has left its essential nature and lapsed into existence. Thereby it forfeited its theonomy and asserted its autonomy. The estrangement from its essential nature is overcome for human existence through an ecstatic experience that gives birth to theonomy. This is accomplished in the experience of the New Being "as symbolized in Jesus who is the Christ."[84] Jesus is this New Being insofar as in him there is the undistorted manifestation of his essential being within and under the conditions of existence (*ST* 2:119). Christ is the end of existence lived out in estrangement, con-

---

82. Paul Tillich, *Systematic Theology*, vol. 2, *Existence and the Christ* (Chicago: University of Chicago Press, 1975 [1957]), 2:3; hereafter *ST*. References are placed in the text.

83. So rightly A. T. Mollegen, "Christology and Biblical Criticism in Tillich," in *The Theology of Paul Tillich*, 269.

84. Carl J. Armbruster, *The Vision of Paul Tillich* (New York: Sheed and Ward, 1967), 168.

flict, and self-destruction. "The Christ is essential man. He represents man to man, that is, he shows what man essentially is. But he also represents God to man, because essential man has embedded within him the image of God. Therefore, essential manhood and essential God-manhood are identical."[85]

For Tillich, similar to Barth, Christ is the perfected human being. Yet Tillich was very hesitant to accept the paradigm of the incarnation, because he was convinced that its intention (to say that God changed into something that is not God) cannot be maintained theologically. Rather, he opted for the Johannine metaphor that the logos became flesh. "Flesh" signifies historical existence, and "becoming" indicates that God participates in that which is estranged from him.

In Jesus the New Being was and is actualized, and estrangement of existence has been overcome. Jesus Christ as the New Being rescues us from our estranged human situation. The expression of the New Being in Jesus as the Christ can be seen in Christ's words, in his deeds, and in his suffering (ST 2:121-23). With regard to the last item we are surprised to hear Tillich declare: "The suffering on the Cross is not something additional which can be separated from the appearance of the eternal God-Manhood under the conditions of existence; it is an inescapable implication of this appearance" (ST 2:123).[86] Christ's suffering on the cross is a mere consequence of his becoming human. The salvific function of Christ is no longer centered in cross and resurrection but in Jesus as the Christ, because in him "the conflict between the essential unity of God and man and man's existential estrangement is overcome" (ST 2:125). This was the biblical picture of Jesus as the Christ that Tillich gleaned from the New Testament.

Tillich saw in the cross of Christ and in his resurrection central symbols of the universal significance of Jesus. The resurrection becomes "the decisive test of the Christ-character of Jesus of Nazareth. A real experience made it possible for the disciples to apply the known symbol of resurrection to Jesus, thus acknowledging him definitely as the Christ" (ST 2:154). Tillich interpreted the resurrection of Jesus as the Christ with the help of the restitution theory. This restitution "is rooted in the personal unity between Jesus and God and in the impact of this unity on the minds of the apostles. . . . In an ecstatic experience the concrete picture of Jesus of Nazareth became indissolubly united with the reality of the New Being. He is present wherever the New Being is present" (ST 2:157). While Tillich rejected the interpretation of the resurrection as a spiritu-

---

85. So the fitting summary of Tillich's position in Armbruster, *Vision of Paul Tillich*, 179.

86. See also Armbruster, *Vision of Paul Tillich*, 198, who rightly cautions that this close connection of the cross with the significance of Jesus the Christ allows for "no room whatsoever for the sacrificial aspect of the crucifixion."

alistic or psychological event, one wonders whether his own restitution theory does not ultimately issue from his positing a psychological event that occurred in the minds of the disciples and continues to occur in each Christian who recognizes the significance of Jesus as the Christ.

The problem seems to stem from Tillich's own Christology. While he agreed with the decisions of Nicea and Chalcedon, that Christ is truly divine and that in him the human and the divine are equally present, the human being Jesus only serves as the paradigm of the manifestation of the New Being (*ST* 2:145). Especially since his visit to Japan in 1960, Tillich had become more and more open to the manifestation of the New Being in other religions, as we can gather from his last public lecture where he stated: "There are revealing and saving powers in all religions."[87] Jesus the Christ can be used as symbol; the question is whether it is *the* symbol.

Yet before pushing Tillich into the corner of liberal theology or accusing him of syncretism, we should read the first sentences of his *Systematic Theology*, where he stated how he understood his task as a theologian: "Theology, as a function of the church, must serve the needs of the church. A theological system is supposed to satisfy two basic needs: The statement of the truth of the Christian message and the interpretation of this truth for every new generation" (*ST* 1:3).[88] This is exactly what Tillich had in mind throughout his long career, to discern what the Christian message is and to interpret it in the context of his own time. To accomplish this he used two tools: the method of correlation and the concept of symbol. "In using the method of correlation, systematic theology proceeds in the following way: it makes an analysis of the human situation out of which existential questions arise, and it demonstrates that the symbols used in the Christian message are the answers to these questions" (*ST* 1:62). For this analysis one employs all materials made available by our creative self-interpretation in culture. This was one of the reasons why Tillich was interested in virtually everything that humanity did and produced, whether drama, poetry, art, philosophy, or science. Tillich claimed that this analysis is actually the task of the philosopher. The Christian message then provides the answers to the questions implied in the human existence, meaning answers to issues like hubris, anxiety, estrangement, etc.

Tillich was adamant that the answers theology provides are not derived from human existence, but from the notion of God, who is the infinite ground

87. Paul Tillich, "The Significance of the History of Religions for the Systematic Theologian" (1965), in Paul Tillich, *The Future of Religions*, ed. Jerald C. Brauer (New York: Harper and Row, 1966), 81.

88. Paul Tillich, *Systematic Theology*, vol. 1, *Reason and Revelation: Being and God* (Chicago: University of Chicago Press, 1951).

of courage and "the infinite power of being which resists the threat of non-being" (*ST* 1:64). This method of correlation allowed him and even forced him to be open to all expressions of culture and to integrate them into his theological system. The actual theological task is then to show how the symbols of the Christian message are the answers to these questions. Again, Tillich distinguished between sign and symbol: "The sign bears no necessary relation to that to which it points, the symbol participates in the reality of that for which it stands" (*ST* 1:239). Similar to the icon in Orthodox theology, the symbol therefore is an avenue to get in touch with what it stands for, meaning ultimately the ground of being. All statements about God and the divine reality are not descriptive but symbolic, they are not photographs but pointers, allowing for participation in that to which they point. Therefore Tillich asserted in volume 1 of his *Systematic Theology* that all statements about God are of symbolic nature. Only "the statement that God is being-itself is a non-symbolic statement. It does not point beyond itself. It means what it says directly and properly" (*ST* 1:238).

In volume 2, however, Tillich remembered that he grew up with the neoorthodox dialectic of the human and divine. They cannot be mixed or too closely associated. He then stated: "Thus it follows that everything religion has to say about God, including his qualities, actions, and manifestations, has a symbolic character and that the meaning of 'God' is completely missed if one takes the symbolic language literally." Asking himself whether there is a nonsymbolic statement about God that is possible, he concluded: "There is a point at which a non-symbolic assertion about God must be made. . . . Namely, the statement that everything we say about God is symbolic" (*ST* 2:9). This means that Tillich affirmed, with Barth, that God is the totally other. And he concluded that anything we say about God or God's manifestation must be expressed in symbolic language. This then allowed the freedom for both the liberals and the conservatives to take the symbols to be either more metaphoric or more literal. Tillich had the unique gift to speak to both and to be understood by both.

Langdon Gilkey (1919-2004) was, chronologically speaking, almost a successor to Tillich at the University of Chicago Divinity School. This was most fitting because both can be understood as interpreters of culture. While Tillich correlated culture with the Christian message, Gilkey followed culture as it unfolded in his own life and around him.[89] Gilkey was born near the University of

---

89. Cf. for his own interpretation, Langdon Gilkey, "A Retrospective Glance at My Work," in *The Whirlwind in Culture: Frontiers in Theology; In Honor of Langdon Gilkey*, ed. Donald W. Musser and Joseph L. Price (Bloomington, Ind.: Meyer-Stone Books, 1988), 1-35.

Chicago, his father being pastor of Hyde Park Baptist Church and his mother active in the YMCA. He went to Harvard for college, majoring in philosophy. Upon graduation in 1940, he traveled to Peking to teach English at an American-British university for Chinese students. But war began in December 1941, and the foreigners were rounded up and put under a form of house arrest. A year and a quarter later they were sent to an internment camp in Shantung province. From this experience resulted Gilkey's book *Shantung Compound* (1966). This experience also convinced him of the relevance of the symbols of sin and estrangement and the necessity of moral awareness and responsibility, of spiritual self-understanding and repentance, and of a deep trust in God if creative personal and communal life is to be possible. He was continuously confronted with the pettiness and the collapse of virtue under the trying circumstances of life in a forced camp.

In the internment camp he also read the first volume of Reinhold Niebuhr's *Nature and Destiny of Man*. When he returned to the States in 1945, it was clear for Gilkey that he would study with Niebuhr at Union Theological Seminary in New York. A result of his doctoral thesis was his 1959 book *Maker of Heaven and Earth: A Study of the Christian Doctrine of Creation*. Upon obtaining his Ph.D. from Columbia University (in conjunction with Union Theological Seminary), he taught at Vassar (1951-54) and then at Vanderbilt. There he got into the civil rights struggle over the dismissal of a black student from the divinity school, which showed him the truth of what Niebuhr had described in *Moral Man and Immoral Society*. In 1963, after this conflict had been resolved through the pressure of most of the faculty of the university, he received a call to teach at the University of Chicago Divinity School, where he stayed until retirement. He hardly had established himself there when the death-of-God theology originated in his immediate environment, since William Hamilton had been a friend of his and Thomas J. J. Altizer had studied there, too. But Gilkey did not become one of its proponents, since, as he declared: "My cumulative experience of twenty-five years had assured me in countless ways of the reality, the power, and the grace of God. In addition, personal and social experience had also far too thoroughly convinced me of the relevance and validity of the classical symbols of theology for this."[90]

Gilkey wrote three books counteracting that move of utter secularity, the first being *Naming the Whirlwind: The Renewal of God-Language* (1969). In that he analyzed the then present situation, saying the new move of the death-of-God theology "seems to question the very roots of any form of religious beliefs at all," not just the orthodox or fundamentalist beliefs as had been the case so

---

90. Gilkey, "Retrospective Glance," 23.

far.[91] The reason for the radicality of this movement, though Gilkey did not expressly say so, was that America was largely a religious foundation. As the United States became more and more secular, this secularity seemed to replace the religious undergirding of this country. Yet both liberal and neoorthodox theology were ill prepared to accept the challenge of growing secularity. For liberal theology, God had receded so much into the background that when the turbulence of two world wars and the Great Depression challenged the notion of the moral perfectibility of humanity and of continual progress, there was very little left to offer to secular humanity. Yet in neoorthodoxy God was so totally other that what was beheld there as fundamental Christian doctrines had very little relevance for everyday life. Therefore the death-of-God theologians could talk about the meaninglessness of God-language and pronounce the death of God.

Since the radical theologians mainly raised problems about God but did not solve them, Gilkey looked to secular humanity itself and found that "secular man on the level of his existence is not as 'unreligious' and so free of the need for mythical language in his self-understanding as he thinks. Thus many of the religious symbolic forms characteristic of former generations remain relevant to the way man actually lives."[92] For instance, the category of ultimacy arises both in the guise of fanaticism and in the experience of despair.

As Gilkey showed in *Religion and the Scientific Future: Reflections on Myth, Science, and Theology,* published just a year later, there is a paradox in humanity because humanity "is seen as an initiating moral and rational *cause* as well as the determined *effect* of natural and historical forces" to solve our problems. However, this same human being is then understood "as the determined *object* of inquiry" as if humanity would have no freedom at all.[93] How can a human being be free on the one hand to objectively investigate and on the other hand not free at all so that it can be objectively examined? Gilkey therefore concluded: "For if man has still great difficulty in controlling himself, even when he means well, then surely we must be much more realistic about ourselves and hence more careful when we embark socially on programs designed to control ourselves and thus our destiny and ourselves through scientific knowledge."[94] He even ventured to say: "Man cannot believe himself to be the sole arbiter of his own destiny without intellectual contradiction and historical self-

91. Langdon Gilkey, *Naming the Whirlwind: The Renewal of God-Language* (Indianapolis: Bobbs-Merrill, 1969), 4.

92. Gilkey, *Naming the Whirlwind,* 248-49.

93. Langdon Gilkey, *Religion and the Scientific Future: Reflections on Myth, Science, and Theology* (New York: Harper and Row, 1970), 81-82.

94. Gilkey, *Religion,* 95.

destruction."[95] Since we are presently in a volatile situation and since humanity is unable to chart the course toward the future because of humanity's intrinsic finitude, "we need symbols of ultimacy with which these intense reactions and perilous ventures into the unknown can be illumined, channeled, strengthened and tempered."[96]

Gilkey therefore set forth a Christian interpretation of history in his *Reaping the Whirlwind* (1976). Discerning the biblical symbols, he concluded that providence cannot simply be the continuation of finite being and the ups and downs of human creativity, sin, and catastrophe. Instead providence must "be supplemented by incarnation and atonement, and ultimately by eschatology" (266). We cannot just go in cycles, but there must be ground for hope in terms of ultimate hope. He sees reason for this in the loneliness and suffering of Jesus through which God participates in our alienation and misery. This shows God's love for his creatures and is a continuing basis for our participation in God's future history. Therefore Gilkey even stated: "All of creaturely life participates in God: in its being, its continuing being, its spontaneity, its freedom, its novel possibilities, its responsibilities" (283). Yet beyond powerlessness and suffering there is the resurrection where the final hope of reunion and completion find their ground and their ultimate expression. This means that history does not oscillate between hope and despair, between forgiveness and sin, but the divine love will be united "with the divine power of being and with the divine goal for creation into a love that triumphs over the conditions of our finitude as well as over our sin, and brings us, as all love does, into reunion and communion again" (318).

Gilkey is a theologian of history, yet in contrast to those of the nineteenth century he is not one of progress and human perfection, but also not one of the decline of history. Upheld by God's grace, the historic process reflects human triumphs in failure, yet ultimately it will be elevated into God's kingdom through God's grace and all-encompassing love. Therefore Gilkey is not a prophet of pessimism, but reminds us of God's never-ending love. Yet on history and the role humans play in it, he perceptively states: "Although the level of knowledge, theoretical and technical, may steadily rise, our ability to use it creatively does not, nor do self-concern and irrationality recede. Thus civilization remains as ambiguous and precarious a venture as ever."[97]

To the history of human ambiguity also belong the rise of creationism, on

95. Gilkey, *Religion*, 98.
96. Langdon Gilkey, *Reaping the Whirlwind: A Christian Interpretation of History* (New York: Seabury Press, 1976), 239. The parenthetical page references in the next paragraph are to this work.
97. Gilkey, "Retrospective Glance," 26.

which Gilkey commented in *Creationism on Trial: Evolution and God in Little Rock* (1985), and the rising self-consciousness of religions outside Christianity. He was confronted with this latter issue existentially when he taught for one semester at the University of Kyoto in Japan in 1975 and pondered how we can talk to each other representing various religious faiths. He suggested that "not just our response to revelation . . . is relative; it is the revelation to which [I am] responding that is now roughly equal to the others."[98] He surmises that perhaps this would lead to a more fruitful dialogue without abandoning one's own position. Whether here the relativity does not ultimately gain the upper hand remains to be seen. On our view of nature, one could question Gilkey's surmise, for instance, that we could gain much from Buddhism, especially since Buddhist countries have not fared any better in ecological issues than have "Christian" countries. Yet Gilkey is certainly correct that any dialogue, whether ecumenical or interreligious, cannot start with the assumption of arrogance, but in the genuine attitude of humility, realizing that all of humanity are children of God. Similar to Tillich, it has been characteristic of Gilkey and his theology that it continued to reach out to others. This also showed in his unparalleled popularity as an adviser of doctoral candidates in Chicago.

Christ and Culture; or, The Long Shadow of Karl Barth: The Niebuhr Brothers

Neither Reinhold Niebuhr nor his brother Richard was a student or follower of Karl Barth, though Richard had followed Barth's literary output since the early 1930s.[99] Yet, similar to Barth, they started out in the liberal camp and then, as Barth had done, Reinhold arrived at social involvement and an assessment of society that was both realistic and Christ centered while Richard traveled from a monotheistic interpretation of the world, betraying the influence of Ernst Troeltsch, to a more and more christocentric view. To some extent they did for American theology what Barth did for European theology, bringing Christ to theology and to the world. While for Barth the turning point was the crisis ensuing from World War I, for the Niebuhrs it was the Great Depression and the resulting economic plight and inestimable human misery that

---

98. Langdon Gilkey, "Plurality: Christianity's New Situation," in Langdon Gilkey, *Through the Tempest: Theological Voyages in a Pluralistic Culture,* selected and edited by Jeff B. Pool (Minneapolis: Fortress, 1991), 31, where he also reflected on his visit in Kyoto.

99. So James M. Gustafson, "Niebuhr, Karl Paul Reinhold," in *Theologische Realenzyklopädie,* 24:469.

showed them the fallacy of liberal theology and its optimistic portrayal of humanity and its future.

The ethicist James M. Gustafson (b. 1925) wrote: "No other American theologian of the 20th century had during his life such a far-reaching and deep influence as Reinhold Niebuhr. His articles on political, religious, and cultural issues were published both in religious and also in secular journals."[100] And Richard Fox (b. 1945), who wrote a detailed biography of Niebuhr, said he was a "political organizer and commentator, religious thinker, social critic, seminary teacher. . . . Forty or more weekends a year, for more than a quarter century, he bolted from one state to another, preaching at colleges, addressing student conferences, conferring at political meetings."[101] Gabriel Fackre (b. 1926) added: "There are in America more doctoral dissertations about Niebuhr than any other twentieth-century theologian. . . . Every canyon and crevice of his story has been explored, including the paths of his intellectual and personal pilgrimage."[102]

Who was **Reinhold Niebuhr** (1892-1971), what caused his restlessness, and what made him so important? Fame was not laid into his crib. To the contrary. His father had emigrated from Germany and was a pastor of the German Evangelical Synod. His mother also was the daughter of an emigrant, a pastor. Niebuhr attended Elmhurst College in Illinois and went to Eden Theological Seminary in St. Louis for theological studies. At Eden he was dissatisfied with being German and gravitated toward the one professor who taught in English. In 1913, as he was looking for graduate education at Yale, his father suddenly died and he had to preach the funeral sermon in his father's congregation. The members wanted him to succeed his father, but he had set his eyes on further education. While at Yale he realized that he had no command of English and no B.D., since Eden had not been accredited. He became aware of how truncated his education was. To remedy the situation he wrote his B.D. thesis and, in the fall of 1914, became a bona fide graduate student at Yale Divinity School. Though his academic average had not been high enough, he nevertheless obtained the master's degree in 1915 and then, because he was in dire financial straits and also tired of academia, he looked for a church to pastor. Just like his education, the church he obtained was not what he actually desired. It was a very small church, Bethel Evangelical Church in Detroit, to which he had been assigned. The congregation was predominantly German American. But in this charge he had to support his family; his mother helped him in church work as

---

100. Gustafson, "Niebuhr, Karl Paul Reinhold," 24:471.

101. Richard W. Fox, *Reinhold Niebuhr: A Biography* (San Francisco: Harper and Row, 1987 [1985]), x.

102. Gabriel Fackre, *The Promise of Reinhold Niebuhr* (Philadelphia: Lippincott, 1970), 15.

she had done for his father. Here he also began his life as an incessant writer of letters, articles, and short editorials.

To fit in with the American mix, he advocated that the German Americans show their loyalty even to the point of his synod dropping the term "German" from its name, especially as America entered the war against Germany in 1917. Yet there were also other issues he picked up, such as the policies of the automobile manufacturers, which supposedly were very humanitarian but at the bottom line were geared toward high profits. Mass layoffs, long factory shutdowns with no pay when retooling occurred, the firing of older workers and an antiunion policy were some of the issues that raised Niebuhr's social consciousness and realism. Some of them made it into the *Christian Century*, of which he was an editor. When the war cut off the supply of European emigrants, the automobile industry drew large numbers of black citizens from the South, which increased racial tensions. Niebuhr got involved in the labor conflict and also in the issue of racial justice. Soon his congregation was open to black members. In 1923 Sherwood Eddy, a YMCA evangelist, invited Niebuhr to join him on a tour of Germany. When they arrived at the Ruhr Valley and saw how the Germans were treated there by the French, who had occupied this region to exploit its heavy industry and its coal mines, Niebuhr became a declared pacifist.[103] He also stirred up enough sentiment back home that the U.S. government took up relief action. Eddy also provided funds allowing Niebuhr to hire an assistant at Bethel Church, so he could accept the growing number of invitations for speaking engagements in colleges and churches.

As Detroit was growing in the early twenties at an explosive rate, Niebuhr's congregation increased in numbers. Thanks to a wealthy parishioner who had joined the church, Bethel relocated and was able to afford an imposing English Gothic church building and a modern parsonage. In 1927 Niebuhr's first book appeared, *Does Civilization Need Religion?* Again, most of its content had appeared earlier in the *Christian Century*. While religion had not fared well in modern industrial society, he contended that the future of religion and the future of civilization are inseparable because "the future of religion is involved in the ethical reconstruction of modern society."[104] The contribution religion makes to this reconstruction is "its reverence for human personality and its aid in creating the type of personality which deserves reverence."[105] Niebuhr picks

103. Fox, *Reinhold Niebuhr*, 78. Cf. also Reinhold Niebuhr, "Germany in Despair" (1923), in *Young Reinhold Niebuhr: His Early Writings, 1911-1931*, edited with an introduction by William G. Chrystal, foreword by John C. Bennett (St. Louis: Eden, 1977), 128-31.

104. Reinhold Niebuhr, *Does Civilization Need Religion? A Study in the Social Resources and Limitations of Religion in Modern Life* (New York: Macmillan, 1928 [1927]), 17.

105. Reinhold Niebuhr, *Does Civilization Need Religion?* 62.

up here Schweitzer's call for reverence for life. Niebuhr preferred the ethical rather than the intellectual aspect of religious faith in order to create a religious spirit sufficiently vigorous to effect changes necessary in modern society. He called for a Christian idealism that makes religion socially effective and detaches itself "from the dominant secular desires of the nations as well as from the greed of economic groups."[106] In conclusion, he picked up Troeltsch's claim that the fate of Western society is inextricably intertwined with the Christian faith. Therefore he saw in the Christian religion the inevitable basis for a spiritual regeneration of our civilization.

By now he was famous enough to obtain a teaching position. Yale very much wanted to lure him to their rejuvenated divinity school, but in 1928 he was appointed professor of applied Christianity at Union Theological Seminary in New York and remained there until his death. As Tillich had experienced, too, teaching at Union in New York City brought one into contact with a continuous stream of visitors from other parts of America and also from overseas. This new position considerably increased Niebuhr's possibilities for involvement. He helped found the Fellowship of Socialist Christians and joined the Socialist Party. He even appeared on its ballot as a congressional candidate from a local New York district in 1930. Moreover, from his pen now came a stream of books.

In *Moral Man and Immoral Society* (1932), Niebuhr showed that our industrial society creates instability and aggravates the injustices from which people already suffer. It also unites the whole of humanity into a system of economic interdependence. In this situation he differentiated between the morality of individuals and that of society or societies. He asserted that "from the perspective of the individual the highest ideal is unselfishness. Society must strive for justice even if it is forced to use means, such as self-assertion, resistance, coercion and perhaps resentment, which cannot gain the moral sanction of the most sensitive moral spirit."[107] While this unselfish spirit that appears for instance in pacifism certainly can be impressive and can win some people over, in group relations this always results in failure. If a group practices only its pure moral principles, it will never realize its hopes because the other side might easily understand this as a kind of resignation or weakness and dictate its own terms. While there are possibilities for individual unselfishness, especially as one works within a group, the matter is different with a group asserting its rights and interests against other communities. Therefore Niebuhr could advo-

---

106. Reinhold Niebuhr, *Does Civilization Need Religion?* 229.

107. Reinhold Niebuhr, *Moral Man and Immoral Society: A Study in Ethics and Politics* (New York: Charles Scribner's, 1960), 257.

cate a class struggle resisting the Nazis and welcome leaders of the resistance movement, such as Tillich, to America. In 1940 Niebuhr resigned from the Socialist Party and later helped found the Liberal Party. He became now more and more engaged in politics, especially with his association with government policy makers in the State Department, and wrote many political commentaries in the *New Republic, Harper's, Life,* and in his own publication, *Christianity and Crisis,* which he founded in 1941.

In 1941 and 1943 his two-volume *Nature and Destiny of Man* appeared, which was the Gifford Lectures of 1939-40. The work provides a good portrait of the final stage of his theology and ethics. In the first volume he covered the different understandings of humanity from Greek antiquity to modern naturalism. Then he focused on the Christian understanding of humanity. There he started with general revelation as the point of contact and stated that, as a personal human experience, this provides for "the sense of reverence of a majesty and of dependence upon an ultimate source of being, . . . the sense of moral obligation laid upon one from beyond oneself and of a moral unworthiness before a judge, . . . the longing for forgiveness."[108] From that foundation, then, the biblical historical revelation can proceed, according to Niebuhr. He then described humanity as created in the image of God, as a sinner, and nevertheless being responsible. In the second volume, *Human Destiny,* Niebuhr started with the Christ event. He showed that the double assertion of the kingdom of God that has come and is coming leads to the implication that history is an interim.[109] Then he outlined the dynamics of this interim, mainly focusing on nature, grace, and love. His ethical interests came to the fore when he stated that nature represents the historical possibilities of justice, while grace corresponds to the ideal possibility of perfect love. Yet love stands in a dialectic relationship to justice, since it is "both the fulfillment and the negation of all achievements of justice in history."[110] This means there are events in history that have significance in relation to the ultimate fulfillment in love. But seen from the perspective of our destiny, they are still incomplete. We can therefore detect only "partial fulfillments and realizations" of history in civilization and culture and in the life of individuals as well, when we view history from the end.[111] History is not meaningless, but it is not simply a process that leads to a clearly discernible goal, unless beheld in the eyes of faith.

---

108. Reinhold Niebuhr, *The Nature and Destiny of Man: A Christian Interpretation,* vol. 1, *Human Nature,* introduction by Robin W. Lovin (Louisville: Westminster John Knox, 1996 [1941]), 131.

109. Cf. Reinhold Niebuhr, *The Nature and Destiny of Man: A Christian Interpretation,* vol. 2, *Human Destiny* (Louisville: Westminster John Knox, 1996 [1943]), 48.

110. Reinhold Niebuhr, *Nature and Destiny,* 2:246.

111. Reinhold Niebuhr, *Nature and Destiny,* 2:301.

Gone here is the revolutionary optimism of earlier days. We are confronted with a sober realism that also reflects the unsettling times of World War II. Not by accident are we confronted on the last pages of his two-volume work with the concept of the anti-Christ. Some of this can already be sensed in an earlier writing, *Beyond Tragedy* (1937), where he stated that "the Christian view of history passes through the sense of tragic to a hope and an assurance which is 'beyond tragedy.' The cross, which stands at the center of the Christian world view, reveals both the seriousness of human sin and the purpose and power of God to overcome it."[112]

Niebuhr was not a prophet of doom, but an astute interpreter of history from a more and more christocentric angle. While at Union, in 1931 he married one of his students who later taught at Barnard College and headed there the department of religion. Ursula Niebuhr was a positive influence on her husband's thinking and also the provider for the once-a-week evening living-room dialogues between students and her husband. Besides his increasing involvement in political and public affairs, being a consultant for many people in public life, he was also active in ecumenical affairs, including the first assembly of the World Council of Churches at Amsterdam in 1948, and the consultant to the National Council of Churches. The Christian realism he represented influenced many emerging church leaders and theologians, regardless of their denominational or ethnic affiliation. Next to him one should also not forget his sister Hulda Niebuhr (1889-1962), who for many years taught Christian education at New York University and McCormick Theological Seminary in Chicago. Yet there was also his brother H. Richard Niebuhr. While Reinhold was very much a theologian of the public square, starting as liberal pacifist, pursuing the line of the Social Gospel, and finally advocating a biblical realism, Richard too reached to the events of his time. Yet much more than his brother did this Niebuhr take up the challenge of historical and cultural relativism to advocate amidst the plurality of culture and religion a radical monotheism.

H. Richard Niebuhr (1894-1962), younger brother of Reinhold, was also born in Wright City, Missouri. In 1908 he entered Elmhurst College, as his brother had done, and graduated from the unaccredited college in 1912. Then he went to Eden College, graduating there in 1915. Like his brother, he was influenced at Eden by Professor Samuel D. Press, the school's first American-born professor, but who had studied in Germany with Harnack and the church historian and systematician Reinhold Seeberg (1859-1935). Since Niebuhr's father died in 1913, Niebuhr had to support himself after that. Upon graduation from seminary, he

---

112. Reinhold Niebuhr, *Beyond Tragedy: Essays on the Christian Interpretation of History* (New York: Charles Scribner's, 1946 [1937]), x.

worked as a newspaper reporter and was ordained in 1916 at the age of twenty-two. Then he served Walnut Park Evangelical Church in St. Louis for two years. Since his finances were meager but he nevertheless wanted a good education, he sought out every opportunity to further himself. When the United States entered World War I, he enlisted as an army chaplain, but the war ended before he was sent overseas. After the war he enrolled at Union Theological Seminary and Columbia University in New York, but then was called back to Eden to teach. Press, by then president at Eden Seminary, called him in 1919 to teach theology and ethics at the seminary. He earned an M.A. in German, philosophy, and psychology, while serving Walnut Park Evangelical Church. It was only in 1922 that he finally could pursue graduate work in a more uninterrupted fashion at Yale University Divinity School. However, he still simultaneously served a congregation. Within only two years he had earned a B.D. and a Ph.D., his doctoral dissertation being "Ernst Troeltsch's Philosophy of Religion." Then he was invited to become president at Elmhurst, and in 1927 to return to Eden as its academic dean.

While he was there his first book appeared, *The Social Sources of Denominationalism* (1929), a result of his teaching experience. The publication was heavily influenced by Ernst Troeltsch and Max Weber. Niebuhr stated that Christendom has often compromised the message of the gospel by aligning itself with prevalent trends in society. Therefore he decried the evil of denominationalism that lies "in the failure of the churches to transcend the social conditions which fashion them into caste-organizations." They adhere to standards and institutions that are only remotely similar to the Christian ideal and are primarily concerned with self-preservation and expansion. "The domination of class and self-preservative church ethics over the ethics of the gospel must be held responsible for much of the moral ineffectiveness of Christianity in the West."[113] Then Niebuhr outlined a history of denominationalism in the United States that included the immigrant and black churches. While he saw the history of schism as a history of Christianity's defeat, he found no remedy in neo-Reformation theology, because this, for Niebuhr, is an escape from the world. He rather opted, in line with the Social Gospel, for the fatherhood of God and the brotherhood of all people. He saw this interconnecting bond made transparent in the life of Christ. "His sonship and his brotherhood, as delineated in the gospel, are not the example which men are asked to follow if they will, but rather the demonstration of that character of ultimate reality which they can ignore only at the cost of their souls."[114] Therefore Christ inspired us to Christ-

113. H. Richard Niebuhr, *The Social Sources of Denominationalism* (Cleveland: World Publishing, 1968 [1929]), 21.

114. H. R. Niebuhr, *Social Sources of Denominationalism*, 278-79.

like fellowship with people of other social status and other color. Niebuhr concluded: "The increase of that fellowship today is the hope of Christendom and of the world."[115]

We notice in this book already something of what accompanied Niebuhr's whole life, a passion for the church. That did not cease when he was invited to join the faculty at Yale Divinity School, an invitation he reluctantly accepted because it meant leaving his denominational seminary in 1931 to become associate professor of Christian ethics. In 1938 he became full professor, and later he occupied the prestigious Sterling chair of theology and Christian ethics. In 1930 he was awarded an eight-month sabbatical to study in Germany. He spent most of his time in Tübingen and Frankfurt, where at the latter place he got acquainted with Tillich. This resulted in translating Tillich's *Die religiöse Lage der Gegenwart* (1926), which was published in 1932 under the title *The Religious Situation*.

Another book of the 1930s, which was from his own pen and became a classic, was *The Kingdom of God in America* (1937). While in *The Social Sources of Denominationalism* he had described more how the social context molded or corrupted the gospel, now he wanted to show the other side, how the vision of the kingdom shaped America's culture. He had discovered that "the idea of the kingdom of God had indeed been the dominant idea in American Christianity, . . . but that it had not always meant the same thing."[116] He showed how this idea was at work throughout American history, yet he was also adamant to assert that this idea cannot be understood at all "save on the basis of faith in the sovereign, living, loving God."[117] This shows another important point in Niebuhr's outlook. Though he was very much interested in interpreting history, for him history made no sense unless there was someone who ultimately guided history as its creator, ruler, judge, and redeemer.

This is demonstrated more clearly in his next significant publication, *The Meaning of Revelation* (1941). In Barthian fashion Niebuhr stated: "Christian theology must begin today with revelation."[118] But then he continued with a sentence that might lead into relativism, betraying his indebtedness to Troeltsch: "It [i.e., Christian theology] knows that men cannot think about God save as historic, communal beings and save as believers." Christian theology must begin with revelation, and this revelation can be found only in its his-

115. H. R. Niebuhr, *Social Sources of Denominationalism*, 283.
116. H. Richard Niebuhr, *The Kingdom of God in America*, with a new introduction by Martin E. Marty (Middletown, Conn.: Wesleyan University Press, 1988 [1937]), xxii.
117. H. R. Niebuhr, *Kingdom of God*, xxvi.
118. H. Richard Niebuhr, *The Meaning of Revelation* (New York: Macmillan, 1967 [1941]), 30.

toric manifestation, namely, in the experience of the believers. This is the sphere of the internal history over against the external one, "the story of what happened to us, the living memory of the community."[119] Revelation is not some kind of hypothesis which then must be shown to be true, but through revelation something happens to us "in our history which conditions all our thinking and . . . through this happening we are enabled to apprehend what we are, what we are suffering and doing and what our potentialities are."[120] Revelation therefore is existential illumination of our own self, and in this way it brings us in touch with the one from whom and to whom we are. This means there is a transforming power in revelation, which at the same time is the self-disclosure of God.

This transformative power was also brought forth in *Christ and Culture* (1951). Yet before that work was published there occurred the agony of World War II, in which Niebuhr suffered under the ambivalence and the nightmare of war.[121] He was critical of both the pacifists and the just-war theorists, since neither really understood the suffering which that war caused. In *Christ and Culture* he addressed the enduring issue of how Christianity and civilization are to be related to each other. Throughout history he discerns five different possibilities: Christ against culture, the Christ of culture, Christ above culture, Christ and culture in paradox, and Christ the transformer of culture. While he certainly preferred Christ as the transformer of culture, he concluded that there is not one Christian answer. The reason for this is simply that we are in society and not outside of it. Therefore we cannot determine objectively what to do. We must decide as Christians in the midst of our cultural history. Yet recognizing this relativity does not mean that we are without an absolute, because in all our doing and thinking we are related to the ultimate absolute, God in Christ. This means the question is whether in our dependent freedom "we will choose with reasoning faithlessness or reasoning faith" which direction we will go.[122] The relationship of Christians to God as agents in culture was decisive for Niebuhr. He had learned from Troeltsch that Western culture and Christian faith belong together.

Therefore he entitled one of his last publications *Radical Monotheism and Western Culture* (1960), in which he claimed that "radical monotheism de-

---

119. H. R. Niebuhr, *The Meaning of Revelation*, 66.

120. H. R. Niebuhr, *The Meaning of Revelation*, 101.

121. Cf. for details the brief but illuminating biography of H. R. Niebuhr by William Stacy Johnson, in H. Richard Niebuhr, *Theology, History, and Culture: Major Unpublished Writings*, ed. William Stacy Johnson, foreword by Richard R. Niebuhr (New Haven: Yale University Press, 1996), xvii.

122. H. Richard Niebuhr, *Christ and Culture* (New York: Harper Torchbook, 1951), 251.

thrones all absolutes short of the principle of being itself. At the same time it reverences every relative existent."[123] He could even accept naturalism and humanism as critiques of both religion and culture, but not as exclusive systems of closed societies, since, as he rightly saw, they could only emerge within the freedom provided by radically monotheistic faith.

Before he could put into print his last lecture series *(The Responsible Self)* — most of his important publications resulted from lecture series he delivered on various university campuses — Niebuhr suddenly died of a heart attack. Yet a statement from his conclusion summarizes what his main concern was, to show that God in Christ is active in culture and history and to elicit our response commensurate with the example Christ has given: "The responsible self we see in Christ and which we believe is being elicited in all our race is a universally and eternally responsive I, answering in a universal society and in a time without end, in all actions upon it, to the action of the One who heals all our diseases, forgives all our iniquities, saves our lives from destruction, and crowns us with everlasting mercy."[124] Here it is not simply God and culture as in earlier American theological positions. But Christ has now become central for culture as both its judge and also its hope. This central concern gleaned from neo-Reformation theology had been forcefully advanced by America's theologians who were most influential on society.

For Further Reading

Shailer Mathews (1863-1941)

Krumbine, Miles H. *The Process of Religion: Essays in Honor of Dean Shailer Mathews.* New York: Macmillan, 1933.

Lindsey, William D. *Shailer Mathews's Lives of Jesus: The Search for a Theological Foundation for the Social Gospel.* Albany: State University of New York Press, 1997.

Mathews, Shailer. *The Church and the Changing Order.* New York: Macmillan, 1908.

———. *The Growth of the Idea of God.* New York: Macmillan, 1931.

———. *Jesus on Social Institutions.* Edited with an introduction by Kenneth Cauthen. Philadelphia: Fortress, 1971.

———. *New Faith for Old: An Autobiography.* New York: Macmillan, 1936.

———. *The Social Teaching of Jesus: An Essay in Christian Sociology.* New York: Macmillan, 1910 [1897].

123. H. Richard Niebuhr, *Radical Monotheism and Western Culture: With Supplementary Essays,* foreword by James M. Gustafson (Louisville: Westminster John Knox, 1993 [1960]), 37.

124. H. Richard Niebuhr, *The Responsible Self: An Essay in Christian Moral Philosophy,* introduction by James M. Gustafson, foreword by William Schweiker (Louisville: Westminster John Knox, 1999 [1963]), 144-45.

Shirley Jackson Case (1872-1947)

Case, Shirley Jackson. *The Christian Philosophy of History*. Chicago: University of Chicago Press, 1943.

————. *The Social Origins of Christianity*. New York: Cooper Square, 1975 [1923].

Hynes, William J. *Shirley Jackson Case and the Chicago School: The Socio-Historical Method*. Chico, Calif.: Scholars, 1981.

Peden, W. Creighton, and Jerome A. Stone, eds. *The Chicago School of Theology — Pioneers in Religious Inquiry*. Vol. 1, *The Early Chicago School, 1906-1959: G. B. Foster, E. S. Ames, S. Mathews, G. B. Smith, S. J. Case*. Lewiston, N.Y.: Edwin Mellen, 1996. Pp. 243-331.

Henry Nelson Wieman (1884-1975)

Bretall, Robert, ed. *The Empirical Theology of Henry Nelson Wieman*. Carbondale: Southern Illinois University Press, 1963.

Peden, Creighton. *Wieman's Empirical Process Philosophy*. Washington, D.C.: University Press of America, 1977.

Shaw, Martin. *Nature's Grace: Essays on H. N. Wieman's Finite Theism*. New York: Peter Lang, 1995.

Wieman, Henry Nelson. *Religious Experience and Scientific Method*. Westport, Conn.: Greenwood, 1970 [1926].

————. *Religious Inquiry: Some Explorations*. Boston: Beacon Press, 1968.

————. *Science Serving Faith*. Edited by Creighton Peden and Charles Willig. Atlanta: Scholars, 1987.

Bernard Meland (1899-1993)

Inbody, Tyron. *The Constructive Theology of Bernard Meland: Postliberal Empirical Realism*. Atlanta: Scholars, 1995.

————. "The Contribution of Bernard Meland to the Development of a Naturalistic Historicist Concept of God." *American Journal of Theology and Philosophy* 20 (Summer 1999): 259-79.

Meland, Bernard. *The Realities of Faith: The Revolution in Cultural Forms*. New York: Oxford University Press, 1962.

————. *Seeds of Redemption*. New York: Macmillan, 1947.

————, ed. *The Future of Empirical Theology*. Chicago: University of Chicago Press, 1969.

Mueller, J. J. *Faith and Appreciative Awareness: The Cultural Theology of Bernard E. Meland*. Washington, D.C.: University Press of America, 1981.

Rogers, Dolores. *The American Empirical Movement in Theology*. New York: Peter Lang, 1990.

Stone, Jerome A. "Bernard Meland and the New Formative Imagery of Our Time." *Zygon* 30 (Summer 1995): 435-49.

Towne, Edgar A. "God and the Chicago School in the Theology of Bernard Meland." *American Journal of Theology and Philosophy* 10 (Jan. 1989): 3-19.

Bernard M. Loomer (1912-85)

Dean, William, and Larry E. Axel, eds. *The Size of God: The Theology of Bernard Loomer in Context.* Macon, Ga.: Mercer University Press, 1987.

Fox, Douglas. "Bernard Loomer's Concept of 'Interconnectedness': A Pious Naturalism." In *God, Values, and Empiricism: Issues in Philosophical Theology,* edited by W. Creighton Peden and Larry E. Axel, 53-63. Macon, Ga.: Mercer University Press, 1989.

Peden, W. Creighton, and Jerome A. Stone. *The Chicago School of Theology — Pioneers in Religious Inquiry.* Vol. 2, *The Later Chicago School, 1919-1988: A. E. Haydon, H. N. Wieman, D. D. Williams, B. E. Meland, B. M. Loomer, J. L. Admas.* Lewiston, N.Y.: Edwin Mellen, 1996. Pp. 285-384.

Daniel D. Williams (1910-73)

Williams, Daniel D. *Essays in Process Theology.* Edited by Perry LeFevre. Chicago: Exploration Press, 1985.

——. *God's Grace and Man's Hope.* New York: Harper and Brothers, 1949.

——. *The Spirit and the Forms of Love.* New York: Harper and Row, 1968.

Alfred North Whitehead (1861-1947)

Hartshorne, Charles. *Whitehead's View of Reality.* New York: Pilgrim Press, 1981.

Hosinski, Thomas. *Stubborn Fact and Creative Advance: An Introduction to the Metaphysics of Alfred North Whitehead.* Lanham, Md.: Rowman and Littlefield, 1993.

Leclerc, Ivor, ed. *The Relevance of Whitehead: Philosophical Essays in Commemoration of the Centenary of the Birth of Alfred North Whitehead.* London: George Allen and Unwin, 1961.

Lowe, Victor, Charles Hartshorne, and A. H. Johnson, eds. *Whitehead and the Modern World: Science, Metaphysics, and Civilization; Three Essays on the Thought of Alfred North Whitehead.* Freeport, N.Y.: Books for Libraries Press, 1972 [1950].

Pols, Edward. *Whitehead's Metaphysics: A Critical Examination of "Process and Reality."* Carbondale: Southern Illinois University Press, 1967.

Whitehead, Alfred North. *Process and Reality: An Essay in Cosmology.* New York: Macmillan, 1960.

——. *Religion in the Making.* New York: Macmillan, 1926.

——. *Science and the Modern World.* New York: Macmillan, 1960 [1925].

Charles Hartshorne (1897-2000)

Gragg, Alan. *Charles Hartshorne.* Peabody, Mass.: Hendrickson, 1991 [1973].

Hartshorne, Charles. *Beyond Humanism: Essays in the Philosophy of Nature.* Lincoln: University of Nebraska Press, Bison Books, 1968 [1937].

——. *The Darkness and the Light: A Philosopher Reflects upon His Fortunate Career and Those Who Made It Possible.* Albany: State University of New York Press, 1990.

———. *The Logic of Perfection and Other Essays in Neo-Classical Metaphysics.* La Salle, Ill.: Open Court, 1962.

———. *Man's Vision of God and the Logic of Theism.* Chicago: Willett, Clark & Co., 1941.

———. *A Natural Theology for Our Time.* La Salle, Ill.: Open Court, 1967.

———. *The Philosophy of Charles Hartshorne.* Edited by Lewis Edwin Hahn. Library of Living Philosophers Series, vol. 20. La Salle, Ill.: Open Court, 1991.

James, Ralph E. *The Concrete God: A New Beginning for Theology — the Thought of Charles Hartshorne.* Indianapolis: Bobbs-Merrill, 1967.

Reede, William L., and Eugene Freeman, eds. *Process and Divinity: Philosophical Essays Presented to Charles Hartshorne.* La Salle, Ill.: Open Court, 1964.

John B. Cobb, Jr. (b. 1925)

Bube, Paul Custodio. *Ethics in John Cobb's Process Theology.* Atlanta: Scholars, 1988.

Caraway, James. *God as Dynamic Actuality: Preliminary Study of the Process Theologies of John B. Cobb, Jr., and Schubert M. Ogden.* Washington, D.C.: University Press of America, 1978.

Cobb, John B., Jr. *A Christian Natural Theology: Based on the Thought of Alfred North Whitehead.* Philadelphia: Westminster, 1965.

———. *Christ in a Pluralistic Age.* Philadelphia: Westminster, 1975.

———. *Living Options in Protestant Theology: A Survey of Methods.* Philadelphia: Westminster, 1962.

———. *The Structure of Christian Existence.* Philadelphia: Westminster, 1967.

Griffin, David Ray, and Joseph C. Hough, Jr., eds. *Theology and the University: Essays in Honor of John B. Cobb, Jr.* Albany: State University of New York Press, 1991.

Griffin, David Ray, and Thomas Altizer, eds. *John Cobb's Theology in Process.* Philadelphia: Westminster, 1977.

David Ray Griffin (b. 1939)

Basinger, David. "Divine Power: Do Process Theists Have a Better Idea?" In *Process Theology,* edited by Ronald Nash, 201-13. Grand Rapids: Baker, 1987.

Blaisdell, Charles R. "Griffin's Theodicy." *Encounter* 50 (Autumn 1989): 367-78.

Griffin, David Ray. *Evil Revisited: Responses and Reconsiderations.* Albany: State University of New York Press, 1991.

———. *A Process Christology.* Philadelphia: Westminster, 1973.

———, et al. *Varieties of Postmodern Theology.* Albany: State University of New York Press, 1989.

Schubert M. Ogden (b. 1928)

Caraway, James. *God as Dynamic Actuality: Preliminary Study of the Process Theologies of John B. Cobb, Jr., and Schubert M. Ogden.* Washington, D.C.: University Press of America, 1978.

Devenish, Philip E., and George L. Goodwin, eds. *Witness and Existence: Essays in Honor of Schubert M. Ogden.* Chicago: University of Chicago Press, 1989.

O'Donnell, John J. *Trinity and Temporality: The Christian Doctrine of God in the Light of Process Theology and the Theology of Hope.* New York: Oxford University Press, 1983.

Ogden, Schubert M. *Christ without Myth: A Study Based on the Theology of Rudolf Bultmann.* New York: Harper, 1961.

————. *The Reality of God and Other Essays.* New York: Harper, 1966.

Paul Tillich (1886-1965)

Kelsey, David H. *The Fabric of Paul Tillich's Theology.* New Haven: Yale University Press, 1967.

Pauck, Wilhelm, and Marion Pauck. *Paul Tillich: His Life and Thought.* New York: Harper and Row, 1976.

Tillich, Paul. "Autobiographical Reflections." In *The Theology of Paul Tillich,* edited by Charles W. Kegley. New York: Pilgrim Press, 1982.

————. *The Future of Religions.* Edited by Jerald C. Brauer. New York: Harper and Row, 1966.

————. *Paul Tillich: Theologian of the Boundaries.* Edited by Mark Kline Taylor. Minneapolis: Fortress, 1991.

————. *Systematic Theology.* 3 vols. in 1. Chicago: University of Chicago Press, 1967.

Langdon B. Gilkey (1919-2004)

Gilkey, Langdon. *Naming the Whirlwind: The Renewal of God-Language.* Indianapolis: Bobbs-Merrill, 1969.

————. *Reaping the Whirlwind: A Christian Interpretation of History.* New York: Seabury Press, 1976.

————. *Religion and the Scientific Future: Reflections on Myth, Science, and Theology.* New York: Harper and Row, 1970.

————. *Shantung Compound: The Story of Men and Women under Pressure.* New York: Harper and Row, 1966.

————. *The Theology of Langdon B. Gilkey: Systematic and Critical Studies.* Edited by Kyle A. Pasewark and Jeff B. Pool. Macon, Ga.: Mercer University Press, 1999.

————. *Through the Tempest: Theological Voyages in a Pluralistic Culture.* Selected and edited by Jeff B. Pool. Minneapolis: Fortress, 1991.

Musser, Donald W., and Joseph L. Price, eds. *The Whirlwind in Culture: Frontiers in Theology; In Honor of Langdon Gilkey.* Bloomington, Ind.: Meyer-Stone Books, 1988.

Walsh, Brian. *Langdon Gilkey: Theologian for a Culture in Decline.* Lanham, Md.: University Press of America, 1991.

Reinhold Niebuhr (1892-1971)

Bingham, June. *Courage to Change: An Introduction to the Life and Thought of Reinhold Niebuhr.* New York: Charles Scribner's, 1972.

Brown, Charles C. *Niebuhr and His Age: Reinhold Niebuhr's Prophetic Role and Legacy.* Foreword by Arthur M. Schlesinger, Jr. New ed. Harrisburg, Pa.: Trinity, 2004.

Fackre, Gabriel. *The Promise of Reinhold Niebuhr.* Philadelphia: J. B. Lippincott, 1970.

Fox, Richard W. *Reinhold Niebuhr: A Biography.* San Francisco: Harper and Row, 1987 [1985].

Gilkey, Langdon. *On Niebuhr: A Theological Study.* Chicago: University of Chicago Press, 2001.

Niebuhr, Reinhold. *Beyond Tragedy: Essays on the Christian Interpretation of History.* New York: Charles Scribner's, 1946 [1937].

———. *Does Civilization Need Religion? A Study in the Social Resources and Limitations of Religion in Modern Life.* New York: Macmillan, 1928 [1927].

———. *Moral Man and Immoral Society: A Study in Ethics and Politics.* New York: Charles Scribner's, 1960.

———. *The Nature and Destiny of Man: A Christian Interpretation.* Vol. 1, *Human Nature.* Introduction by Robin W. Lovin. Louisville: Westminster John Knox, 1996 [1941].

———. *The Nature and Destiny of Man: A Christian Interpretation.* Vol. 2, *Human Destiny.* Louisville: Westminster John Knox, 1996 [1943].

———. *Young Reinhold Niebuhr: His Early Writings, 1911-1931.* Edited with an introduction by William G. Chrystal. Foreword by John C. Bennett. St. Louis: Eden, 1977. Pp. 128-31.

Rasmussen, Larry, ed. *Reinhold Niebuhr: Theologian of Public Life.* Minneapolis: Fortress, 1991.

H. Richard Niebuhr (1894-1962)

Fowler, James. *To See the Kingdom: The Theological Vision of H. Richard Niebuhr.* Lanham, Md.: University Press of America, 1985 [1974].

Irish, Jerry. *The Religious Thought of H. Richard Niebuhr.* Atlanta: John Knox, 1983.

Niebuhr, H. Richard. *Christ and Culture.* New York: Harper Torchbook, 1951.

———. *The Kingdom of God in America.* With a new introduction by Martin E. Marty. Middletown, Conn.: Wesleyan University Press, 1988 [1937].

———. *The Meaning of Revelation.* New York: Macmillan, 1967 [1941].

———. *Radical Monotheism and Western Culture: With Supplementary Essays.* Foreword by James M. Gustafson. Louisville: Westminster John Knox, 1993 [1960].

———. *The Responsible Self: An Essay in Christian Moral Philosophy.* Introduction by James M. Gustafson. Foreword by William Schweiker. Louisville: Westminster John Knox, 1999 [1963].

———. *The Social Sources of Denominationalism.* Cleveland: World Publishing, 1968 [1929].

———. *Theology, History, and Culture: Major Unpublished Writings.* Edited by William Stacy Johnson. Foreword by Richard R. Niebuhr. New Haven: Yale University Press, 1996.

Ramsey, Paul. *Faith and Ethics: The Theology of H. Richard Niebuhr.* New York: Harper and Row, 1965.

12 Europe's Emphasis on Relating Christ to the World

It was not just the overpowering figure of Karl Barth that swayed European Protestant theology more toward a christocentric position. In Europe virtually all theological education, i.e., for future professors and future pastors, occurs in the same institution. While these institutions are not always affiliated with denominations, the churches usually have a say over appointment and curricula. Therefore in general, theological education in Europe is much more geared toward the perceived needs of the church and also more Christ centered, since future leaders of the Christian churches are educated in these theological schools. In the United States, however, the (denominational) seminaries train future clergy, while graduate schools train future teachers for both seminaries and religion departments. Since the demand for teachers in religion departments is much larger than the demand in seminaries, the graduate schools also train for areas that cover the whole spectrum of the world's religions, something that is hardly done in European theological faculties. It is not accidental therefore that two European theologians so far apart in their starting points as Karl Barth and Paul Tillich claimed that theology is a function of the church. Moreover, in many European countries there is a clear distinction between the philosophy of religion, which has a clearly theistic focus, and systematic theology, which is much more christocentric.

Scottish Christocentrism

The Gospel Matters: Peter T. Forsyth

Peter T. Forsyth (1848-1921) has been called "an English forerunner of Karl Barth."[1] He was born in Aberdeen, Scotland, as son of a postal carrier in a household of meager income. Despite his disadvantage of background, he managed to enter Aberdeen University in 1864 and graduated with first-class honors in classics. After a time as assistant lecturer and tutor, he spent a semester studying under Ritschl at Göttingen University in 1870. He returned again to college, but had to quit because of ill health. He was ordained to the ministry of the Congregational Church in 1876 and served in several pastorates till 1901. Then he became principal of Hackney Theological College in London, and later, dean of the faculty of theology in the University of London. In 1905 he also served as chairman of the congregational union of England and Wales. He wrote more than twenty-five books and hundreds of articles on a wide range of subjects, such as *Christian Perfection* (1899), *The Person and Place of Jesus Christ* (1909), *Justification and God* (1916), *Lectures on Church and Sacraments* (1917), etc. He gradually moved from a liberal position to a more "positive" one. This perspective was especially evident in the "new theology" controversy of 1907, when R. J. Campbell, pastor of City Temple in London and one of the most influential of the Nonconformists, published a manifesto of this new theology in which he declared: "The starting-point of the New Theology is belief in the immanence of God, and the essential oneness of God and man. . . . We believe that Jesus is and was divine, but so are we. His mission was to make us realize our divinity and our oneness with God."[2] Forsyth attacked this new theology and its central weakness, charging that it offered virtual self-salvation rather than insisting upon the divine act of God.

Forsyth's position can be gleaned very well from *Positive Preaching and Modern Mind*, the Lyman Beecher Lectures on preaching of 1907 he had been invited to give at Yale University. He started off his lectures by declaring that "with its preaching Christianity stands or falls."[3] This means that the center of

---

1. So Geoffrey Wainwright, foreword to *A Sense of the Holy: An Introduction to the Thought of P. T. Forsyth through His Writings*, by P. T. Forsyth (Pasadena, Calif.: Wipf and Stock, 1996), ix.

2. As quoted by Robert McAfee Brown, *P. T. Forsyth: Prophet for Today* (Philadelphia: Westminster, 1952), 27.

3. See Peter T. Forsyth, *Positive Preaching and Modern Mind* (Cincinnati: Jennings and Graham, 1907), 3, for this and the following quote. For following quotes from this book the page numbers appear in the text.

the Christian faith is the kerygma, or the proclamation of the gospel. Yet Forsyth leaves no doubt that "the Christian preacher is not the successor of the Greek orator, but of the Hebrew prophet. The orator comes with but an inspiration, the prophet comes with a revelation." Central for the kerygma is revelation initiated by God's doing. One does not proclaim what is one's opinion, but rather the gospel. The gospel focuses on grace, namely, God's "undeserved and unbought pardon and redemption of us in the face of our sin, in the face of the world-sin, under such moral conditions as are prescribed by His revelation of His holy love in Jesus Christ and Him crucified" (5-6). Here we have in a nutshell Forsyth's whole theology. He believed that though we are sinful God redeems us out of his free grace. God does this through Jesus Christ who on our account was crucified.

The Bible is kerygma, "not the history of an idea, but of a long divine act" (10). Forsyth had no problem with the issue of historicity. He conceded that the Bible is not God's word "but the *record* of God's Word" (12). Nevertheless, "it is a direct record not of Christ's biography, but of Christ's gospel" (13). Almost in the vein of Kähler, Forsyth declared: "Remember that Christ did not come to bring a Bible, but to bring a Gospel. The Bible arose afterwards from the Gospel to serve the Gospel" (15). The Bible is the medium of the gospel and was created by faith in the gospel and in turn creates faith among us. Faith comes from listening to the kerygma, as Forsyth emphasized together with the Reformers. Yet Forsyth was not a biblicist, as he showed by treating the issue of the virgin birth of Jesus. While he did not want to decide whether the virgin birth was indispensable for Christ's entry into the world, he insisted that if it were, that would also necessitate that it was a requirement for Christ's work of redemption. Forsyth did not argue historically, but theologically. Instead of an orthodox theology he proposed an evangelical theology, by which he meant a "theology which does full justice to the one creative principle of grace" (205). In contrast to liberal theology, it begins with the word and not with the world, with faith and not with thought, with grace and not with love, with holiness and not with kindness (cf. 248). It does not bring the world to the word, but the word to the world, because its task is to proclaim the word. And it emphasizes God's holiness and not his kindness, which often was the trademark of liberalism.

Three points are essential for modern theology according to Forsyth. (1) *"It is a Gospel of Jesus the Eternal Son of God."* This means that Christ is the center of any theology. And again just like Kähler, Forsyth emphasized: "The historic Jesus is personally identical with the Christian principle or with the Eternal Christ." The unique relationship to God constituted his person, and "the idea of a metaphysical sonship is not absurd" (251). (2) *"It is a Gospel of Jesus the Mediator."* He is the mediator between God and us and mediates the holy grace of God. "He is the Redeemer, not the champion, of mankind" (253). (3) "*Christianity is a Gospel of Christ's resurrection.* The same Jesus who died also rose, and lives as the King of heavenly Glory and Lord of human destiny" (255). The resurrection of Christ is no proof or evidence in the same way that Jesus never used his miracles to prove something, but the resurrection shows his divine power. "The resurrection of Christ, is thus not evidential, but it is real. It is not the surest thing in scientific history, but it is an essential fact to Christian faith" (257). He rightly claimed that the apostles did not critically examine the evidence for the resurrection, because what impressed them was the returned savior.

Forsyth wanted to get away from the scientific objections to the central tenets of the Christian faith and instead emphasized that revelation and resurrection evidence themselves in the Christian faith. Therefore he claimed that the "present fertile obsession by 'the historical Jesus'" amounts to nothing for the Christian faith. "It is impossible to treat Christ adequately, except theologically and personally."[4] The historical-critical investigation cannot threaten or endanger the Christian faith, because that faith is evidenced internally through the Word. Forsyth was in touch with German theology and knew both its dangers and promises. He anticipated Barth's emphasis on revelation as God's self-disclosure and on a christocentric faith. Since the cross remained central for him, he escaped Barth's triumphalism.

Christ-Centered Knowledge of God: The Baillie Brothers

Another Scottish theologian in close touch with Continental theology was **John Baillie** (1886-1960). He was born in a Scottish Presbyterian parsonage in the highlands of Scotland. There prevailed a deep and sincere faith with a heavy emphasis on the sense of the holy in the twice-a-year celebrations of the Lord's Supper.[5] He attended Edinburgh University, where he received a good introduction to philosophy, and then had four years of theological training at New College in Edinburgh.

During this time he spent a summer in Germany, where he was especially attracted by Wilhelm Herrmann at Marburg. Through the influence of Kant and Schleiermacher he gradually realized while he was in seminary that religion

4. Peter T. Forsyth, *The Cruciality of the Cross* (London: Hodder and Stoughton, 1910), 169.

5. Cf. John Baillie, "Confessions of a Transplanted Scot," in *Contemporary American Autobiographies*, ed. Vergilius Ferm (New York: Round Table, 1933), 2:34.

is in possession of an insight into reality that is all its own and cannot be reached by any other means. Yet he did not accept the subjectivistic line in Schleiermacher's understanding of religion, nor did he equate religion with feeling, nor with the psychologizing he sensed in William James. For him religious faith became "a way of knowledge which is at least equal to any other in point of reliability and which leads us into the presence of a Reality that is not discoverable by any other means."[6] In this way he also felt an affinity to Barth, who most likely was at Marburg at the same time he was, but who picked up very different things from Herrmann. In contrast to Barth, Baillie did not reject a point of contact in our world with God. Another insight, which Baillie gleaned from Herrmann, was the intimate relation between faith and morals, between our religious belief and our consciousness of obligation.

Having finished his theological training, he had to serve four years in France during World War I. This experience forced him to abandon his sheltered existence, a move that helped him better understand the spiritual needs and capacities of normal humanity. Baillie held several positions in North America, following calls to professorships at Auburn Theological Seminary in New York, Immanuel College in Toronto, and Union Theological Seminary in New York, before returning to his native Scotland in 1934. There he became professor of divinity in Edinburgh till his retirement in 1956. He also served as principal of New College and dean of the faculty of divinity at Edinburgh University, was one of the presidents of the World Council of Churches, worked also on the Faith and Order Commission, and served as chaplain to the queen in Scotland.

Of his more than twenty books, we refer to three that are typical of his thinking: *Our Knowledge of God* (1939), *The Belief in Progress* (1951), and *The Idea of Revelation in Recent Thought* (1956). In *Our Knowledge of God* Baillie started out by contrasting Barth with Brunner, which is not surprising because he wrote a preface to the English translation of the literary exchange between the two. He sided with Brunner and quoted Calvin against Barth because Barth's denial of any knowledge of God would also mean a total obliteration of our humanity. He questioned whether "the denial to man of all participation in the divine nature, and of even a delegated creativity, does not tend to issue in a denial of all liberty in human action."[7] Baillie preferred the dialectic that "though all that is in us good or of responsiveness is His, and in the last resort even His *alone,* yet it is truly our own *as well.*"[8] We are always creatures of

---

6. John Baillie, "Confessions," 51.

7. John Baillie, *Our Knowledge of God* (London: Oxford Paperbacks, 1963 [1939]), 233.

8. John Baillie, *Our Knowledge of God,* 234.

God, and therefore whatever we have is God's. Because of our creatureliness there is something in us that corresponds to God.

In *The Belief in Progress* (1951) Baillie traced the notion of progress throughout history, showing that in antiquity there was a profoundly pessimistic outlook on history. The early fathers of the Christian church initially assumed this perspective, but little by little they replaced it with a more optimistic assessment. Augustine in particular showed that history is moving forward to the God-destined completion. "For the Christian, terrestrial history is a forward-moving process of a very special kind. . . . A definite beginning, a middle or focal point, and a definite end."[9] God created the world, then came the fall, and therefore God sent Jesus the Savior. This event marks the watershed of history and provides the key to the whole of it. From there on, Christians look forward to his coming. Therefore the time in which we live now is the final era. The modern idea of progress, however, which has arisen only within Christian civilization, is "a heresy" forgetting much of what has been vitally Christian.[10] It ascribes to humanity an autonomous dignity and importance that had been denied to it by traditional Christian understanding. If history is left to itself, it will never come to an end, or if it does, it will again end in finitude. This is very different from the progress for which Christians may hope, radiating from the Christian center of history and moving toward Christ as its fulfillment.

In *The Idea of Revelation in Recent Thought* (1956), Baillie shows again that he attentively listened to the Continental theological discourse. With Barth he understands revelation as divine self-disclosure that occurs from the divine subject to the human. According to the Bible, it is not a propositional revelation, but it discloses "nothing less than God's own will and purpose."[11] In revealing his will and purpose, God always reveals himself in actions, as we can see in the Bible. It is essentially the story of the acts of God. Since the message of the prophets arises out of the course of events they have experienced and interpreted, event and interpretation together is God's word to us. The Word was then made flesh in Jesus Christ. "This is the full and final revelation that gathers up all other revelation into itself."[12] Therefore this revelation stands out most clearly. It elicits our response, and "the Christian name for this response is faith."[13] Faith is not primarily assent, as it was understood during a great part of Christian history. Though that element dare not be neglected, faith is particu-

---

9. John Baillie, *The Belief in Progress* (New York: Charles Scribner's, 1951), 84.

10. John Baillie, *The Belief in Progress,* 95.

11. John Baillie, *The Idea of Revelation in Recent Thought* (New York: Columbia University Press, 1965 [1956]), 28.

12. John Baillie, *The Idea of Revelation,* 69.

13. John Baillie, *The Idea of Revelation,* 85.

larly trust, a reliance on Christ for our salvation; it allows us to let our lives be shaped by our response to that grace. We see in Baillie's approach a consistent attempt to mediate both the biblical witness and the insights of the Christian tradition and apply them to issues of the present. In this approach he is not very different from his brother Donald.

Donald M. Baillie (1887-1954) was born, like his brother John, in the Scottish highlands. When his father died, his mother moved to Inverness, where the boys received their first education. Donald enrolled at Edinburgh University, where he excelled in moral philosophy and metaphysics, and he went on to New College to study theology. Similar to his brother, he spent summers in Heidelberg and Marburg studying with Herrmann and Johannes Weiss. In 1913 he graduated, was licensed, and served as an assistant pastor. Since for health reasons he could not do his duty in the army, he served in parishes. In 1918 he was ordained and was called by the United Free Church to a parish in a small coastal town. In 1921 he was already an examiner for theology at St. Andrews, and from 1923 to 1930 he served in a second pastorate.

In 1926 he was asked to conduct the Kerr Lectures at Glasgow College of the United Free Church of Scotland, which resulted in his first book, *Faith in God and Its Christian Consummation*. In a long introductory chapter, he traced the history of the concept of faith all the way through Greek antiquity and the Old Testament up to the New Testament. Faith is neither custom nor is it dependent on reason, Baillie asserted, and in contrast to what Schleiermacher and William James had taught, it cannot be based on religious experience either. Faith is also not a human activity by which we will to believe, because this would exclude faith as a gift from God. Yet one can understand faith as based upon our moral consciousness, because "it is the elemental sense of the Divine which expresses itself in all our values, though not completely in any of them or in all of them put together."[14] This means there is a religious a priori that comes to expression in the practical moral lives of the people. But in taking the moral faith as a starting point, Baillie rejected the idea of the origin of faith or religion in animism by some kind of primitive speculation or in fear, demarking his position from Söderblom and from the British social anthropologist Robert R. Marett (1866-1943) and their notions of religion. He was also critical of Rudolf Otto and his theory of the numinous. The object of faith, however, can be found in a religion, because religion gives us God and "God is what we really desire in every simple, spontaneous, disinterested choice of the ideal in our daily lives. God is what we really love and wherever we truly love our fellows.

14. Donald M. Baillie, *Faith in God and Its Christian Consummation*, foreword by John MacIntyre, new ed. (London: Faber and Faber, 1964 [1927]), 194.

God is what we dimly know, even in apprehending our duty in the common-place details of practice."[15] Finally, Baillie moved to Jesus whom we encounter in the Gospels. "It is only through Jesus Himself that we can ever believe His Gospel of the love of God, and so Christian faith in God is faith 'in Christ.'"[16] But then, Baillie tells us, in Jesus we are faced with the paradox that he who shows us God and his love ends himself in suffering and death on the cross. There is neither logical consistency in the Christian faith, nor pessimism, nor an easy optimism. Baillie concluded: "We will rather rejoice in an 'optimism which is grounded in pessimism,' acknowledging the terrible reality of evil, yet committing our way entirely to the personal God of infinite power and wisdom and love who is revealed to us in the Gospel of Jesus as our Father."[17]

In *God Was in Christ* (1947), Baillie focused more directly on God's self-disclosure in Jesus Christ and went beyond the paradox of the cross by explaining this as Christ's atoning death, with extensive recourse to the early fathers of the Christian faith. He picked up the dialogue with Continental theology, here especially with the form critics. Drawing on the insights of C. H. Dodd and others, he did not give in to historical defeatism, but assured "that the historical personality of Jesus comes to stand out unmistakably."[18] But the Jesus of history is not sufficient because Jesus is not simply the way to God, contrary to what Harnack had emphasized. God acted in him and therefore God is not just like Christ, but God was in Christ. This means that "christology stands for a Christian interpretation of history, but it can stand for that only because it stands for the conviction that God became man in the historical person of Jesus."[19] In contrast to other interpretations of histories, Christian history does not go in circles nor is it a continuous up and down with highs and lows incessantly following each other as when one treads water, but it has a definite goal, the entrance into heaven made possible through Christ's atoning action.

In 1934 Baillie was appointed to the chair of systematic theology in the University of St. Andrews, which had conferred on him an honorary doctorate of divinity the previous year. He enjoyed now a constant stream of visitors who stayed with him, from Karl Barth and Paul Tillich, to Rudolf Bultmann and Emil Brunner, and many others. Students also came, especially from the United States, to study under him. Yet the only book of any size that he wrote during

15. D. M. Baillie, *Faith in God*, 227-28.

16. D. M. Baillie, *Faith in God*, 260.

17. D. M. Baillie, *Faith in God*, 301.

18. Donald M. Baillie, *God Was in Christ: An Essay on Incarnation and Atonement* (London: Faber and Faber, 1961 [1947]), 58.

19. D. M. Baillie, *God Was in Christ*, 79.

this period was *God Was in Christ*. This work immediately established his reputation, both on the Continent, being translated into German, and in America.

Donald Baillie was concerned for Christian unity and worked in the Faith and Order Commission of the World Council of Churches, taking part in many of its conferences. He was also the convener of the Inter-Church Relations Committee of the Church of Scotland, and one of the representatives to confer with the Church of England with a view to closer relations. He was also active in the Student Christian Movement. When Bultmann heard of his early death, he wrote to his brother John — Donald Baillie was never married — "That I should have been permitted to know him remains as one of the most important and significant of my experiences. . . . *[God Was in Christ]* is the most significant book of our time in the field of Christology. It is a model of versatile and understanding dialogue with other theological and religious outlooks, and above all of interpretation of the dogmatic tradition."[20] The Baillie brothers, being typical of much mid-twentieth-century British theology, were mediators between Continental theology, the tradition of the Fathers, and the philosophical trends on the British Isles. This can also be said, to a large extent, for Thomas F. Torrance.

Theology as a Science of the Triune God: Thomas F. Torrance

Thomas F. Torrance (b. 1913) is one of the leading Reformed theologians in the Anglo-Saxon world. He was born in China of missionary parents, his father from the Church of Scotland and his mother an Anglican. In 1927 he, his siblings, and his mother moved back to Scotland, while his father stayed in China for another seven years. Thomas entered Edinburgh University in 1931 and studied classics and philosophy, one of his teachers being Norman Kemp Smith (1872-1958), the well-known Kant expert. Three years later he entered New College in Edinburgh to study theology. There he became acquainted with the theology of Karl Barth. Once he had obtained a scholarship, he pursued his doctoral studies in Basel under Barth, from 1937 onward. His Ph.D. thesis was entitled "The Doctrine of Grace and the Apostolic Fathers" and was published in book form in 1948. After only one year of studies at Basel, John Baillie persuaded him to accept a position at Auburn Theological Seminary in New York City. The following year Princeton University offered the just twenty-six-year-

---

20. As quoted by John Baillie, "Donald: A Brother's Impression," in Donald M. Baillie, *The Theology of the Sacraments and Other Papers*, with a biographical essay by John Baillie (London: Faber and Faber, 1957), 35.

old Torrance a position in their new department of religion. Since it was 1939 and a war was imminent, Torrance decided to return to Scotland to become an army chaplain. There was a waiting list, however, and he spent one year at Oriel College in Oxford working on his thesis. Then he served a small country town parish in Scotland, and only in 1944 could he serve as an army chaplain in the Middle East and then in Italy. In 1947 he could finally complete his doctoral studies, and upon that moved to Aberdeen to become pastor of the large Beechgrove Parish Church.

In 1949 his first book, *Calvin's Doctrine of Man*, appeared. In it he skillfully arranged Calvin's own assertions, concluding that "Calvin's position would seem to be that God allows sufficient light to reach man in his perverse will that he may see the distinctions between good and evil, but he cannot see his way out to God so long as he remains in his perversity."[21] This means that humanity cannot reach God on its own, but it knows the difference between good and evil. To that Torrance added: "Calvin insists upon the necessity of the Word for the understanding of nature, and of God who manifests Himself in nature."[22] Neither nature nor God can be understood correctly without God's word, meaning God's self-disclosure. Torrance conceded that, as a follower of Calvin, Barth was basically correct in insisting on the word of God to adequately understand both God and nature. Nevertheless, he saw that Barth overstated his case in eliminating any knowledge of God, even to the point that humanity could not distinguish between good and evil. This book was the first of more than thirty books Torrance wrote, covering virtually every significant topic in theology.

Torrance also founded the Scottish Church Theological Society and started the *Scottish Journal of Theology*, which he edited for more than thirty years. In 1950 he was called to the New College in Edinburgh for a professorship in church history. Two years later he switched to Christian dogmatics at the same institution. In 1952 he also began the immense task of overseeing the English translation of Barth's *Church Dogmatics*, which even more intimately acquainted him with Barth's later theology. He served on the Faith and Order Commission from 1952 to 1962, was one of the representatives of the Reformed churches in the dialogue with the Eastern Orthodox Church, and was moderator of the Church of Scotland in 1976/77.

Though he came from a christocentric trinitarian perspective, it became more and more important for Torrance to show that Christian theology is an enterprise that is on par with other scientific enterprises. It is not an esoteric pursuit. For instance, in his 1996 publication *The Christian Doctrine of God:*

---

21. T. F. Torrance, *Calvin's Doctrine of Man* (Grand Rapids: Eerdmans, 1957 [1949]), 158.
22. Torrance, *Calvin's Doctrine of Man*, 171.

One Being Three Persons, Torrance stated in the first sentence of the introduction: "The Christian doctrine of God is to be understood from within the unique, definitive and final self-revelation of God in Jesus Christ his only begotten Son, that is, from within the self-revelation of God as God became man for us and our salvation, in accordance with its proclamation in the Gospel and its actualization through the Holy Spirit in the apostolic foundation of the Church."[23] There is nothing beyond or outside God's self-disclosure that could rival it. In talking about a Christian doctrine of God, we must start with that self-revelation that also had a purpose, namely, our salvation. A Christian doctrine of God, however, cannot be elaborated without being in accordance with its proclamation in the gospel. Otherwise, Torrance contends, it is not just unbiblical, but also not Christian. And furthermore, this Christian doctrine is actualized through the Holy Spirit in the apostolic foundation of the church. The church, not being a historical accident, but founded by the apostles, actualizes this doctrine of God through its worship (creeds) and through its theology.

To arrive at an adequate Christian doctrine of God, three components are necessary: God's self-disclosure in Jesus Christ, the apostolic tradition, and the church's witness. It is peculiar for the Christian faith that according to it God communicated himself to us through God's word. This word was incarnate in Jesus and imparted to us God's spirit, so that we can really know God, not just for himself, but primarily as God is in the saving activity in history. It goes without much saying that Torrance shows his indebtedness to Barth, but beyond that, especially in his trinitarian nod to Athanasius and the Greek Fathers, and with his references to the biblical testimony to the Reformed theology. In contrast to Barth, who did not have such an explicit interest in patristics, Torrance also wanted to show that theology is a scientific enterprise and, contrary to what Barth would say, that it has something to do with science. Perhaps here we also see that we are in a different era. Living within the closed scientific worldview of the nineteenth century, Barth was convinced that any openness to science would ultimately suffocate theology. But for Torrance the situation was different. He realized that even natural science is no longer so sure that it can provide an objective view of its object under investigation.

Torrance defined theology as "the unique science devoted to the knowledge of God, differing from other sciences by the uniqueness of its object which can be apprehended only on its own terms and from within the actual situation it has created in our existence in making itself known."[24] Theology is the

23. Thomas F. Torrance, *The Christian Doctrine of God: One Being Three Persons* (Edinburgh: T. & T. Clark, 1996), 1.

24. Thomas F. Torrance, *Theological Science* (Edinburgh: T. & T. Clark, 1996 [1969]), 281.

unique science devoted to the knowledge of God, just as biology is the unique science devoted to the knowledge of the biosphere, the sphere of living things. (This aspect of theology as a science was later picked up by Wolfhart Pannenberg [see chap. 15].) As a science theology is a human endeavor in quest for truth to apprehend God as far as it can, to understand what it apprehends, and to speak clearly and carefully about that. Therefore it has in common with all other sciences that it is a human inquiry that moves forward toward active exploration and tests the truthfulness of the knowledge it gained by tracing it back to the reality it already knows. Like all other science, it proceeds by the reference to an externally given reality. And like other science, it operates without a preconceived metaphysics, meaning that any metaphysics it carries with it may be called into question, such as traditional natural theology. Yet it must then develop and use appropriate metaphysical conceptions, because it must clarify the nature and the status of the realities to which its statements refer. And finally, similar to other sciences, theology as a special science comes up against a line through which it "cannot penetrate and cannot even attempt to pass without inconsistency and error."[25]

Even theology is limited in its results. It does not know everything, and what it knows it does not know definitely. Otherwise it would be a science *by* God and not *of* God. But there are also differences between theology and other sciences, such as the proximate objectivity in theology, meaning that we can know God only insofar as God objectifies himself within the structured objectivities of our world. How God is in God's self, we do not know. This is different with other sciences where the object investigated is even ultimately an object within our world. Another difference is the issue of truth, because for the other sciences a scientific fact is always communicable because it is one of many comparable facts. "Theological truth . . . is unique, and cannot be abstracted from its concrete particularity and be generalized, or interpreted as an instance of general truth."[26] If we were to neglect its concrete particularity, meaning revelation in Jesus Christ, we would move from theology to comparative religion.

Then there is also a difference in subjectivity. While in other sciences the subjective moment should be excluded as much as possible, in theological science "the personal is a predicate of the object and . . . the object demands reciprocity from the person of the theologian."[27] This means that we do not start with a disjunction between subject and object, but with a union of object and subject right from the beginning. Especially with the last point of the difference

25. Torrance, *Theological Science*, 290.
26. Torrance, *Theological Science*, 302.
27. Torrance, *Theological Science*, 305.

in subjectivity, we notice again how important it is for Torrance that though theology is a human enterprise, its actual subject that makes it possible is not the human person but God. Only through God can God be known. While we notice in this approach an affinity to the scholasticism of Barth, Torrance is much more open in his system, since he realizes that the modern scientific enterprise of which theology is part could only arise from the Judeo-Christian context. Therefore theology is decisive for him since it is "the bond of cultural unity" that on a deeper level brings all pursuit of knowledge and learning together.[28]

English Conservative Criticism

Theology on the British Isles is not confined to Scotland. We must remember, for instance, the famous Cambridge trio of the nineteenth century. B. F. Westcott (1825-1901), F. J. A. Hort (1828-92), and J. B. Lightfoot (1829-89) introduced wider circles of British theology to new developments in historical and critical biblical research. Their work was on a high scholarly level. They reached rather conservative conclusions, confining themselves to textual criticism and historical research in Paul, the early fathers, and the development of the ecclesial office, while the source theory of the Gospels or literary criticism was not yet in their view. In 1881 Westcott and Hort issued a Greek edition of the New Testament. Their work was continued in the twentieth century by Dodd, Moule, and Nineham.

The Biblical Basis: Charles H. Dodd, Charles F. D. Moule, D. E. Nineham

Charles Harold Dodd (1884-1973), a Welshman and a Congregationalist, studied in Berlin in 1907 and attended lectures there by Adolf von Harnack. In 1930 he began to serve as Rylands Professor of Biblical Criticism and Exegesis in Manchester, and after 1935 as Norves-Holse Professor in Cambridge. He is especially known for his studies in the Gospel of John and for his "realized" eschatology, a concept picked up later by John A. T. Robinson (1913-83).

With the concept of a "realized eschatology" Dodd wanted to answer the question Albert Schweitzer had posed: How was it possible that the false hope

---

28. Thomas F. Torrance, "The University within a Christian Culture," in Thomas F. Torrance, *The Christian Frame of Mind: Reason, Order, and Openness in Theology and Natural Science,* introduction by W. Jim Neidhardt (Colorado Springs: Helmers and Howard, 1989), 143.

of an early return of Christ in glory could not touch the substance of the Christian hope? He suggested that the first Christians expected the last judgment and the coming of Christ almost any day. "During the first century events occurred from time to time which raised hopes that it was at hand; but they were always disappointed, as similar hopes have been disappointed many times since."[29] Though their hopes for an early return of Jesus Christ proved to be an illusion, gradually they realized that the decisive event had already happened: Christ had come. God had confronted the Jewish people in his kingdom, power, and glory. This world had become the scene of the divine drama, in which the eternal issues were laid bare. It was the hour of decision. It was "realized eschatology"[30] because in Jesus the eternal entered decisively into history. This means that while Jesus used the traditional apocalyptic symbolism to indicate the "otherworldly" or absolute character of the kingdom of God, he used parables to enforce and illustrate the idea that the kingdom of God had come upon people then and there. The coming of the kingdom of God even implied a judgment because those who censured Jesus for his work and teaching pronounced judgment upon themselves. They excluded themselves from the kingdom. "The act of acceptance or of rejection determines the whole direction of a man's life, and so of his destiny."[31]

Finally, the first Christians realized that God's victory was won by Christ, and that they already shared in it. They did not, however, discard the hope for another coming of Christ. They knew about the tensions between realization and expectation: God's victory was won, yet there were many difficulties to overcome. But how was the victory won? Dodd pointed to the characteristic signs of the Day of the Lord. Jesus, as presented by the Gospel writers, had announced threatening catastrophes that were more than mere personal disasters. And he proclaimed a final triumph. He would rise from the dead, the kingdom of God would come with power, and the Son of Man would come with the clouds of heaven. All this points to the same thing: immediate victory out of apparent defeat.[32] He returned to life after his death, gathered his disturbed followers, empowered them with his Holy Spirit, and sent them out into the world.[33] So a new

---

29. C. H. Dodd, *The Coming of Christ — Four Broadcast Addresses for the Season of Advent* (Cambridge: Cambridge University Press, 1951), 7.

30. C. H. Dodd, *Parables of the Kingdom* (Glasgow: Fount Paperbacks, 1978), 151.

31. Dodd, *Parables of the Kingdom*, 150.

32. Cf. Dodd, *The Coming of Christ*, 12-14.

33. Cf. C. H. Dodd, *The Interpretation of the Fourth Gospel* (Cambridge: University Press, 1968 [1953]), 405-7, where he emphasizes that already John (13:31–14:31) understood Christ's return "in a sense different from that of popular Christian eschatology." After the death of Jesus, and because of it, Jesus' followers will enter into union with him as their living Lord. Thus death

era started with the kingdom of Christ on earth. Christ's resurrection invested him with power and glory, and he became the invisible king of all people. This source of power kept the church alive throughout the centuries.

> The Church prays, "Thy Kingdom come"; "Come, Lord Jesus." As it prays, it remembers that the Lord did come, and with Him came the Kingdom of God. Uniting memory with aspiration, it discovers that He comes. He comes in His Cross and Passion; He comes in the glory of His Father with the holy angels. Each Communion is not a stage in the process by which His coming draws gradually nearer, or a milestone on the road by which we slowly approach the distant goal of the Kingdom of God on earth. It is a re-living of the decisive moment at which He came.
>
> The preaching of the Church is directed towards reconstituting in the experience of individuals the hour of decision which Jesus brought. . . . It assumes that history in the individual life is of the same stuff as history at large; that is, it is significant so far as it serves to bring men face to face with God in His Kingdom, power and glory.[34]

Dodd's magnificent interpretation of the existential impact of eschatology also wrestled with another line of thought in the New Testament. Dodd had realized that some passages in the New Testament mention a breakdown of the physical universe before Christ's coming. Though he did not want to take the imagery of falling stars and darkening sun literally, he knew that the most elegant symbolic interpretation cannot do justice to the reality behind it. Thus he asserted that the final coming of Christ will not be a coming in history, because the coming of Christ in history has already been fulfilled in his resurrection, but "*beyond* history."[35] If we were to hope for it as an event in history, Dodd realized, we might be tempted to see it too close in parallel to the restoration of the kingdom of David, which was the utopia of popular Jewish hopes at the time of Jesus. But Jesus expressly rejected such thought, and no alternative utopia is suggested. "There is no hint that the Kingdom of God is Utopia."[36]

The attempt to escape both from an antiquated cosmology and from seeking the coming of the kingdom in an earthly utopia led Dodd to a

---

marks his departure from this earth, while resurrection stands for his enthronement in power and his return.

34. Dodd, *Parables of the Kingdom,* 151-52. Cf. also his *The Founder of Christianity* (New York: Macmillan, 1970), 172, where he again emphasizes the experience of a new corporate life, made possible because God himself had come to humanity in a way altogether new.

35. Cf. Dodd, *The Coming of Christ,* 17.

36. Dodd, *Parables of the Kingdom,* 154.

transcendentalistic approach that asserts the eschaton in the future but beyond history. Dodd did not absolutize this approach but tried to balance it with an equal emphasis on the existential now of the aspired eschaton. He concluded that when John emphasized in his Gospel that *now* the judgment of this world had come, he was not mistaken, and whenever people believed that the Lord was near and the judgment was to come, they were not mistaken, because Christ comes beyond space and time. Although the blessedness of God's kingdom may be enjoyed here and now, "it is never exhausted in any experience that falls within the bounds of space and time."[37] But when all history is taken up into the larger whole of God's eternal purpose, Christ will come the last time, everything will reach its fulfillment, and we will see our lives the way God sees them. Dodd employed the methodological insights of form criticism in search of the historical Jesus and arrived at conservative results regarding the historical authenticity of the scriptural tradition.

Charles F. D. Moule (b. 1908) continued the tradition of critical orthodoxy but was also influenced by the German schools of interpretation. From 1951 to 1973 he occupied the Lady Margaret Chair of Divinity at Cambridge and was especially interested in the origins of the Christology of Paul, for whom he believed Christ is a corporate figure. New Testament Christology is not the result of the general impact of the religious environment. There is a direct line of continuity between Jesus' self-understanding and the church's christological interpretation of him.

British New Testament scholarship was not simply critically conservative, however. **D. E. Nineham** (b. 1920), for instance, emphasized in his published lectures, *The Use and Abuse of the Bible* (1976), that the New Testament past is irretrievable. Though a tentative historical outline of a reconstructed life of Jesus might be given, it does not support contemporary Christian apologetic.

Connecting the Classical Tradition with Modernity: John Macquarrie, Richard G. Swinburne, John H. Hick

The predominance of the Anglican and Catholic tradition with its strong influence on classical and historical training produced a number of significant historians and patristic scholars in England. Geoffrey William Hugo Lampe (1912-80), an Anglican theologian and professor of theology at the University of Birmingham after 1953, was but one. He moved from a Barthian neoorthodoxy to an outspoken theological liberalism in which he advocated the meaninglessness

---

37. Dodd, *Parables of the Kingdom,* 169, and *The Coming of Christ,* 19-25.

of the trinitarian orthodoxy of the Athanasian Creed. He said modern theologians should not simply be content to accumulate fresh insights from the past, but should also be prepared to modify or abandon earlier conclusions. Maurice F. Wiles (b. 1929), regius professor of divinity at the University of Oxford, also a patristic scholar, followed lines similar to Lampe's and contributed with Nineham to the volume *The Myth of God Incarnate* (1977), edited by the philosopher of religion John Hick. Here he showed in the introductory essay that the abandonment of the incarnation as a metaphysical claim about the person of Jesus would not lead to discarding the truth of God's self-giving love, and the role of Jesus in bringing that vision to life in the world. This volume created quite a stir and was countered by more conservative theologians with *The Truth of God Incarnate,* published the same year.

When logical positivism became the dominant stream in mid-twentieth-century England, there was a group at Oxford, the metaphysicals, who attempted to develop a full Christian response to that philosophical climate. The group included Austin Farrer (1904-68), Michael Foster (1903-59), Richard Hare (1904-66), Eric Mascall (1905-93), and Basil Mitchell (b. 1917). They produced *Faith and Logic* (1957), edited by Mitchell, as a public demonstration that faith was philosophically not indefensible. Faith can neither be established nor refuted by empirical evidence, though it has empirical application. Later Mitchell argued in *The Justification of Religious Belief* (1973) that the Christian view was sustainable cumulatively because of its capacity to make sense of all the evidence.

John Macquarrie (b. 1919), a Presbyterian by birth and a Scot, became an Anglican while teaching at Union Theological Seminary in New York (1962-69). In 1969 he accepted a call to Oxford, to the Lady Margaret Professorship of Divinity of Oxford, which he occupied from 1970 to 1986 while serving simultaneously as canon of Christ Church. Macquarrie was first influenced by Bultmann's existential interpretation of the New Testament, which resulted in his Ph.D. thesis at Glasgow University (1955: "An Existentialist Theology: A Comparison of Heidegger and Bultmann"). Macquarrie refined it to an existential ontological theism that was to replace traditional metaphysical theism. He thereby investigated the universal conditions for the possibility of religion and theology, including God-talk and particular revelations, to prepare for the special symbolic theology of the Christian faith (1967: *God-Talk: An Examination of the Language and Logic of Theology*). In contrast to both Torrance and Bultmann, he operates from a general religious experience. Throughout his writings the issue of human self-transcendence persists, which is constrained by finitude but open to God. He discerns a dynamic spirit in human life through which we are called to yet unrealized possibilities to become self-aware and to act creatively and responsibly in a fuller way of life (1985: *In Search of Deity: An Essay in Dialectical Theism*, the Gifford Lectures of 1983).

As shown in his magisterial study *Twentieth-Century Religious Thought: The Frontiers of Philosophy and Theology, 1900-1970* (first published 1963), Macquarrie wrote from a historically informed perspective. Therefore it comes as no surprise that he is unhappy with *The Myth of God Incarnate*, charging it with "dissatisfaction with traditional doctrines of incarnation" without offering a "common reconstruction of belief."[38] He noted that Christian doctrines are so closely interrelated that if you take away one, several others tend to collapse. One may wonder whether this domino theory always holds true. Yet incarnation is indeed closely associated with Christology proper, so that the latter would not remain unscathed. But even Macquarrie could not escape the kind of theological reductionism with which he charged the authors of *The Myth of God Incarnate.*

In 1990 Macquarrie published *Jesus Christ in Modern Thought*, in which he showed how through the centuries classical Christology had come under critique, and illustrated what attempts had been made to provide alternatives, such as a rationalist Christology by Kant or liberation Christologies. Then he asked who Jesus Christ is really for us today. In providing his own reconstruction, he posed first the historical question and conceded that critical scholarship has eroded much of the historical material of the New Testament. Yet he found "that historical criticism of the gospels is far from being negative.... The one who confronts us in the gospels is no mythological demigod but a genuine human being in the fullest sense."[39] Since Macquarrie understood incarnation not as an instantaneous moment but as a gradual process, he also understood Jesus not as being perfect in every respect, but "in a process of becoming perfect" (374). Adopting a dynamic understanding of human nature for which he found support in some of the early fathers, he sees "Jesus Christ as the revelation of the fulfilment for which humanity is destined" (385). But then Macquarrie arrives at two endings for Christology. There is a happy ending that concludes in the death and resurrection of Jesus Christ, and his descent and his ascension. His coming again and the destined fulfillment are modified to the "gradual processes of history" (411). The austere ending, however, for which Macquarrie seeks support from the Gospel of John and from Bultmann, sees the resurrection and the saving efficacy of the cross as being one and the same.

---

38. John Macquarrie, "Christianity without Incarnation? Some Critical Comments," in *The Truth of God Incarnate*, ed. Michael Green (Grand Rapids: Eerdmans, 1977), 144.

39. John Macquarrie, *Jesus Christ in Modern Thought* (London: SCM, 1990), 358. Page references to this work are placed in the text.

Macquarrie concludes: "Resurrection is an event in the believers, it is indeed the event of the church, which is Christ's living body, and which in its preaching and the sacraments and community continues his life and work" (412). Both endings conserve for him the essential truths of the Christian faith. Bultmann's influence seems to have taken a lasting hold of Macquarrie's theological outlook.

Richard G. Swinburne (b. 1934), professor of philosophy at Oxford, is a philosopher concerned with phenomena, and the meaning and justification of theories that explain them. He uses modern natural science, analyzes it through modern philosophy, and shows the meaningfulness and justification of Christian theology. His concern is with the consistency of Christian doctrines, the a priori evidence for and against them and the criteria that must be met by the evidence of the historical occurrences involved. He concludes that God has revealed certain truths which it matters that human beings believe and which are found in Scripture, creeds, and church practice, and are centered on the belief in the trinitarian God incarnate.

John H. Hick (b. 1922), whose theological position we will describe more extensively later (see chap. 15), began like Swinburne as an evangelical Christian, but then became more and more theocentric and universalistic. He was professor in Birmingham from 1967 to 1982, and subsequently professor at the Claremont School of Theology in the United States. Before we leave the English scene, we should also take note of Alister McGrath (b. 1953), one of the younger promising theologians with an evangelical bent.

Scandinavian Revivalism

Apart from the Dane Søren Kierkegaard, no Scandinavian theologian decisively influenced the general European theological development. As we have seen, however, theology in the Scandinavian countries was not isolated. It followed closely general European trends and, until recently, had its closest contact with German theology. Besides its strong emphasis on motif research, the context of theology in Nordic countries has been decisively shaped by pietism. In the nineteenth century the leaders of that movement strongly influenced the ecclesial and theological situation in the almost exclusively Lutheran countries there. Important figures of the pietistic movements were Hans Nielsen Hauge in Norway, Paavo Ruotsalainen in Finland, Carl Olof Rosenius in Sweden, and the Association for Home Mission (Forening for Indre Mission), after 1861 under the leadership of Vilhelm Beck (1829-1901) in Denmark. But in that country one must also consider the impact of Nikolai Frederik Severin Grundtvig.

Evangelical Lay Piety: Paavo Henrik Ruotsalainen, Hans Nielsen Hauge, and Carl Olof Rosenius

"No other man in the history of the Church of Finland occupies a more commanding position than the lay evangelist" **Paavo Henrik Ruotsalainen** (1777-1852).[40] He was born in a small farmer's cottage and, as is customary, helped with the farm chores at a very early age. This obligation gave him little opportunity for education. He learned to read but never to write, and throughout his lifetime had to rely on others to transcribe what he dictated. At his time revivals were sweeping through Sweden, Norway, and Denmark as a spontaneous reaction of the spiritually hungry people against the state church, which frequently seemed to be indifferent to the religious needs of its people. Ruotsalainen also actively participated in these revival sessions, which were often conducted in his home village. He received clarity of faith when he was told he needed "the inner awareness of Christ."[41] From thereon he pursued even more diligently prayer and Bible study, and soon became known in ever widening circles as a person of astounding Bible knowledge and the ability to lead other Christians to spiritual clarity. Within a few years he was *the* leader of the revival movement in his own country, crisscrossing the land and instilling in the people a living faith through which Christianity became practically the norm for the Finns. He always had a respect for pastors and worshiped faithfully in his home church when he was not away for revivals. In turn, many pastors saw in him their spiritual leader.

The only writing of his that was published is *A Few Words to the Awakened among the Peasants* (1846). There he took his cue from 1 Peter 5:6: "Humble yourselves therefore under the mighty hand of God, that in due time he may exalt you."[42] For him the Christian faith did not mean to follow a set of prescriptions, for instance abstinence or frequent prayer, but he was convinced that "by means of his Word God takes charge, convicts of sin, reveals Jesus Christ to the sinner, justifies the ungodly by grace through faith in Christ, and gives his Holy Spirit."[43] Since it was God's own doing to take charge of one's life, the Christian could not push for it, but simply had to wait for Christ to enter one's life.

---

40. So G. Everett Arden, *Four Northern Lights: Men Who Shaped Scandinavian Churches* (Minneapolis: Augsburg, 1964), 21.

41. Arden, *Four Northern Lights*, 25.

42. Paavo Ruotsalainen, *A Few Words to the Awakened among the Peasants* (1846), in Paavo Ruotsalainen, *The Inward Knowledge of Christ: The Letters and Other Writings*, translated with an introduction by Walter J. Kuhkonen (Helsinki: Luther-Agricola Society, 1977), 74.

43. Kuhkonen, in Ruotsalainen, *A Few Words*, 13-14.

What Ruotsalainen did for Finland, **Hans Nielsen Hauge** (1771-1824) accomplished for Norway. Yet his life was much more complicated. He was born on a farm in southeastern Norway in a Christian home marked by deep piety. From early on he was concerned about the rationalism that had left its mark on many pastors and was influencing the people. In 1796 he had a spiritual experience that he interpreted as coming from God himself, who called him "to proclaim God's name to others, urging them to repent of their sins and turn to the Light."[44] Immediately after this experience, Hauge sought to lead others to Jesus as their savior and guide in their lives. This coincided with the revival movements sweeping through all Scandinavian countries.

Hauge was a man of many skills, who not only led people to reconciliation with and obedience to God, namely, an inward religiosity, but showed that this also involved political responsibility, high moral conduct, and economic initiative. In other words, being a Christian meant a whole different way of thinking and living. He launched several business ventures, and urged other peasants to follow his example to achieve a better living standard. He also urged them to actively engage in political affairs. This was all before 1814, the year Norway proclaimed its independence from Danish domination. In 1796 he also published his first book, *Meditation on the Folly of the World*, after which more than thirty additional books followed. He warned people of the danger of a false Christianity that relies on forgiveness without genuine repentance.[45] In his endeavors to reach the people, he crisscrossed Norway and covered more than ten thousand miles in eight years. Yet there was also opposition to him, since he, as an ignorant farm boy, encroached upon a field reserved for educated pastors. This was compounded by his attacks on pastors who, he felt, were not doing their duty and who exhibited pride and greed. Hauge and the established church were soon on a collision course.

An ordinance of 1741 required, among other things, that the local pastor be informed when and where a religious meeting was held in his parish. This ordinance also allowed the pastor to forbid such meetings. While initially Hauge informed the pastors of his meetings, he soon stopped, because more and more pastors felt threatened and did not want him to be in their parish and interfere with their way of doing things. So in eight years he was arrested ten times, always for violating this ordinance. Finally he was arrested in 1804 on charges of "spreading harmful religious ideas among the common people, establishing a separate sect, making himself rich, and violating the laws of the

44. So Joel M. Njus in his biographical sketch in *Autobiographical Writings of Hans Nielsen Hauge*, trans. Joel M. Njus (Minneapolis: Augsburg, 1954), 5.
45. Cf. Arden, *Four Northern Lights*, 58-59.

State."[46] He was brought to the prison in Christiana, now Oslo. He used his time in prison productively. By knitting mittens that he sold to the people in town, he earned enough money to buy books and read a variety of subjects. In 1809 war broke out with England, and since salt became extremely scarce, Hauge offered his services to help people secure salt from ocean water. He was released for that service, but soon again put under arrest. In 1811 he was finally permitted to move to a small farm just outside the city. In 1813 he was eventually sentenced, but since that sentence was too harsh, he appealed and the following year all the charges were dropped except that he had violated the ordinance of holding religious meetings. After paying a fine, he was a free man again.

Through the lengthy imprisonment his health was broken. Friends helped him buy a farm on which he could earn his own living. He now wrote his travel accounts, saying, "I enjoy the respect and friendship of the most enlightened and respected men of our country."[47] Indeed, Hauge had earned the respect of his people. He had shown them that to proclaim Christ as savior is not the prerogative of the ordained pastors, but every Christian's calling. Therefore he urged the people to follow his example by making Christian evangelism part of their daily lives. The terms "Haugeanism" and "lay evangelism" became virtually synonymous. For Hauge, emotionalism was not the sign of true Christianity. Conversion must be honest, deep, and thoroughgoing, and measured in spiritual balance, perseverance, and continued growth in godly living. Faith, according to Hauge, is also more than science and head knowledge. Faith is not acquired, but "given in regeneration. This gift of God, which comprehends Christ, and in Him the righteousness by grace alone (Eph 2:7-8), changes and cleanses our hearts."[48] While faith frees us from the curse of the law, it never relieves us from the obedience to the law. This does not mean works righteousness, of which Hauge was occasionally accused, but that faith is active in love and that from appeal and upright heart flow, "as from a spring, good works and deeds to the glory of God and to the blessing of our neighbor."[49]

Hauge was influential not only for laypeople, but more and more also for the clergy. His legacy was carried on by Gisle Johnson (1812-94), who had deep roots in the pietistic movement. He was appointed to the theological faculty at the University of Oslo in 1849 as lecturer, and the following year as professor. With his teaching duties at the university in biblical scholarship, he combined

---

46. Hans Nielsen Hauge, "My Travels," in *Autobiographical Writings of Hans Nielsen Hauge*, 124.

47. Hauge, "My Travels," 142.

48. "Hauge's Religious Convictions," as translated in Joseph M. Shaw, *Pulpit under the Sky: A Life of Hans Nielsen Hauge* (Minneapolis: Augsburg, 1955), 216.

49. Shaw, *Pulpit under the Sky*, 218.

preaching and Bible studies in one of Oslo's largest churches. It soon became known as the center of a renewed religious revival. This movement then spread beyond Oslo and reached into the countryside, where it merged with the Haugean movement. When at the end of the nineteenth century a tendency toward historical critical exegesis and liberal systematic theology developed in the theological faculty, increased tensions developed with the revival movement. To conserve the pietistic confessional Lutheranism in Norway and to enable ministerial training in that direction, the *Menighetsfakultet,* literally meaning a faculty for the people and the congregations, was started in 1908 and given official government recognition in 1913. Its most prominent representative was Ole Hallesby (1879-1961), who was theologically indebted also to Erlangen theology. While the two theological faculties often opposed each other, they now peacefully coexist and draw their students from different streams of piety deeply anchored in the Church of Norway.

Carl Olof Rosenius (1816-68) was born in a Swedish parsonage to parents deeply influenced by the revival movement. Since the Swedish church was a state church, the church had difficulty maintaining the kind of freedom needed to care for the people. Moreover, the church had absorbed elements of rationalism, secularism, and a form of ritualism. When Rosenius studied theology at Uppsala University, he encountered the usual spiritual and theological doubts that come with such study. As he was looking for guidance he found George Scott (1804-74), an English Methodist missionary headquartered in Stockholm, sent there to revive the faith of the Swedish people. Soon Rosenius and Scott became friends and Rosenius found spiritual clarity and renewed faith in God and in his word. Scott recognized the potential of Rosenius, who was granted "an annual salary from the Foreign Evangelical Society of New York City, as a city missionary in Stockholm."[50] Rosenius could now work as an evangelist without waiting to be ordained by his church. Since mission societies were working in many countries, the origin of his financial support was not unusual. For the rest of his life, Rosenius was employed as a lay evangelist, working as a city missionary in Stockholm, with his activities centered at Bethlehem Chapel, Scott's church.

In 1842 Scott and Rosenius founded the periodical *Pietisten (The Pietists),* a monthly magazine that gave the evangelical movement in Sweden a clear voice and soon became one of the most widely read papers in the nation. Rosenius also wrote numerous devotional books that were translated into many languages and sold approximately two million copies in Sweden alone. Though in 1856 the national evangelical foundation (Evangeliska Fosterlands-

---

50. So Arden, *Four Northern Lights,* 123.

Stiftelsen) was started as an umbrella organization for evangelical activities, Rosenius was not separatistic but worked for renewal within the church. The center of his faith was the awareness of the majesty and holiness of the living God who demanded fulfillment of the law that humanity could not accomplish because it had misused its freedom. Here Christ substituted and earned the punishment for humanity's misdoings. A Christian should never forget this atoning work of Christ, because through it Christ gained victory not only over death, but over every evil power. Yet a Christian can never have confidence that he or she is on the safe side, because as Rosenius wrote: "There has never on earth existed, nor does there now exist, any saint that is not every hour guilty before the holy Law of God."[51] This means that though a Christian is always in danger of sinning again, he or she is both justified and sinner. Similarly, the sinner's faith need not be exceptionally strong, because it is compared to "the hand that lays hold of that which is offered in Christ; faith is, so to speak, the open door through which Christ with his gift of salvation, comes to the penitent and believing sinner."[52] There can be no Christian pride, just humility. The piety of Rosenius shaped not just the Lutheran community in Sweden, but also the faith of many immigrants who came to this country. One of his hymns, "With God as our friend," is found in the present-day *Lutheran Book of Worship* (hymn no. 371).

The Ecclesial and Sacramental Piety of Nikolai Frederik Severin Grundtvig

Nikolai Frederik Severin Grundtvig (1783-1872) was also born in a parsonage of parents with a conservative Lutheran piety. At the age of nine, Frederik entered a boarding school for six years, and then the *Gymnasium* at Aarhus, where he mastered the Latin language. In 1800 he began to study theology at the University of Copenhagen. There he shed the traditional Christianity of his parents and accepted a rationalistic faith in God, virtue, and immortality. After his theological exam in 1803, he spent some time at home pursuing his interest in poetry and historical studies. From 1805 to 1808 he served as a tutor in one of the large estates and fell hopelessly in love with the twenty-six-year-old wife of his employer. To overcome this he immersed himself in romantic philosophy and Nordic mythology.

---

51. Carl O. Rosenius, *The Believer Free from the Law*, translated with an introduction by Adolf Hult (Rock Island, Ill.: Augustana Book Concern, 1923), 46.

52. So Arden, *Four Northern Lights*, 138.

Upon his return to Copenhagen, Grundtvig published in 1808 his first important literary and scholarly work, *The Mythology of the North.* He traced the sources of the ancient Eddas, a collection of ancient, partly mythological Nordic tales written down in the thirteenth century, and claimed that this pre-Christian literature contained a dramatic presentation of the whole drama of human existence in the form of myth. Yet his career as poet and historian was interrupted in 1810 when his ailing father asked him to help him in his parish. The probational sermon he preached to the consistorial authorities in Copenhagen was entitled "Why Has the Lord's Word Disappeared from His House?"[53] This sermon contained such a strong attack on the clergy and the national church of Denmark that he was officially rebuked and his endorsement delayed. Grundtvig thought of himself as a prophet called to awaken Denmark to a new life, and therefore he asked himself whether he was really awakened. He confessed: "Suddenly it was as if scales have fallen from the eyes of my mind, my pride and uncharitableness stood incarnate before me, and no remorse or repentance was to be found in me for my past sins. Now was I nigh to despair, my reason trembled, but my heart remained hard and cold."[54] Under the care of his father he slowly recovered, but now he was a new and different person, because he had a new sense of humility. For the first time he saw himself as an utterly lost, helpless sinner, saved alone by the grace and mercy of God.

Grundtvig was ordained in 1811 and served in his father's parish until his father's death in 1813. Then he moved back to Copenhagen and translated from the Latin a Danish history and from old Nordic a Norwegian history, as well as the Anglo-Saxon Beowulf epos. Altogether, six volumes appeared between 1818 and 1822. In 1821 he finally was called to a small parish, and in 1822 went to Our Savior's Church in Copenhagen. Both times he was appointed because King Frederick VI (1768-1839) appreciated Grundtvig's old Nordic research, and therefore he prevailed over the objections of bishop and consistory. On account of difficulties with some of his associates, Grundtvig resigned in 1826. For the next thirteen years he lived without a pastoral office, deriving his livelihood from continued research and publications, partially financed by the king. In 1839 he was finally called to Vartov, to a chaplain's position in a home for aged women, where he worked until his death. There he also began to experiment with educational ideas in terms of adult education and attempted to renew the church's hymnody. Throughout his life he composed approximately fifteen hundred hymns. Still about one-third of the hymns in the hymnal of the Dan-

---

53. Cf. for the following Arden, *Four Northern Lights*, 90-91.

54. Nikolai Grundtvig, as quoted in Hal Koch, *Grundtvig*, translated with introduction and notes by Llewellyn Jones (Yellow Springs, Ohio: Antioch, 1952), 47.

ish church from 1953 are from Grundtvig,[55] and in the present *Lutheran Book of Worship* seven hymns have Grundtvig as their author. The Vartov home soon became the gathering place for a growing circle of Grundtvig's followers, and a congregational life was developed there that exerted wide influence throughout Denmark.

As a contemporary of Kierkegaard, Grundtvig became the founder of Grundtvigianism. Influenced by the Lutheran theology of the awakening, which again was influenced by romanticism and idealism, he developed an ecclesial and sacramental Christianity, the center of which was Word and faith, founded in baptism and nourished by the Eucharist. While this kind of theology was rejected by the theologians of Copenhagen University, Søren Kierkegaard's brother Peder (1805-88), who was bishop and secretary of church affairs, appreciated it. Against Protestant orthodoxy and its legalistic understanding of Scripture, Grundtvig rejected any kind of biblicism and claimed that the Apostles' Creed enunciated at baptism is the fully valid witness of the true and original faith in Christ. Since the church of Christ is invisible and so is the work of the Holy Spirit, objective knowledge about Christ and about the content of the Christian faith is totally inadequate to attain a Christian life. Grundtvig opted for complete freedom of what is taught and also for a change from the confessional state church to a people's church. The church should correspond to the present forms of religious faith and devotion to God. With this, Grundtvig did not want to question Christian proclamation, but to further the spiritual development within the church. Christians should be allowed to choose their own congregations and their own pastors. In Denmark during World War II this led to a renaissance of Grundtvig that opted against any confessional strictures and hierarchic tendencies in the church. At the same time, the eucharistic services have until now enjoyed renewed appreciation. The Danish Evangelical Lutheran Church in America, organized in 1872, owed its existence in part to Grundtvigianism. Grundtvig's influence extended far into society and shaped the religious, cultural, and ecclesial identity of many Danes, especially in terms of openness that gave rise to a Grundtvigianism with an ecclesial sacramental piety and an emphasis on national identity. This movement is still vigorous to this day. Even in the United States Haugeanism and Grundtvigianism continue to exert considerable influence on Christians and Christian denominations with Scandinavian backgrounds.

---

55. So Christian Thodberg, "Grundtvig, Nikolaj Frederik Severin," in *Theologische Realenzyklopädie*, 14:286.

For Further Reading

Peter T. Forsyth (1848-1921)

Brown, Robert McAfee. *P. T. Forsyth: Prophet for Today.* Philadelphia: Westminster, 1952.

Forsyth, Peter T. *The Cruciality of the Cross.* London: Hodder and Stoughton, 1910.

————. *Positive Preaching and Modern Mind.* Cincinnati: Jennings and Graham, 1907.

————. *A Sense of the Holy: An Introduction to the Thought of P. T. Forsyth through His Writings.* Foreword by Geoffrey Wainwright. Pasadena, Calif.: Wipf and Stock, 1996.

Hart, Trevor, ed. *Justice the True and Only Mercy: Essays on the Life and Theology of Peter Taylor Forsyth.* Edinburgh: T. & T. Clark, 1995.

Pitt, Clifford. *Church, Ministry, and Sacraments: A Critical Evaluation of the Thought of Peter Taylor Forsyth.* Washington, D.C.: University Press of America, 1983.

John Baillie (1886-1960) and Donald M. Baillie (1887-1954)

Baillie, Donald M. *Faith in God and Its Christian Consummation.* Foreword by John MacIntyre. New ed. London: Faber and Faber, 1964 [1927].

————. *God Was in Christ: An Essay on Incarnation and Atonement.* London: Faber and Faber, 1961 [1947].

————. *The Theology of the Sacraments and Other Papers.* With a biographical essay by John Baillie. London: Faber and Faber, 1957.

Baillie, John. *The Belief in Progress.* New York: Charles Scribner's, 1951.

————. *The Idea of Revelation in Recent Thought.* New York: Columbia University Press, 1965 [1956].

————. *Our Knowledge of God.* London: Oxford Paperbacks, 1963 [1939].

Baillie, John, and Donald Baillie. *John and Donald Baillie: Selected Writings.* Edited by David Fergusson. Edinburgh: Saint Andrew, 1997.

Fergusson, David. *Christ, Church, and Society: Essays on John Baillie and Donald Baillie.* Edinburgh: T. & T. Clark, 1993.

Newlands, George. *John and Donald Baillie: Transatlantic Theology.* New York: Peter Lang, 2002.

Thomas F. Torrance (b. 1913)

Colyer, Elmer. *The Promise of Trinitarian Theology: Theologians in Dialogue with T. F. Torrance.* Lanham, Md.: Rowman and Littlefield, 2001.

McGrath, Alister E. *Thomas F. Torrance: An Intellectual Biography.* Edinburgh: T. & T. Clark, 1999.

Torrance, Thomas F. *Calvin's Doctrine of Man.* Grand Rapids: Eerdmans, 1957 [1949].

————. *The Christian Doctrine of God: One Being Three Persons.* Edinburgh: T. & T. Clark, 1996.

————. *The Christian Frame of Mind: Reason, Order, and Openness in Theology and*

Natural Science. Introduction by W. Jim Neidhardt. Colorado Springs: Helmers and Howard, 1989.

———. *Theological Science*. Edinburgh: T. & T. Clark, 1996 [1969].

Weightman, Colin. *Theology in a Polanyian Universe: The Theology of Thomas Torrance*. New York: Peter Lang, 1994.

Charles Harold Dodd (1884-1973)

Dodd, C. H. *The Coming of Christ — Four Broadcast Addresses for the Season of Advent*. Cambridge: Cambridge University Press, 1951.

———. *The Founder of Christianity*. New York: Macmillan, 1970.

———. *The Interpretation of the Fourth Gospel*. Cambridge: University Press, 1968 [1953].

———. *Parables of the Kingdom*. Glasgow: Fount Paperbacks, 1978.

See also chapter 9.

Charles F. D. Moule (b. 1908)

Berkey, Robert F. "Christological Perspectives: The Context of Current Discussions." In *Christological Perspectives: Essays in Honor of Harvey K. McArthur*, edited by Robert Berkey and Sarah Edwards, 3-23. New York: Pilgrim Press, 1982.

Lemcio, Eugene E. "The Intention of the Evangelist, Mark." *New Testament Studies* 32, no. 2 (Apr. 1986): 187-206.

Moulder, James. "Some Questions about the Origins of Christology." *Journal of Theology for Southern Africa* 30 (Mar. 1980): 39-52.

D. E. Nineham (b. 1920)

Abba, Raymond. "Historical Scepticism in Recent Biblical Studies." *Colloquium* 17, no. 2 (May 1985): 23-32.

Houlden, Leslie. "In Honour of Dennis Nineham." *Theology* 89 (Summer 1986): 339-41.

Houston, Joe. "Objectivity and the Gospels." in *Objective Knowledge: A Christian Perspective*, edited by Paul Helm, 147-65. Leicester: Inter-Varsity, 1987.

John Macquarrie (b. 1919)

Cummings, Owen. *John Macquarrie: A Master of Theology*. New York: Paulist, 2002.

Long, Eugene. *Existence, Being, and God: An Introduction to the Philosophical Theology of John Macquarrie*. New York: Paragon, 1985.

Macquarrie, John. *Christology Revisited*. London: SCM, 1998.

———. *God-Talk: An Examination of the Language and Logic of Theology*. New York: Harper and Row, 1967.

———. *In Search of Deity: An Essay in Dialectical Theism*. London: Xpress Reprints, 1993 [1984].

———. *Jesus Christ in Modern Thought*. London: SCM, 1990.

———. *On Being a Theologian*. Edited by John Morgan. London: SCM, 1999.

————. *Principles of Christian Theology.* 2nd ed. New York: Charles Scribner's 1977.

————. *Studies in Christian Existentialism.* London: SCM, 1966.

Paavo Henrik Ruotsalainen (1777-1852)

Arden, G. Everett. *Four Northern Lights: Men Who Shaped Scandinavian Churches.* Minneapolis: Augsburg, 1964.

Nyman, Helge. "Lutheran Piety in Finnish Pietism." In *Ecclesia, Leiturgia, Ministerium,* edited by M. Parvio et al., 89-102. Helsinki: Loimaan Kirjapaino, 1977.

Ruotsalainen, Paavo. *The Inward Knowledge of Christ: The Letters and Other Writings.* Translated with an introduction by Walter J. Kuhkonen. Helsinki: Luther-Agricola Society, 1977.

Hans Nielsen Hauge (1771-1824)

Aarflot, Andreas. *Hans Nielsen Hauge: His Life and Message.* Minneapolis: Augsburg, 1979.

Hauge, Hans Nielsen. *Autobiographical Writings of Hans Nielsen Hauge.* Translated by Joel M. Njus. Minneapolis: Augsburg, 1954.

Nodtvedt, Magnus. *Rebirth of Norway's Peasantry: Folk Leader Hans Nielsen Hauge.* Tacoma, Wash.: Pacific Lutheran University Press, 1965.

Shaw, Joseph M. *Pulpit under the Sky: A Life of Hans Nielsen Hauge.* Minneapolis: Augsburg, 1955.

Carl Olof Rosenius (1816-68)

Arden, Gothard. *Four Northern Lights: Men Who Shaped Scandinavian Churches.* Minneapolis: Augsburg, 1964. Pp. 115-50.

Rosenius, Carl O. *The Believer Free from the Law.* Translated with an introduction by Adolf Hult. Rock Island, Ill.: Augustana Book Concern, 1923.

Nikolai Frederik Severin Grundtvig (1783-1872)

Allchin, A. N. *N. F. S. Grundtvig: An Introduction to His Life and Work.* London: Darton, Longman and Todd, 1997.

————, ed. *Heritage and Prophecy: Grundtvig and the English-Speaking World.* Norwich: Canterbury, 1994.

Knudsen, Johannes. *Danish Rebel: A Study of N. F. S. Grundtvig.* Philadelphia: Muhlenberg, 1955.

Koch, Hal. *Grundtvig.* Translated with introduction and notes by Llewellyn Jones. Yellow Springs, Ohio: Antioch, 1952.

13 Theology Is More than Protestant

The 1960s were not only tumultuous years with worldwide student protests against the full-scale U.S. involvement in Vietnam after 1965, with the new leftist movement in politics, and even a new sound in music with the Beatles. They were also exciting years in theology, with the aggiornamento of Pope John XXIII (1881-1963), the call to get moving, and the Second Vatican Council (1962-65) through which the Roman Catholic Church not only squarely faced the twentieth century but also officially entered the ecumenical scene. While we have occasionally mentioned Roman Catholic theologians at places in this book where they made important contributions, we take Vatican II as the opportunity to tell the story of Roman Catholic theology. This also gives us a chance to view the different strands of Roman Catholic theology more coherently without forgetting that they often interacted with Protestant theologians and movements.

Orthodox theology, especially from Greece, had contact with both Roman Catholic and Protestant theology for quite a while. The same was true for many Orthodox theologians from the Soviet empire because many had fled to the West or had been exiled. But it was only through the collapse of Soviet Communism in the late 1980s that Orthodox theologians could freely travel in larger numbers and share their traditions and their insights with representatives from other denominations. This means that during the latter half of the twentieth century, theological discourse became truly ecumenical, including the great traditions of the East and the West.

The Entrance of Roman Catholic Theology
into the Ecumenical Fold

Considering only the number of Roman Catholic institutions at which theologians work, it seems unfair to allot only a few pages to Roman Catholic theology. Indeed, one hundred years from now the story may be very different. Yet with the concentration of the teaching office in one person, namely, the pope, or one institution, namely, the Vatican, the official trademark of Roman Catholic theology has not been creativity, but fidelity to the teaching office. Only with Vatican II and the exoneration of many of the most creative and productive minds in recent Roman Catholic theology did the picture change. Even then academic freedom was still understood differently in Roman Catholic quarters than in Protestant, and sometimes also among Roman Catholics, depending on their geographic proximity to or distance from Rome. Apologizing for brevity, we want to draw out some developmental lines in Roman Catholic theology. A good place to start is France, because it has had considerable influence on Rome and also produced many significant theologians.

A Reformer without a Home: Hugues Félicité Robert de Lamennais

Hugues Félicité Robert de Lamennais (1782-1854) came from a well-to-do, upper-middle-class family of Brittany and pursued theology through private study. He was ordained a priest in 1816 without having attended a seminary. His aim was first to restore to the church the self-confidence it had lost during the French Revolution of 1789 when through the demise of the royal house the church was deprived of its political support. In his four-volume *Essay on the Indifference in Matters of Religion* (1817-23; Eng. trans. 1895), he claimed that certitude must be sought in general reason or common sense. Both participate in divine omniscience, and therefore are infallible. The highest expression of this certitude is found in the church and embodied in the pope. This publication was a powerful attack on widespread religious indifference and was appreciated by Pope Leo XII (b. 1760, 1823-29). From his study of history, Lamennais concluded that a union with the political powers did not help the cause of religion. In *On the Progress of the Revolution and the War against the Church* (*Des progrès de la révolution et de la guerre contre l'Eglise*, 1828), Lamennais insisted that the church utilize its fundamental liberties granted by the government and abandon all claims to a privileged position. Thereby it accepts the separation of state and church. The revolution of 1830, through which Napoleon III (1808-73) came to power in France, convinced Lamennais of the correctness of this idea.

To propagate his stance, in the same year he started a newspaper, *L'Avenir (The Future)*, which became the voice of Roman Catholic liberalism with its motto "God and liberty."

Lamennais advocated religious liberty, freedom for the church and for education, and freedom of the press. Yet the French government did not intend to sever its ties to the church, and the French bishops wanted to preserve some independence from Rome through their connection with the government. Therefore both opposed Lamennais's ideas and applied pressure on Rome to condemn him. In an encyclical of 1832 Pope Gregory XVI (b. 1765, 1831-46) warned against the evils of the age, which implied a censure of *L'Avenir*. Lamennais then drafted an act of submission on behalf of the editors of *L'Avenir* and avoided covering any theological aspects of the relation between church and state. Yet this truce did not last long: *L'Avenir* ceased and several of Lamennais's works were put on the index of forbidden books. Lamennais finally broke with the church (1836), and when he died he was buried according to his own directions without funeral rites. Nevertheless, he was mourned by countless admirers.

Neo-scholasticism: Joseph Kleutgen, Matthias Scheeben, Johann Baptist Heinrich, Désiré Joseph Mercier, and Jacques Maritain

The same reactionary trend Lamennais encountered emerged in neo-scholasticism. Its main head was the German Jesuit **Joseph Kleutgen** (1811-83), who taught in Rome and preferred the new scholasticism over the old one, since it no longer dared to contradict Thomas Aquinas (1224/26–1274). In fact, like him, it was concerned about the purity of doctrine. Yet this neo-Thomism was not concerned about critical historical research in contrast to the Catholic Tübingen School (see below), but treated Thomas as having provided a time-less truth that only needed to be appropriated. This movement was not just about repristination. It attempted to secure a space within which a pious spirituality could develop and theological thinking could work constructively. Characteristic for this movement is *A Manual of Catholic Theology* (1873-87; Eng. trans., 2 vols., 2nd ed., 1899-1901), composed by **Matthias Joseph Scheeben** (1835-88), professor of dogmatics and moral theology at the diocesan seminary in Cologne. Only three volumes appeared (1873-87) of his *Manual,* which was never completed. Scheeben had an organic view of the mysteries of faith that he unfolded from the Trinity and the incarnation.

One of the centers for neo-scholasticism was Mainz. **Johann Baptist Heinrich** (1816-91) taught dogmatic theology at the diocesan seminary there. Drawing on Scripture and tradition, he put forth a ten-volume *Dogmatic The-*

ology (*Dogmatische Theologie*, 1881-1904) — four of the volumes being completed by his friend Constantin Gutberlet — that set forth a reasonable understanding of faith in clear conceptuality. The Jesuits at the theological faculty in Innsbruck also advocated neo-scholasticism, as did, until Vatican II, many representatives at the Papal Theological Institutes in Rome such as the Collegium Romanum, the Collegium Angelicum, and the Benedictines at San Anselmo.

Neo-scholasticism was by no means monolithic but was willing to assimilate influence from outside its own tradition. **Désiré Joseph Mercier** (1851-1926) was professor of philosophy at Louvain (1882-1906), archbishop of Mechelen, Belgium (1906-26), and elevated to cardinal in 1907. Alarmed by the isolation of the Roman Catholic faith from the scientific community, he founded the Institut Supérieur at Louvain in 1889 "to bridge the gap between modern science and philosophy, particularly with respect to the problem of knowledge."[1] Then there were the French Dominicans who made important contributions both in critical research and in the popularization of domestic philosophy, especially through their periodicals *Revue des Sciences Philosophiques et Théologiques* and *Revue Thomiste*.

Mention must also be made of **Jacques Maritain** (1882-1973), who was professor of philosophy at the Institut Catholique in Paris (1914-33), professor at the Toronto Institute for Medieval Studies (1933-45), ambassador of France to the Vatican (1945-48), and after that professor at Princeton University, where he became emeritus in 1956.[2] Though born in Paris in a liberal Protestant family, he converted to Roman Catholicism in 1906 and through Dominican influence became acquainted with Thomas Aquinas. While initially following Henri Bergson's dynamic philosophy, he turned upside down the positivistic scheme of Auguste Comte, who had claimed that in an ascending line there were three stages to human understanding: the theological, the metaphysical, and the positive or scientific. For Maritain there is first scientific knowledge in the world of reflection, then metaphysical knowledge, and finally the suprarational knowledge that belongs to mystical experience. Rational metaphysics can indeed obtain a knowledge of God. It can know about God's existence and attributes. But the concepts of metaphysical knowledge are still inadequate to their object. At the suprarational level, however, reason is illuminated by divine revelation and therefore God can be known in his essence without the mediation of any analogy or concept. Yet Maritain did not stay with philosophical and theological

1. Thomas Gilby, "Thomism," in *The Encyclopedia of Philosophy*, ed. Paul Edwards (New York: Macmillan, 1967), 8:121.

2. For Jacques Maritain see Aidan Nichols, "Maritain, Jacques," in *Theologische Realenzyklopädie*, 22:162-64, and John Macquarrie, *20th Century Religious Thought: The Frontiers of Philosophy and Theology, 1900-1970*, rev. ed. (London: SCM, 1971), 284-86.

speculation, but also went into the field of political ethics where he influenced the formulation of Christian democratic programs especially in Latin America and Italy.

The Catholic Tübingen School: Johann Sebastian von Drey, Johann Adam Möhler, Johann Baptist Hirscher, and Karl Adam

Other movements were more progressive, such as the Tübingen School, whose members were fascinated by idealistic philosophy but did not want to steer away from Catholic orthodoxy. The founder of this school was **Johann Sebastian von Drey** (1777-1853), who taught in Tübingen from 1817 to 1846 and was influenced by Schelling and Schleiermacher. He endeavored to integrate the results of Protestant historical investigations into theology and develop a perspective of transcendental idealism. Catholicism could then be traced back to a foundational and comprehensive idea. This idea, however, was not an a priori of reason as found in philosophy, but a seed planted by Christ, the eternal plan of God that unfolds itself in time. Catholicism understands itself, according to Drey, as the truly objective, uninterrupted, pure and consequent continuation of early Christendom. There are an organic unity of the church, a progressive development, and a community inspired by the Holy Spirit. Revelation is not handed on, but it hands itself on in the church. According to Drey, the original Christian fact, given in Jesus, is still present in modern Catholicism. This concept is developed in his *Geschichte des katholischen Dogmensystems* (*History of the Catholic System of Dogma*, 1812/13).

Johann Adam Möhler (1796-1838), the most significant representative of the Roman Catholic Tübingen School, is still well-known today, especially through the ecumenical work of the Johann Adam Möhler Institute at Paderborn. In 1822 Möhler was offered a position in church history and related disciplines at the Roman Catholic faculty in Tübingen, and in 1835 he became full professor at the University of Munich, lecturing in church history and related topics, including the epistles of Paul. Only three years later he died of cholera. Möhler wrote sixty-five reviews for the *Tübinger Theologische Quartalschrift*, which had been established by Drey, and a commentary on Paul's epistle to the Romans. Most significant, however, was his 1825 book *Unity in the Church or the Principle of Catholicism: Presented in the Spirit of the Church Fathers of the First Three Centuries*. While he was still Privatdozent at Tübingen, he undertook a study tour of northern Germany in 1822-23 to visit Göttingen and Berlin and to acquaint himself with other theological faculties. He was especially impressed with the Protestant church historian August Neander (1789-

1850), of whom he wrote: "I will never forget Neander's lectures. They will have a decisive influence on my studies of Church history. In addition his private life is penetrated by illuminating religiosity, simple like the bearing of a local school-teacher. . . . Origen, Tertullian, Augustine, Chrysostom, St. Bernard, the letters of Boniface, and many others, he knows by heart."[3]

His book on the unity of the church, while following New Testament lines, betrays the influence of Neander and Schleiermacher, using organic images of the body to describe the church, as they did. This book had an immense impact and was also translated into French. Especially noteworthy is his emphasis on unity and diversity: "Although the Catholic principle binds all believers into one unity, the individuality of each is not suspended, for each individual is to continue as a *living* member of the whole body of the Church."[4] Only through the manifold characteristics of single individuals, their free development and unhindered movement, does the church become a living organism that can flourish and blossom. His well-balanced and internally consistent theology strives for a theological renewal. According to Möhler, the church is identified with the bishop as the bishop is identified with the church. Möhler left open whether the church is structured from below or from above. He drew heavily on the church fathers, but little on New Testament exegesis. Strongly influenced by Romantic thinking, he emphasized the community of the faithful but recognized a prevalence of the hierarchy of offices.

Johann Baptist Hirscher (1788-1865), another representative of this school, was professor of moral and pastoral theology at Tübingen from 1817 to 1837, when he became professor of moral theology and catechesis at the University of Freiburg. He was a reformer in catechesis and pastoral care. His theology was biblically oriented, influenced by Augustine, and strove for a realization of the kingdom of God in humanity. He was instrumental in renewing moral theology by taking into consideration the social issues of his time and connecting them to dogma and spirituality. This shows that even the open-minded Tübingen School endeavored a consolidation of the church after the French Revolution and its aftermath.

Karl Adam (1876-1966) can only indirectly be counted as a representative of the so-called Tübingen School. Similar to that school, for him ecclesiology and therewith Christology were central areas of concern. In 1900 he became a consecrated priest in the Regensburg diocese, and in 1917 was called to be pro-

---

3. Johann Adam Möhler, in a letter cited extensively in *Unity in the Church or the Principle of Catholicism: Presented in the Spirit of the Church Fathers of the First Three Centuries*, edited and translated with an introduction by Peter C. Erb (Washington, D.C.: Catholic University, 1996), 28-29.

4. Möhler, *Unity in the Church*, 166.

fessor of moral theology at Strassbourg University. When after World War I Strassbourg became again French, Adam had to leave and taught as professor of dogmatics at Tübingen from 1919 to 1947. Next to his books on Christology (*Jesus Christus*, 1933; Eng. trans. *Son of God*, 1934; *Christ Our Brother*, 1929; Eng. trans. 1931; and *The Christ of Faith: The Christology of the Church*, 1954; Eng. trans. 1957), his book *The Spirit of Catholicism* (1924; Eng. trans. 1929) was most well-known and appeared in many editions.

Adam opened his theology with reflections on the church. For him the conviction that "the Church is permeated by Christ, and of necessity organically united with Him, is a fundamental point of Christian teaching."[5] Since Christ does not become visible in one person, but in the community as communion, there is an organic unity in this body of Christ where the individual members and organs have their own functions, but as in a body they exist for each other.[6] God, Christ, and the church belong together for Adam, because "I come to a living faith in the Triune God through Christ in His church. I experience the action of the living God through Christ realizing Himself in His church."[7] It comes as no surprise that Adam faced no problems with the church. His *Spirit of Catholicism* was one of the most widely read books of German Catholicism in the early twentieth century.[8] The Protestant faculty at Tübingen even asked Karl Heim, his colleague on the Protestant side, to respond to it with a lecture series, which was then published as *The Nature of Protestantism* (1925; Eng. trans., Philadelphia, 1963; also translated as *Spirit and Truth: The Nature of Evangelical Christianity* [London, 1935]), which, however, carried with it a certain degree of polemical overkill that did not do justice to Adam. Some of Adam's concerns about the church were picked up again at Vatican II in the dogmatic constitution *Lumen Gentium*.

Facing the Challenge of the Times: Anton Günther, Antonio Rosmini, and Johann Michael Sailer

Although **Anton Günther** (1783-1863) did not found a school in its own right, around 1850 his opponents coined the term "Güntherianism" to refer to state-

---

5. Karl Adam, *The Spirit of Catholicism*, trans. Dom Justin McCann, rev. ed. (New York: Macmillan, 1943), 16.

6. Cf. Adam, *The Spirit of Catholicism*, 40.

7. Adam, *The Spirit of Catholicism*, 51.

8. Rudolf Graber, *Karl Adam (1876-1966) zum 100. Geburtstag* (Regensburg: Erhardi, 1976), 17, mentions that Adam's book is one of the most widely read books in more recent Catholicism.

ments that deviated from orthodox Catholicism. Günther's friends and students were accorded the same label with the charge, as for instance by Joseph Kleutgen, that Güntherianism is semirationalism. Only the Old Catholics, who split from the Roman Catholic Church in response to Vatican I, saw in Güntherianism something positive, the Catholic answer to the challenge of German idealism that often veered toward a pantheistic concept of the world or even atheism. This latter, positive sense of Güntherianism coincided to some extent with Günther's own direction.

Günther was born in Bohemia, then part of the Austrian-Hungarian Empire.[9] He studied philosophy and law at Prague and theology at the Theological Academy at Raab, Hungary. In 1820 he was consecrated a priest, and two years later he joined the Jesuits. After serving for two years his novitiate in Galicia, he spent the rest of his life in Vienna. As an educator of princes, he received a small pension. Thereby he was free for the rest of his life to devote himself to his project to reconcile faith and knowledge and to place the dogmas of the Roman Catholic Church on a firm philosophical foundation, similarly to Teilhard de Chardin a century later. However, while Teilhard pursued a monistic and evolutionary track, Günther, influenced by Hegel, thought in dualistic and dialectic terms.

Günther, for instance, claimed: "Nature is the image of the spirit, its mirror. The spirit finds in nature its own dynamic being, drawn out in its manifoldness to reflect itself everywhere wherever the spirit may touch nature. Yet reason also states an infinite chasm and a qualitative difference between spirit and nature."[10] This Hegelian dialectic again shows when he claims that there is a coexistence of the "lights," i.e., the revelatory insights from a primary revelation in creation and a secondary one in the historical revelation in salvation. "And it is the task to determine the relationship between the two lights. We must move beyond the negative criterion of reason, which is characterized as non-contradictory, to the positive criterion which consists in the congruence of the revealed content with reason."[11]

Günther was opposed to the pervasive pantheism and atheism of his time and wanted to combat them with Hegel's synthesis, and yet distinguish between nature and spirit. Since Hegel's ideas resonated not only with Protestants, Günther found many Roman Catholic followers and also much support and appreciation for his own work. Twice Bavaria wanted to win him for a profes-

9. Cf. for the following the extensive biography in Joseph Pritz, *Glaube und Wissen bei Anton Günther. Eine Einführung in sein Leben und Werk mit einer Auswahl seiner Schriften* (Vienna: Herder, 1963), 16-114.

10. Günther, in Pritz, *Glaube und Wissen*, 151 (selections from his writings).

11. Günther, in Pritz, *Glaube und Wissen*, 125.

sorship in theology at the University of Munich, which even conferred on him an honorary doctorate in 1832. Prussia too wanted him for Bonn, and he was later offered positions at the universities of Breslau, Giessen, and Tübingen (as the successor to Drey). Yet Günther preferred the solitary life of an independent scholar and remained in Vienna.

His growing circle of friends and disciples, who often were more audacious than he himself, also brought his neoscholastic opponents to the fore. In January 1857 all of Günther's books were put on the index of forbidden books. But even then Pope Pius IX (1792-1878) was not opposed to him, since Günther immediately submitted to ecclesiastical authority. Among other things, his opponents claimed his work was rationalistic and he did not accord enough appreciation to scholastic theology and the fathers of the church.[12] It is not without irony that Vatican I also rejected materialism and pantheism as Günther had done. Nevertheless, many of his influential followers joined the Old Catholic movement after Vatican I.

Similar to Günther, **Georg Hermes** (1775-1831), who taught dogmatics at Münster and after 1819 at Bonn, was a faithful son of this church who attempted to reconcile faith and reason by using Kant's system while at the same time combating Kant's criticism. More than thirty of his students received calls to professorships in philosophy and theology. While he died in peace, neoscholastic colleagues, especially from Mainz, attacked "Hermesianism" as a Pelagian and rationalistic heresy.[13] A papal dictum of 1835 called his writings "absurd" and "alien" to Roman Catholic teachings. Eventually German bishops succeeded to "purify" the centers of Hermesian thought such as Bonn, Munich, and Breslau.

Antonio Rosmini (1797-1855) was one of the most important Italian theologians of the last two centuries and was the oldest son of a family of noble blood whose ancestors lived for centuries in Rovereto (Trentino), which at that time still belonged to Tyrol as part of the Austrian Empire. Against the wishes of his parents he studied theology in Padua, was consecrated a priest in 1821, and in the following year received his doctorate in theology and canon law. In the knowledge of his own sinfulness he strove for perfection, and he was convinced that any work that providence would suggest to him he should perform as a tool of God to help the weak. In 1828 he founded the Institute of Charity (Istituto della Carità), the rules of which were approved in 1839 through Pope Gregory XVI.

12. Cf. Pritz, *Glaube und Wissen*, 58.

13. For more details cf. Hubert Jedin, ed., *Handbuch der Kirchengeschichte* (Freiburg: Herder, 1971/85), 6/1:448-52.

The basic rules of the institute were to strive for one's own perfection through prayer and meditation in a life withdrawn from the world but connected with it through works of charity, to participate in the culture of one's time, and to engage in scholarly pursuits.[14] When the national movement took hold for unification of Italy, a country that consisted mainly of small principalities, Rosmini was called to the aid of Pope Pius IX in 1848 to help. Rosmini advocated a confederation of the Italian principalities under the honorary primacy of the pope with the papal states to be retained. Yet Austria intervened, unification plans came to a halt, and the pope had to flee. In 1848 Pius still thought to elevate Rosmini to cardinal and appoint him secretary of state. But now the tides had changed, and already the following year his books *The Constitutions of the Society of Charity* (Eng. trans. 1988) and *The Five Wounds of the Holy Church* (1832; Eng. trans. 1883) were put on the index without a word of explanation. Similar to Günther, Rosmini accepted this verdict.

It is no surprise that secular authorities saw *The Five Wounds of the Holy Church* as an especially dangerous publication and put pressure on the pope to silence Rosmini. For instance, as one of the five wounds he pronounced the appointment of the bishops through nonecclesial powers. For many countries, however, bishops were important administrators, and therefore such an idea ran contrary to long-standing customs. Concerning the third wound, the disunity of the bishops, Rosmini observed that in a national church such as the Roman Catholic Church in France, the episcopate no longer regarded itself as a community of shepherds but as the premier class, "when it has become a political magistracy, a council of State, an assembly of courtiers. And this nationalism of Churches, which existed in fact before it was formally acknowledged, is opposed to, and destructive of all Catholicity."[15] Rosmini advocated a church that is not separated from the state but is independent of governmental interference, and that emulates its Lord and the apostles in simplicity of lifestyle and poverty. Advocating this kind of lifestyle, Rosmini had many cardinals against him too.

Another wound Rosmini observed is the separation of the people from the clerics in public worship. He noted: "That worship, to which God had annexed His grace, in order to render men able to practise the moral lessons in-

---

14. For his foundational teachings, see Antonio Rosmini, *Grundlehren der christlichen Vollkommenheit*, translated with a postscript by Hubert Schiel (Burg Rothenfels am Main: Deutsches Quickbornhaus, 1925). A good English summary of his life and his teachings is provided by Denis Cleary, *Antonio Rosmini: Introduction to His Life and Teaching* (Durham: Rosmini House, 1992).

15. Antonio Rosmini, *The Five Wounds of the Holy Church* (69), edited with an introduction by H. P. Liddon (New York: Dutton, 1883), 119-20.

culcated on them, was not merely a spectacle set before the eyes of the people. The people were not to be only lookers-on without any active part or share in the devotional scene."[16] For Rosmini all the faithful, clerics and laity, form a unity. Sometimes the clerics represent God and speak and act for the people in the name of God, and at other times the clerics are in the midst of the people, together speaking to God and expecting his salvific activity. Many of Rosmini's suggestions sound very modern and found serious consideration in Vatican II. Along with these practical writings Rosmini also composed treatises on theological issues, theological anthropology, Christology, and eschatology. His complete works, which have been edited since 1975, will comprise approximately eighty volumes when complete. "No other single person in Italian Catholicism of modernity has had such a lasting impact."[17]

Johann Michael Sailer (1752-1832) has been called the "Church Father of Bavaria."[18] Yet similar to Günther and Rosmini, his work did not meet with unanimous approval. Those who fought for the legacy of the Enlightenment saw in him a crypto-Jesuit, and the papal delegate in Munich considered him a mystic enthusiast or even a clandestine Protestant.[19] Sailer worked for the renewal of Catholicism at the beginning of the nineteenth century. He wanted to overcome the shallow Enlightenment ideas concerning religion and morals and wanted to deepen the religiosity in southern Germany. He sensed that romanticism, dominant at that time, reawakened a yearning for religion and the church.

Sailer was born to rather poor parents in the village of Aresing near Schrobenhausen, Upper Bavaria. He graduated from the Jesuit high school *(Gymnasium)* at Munich in 1770 and joined the Jesuits. After his novitiate he began philosophical theological studies at the University of Ingolstadt, where he obtained his Ph.D. in 1774. When the Jesuit Order was banned, he became a priest in 1775 in the diocese of Augsburg. Then he returned for further studies to Ingolstadt and obtained his theological doctorate. As a former Jesuit, however, he had to leave the university in 1781. That year the elector of Bavaria also decreed that no book of prayer or devotion was to be sold in the electorate of Bavaria without approval of the theological faculty in Ingolstadt. Since Sailer was the youngest professor in the faculty, it became his task to approve these

16. Rosmini, *The Five Wounds* (14), 12.

17. So rightly Victor Conzemius, "Rosmini-Servati," in *Lexikon für Theologie und Kirche,* 8:1312.

18. Cf. the title of the book by Georg Schwaiger, *Johann Michael Sailer. Der bayerische Kirchenvater* (Munich: Schnell & Steiner, 1982).

19. So Bishop Josef Stimpfle, preface to *Johann Michael Sailer 1751-1832. Von Aresing nach Regensburg,* ed. Gemeindeverwaltung Aresing (Pfaffenhofen a.d. Ilm: Hans Prechter, 1982), 9.

books. In so doing he found that virtually all the devotional material was full of legends that were inappropriate, even sometimes offensive to an inquiring mind. Therefore he himself composed and published a *Complete Book of Devotion and Prayer for Use by Catholics* (*Vollständiges Gebetbuch für katholische Christen*, 1783). This publication made Sailer famous, but at the same time it brought him the charge from the Protestant side of proselytism and from the Roman Catholic of being a representative of the Enlightenment. Already the following year he was appointed professor of ethics and pastoral theology at the University of Dillingen.

Within ten years he was discharged again because of his alleged Enlightenment tendencies. He used this second retirement productively, translating the *Imitation of Christ* by Thomas à Kempis (ca. 1379-1471), a medieval mystic; publishing a collection of Christian letters throughout the centuries; and adapting to his own time the spiritual exercises of Ignatius of Loyola (1491-1556), the founder of the Jesuit Order. When the University of Ingolstadt was transferred to Landshut in 1800, he again obtained a professorship, since he had been a victim of the Jesuit party.[20] Until 1821 he taught there moral and pastoral theology, pedagogy, liturgics, and catechetics. He also served as university preacher. Moreover, he offered lecture series for general studies and impacted a whole generation of priests with his living Christianity. King Max I Joseph of Bavaria (1756-1825) wanted him to become bishop of Augsburg, but Sailer's conservative ecclesiastical opponents thwarted that attempt.

In 1821 Sailer finally became a member of the Regensburg cathedral chapter, the following year deputy bishop, and in 1829 finally bishop of Regensburg. At the 150th anniversary of his death, Pope John Paul II called Sailer a "successful originator of Catholic renewal in his mother country, an incisive defender of true doctrine, finally almost a herald of the more recent ecumenical movement."[21] Indeed, his devotional materials were appreciated by both Roman Catholics and Protestants, and he was not afraid to maintain good contacts with Protestants. With Immanuel Kant, Sailer attempted to answer the three basic questions of humanity: What can we know? For what may we hope? What shall we do? His answer came from his faith: we know about God, we have salvation in Christ, and we should act in love.[22] This answer did not remain ab-

20. For the following cf. Anton Landersdorfer, "Sailer, Johann Michael," in *Theologische Realenzyklopädie*, 29:639.

21. "Wort des Hl. Vaters zur Feier der Bischof Sailer-Gedenkwoche 14. bis 20. Mai 1982," in *Amtsblatt für die Diözese Regensburg*, May 28, 1982, 85.

22. Cf. Johann Hofmeier, "Gott in Christus, das Heil der Welt — Die Zentralidee des Christentums im theologischen Denken Johann Michael Sailers," in *Johann Michael Sailer. Theologe, Pädagoge und Bischof zwischen Aufklärung und Romantik*, ed. Hans Bungert

stract for Sailer, because his deep mystic piety was informed by a knowledge of both Scripture and the fathers of the church. This organic unity of Scripture and the Fathers assured for him that tradition did not mean something that is added on to Scripture, but rather is a living tradition that as the life-giving spirit carries the church through the centuries.[23] All animosities against him notwithstanding, Sailer therefore always remained faithful to his church.

Caught by the Reaction of Vatican I: *Johann Josef Ignaz von Döllinger and Karl Joseph von Hefele*

An inner consolidation, albeit under the leadership of Rome, was especially promulgated under the pontificate of Pius IX (1846-78). The *Syllabus Errorum* of 1864 counted eighty errors that culminated in the liberalism of that day. But there were others who tried to reconcile the church with modern society, such as Count Charles Forbes René de Montalembert (1810-70), a pious Roman Catholic but an ardent liberal in politics, who strove for the freedom of conscience, the separation of church and state, and the freedom of press, among many other things. Important are his two 1863 speeches at the international Catholic congress in Mechelen, Belgium, where he called for a free church in a free state, a stance that was promptly rejected by Pius IX.

Johann Josef Ignaz von Döllinger (1799-1890), a historian and theologian, met with a similar fate. He taught church history and canon law starting in 1826 at the newly founded University of Munich. Similar to the French movement of liberal Catholicism, Döllinger sought to restore social and religious life on Roman Catholic principles. At a gathering of the German bishops (1848), he advocated the idea of a national church and was convinced that they should meet regularly. He also encouraged the growth of a Catholic press. After a dispute with King Ludwig I of Bavaria (1786-1868) over the dismissal of four professors, Döllinger was dismissed too in 1847, but restored in 1850. Similar to Johann Adam Möhler, he saw an organic growth and consistent development in the church. Therefore Protestantism marked a break with the past. Also, the concept of tradition played an important role in his thinking. Therefore he judged the Reformation initially rather negatively, but later came to a more positive understanding. Yet Luther's emphasis on justification by grace alone remained alien to him. By 1850 he had become more nationalistic, calling for

---

(Regensburg: Mittelbayerische Druckerei- und Verlagsgesellschaft, 1983), 39, who extensively deals with the affinity between Kant and Sailer.

23. Cf. Schwaiger, *Johann Michael Sailer*, 171.

episcopal independence from Rome with the Catholic Church in Germany headed by a German metropolitan. Education for the priesthood should occur in universities rather than in ecclesial seminaries. He argued that scholars in their research must be free from arbitrary interference by church authorities, a position that was rejected by the publication of the *Syllabus of Errors* in 1864. Freedom in research was especially important for him, since he was a dedicated historian who was very much interested in the patristic era and in the formation of the church in the first centuries.

Döllinger sensed that at the First Vatican Council (1869-70) the infallibility of the pope was to be established. To counteract this idea, in 1869 he wrote a book, anonymously, called *The Pope and the Council,* in which he demonstrated from the history of the papacy that such infallibility is not warranted. For the council, however, he claimed the following:

> Complete and real freedom for every one, freedom from moral constraint, from fear and intimidation, and from corruption, belongs to the essence of a Council. In assembly of men bound in conscience by the oaths to consider the maintenance and increase of Papal power their main object, — men living in fear of incurring the displeasure of the *Curia,* and with it the charge of perjury, and the most burdensome hindrances in the discharge of their office — cannot certainly be called free in all those questions which concern the authority and claims of the See of Rome, and very few at most of the questions that would have to be discussed at a Council do not come under this category.[24]

Small wonder that Döllinger was not asked to participate in the proceedings of Vatican I and that his book was immediately placed on the index. Yet he was kept informed of the discussions of the council through bishops who shared his concerns.

When papal infallibility was declared in 1870, Döllinger fought with all his scholarly reputation against it, but without success. When he refused to subscribe to it, he was excommunicated in 1871 by the archbishop of Munich, and lost his professorship the following year. But King Ludwig II (1845-86) of Bavaria thought this was unjust and the same year appointed him *Rektor* of the University of Munich and president of the Bavarian Academy of the Sciences. Döllinger no longer celebrated Mass, but regularly attended the liturgy. Now he devoted himself to promoting Christian unity by attacking its main stumbling

---

24. Janus [Ignaz Döllinger], *The Pope and the Council* (London: Rivingtons, 1869), 423-24.

block when he contended that the infallibility cannot be maintained and the Jesuits who stood behind it would also lose their influence. In the *Lectures on the Reunion of the Churches* of 1872, he substantiated his hope for a reunion of the churches in the following way: "If we look closer, we shall be able to assume a disposition and readiness for union among all those who admit that the communion they belong to is not absolutely the Church, and the one and single Church complete in itself, but only a branch Church, which cannot claim to be itself that One Holy Catholic and Apostolic Church whereof the Creed speaks."[25] Indeed, that was a wish that is still carrying promise among many who are working in the ecumenical movement today.

Karl Joseph von Hefele (1809-93) was the successor to Möhler at the University of Tübingen in church history, first as Privatdozent in 1836 and then as professor in 1840. In 1852/53 he became rector of the university, and in 1869 was made bishop at Rottenburg. He was industrious in carefully studying the sources of dogma. He published a seven-volume *History of the Councils of the Church. From the Original Documents* (1855-74; Eng. trans. 1894-96, in 5 vols.) and was one of the consultants in preparation for Vatican I. He, too, objected to papal infallibility, especially for historical reasons. He voted against it in the decisive session and left Rome early so he would not have to vote in the public session. Nevertheless, as the lone German bishop to have not accepted the doctrine, he yielded to the pressure of Rome and of the priests of his diocese to accept the new dogma in 1871. Yet he also maintained a friendly relationship with both the government and the Protestants.

Modernistic Tendencies? Alfred Loisy, George Tyrrell, and Maurice Blondel

While Protestant theology in Europe was conducted largely in German in the nineteenth and first part of the twentieth century, Catholic theology of that period was to a large extent promoted in French. There was also a decided difference between Germany and France with regard to Roman Catholic theology. After the French Revolution Catholic education had been outlawed and was not condoned until 1875 when the Instituts Catholiques were established at various universities. While the historical-critical investigation of biblical documents flourished in Germany through theological faculties at state universities, this was not the case in France. There theological education was a church matter.

---

25. Johann Josef Ignaz von Döllinger, *Lectures on the Reunion of the Churches*, translated with a preface by Henry Nutcombe Oxenham (London: Rivingtons, 1872), 150.

When, for instance, **Alfred Loisy** (1857-1940), who studied at the Institut Catholique in Paris, submitted his doctoral dissertation on the doctrine of inspiration, he was told that such a piece could not be published because he had conceded that "the element of the divine which might be added by inspiration changed not at all the nature of the writings to which it pertained."[26] Only when he wrote a new thesis on a less touchy topic, the history of the Old Testament canon, did he receive his doctorate from the Institut in 1890 while already a professor at the same institution. Loisy also studied with Ernest Renan at the Collège de France and served as professor of Hebrew and exegesis (1885-93) at the Institut. Yet when he stated in 1893 that the Pentateuch is not the work of Moses, the first chapters of Genesis are not a literal account of the beginnings of humanity, and the books of the Old and New Testament do not possess equal historical value, the board of the governors of the Institut decided to expel him. He then served as chaplain at a convent of Dominican nuns in Paris, where he stayed till 1899 when he resigned because of illness.

In 1902 his book *The Gospel and the Church* appeared, which set off a storm unlike any other theological publication in the twentieth century. Because of the color of its cover, it was called "the little red book." Loisy saw the church in continuity with the gospel. The church is the historical development of the gospel, and without the church the gospel could not be preached and would no longer be present in history. The church is the gospel in history, it has explained the gospel, and adapted it to different peoples under various conditions of history. In this book we also find the often misquoted sentence: "Jesus foretold the kingdom, and it was the Church that came."[27] This did not mean for Loisy that Jesus intended something different from what developed. For him there was a historical continuity between the gospel and the church. But even for Loisy there was a discontinuity between the Jesus of history and the Gospels, because Jesus must be understood in the context of Judaism, a context that has changed since then. Loisy was charged with modernism and excommunicated in 1908. Thereafter he continued to teach at the Collège de France (1909-26) and the École des Hautes Études (1924-27). He died in 1940 without being reconciled with his church.

The modernist movement extended beyond France, as we have seen, into Germany and also to England and Italy.[28] In England, one should mention

26. Alfred Loisy, as quoted more extensively in Bernard B. Scott, introduction to *The Gospel and the Church*, by Alfred Loisy, trans. Christopher Home (Philadelphia: Fortress, 1976 [1903]), xviii.

27. Loisy, *Gospel and the Church*, 166.

28. Cf. more extensively Alec R. Vidler, *The Modernist Movement in the Roman Church: Its Origins and Outcome* (Cambridge: At the University Press, 1934).

Baron Friedrich von Hügel (1852-1925) and the Irish Jesuit **George Tyrrell** (1861-1909), a convert from the Anglican Church of Ireland, who also wrote the introduction to the English translation of Loisy's *Gospel and the Church*. For Tyrrell dogma was second to religious experience and Christianity was the kernel of a universal religion of the future.

While Tyrrell affirmed that the Catholic Church "alone can answer firmly and infallibly what all are asking," he was not convinced that this should be done through "speculative considerations," but rather "through an insight into the high and all-satisfying ethical conceptions of the Catholic religion."[29] Ethics meant for him not primarily social action, but a formation of the heart. The title of his book *Hard Sayings* reveals this claim, because it does not refer to things that are difficult intellectually to comprehend, but to God's love for us that transcends our imagination.[30] Therefore in *Lex Orandi,* a treatise on the Christian creed, he tried to show that it is not enough "to connect the truths of theology with the truths of history and science," but "to connect the life of religion with the rest of our life, and to show that the latter demands the former."[31] Revelation offers the mysteries of faith in the language of prophecy, while theology endeavors to translate them into the language of science and to harmonize "these translations with the whole system of our understanding."[32]

In *Lex Credendi*, the sequel to *Lex Orandi*, Tyrrell views the Lord's Prayer as the rule and criterion of pure doctrine. He is not interested in building "a coherent intellectual system," but rather in testing the truths of Christianity "by the criterions of life, of spiritual fruitfulness."[33] The Roman Church at the beginning of the twentieth century, however, saw its main task to oppose with intellectual clarity "dangerous modern ideas." Since Tyrrell stood up for Loisy, Tyrrell was expelled from the Jesuit Order in 1906. When Pope Pius X published the encyclical *Pascendi* the following year, in which he condemned any modernistic ideas in philosophy and theology, and forbade any criticism from a historical perspective, Tyrrell spoke sharply against it and was promptly excommunicated.[34] According to his own thinking, Tyrrell never left his church, because

---

29. George Tyrrell, *Hard Sayings: A Selection of Meditation and Studies,* 6th ed. (London: Longmans, Green, 1904 [1898]), xiii.

30. Cf. Tyrrell, *Hard Sayings,* xvii-xviii.

31. George Tyrrell, *Lex Orandi or Prayers and Creed* (London: Longmans, Green, 1907 [1903]), viii.

32. George Tyrrell, *Lex Credendi* (London: Longmans, Green, 1907 [1906]), viii.

33. Tyrrell, *Lex Credendi,* 251.

34. Cf. Ernst Erasmi in George Tyrrell, *Das Christentum am Scheideweg,* trans. Ernst Erasmi, ed. Friedrich Heiler (Munich: Ernst Reinhardt, 1959), 32, in his extensive introduction where he also relates that Tyrrell's bishop did not allow a church burial (9).

that church for him mediated "between God and the soul, as a mystical body in union with which alone salvation is possible."[35] It came as no surprise that Vatican II picked up some of his ideas, such as the church as a sacrament, and the church's service in the world. Influenced by the deep piety of John Newman and by Maurice Blondel in his apologetic concern for the Christian faith, Tyrrell was ahead of his time, because the attempt to connect the church to the modern times emerged virtually everywhere. In Italy modernism is connected in the social area with Romolo Murri (1870-1944), in the area of culture with Ernesto Bonaiuti (1881-1946), and in the literary area with Senator Antonio Fogazzaro (1842-1911), a novelist and poet.

Maurice Blondel (1861-1949), professor of philosophy at Lille and later at Aix-en-Provence, attempted to bridge the gap between modern thought and Catholicism through a new method of apologetics. In his doctoral thesis "L'Action" of 1893, "a masterpiece of the late 19th century," he shows that human conduct always employs metaphysical views.[36] Therefore the question of humanity's supernatural destiny must be left open. Blondel wrote:

> To think that we can arrive at being and legitimately affirm any reality whatsoever without having reached the very end of the series which extends from the first sensible intuition to the necessity of God and of religious practice, is to remain in illusion: we cannot stop at an object in the middle to make an absolute truth of it without falling into the idolatry of the understanding; every premature affirmation is illegitimate and, in the eyes of science, false, even when we will have to come back to it later on, but by a different way, and with a different meaning. — To think, on the contrary, that human conduct is independent of all metaphysical views, that practice is sufficient unto itself, and that it is possible to live without any concern for being, is equally an error.[37]

Such an unashamed defense of a supernatural religion did not go over well in secular France, and after defending his thesis for over four hours he was refused a university post. Only by direct appeal to the minister of education two years later was this refusal overcome.[38] Some of Blondel's deliberations were picked up by the so-called *nouvelle théologie* (new theology).

---

35. Tyrrell, *Hard Sayings*, 415.

36. So J. M. Somerville, "Blondel, Maurice," in *New Catholic Encyclopedia*, 2:617.

37. Maurice Blondel, *Action* (1893), *Essay on a Critique of Life and a Science of Practice*, trans. Olivia Blanchette (Notre Dame: University of Notre Dame Press, 1984), 392.

38. So Blanchette, preface to *Action*, xiv.

A New Theology: Marie-Dominique Chenu and
Yves Marie Joseph Congar, Pierre Teilhard de Chardin,
Henri de Lubac, and Jean Daniélou

In 1907, the same year the encyclical *Pascendi* condemned modernism, a new theological school was started in Le Saulchoir, near the Belgian town of Tournai. This institution was to become a center for the renewal of Catholic theology in the first half of the twentieth century. It was run by Dominicans with the intention of continuing the Thomistic tradition. Its first rector was Ambroise Gardeil (1859-1931). While steering clear of the discussion about modernism, they undertook the task of reforming theology. The new theology wanted to overcome modernistic historicism by showing a continuity between revelation, dogma, and theology, while maintaining the primacy of revelation. It was important that theology stay in contact with its living source, the re-vealed Word of God. Theology should use biblical and historical criticism as in-struments to tie it even more closely to its actual object matter, which has been entrusted to it according to the progressive economy of revelation. Theology also has a speculative function, but should not give in to baroque embellish-ments. Theology should express a faith that shows solidarity with its respective time; this means being present for the revealed Word of God in the life of the church and the actual experiences of the Christians.

Marie-Dominique Chenu (1894-1989) was professor of the history of dogma at the Dominican School at Le Saulchoir (1920-42) and rector of the same school (1932-42). He wrote a small booklet in 1937 about Le Saulchoir, *Une école de théologie: Le Saulchoir (A School of Theology: Le Saulchoir),* in which he laid out a plan for a reform of theology claiming the primacy of the revealed Word of God, acceptance of biblical and historical criticism, an open-minded Thomism, and an openness toward the problems of the present. In the middle of World War II, in 1942, this little booklet was put on the index of outlawed works, since the *Osservatore Romano,* the official newspaper of the Vatican, claimed in an official commentary that it was an expression of the *nouvelle théologie,* lean-ing toward semimodernism, relativism, and subjectivism. Consequently, Chenu lost his rectorate and also his chair at Le Saulchoir and withdrew to a Dominican monastery in Paris. In informing him of the Roman decision, Emmanuel Célestin Cardinal Suhard of Paris (1874-1949) tried to comfort Chenu with the remark that within twenty years everybody would echo his teachings. Little did the cardinal know that this would indeed come true. But before this happened, Chenu suffered another blow. He had also been an adviser and a theological ex-pert concerning the worker-priest movement in France, which had as its goal a missionary objective and solidarity with blue-collar workers. In 1953 the Vatican decided that worker-priests were not allowed in factories and other places. Chenu had to leave Paris. He returned in 1959, the year Pope John XXIII announced Vatican II. He then became an adviser for the council.

Later, Pope Paul VI used a text by Chenu in his encyclical *Populorum Progressio* (1968), when talking about the humanistic and Christian significance of work, which earlier had been criticized by Rome.[39]

In his small book on the school of theology at Le Saulchoir, Chenu had mentioned the need for a theology that recognized the signs of the times. This term was used during Vatican II in the pastoral constitution *Gaudium et Spes* and in John XXIII's encyclical *Pacem in Terris* of 1963. Chenu stated that the present time signals to the church the coherence and timeliness of the gospel when confronted with the problems of humanity. For a theologian discerning the signs of the times and who is interested in concrete experiences, history reveals the plan of God. Events in history are signs for that which is contained in the gospel. The new values that come to the fore in the history of humanity are material for the gospel, and the true tradition is permeated through the Word of God. A theologian, so Chenu claimed, sees history and God's way with this world as belonging together — both refer to each other.

Yves Marie Joseph Congar (1904-95) was a student of Chenu at Le Saulchoir and taught there fundamental theology and dogmatics from 1931 to 1954, interrupted only by World War II when he became prisoner of war in Germany. This also saved him from sharing the same fate as Chenu. When Le Saulchoir moved in 1939 to Etiolles near Paris, Congar became involved with the worker-priest movement. Since this seemed to be suspicious work in the eyes of the church, because the workers movement was seen as infiltrated by Marxists, the church hierarchy exiled him in 1954 to Israel and then to Cambridge for further study. In 1956 he was allowed to return to France, where he taught at the University of Strasbourg till 1968. Vatican II meant for him rehabilitation, and in the preface of 1968 to the new edition of his book *Vraie et Fausse Réforme dans l'église (True and False Reforms in the Church)*, which had been deemed suspicious in 1950, Congar confessed: "John XXIII had within only a few weeks created a new ecclesial climate as he had done later at the council. The decisive openness had come from above. With one stroke, the forces of renewal which did not dare to come into the open, could now unfold their wings." In 1994 he was even elevated to cardinal.

---

39. Cf. Marie-Dominique Chenu, *The Theology of Work: An Exploration*, trans. Lilian Soiron (Chicago: Henry Regnery, 1966), and Pope Paul VI, *On the Development of Peoples: Populorum Progressio* (Washington, D.C.: United States Catholic Conference, 1967), 37 n. 29, where Chenu's book is cited.

Congar founded the series Unam Sanctam (One Holy Church) in 1937, which showed his "premature" interest in ecumenical work. He opened this series with his own publication, *Divided Christendom: A Catholic Study of the Problem of Reunion* (*Chrétiens désunis. Principes d'un "Oecuménisme" Catholique*, 1937; Eng. trans. 1939). For the first time the attempt was made to theologically define ecumenism and to put it within the theological enterprise. In *True and False Reforms in the Church* he does not plead for a reform *of* the church, but *in* the church, one that unfolds itself in the concrete life of the church. This means reform as renewal. More and more he became convinced that catholicity must also allow for differences. As the most prominent ecumenical scholar of his church in the twentieth century, he distinguished between true and false tradition in history and pointed to wrong developments. While initially he thought that catholicity means enclosing all the differences, toward the end of his life he realized that there is a common origin that ties us together.

Pierre Teilhard de Chardin (1881-1955), a Jesuit theologian and paleontologist who taught theology at the Institut Catholique in Paris, also encountered difficulties. When he tried to reconcile the traditional doctrine of original sin with a modern evolutionary vision, he was dismissed from his academic post. From 1926 to 1946 he was in China, where he was involved in discovering the Peking man. Upon his return, he stayed briefly in Paris and was transferred again to other parts of the world. After World War II he returned to Paris, but as a consequence of the encyclical *Humani Generis* he was again barred from both teaching and publishing and moved to New York in 1951, where he died four years later. During his life he was allowed to publish hardly any of his writings that proposed a philosophical, evolutionary religious vision of the course of the world from creation to the parousia. His works were published posthumously from 1955 to 1976 in thirteen volumes.

Though he worked mainly in paleontology, Teilhard was an immensely spiritual person. This can be seen from *The Divine Milieu,* written in 1926/27 and published in 1957, where he proposed a spirituality for Christians in the modern world. In mystic fashion he declared that "at the heart of our universe, each soul exists for God, in our Lord."[40] Then he talked about Christian perfection and about the universal Christ and the great communion before he arrived at the parousia. He wrote: "The Messiah, who appeared for a moment in our midst, only allowed himself to be seen and touched for a moment before vanishing once again, more luminous and ineffable than ever, into the depth of the

---

40. Pierre Teilhard de Chardin, *The Divine Milieu* (New York: Harper Torchbooks, 1968), 56.

future. He came. Yet now we must expect him — no longer a small chosen group among us, but all men — once again and more than ever. The Lord Jesus will only come soon if we ardently expect him."[41]

"*The Phenomenon of Man* is certainly the most important of Père Teilhard's published works."[42] It was written between 1938 and 1940, reworked and completed in 1947-48, and finally published in 1955. For Teilhard there is an upward movement from the cosmosphere (the universe) via the biosphere (the sphere of life) and the noosphere (the realm of human thinking) to the Christosphere (the realm of Christ). The whole cosmos will eventually find its fulfillment in Christ, who through his incarnation has already penetrated the world and moves it to its final destiny. Teilhard proposed a universal Christ who is alpha and omega, the beginning and end of all things. Theology and the natural sciences converge in Teilhard's thoughts in the same way our own striving and God's gift of the kingdom converge. Having been called the greatest apologist of Christianity after Blaise Pascal (1623-62), Teilhard shared Pascal's fate, because in 1962 the Holy Office in Rome published an admonition against "the errors and ambiguities" in the writings of Teilhard. Henri de Lubac attempted a defense of his fellow Jesuit showing the fundamentally positive directions of his thoughts as well their limitations. Jean Daniélou came to his aid, too, and finally Teilhard was rehabilitated at Vatican II.

The second phase of *nouvelle théologie* was primarily influenced by the Jesuit school in Lyon-Fourvière. This center for the renewal of theological research devoted itself especially to translating patristic texts under the leadership of Daniélou, Lubac, as well as Hans Urs von Balthasar and Hugo Rahner. **Henri de Lubac** (1896-1991), a Jesuit who taught fundamental theology and history of religion at the Institut Catholique at Lyon, was initiator and coeditor of the Sources Chrétiennes, a series of editions of patristic texts that he had started together with Daniélou in 1942, as well as a series of theological monographs starting at 1944 with the title Théologie. Again, because of *Humani Generis* he was not allowed to teach for the next ten years and had to leave Lyon. His books were removed from the libraries of the Jesuits and were barred from sale. Through Pope John XXIII he was rehabilitated and appointed as consultant working in the theological commission that prepared Vatican II. His fault was that he tried to make better known the treasures of the Catholic tradition. The pursuit necessitated uncomfortable questions, for instance, whether Origen should not be exonerated or whether the correlation between nature and grace

41. Teilhard, *The Divine Milieu*, 151.

42. So Julian Huxley, introduction to *The Phenomenon of Man*, by Pierre Teilhard de Chardin, trans. Bernard Wall (New York: Harper and Row, 1965), 12.

in Roman Catholicism was correct. For Lubac catholicity is a gift and a task. It is dynamic and missionary with the goal of planting the church. He believed that catholicity is also the search for a living synthesis between the symbolic theology of the patristic era and the dialectic theology of high scholasticism. Both perspectives can be brought together in the wider horizon of catholicity.

In his work *The Mystery of the Supernatural* of 1946, Lubac showed that humanity is drawn to God and has a desire to vision God. This desire is no wishful thinking, but a natural desire toward the supernatural with no innate power to fulfill its yearning for a gift, the *donum perfectum*, the perfect gift that is God's self.[43] It is the paradox of humanity that as a finite spirit humanity is open toward the infinite. Though humanity desires a vision of God, Lubac makes it clear that this desire does not determine God actually giving that vision. "God is not governed by our desire."[44] This means that although there is no direct way to God, God's free will awakens that desire in us. Once this desire exists in us, it becomes a sign of a certain gift, namely, of God's self-giving to us, of his self-disclosure. This also implies that we are created for the vision of God, because, as Lubac confessed, reiterating the words of Augustine: "You have made us towards you, o God."[45] Lubac wanted to enliven the sense for the mystery by mining the great catholic tradition. To this end, he studied the history of theology by working on Origen in the early period of the church, but also delving into medieval exegesis, which resulted in a four-volume opus (*Medieval Exegesis*, 1959-63; Eng. trans. in 2 vols., 1998-2000). Through this kind of research he showed that the symbolism of tradition is in the service of the mystery. Being fully exonerated, Lubac was finally elevated to cardinal in 1983.

Jean Daniélou (1905-74), a Jesuit and student of Lubac, who from 1944 taught early Christianity at the Institut Catholique in Paris, published an article in 1946 on the present orientations in religious thought. Here he claimed that instead of bringing renewal, modernism has led to a hardening of positions. To remedy the situation we should return to the foundational sources of Christianity: the Bible, the church fathers, and the liturgy. Contact should also be made with the different streams of contemporary thought to enrich and widen the horizon of theology. Then one should maintain contact with life in meeting the needs of the souls. Again, discussion started and his opponents saw this article as a manifesto of the *nouvelle théologie*. Subsequently one of his first books was banned from bookstores, since after World War II one suspected heresies

43. Cf. Henri de Lubac, *The Mystery of the Supernatural,* trans. Rosemary Sheed (London: Geoffrey Chapman, 1967), 97-98.

44. Lubac, *Mystery of the Supernatural,* 272.

45. Lubac, *Mystery of the Supernatural,* xiv.

everywhere. Then came in 1950 *Humani Generis,* the papal encyclical of Pope Pius XII that analyzed and criticized the new tendencies in theology. This meant the eventual end of the group of theologians in Le Saulchoir and Fourvière who had attempted to establish a theology of renewal. But Daniélou maintained his teaching position after the publication of *Humani Generis,* and was even named dean of the Institut Catholique in 1961. With Vatican II the whole climate changed. Daniélou was influential at that council, and in 1969 he was even elevated to cardinal. In that position he was elected to the Académie Française in 1972/73 and became a formative mind of theology in the second part of the twentieth century.

In his book *The Lord of History* (1953), which characterizes his theology, Daniélou presented a Christian vision of history. "It is this belief in the irreversibility of salvation that gives rise to the Christian virtue of hope, in contrast to the characteristic melancholy which flows from the Greek acceptance of endless repetition."[46] He introduced the category of progress in the sense of a progressive economy of salvation in which the Old Testament and the New are two successive stages in development. In contrast to modern philosophy, which has forgotten the concept of the end and goal of history, Christian theology maintains that finality because of its eschatological persuasion. History is neither repetitive, nor cast in stone, nor simply meandering here and there, but is characterized by eventfulness, progressiveness, and goal-orientation, and therefore hope. "The object of hope is the final destiny of the world and of the whole human race."[47]

Proclamation in a New Key: Hugo and Karl Rahner, Romano Guardini, Odo Casel, Erich Przywara, and Hans Urs von Balthasar

While the Dominican theologians of Le Saulchoir wanted to reform theology, and the Jesuits at Lyon-Fournière attempted to enliven theological research, the Jesuits of the theological faculty of Innsbruck attempted a theological renewal through a more effective proclamation of the Christian message. That venture resulted in a theology of proclamation, or a kerygmatic theology. It was developed in the second half of the 1930s and was especially connected with Josef Andreas Jungmann (1889-1975) and **Hugo Rahner** (1900-1968). They were convinced that the emphasis on traditional Christianity no longer allowed the

---

46. Jean Daniélou, *The Lord of History: Reflections on the Inner Meaning of History,* trans. Nigel Abercrombie (London: Longmans, 1958), 2.

47. Daniélou, *The Lord of History,* 353.

Christian faith to be experienced as the good news and to have an enlivening effect on our lives. Therefore a renewal of proclamation was needed. While scholarly theology sought to discern the revealed truth, a theology of proclamation wanted to make these truths transparent, so one could agree with them. Scholarly theology has truth as its object matter, but a theology of proclamation looks for the visual and concrete perception of the truth of revelation and unfolds primarily its motifs that can arouse our consent. We do not look for Christ only in history and doctrine, but also in life. (Hugo's brother, Karl Rahner, however, had little interest in this movement, because he saw the need not just for a new approach within theology, but for an altogether new theology in which he proposed the "anthropological turning-point." This means that, similar to Tillich's method of correlation, Karl started with humanity's own experience and then asked how the Christian truth corresponds to that experience.)

Hugo Rahner published a *Theology of Proclamation* (1938) to show a possible way of relating theory and proclamation with continuous reference to the proclamation of the Fathers. The kerygmatic focal point for him is the divinity of Christ. Rahner wrote: "Faith is continually an affirmation of an intellectual content to that which we call the word of God, to a truth and to a 'theory' in the sense of the Church Fathers. If we fail to reiterate this fact in our preaching of the divinity of Christ, and fail to illumine it by the internal clarity of faith itself, then in the development of Christian belief we are quite apt to fall into error."[48] Especially in looking at the Protestant life-of-Jesus research, Rahner was not content with proclaiming the New Testament kerygma, since that must be seen in its unfolding in the dogmatic interpretation of the early church. Rahner not only saw the church in continuity with the eternal word, but as "the continuation of the eternal Word, proceeding from the mouth of the Father."[49] The one who preaches therefore stands in this kind of continuity, "if he models himself upon the speaking God, if he speaks as his master speaks, hence if his preaching today is revitalized by an ever renewed contact with the tradition in Scripture, the Fathers, the liturgy, and in the writings of the saints of every century."[50] This should lead to a theology of the heart that is grasped by the mystery of Christ. The one who proclaims does not simply proclaim, but is drawn into that mystery. We become part of the magnificent drama of salvation.

The Italian-born theologian **Romano Guardini** (1885-1968) taught philosophy of religion and Catholic worldview successively at the universities of

---

48. Hugo Rahner, *A Theology of Proclamation*, trans. Richard Dimmler et al. (New York: Herder and Herder, 1968), 64.

49. Hugo Rahner, *A Theology of Proclamation*, 136.

50. Hugo Rahner, *A Theology of Proclamation*, 15.

Berlin (1923-39), Tübingen (1945-49), and Munich (1948-62). He was not part of a movement but was active in movements, for instance, in the movement for liturgical renewal and in the youth movement after World War I, and was a popular preacher and author. He became well known through his inspirational books *The Church and the Catholic* (1935) and *The Spirit of the Liturgy* (1918). He picked up on the renewed sense of community following the disintegration caused by World War I, showing that this community is not a collection of self-contained individuals, "but the reality which comprehends individuals — the Church. She embraces the people; she embraces mankind. She draws even things, indeed the whole world, into herself. Thus the Church is regaining that cosmic spaciousness which was hers during the early centuries and the Middle Ages."[51] By pointing to the church, he went beyond the community that ends at national boundaries to one that comprises all of humanity and the whole cosmos. Guardini furthered a renewed appreciation of popular piety. While working for authentic liturgical education, he sensed the concerns of the people. Therefore he realized that the church becomes alive in the souls of the people.

On liturgy, Guardini emphasized that it has very little to do with the individual as such, because "in the liturgy God is to be honored by the body of the faithful, and the latter is in its turn to derive sanctification from this act of worship."[52] Only insofar as the individual is part of the body does he or she really participate in the liturgy and therefore in its benefits. Liturgy is not an individualistic enterprise for private edification. This does not diminish the prayers of the individual, but the forms of popular piety geared toward the individual exist side by side with those of the liturgy. As an astute observer of his time, he organized educational activities for the youth and recovered texts and figures of world literature by creating in theology a sensibility for actual life.

Odo Casel (1886-1948), a Benedictine monk of the monastery Maria Laach, Germany, a center of liturgical renewal, endeavored to renew liturgy and with it theology through introducing mysticism and the mysterious. He was convinced that holistic thinking for which humanity yearns looks more favorably to the mysterious than does modern rationalistic and subjectivistic thought.[53] Therefore he develops a theology of the mystery that leads to a nonrational apprehension of reality, especially of God's saving activity in the cult of the church. The cultic mystery is for Casel "the objective and necessary representation and actualization of the saving work of Christ. . . . In the cultic

51. Romano Guardini, *The Church and the Catholic,* in *"The Church and the Catholic" and "The Spirit of the Liturgy,"* trans. Ada Lane (New York: Sheed and Ward, 1935), 23.

52. Romano Guardini, *The Spirit of the Liturgy,* in *"The Church and the Catholic" and "The Spirit of the Liturgy,"* 122.

53. So Odo Casel, *Glaube, Gnosis, Mysterium* (Münster: Aschendorff, 1941), iv.

mystery the mystery of Christ becomes visible and efficacious; thereby it is a kind of continuation and further unfolding of the economy of Christ. Without the cultic mystery it could not be mediated to all generations of the community of salvation as this community extends through space and time."[54] Liturgy for Casel is holy action in which Christ becomes present with what he has done for us, but it is not a repetition of what has happened there and then in the life of Jesus.

Since Casel did not shy away from quoting theologians of the early church, such as Origen, to support his arguments, and since he pointed to the affinity of the Christian mystery with the Hellenistic mystery religions, his work did not remain uncontested. Yet saving one's soul and attaining eternal bliss, this tremendous yearning, as we find in the mystery cults, was for Casel "a preparatory discipline."[55] It finds its fulfillment in the mysteries of Christ. Casel was convinced that the analogy to the mysteries of antiquity "teaches us to recognize and discern many of the Christian truths in a deeper manner."[56] Similar to the history of religion school on the Protestant side, Casel mined the insights of the pre-Christian environment. He also showed a remarkable affinity to Rudolf Otto, who also pointed to analogies and to differences between the Christian faith and its religious environment. Important was his notion that in the Eucharist we have a representation of Christ's salvific activity, something that has also been pointed out by Protestant liturgists.

Erich Przywara (1889-1972) was also concerned about Catholic renewal. Catholicism is confronted with opposing poles of modernism, on the one hand the continuously new, and on the other unalterable tradition.[57] Przywara was born in Kattowitz, Upper Silesia, and joined the Jesuit Order in 1908. Since this order was outlawed in the German Empire, he received his education and had his novitiate in the Netherlands. From 1922 to 1941 he worked for the journal *Voices of the Time (Stimmen der Zeit)* in Munich, until it was discontinued by the Nazi secret police. After World War II he concerned himself primarily with caring for academically educated Roman Catholics. He had more than 800 publications to his name, 15 of which were books.

Similar to Karl Barth, Przywara emphasized that God cannot be grasped

---

54. Casel, *Glaube, Gnosis, Mysterium*, 40.

55. Odo Casel, *Die Liturgie der Mysterienfeier* (Freiburg im Breisgau: Herder, 1922), 45, with reference to Clement of Alexandria, *The Stromata* (6.17), where Clement mentions Greek philosophy as a "preparatory discipline" for the Christian message.

56. Casel, *Die Liturgie*, 98.

57. Cf. Erich Przywara, "Kirche als Volk und Volk als Kirche. Der Sinn des Zweiten Vatikanischen Konzils" (1966), in Erich Przywara, *Katholische Krise*, ed. Berhard Gertz (Düsseldorf: Patmos, 1967), 251-52.

since he is totally beyond us. Yet at the same time God is also in his creation. "God in us *and* above us."[58] The transcendence and immanence of God related to each other in a polar way. Against the presumed Kantian theoretical unknowability of God and the nominalistic Lutheran postulate that God's will is revealed to our own will, Przywara asserted an *analogia entis,* an analogy of being that bridged the polarity of similarity and difference between God and the created.[59] Yet Przywara denies that we can reach up to God. On the contrary, we are radically dependent on God. "Through all the 'God-equality' of the creature regardless how strong this equality may be, from the natural 'God-equality' of the human as 'created according to the similarity with God' to the supernatural 'participation in the divine nature' to the 'being made like God in Christ' the son of God, the 'even bigger unequality' with God pervades through all of this [equality]."[60] Przywara did not work in isolation, but was a conversation partner of Barth, which is noticeable in his work, and also of the phenomenologist Edmund Husserl. While his work with the educated class exerted considerable influence, and even colleagues such as Karl Rahner appreciated his work, he had no lasting influence.[61] But he did show that Catholicism need not be afraid of modernity.

When Romano Guardini retired in 1964 from the University of Munich, he was succeeded by the Jesuit **Karl Rahner** (1904-84). After 1961 Rahner was instrumental in the preparations for Vatican II, and he was an official and quite influential theologian later for that council. In 1967 he moved to the University of Münster. Through his numerous publications and lectures he had an immense influence as a theologian, and his books had a combined sale of more than one million copies. Fifteen honorary doctorates witness to the impact he made on academia. At least in literary output if not in influence, Rahner is to Roman Catholic theology what Karl Barth is to Protestantism. "Karl Rahner had been hailed as *the* religious thinker who had contributed more than any other to the renewal of Catholic theology in the twentieth century."[62] As he wrote: "I am envisaging a Catholic theology that is courageous and does not shun relative and restricted conflicts with Church authorities. . . . I envisage a theology which in the Church at large must be a theology of the worldwide

---

58. Erich Przywara, *Gottgeheimnis der Welt: Drei Vorträge über die geistige Krisis der Gegenwart* (Munich: Theatiner, 1923), 106.

59. Cf. Przywara, *Gottgeheimnis,* 129 and 135.

60. Erich Przywara, "Die religiöse Krisis der Gegenwart und der Katholizismus" (1925), in *Katholische Krise,* 52.

61. So Eva-Maria Faber, "Przywara, Erich," in *Theologische Realenzyklopädie,* 27:609.

62. So Geffrey B. Kelly, ed., introduction to *Karl Rahner: Theologian of the Graced Search for Meaning* (Minneapolis: Fortress, 1992), 1.

Church. That means a theology which does not only recite its own medieval history but, one that can listen to the wisdom of the East, to the longing for freedom in Latin America, and also to the sound of African drums."[63]

Rahner was loyal to his church, but he also had a creative tension with church authority. One of his trademarks was that in public he never wore a clerical collar. He envisioned a church theology that was in tune with the whole world and not simply with the European tradition. It is not accidental that his philosophical mentor was Martin Heidegger (1889-1976), not so much on specific material notions but in style of thinking and of investigating. Rahner attempted to construct a synthesis by taking the various dogmatic propositions, reducing them to certain fundamental principles and then establishing an internally coherent body of dogmatic truth. This means that he went beyond proof texting from the authority of tradition or from the biblical witness. He left a legacy of over four thousand entries in his bibliography, including the twenty-two volumes of *Theological Investigations* in which he covered nearly every aspect of religious thought.

Rahner was born in Freiburg im Breisgau, Germany, the city where Heidegger later taught. The family in which he grew up was traditionally pious and Roman Catholic. Upon graduation from the *Gymnasium* (1922), he entered the Society of Jesus as his brother Hugo had done earlier. Rahner studied philosophy from 1924 to 1927 and then taught Latin. In 1929 he began his four years of theological studies and later was ordained to the priesthood. In 1934 his superiors sent him to the University of Freiburg to obtain a doctorate in philosophy. He had already been interested in Immanuel Kant and Joseph Maréchal (1878-1944), a Jesuit philosopher at Louvain, Belgium, who has been called the father of transcendental Thomism. (While Maréchal agreed with Kant that we have no intellectual intuition of the noumenal, he contended with Thomas that there is in humanity an innate dynamism to Absolute Being. This means that God implanted in us a yearning toward Godself. This yearning needs to be clarified and answered.) At Freiburg he studied with Heidegger, among others. Rahner's thesis was on Thomas, entitled "Spirit in the World" (Eng. trans., 2nd ed., 1957).

In this dissertation of 1936 Rahner was fascinated with the congruence between Heidegger's concept of *Dasein* (being in the world) and Aquinas's concept of the dynamism of the human mind. The problem with his thesis, however, was that it was too Heideggerian and not Catholic enough. Therefore Rahner left Freiburg without a doctorate and was sent in 1936 to Innsbruck,

---

63. So Karl Rahner, foreword to *Theology and Discovery: Essays in Honor of Karl Rahner, S.J.*, ed. William J. Kelly (Milwaukee: Marquette University Press, 1980), 1.

where he completed his doctorate in theology in the same year. This time the thesis was research-based on patristic texts concerning the origin of the church. The following year he was appointed Privatdozent at the University of Innsbruck, and when the National Socialists closed the faculty of theology in 1939, he worked in a pastoral institute in Vienna. When the pressure of the National Socialists became too strong, he did pastoral work in a parish ministry in Bavaria. After the war he taught dogmatic theology to young Jesuits in Munich, and in 1949 he was appointed professor of dogmatics at the theological faculty of the University of Innsbruck. In 1964 he was called to Munich, but left after three years to assume a professorship in dogmatics and history of dogma in Münster, from where he retired in 1971.

In 1983 he published, together with Heinrich Fries (1911-99), *The Unity of the Churches: An Actual Possibility* (Eng. trans. 1985). They start with this telling thought: "The unity of the Church is the commandment of the Lord of the Church, who will demand from the leaders of the churches an accounting as to whether or not they have really done everything possible in this matter. This unity is a matter of life or death for Christendom."[64] There they set forth eight theses, of which the first one reads: "The fundamental truths of Christianity, as they are expressed in Holy Scripture, in the Apostles' Creed and in that of Nicaea and Constantinople are binding on all partner churches of the one Church to be." And in thesis 2 they add: "Beyond that, a realistic principle of faith should apply: Nothing may be rejected decisively and confessionally in one partner church which is binding dogma in another partner church."[65] The theses and the whole book attracted considerable attention. Joseph Cardinal Ratzinger (b. 1927), prefect of the Sacred Congregation for the Doctrine of the Faith, the present Pope Benedict XVI, rejected the whole proposal and accused Rahner and Fries of "theological acrobatics," and of being out of touch with reality.[66] Rahner had been active in ecumenical work since 1948 and certainly did not like being accused of thin-air acrobatics. Yet he was not worried about any possible consequences, because, as he stated: "They will not go after me. They will just say, 'he is an old man.'"[67] Rahner was not the church's theologian but a theologian for the church.

Rahner's *Foundations of Christian Faith: An Introduction to the Idea of Christianity*, first published in German in 1976 (Eng. trans. 1978), is one of the most important texts of Catholic theology in the twentieth century. Rahner was

---

64. Heinrich Fries and Karl Rahner, *The Unity of the Churches: An Actual Possibility*, trans. Ruth C. L. Gritsch and Eric W. Gritsch (Philadelphia: Fortress, 1985), 1.

65. Fries and Rahner, *Unity of the Churches*, 7.

66. Cf. Geffrey B. Kelly, introduction to *Karl Rahner*, 17.

67. Rahner shared his assessment at a luncheon after a public lecture at the University of Regensburg in 1984.

dissatisfied with the scholastic method that started with formulations from above. Instead he proposed an anthropological method that started with the human condition from below and attained a correspondence between life and truth, between experience and conceptuality. He discerned humanity's own experience and asked how the Christian truth can correspond to that experience. This transcendental anthropological method shows that there is an a priori structure of the finite spirit in the world that does not just experience certain categorical structures in the world, but because of its openness toward being in general it makes experiences toward the infinite and the mystery. His concern with being shows his indebtedness to Heidegger, whose student he had been in Freiburg. The human being is for Rahner a "transcendent being."[68] Through the power of the transcendentality of its spirit, the human being lives at the shore of an infinite sea of mystery, and categorical experience — be it in science or in everyday life — is only a tiny island in an infinite sea of the unnamed mystery. Any proof for the existence of God therefore cannot come from outside but must come from within humanity itself.

Rahner's theology is a transcendental theology with an existential base. Grace, for instance, is an existential reality given from God in a supernatural way. Yet at the same time, it is a reality given in the midst of human existence in knowledge and freedom as an offer to which humanity can respond with acceptance or rejection. Humanity cannot abandon this transcendental peculiarity of its being. Therefore Rahner arrived at the term "anonymous Christians," because he was convinced that there is no religion in which there is not some trace of God's grace.[69] In his *Foundations* he did not use the term, because it caused a lot of controversy. Yet he still affirmed that "in this Spirit of his he [Christ] is present and operative in all faith."[70] Rahner realized that Christian doctrines are no longer self-evident in a secular and pluralistic world. Therefore it is necessary to treat all theological doctrines with the transcendental anthropological method so that in each one there is a corresponding anthropological starting point to which one can refer in the dialogue with present-day humanity. Rudolf Bultmann, with his existential interpretation of the New Testament, and Paul Tillich, with his method of correlation, pursued a similar anthropological turn. Yet one need not be surprised that in many ways Rahner's rather complicated method and terminology was also a cause for suspicion and misunderstanding.

The Swiss **Hans Urs von Balthasar** (1905-88) was another solitary but in-

---

68. Karl Rahner, *Foundations of Christian Faith: An Introduction to the Idea of Christianity,* trans. William V. Dych (New York: Crossroad, 1990), 31.

69. Karl Rahner, "Christianity and the Non-Christian Religions," in *Theological Investigations,* vol. 5, *Later Writings,* trans. K. H. Kruger (Baltimore: Helicon, 1966), 131.

70. Karl Rahner, *Foundations of Christian Faith,* 318.

sightful figure. He was born into a long-established patrician family in Luzern, Switzerland. In his childhood and youth he showed a remarkable interest in music and literature. He studied German literature at the University of Zürich, where he submitted his thesis in 1929 on a topic in modern German literature. The same year, he joined the Society of Jesus in Bavaria. Balthasar received his theological training near Munich and in Fourvières near Lyon, where he came under the influence of Henri de Lubac. He wanted to pursue a career in pastoral work and writing, and became student chaplain at the University of Basel in 1940. There he met Adrienne von Speyr (1902-67), a medical doctor and a mystic, who was brought up Protestant but through Balthasar's influence joined the Roman Catholic Church, with Balthasar becoming her spiritual guide. Together with von Speyr he founded the Institute of St. John, a community in which the members take vows of poverty, chastity, and obedience but live in the world and follow a secular profession. When Balthasar assumed the role of director of the institute, he had to leave the Jesuit Order. This decision was very painful, because it also meant he was excluded from the official world of the church and could not obtain a professorship in theology or participate in the Second Vatican Council. He lived then as an independent writer. But after the Second Vatican Council his work gradually was recognized, and in 1969 he became a member of the international papal commission of theologians and died two days before he was to be elevated to cardinal.

Being faithful to tradition did not mean for Balthasar a repetition or a literal handing on of philosophical or theological theses, but the attitude of inner reflection and courageous creativity as a necessary prelude to actual spiritual faithfulness. Balthasar felt that the cosmological way of antiquity and the more recent anthropological way to communicate the Christian faith were reductionistic, and therefore he proposed the way of love. In Christian revelation the absolute love of God meets humanity in Jesus Christ. Though Jesus also taught, he primarily discloses himself in his life of passion and death, which reveals the absolute love of God. One can perceive this absolute love in itself and needs neither the cosmos nor humanity to mediate it. Either one sees it or one does not. As an answer to that love, we see the faithful love of the church and in the church the answer of the individual persons.

Balthasar unfolded a trinitarian theology. The specific principle of Catholicism is that revelation has its center in itself and from there it unfolds itself. He confined himself to portraying revelation's own shape in its beauty, compassion, and truth through which it draws us into it to assent to it and to act appropriately. We can glean this approach from his four volumes of *Explorations in Theology* (1960-74). He started in volume 1 *(The Word Made Flesh)* with word and revelation and word and redemption. In volume 2, under the title *Spouse of the Word,* he unfolded his ecclesiology beginning with a contemporary experience of the church and concluding with the liturgy and the sacraments. The third volume *(Creator Spirit)* focused on the Holy Spirit, where he drew heavily on secular literature. And finally under the title *Spirit and Institution,* he dealt with various topics such as the church, anthropology, and eschatology. Many of the items are quite insightful. For instance, under the title of "Loneliness in the Church" he stated: "Many Christians today feel lonely in their Church. In fact, it would not be too much to say: They feel isolated *from* the Church."[71] Then he talked about Jesus as the one who gathers people out of their loneliness, and came to his concern of church renewal, saying: "The true Church of Jesus Christ is something quite different from and more mysterious than the Church that sociologists investigate. Church history has shown over and over again that true renewal in the Church always comes from courageous individuals who are not afraid of loneliness (and who *for that very reason* gain followers!)."[72] Reform in the church meant for him a rejection of loneliness, solitude, and holiness, because the saints continually found and renew the church.

In Reaction to Vatican II: Johann Baptist Metz, Hans Küng, and Edward Schillebeeckx

Ecclesiological concerns became a matter of prime importance in the wake of Vatican II (1962-65). But soon in both Roman Catholic and Protestant quarters, a political theology emerged. On the Catholic side, the leading voice was **Johann Baptist Metz** (b. 1928), professor of fundamental theology at the University of Münster. As a student of Karl Rahner, he published in 1968 *Theology of the World,* in which the relationship between church and world provided the context for the social reality in its historical development. It was meant as a corrective against the privatization of theology and pointed to the public and social consequences of the Christian message. The problems that came to the fore with the Enlightenment and Marxism should not be circumvented as in a metaphysical, existential, and transcendental theology, but they should be critically addressed and a new relationship between theology and praxis established.

Metz contended that we have no reason to shun the world, because through the incarnation God had accepted the world, and *"the secularity of the*

---

71. Hans Urs von Balthasar, *Explorations in Theology,* vol. 4, *Spirit and Institution,* trans. Edward T. Oakes (San Francisco: Ignatius, 1995), 261.

72. Balthasar, *Explorations in Theology,* 4:284.

world, as it has emerged in the modern process of secularization and as we see it to-day in a globally heightened form, has fundamentally, though not in its individual historical forms, arisen not against Christianity but through it."[73] Putting all its hope in the one God, the Christian faith has rendered the world secular. While this positive acceptance of modern secularity reminds us of Gogarten, Metz puts more emphasis on eschatology than did Gogarten. Metz stated: "Since the hope of the Christian faith is oriented toward the future, it cannot fulfill itself in bypassing the world and the future of the world."[74] This means that the eschatological outlook of the Christian faith necessitates an interaction with the world.

This involvement in the affairs of the world is even more necessary since the eschatological promises of freedom, peace, justice, and reconciliation have a public dimension that in its critical and liberating function must be asserted in the face of historical social processes. Political theology, for which Metz opted, is not a new discipline. Metz wanted to make Christian proclamation societally effective and searched for categories that serve to shape and change public and private consciousness. Because of the eschatological proviso, meaning that the completion of the kingdom is at the eschaton, the church has a critical and liberating function in society. It is not surprising that through the restorative tendencies toward the close of the twentieth century, liberation theology in general and Metz's own agenda were met with increasing suspicion by Rome.

Metz was more fortunate than the Swiss **Hans Küng** (b. 1928), who taught fundamental theology and dogmatics at the University of Tübingen (1963-80). In 1979 the church withdrew its endorsement for him to teach in a Roman Catholic theological faculty. Subsequently, a new professorship in ecumenical theology was established for him at Tübingen (1980-95). The latter appointment was more fitting for Küng, because already his 1957 doctoral thesis, "On Justification," bore the subtitle "The Doctrine of Karl Barth and a Catholic Reflection."

Hans Küng was born near Luzern, Switzerland, and after graduation from high school went to Rome to study theology at the Pontifical Gregorian University in 1948. He received his licentiate in philosophy three years later with a thesis on the existentialist Jean-Paul Sartre (1905-80). In 1955 he obtained his licentiate in theology with a thesis on Barth's doctrine of justification. Two years later he received his doctorate on the same subject at the Institut Catholique in Paris. Balthasar had been influential in steering Küng toward

---

73. Johann B. Metz, *Theology of the World,* trans. William Glen-Doepel (New York: Herder and Herder, 1969), 19-20.

74. Metz, *Theology of the World,* 91-92.

Barth, since Balthasar was very impressed with Barth's neoorthodox outlook. While in Paris Küng got acquainted with the work of Yves Congar. The argument of his thesis was twofold, namely, that "living Catholic theology takes justification seriously as God's act of sovereignty in Jesus Christ. The God who is gracious to us in Jesus Christ is beginning, middle, and end of everything," and "Barth does in fact take the justification of man seriously."[75] He concludes his thesis with the affirmation: "It is without any doubt, then, significant that today there is a fundamental agreement between Catholic and Protestant theology, precisely in the theology of justification — the point at which Reformation theology took its departure."[76]

(While we cannot discuss the issue of who had deviated from the proper interpretation of justification at the time of the Reformation, we should note that on Reformation Day, October 31, 1999, the Lutheran World Federation and the Roman Catholic Church signed at Augsburg a *Joint Declaration on the Doctrine of Justification* that shows a "consensus in basic truths of the doctrine."[77] Here the conclusion of Küng's thesis was finally vindicated.)

Since Barth concurred with Küng that he had correctly interpreted Barth's own position and Rahner also mentioned that Küng had correctly interpreted the Roman Catholic position, Küng's dissertation immediately aroused immense interest. In 1962 Pope John XXIII designated him an official theological consultant to the Second Vatican Council, and for some time he worked with the commission to draft the *Dogmatic Constitution on the Church (Lumen Gentium)*. When Küng wrote his next major work, *The Church* (1967), he attempted to see the church primarily from its New Testament origins, and from there he made the connection to the present.[78] This historical and exegetical approach relativized many of the absolutistic dogmatic statements on the church. For Küng the real essence of the church becomes concrete in its historical form, yet it can also assume wrong and distorted forms. Therefore one should return to the original source of the New Testament and one will see that there are different lines that developed according to the gospel, next to or outside the gospel, and contrary to the gospel. While the first one is legitimate, the second can at the most be tolerated, and the third must be rejected. Küng

---

75. Hans Küng, *Justification: The Doctrine of Karl Barth and a Catholic Reflection, with a Letter from Karl Barth,* trans. Thomas Collins et al. (London: Burns and Oates, 1964), 263 and 264.

76. Küng, *Justification,* 271.

77. *Joint Declaration on the Doctrine of Justification,* in Anthony N. S. Lane, *Justification by Faith in Catholic-Protestant Dialogue: An Evangelical Assessment* (London: T. & T. Clark, 2002), 239.

78. Cf. Hans Küng, *The Church* (Garden City, N.Y.: Doubleday Image Book, 1976), 337.

contended that a critical ecclesiology would demonstrate that the charismatic structure of the church was absorbed in an absolutistic and overly centralized structure of the office.

It came as no surprise that in his work *Infallible? An Inquiry* (1970) he showed with his historic approach that "'the teaching office' is a concept that was introduced at a late stage in time and its content is far from clear."[79] It is neither directly found in Scripture nor in tradition. Within the church there are shepherds and teachers, leaders and theologians who have their own specific charisma, their own specific calling, and their own specific function. There is no infallibility. But if believing persons rely on the Christian message as a whole, there is only an indefectibility of the church, because "the revelation of the Spirit is and remains always the source and norm of the Church's sense of faith" and not the teaching authority.[80] This means that we are held in truth but we do not have the truth. The church, however, reacted quickly against these conclusions. The Roman Papal Congregation for the Propagation of the Faith summoned Küng to appear in Rome. Küng refused to comply and therefore lost his approval as a teacher of Roman Catholic theology. Yet the dialogue beyond the Roman Catholic denominational borders that Küng had started did not stop, but rather increased.

More recently Küng also engaged in dialogue with other world religions. *Ecumene,* he claimed, is not just the community of Christian churches, but in its original meaning signifies the whole inhabited earth, which implies the community of the great religions of the world. In a project on a global ethos (*Global Responsibility: In Search of a New World Ethic;* Eng. trans. 1990), he continued his engagements in ecumenism to develop an ecumenical theology for peace. Humanity cannot live together without a global ethos of nations. There is no peace among nations without peace among religions, and no peace among religions without dialogue among them. Though Roman Catholic theological faculties are usually off-limits for Küng, he is widely read and discussed by both theologians and laypersons. Küng's amazing literary output and his ability to feel the pulse of the time and to translate the Christian message into simple terms make him one of the most well-known Roman Catholic theological communicators.

Another theologian who works for renewal is the Belgian Dominican **Edward Schillebeeckx** (b. 1914), who was born in Antwerp and studied from 1935 to 1945 in Gent and Louvain, and from 1946 to 1947 in Paris. Chenu and Congar

---

79. Hans Küng, *Infallible? An Inquiry,* trans. Edward Quinn (Garden City, N.Y.: Doubleday, 1971), 221.

80. Küng, *Infallible?* 190.

were some of his mentors. From 1947 to 1957 he taught at the Dominican Seminary in Louvain, and from 1957 till his retirement in 1983 as Professor of Dogma and the History of Theology at the theological faculty of the Catholic University in Nijmegen, Netherlands. He was one of the theological advisers of the Dutch bishops at the Second Vatican Council, and in the spirit of that council he has been one of the leaders pushing for reform within the church. But at Vatican II he was denied the official status as *peritus* by the Roman Curia because his theological reflections were found too liberal. While he initially rejoiced in the freedom that the council provided, he then realized: "When this Christian freedom recognized by the council was not subsequently guaranteed and protected by church law, this promise became an empty gesture, without any evangelical influence on our history. Then the breadth of the council was cut off and its spirit, the Holy Spirit, was extinguished. . . . Church hierarchies achieved an uncontrolled power over men and women of God."[81] Nevertheless, in 1965 Schillebeeckx founded *Concilium* together with Yves Congar, Karl Rahner, and Hans Küng, and served as its general editorial director for many years. That journal brought the new spirit of Vatican II into the theological world far beyond Roman Catholicism. Regardless of his problems with the Roman hierarchy, and in contrast to Küng, Schillebeeckx never lost his ecclesial standing, and is "one of the greatest theologians of the twentieth century."[82]

One can distinguish two periods in Schillebeeckx's work. In the first phase he followed an open-minded Thomism, while he worked on the sacraments and on a historical study about marriage. First he traced the history of a doctrine and then elaborated on it systematically. In the second period, which followed Vatican II, he abandoned Thomism and picked up modern hermeneutics to engage in an immediate dialogue with the experience of secular humanity. Schillebeeckx is convinced that Catholic theology needs a hermeneutic. Theological hermeneutics interprets the Old and the New Testament as texts of revelation, which themselves are already interpretations of those events to which they refer. This results in a hermeneutics of an interpretation of an interpretation. To understand a tradition means to interpret it anew by interpreting texts of the past, while starting from the present of a new cultural situation. A hermeneutics of experience and a hermeneutics of praxis ensue from this approach. The interpretation contained in the texts yields an experience that must be interpreted and handed on so that the original experience shown in the text

---

81. Edward Schillebeeckx, *Church: The Human Story of God,* trans. John Bowden (New York: Crossroad, 1990), xiv.

82. Robert J. Schreiter, introduction to *The Language of Faith: Essays on Jesus, Theology, and the Church,* by Edward Schillebeeckx (London: SCM, 1995), ix.

can call forth new experiences in the interpreter and the community for whom it is interpreted. This hermeneutic of experience then must be drawn out into a hermeneutic of praxis that allows one to experience the experience interpreted in the text in a new way and to concretize it in praxis in a radical engagement for humanity. It also compels the community to humanize the world and to urge it toward the eschaton. For this hermeneutic of praxis, Schillebeeckx dialogues with the new critical theory of the Frankfurt School represented by the philosopher Jürgen Habermas (b. 1929).

Schillebeeckx reflects the postconciliar theology that has started to dialogue with secular culture and has realized that there are two sources for the human situation, revelation and Christian tradition on the one side, and human experience on the other. In correlating the two, he published a three-volume sequence on Christology (1974-89).[83] He did not follow in it the stream of the ecclesial tradition, but employed a radical historical critical method to discern with certainty or a high degree of probability what we know about the historical Jesus. Yet he did not pursue a dogmatic reductionism, but wanted to present our historical knowledge as truthfully as possible to trace the origin of the christological confessions of the church and their enduring significance for today. Therefore he concluded that according to the Christian faith, Jesus is the decisive and definitive revelation of God. As this revelation, Jesus shows us what we actually could and should be. This result is indicative of Schillebeeckx's intention. Dogmatic statements must result in action, and thereby the aggiornamento of Pope John XXIII was a summons for Schillebeeckx.

Coping with Tradition and Modernity: David Tracy

A Roman Catholic theologian who is also very much concerned with hermeneutics and who is especially well known in the USA is **David Tracy** (b. 1939), who was born in Yonkers, New York, and had his initial theological training there at St. Joseph's Seminary. He obtained his licentiate (1964) and his doctorate (1969) at the Gregorian University in Rome. In 1963 he was ordained to the priesthood, and in 1967 he secured his first teaching position as instructor in theology at the Catholic University in America in Washington, D.C. Two years later he became professor of theology at the University of Chicago Divinity School, and has taught there ever since. His first book was *The Achievement of*

---

83. Edward Schillebeeckx, *Jesus: An Experiment in Christology,* trans. Hubert Hoskins (London: Collins, 1979); *Christ: The Experience of Jesus as Lord,* trans. John Bowden (New York: Seabury Press, 1980); and *Church.*

Bernard Lonergan (1970), a result of his doctoral dissertation on Lonergan's method while he studied with him at Rome.[84] Lonergan's method of doing theology also influenced his further publications, as we can see from his *Blessed Rage for Order* (1975) and *The Analogical Imagination* (1981).

Similar to Paul Tillich, Tracy opted for a method of correlation in his *Blessed Rage for Order*, a correlation of Christian texts and common human experience and language. Yet he rejected the question-and-answer method of Tillich, saying that if the Christian message would have an answer applicable to every human situation, this would demand a comparison of the Christian answer with all other answers. In looking at the common human experience and language, he noticed a religious dimension similar to what Langdon Gilkey had pointed out.[85] Hermeneutic phenomenology investigates the religious dimension in common human experience and language, while historical and hermeneutical investigations elucidate the meanings referred to by Christian texts. The religious dimension and the meanings should then be correlated "to determine their significant similarities and differences and their truth-value."[86] So we arrive at meanings, from common human experience and from the primary texts of the Christian tradition. Systematic theology is then concerned "with the construction of the *present* meaning, meaningfulness, and truth of the Christian tradition," by comparing these meanings in their religious, theistic, and christological aspects.[87]

In *The Analogical Imagination* Tracy advocated basically the same hermeneutical method, an analogical imagination through which one spots the similar in the dissimilar and thereby brings order in the chaos through a communal analogical imagination. In a more recent publication, *On Naming the Present: Reflections on God, Hermeneutics, and Church* (1994), he wanted to move from the historical context to the social location in the development of hermeneutics and shift therefore the emphasis from text to discourse.[88] The present problems are not concerned with how one retrieves the past, but with history, tradition, and interpretations. Therefore Tracy seeks to move hermeneutics beyond foundationalism and relativism as we see, for instance, in liberation theology.

---

84. Cf. David Tracy, *The Achievement of Bernard Lonergan* (New York: Herder and Herder, 1970).

85. Cf. for this David Tracy, *Blessed Rage for Order: The New Pluralism in Theology* (New York: Seabury Press, 1975), 46-47.

86. Tracy, *Blessed Rage for Order*, 53.

87. Tracy, *Blessed Rage for Order*, 240.

88. Cf. David Tracy, *On Naming the Present: Reflections on God, Hermeneutics, and Church* (London: SCM, 1994), 135.

The Recovery of the Orthodox Tradition

Though Orthodox theology has some branches in western Europe and more strongly in the United States, its fertile origin is in eastern Europe and Greece. Through the efforts of the World Council of Churches (WCC), Orthodox theologians from Eastern Europe were able to participate in ecumenical discussions during the Soviet rule. But since then we have come to realize more and more how their deliberations were influenced, if not outright orchestrated, by the Communist political powers in their own countries. This left only Greece to voice the concerns of Orthodoxy, and being intimidated by the sheer number of non-Orthodox theologians and the diversity of non-Orthodox theological traditions, Greek theologians often resorted to ultra-Orthodox standpoints in order to be heard.

Historically speaking, Orthodox theology of eastern Europe and Greece is the theology of a martyr church. By the end of the fourteenth century, the Turkish Ottoman Empire incorporated Greek areas into its rule. It was only in 1821 that the Greeks started their war of liberation against the Turkish supremacy, resulting in the death of Patriarch Gregorios V in Constantinople and several bishops. Young Otto of Bavaria (1815-67), the first king of modern Greece (1832-62), founded the University of Athens (1837) and with it a theological faculty. When in the latter nineteenth and early twentieth centuries the Balkan states emancipated themselves from the Ottoman Empire, they founded national universities with Orthodox faculties. Their professors studied predominantly in Athens, and the faculty there became the mother faculty of the Balkans. While there were soon three theological faculties for the Greeks, in Athens, Thessaloníki, and Chalki near Istanbul, the one in Chalki was closed by the Turkish government in 1971.

In Russia, the Communist government wanted to annihilate Christendom completely and decreed on December 11, 1917, that all theological teaching institutes must be closed and their buildings, money, and libraries confiscated. Since Stalin needed the church during World War II to support his struggle with the Nazi invaders, two academies and eight seminaries were opened again, yet they were under tight government control. After the collapse of the Soviet Union, the Russian Orthodox Church in 1997 had again four academies, twenty-one seminaries, twenty-three spiritual schools, and six pastoral courses. The Orthodox in other Communist countries fared somewhat better, but even there the stated goal of the Communist governments was to make theological education as difficult as possible. Theological faculties were usually separated from state universities and carefully monitored by the state. But prior to the Marxist rule, Orthodox theology flourished, especially in Russia.

Russia Opens to the West: Makarii Bulgakov

One of the most prominent theologians of the nineteenth century in Russia and the author of a classical compendium of theology was **Makarii Bulgakov** (1816-82). Before he was made *Rektor* at the St. Petersburg Academy, he studied and then taught at the academy in Kiev. Later he also served as metropolitan of Moscow. His twelve volumes on the history of the Russian church are a pioneer study based on original sources. Besides writing an introduction to theology (1847), he wrote a dogmatics in five volumes (1849-53) that made him famous. "It was quickly translated into French and remained in use from that time onward."[89] Yet it was not very original, because for once Bulgakov relied very much on Western sources and often even gathered his patristic citations from there, thinking there was no need to research it all over again. He also was very detached and had no sense for the religious and social problems of his time. The theological and philosophical fervor that was alive at the Kiev Academy when he studied there did not affect him. Besides his five-volume dogmatics, Bulgakov also composed a concise dogmatics to be used as a textbook in schools. Florovsky critically commented that "Markarii's book was outdated the day it first saw the light, and it remained unneeded and without a role to play in Russian theological consciousness."[90] Nevertheless, his works established him as one of the leading theologians in the Orthodox world. While Bulgakov was open to the West and learned from both Roman Catholic and Protestant theologians and also from Kant, there was another tendency in the nineteenth century: Slavophilism.

Turning In upon Itself: The Slavophile Movement; Aleksei Khomiakov and Vladimir Solovyev

Though the Slavophile movement did not escape German and French idealism, its representatives did not see the future of Russia in an openness to the West, because they felt that the West was decadent. They returned to an ideology that was centered around Moscow. "Basically conservative and traditional, the Slavophiles supported the Orthodox Church as synonymous with Russian native culture in opposition to Western Catholicism or Protestantism."[91] **Aleksei S. Khomiakov** (1804-60) is the most prominent theologian of the Slavophile move-

89. Georges Florovsky, *Ways of Russian Theology*, pt. 1 (Belmont, Mass.: Nordland, 1979), 257.

90. Florovsky, *Ways of Russian Theology*, pt. 1, 259.

91. George A. Maloney, *A History of Orthodox Theology since 1453* (Belmont, Mass.: Nordland, 1976), 57.

ment. He was well versed in the writings of the early fathers and sought a return to the unity in love that formed the bond of community of the early church. His travels throughout Europe and his contacts with many leading intellectuals strengthened his conviction of the corruption of the West and the superiority of the Russian culture and religion. Though reacting against the excessive use of Hegelian philosophy and German liberalism, he himself drew heavily on German idealism. This helped him develop a concept of philosophy of history that shows the dialectic between the primacy of the spirit, of freedom and love, and the organic necessity that is based on ironclad logical laws. Khomiakov saw on one side the principle of the spirit and on the other side the legalism of Rome and the rationalism of Protestantism.

Most important was Khomiakov's understanding of the one church. The unity of the church follows necessarily from the unity of God. The church is not an aggregate of individuals, but a unity of divine grace that in its manifoldness lives through reasonable human beings subject to that grace. Significant is also his concept of *sobornost,* which means both catholicity and conciliarity, a concept that furthered the demand for the participation of the laity in ecclesial decisions. The unity of the church is not maintained through some kind of teaching office or institution such as the synod, but through the mystical charisma of the Holy Spirit that conserves and unites all members in unity and faith through love. No wonder this was understood as being too idealistic and undermining the teaching hierarchy of the Orthodox Church and its visible structure. Khomiakov's works "were censured and were allowed to be printed in Russia only in 1879, but with due warning to the readers that Khomiakov's works contain errors, due to Khomiakov's lack of education in theological matters."[92]

Vladimir S. Solovyev (1853-1900), philosopher, theologian, and poet, also came from the Slavophile movement but then went his own way. His rejection of Western Christendom and especially of the Roman Catholic Church merged with an advocacy of a theocratic system. But he moved beyond that. He read and traveled widely and came across David Friedrich Strauss's and Ernest Renan's lives of Jesus, and also the materialistic writings of Ludwig Büchner (1824-99). He was also influenced by Auguste Comte's positivistic philosophy, as well as German idealism and the mystic writings of the West. Solovyev developed a mystical philosophy called sophiology. Sophia is the eternal idea that God realizes in creation. Therefore human activity must consist in realizing the union between the sophia as the female face of the deity and the world as logos, the masculine face of the deity, through the all-unity that pervades God's created world. Through his incarnation Christ's mission was to effect the union

---

92. Maloney, *History of Orthodox Theology,* 60-61.

between God and humanity by his beauty, goodness, and harmony that reflect perfectly the mind of God. With these ideas, Solovyev was occasionally accused of introducing sophia as a fourth principle in the Trinity, or even of pantheism.

Eventually he went beyond his sophiology and in 1896 became a Roman Catholic priest. Nevertheless, he thought of himself not as having left the Orthodox Church, "but as entering into the fullness of the universal Church by joining together the traditions of the Christian East and the West. He maintained that the two Churches, the Orthodox and the Roman Catholic, had remained mystically united despite the extrinsic, legalistic separation."[93] How such an ideal of uniting the East and the West was deemed possible we can glean from his book *Russia and the Universal Church.* There he wrote: "The fundamental truth and distinctive idea of Christianity is the perfect union of the divine and the human individually achieved in Christ, and finding its social realization in Christian humanity, in which the divine is represented by the Church, centered in the supreme pontiff, and the human by the State. This intimate relation between Church and State implies the primacy of the former, since the divine is previous in time and superior in being to the human."[94] The union between the human and divine should be achieved also on earth by church and state cooperating and uniting into what many Western theologians called the kingdom of God. Yet in Solovyev this was also an ideal synthesis that gained its inspiration from Hegel. In his programmatic *Lectures on the Humanity of God* (1877-81), he showed that in the French Revolution and German philosophy modern rationalism broke down.[95] One cannot satisfy the material needs once the religious foundation has been lost. Humanity as unconditionally significant is destined to be united with God in Jesus Christ, the divine-human being, and obliged to realize this unity in social and ecclesial life.

Progressiveness of Russian Theology: Dimitri Merezhkovskii and Michail Tareev

Around the turn to the twentieth century, theological work flourished in Russia. Historical research gained influence and the controversial question emerged as to the possibility of a theological development of doctrine. Interest-

93. Maloney, *History of Orthodox Theology,* 63.

94. Vladimir Solovyev, *Russia and the Universal Church,* trans. Herbert Rees (London: Geoffrey Bles, 1948), 14.

95. For a good summary on the *Lectures* see Paul Valliere, *Modern Russian Theology: Bukharev-Soloviev-Bulgakov; Orthodox Theology in a New Key* (Grand Rapids: Eerdmans, 2000), 143-71, who however leaves unmentioned Hegel's influence on Solovyev's "positive religion."

ing is also the emphasis on salvation advocating a kenotic theology and a theology of the cross. Important are Antonii Khrapovitskii (1864-1936), for whom the suffering redeemer is the true God. The example of Christ shows the suffering love and the salvific power of the suffering of God. Pavel J. Svetlov (1862-1945), professor of apologetics at the University of Kiev, emphasized in his book *The Cross of Christ* (1893) that the Christian religion is the religion of the cross, namely, the suffering of the good for its victory over evil.

At the beginning of the twentieth century, there were also attempts to dialogue with the Christian intelligentsia. The Petersburg Religious-Philosophical Meetings of 1901-3 served as a platform for these encounters between the church and the educated class. The philosopher of culture **Dimitri S. Merezhkovskii** (1865-1941) called for a new revelation and proclaimed a Johannine church with a dynamic apocalyptic principle in which the three main groups of Christendom — Orthodoxy, Catholicism, and Protestantism — should be integrated "as one catholic and apostolic genuinely universal Church of the Holy Sophia."[96] This demand exceeded the possibilities of Orthodox theologians. Yet those who participated in the meetings realized a common spiritual task and a social responsibility. Such was the "new theology" or "philosophy of the heart" of **Michail M. Tareev** (1866-1934).[97] He served as professor of ethics at the Moscow spiritual academy until the academy was shut down by the state in 1918. Tareev emphasized that people are primarily interested in what Christianity can contribute to aspects of life such as economic needs, social demands, married life, the community of workers, and a brotherly and sisterly life in society. We notice here influences of the American Social Gospel, of the German philosophy of life, and of Kierkegaard. Marxist socialism was decidedly rejected by Tareev. But the Marxists had the upper hand, and theology was effectively silenced except on foreign shores.

Russian Theology in Exile: Sergius Bulgakov, Vladimir Losskii, and Georges Florovsky

Sergius N. Bulgakov (1871-1944) showed that Orthodox theology can be progressive.[98] He was born south of Moscow, came from a family of six generations

96. Georges Florovsky, *Ways of Russian Theology,* pt. 2 (Vaduz, Liechtenstein: Büchervertriebsanstalt, 1987), 239.

97. For more information on Tareev, see Reinhard Slenczka, "Lehre und Bekenntnis der Orthodoxen Kirche. Vom 16. Jahrhundert bis zur Gegenwart," in *Handbuch der Dogmen- und Theologiegeschichte,* ed. Carl Andresen (Göttingen: Vandenhoeck & Ruprecht, 1980), 2:543-44.

98. For a helpful biography see Michael Plekon, *Living Icons: Persons of Faith in the East-*

of priests and deacons, and was brought up as a devout Orthodox child. Soon he rebelled against this religious sphere and associated with the Marxist intelligentsia for fifteen years. He studied successively in Moscow, Berlin, Paris, and London, and from 1901 to 1906 occupied the chair of political economy at Kiev Polytechnic Institute. At that time he had already been disillusioned by the religion of progress and the glamour of the West. While before he had written on market economy and agriculture under capitalism, now he became a leader of the young movement of religious intelligentsia. In 1906 he was appointed professor of political economy at the Moscow University Institute of Commerce. He continued to publish a great number of articles and studies in political and economic theory.

In 1912 he wrote *Philosophy and Economics,* expounding his first systematic treatment of sophiology. In this work he contended that the world is a manifestation of Sophia, the Divine Wisdom. In 1917 he was made professor of the University of Moscow and was also one of two laypeople elected to the advisory council of the patriarch of Moscow. The following year he accepted ordination to the priesthood and was consequently expelled from the university by the Communists. He still taught at a university in the Crimea, but being exiled from Russia in 1923 effectively canceled that job. Via Constantinople he came to Prague, then the center of the Russian émigré community. He became instrumental in forming the Russian Student Christian Movement, a distinctly Orthodox movement. He served as a lecturer in the Russian Law Institute, which had been founded by the émigrés in Prague, but when in 1925 it was decided that a Russian Orthodox theological academy should be founded in Paris, which was to become St. Sergius Theological Institute, Metropolitan Eulogius invited him to become professor of dogmatics and dean of the new school. There he stayed and taught for the rest of his life. He was still active in the Russian Student Christian Movement and also participated in ecumenical conferences and was active in the Faith and Order Movement. In 1934 he made an extensive lecture trip to the United States and Canada arranged by the Episcopal Church.

For Bulgakov sophiology was not *the* theme, but *a* significant theme in Orthodox theology. This sophia theology is directed against a world-denying attitude in Christianity or a secularization of the world. The sophia is not a fourth manifestation of God that would transform the Holy Trinity into a quaternity. Instead, "the divine *Sophia,* as the revelation of the Logos, is the all-embracing unity which contains within itself all·the fullness of the world of

---

ern Church, foreword by Lawrence C. Cunningham (Notre Dame: University of Notre Dame Press, 2002), 29-40.

ideas."[99] "Wisdom in creation is ontologically identical with its prototype, the same Wisdom as exists in God. The world exists in God: 'For in him, and through him, and to him, are all things.'"[100] Sophiology affirms God's relation to the world that is so intimate that ideally it mirrors God. Therefore this kind of thinking can be understood as an apophatic theology, meaning a theology reaching up to God because he has reached down to us. Bulgakov was a prolific writer. Best known among his works are the large trilogy of 1933-46, *The Lamb of God* (on Christ), *The Comforter* (on the Holy Spirit; Eng. trans. 2004), and *The Bride of the Lamb* (on the church; Eng. trans. 2002), and his smaller trilogy of 1927-29, *The Burning Bush* (on Mary), *The Friend of the Bridegroom* (on John the Baptist; Eng. trans. 2003), and *Jacob's Ladder* (on angels).

Closely associated with him in this plea for a renewal of Orthodox theology was his friend **Pavel A. Florenskii** (1882-1943), a scientist, philosopher, and theologian who was shot to death in a Russian prison camp. He developed a metaphysics of love nourished by the sources of antiquity as well as of modern philosophers. Florenskii also developed a sophiology that thematized God's presence in the world, in terms not only of grace and salvation but also of creation and preservation. Humanity participates in the sophia which, as the link connecting God and the created world, is effective on the boundary between cosmos and chaos. The sophia is the *natura naturans,* the divine logos as an ontological principle. Florenskii's highly original work was cut short by the revolution of October 1917.

Vladimir N. Losskii (1903-58), son of the philosopher Nikolaii Losskii (1870-1965), met with a similar fate to Bulgakov's. He was born in Petersburg and died — like his father — in exile in France. He taught at the St. Sergius Theological Institute in Paris and advocated a mystical theology and was opposed to Bulgakov's sophiology as irreconcilable with Orthodox dogma. Decisive for him was the connection between theology and mysticism. A mystic theology showed him that talking about God is not only a matter of language and text, but an encounter with the reality of God in this world. His best-known work is *The Mystical Theology of the Eastern Church* (French 1944; Eng. trans. 1957).

With the last few theologians we have touched on the demise of Russian Orthodox theology. After the Soviet revolution there was no longer place for theologians in Russia to think, teach, and write. Until the Moscow Academy was reopened in 1944, the Orthodox theological institute in Paris was the only

---

99. Sergius Bulgakov, "The Wisdom of God," in Sergius Bulgakov, *A Bulgakov Anthology,* ed. James Pain and Nicolas Zernov (Philadelphia: Westminster, 1976), 154.

100. Bulgakov, "The Wisdom of God," 155.

Russian theological academy at a university level in the world, and surely the first institution completely free of government interference where Orthodox theology could be pursued. Next to Bulgakov there were Georges W. Florovsky, Alexander Schmemann, and John Meyendorf, among others. The Russian theologians at the institute attended the first meeting of the Life and Work Conference at Stockholm (1925) under Bishop Söderblom, and also took a leading part in further conferences, including the initial conference of the WCC in Amsterdam in 1948, since no theologians from within Soviet Russia could participate. Some émigré theologians eventually moved on to the United States.

The best known of them is the archpriest **Georges Florovsky** (1893-1979). He was born in Odessa where his father was *Rektor* of the local seminary. He studied at the University of Odessa and taught philosophy there for a short time before Marxist pressure forced him to emigrate to Bulgaria in 1920. The following year he moved to Prague, and finally in 1926 he ended up in Paris, where he received the chair of patrology at the newly founded Orthodox Theological Institute (St. Sergius). In 1932 he was ordained to the priesthood, and in 1948 he went to New York to teach at the newly opened St. Vladimir's Orthodox Seminary. There he also became dean and founded the *St. Vladimir's Seminary Quarterly,* which had a great influence in Orthodox theology. In 1955 he moved to Holy Cross Greek Orthodox Theological School in Brookline, Massachusetts, and the following year he was appointed lecturer at Harvard Divinity School for Eastern church history, and subsequently professor. Upon his retirement in 1964 he was invited to Princeton as visiting professor in the departments of history and Slavic studies. He was active in the Central Committee of the WCC and in other ecumenical organizations.

Florovsky fought for a return to the living tradition of the Fathers and was convinced of the necessity of a rebirth of Christian Hellenism. He was a prolific writer living in the West, and it was understandable that he interpreted the Orthodox tradition to the West. We see this, for instance, in his two-volume history *Ways of Russian Theology* (1979-87) and *The Byzantine Fathers of the First Century* (1987) and *Byzantine Fathers of the Sixth to the Eighth Century* (1987), which were part of his *Collected Works* that comprise more than a dozen volumes. Being confronted with Western historicism, he also took up the issue of historical interpretation while still convinced that there is a — though hidden — providential course in history.[101] Central to Florovsky's thinking was his ecclesiology and therefore the catholicity of the church. The church as the new

---

101. So Jaroslav Pelikan, "Puti Russkogo Bogoslava: When Orthodoxy Comes West," in *The Heritage of the Early Church: Essays in Honor of Georges Vasilievich Florovsky,* ed. David Neiman and Margaret Schatkin (Rome: Pont. Institutum Studiorum Orientalium, 1973), 16.

community of the Spirit constitutes the active nucleus of the new creation. This is where our salvation and divinization are realized. Therefore a catholic unity "begins and ends with the regeneration of the redeemed in Christ and the Spirit."[102] To that end he was involved in the ecumenical dialogue, where he also showed the West the riches of Eastern patristic theology.

Russian Theology on Foreign Soil: Alexander Schmemann and John Meyendorff

Now we come to the second generation of Russian émigrés. **Alexander Schmemann** (1921-83) was born into a Russian family with Baltic German ancestors on his father's side. The family moved from Estonia to Paris while he was still quite young. He had a Russian education in exile, attending a Russian military school in Versailles and then a *Gymnasium,* after which he studied at the Orthodox Theological Institute in Paris (1940-45), specializing in church history. His thesis was on Byzantine theocracy. He became an instructor in church history at the institute, first as a layperson, and after his ordination in 1946 as a priest. The church was the focus of his spiritual and intellectual interests; not so much the church of the past, but of the present, and how it was alive and survived in and through the liturgy.[103]

Once Florovsky left for America, Schmemann soon left too (1951) and joined the faculty at St. Vladimir's, where he became dean in 1962, a position he held until his death. During his tenure the priests who were educated at St. Vladimir's did not serve only the Russian church, but also the Antiochian and the Serbian churches. Through his leadership the seminary became a center of liturgical and eucharistic revival. He did not sever his links, however, with Europe, since in 1959 he obtained his doctorate from St. Sergius.

Schmemann saw three functions of Orthodox theology in the West. First was a pastoral one: to be attentive to the religious and social needs of the people. Secondly, he perceived a missionary function "to make Orthodoxy known, understood and, with God's help, accepted in the West."[104] This conviction stemmed from his belief that the Orthodox Church is the true church and there-

---

102. Aidan Nichols, *Theology in the Russian Diaspora: Church, Fathers, Eucharist in Nikolai Afanas'ev (1893-1966)* (Cambridge: Cambridge University Press, 1989), 157.

103. So John Meyendorff, "A Life Worth Living," in *Liturgy and Tradition: Theological Reflections of Alexander Schmemann,* ed. Thomas Fisch (Crestwood, N.Y.: St. Vladimir's Seminary Press, 1990), 148.

104. Alexander Schmemann, *Church, World, Mission: Reflections on Orthodoxy in the West* (Crestwood, N.Y.: St. Vladimir's Seminary Press, 1979), 123.

fore incompatible with any provincialism in thought or vision. Thirdly, the task of Orthodox theology is to be prophetic by reminding the people of the true mission and denouncing their betrayals of the divine will. Here theology must refer to the life of the church, to the absolute truth of the church's own tradition, to keep alive and operative a criterion by which the church judges itself.

The life of the church, however, is embodied and felt in the liturgy. Schmemann pointed out the cosmic and eschatological dimension of the liturgy. For instance, he remarked that the Eucharist had been reduced in the West to the means of grace leading to individual edification and sanctification, to the virtual exclusion of all other aspects. One must recover, however, that the Eucharist is not an individual or communal act. Instead, it has a cosmic and eschatological dimension being sustained by and leading to the Lord of the cosmos and to the communion with all the saints. "The liturgy of the Church is cosmic and eschatological because the Church is cosmic and eschatological; but the Church would not have been cosmic and eschatological had she not been given, as the very source and constitution of her life in faith, the *experience* of the new creation, the experience and *vision* of the Kingdom which is to come. And this is precisely the *leiturgia* of the Church's cult, the function which makes it the source and indeed the very *possibility* of theology."[105] Liturgy is not static, but has an inner dynamic pushing forward to the kingdom of God. If theology is a function of the church, as Karl Barth claimed, then Schmemann was certainly correct to say that theology is derived from the church's innermost activity, the liturgy of the worship.

John Meyendorff (1926-92) was born in France of Russian émigré parents of Baltic German aristocratic origin. In contrast to Schmemann, he went to French schools and then graduated from the Orthodox Theological Institute in Paris in 1949. He earned his Ph.D. in 1958 from the Sorbonne with a critical edition, translation, and commentary of the Byzantine monastic theologian Gregory Palamas (ca. 1296-1359) and his work *Defense of the Holy Hesychasts*. The following year he was ordained a priest and left France to join the faculty of St. Vladimir's Orthodox Theological Seminary as professor of patristics and church history. He stayed there until his death. He also served as seminary dean and *Rektor* of the seminary chapel from 1984 till shortly before he died. Before coming to St. Vladimir's, he had taught church history and patristics at St. Sergius in Paris. In America he also served on the faculty of Harvard University's Dumbarton Oaks Byzantine Research Center in Washington, D.C., until 1967, when he took on a position as professor of Byzantine history at Fordham University, which he served concurrently with his position at St. Vladimir's.

---

105. Alexander Schmemann, "Liturgy and Theology," in *Liturgy and Tradition*, 58.

Together with Schmemann he helped transform the Russian Orthodox Missionary Metropoly in North America into the self-governing Orthodox Church in America comprised of Orthodox believers of various nationalities and ethnic origins. He was also deeply involved in the ecumenical movement, served as a moderator of the Faith and Order Commission of the WCC (1967-75), and represented the Orthodox Church in America at the Central Committee of the WCC. Unlike Schmemann, he was fortunate to see the dissolution of Marxism in Russia and was able to travel there, freely lecturing in many universities, theological academies, and scholarly institutes that were again open to the message and the propagation of Orthodox theology.

Meyendorff's literary output was considerable, including three volumes of *Christian Spirituality* (*Origins to the Twelfth Century,* 1985; *High Middle Ages and Reformation,* 1987; *Post-Reformation and Modern,* 1989), the continuation of his study on Gregory Palamas (*St. Gregory Palamas and Orthodox Spirituality,* 1974; *A Study of Gregory Palamas,* 2nd ed., 1974; *The Triades: Gregory Palamas,* 1983), and many other significant studies. Interesting is *The Vision of Unity* (1987), which contains his editorials from the church monthly he edited, *The Orthodox Church.* In the editorials he advocated the establishment of the autocephaly of the Orthodox Church in America, which was established in 1970. Meyendorff basically interpreted the richness of the Orthodox tradition for the West by distinguishing carefully in this heritage "between that which founds part of the Church's Holy Tradition, unalterable and universally binding, received from the past, and that which is a mere relic of former times, venerable, no doubt in many respects, but sometimes also sadly out of date and even harmful to the mission of the Church."[106] His erudition notwithstanding, this tradition left him convinced that the Orthodox Church needs to summon all Christians to "return to the faith of the Fathers and Apostles, which she is conscious of having preserved in its fullness."[107] Indeed, the Orthodox tradition did not face the painful split at the Reformation and the further splits amongst the churches of the Reformation. Nevertheless, it also needs to come to terms with the split that occurred much earlier, that between East and West.

---

106. John Meyendorff, *The Orthodox Church: Its Past and Its Role in the World Today,* revised and expanded by Nicholas Lossky (Crestwood, N.Y.: St. Vladimir's Seminary Press, 1996), 173.

107. Meyendorff, *The Orthodox Church,* 201.

Orthodox Theology in Eastern Europe and Greece: Dumitru Staniloae and Justin Popovic, Nikos Nissiotis, Joannis Zizioulas, and Christos Yannaras

When we look for Orthodox theologians beyond Russia, we must note the Romanian Orthodox theologian **Dumitru Staniloae** (1903-93), who studied theology at the theological faculty of Cernauti (1922-27), which was then in the Romanian Bucovina.[108] He wrote his doctoral dissertation on the life and activity of the Orthodox patriarch Dositheos II of Jerusalem (1641-1707), who is the author of the Orthodox Confession of 1675, which was formulated in reaction to the Calvinistic confession of the patriarch of Constantinople, Cyril Loukaris (1572-1638). Staniloae then continued his studies at the universities of Athens, Munich, Berlin, and Paris. After that he taught at the Orthodox Theological Faculty of Sibiu in Transylvania (1929-46), where he also became *Rektor* of the faculty.[109] In 1938 he wrote the short but well-documented book *The Life and Teaching of St. Gregory Palamas,* and in 1943 he wrote *Jesus Christ, or the Restoration of Man.* In 1946 he began teaching at the Theological Institute of Bucharest, which allowed him to publish a Romanian version of the *Philocalia,* the well-known compendium of patristic writings of prayer that influenced the monastic revival of postwar Romania. By 1948 he had published the first three volumes. In the following years he also published his important theological works *Orthodox Christian Doctrine* (1952) and *Textbook of Dogmatic and Symbolic Theology* (2 vols., 1958).

In 1958 he was charged with "attempts against the proletarian Romanian State" and was imprisoned for five years. In 1965 he regained tenure at the Theological Institute in Bucharest. Through his *Orthodox Dogmatic Theology* (3 vols., 1978; Eng. trans. 1994), Staniloae became one of the most prominent Orthodox theologians of the second half of the twentieth century. Similar to the Serbian theologian Justin Popovic (1894-1979), who taught at the University of Belgrade until he was removed in 1934, and who also wrote *Dogmatic of the Orthodox Church* (3 vols., 1932-78), Staniloae attempted a patristic renewal and endeavored to show the relevancy of the Christian doctrine for human existence. Staniloae was ecumenically minded, as can be seen from the German edition of his *Dogmatics* (1984/90), which was translated by a Lutheran colleague from Romania (Hermann Pitters) and for which Jürgen Moltmann wrote the preface.

108. For Dumitru Staniloae cf. Ioan Vasile Leb and Valer Bel, "Dumitru Staniloae. Geisterfahrung und Spiritualität," in *Theologen des 20. Jahrhunderts. Eine Einführung,* ed. Peter Neuner and Gunther Wenz (Darmstadt: Wissenschaftliche Buchgesellschaft, 2002), 145-56.

109. John Meyendorff, foreword to *Theology and the Church,* by Dumitru Staniloae, trans. Robert Barringer (Crestwood, N.Y.: St. Vladimir's Seminary Press, 1980), 8-9.

Greek theologians could work in their own country unhindered by Communism and could also maintain meaningful international contacts. A prominent example of this is **Nikos Nissiotis** (1924-86), professor at the theological faculty of the University of Athens, who "was born in a very strict orthodox family," his father being an Orthodox priest.[110] From childhood he was firmly rooted in the Greek Orthodox ecclesial tradition and maintained a strong commitment to his church.[111] Having studied in Basel with Barth and in Zürich with Emil Brunner, as well as in Louvain, but doing his doctorate in Athens (1956), he became exposed to Western theology and from then on maintained an ecumenical commitment throughout his life. He was director of the Ecumenical Institute in Bossey, Switzerland (1958-74), an observer at Vatican II as a permanent representative of WCC, associate general secretary to the WCC (1968-72), and moderator of the WCC Commission on Faith and Order (1975-83), in which capacity he also chaired the Lima, Peru, conference in 1982 that produced the ecumenically significant document *Baptism, Eucharist, and Ministry*. Beyond his ecumenical, theological involvements, he was very much interested in sports and became the vice chairman of the National Olympic Committee of Greece. His life was cut short by a car accident in 1986, an event that was reported in our (Regensburg) daily newspaper on the sports page.

Nissiotis was "a bridge-builder between the Eastern and Western traditions."[112] It was not by accident that he, a Greek Orthodox, and Heinrich Fries, a Roman Catholic, each contributed a preface to the *Ecumenical Dogmatics* (*Ökumenische Dogmatik,* 1983) of the Lutheran systematician and teacher of Wolfhart Pannenberg, Edmund Schlink (1903-84). Yet he was a genuine representative of Orthodox theology. His theological reflections were deeply embedded in the biblical and Eastern patristic basis. He always argued historically, for instance, when he claimed that for the church fathers of the first centuries the Greek tradition was a decisive help for communicating the gospel. Contrary to Harnack, he said "the essence of the Gospel was not compromised through this connection." He contended that "classical education cannot be absorbed by a faith which is founded on the absolute uniqueness of the personal self-disclosure of God, and the Christian faith on the other hand cannot be assimilated by philosophical systems."[113]

110. Joseph Kallarangatt, "The Ecumenical Theology of Nikos A. Nissiotis," *Christian Orient* 11 (Dec. 1990): 173.

111. For Nikos Nissiotis cf. Marios Begzos, "Zukunft aus Herkunft — Zur ökumenischen Tragweite der Ostkirche," in *Theologen des 20. Jahrhunderts,* 204-16.

112. So Kallarangatt, "The Ecumenical Theology," 174.

113. Nikos Nissiotis, "Ost und West in der Begegnung und Gemeinschaft der Kirchen," *Reformatio* 1 (1980): 486.

Nissiotis, however, did not obliterate actual discrepancies. He noted that there are significant differences between theology in the East and the West. While the Eastern liturgy emphasizes Christ's victory as the resurrected One and therefore theology derived from that liturgy focuses on how humanity can participate in the event of the incarnation of the logos, Western liturgy interprets Christ's victory as a salvific activity. Therefore the theology derived from this promise of redemption centers on humanity as a fallen creature that is saved by Christ's salvific activity. Furthermore, there is a different understanding of the church in the East and the West. For the East the church as a transcendental unity is an ontological reality in which those are included who participate in the liturgy, while in the West the church is much more an institution with a peculiar historical reality. In the Eastern Church there is also a much more vertical expectation of the future by which in the liturgy the future reality can already be anticipated, while in the West the future is much more seen as something beyond our historical reality. From his involvement with the WCC Nissiotis realized that these different emphases are not exclusive but "complementary. . . . One cannot exist without the other. They are the two sides of one and the same coin."[114] He also refuted the idea that only Western theology is European, because in the first centuries there was a political and cultural unity of Europe. Therefore "Eastern Orthodoxy is also European theology."[115] With theologians such as Nissiotis Orthodox theology decisively entered the ecumenical dialogue without abandoning its own heritage; it contributed from its heritage to this dialogue.

With **Joannis D. Zizioulas** (b. 1931) we can also notice this bridge-building tendency. He did his theological studies at the University of Athens, where he received his doctorate in theology with a thesis entitled "The Unity of the Church in the Holy Eucharist and the Bishop during the First Three Centuries" (1965). But he also studied patristics at Harvard and was a fellow at the Dumbarton Oaks Byzantine Research Center. For several years he worked on the staff of the Commission for Faith and Order of the WCC in Geneva. He was a professor of the theological faculty of the University of Thessalonica, Greece, and prior to that professor of theology at the University of Glasgow, Scotland. In 1986 he was consecrated bishop and is now metropolitan of Pergamon. He started developing a eucharistic theology with his doctoral thesis and has continued developing it in *Being as Communion: Studies in Personhood in the Church* (1985). In the center of his ecclesiology is the Eucharist as the sacrament of unity par excellence, and therefore the expression of the mystery of the church itself.

114. Nissiotis, "Ost und West," 493.
115. Nissiotis, "Ost und West," 494.

Finally we must mention **Christos Yannaras** (b. 1935), who is professor of philosophy at the Pantion University of Social and Political Science in Athens. For him the personal relation between God and humanity as well as that among humans in the church betray an "erotic" dynamic meaning and ascetic self-denial and self-sacrifice.[116] He also wrote, among other works, a primer of the Christian Faith (*Elements of Faith: An Introduction to Orthodox Theology*, 1991 [1983]) and an ethics (*The Freedom of Morality*, 1984).

For Further Reading

Hugues Félicité Robert de Lamennais (1782-1854)

Hastings, C. B. "Hugues-Félicité Robert de Lamennais: A Catholic Pioneer of Religious Liberty." *Journal of Church and State* 30 (Spring 1988): 321-39.

O'Connell, Marvin R. "Politics and Prophecy: Newman and Lamennais." In *Newman after a Hundred Years*, edited by Ian Kerr and Alan G. Hill, 175-91. New York: Oxford University Press, 1990.

Roe, W. G. *Lamennais and England: The Reception of Lamennais's Religious Ideas in England in the Nineteenth Century*. Oxford: Oxford University Press, 1966.

Matthias Joseph Scheeben (1835-88)

Burke, T. Patrick. *Faith and the Human Person: An Investigation of the Thought of Scheeben*. Chicago: John XXIII Institute, 1968.

Murray, John Courtney. *Matthias Scheeben on Faith*. Lewiston, N.Y.: Edwin Mellen, 1987.

Jacques Maritain (1882-1973)

Allen, Edgar. *A Guide to the Thought of Jacques Maritain*. London: Hodder and Stoughton, 1950.

Doering, Bernhard. *Jacques Maritain and the French Catholic Intellectuals*. Notre Dame: University of Notre Dame Press, 1983.

Nottingham, William. *Christian Faith and Secular Action: An Introduction to the Life and Thought of Jacques Maritain*. St. Louis: Bethany, 1968.

Johann Sebastian von Drey (1777-1853)

Burtchaell, James T. "Drey, Möhler and the Catholic School of Tübingen." In *Religious Thought in the West*, edited by Ninian Smart, John Clayton, et al., 111-39. Cambridge: Cambridge University Press, 1985.

---

116. Cf. Christos Yannaras, *Person and Eros. Eine Gegenüberstellung der Ontologie der griechischen Kirchenväter und der Existenzphilosophie des Westens*, trans. Irene Hoening (Göttingen: Vandenhoeck & Ruprecht, 1982 [1976]).

Fehr, Wayne. *The Birth of the Catholic Tübingen School: The Dogmatics of Johann Sebastian Drey*. Chico, Calif.: Scholars, 1981.

Hinze, Bradford. *Narrating History, Developing Doctrine: Friedrich Schleiermacher and Johann Sebastian Drey*. Atlanta: Scholars, 1993.

Johann Adam Möhler (1796-1838)

Fitzer, Joseph. *Moehler and Baur in Controversy, 1832-38: Romantic-Idealist Assessment of the Reformation and Counter-Reformation*. Tallahassee, Fla.: American Academy of Religion, 1974.

Franklin, R. W. *Nineteenth-Century Churches: The History of a New Catholicism in Württemberg, England, and France*. New York: Garland, 1987.

Möhler, Johann Adam. *Unity in the Church or the Principle of Catholicism: Presented in the Spirit of the Church Fathers of the First Three Centuries*. Edited and translated with an introduction by Peter C. Erb. Washington, D.C.: Catholic University, 1996.

Savon, Hervé. *Johann Adam Möhler: The Father of Modern Theology*. Translated by Charles McGrath. Glen Rock, N.J.: Paulist, 1966.

Johann Baptist Hirscher (1788-1865)

Mitchel, Nathan. "The Problem of Authority in Roman Catholicism." *Review and Expositor 75* (Spring 1978): 195-210.

Karl Adam (1876-1966)

Adam, Karl. *The Christ of Faith: The Christology of the Church*. New York: Pantheon Books, 1957.

———. *Christ Our Brother*. Translated by Justin McCann. London: Sheed and Ward, 1931.

———. *One and Holy*. Translated by Cecily Hastings. New York: Sheed and Ward, 1951.

———. *The Spirit of Catholicism*. Translated by Dom Justin McCann. Introduction by Robert A. Krieg. New York: Crossroad, 1997 [1929].

Krieg, Robert. *Karl Adam: Catholicism in German Culture*. Notre Dame: University of Notre Dame Press, 1992.

Anton Günther (1783-1863)

Bunnell, Adam. *Before Infallibility: Liberal Catholicism in Biedermeier Vienna*. Rutherford, N.J.: Fairleigh Dickinson University Press, 1990.

Antonio Rosmini (1797-1855)

Cleary, Denis. *Antonio Rosmini: Introduction to His Life and Teaching*. Durham: Rosmini House, 1992.

Leetham, Claude Richard Harbord. *Rosmini: Priest and Philosopher*. New York: New City Press, 1982.

Rosmini, Antonio. *A Selection from the Ascetical Letters of Antonio Rosmini.* Translated and edited by John Morris. Loughborough: John Morris, 1993-95.

Johann Michael Sailer (1752-1832)

Dietrich, Donald J. "German Historicism and the Changing Image of the Church: 1780-1820." *Theological Studies* 42 (Mar. 1981): 46-73.
Dru, Alexander. *The Contribution of German Catholicism.* New York: Hawthorn, 1963. Pp. 41-47.

Johann Josef Ignaz von Döllinger (1799-1890)

Boudens, Robrecht, ed. *Conversations with Dr. Döllinger, 1870-1890.* Leuven: Leuven University, Peeters, 1985.
Döllinger, Johann Josef Ignaz von. *Lectures on the Reunion of the Churches.* Translated with a preface by Henry Nutcombe Oxenham. London: Rivingtons, 1872.
Janus [Ignaz Döllinger]. *The Pope and the Council.* London: Rivingtons, 1869.

Karl Joseph von Hefele (1809-93)

Hefele, Karl Joseph von. *A History of the Christian Councils of the Church. From the Original Documents.* Translated and edited by William R. Clark. 2nd rev. ed. 5 vols. Edinburgh: T. & T. Clark, 1872-96.

Alfred Loisy (1857-1940)

Hill, Harvey. *The Politics of Modernism: Alfred Loisy and the Scientific Study of Religion.* Washington, D.C.: Catholic University of America Press, 2002.
Loisy, Alfred. *The Gospel and the Church.* Translated by Christopher Home. Philadelphia: Fortress, 1976 [1903].
Petre, Maude Dominica. *Alfred Loisy: His Religious Significance.* Cambridge: Cambridge University Press, 1944.
Ratté, John. *Three Modernists: Alfred Loisy, George Tyrrell, William L. Sullivan.* New York: Sheed and Ward, 1967.

George Tyrrell (1861-1909)

Sagovsky, Nicholas. *On God's Side: A Life of George Tyrrell.* New York: Oxford University Press, 1990.
Tyrrell, George. *Autobiography and Life of George Tyrrell.* London: E. Arnold, 1912.
————. *Hard Sayings: A Selection of Meditation and Studies.* 6th ed. London: Longmans, Green, 1904 [1898].
————. *Lex Credendi.* London: Longmans, Green, 1907 [1906].
————. *Lex Orandi or Prayers and Creed.* London: Longmans, Green, 1907 [1903].
Wells, David. *The Prophetic Theology of George Tyrrell.* Chico, Calif.: Scholars, 1980.

Maurice Blondel (1861-1949)

Blondel, Maurice. *Action* (1893). *Essay on a Critique of Life and a Science of Practice.*

Translated by Olivia Blanchette. Notre Dame: University of Notre Dame Press, 1984.

Conway, Michael. *The Science of Life: Maurice Blondel's Philosophy of Action and the Scientific Method.* New York: Peter Lang, 2000.

Lacroix, Jean. *Maurice Blondel: An Introduction to the Man and His Philosophy.* Translated by John C. Guinness. New York: Sheed and Ward, 1968.

McNeill, John. *The Blondelian Synthesis: A Study of the Influence of German Philosophical Sources on the Formation of Blondel's Method and Thought.* Leiden: Brill, 1966.

Marie-Dominique Chenu (1894-1989)

Chenu, Marie-Dominique. *The Theology of Work: An Exploration.* Translated by Lilian Soiron. Chicago: Henry Regnery, 1966.

Komonchak, Joseph A. "Returning from Exile: Catholic Theology in the 1930s." In *The Twentieth Century: A Theological Overview,* edited by Gregory Baum, 35-48. New York: Orbis, 1999.

Potworowski, Christophe F. *Contemplation and Incarnation: The Theology of Marie-Dominique Chenu.* Montreal: McGill-Queen's University Press, 2001.

Principe, Walter H. "Changing Church Teachings." *Grail,* Summer 1990, 13-40.

Yves Marie Joseph Congar (1904-95)

Dunne, Victor. *Prophecy in the Church: The Vision of Yves Congar.* New York: Peter Lang, 2000.

Henn, William. *The Hierarchy of Truths according to Yves Congar, O.P.* Rome: Editrice Pontificia Università Gregoriana, 1987.

MacDonald, Charles. *Church and World in the Plan of God: Aspects of History and Eschatology in the Thought of Père Yves Congar, O.P.* Frankfurt am Main: Peter Lang, 1982.

Pierre Teilhard de Chardin (1881-1955)

Hefner, Philip. *The Promise of Teilhard: The Meaning of the Twentieth Century in Christian Perspective.* Philadelphia: Lippincott, 1970.

King, Ursula. *Spirit of Fire: The Life and Vision of Teilhard de Chardin.* Maryknoll, N.Y.: Orbis, 1996.

Lubac, Henri de. *Teilhard de Chardin: The Man and His Meaning.* New York: New American Library, 1965.

Teilhard de Chardin, Pierre. *The Divine Milieu.* New York: Harper Torchbooks, 1968.

———. *The Phenomenon of Man.* Translated by Bernard Wall. New York: Harper and Row, 1965.

Henri de Lubac (1896-1991)

Balthasar, Hans Urs von. *The Theology of Henri de Lubac: An Overview.* San Francisco: Ignatius, 1991.

Lubac, Henri de. *At the Service of the Church: Henri de Lubac Reflects on the Circumstances That Occasioned His Writings*. San Francisco: Ignatius, 1993.

——. *The Mystery of the Supernatural*. Translated by Rosemary Sheed. London: Geoffrey Chapman, 1967.

Wood, Susan. *Spiritual Exegesis and the Church in the Theology of Henri de Lubac*. Grand Rapids: Eerdmans, 1998.

Jean Daniélou (1905-74)

Chaney, Charles. "An Introduction to the Missionary Thought of Jean Daniélou." *Occasional Bulletin of Missionary Research* 17 (May 1966): 1-10.

Daniélou, Jean. *The Lord of History: Reflections on the Inner Meaning of History*. Translated by Nigel Abercrombie. London: Longmans, 1958.

John, Eric. "Daniélou on History." *Downside Review* 72, no. 227 (1953): 2-15.

Kraft, Robert A. "In Search of Jewish Christianity and Its Theology: Problem of Definition and Methodology." *Recherches de Science Religieuse* 60 (Jan./Mar. 1972): 81-92.

Hugo Rahner (1900-1968)

Rahner, Hugo. *A Theology of Proclamation*. Translated by Richard Dimmler et al. New York: Herder and Herder, 1968.

Romano Guardini (1885-1968)

Guardini, Romano. *"The Church and the Catholic" and "The Spirit of the Liturgy."* Translated by Ada Lane. New York: Sheed and Ward, 1935.

Krieg, Robert. *Romano Guardini: A Precursor of Vatican II*. Notre Dame: University of Notre Dame Press, 1997.

——, ed. *Romano Guardini: Proclaiming the Sacred in a Modern World*. Chicago: Liturgy Training Publications, 1995.

Scola, Angelo. "Freedom, Grace, and Destiny." *Communio* (U.S.) 25 (Fall 1998): 439-61.

Odo Casel (1886-1948)

Dalmais, Irénée Henri. "The Liturgy as Celebration of the Mystery of Salvation." In *Principles of the Liturgy*, edited by Irénée Dalmais et al., 253-72. Collegeville, Minn.: Liturgical Press, 1987.

Hart, James G. "Cult-mystery Revisited." *Downside Review* 91 (Apr. 1973): 141-53.

Neunheuser, Burkhard. "Odo Casel in Retrospect and Prospect." *Worship* 50 (Nov. 1976): 489-504.

Erich Przywara (1889-1972)

Zeitz, James V. "Erich Przywara on Ultimate Reality and Meaning: Deus semper major 'God Ever Greater.'" *Ultimate Reality and Meaning* 12 (Summer 1989): 192-201.

————. "God's Mystery in Christ: Reflections on Erich Przywara and Eberhard Jüngel." *Communio* (U.S.) 12 (Summer 1985): 158-72.

Karl Rahner (1904-84)

Fries, Heinrich, and Karl Rahner. *The Unity of the Churches: An Actual Possibility.* Translated by Ruth C. L. Gritsch and Eric W. Gritsch. Philadelphia: Fortress, 1985.

Kelly, Geffrey B., ed. *Karl Rahner: Theologian of the Graced Search for Meaning.* Minneapolis: Fortress, 1993.

Kelly, William J., ed. *Theology and Discovery: Essays in Honor of Karl Rahner, S.J.* Milwaukee: Marquette University Press, 1980.

Kress, Robert. *A Rahner Handbook.* Atlanta: John Knox, 1982.

Rahner, Karl. *Foundations of Christian Faith: An Introduction to the Idea of Christianity.* Translated by William V. Dych. New York: Crossroad, 1990.

Taylor, Mark Lloyd. *God Is Love: A Study in the Theology of Karl Rahner.* Atlanta: Scholars, 1986.

Hans Urs von Balthasar (1905-88)

Balthasar, Hans Urs von. *Engagement with God.* London: SPCK, 1975.

————. *Explorations in Theology.* Translated by Alexander Dru et al. 4 vols. San Francisco: Ignatius, 1989-95.

Gardner, Lucy, ed. *Balthasar at the End of Modernity.* Edinburgh: T. & T. Clark, 1999.

Riches, John, ed. *The Analogy of Beauty: The Theology of Hans Urs von Balthasar.* Edinburgh: T. & T. Clark, 1986.

Johann Baptist Metz (b. 1928)

Ashley, James. *Interruptions: Mysticism, Politics, and Theology in the Work of Johann Baptist Metz.* Notre Dame: University of Notre Dame Press, 1998.

Downey, John. *Love's Strategy: The Political Theology of Johann Baptist Metz.* Harrisburg, Pa.: Trinity, 1999.

Johns, Roger Dick. *Man in the World: The Political Theology of Johannes Baptist Metz.* Missoula: Scholars Press for the American Academy of Religion, 1976.

Metz, Johann B. *Theology of the World.* Translated by William Glen-Doepel. New York: Herder and Herder, 1969.

Hans Küng (b. 1928)

Häring, Hermann. *Hans Küng: Breaking Through.* London: SCM, 1998.

Jens, Walter. *Dialogue with Hans Küng.* London: SCM, 1997.

Küng, Hans. *The Church.* Garden City, N.Y.: Doubleday Image Book, 1976.

————. *Infallible? An Inquiry.* Translated by Edward Quinn. Garden City, N.Y.: Doubleday, 1971.

————. *Justification: The Doctrine of Karl Barth and a Catholic Reflection, with a Let-*

ter from Karl Barth. Translated by Thomas Collins et al. London: Burns and Oates, 1964.

Kuschel, Karl-Josef. *Hans Küng: New Horizons for Faith and Thought*. London: SCM, 1993.

Edward Schillebeeckx (b. 1914)

Bowden, John. *Edward Schillebeeckx: Portrait of a Theologian*. London: SCM, 1983.

Schillebeeckx, Edward. *Christ: The Experience of Jesus as Lord*. Translated by John Bowden. New York: Seabury Press, 1980.

————. *Church: The Human Story of God*. Translated by John Bowden. New York: Crossroad, 1990.

————. *I Am a Happy Theologian*. London: SCM, 1994.

————. *Jesus: An Experiment in Christology*. Translated by Hubert Hoskins. London: Collins, 1979.

————. *The Language of Faith: Essays on Jesus, Theology, and the Church*. London: SCM, 1995.

Schreiter, Robert J., and Mary Catherine Hilkert, eds. *The Praxis of Christian Experience: An Introduction to the Theology of Edward Schillebeeckx*. San Francisco: Harper and Row, 1989.

David Tracy (b. 1939)

Jeanrond, Werner G., and Jennifer L. Rike, eds. *Radical Pluralism and Truth: David Tracy and the Hermeneutics of Religion*. New York: Crossroad, 1991.

Le Roux, Charl. "The Postmodern — Tracy, Taylor and Dogen." *Religion and Theology* 3, no. 2 (1996): 93-108.

Massa, Mark S. "The New and Old Anti-Catholicism and the Analogical Imagination." *Theological Studies* 62, no. 3 (Summer 2001): 549-70.

Tracy, David. *The Achievement of Bernard Lonergan*. New York: Herder and Herder, 1970.

Makarii Bulgakov (1816-82)

Florovsky, Georges. *Ways of Russian Theology*. Part 1. Belmont, Mass.: Nordland, 1979.

Aleksei S. Khomiakov (1804-60)

O'Leary, Paul Patrick. *The Triune Church: A Study in the Ecclesiology of A. S. Xomjakov*. Freiburg: Universitätsverlag Freiburg, Switzerland, 1982.

Riasanovsky, Nicholas V. "A. S. Khomiakov's Religious Thought." *Saint Vladimir's Theological Quarterly* 23, no. 2 (1979): 87-100.

Ritchey, Mary G. "Khomiakov and His Theory of Sobornost." *Diakonia* 17, no. 1 (1982): 53-62.

Vladimir S. Solovyev (1853-1900)

Bercken, Wil van den, Manon de Courten, and Evert van der Zweerde, eds. *Vladimir*

Solov'ëv: Reconciler and Polemicist; Selected Papers of the International Vladimir Solov'ëv Conference Held at the University of Nijmegen, the Netherlands, September 1998. Sterling, Va.: Peeters, 2000.

Copleston, Frederick. *Russian Religious Philosophy: Selected Aspects*. Notre Dame: University of Notre Dame Press, 1988.

Solovyev, Vladimir. *Russia and the Universal Church*. Translated by Herbert Rees. London: Geoffrey Bles, 1948.

Sutton, Jonathan. *The Religious Philosophy of Vladimir Solovyov: Towards a Reassessment*. New York: St. Martin's Press, 1988.

Dimitri S. Merezhkovskii (1865-1941)

Bedford, Charles. *The Seeker: D. S. Merezhkovskiy*. Lawrence: University Press of Kansas, 1975.

Florovsky, Georges. *Ways of Russian Theology*. Part 2. Vaduz, Liechtenstein: Büchervertriebsanstalt, 1987.

Sergius Bulgakov (1871-1944)

Bulgakov, Sergius. *A Bulgakov Anthology*. Edited by James Pain and Nicolas Zernov. Philadelphia: Westminster, 1976.

Evtuhov, Catherine. *The Cross and the Sickle: Sergei Bulgakov and the Fate of Russian Religious Philosophy*. Ithaca, N.Y.: Cornell University Press, 1997.

Graves, Charles. *The Holy Spirit in the Theology of Sergius Bulgakov*. Geneva: Printed privately at the World Council of Churches, 1972.

Plekon, Michael. *Living Icons: Persons of Faith in the Eastern Church*. Foreword by Lawrence S. Cunningham. Notre Dame: University of Notre Dame Press, 2002. Pp. 29-58.

Williams, Rowan, ed. *Sergii Bulgakov: Towards a Russian Political Theology*. Edinburgh: T. & T. Clark, 1999.

Vladimir N. Losskii (1903-58)

Laats, Alar. *Doctrines of the Trinity in Eastern and Western Theologies: A Study with Special Reference to K. Barth and V. Lossky*. New York: Peter Lang, 1999.

Levitzky, Sergei. "Patriarch of Russian Philosophy: Nicholas Lossky and His Teaching." *St. Vladmir's Seminary Quarterly* 7, no. 2 (1963): 73-83.

Sherwood, Polycarp. "Debate on Palamism: Reflections on Reading Lossky's *The Vision of God*." *St. Vladimir's Seminary Quarterly* 10, no. 4 (1966): 195-203.

Georges Florovsky (1893-1979)

Blane, Andrew, ed. *Georges Florovsky: Russian Intellectual and Orthodox Churchman*. Crestwood, N.Y.: St. Vladimir's Seminary Press, 1993.

Cavarnos, Constantine. *Father Georges Florovsky on Ecumenism*. Etna, Calif.: Center for Traditionalist Orthodox Studies, 1992.

Neiman, David, and Margaret Schatkin, eds. *The Heritage of the Early Church: Essays in Honor of Georges Vasilievich Florovsky.* Rome: Pont. Institutum Studiorum Orientalium, 1973.

Alexander Schmemann (1921-83)

Fisch, Thomas, ed. *Liturgy and Tradition: Theological Reflections of Alexander Schmemann.* Crestwood, N.Y.: St. Vladimir's Seminary Press, 1990.

Morrill, Bruce T. *Anamnesis as Dangerous Memory: Political and Liturgical Theology in Dialogue.* Collegeville, Minn.: Liturgical Press, 2000.

Plekon, Michael. *Living Icons: Persons of Faith in the Eastern Church.* Notre Dame: University of Notre Dame Press, 2002. Pp. 178-202.

Schmemann, Alexander. *Church, World, Mission: Reflections on Orthodoxy in the West.* Crestwood, N.Y.: St. Vladimir's Seminary Press, 1979.

———. *The Journals of Father Alexander Schmemann, 1973-1983.* Crestwood, N.Y.: St. Vladimir's Seminary Press, 2000.

John Meyendorff (1926-92)

Meyendorff, John. "Father John Meyendorff: Orthodox Scholar." In *Between Peril and Promise,* edited by James Newby and Elizabeth Newby, 56-66. Nashville: Thomas Nelson, 1984.

———. *The Orthodox Church: Its Past and Its Role in the World Today.* Revised and expanded by Nicholas Lossky. Crestwood, N.Y.: St. Vladimir's Seminary Press, 1996.

Plekon, Michael. *Living Icons: Persons of Faith in the Eastern Church.* Notre Dame: University of Notre Dame Press, 2002. Pp. 203-33.

Shaw, Lewis. "John Meyendorff and the Heritage of the Russian Theological Tradition." In *New Perspectives on Historical Theology: Essays in Memory of John Meyendorff,* edited by Nassif Bradley, 10-42. Grand Rapids: Eerdmans, 1996.

Slesinski, Robert. "John Meyendorff: A Churchman of Catholic Outreach." *Diakonia* 27, no. 1 (1994): 5-17.

Dumitru Staniloae (1903-93)

Bartos, Emil. *Deification in Eastern Orthodox Theology: An Evaluation and Critique of the Theology of Dumitru Staniloae.* Carlisle, Cumbria: Paternoster, 1999.

Miller, Charles. *The Gift of the World: An Introduction to the Theology of Dumitru Staniloae.* Edinburgh: T. & T. Clark, 2000.

Roberson, Ronald. *Contemporary Romanian Orthodox Ecclesiology: The Contribution of Dumitru Staniloe and Younger Colleagues.* Rome: Pontificium Institutum Orientale, 1988.

Staniloae, Dumitru. *Theology and the Church.* Translated by Robert Barringer. Crestwood, N.Y.: St. Vladimir's Seminary Press, 1980.

Nikos Nissiotis (1924-86)

Kallarangatt, Joseph. "The Ecumenical Theology of Nikos A. Nissiotis." *Christian Orient* 11 (Dec. 1990): 173-86.

Stransky, Thomas, et al. "Nikos Nissiotis: Three Sketches." *Ecumenical Review* 48 (Oct. 1996): 466-75.

Joannis D. Zizioulas (b. 1931)

Collins, Paul. *Trinitarian Theology, West and East: Karl Barth, the Cappadocian Fathers, and John Zizioulas.* New York: Oxford University Press, 2001.

Fox, Patricia. *God as Communion: John Zizioulas, Elizabeth Johnson, and the Retrieval of the Symbol of the Triune God.* Collegeville, Minn.: Liturgical Press, 2001.

McPartlan, Paul. *The Eucharist Makes the Church: Henri de Lubac and John Zizioulas in Dialogue.* Edinburgh: T. & T. Clark, 1993.

Christos Yannaras (b. 1935)

Fisher, David A. "The Freedom of a Christian: The Thought of Christos Yannaras." *Diakonia* 30, no. 2 (1997): 119-26.

Harrison, Verna. "Yannaras on Person and Nature." *St. Vladimir's Theological Quarterly* 33, no. 3 (1989): 287-96.

In addition to the appearance of Roman Catholic and Orthodox theology on the ecumenical national and international scene, the 1960s also saw the emergence of black liberation theology in the United States, which other liberation theologies in Latin America, Africa, and Asia soon followed. With newly won independence and self-respect, theological voices from former colonies in Africa and Asia entered the *ecumene*. With the rise of feminist theology, soon the other half of humankind asked for its rightful place in theological discourse.

The Quest for Liberation

The quest for liberation persists wherever people are oppressed and underprivileged. While it may be a gender issue, as with women's liberation, it is also associated with color, and with economic and class issues. In the United States it began with black liberation theology, prompted through James Cone and his book *Black Theology and Black Power* of 1969.

Black Theology: James H. Cone, Deotis Roberts, and Cornel West

James H. Cone (b. 1938) was born in Fordyce, Arkansas, about sixty miles south of Little Rock. In the small rural community in which he grew up he encountered the cultural and social hegemony of white supremacy and the spiritual depth of the black church. At the age of ten he joined the Macedonia African

Methodist Episcopal Church, and at age sixteen he entered the ministry. In 1958 he received his B.A. from Philander Smith College in Little Rock, and in 1961 his B.D. from Garrett Biblical Institute, now Garrett-Evangelical Theological Seminary, in Evanston, Illinois. Two years later he received his M.A. from Northwestern University, and in 1965 his Ph.D. with the thesis "The Doctrine of Man in the Theology of Karl Barth." Cone became the first African American to graduate with a doctorate in theology from Garrett-Northwestern. He returned to Philander Smith to teach as assistant professor of religion and philosophy (1964-66), then taught for another three years as assistant professor of religion at Adrian College in Michigan. After that he was called to Union Theological Seminary in New York, first as assistant professor (1969-70), then as associate professor, in 1973 as full professor, then as the Charles A. Briggs Professor of Systematic Theology (1977), and finally as the Briggs Distinguished Professor (1987). He has been visiting professor at numerous campuses in the USA, and his books have been translated into many languages.

On July 31, 1966, a full-page advertisement appeared in the *New York Times,* a statement on black power by the National Committee of Negro Churchmen. It stated that "the future of America will belong to neither white nor black unless all Americans work together at the task of rebuilding our cities. We must organize not only among ourselves but with other groups in order that we can, together, gain power sufficient to change this nation's sense of what is *now* important and what must be done *now.*"[1] This was the first assertion of black independence and of a black power movement. Then came in 1969 the Black Manifesto, presented by James Forman (b. 1928) to the National Black Economic Development Conference in Detroit, which demanded a social revolution and self-determination of black institutions. The way was now paved for Cone to assert that "Black Power is the most important development in American life in this century," and "there is a need to begin to analyze it from a theological perspective."[2] According to Cone, black power meant *"complete emancipation of black people from white oppression by whatever means black people deem necessary"* (6). This goes beyond integration, because integration would mean accepting the values of the white people. Black theology, however, is not ethnically determined. As Cone explained, "Being black in America has little to do with skin color. To be black means that your heart, your soul, your mind, and your body are where the dispossessed are" (151). What Cone was asking for

---

1. "Black Power, Statement by the National Committee of Negro Churchmen, July 31, 1966," reprinted in James H. Cone and Gayraud S. Wilmore, eds., *Black Theology: A Documentary History,* vol. 1, *1966-1979,* 2nd rev. ed. (Maryknoll, N.Y.: Orbis, 1993), 23.

2. James H. Cone, *Black Theology and Black Power* (Maryknoll, N.Y.: Orbis, 1999 [1969]), 1. Page references to this work have been placed in the following text.

was equality with whites and not integration into their system, because blacks were already experiencing the latter in their oppressed state. They were allotted their place in society through white supremacy. If black people were willing to die in a riot, then, Cone concluded, this was not out of despair but in hope of "their own dignity grounded in God himself" (30).

"Unless theology can become 'ghetto theology,' a theology which speaks to black people, the gospel message has no promise of life with the black man — it is a lifeless message" (32). This means that theology has to speak to the situation in which black people find themselves and affirm them through the gospel. Cone states the obvious in saying that it is ironic that America with its history of injustice to the poor — especially to those who are black and of Native American descent — prides itself on being a Christian nation. In contrast, Jesus has the poor at the center of his mission. Therefore black power and Christianity have the liberation of humanity in common. The churches must fall into step, either embracing the cause of liberation and proclaiming the gospel of Christ in word and deed, or continuing to be chaplains to the forces of oppression. Yet, the question must be asked whether this would not lead to violence. Cone does not sidestep this issue, but reminds us that violence already exists — it is being done to blacks. He even states that "we can be certain that black patience has run out, and unless white America responds positively to the theory and activity of Black Power, then a bloody, protracted civil war is inevitable. There have occasionally been revolutions — massive redistributions of power — without warfare. It is passionately to be hoped that this can be one of them. The decision lies with white America and not least with white Americans who speak the name of Christ" (143). This means that Cone was not advocating violence, but would understand if it arose. Again, the question was put to whites how to respond to the demand of equality. It was no surprise that this book immediately aroused the attention of many and was translated into several foreign languages.

Cone then became the key drafter of the statement on black theology written by the National Conference of Black Christians' Committee on Theological Prospectus of June 13, 1969. It stated: "Black Theology is a theology of black liberation. . . . The demand that Christ the Liberator imposes on all men *requires* all blacks to affirm their full dignity as persons and all whites to surrender their presumptions of superiority and abuses of power."[3] This document alerts its readers that repeated requests had been made for significant programs of social change, but they were always refused, even by the churches. Therefore,

3. "Black Theology: Statement by the National Committee of Black Churchmen, June 13, 1969," reprinted in Cone and Wilmore, *Black Theology*, 1:38.

reparations must now be made. It also asserted that the black community would be willing to suffer in order to affirm the dignity of black personhood.

In a second book, called *A Black Theology of Liberation* (1970), Cone stated in the first sentence that "Christian theology is a theology of liberation."[4] Since, however, "white theology has consistently preserved the integrity of the community of oppressors, I conclude that it is not Christian theology at all."[5] This means that to be Christian a theology must take seriously the task of liberation. Since a theology cannot be separated from the community it represents, a black theology uses black experience, black history, and black culture as its sources. Only then does revelation enter the picture. But from a black theological perspective, revelation is not comprehensible "without a prior understanding of the concrete manifestation of revelation in the black community as seen in the black experience, black history, and black culture."[6] Revelation must always be understood in the context to which it speaks. Too, theology must neglect neither Scripture nor tradition as the theological reflection of the church upon the nature of Christianity from the beginning to the present day. Having established these parameters for doing theology, Cone develops a black theology covering the traditional topics of God, humanity, Christ, and the church.

Cone has been a prolific writer. In 1972 he wrote *The Spirituals and the Blues: An Interpretation;* in 1975 *God of the Oppressed,* with a revealing introductory autobiography; then on Martin Luther King and Malcolm X in *Martin and Malcolm and America: A Dream or a Nightmare?* (1991). He also published other works. Cone has been the most influential black theologian writing on black liberation. Yet others also assert the necessity of black liberation, such as J. Deotis Roberts and Cornel West.

J. Deotis Roberts (b. 1927), the grand seigneur of black theology, has taught at many places. He was dean of theology at Virginia Union University in Richmond, Virginia; Commonwealth Professor of religious studies at the University of Virginia, George Mason Campus; and distinguished professor of philosophical theology at Eastern Baptist Theological Seminary in Philadelphia, professor of religion at Howard University, as well as professor of theology at the Divinity School of Duke University. Right at the beginning of *A Black Political Theology* (1974) he stated: "Theology is *reasoned* interpretation of the intellectual content of the Christian faith. This is an aspect of theology which is satisfying to the mind. Theology is a reflection upon experience as well. This is

---

4. James H. Cone, *A Black Theology of Liberation* (Maryknoll, N.Y.: Orbis, 1995 [1970]), 1.

5. Cone, *Black Theology of Liberation*, 9.

6. Cone, *Black Theology of Liberation*, 29.

the approach to theology which moves the heart and will. . . . Theology has to do with divine revelation. It is not based upon a human quest for God. We have been found by God."[7]

Roberts opts for a political theology and therefore is not primarily interested in the repetition of creeds and norms. Political theology, as he states, "enrolls itself in the attempt to impart the *kerygma* by means of involvement in the human quest for liberation. . . . The situation of man in the world is normative for political theology, of which black theology is an expression."[8] Thereby political theology perceives existence as sociopolitically conditioned and opts for a coming together of theory and praxis. He therefore sees black power as an alternative to nonviolence, which was primarily advocated by Martin Luther King, Jr. While Roberts does not opt for violence, he also believes that love and justice cannot be attained without power. Therefore he looks to the black Christ who liberates and a universal Christ who reconciles. "The Jesus of the disinherited sets us free. The Jesus who breaks through the color line reconciles all men. . . . We cannot fully know Jesus in the role of reconciler until we know him in his role as liberator. . . . *Jesus means freedom!*"[9] In *A Black Political Theology* Roberts wanted to provide a theological foundation for an action-oriented people who are determined to be black and free. For Roberts black theology is contextual theology arising from the black experience, just as Karl Barth's theology came out of the European crisis in the first quarter of the twentieth century.[10] Therefore black theology must address the fact of poverty in the black community, and it must be involved with the educative process for blacks, in terms of both their religious consciousness as well as academia. This means there has to be cooperation between this theology and ministry, because black theology is deeply anchored in the black culture.[11]

Cornel West (b. 1953) did his undergraduate studies at Harvard and received his Ph.D. from Princeton (1980) with a thesis entitled "Ethics, Historicism, and the Marxist Tradition." He taught at Yale University, was professor of philosophy and Christian practice at Union Theological Seminary in New York, and chaired the department of Afro-American studies at Princeton University (1988-94), was then University Professor at Harvard, and has been since 2002 University Professor of Religion at Princeton. Although his under-

---

7. J. Deotis Roberts, *A Black Political Theology* (Philadelphia: Westminster, 1974), 19.

8. Roberts, *A Black Political Theology,* 190.

9. Roberts, *A Black Political Theology,* 138.

10. So J. Deotis Roberts, "Black Consciousness in Theological Perspective," in *Quest for a Black Theology,* ed. James Gardiner and J. Deotis Roberts (Philadelphia: Pilgrim Press, 1971), 66.

11. Cf. J. Deotis Roberts, in his chapter "The Future of Black Theology," in J. Deotis Roberts, *Black Theology in Dialogue* (Philadelphia: Westminster, 1987), esp. 115-17.

graduate degree was in Semitic languages (1973), he was the first African American to complete a Ph.D. program in philosophy at Princeton University.

West is more abstract in his reflections and at the same time more descriptive and analytical than both Roberts and Cone. He sees two sources that shape black American thinking: the prophetic Christian thought as seen in evangelical and pietistic Christianity, and American pragmatism that conceives of knowledge as occurring within the framework of intersubjective, communal inquiry. He opts for a dialogical encounter between black Christian thinking and progressive Marxist social analysis, because the fundamental thrust of Marxism, "despite the numerous brutalities perpetrated by Marxist regimes, is the self-fulfillment, self-development, and self-realization of harmonious personalities."[12] Ultimately he sees the task of black religious philosophy to provide a political prescription for the specific praxis in a struggle for liberation. To that extent he contends: "The revolutionary Christian perspective and praxis must remain anchored in the prophetic Christian tradition in the Afro-American experience which provides the norms of individuality and democracy; guided by the cultural outlook of the Afro-American humanist tradition which promotes the vitality and vigor of black life; and informed by the social theory and political praxis of progressive Marxism which proposes to approximate as close as is humanly possible the precious values of individuality and democracy as soon as God's will be done."[13] West attempts to wed together the black church, the black humanist tradition, and progressive Marxism. To that extent, he deals with social and political theory and history, engaging in the dialogue from a decidedly black perspective.

Other black theologians saw no need for a separate black theology. For instance, Charles H. Long (b. 1926) was a student of the historian of religion Mircea Eliade (1907-86). He served as professor of history of religion at the University of North Carolina at Chapel Hill and then at Syracuse University, was a past president of the American Academy of Religion, and saw himself primarily as a historian of religion who contributed to his own field of inquiry without taking into account a decidedly black perspective.[14]

Native Americans have had their struggle of liberation as well. Though a significant number of them have been educated and have returned to their

---

12. Cornel West, *Prophesy Deliverance! An Afro-American Revolutionary Christianity* (Louisville: Westminster John Knox, 2002 [1982]), 16.

13. West, *Prophesy Deliverance!* 146.

14. For details on Long, cf. Dwight N. Hopkins, *Black Theology: USA and South Africa* (Maryknoll, N.Y.: Orbis, 1990), 70-76, and the books by Charles H. Long, such as *Alpha: The Myths of Creation* (Chico, Calif.: Scholars, 1983 [1963]), and *Significations: Signs, Symbols, and Images in the Interpretation of Religion* (Philadelphia: Fortress, 1986).

communities to advocate new economic, legal, political, and social initiatives, their struggle has been even more difficult.[15] Since they are fewer in number than the blacks, they could not exert the same power, and since they often live on remote reservations, they were even more out of sight than blacks in their urban ghettos. Because the church did not play the same central role for them as it has in Afro-American communities, they also did not pursue a Christian Native American theology. This can be seen, for instance, with **Vine Deloria** (b. 1933), whose grandfather, a Yankton chief, converted to Christianity and became an Episcopal priest. His father then became an Episcopal archdeacon, while Deloria received a B.D. degree from the Lutheran Augustana Theological Seminary, now part of the Lutheran School of Theology at Chicago. But then he earned a law degree at the University of Colorado.[16] Deloria is no longer sure about his Christianity, since the Native American tribal religion "provided for a meaningful existence for a people facing a world far different than the one presently experienced."[17] Christianity is unable to speak to certain problems of the Indians without facing internal collapse of its doctrinal structure. It can simply not be true, Deloria argues, that other peoples spent centuries in the state of delusion, just because their experiences of God were radically different from those of Western peoples. What is important, he suggests, is the place where religious experience occurs. For whites it is their religious edifices, for Native Americans it is nature. To the Native American, land and that which lives on it are therefore important. But Western Christianity has neglected this context. Therefore Deloria cannot make use of his Christian faith and contends that American Indians will find peace with the land only "when the invaders of the North American continent will finally discover that for this land, God is red."[18] In the struggle for liberation many Native Americans are returning to their own tribal religions, since they feel that the "white man's religion" is a religion of oppression and exploitation. In contrast to the Afro-Americans, they are yet unable to arrive at a positive interpretation of the Christian faith.

15. For details cf. Vine Deloria, Jr., *Behind the Trail of Broken Treaties: An Indian Declaration of Independence* (New York: Dell, 1974).

16. Cf. for details, also for Deloria's struggle with the Christian faith, Benjamin A. Reist, *Theology in Red, White, and Black* (Philadelphia: Westminster, 1975), 53.

17. Vine Deloria, Jr., *God Is Red: A Native View of Religion*, 2nd ed. (Golden, Colo.: Fulcrum, 1994), 283.

18. Deloria, *God Is Red*, 292.

The Struggle of Liberation Theology: Clodovis and Leonardo Boff and the Vatican; Gustavo Gutiérrez

Since black theology is a contextual regional theology, considering the black experience in the United States, we must also look to other regional contexts, such as Latin America and its liberation theology, which came to the notice of black theologians, especially through Gustavo Gutiérrez's 1973 English translation of *A Theology of Liberation*.[19] Out of this originated the 1975 Detroit Conference on "Theology in the Americas," organized by Father Sergio Torres, with the intention of establishing a dialogue between Latin American liberation theologians and North American black theologians to initiate a process of evaluation of the North American reality from the viewpoint of the poor and the oppressed. Yet the discussions did not go very far, since the black theologians talked about race oppression while the Latin Americans emphasized the significance of class oppression. This also shows that regional contextual theology often has difficulty transcending its own contextual horizon.

Since Latin American liberation theology originated in a predominantly Roman Catholic context, it immediately got a hearing in the Roman Catholic global community, far transcending the Latin American location. Even Pope John Paul II picked up the concerns of liberation theology. When he addressed the Third General Conference of the Latin American episcopate in Puebla, Mexico, in 1979, millions of people listened to his words. He said violence, whether committed by those on the left or on the right of the political spectrum, is unchristian and therefore must be condemned. He further emphasized that a theology of liberation not founded on the gospel but on the Marxist analysis of reality is a false theology. Yet he recognized that many liberation theologies are not ideologically twisted, but integrate Christian values and therefore are true theology. This three-part analysis shows in a nutshell the problematic nature as well as the promise of liberation theology. It is a response to violence committed in word and deed and recognizes Christian values. It propagates and hopes for an evangelically grounded liberation. Yet often those who are concerned about liberation are similar to many of the earliest followers of Jesus. They attempt to take the inauguration of the kingdom in their own hands.

To channel liberation concerns into the ecclesially appropriate direction, the Sacred Congregation for the Doctrine of the Faith, of the Vatican, has also ad-

---

19. For the interaction between black theology and Latin American liberation theology, see James H. Cone, "From Geneva to São Paulo: A Dialogue between Black Theology and Latin American Liberation Theology," in *Black Theology: A Documentary History*, vol. 2, *1980-1992*, ed. James H. Cone and Gayraud S. Wilmore (Maryknoll, N.Y.: Orbis, 1993), 371-87.

dressed several times the issue of a theology of liberation. In 1984, for instance, it acknowledged that the yearning for liberation agrees with a deep-seated theme of the Old and the New Testaments. "In itself, the expression 'theology of liberation' is a thoroughly valid term: it designates a theological reflection centered on the biblical theme of liberation and freedom, and on the urgency of its practical realization."[20] At the same time, the congregation noted that some liberation theologians "are tempted to emphasize, unilaterally, the liberation from servitude of an earthly and temporal kind."[21] Furthermore, concepts that are "uncritically borrowed from marxist ideology and recourse to theses of a biblical hermeneutic marked by rationalism are at the basis of the new interpretation."[22] Where this occurs, the revolutionary praxis becomes the highest criterion of theological truth.

Since these summary accusations concerning some aspects of liberation theology caused much dismay especially in Latin America, the congregation issued the instruction *On Christian Freedom and Liberation,* on March 22, 1986.[23] There we find a more discerning discourse concerning liberation theology. The congregation states: "Human history, marked as it is by the experience of sin, would drive us to despair if God had abandoned His creation to itself. But the divine promises of liberation, and their victorious fulfillment in Christ's death and resurrection, are the basis of the 'joyful hope' from which the Christian community draws the strength to act resolutely and effectively in the service of love, justice and peace. The Gospel is a message of freedom and a liberating force."[24] It becomes clear from the instruction that liberation must be understood first of all in a salvational way. Only then does it find its continuation in the concrete and liberating tasks that result from an ethical demand. But this order seems to have often been lost in liberation theology, so that the emphasis was not just placed on orthopraxis over against orthodoxy, but right doctrine was accorded only secondary significance. This kind of admonition may be justified against some representatives of liberation theology. Yet one is surprised that the deliberations by the congregation show little appreciation for the eschatological emphasis of liberation.[25]

---

20. Sacred Congregation for the Doctrine of the Faith, *Instruction on Certain Aspects of the "Theology of Liberation"* (III/4) (Aug. 6, 1984) (Boston: St. Paul, 1984), 8.

21. Sacred Congregation, *Instruction on Certain Aspects* (introduction), 3.

22. Sacred Congregation, *Instruction on Certain Aspects* (VI/10), 16.

23. For a direct response to this first instruction, see Juan Luis Segundo, *Theology and the Church: A Response to Cardinal Ratzinger and a Warning to the Whole Church,* trans. John W. Diercksmeier (New York: Winston, 1985).

24. The Congregation for the Doctrine of the Faith, *Instruction on Christian Freedom and Liberation* (3/43) (Mar. 22, 1986) (Boston: St. Paul, 1986), 26.

25. Though much is said in it about salvation, the term "eschatological" appears only in a

The congregation did not want to have its criticism of liberation theology interpreted as "setting [it]self up as an obstacle on the path to liberation."[26] Its pronouncements were also not intended to be an indirect approval of those who contribute to the continuation of the misery of the nations who profit from it, and who are accomplices in it, or who remain untouched by this misery. In many countries, any criticism against the prevailing practice of injustice is brutally suppressed and the rich are privileged at the expense of the poor. Such conditions call for liberation, a redistribution of the riches and a radical social and economic reorientation. The modern technological resources of the industrial nations were originally readily adopted by almost all countries since they brought the industrialized countries widespread affluence. But now these resources are regarded more and more as dubious means, since at the same time they dehumanize the lives of people in these countries and suffocate eternal values. The insight is growing that an opulent lifestyle in one part of the world is made possible by people who live in another part of the world. These laborers create this affluence by working for little money and under conditions that are nearly unbearable. By following the biblical admonition to care for the poor and powerless, Christians become more and more responsive to the needs of the exploited, oppressed, and underprivileged. While the congregation was not blind to the plight of the people, it reminded liberation theology that "The salvific dimension of liberation cannot be reduced to the socio-ethical dimension, which is a consequence of it. By restoring man's true freedom, the radical liberation brought about by Christ assigns to him a task: Christian practice which is the putting into practice of the great commandment of love."[27] This suspicion, that liberation theology reduces soteriology to social-ethical activism, caused uneasiness in the congregation and resentment among the representatives of liberation theology. This can be seen especially dramatically in the difficulties that the brothers Clodovis and Leonardo Boff encountered.

Clodovis Boff (b. 1944) was born in Concórdia, Santa Catarina, Brazil, and studied philosophy in Rio de Janeiro. He was ordained a Servite priest and received his doctorate from the Catholic University of Louvain, Belgium, in 1976 with a thesis entitled "Theology and Praxis: Epistemological Foundations" (Eng. trans. 1987). (He also received a licentiate in philosophy from the Univer-

---

side reference. In this situation the opinion of Johann Baptist Metz makes sense, when he claims that the defense of "a culturally monocentric church of the west" is more at stake here than the propagation of the "messianic church of its origin" ("Thesen zum theologischen Ort der Befreiungstheologie," in *Die Theologie der Befreiung. Hoffnung oder Gefahr für die Kirche?* ed. Johann Baptist Metz [Düsseldorf: Patmos, 1986], 154).

26. Congregation, *Instruction on Christian Freedom* (20), 11.

27. Congregation, *Instruction on Christian Freedom* (71), 46.

sity of São Paulo in 1970.) Upon his return to Brazil, he became professor of theology at the Franciscan Theological Institute in Petrópolis, and in 1978 professor of theology at Our Lady of the Assumption in the Faculty of Theology at the Catholic University of São Paulo.

In direct response to the 1984 instruction, Boff pointed out that "*The fundamental question of liberation theology is not theology but liberation.* Theology does not occupy the center, but the poor."[28] We are confronted here with a decidedly contextual theology that wants to demonstrate that the kingdom has not just a personal dimension (the soul) or a transcendental dimension (heaven) but a historical dimension, the relationship between people and the structures of society. Liberation theology strives to overcome the dichotomy between this world and the world to come. Boff claims that the transcendental dimension of faith has been treated sufficiently by classical theology and is accepted and presupposed by the theology of liberation. Yet liberation theology intends to "connect the mystery of God with the history of humanity."[29] It seeks to accomplish a living unity of the experience of salvation with the experience of liberation. As Leonardo Boff stated: "The historical process anticipates and paves the way for definitive liberation in the kingdom. Thus human forms of liberation acquire a sacramental function. They have a weight of their own, but they also point toward, and embody in anticipation, what God has definitively prepared for human beings."[30]

Leonardo Boff (b. 1938), brother of Clodovis, was also born in Concórdia and received his graduate degree in philosophy in Curitiba (1961) and in theology in Petrópolis (1965) and then earned a doctorate from the Roman Catholic faculty of the University of Munich (1970). He is a Franciscan priest and has been professor of systematic theology in Petrópolis since 1970. The critical attitude of the Sacred Congregation for the Doctrine of Faith in its first pronouncement on liberation theology was most likely caused by his book *Church: Charism and Power; Liberation Theology and the Institutional Church* (1981).

Because the feudal society in Latin America very much reflects the hierarchical structure of the church, Boff directly addressed this issue, writing: "In spite of the inevitable gap between proclamation and implementation, there is today another gap that results from power structures, institutional deficiencies, and distortions — both practical and theoretical — inherited from models that no longer reflect reality. There are violations of human rights within the

---

28. Clodovis Boff, *Die Befreiung der Armen: Reflexionen zum Grundanliegen der lateinamerikanischen Befreiungstheologie* (Freiburg, Switzerland: Edition Exodus, 1986), 16.

29. Clodovis Boff, *Die Befreiung der Armen,* 27.

30. Leonardo Boff, *Liberating Grace,* trans. John Drury (Maryknoll, N.Y.: Orbis, 1979), 152.

Church itself."[31] The reason for this is the centralization of all decisions in a small hierarchical elite through the absolutizing of doctrine, cultural forms, and the distribution of power within the community. Boff claimed: "The absolutizing of a form of the Church's presence in society led to the oppression of the faithful."[32] Boff has no intention of calling for an abolition of the present form of church with dioceses and bishops, parishes and priests. Yet for him there are two expressions of the one church of Christ and of the apostles: the institutional church and the ecclesial base communities. "The institutional Church supports and encourages the basic ecclesial communities; through them it is able to enter the popular sector and be made concrete by sharing in the painful passion as well as the hopes of the people. These ecclesial communities, in turn, are in communion with the institutional Church; they want their bishop, their priests and religious. In this way, the communities are put in touch with the grand apostolic tradition, guarantee their catholicity, and reaffirm the unity of the Church."[33] Boff left no doubt that these base communities are truly the church of Christ and of the apostles at the grassroots level.

There is a new type of society taught within these communities by learning to overcome the unjust relationships that dominate the larger society. This is done "through the direct participation of all the members of the group, the sharing of responsibilities, leadership, and decision-making, through the exercise of power as service."[34] Boff now called for an end of the dichotomy between the teaching and learning church, a dichotomy that resulted in the pathological view of the church's reality. There is not one part that knows everything and another that knows nothing, but there must be a mutual sharing, listening, and learning from each other. Such suggestions that lean toward democracy were not welcomed by the prefect of the Congregation for the Doctrine of the Faith at the Vatican, Joseph Cardinal Ratzinger (b. 1927), the present Pope Benedict XVI. As a result, Boff was summoned to appear before the congregation in 1984. While in Rome he was strongly supported by his Franciscan co-*fratres* and the Brazilian episcopate. Nevertheless, in the following year Rome imposed on him "a period of silence under obedience . . . of sufficient duration to afford him a space for adequate reflection."[35] Yet the father general of the Franciscans specified that the homilies at the Eucharist and the lectures

---

31. Leonardo Boff, *Church: Charism and Power; Liberation Theology and the Institutional Church*, trans. John W. Diercksmeier (New York: Crossroad, 1985), 33.

32. Leonardo Boff, *Church*, 85.

33. Leonardo Boff, *Church*, 126.

34. Leonardo Boff, *Church*, 129.

35. Clodovis Boff, in Leonardo Boff and Clodovis Boff, *Liberation Theology: From Dialogue to Confrontation*, trans. Robert R. Barr (San Francisco: Harper and Row, 1986), 94-95.

on theology to Franciscan seminarians in Petrópolis would not fall under this ban, since they were not open to the public. Boff accepted the decision of the Vatican, despite the loud public outcry in Brazil and throughout the world, and entered his period of penitential silence.

Unlike in the USA, no certain ethnic group, such as the Afro-Americans, was excluded from its share in society, but rather in Latin America vast masses of people were exploited by a few exceedingly rich people, absentee landholders and financial investors. To remedy the situation, the local Roman Catholic Church, including the hierarchy, began to empower the people through what Brazilian educator Paulo Freire (1921-77) called the *Pedagogy of the Oppressed* (New York: Seabury Press, 1970). They encouraged the study of Scripture and helped the poor to demand their own share in society. To some extent, liberationists also relied on the social analysis of Karl Marx to understand what had happened in society and to look for solutions.[36] Yet most Latin American liberation theologians never adopted a Marxist ideology. Though many representatives of liberation theology could be named, we want to turn our attention to only one more, Gustavo Gutiérrez, whose *Theology of Liberation* (1972; Eng. trans. 1973) became a classic of liberation theology.[37]

Gustavo Gutiérrez (b. 1928) was born in Lima, Peru. Intending to become a doctor, he studied medicine at San Marcos University in Lima, where he received a degree in medical science. At the same time he studied the writings of Karl Marx, and then studied philosophy at the Catholic University in Lima. Gradually he became more interested in theology and the priesthood, and after completing theological studies in Santiago, Chile, he studied philosophy and psychology at Louvain, Belgium, and obtained a Ph.D. in theology at the University of Lyons, France, in 1959. Still his interest in Marx continued unabated. The same year he received his Ph.D. he was ordained a priest and studied at the Gregorian University in Rome. In the early 1960s, he returned to Lima to serve as a parish pastor and instructor in the department of theology and social sciences at the Catholic Pontifical University of Lima. Then he came under the influence of Che Guevara (1928-67), an Argentinian Marxist revolutionary and medical doctor who died in Bolivia as a guerrilla fighter, and who had been a fellow student at Louvain, and of the Colombian theologian and revolutionary Camilo Torres (1929-66), who met the same fate as Che. This identified Gutiérrez even more with the poor people of his own country. In 1968 he served

36. Cf. José Profirio Miranda, *Marx and the Bible: A Critique of the Philosophy of Oppression,* trans. John Eagleson (Maryknoll, N.Y.: Orbis, 1974).

37. For helpful portraits of liberation theologians on a global scale, see Deane William Ferm, *Profiles in Liberation: 36 Portraits of Third World Theologians* (Mystic, Conn.: Twenty-Third Publications, 1988).

as theological adviser at the Medellín, Colombia, conference of Latin American bishops advocating "a preferential option for the poor." He also participated in the Theology in the Americas conference in Detroit and served as visiting professor at Union Theological Seminary in 1976/77, where he became a dialogue partner of James Cone. While never becoming a Marxist, he did not hesitate to use Marxist social analysis in his effort to understand the plight of the poor. Gutiérrez is a highly pastoral person with a deep spirituality.

For Gutiérrez the theology of liberation is a theology of salvation incarnated in the concrete historical and political conditions of today. That theology is seen here under the aspect of salvation is understandable in light of the situation to which liberation theology primarily speaks. The situation of the oppressed calls for a revolutionary transformation of the very basis of a dehumanizing society. Though liberation theologians have often employed Marxist terminology, there is no conceptual panacea that would safeguard such a revolutionary transformation. Christians involved in the process of liberation proceed by trial and error in their attempt to build a different social order and to establish a new way of being human. While hope is central to a theology of liberation, one does not pursue its goal in euphoria. The joy of the resurrection first requires death on the cross.

But in his comprehensive *Theology of Liberation,* Gutiérrez made it clear that "it is important to keep in mind that beyond — or rather, through — the struggle against misery, injustice, and exploitation the goal is the *creation of a new humanity.*"[38] Gutiérrez learned from the Old Testament that God is a history-making God and that salvation is there spoken of in terms of a re-creation of history. The God who creates the cosmos out of chaos is the same God who leads Israel from alienation to liberation. Similarly, in the New Testament we hear of a new creation. Creation and salvation therefore belong together. By means of our labor we participate in the all-embracing salvific process, thereby engaging ourselves in the work of creation. By transforming this world we become human and build a human community. In our struggle against misery and exploitation and in our attempt to build a just society, we become part of the saving action that is on its way toward complete fulfillment. Salvation is not a return to the days of old, but a striving forward toward something new and unprecedented. In talking about the new creation, Gutiérrez rightly emphasized Christ as its center and goal.

The vision of salvation and new creation would lose its driving force

---

38. Gustavo Gutiérrez, *A Theology of Liberation: History, Politics, and Salvation,* trans. and ed. C. Inda and J. Eagleson, 15th anniversary edition with a new introduction by the author (Maryknoll, N.Y.: Orbis, 1988), 81.

without the eschatological promises that permeate virtually the whole Bible. Gutiérrez appropriately distinguished between the promises made by God throughout history and the "Promise" that unfolds and becomes richer and more definite in these individual promises. "The Promise is not exhausted by these promises nor by their fulfillment; it goes beyond them, explains them, and gives them their ultimate meaning. But at the same time, the Promise is announced and is partially and progressively fulfilled in them."[39] The promises replacing each other urge history on to new horizons and new possibilities. The Promise is gradually revealed in its fullness. Since it is already fulfilled in historical events, yet not completely, it incessantly projects itself into the future and creates a permanent historical mobility. Gutiérrez knows that both the present and the future aspects are indispensable for properly aligning the relationship between the Promise and history.

When one asks what this Promise might be, Gutiérrez points to the efficacious self-disclosure of God's love and God's consequent self-communication. This Promise, which is both revelation and good news, is at the heart of the Bible, and enters into a decisive stage in the incarnation of the Son and the sending of the Spirit. Since the Promise is intimately connected with salvation and with the time of fulfillment, it is clear for Gutiérrez that in the Bible eschatology is "the driving force of salvific history radically oriented toward the future. Eschatology is thus not just one more element of Christianity, but the very key to understanding the Christian faith."[40]

Gutiérrez is adamant in pointing out that the intrinsic eschatological structure of the Christian faith is not to be spiritualized. Neither its present nor its future aspects should be related merely to spiritual realities, since their origin and goal have definite historical bearings. For instance, when the prophets announce the kingdom of peace, this presupposes the establishment of justice on earth. Similarly, the coming of the kingdom and the expectation of the parousia necessarily imply historical, temporal, earthly, social, and material realities. A spiritualization, however, would tend to forget the human consequences of the eschatological promises and the power to transform the unjust social structures they imply. The elimination of misery and exploitation therefore can be understood as a sign of the coming kingdom.

Gutiérrez emphasizes that the eschatological promises are being fulfilled throughout history. And he cautions that they cannot be clearly and completely identified with a specific social reality. Yet we are somewhat bewildered when we read: "The complete encounter with the Lord will mark an end to history,

39. Gustavo Gutiérrez, *A Theology of Liberation*, 92.
40. Gustavo Gutiérrez, *A Theology of Liberation*, 93.

but it will take place in history."[41] Does this mean that we are evolving toward a state of eschatological fulfillment, a state that, because it is eschatological, will not be just another point on the map of history? If that is the case, Gutiérrez would burden us with the impossible task of demonstrating that we are evolving toward that state. Gutiérrez is right when he claims that the liberating action of Christ is not marginal to the real life of humanity but strikes at its very heart. The struggle for a just society can in its own right also be considered a part of salvation history. But Gutiérrez seems to neglect the fact that the immense depravity of humanity not only causes the conditions that cry out for liberation but also prevents liberation from becoming a historical event. That is why salvation calls for a totally new creation that cannot be realized by us. Notwithstanding all good endeavors to which Gutiérrez summons us, we are always confronted with the dilemma of Romans 7:19 ("For I do not do the good I want, but the evil I do not want is what I do"). Yet this cannot serve as an excuse, but must be seen as our limitation.

Liberating the Other Half of Humanity (Feminist Theology)

Feminist theology emerged about the same time Latin American liberation theology came to the fore. It is striving for adequate representation in language, on all levels of society and church, and in theological reflection. Some female theologians, though sensitive to women's issues in their own field, do not propagate their own variety of feminist theology. They are predominantly contributors in their own field of expertise, such as Sallie McFague (b. 1933), the former E. Rhodes and Leona B. Carpenter Professor of Theology at Vanderbilt University, or Annemarie Schimmel (b. 1922), professor emeritus in the department of Near Eastern languages at Harvard University who, even in Muslim countries, is an acknowledged expert on Islam. Others, however, are more interested in mining the riches of feminist experience and drawing attention to the problems still existing there. Yet "*the* feminist theology does not exist!"[42] Its diversity is even more noticeable than with liberation theology. It ranges from representa-

---

41. Gustavo Gutiérrez, *A Theology of Liberation*, 97. While we cannot agree with the claim of Juan Gutiérrez, *The New Libertarian Gospel: Pitfalls of the Theology of Liberation*, trans. P. Burns (Chicago: Franciscan Herald Press, 1977), 97, that Gustavo Gutiérrez has emptied theology of its content, we agree with Juan Gutiérrez that in liberation theology evangelization in terms of conversion as the specific mission of the church certainly loses significance at the expense of sociopolitical reforms.

42. So correctly Lucia Scherzberg, *Grundkurs feministischer Theologie* (Mainz: Matthias Grünewald, 1995), 11.

tives who have discarded the Judeo-Christian tradition as normative and advocate those religions that emphasize the life-giving power of goddesses to scholars who rely on solid theological exegesis of biblical texts.[43]

A Biblical Hermeneutics: Luise Schottroff and Elisabeth Schüssler Fiorenza

With the biblical texts, feminist exegesis can arrive at surprising conclusions. For instance, we are told: "It is unmistakably men who speak in the visions of the apocalypse of John."[44] Otherwise the martyrs could not be adorned with victory wreaths and assume the heritage of force. There are no visions in the book of Revelation that describe mutuality, community in relationships, and interdependence. This stands in stark contrast to the Synoptic Gospels and the stories about Jesus. In Revelation the elect are related to God but not to each other. As the German New Testament scholar **Luise Schottroff** (b. 1934) notes:

> the apocalypse is a book about power and violence written from the perspective of men who resist (at the risk of their lives) the inimical and anti-Godly power of Rome. All relationships mentioned in this book are described as relationships of power, be it the power of the animal from the sea, the dragon, or be it the power of the lamb that is victorious over these powers and who has started, with its suffering, the process by which God gains rule over the earth and through which it becomes a new earth. History is understood as a struggle for the liberation of the earth. These relationships of power are almost exclusively those of power.[45]

Instead of those symbols of power one should look to Jesus, who is portrayed in the Gospels as the eschatological gatherer of the dispersed, and to Paul, who in Romans 12:12 encourages the Christians in Rome: "Rejoice in

---

43. Cf. Maria Kassel, "Tod und Auferstehung," in *Feministische Theologie: Perspektiven zur Orientierung*, ed. Maria Kassel (Stuttgart: Kreuz Verlag, 1988), 191-225, where she weds together "the pre-patriarchal" Sumerian myth of Inanna's descent into the netherworld with the Judeo-Christian tradition of death and resurrection whereby the former becomes normative for the latter.

44. Luise Schottroff, "Die befreite Eva: Schuld und Macht der Mächtigen und Ohnmächtigen nach dem Neuen Testament," in *Schuld und Macht: Studien zu einer feministischen Befreiungstheologie*, ed. Christine Schaumberger and Luise Schottroff (Munich: Chr. Kaiser, 1988), 93.

45. Schottroff, "Die befreite Eva," 97-98.

hope, be patient in suffering, persevere in prayer." Such perseverance has nothing to do with passivity.[46] This is the attitude of the martyrs in the Jewish and then the Christian tradition who take the conflicts of society upon themselves because they are expecting the kingdom of God on this earth and draw the consequences for their lives from this hope. Perseverance betrays an eschatological orientation through which the hope engendered causes them to resist the praxis and goals of society. The expectation of God as an eschatological hope does not reconcile them with the atrocities in human history, but it gives the faithful the power not to surrender on account of this violence. They expect the kingdom of God and the resurrection of the dead. From this hope they receive power, the will to resist, and resurrection already now. "Perseverance *(hypomonē)* is the power of the resurrection in the midst of the death structures in which I am entangled as an accomplice."[47]

When we leave the New Testament, we encounter in early Christianity an "extreme ambiguity toward women" as far as the eschaton is concerned. "Female sexuality and giving birth are seen as the antithesis of the escape from mortal life that reborn virginal Christians seek."[48] But the Christian virgins and especially Mary are understood as spiritual beings who bear rich fruit on account of their virtues. At the same time, the feminine is the symbol and expression of the perishable body from which we should flee so that the soul is purified for eternal life. All feminine processes of life, such as pregnancy, birth, and the feminine itself, are impure and carry with them the blemish of decay and death. Symptomatic of this is the gnostic *Gospel of Thomas,* where we read in the conclusion: "Simon Peter said to them, 'Let Mary leave us, for women are not worthy of Life.' Jesus said, 'I myself shall lead her in order to make her male, so that she too may become a living spirit resembling you males. For every woman who will make herself male will enter the Kingdom of Heaven.'"[49]

This line of reasoning was even continued by some of the church fathers. Jerome (ca. 347/48–420), for instance, writes in his *Commentary on Ephesians* in a side comment on Ephesians 5:28: "As long as a woman serves procreation and the children, there exists the same difference between her and a man as between body and soul. But when she wants to serve Christ more than the world, she will stop being a woman and will be called a man, because we desire that all will

46. For the following cf. Schottroff, "Die befreite Eva," 102-4.

47. Schottroff, "Die befreite Eva," 108.

48. Rosemary R. Ruether, *Sexism and God-Talk: Toward a Feminist Theology* (Boston: Beacon Press, 1983), 245.

49. *The Gospel of Thomas* 114, in James M. Robinson, *The Nag Hammadi Library* (San Francisco: Harper and Row, 1977), 130.

be advanced to a perfect man."[50] Augustine also dealt with the issue of whether women can enter eternal life as women, since God made only man from the earth and then took the woman from man. But he arrived at very different results than did Jerome: "For my part, they seem to be wiser who make no doubt that both sexes shall rise. For there shall be no lust, which is now the cause of confusion. . . . And the sex of woman is not a vice, but nature. . . . The woman, therefore, is a creature of God even as the man; but by her creation from man unity is commended."[51] Attempts were still made to consider with Aristotle the woman as a second-rate man and to see in the woman primarily a temptress that needed to be shunned at all cost. But especially the prioresses and nuns of the Middle Ages developed something like a female self-consciousness that no longer accepted the demand to become like men; rather, they considered themselves equal with men.[52] Perhaps the Augustinian dictum that being a woman is not a vice, but nature, proved to be too persuasive.

Elisabeth Schüssler Fiorenza (b. 1938) is a Roman Catholic who was born in Romania and received her education in Germany, obtaining her Ph.D. in New Testament studies from the Roman Catholic faculty at the University of Münster. Having taught at the University of Notre Dame, the Episcopal Divinity School in Boston, and Union Theological Seminary in New York, she is now Krister Stendahl Professor of Divinity at Harvard Divinity School. She was the first woman president of the Society of Biblical Literature (1987) and is married to Francis Fiorenza (b. 1941), a systematic theologian who also teaches at Harvard Divinity School. Her book *In Memory of Her* (1982), a primer in feminist biblical hermeneutics, has been translated into twelve languages.

For Schüssler Fiorenza, feminist theology is "a different way and alternative perspective for doing theology. At the same time it insists that the androcentric-clerical theology produced in Western universities and seminaries no longer can claim to be a Catholic Christian theology if it does not become a theology inclusive of the experiences of all members of the Church, women and men, lay and clergy."[53] This means that as a dedicated Roman Catholic, her ap-

---

50. Jerome, *Commentariorum in Epistolam ad Ephesios*, in J. P. Migne, *Patrologia Latina* 26:533; and cf. Elisabeth Gössmann and Haruko Okano, "Himmel ohne Frauen? Zur Eschatologie des weiblichen Menschseins in östlicher und westlicher Religion," in *Das Gold in Wachs: Festschrift für Thomas Immoos zum 70. Geburtstag,* ed. Elisabeth Gössmann and Günter Zobel (Munich: Indicium Verlag, 1988), 400, who comment on these thoughts of Jerome on Eph. 4:13.

51. Augustine, *The City of God* 22.17, in Nicene and Post-Nicene Fathers, 1st ser., 2:496.

52. Cf. Gössmann and Okano, "Himmel ohne Frauen?" 405-6.

53. Elisabeth Schüssler Fiorenza, "For Women in Men's World: A Critical Feminist Theology of Liberation," in *The Power of Naming: A Concilium Reader in Feminist Liberation Theol-*

proach provides an existential challenge to her own tradition. This challenge becomes evident when she writes: "*Ecclesia* — the term for church in the New Testament — is not so much a religious as a civil-political concept. It means the actual assembly of free citizens gathering for deciding their own spiritual-political affairs. Since women in a patriarchal church cannot decide their own theological-religious affairs and that of their own people — women — the *ecclesia* of women is as much a future hope as it is a reality today."[54] Here the notion of self-governance reminds us of what we will hear from Rosemary Ruether, another leading feminist author. Yet this kind of sentiment got Leonardo Boff in trouble with Rome, when he expressed it about the base communities. But neither Ruether nor Schüssler Fiorenza is teaching at church establishments, and that makes a difference. Therefore they are out of the reach of Rome.

Schüssler Fiorenza starts her hermeneutical considerations with the notion that "a value-free objectivistic historiography is a scholarly fiction. All interpretations of texts depend upon the presuppositions, intellectual concepts, politics, or prejudices of the interpreter and historian."[55] Therefore feminist scholars point out that the Christian tradition was reported and studied by theologians who consciously or subconsciously understood this tradition from a patriarchal perspective of male dominance. A critical theology of liberation, which Schüssler Fiorenza proposes, should uncover and criticize these tendencies that stimulated and perpetuated violence, alienation, and oppression. Thereby also certain myths must be criticized because they have a stabilizing function insofar as they sanction the existing social order and justify its power structure. For instance, Schüssler Fiorenza claims that "the Mary-myth has its roots and development in a male, clerical, and ascetic culture and theology. It has very little to do with the historical woman, Mary of Nazareth."[56] It also separates women from one another, because only those women who represent the humble handmaiden and the ever-virgin Mary are represented by her. On the other hand, Mary of Magdala was indeed a liberated woman, and we see already in the Gospel tradition the beginning of a tendency to play down her role.

Schüssler Fiorenza now develops a multidimensional model of a critical feminist hermeneutics, which is first of all a hermeneutics of suspicion.[57] This

---

ogy, ed. Elisabeth Schüssler Fiorenza (Maryknoll, N.Y.: Orbis, 1996), 11. This reader also provides a wide spectrum of women liberation theologians.

54. Elisabeth Schüssler Fiorenza, *In Memory of Her: A Feminist Theological Reconstruction of Christian Origins* (New York: Crossroad, 1994 [1988]), 344.

55. Elisabeth Schüssler Fiorenza, *Discipleship of Equals: A Critical Feminist Ekklesia-logy of Liberation* (New York: Crossroad, 1993), 62.

56. Fiorenza, *Discipleship of Equals,* 73-74.

57. Elisabeth Schüssler Fiorenza, *Bread Not Stone: The Challenge of Feminist Biblical In-*

hermeneutic of suspicion is now applied to the Bible because for Christian women "the Bible has been used as a weapon against us, but at the same time it has been a resource for courage, hope, and commitment in the struggle." The Bible and tradition cannot simply be trusted or accepted as divine revelation, because the biblical texts "are not the words of God, but the words of *men*" (x-xi). A historical critical scholarship recognizes that the Bible was written by human authors, namely, male authors. The feminist interpretation, therefore, begins with a hermeneutic of suspicion, both of the interpretations of the Bible and of the biblical texts themselves, because they can be patriarchally misinterpreted. As patriarchal texts, they serve to legitimate women's subordinate role and secondary status. The biblical religion, therefore, has to be reclaimed as the heritage of women, too, because the Bible has inspired and continues to inspire women to speak out and struggle against injustice, exploitation, and subordination.

A critical feminist hermeneutics of liberation develops a critical dialectical mode of interpretation showing on the one hand patriarchal authorship and on the other hand women's empowerment and vision in the struggle for liberation. The biblical texts must therefore be critically read and evaluated through a feminist perspective. Schüssler Fiorenza claims: "*The* litmus test for invoking Scripture as the Word of God must be whether or not biblical texts and traditions seek to end relations of domination and exploitation" (xiii). This hermeneutic reminds one to some extent of the criteria used to determine what can be traced back to Jesus; namely, if a text can be explained neither from Judaism nor from Hellenism, it most likely originated with Jesus. For Schüssler Fiorenza, then, the word of God is one that cannot contribute to domination and exploitation.

That her approach is not unwarranted can be seen in her book *In Memory of Her* (1982), in which she attempts to reconstruct Christian origins and points out how in the course of history the female contribution to these origins was more and more excluded. Returning to her book *Bread Not Stone,* she lines out a big agenda when she claims: "A feminist reading of the Bible requires both a transformation of our patriarchal understandings of God, Scripture, and the Church and a transformation in the self-understanding of historical-critical scholarship and the theological disciplines" (xvii). This entails an utterly different way of doing theology. One has to be sensitive to what is said and what is not said, and to what societal realities contribute. But a hermeneutics of suspicion is only the first point to understand what has occurred with the text and its interpretation. Then a hermeneutics of proclamation must be developed, "because the Bible still functions as Holy Scripture in Christian communities to-

---

terpretation (Boston: Beacon Press, 1995 [1984]), xx. Page references for this work are placed in the following text.

day" (15). The Bible as the word of God must be brought to the people. In a third step, a hermeneutics of remembrance is developed that moves from the biblical texts about women to the reconstruction of women's history. Finally, Schüssler Fiorenza calls for a hermeneutics of creative actualization where that which has been reconstructed is articulated in an imaginative way for the ongoing history of women.

Schüssler Fiorenza is a creative, insightful, and certainly industrious theologian who has written or edited nearly two dozen books. Even if one would not follow her hermeneutics of suspicion, one would nevertheless be sensitized to the significance of gender in appropriating the Christian heritage. More than once she claimed that unlike others she did not want to abandon biblical texts. Rightly understood, they are still normative for her. Yet they cannot always be taken as they now stand.

A Community of Equals: Rosemary Radford Ruether

Though she made her voice known on many other issues, too, **Rosemary Radford Ruether** (b. 1936) is certainly the most well-known feminist theologian, if not in the world, then at least in the USA. Ruether grew up in a pious yet ecumenical Roman Catholic family in Georgetown. As an undergraduate she majored in fine arts at Scripps College (1958) and then earned her Ph.D. studying the social and intellectual history of Christian thought at the School of Theology in Claremont, California. While still at Scripps, she married Hermann J. Ruether, a political science student who very much supported her career as a theologian. They are parents of two children. From 1966 to 1976 she taught at a predominantly African American seminary, the School of Religion at Howard University in Washington, D.C. Ruether taught at Garrett-Evangelical Theological Seminary in Evanston, Illinois (1976-2000), and is presently Carpenter Professor of Feminist Theology at the Pacific School of Religion at Berkeley, California, and the author of more than two dozen books.

Ruether's first book on feminist theology was published in 1975, *New Woman, New Earth: Sexist Ideologies and Human Liberation.* In it she starts out with Friedrich Engels's claim that the subjugation of women was the first oppressor-oppressed relation, "the foundation of all other class and property relations."[58] Ruether then leads us through human history, including the his-

---

58. Rosemary Radford Ruether, *New Woman, New Earth: Sexist Ideologies and Human Liberation* (New York: Seabury Press, 1975), 3. Page references for this work are placed in the following text.

tory of the Roman Catholic Church, stating, for instance, that Mariology "has its appeal from males because it enshrines the dominant ego and active principle as masculine in relation to women, who become the symbol of passive dependency upon the male" (56). She points out that "the black liberation movement has been overwhelmingly male oriented in its style and leadership" (120-21). She sees one of the reasons for this lack of equality in black history. The woman was really the center of the family whereas the male was always considered as just a boy by the white slave owner. Therefore the real man was the white slave owner, and black liberation therefore means primarily the liberation of the black male to the status of a man.

Ruether ties the topics of "new woman" and "new earth" together by saying that Western culture has traditionally identified women with nature and nature has been seen as an object of domination by men. In looking at the Old Testament, neither in the psalms nor in the prophets can she see justification for nature to be the sphere of human domination and repression. Furthermore, one finds there no separation between spirit and nature, and therefore no justification to relegate women to nature and to identify men more with the spirit. Apocalyptic thinking and Platonic ideas, however, led the New Testament and Christianity more toward a dualism. In modernity then, "rapid industrialization went hand in hand with the depletion of the economic functions of women traditionally centered around the home. Industrialization also drew many poor women into the factory at exploitative wages, far below those even of the exploited male worker" (196).

Through industrialization and the increasing domination of nature, we confront an immense ecological crisis that demands that the fundamental model of relationships based on domination must be changed. A society no longer bent on conquering the earth has more time for cultivating interiority, contemplation, and artistic work, and also the affirmation of others, "both our immediate neighbors and all humanity and the earth itself" (211). In conclusion, Ruether points to socialized local communities that could greatly alter the traditional role of women by child raising in residential groups, or even in workplaces, that would bring isolated families together and would create minicommunities resembling the clan in tribal culture of days long gone. The emphasis of interdependence instead of domination between men and women and between humanity and the earth is a recurrent theme in Ruether's writings.

In a more recent publication, *Gaia and God: An Ecofeminist Theology of Earth Healing* (1992), Ruether continues her quest for a sustainable society without male domination. Having painted a scenario of the degradation of the environment, she focuses on hypotheses of feminist paleoanthropologists who suggest an original social order in which women and female modes of relationality dominated. Then she comes to the elements necessary for both a sustainable ecological culture and a just society:

1. The rebuilding of primary and regional communities, in which people can understand and take responsibility for the ecosystem of which they are part;
2. just relations between humans that accept the right of all members of the community to an equitable share in the means of subsistence; and
3. an overcoming of the culture of competitive alienation and domination for compassionate solidarity.[59]

Within the biblical tradition she finds two avenues that would sustain these elements and further them, the covenantal tradition and the sacramental tradition. The covenantal tradition emphasizes that "the covenantal relation between humans and all other life forms, as one family united by one source of life, forbids this otherness from being translated into destructive hostility" (227). Under God's covenant humans and other life-forms belong together, and therefore they sustain each other instead of destroying each other and ultimately themselves. In the sacramental tradition, Christ is the cosmic manifestation of God appearing both as the immanent divine source and ground of creation and its ultimate redemptive healing. Ruether points here to the transitoriness of our material makeup: we are composed of parts that were once parts of other forms of life, and once we die, parts of us will again sustain future life-forms.

There is a wellspring of life from which everything is and toward which it again returns. We "know this as the great Thou, the personal center of the universal process, with which all the small centers of personal being dialogue in the conversation that continually creates and recreates the world" (253). Ruether wants to give a sacramental interpretation to the unity of all material substances of life that come from and are ultimately redeemed by Christ. Again, she points to the necessity of building strong base communities that merge and symbolize "a new biophilic consciousness" (269). Because of the fundamental interrelatedness of all components of life, which have their origin and their destiny in God, any dominational exploitation of nature or of women is unfounded.

In her earlier book *Sexism and God-Talk* (1983), she provides a full-fledged feminist theology, where the scant reference to the Judeo-Christian tra-

---

59. Rosemary Radford Ruether, *Gaia and God: An Ecofeminist Theology of Earth Healing* (San Francisco: HarperSanFrancisco, 1992), 201. Page references for this work are placed in the following text.

dition in her other publications is mitigated. She is insistent that our images of God/dess must include female roles and experience. But she does not want to replace God by a Goddess, because this would just replace one form of domination by another. With regard to Jesus, Ruether contends that his maleness has no ultimate significance. "Jesus as liberator calls for a renunciation, a dissolution, of the web of status relationships by which societies have defined privilege and deprivation. He protests against the identification of this system with the favor or disfavor of God. His ability to speak as liberator does not reside in his maleness but in the fact that he has renounced this system of domination and seeks to embody in his person the new humanity of service and mutual empowerment."[60] For her, Jesus is not a person of two thousand years ago, but rather in him "redemptive humanity goes ahead of us, calling us to yet incompleted dimensions of human liberation."[61] This means that Jesus is not simply the present Christ, but a principle of liberation.

As a Roman Catholic, it has been very difficult for her to push for the realization of equality and lay participation to a point where the sacramental dimension is not reserved for a special caste of people. The representatives of her own tradition, to whom she can refer, did not just get in trouble with the church, but usually were excluded from meaningful participation. Nevertheless, Ruether claims: "The Church is where the good news of liberation from sexism is preached, where the Spirit is present to empower us to renounce patriarchy, and where a community committed to the new life of mutuality is gathered together and nurtured, and where the community is spreading this vision and struggle to others."[62] If this statement were the criterion for her own Roman Catholic communion, it would be difficult to attribute to it the title "church." Yet Ruether in her struggle and deliberation does not confine herself in her observations just to one denomination or even to the Christian fold. She wants to draw on all resources available in other traditions, Christian and non-Christian, religious and otherwise.

Beyond God the Father: Mary Daly

Mary Daly (b. 1928) was born a Roman Catholic in Schenectady, New York, and attended only Roman Catholic schools for her entire education. To obtain a

---

60. Rosemary Radford Ruether, *Sexism and God-Talk: Toward a Feminist Theology* (Boston: Beacon Press, 1993 [1983]), 137.

61. Ruether, *Sexism and God-Talk*, 138.

62. Ruether, *Sexism and God-Talk*, 213.

Ph.D. in theology she went to Fribourg, Switzerland, and completed her first doctoral thesis there in 1963: "The Problem of Speculative Theology: A Study in St. Thomas." Three years later, she wrote another doctoral thesis there: "Natural Knowledge of God in the Philosophy of Jacques Maritain." Before returning to the States, she visited the Second Vatican Council in Rome. She started teaching at the Jesuit-founded Boston College in the department of theology, and in 1968 wrote her first book, *The Church and the Second Sex*. She carefully analyzed the problems of sexism in the church and focused especially on the issue of women's ordination, the historical contribution of women in the church, and birth control. The book caught the attention of the public and also of the administration at Boston College, and Daly was fired in 1969. Yet the students demonstrated on her behalf, and the case was reported on the front page of the *New York Times*. Succumbing to public pressure, Boston College promoted her and gave her tenure.

With her next book, *Beyond God the Father* (1973), she abandoned patriarchal Christianity, because "if God is male, then the male is God."[63] The theological traditions in the world religions, Daly contends, "have been formulated by males under the conditions of patriarchy. It is therefore inherent in these symbolic and linguistic structures that they serve the purposes of patriarchal social arrangements" (22). If the men stay in a patriarchal space, they remain in the past. Therefore they should enter their own space and time expressing integrity and transformation. Even if Jesus had been a feminist, as some claim, this would not make any difference, because one would still have to dig through the debris of a long history of oppressiveness to arrive at Jesus and his story. Thereby one would again look backward. Yet Daly is looking forward to the future, to the second coming, but with a twist. "This Second Coming is not a return of Christ but a new arrival of female presence, once strong and powerful, but enchained since the dawn of patriarchy" (96). Women liberate and legitimate themselves. "The power to regain our own life comes from the discovery of the cosmic covenant, the deep harmony in the community of being in which we participate" (177). One might ask by whom this covenant is guaranteed or who makes possible the biophilic attitude, meaning the love of life to which Daly wants to return with her sisters.

It is not surprising, then, that in a more recent publication, *Pure Lust* (1984), Daly talks about a nomadic existence, a meandering through different spheres in the quest "for biophilic participation in Be-ing, transcending the

---

63. Mary Daly, *Beyond God the Father: Toward a Philosophy of Women's Liberation* (Boston: Beacon Press, 1985 [1973]), 19. Page references for this work are placed in the following text.

forces of necrophilic negation of such participation."[64] While she describes patriarchy as necrophilic, essentially life-hating and that which kills the objects of its obsession and aggression, *Pure Lust* speaks of "the high humor, hope, and cosmic accord/harmony of those women who choose to escape, to follow our heart's deepest desire . . . connecting with the auras of animals and plants, moving in planetary communion with the farthest stars."[65] In this desire for union and harmony with all elements of life, which indeed expresses a deep-felt desire in many people, a mystic yearning of oneness seems to have replaced the Christian vision of God the creator, sustainer, and redeemer.

Womanist Theology: Delores Williams

While attempting to encompass all women, Schüssler Fiorenza noted that "as a white educated European woman teaching at Harvard I speak from an 'infinitely privileged position.'"[66] Indeed, there are others who claim that women's liberation is mainly for middle-class white women and reflects their experience. It has nothing in common with those who are much more underprivileged. Here the term "womanist" theology was introduced in 1983 by Alice Walker (b. 1944) in her book *In Search of Our Mothers' Gardens*.[67] James Cone calls womanist theology "the most creative development to emerge out of the Black theology movement during the 1980s and 1990s. It is both an affirmation and a critique of the liberation theology of Black male theologians. Like their brothers, womanists offer a powerful race critique of White supremacy. They separate themselves from the White feminist theologians who ignore racism and join the Black men in the struggle against white supremacy in the church, the academy, and the society."[68]

We want to note here especially **Delores S. Williams.** She grew up in the urban south in the late 1940s and 1950s with her mother and grandmother, and was an active member of the black church. She participated in the civil rights movement in the 1960s, gave birth to four children, went to college and obtained her M.A. from Columbia University in New York with the thesis "The Black

64. Mary Daly, *Pure Lust: Elemental Feminist Philosophy* (Boston: Beacon Press, 2001 [1984]), ix (footnote).

65. Daly, *Pure Lust*, 3.

66. Elisabeth Schüssler Fiorenza, *But She Said: Feminist Practices of Biblical Interpretation* (Boston: Beacon Press, 1992), 8.

67. So Sheila M. Jones, "Womanist Theologians," in *A New Handbook of Christian Theologians*, ed. Donald W. Musser and Joseph L. Price (Nashville: Abingdon, 1996), 513.

68. James Cone, in Cone and Wilmore, *Black Theology*, 2:257.

Woman Portrayed in Selected Black Imaginative Literature and Some Questions for Black Theology." In 1991 she obtained her Ph.D. from Union Theological Seminary in New York with a dissertation entitled "A Study of the Analogous Relation between African-American Woman's Experience and Hagar's Experience: A Challenge Posed to Black Theology." After the sudden death of her husband, Robert C. Williams, she became a single mother. She was Paul Tillich Professor of Theology and Culture at Union and a Presbyterian.

By observing her community, Williams noticed the physical violence done to black women by their own men and the racism and male supremacy in the courts and on the school boards. But it was the African American denominational churches that provided a place where black women could gather, venting their pain and at the same time expressing their love for God and the Spirit that sustain them in their everyday troubles. At the same time, these denominational churches were sexist and biased against black women, and they built beautiful church edifices while thousands of blacks lived in dire poverty. They provided immoral models of male leadership and failed to pull their resources across denominational and class lines to deal effectively with poverty, drug addiction, and other ailments among the blacks.[69] On the other hand, *the* black church, which does not exist as an institution, but only invisibly across various denominations, "is the heart of hope in the black community's experience of oppression, survival struggle and its historic effort toward complete liberation" (205).

Womanist theology, according to Williams, "is a prophetic voice reminding African-American denominational churches of their mission to seek justice and voice for all their people, of which black women are the overwhelming majority in their congregations" (xiii). Womanist theology then attempts to help black women to see, affirm, and have confidence in the importance of their experience and faith to determine the character of the religion in the African American community. It also challenges all oppressive forces that impede black women's struggle for survival and for the development of a positive, productive quality of life. Womanist theology affirms the necessity of responsible freedom for all human beings, but it concerns itself naturally with the faith, survival, and freedom struggle of African American women. While it has no problem cooperating with black male liberation theology, it is critical of white feminist theology and it "critiques white feminist participation in the perpetuation of white supremacy, which continues to dehumanize black women" (xiv).

---

69. Cf. Delores S. Williams, *Sisters in the Wilderness: The Challenge of Womanist God-Talk* (Maryknoll, N.Y.: Orbis, 1993), 206-9. Page references for this work are placed in the following text.

While many biblical traditions can be appropriated to the liberation of the oppressed, such as the stories of Moses, Paul and Silas, there is especially one tradition that Williams emphasizes by returning to her Ph.D. thesis, namely, Hagar, the African slave of the Hebrew woman Sarah. In the opening chapter of her book *Sisters in the Wilderness* (1993), Williams mines this tradition for the black woman's experience and God's response to this experience. Many of the black experiences shine through this Hagar tradition, such as poverty, ethnicity, sexual and economic exploitation, and domestic violence. To pick up on these experiences, a theological methodology for Christian womanists must include at least four elements according to Williams:

1. A multidialogical intent "to advocate and participate in dialogue and action with *many* diverse social, political and religious communities concerned about human survival and productive quality of life for the oppressed."[70]
2. A liturgical intent to select the sources that shape the content of the liturgy that point to justice instead of injustice and oppression.
3. A didactic intent to teach new insights about moral life based on ethics supporting justice for women, survival, and a productive quality of life for poor women, children, and men.
4. An appropriate language to be "an instrument for social and theological change in church and society."[71]

A womanist theology, therefore, complements black liberation theology and — in comparison to feminist and white theologies in general — is usually much more oriented toward the Bible and the church. This is also a reflection of the black experience in which church and Bible played a much more important role than in the often quite secular white environment.

Voices out of Africa

When we now turn to Africa and try to elucidate theological perspectives from there, we embark on a strange and difficult undertaking. It is strange, because some of the best and most well-known theologians of the early church were Africans, such as Origen around 280, Athanasius in the fourth century, and Cyril a

70. Delores S. Williams, "Womanist Theology: Black Women's Voices" (1987), in Cone and Wilmore, *Black Theology,* 2:269.
71. Williams, "Womanist Theology," 2:271.

century later, all coming from Alexandria, present-day Egypt. Then there was Tertullian, again at the beginning of the third century, the first Christian theologian who used Latin in his writings instead of the customary Greek. And finally there is Augustine, spanning the fourth and fifth centuries. But in the seventh century there occurred the Arab conquest. Today in most North African countries, hardly a trace is left of early Christianity, except for Egypt, where the Orthodox Coptic Church still comprises approximately 10 percent of the population, and Ethiopia, where the Coptic Church comprises the vast majority of the population. It seems that Christianity was so much a part of the Roman Empire that when it vanished, Christianity disappeared too, except in the above-mentioned regions. Yet it could also have been that either Islam was too militant to allow for the survival of the Christian church in the long run, or Christianity had not taken sufficient roots in the general populace so that it was swept away. Nevertheless, the Arab conquest and the spread of Islam in North Africa prevented Christianity from spreading down to the middle and southern part of Africa in subsequent centuries.

It was only during the eighteenth and nineteenth centuries that European exploration of the African interior opened the way for Christianity and for commerce. Then colonies were established throughout Africa by the European powers, predominantly Great Britain and France. It was in this colonial context of the nineteenth century that the Christian missions attempted to penetrate the vast African continent. Therefore we have predominantly Roman Catholic Christianity in the former Belgian Congo region, British (Anglican) Christianity in Kenya, and a strong Lutheran church in Namibia. South Africa was settled in the seventeenth century by Dutch immigrants and later conquered by the British, so Anglican and Dutch Reformed churches prevail there. With more than sixty independent African countries each having its own history, it would be difficult in a few pages to draw a complete map of significant theological voices. Therefore we will confine ourselves to only a few of its most significant representatives.

A Practical Theology: Desmond Tutu

The first theologian we turn to is **Desmond Tutu** (b. 1931), born in Klerksdorp, a town west of Johannesburg in western Transvaal.[72] His father was a primary school teacher who belonged to the Methodist church. Tutu attended a boarding school run by a Swedish Lutheran mission. When he was fourteen he con-

---

72. For details on his life see Ferm, *Profiles in Liberation*, 65-66.

tracted tuberculosis and was hospitalized for two years in a hospital supervised by a Roman Catholic community. There he came under the influence of Trevor Huddleston (b. 1913), an Anglican priest, with whom he struck up a long-lasting friendship. Since his family could not send him to medical school, though he wanted to become a physician, he earned a teacher's certificate in 1953, and the following year a B.A. degree from the University of South Africa. He taught school for three years before he entered seminary, attending St. Peter's Theological College in Johannesburg (1955-60). In 1961 he became a priest of the Episcopal Church, and in 1962 he went to England to live there for the next five years and earn a B.D. and an M.Th. in theology at King's College in London. Upon his return to South Africa he served on the faculty of the Federated Theological Seminary in Alice Cape and in the department of theology at the University of Botswana. In the early 1970s he returned again to England to work for three years as the associate director of the Theological Education Fund of the World Council of Churches (WCC). In 1975 he became dean of the cathedral at Johannesburg, the following year bishop of Lesotho, soon thereafter general secretary of the South African Council of Churches, in 1985 bishop of Johannesburg, the following year archbishop of Cape Town, and the next year president of the All-African Conference of Churches. In 1984 he also received the Nobel Peace Prize.

Tutu is a person of the church and not so much an academic theologian. To serve the needs of Africans, theology in his country must be with the people. He cautions: "We are too much concerned to maintain standards which Cambridge or Harvard or Montpellier have set, even when these are utterly inappropriate for our situation."[73] African theology has to touch the depth of the African soul and cannot concern itself with splendid answers to questions that are not asked. Here it is especially an African identity that has to be addressed. In the colonization and evangelization process everything African usually was condemned, since many Western missionaries could not distinguish between the Christian faith and Western civilization. If Christianity takes incarnation seriously, then "Christianity, to be truly African, must be incarnated in Africa. It must speak in tones that strike a responsive chord in the African breast, it must convict the African of his peculiar African sinfulness."[74]

Tutu sees a necessity to address the present-day African issues, the epidemic of coups, military rule, development, poverty, and disease, to name just a

73. Desmond Tutu, "Black Theology and African Theology — Soulmates or Antagonists?" (1975), in *A Reader in African Christian Theology,* ed. John Parratt, rev. ed. (London: SPCK, 1987), 55.
74. Tutu, "Black Theology," 52.

few. Tutu was never afraid to speak out on issues, especially on apartheid, and also suffered consequences for it. But it was clear for him that Christians must be critical of all political systems, "always testing them against Gospel standards."[75] The ultimate authority and obedience of a Christian belong to God, not to a movement, a cause, or a political system. Yet "Christianity can never be a merely personal matter. It has public consequences and we must make public choices." Christians cannot be neutral, because of their allegiance to God. If certain laws are not in line with the gospel, then the Christian must agitate for their removal by all peaceful means. Tutu does not advocate violence. One should also never go so far as to denounce the world as unredeemable, because we should remember that "God loved not the Church, but the world."[76] And therefore the church must claim the world as God's world.

Tutu also remembered that in the early church people were attracted not so much by the preaching as by what they witnessed with the Christians — that they were a community living a new life different from others. This was important for him, especially in shaping the new South Africa nation after the abolition of apartheid. He wrote: "We witness too, by being a community of reconciliation, a forgiving community of the forgiven."[77] That the change from the white minority rule to the black majority rule could be accomplished without bloodshed and vengeance was largely due to Tutu's emphasis on reconciliation and forgiveness, not by ignoring the evils of the past, but by having them confessed and forgiven. In Tutu's "practical theology" we witness in an exemplary way how theology touches the lives of the people and effects a large-scale change. Whether that change has a lasting impact remains to be seen.

The African Cultural-Religious Background: John Mbiti and Kwesi Dickson

John Mbiti (b. 1931) was born in Ketui, Kenya. When in 1951 Mbiti experienced a calling to the Christian ministry in the form of a vision and entrusted this vision to American missionaries, they dismissed it with the reply: "John, you are crazy!"[78] Yet this "crazy" experience completely changed his life. He attended

---

75. See Desmond Tutu, "Politics and Religion" (1978), in Desmond Tutu, *Crying in the Wilderness: The Struggle for Justice in South Africa*, edited and introduction by John Webster, foreword by Trevor Huddleston (Grand Rapids: Eerdmans, 1990), 9, for this and the following quote.

76. Desmond Tutu, "Reflections on Liberation Theology," in *Crying in the Wilderness*, 11.

77. Desmond Tutu, "The Church in the World," in *Crying in the Wilderness*, 7.

78. John S. Mbiti, "Theological Impotence and the Universality of the Church," in *Mis-*

Makerere University in Uganda and Barrington College in Rhode Island, where he received his A.B. and B.D. degrees, and obtained his Ph.D. from Cambridge University in 1963. Upon his return from England, he served as professor of theology and comparative religion at Makerere. Then from 1974 till 1980 he was director and professor at the ecumenical institute in Bossey, Switzerland. He also served in a parish at Burgdorf, Switzerland. Additionally he taught missiology and extra-European theology at the University of Berne.

His Cambridge Ph.D. thesis was entitled "New Testament Eschatology in an African Background: A Study of the Encounter between New Testament Theology and African Traditional Concepts." In the conclusion he points out four items that are essential for an African theology:

1. "Biblical theology must be the basis of any theological reflection."[79]
2. Christian theology must be informed by the major traditions of Christendom, otherwise it will be isolated from the catholicity of the church.
3. A study of African religions and philosophy must be taken seriously as a possible preparation for the gospel.
4. African theology must be a theology "of the living Church as it expands in its Life and Mission in African societies."[80]

In his thesis he points to the difference concerning the understanding of time between the African people, as far as he knows their traditions, and Judeo-Christian thinking. A linear conception of time with a future in the far distance is virtually nonexistent in Africa, because time is considered a two-dimensional phenomenon, with a long past and a dynamic present.[81] Therefore the parousia as something far outstanding is hardly understood. "The *parousia*, which many African Christians cherish and expect to occur soon," therefore is seen as imminent because of signs, such as the wonders of modern technology, or earthquakes, etc. For Africans they signal the soon-approaching end of the world,[82] a phenomenon similar to the time of Martin Luther in medieval Germany.

Out of his teaching experience in Uganda grew his research for *Concepts*

---

sion Trends No. 3: Third World Theologies, ed. Gerald H. Anderson and Thomas F. Stransky (Grand Rapids: Eerdmans, 1976), 13-14.

79. John S. Mbiti, *New Testament Eschatology in an African Background: A Study of the Encounter between New Testament Theology and African Traditional Concepts* (London: SPCK, 1978 [1971]), 189.

80. Mbiti, *New Testament Eschatology*, 190.

81. Cf. Mbiti, *New Testament Eschatology*, 24.

82. John Mbiti, "The Bible in African Culture," in *Paths of African Theology*, ed. Rosini Gibellini (Maryknoll, N.Y.: Orbis, 1994), 35.

of God in Africa. In this book he showed how God was experienced in the African religions and how humanity was separated from God in worship and devotion, and so "the original direct contact and relationship between God and man was broken. The unfortunate consequences for man include the loss of immortality, resurrection, rejuvenation, and free food, in addition to the coming of death and suffering."[83] Yet, as Mbiti emphasizes, "the separation between God and humankind was an ontological and not a moral separation."[84] There is no concept of original sin, or that a person is born a sinner, in African religion. Sin does not occur against God, but is always something that happens within the community.

When Mbiti looks at the God whom he and other African theologians encounter in the African religions, he states: "African theologians themselves are more or less agreed that the God whom African religion acknowledges is the same God as in the Bible" (163). This means that the African peoples know God; the knowledge and acknowledgment of God is the foundation of the African religion. This does not mean that all have identical notions of God, since concepts of God are always dependent on one's own framework whether one lives in the forest or out on the plains. But when Christianity and African religion encounter each other, one can affirm "that there is only one God who is acknowledged and worshipped in both" (164-65). Mbiti does not worry that one could end up in some kind of syncretism. To the contrary, contemporary African Christianity, to a large extent, benefits from the religious foundation already laid down by the African religions. If this understanding of God had not been present, the Christian understanding of God would have been much more difficult for Africans to comprehend. "Because of Jesus Christ, Christianity has received a fuller picture of God than is otherwise possible outside" (165).

What is known in the African religions about God can be compared to what we as Christians know from God through the Old Testament. Yet there are also gaps in the concept of God in the African religion, as we have seen in eschatology or in the concept of original sin. We remember that in African religions salvation is not understood as something far in the future, but as occurring in the present or in the near-present. Africans can also identify this concept of salvation in the person of Jesus, who helped and saved people from various kinds of afflictions. Therefore Mbiti claims that Christian theology and procla-

---

83. John Mbiti, *Concepts of God in Africa* (London: SPCK, 1970), 177.

84. John Mbiti, "God, Sin, and Salvation in African Religion," in *Constructive Christian Theology in the Worldwide Church*, ed. William R. Barr (Grand Rapids: Eerdmans, 1997), 165. Page references in the following text are to this essay.

mation should also speak to the immediate need of salvation, be it from out-dated traditions, from domination by overseas mission societies that have money and power, or from tribalism, corruption, nepotism, and the like.[85] It is decisive for Mbiti that theology is not an academic exercise, but addresses the concrete needs and experiences of the people.

These needs and experiences are also documented by the fact that there are more than five thousand African independent churches, meaning churches out-side of those affiliations that in America are recognized as denominations, and that they often have very independent ideas of how to appropriate Christianity to the context of African religiosity. With his solid scholarship Mbiti has pointed to both the commonality and the difference between African religions and the Judeo-Christian heritage. He has shown that in terms of the Old Testament there certainly is much affinity between the two, though this affinity is less discernible with regard to the New Testament. He rightly emphasizes the need of a point of contact between the people's experience and the challenge of the gospel.

Kwesi A. Dickson (b. 1929) was born in Saltpond, Ghana, as son of a Methodist minister. He received his undergraduate degree at the University College of the Gold Coast in 1956, his B.D. in London, and his Bachelor of Letters at Mansfield College, Oxford University (1959), specializing in the Old Testament. Since 1960 he has served at the University of Ghana at Legon near Accra, first as lecturer, then as professor, and finally as head of the department of the study of religions, and in 1980 as director of the Institute of African Studies at the same university. From 1997 to 2003 he served as president of the All Africa Conference of Churches.

Dickson advocates an African theology and addresses African concerns in a way that Africans can really understand. But this does not mean he advances an African liberation theology. "While socio-economic and political issues must be given the attention they deserve, it is fact, however, that *misrule and mismanagement do not constitute the totality of the situation prevailing in Africa*."[86] But it is important for Christian theology to address itself to the totality of the African experience. Therefore the perspective of liberation theology is too narrow. African theology should be African to serve the peoples of Africa. Dickson is also not negative toward overseas missions, because though many missionaries did not "see anything of value in African life and thought, . . . many European missionaries showed great understanding of African life and

85. So John Mbiti, "Some Reflections on African Experience of Salvation Today," in *Living Faiths and Ultimate Goals: Salvation and World Religions*, ed. S. J. Samartha (Maryknoll, N.Y.: Orbis, 1974), 118.

86. Kwesi A. Dickson, *Theology in Africa* (Maryknoll, N.Y.: Orbis, 1984), 136.

thought and demonstrated a willingness to have their strategy influenced accordingly."[87]

Because today many African Christians, whether they know it or not, hold on to African life and thought and at the same time practice Christianity, "the Churches could serve their members better and be a greater force for good in society if they had a more authentically African character."[88] Here again Dickson points to the independent churches that are even attractive for members of Christian churches, because they use indigenous languages so that all members can participate in worship. They also lean more toward the Old Testament, since that has a particular affinity to Africans, because of the similarity of custom and culture. Therefore African Christianity *"should have such cultural characteristics as would make Africans see it as a faith that speaks to them in the particularity of their life-circumstances."*[89]

In contrast to the European, the African regards death in a positive way, as the fulfillment of earthly life and as the gateway to the ancestors. Dickson writes: "The African believes that death binds up relationships in society, revitalizing the living and underscoring their sense of community."[90] He contends that Paul actually thinks along the same line when he writes in 1 Corinthians 10:16: "The cup of blessing that we bless, is it not a sharing in the blood of Christ?" Then he argues that Paul needs the Jewish background to express the significance of the death of Christ. Why, he asks, could not in a similar way the African background be used to express for the African the significance of Christ's death? A meaningful theology for Africans can only be gathered "when account is taken of the African religio-cultural situation as *one* of the source materials for theologizing."[91] Yet the African religio-cultural situation should not be considered *the* exclusive source material, because for African Christians the first and foremost source is always the Bible. But in some instances the African religious situation can enlighten theological questions that surface in all cultures. That said, theology is done always most meaningfully in particular settings, and for that, cultural particularity is indispensable. Otherwise theology does not speak to the context in which it is executed. We see in Dickson a concern not so much for an independent African theology, though that is on his mind. Instead, he primarily desires a theology for the people he serves, not only in his Methodist church, but beyond that in African culture.

---

87. Kwesi A. Dickson, "Mission in African Countries," in *Christian Mission — Jewish Mission,* ed. Martin A. Cohen and Helga Croner (New York: Paulist, 1982), 192.

88. Dickson, "Mission in African Countries," 196.

89. Dickson, "Mission in African Countries," 201.

90. Dickson, *Theology in Africa,* 196.

91. Dickson, *Theology in Africa,* 124.

Doing Theology as a Woman: Mercy Oduyoye

Mercy A. Oduyoye (b. 1934) was born in Asamankese, Ghana, her father being a Methodist pastor who was also president of the Ghana Methodist Conference. She received a postsecondary certificate of education in 1954 at the University of Kumasi and taught for several years at a Methodist girls middle school. Then she received a B.A. in religion at the University of Ghana (1963). In 1965 she received a B.A. in theology from Cambridge University. Upon her return to Ghana, she served as a high school teacher before assuming the position of secretary of youth education for the WCC in Geneva (1967-73). From 1974 to 1986 she taught in the department of religious studies of the University of Ibadan, Nigeria, and then became one of the deputy general secretaries of the WCC and also a member of the Commission on Faith and Order. Her extensive participation in ecumenical work comes through in her theological reflections. Her writings are also influenced by her membership in the Ecumenical Association of Third World Theologians (EATWOT) and the Ecumenical Association of African Theologians (EAAT). (EATWOT originated in 1976 and is sponsored by the WCC but also includes Roman Catholics. EAAT got started in 1980 and is similarly supported by the WCC.)

Like Dickson, Oduyoye does not want one uniform system of theology, but wishes "that theology reflects awareness of the horizon toward which all believers move."[92] For Oduyoye, as for most African theologians, the Bible is very important and, according to her, the first source of information for Africans, even for those who cannot read but nevertheless are acquainted with it from the oral tradition. Yet next to it comes her own African experience. As she writes in her book of 1986, *Hearing and Knowing:* "In spite of the entrenched patriarchal and ethnocentric presuppositions of the Bible, it is a book I cannot dispense with and indeed may not since I remain in the Christian community and that community means more to me than my personal hurts. For the same reason I cannot be anything else but African" (147). Being faithful to the God who has been active in African history does not allow her to do away with the African experience and simply replace it with the Jewish experience.

Acknowledging a point of contact between our situation and God is very significant for Oduyoye, as it is for all African theologians. This is even more important because the African "primal religious views are similar to those found in the Bible" (64). Therefore it would be foolish to disclaim them. In

---

92. Mercy A. Oduyoye, *Hearing and Knowing: Theological Reflections on Christianity in Africa* (Maryknoll, N.Y.: Orbis, 1986), vii. Page references for this work are placed in the following text.

Oduyoye's reflections sometimes the African religious experience and the Israelite one seem to go together or become interchangeable. For instance, she writes: "God, as the Hebrew and the Akan [i.e., her own tribe] perceive, is not the Impassible One of Greek philosophy" (92). When she comes to liberation concerns, her aspect is not so different from that of African men, because, as she contends: "Our context — oppression, poverty and impoverishment, marginalization from the global technological culture, exploitation that results from unjust global trade and economic arrangements — is a significant area for some African theologians, including both men and women."[93]

There are also specific concerns related to women that Oduyoye voices. She notes that it is impossible in Africa to talk about marriage and women without talking about issues of family and children. But she cautions that marriage should not be seen in terms of trade. As an example, she explains that feminist voices are sensitive to the issue of the bride-price, and she insists together with them that this should not be construed as an economic transaction in which a man buys a woman. Instead, it should be understood as a way "to emphasize the worth of women, to provide community participation and social witness to the coming together of the two persons for the religious duty of procreation" (168). She also notices that since women are in close communion with the soil — most women are the ones that till the soil — they are also in tune with nature and "will not do violence to nature" (173).

Oduyoye has no problems with the emphasis on procreation that in Africa is synonymous with women, but she emphasizes that the concept of mothering means to be concerned and to care, something she believes "both women and men can learn to develop" (176). This shows that in some respect women can be models for men and not simply subservient, as is widely the case in the African culture. She also notes the close association of women with childbearing and nurturing, which again raises the issue of sexuality that so far has not been addressed in relation to religion. This shows that there is still a long road to go before an actual equality between men and women can be attained. Yet at least Oduyoye ventures into this territory.

With these few, and far from exhaustive, glimpses into the African sphere, we indicate the rich diversity of African theology, but also the significance of indigenous religions as a point of contact, something we will see again in India.

---

93. Mercy A. Oduyoye, "Feminist Theology in an African Perspective," in *Paths of African Theology*, 167. Page references in the following text are to this essay.

Theology with an Asian Face

When we turn to a continent as vast as Asia, it is again impossible to provide a comprehensive picture of theology being done there, though contact with Christianity occurred very early in Asia. The Manichean variety of a gnostic Christianity was spread first through Mani (216-277) in his native Iran and then through Manichean missionaries all the way to China, where it stayed in southern China till the sixteenth century. The Nestorians too, who accept only the Councils of Nicea (325) and Constantinople (381) and teach that Mary gave birth to Christ but not to God, spread the gospel all the way to Lake Baikal in Russia and to the Mongols in central Asia. They were present there up to the end of the twelfth century. Later the Jesuits under their cofounder Francis Xavier (1506-52) brought the Christian faith to East India and even Japan. But again the Christian presence did not last. There was a long pause until Christianity came again, usually in the wake of the expansions of European colonial powers. Today, however, there is only one Asian country, the Philippines, that has a Christian majority. Even there theological education, until very recently, had been conducted primarily by expatriates. In most of these countries an indigenous theology is therefore a rather new phenomenon. The growth of Asian theology is also endangered by the fleshpots of the West to which many promising Asian theologians are lured. India, however, is the only Asian country with a long and uninterrupted tradition of Christianity, perhaps going back all the way to the second century and the Syrian Orthodox Church. Therefore we will treat India in a separate section.

The Dialectic and Reality of the Cross:
Kazoh Kitamori and Kosuke Koyama

One of the most interesting theologies in Asia has been developed by **Kazoh Kitamori** (1916-98). He was baptized as a student, studied at the University of Kyoto and the Lutheran Theological Seminary in Tokyo, and then served as professor of systematic theology at Union Theological Seminary in Tokyo. In his *Theology of the Pain of God* (1946) he provides a Japanese rendering of a theology of the cross.[94] Kitamori's theology of the pain of God wants to defend a theology of the cross against the (Barthian) triumphalism of God's grace that makes God's love a divine affair that occurs within the Trinity. He also wants to

---

94. Cf. the chapter "Theology of the Pain of God" in Carl Michalson, *Japanese Contributions to Christian Theology* (Philadelphia: Westminster, 1960), 73-99.

entertain a theology of the pain of God despite those who exclude this metaphor from God's all-embracing love, as it occurred primarily in liberal theology.[95] Kitamori answers these tendencies with Paul: "We must preach Christ crucified." In the vein of Martin Luther, Kitamori argues: "We cannot believe the pain of God unless it is his revelation. Man's thought can never produce such a truth. Accordingly, the pain of God can exist as a truth only in the framework of theology; it cannot spring from man's philosophical or religious thinking" (25). This means the notion that God has pains or is in pain is so unusual that it cannot be a figment of the human mind. It must be a divine reality.

This pain of God presupposes that there really was a historical Jesus, because any docetic form of Christology would exclude the pain of God. If Christ were not truly divine, God would not feel any pain in Christ's suffering. The pain of God is part of God becoming human. Both for Jesus and Paul, the pain of God and the love of God come together because the love of God is rooted in pain. Kitamori distinguishes three orders of love:

1. The immediate love of God on its objects without any hindrance as it existed before the fall or as God the Father loves his completely obedient Son. "Both Christ and man were originally objects of God's love of the first order, but now only Christ is its object. Man has now *fallen* away from this kind of God's love, and has become unworthy of it because of rebellion and sin" (118).
2. Then comes the gospel in the pain of God, the gospel that is hard to believe, because God did not turn away from humanity as one would have expected, but embraced them. In forgiving the sins of humanity, God suffered pain, as is illustrated in Jeremiah 31:20: "Therefore I am deeply moved for him [i.e., for Ephraim]." While there is no pain involved for us, it pains God when he forgives and loves those who should not be forgiven.
3. There is also pain in God sending his only beloved Son to suffer and die. This means that "Christ has separated himself from the love of God the Father and stepped into suffering and death to save lost mankind" (120). This, then, was the pain of God.

When Christ was resurrected from death and was sitting at the right hand of the Father, "then for the first time was God's pain healed" (121). We are al-

---

95. Cf. Kazoh Kitamori, *Theology of the Pain of God,* English translation from the 5th ed. (Richmond: John Knox, 1958), 22-23. Page references for this work are placed in the following text.

lowed to follow this love of God and welcome others to return to us whom we had sent out to suffer instead of keeping them in our love. This means our ethic of pain, our ethic of sinning must become an ethic of love and of grace. When Jesus summons us to take up our own cross, we become witnesses to God's pain through our own pain. In an age of fun and enjoyment, where negativity is either suppressed or liberated away, a reminder of the pain of God, because of the pains we continue to afflict on God, does not lose its timeliness, even if this *Theology of the Pain of God* was written during World War II and published after Japan's own painful defeat and after the pains Japan had inflicted on other countries.[96]

Kosuke Koyama (b. 1929) was born in Tokyo, graduated from Union Theological Seminary (Tokyo) in 1952, received his B.D. from Drew University, New Jersey, in 1954 and a master's and a Ph.D. from Princeton (1959). The United Church of Christ sent him as a missionary to Thailand (1960-68), where he also served as lecturer in systematic theology at Thailand Theological Seminary in Chiang Mai. After that he was director of the Association of Theological Schools in Southeast Asia and dean of the Southeast Asia Graduate School of Theology (1968-74), and senior lecturer in phenomenology of religion at the University of Otago, in New Zealand (1974-79). From 1980 until his retirement in 1996 he served as professor of ecumenics and world Christianity at Union Theological Seminary in New York.

Koyama became well-known through his *Waterbuffalo Theology* of 1974. He closed this book with the sentence: "In this eschatological hour, we are called to share the pathos of God, God's *pathos* toward all scattered things which are held together in the *glory* of the *crucified* Lord."[97] This statement summarizes his theology in a nutshell and also shows him as a student of Kitamori. Theology in Asia, Koyama contends, must bear "the marks of Jesus" (Gal. 6:17). In the plurality and brokenness of Asia the word of the cross must be the foundation of theology. In the face of widespread denominationalism, such theology must be brought forth humbly (cf. 195). In a theology of the cross the two disjunctive elements can be brought together, namely, that in Christ all things are held and that in earthly reality all things are confounded, scattered, and sick. The stumbling block is the eschatological not-yet. "As we live in the turbulent history of mankind today we confess that Christ, the crucified and

96. Cf. Kitamori in his introduction to the German edition: Kazoh Kitamori, *Theologie des Schmerzes Gottes* (Göttingen: Vandenhoeck & Ruprecht, 1972), 13.

97. Kosuke Koyama, *Waterbuffalo Theology* (Maryknoll, N.Y.: Orbis, 1974), 238. Page references for this work are placed in the following text. Cf. also 116, where Koyama refers to his teacher's book *Theology of the Pain of God*, of which he was asked to bring a section to the publisher.

hidden Lord, stands at the center of history" (229). Christians who follow the cross are saved from triumphalism, and in seeing the discomfort of the crucified Christ they point to him as the source of all comfort, since "Christ suffered because he was involved with others. He died for others" (233). This not only comforts us with the knowledge that we are saved because he was destroyed, but also tells us that we live and share our lives with the painful pathos of God's saving will. A theology in Asia is a theology of solidarity with the suffering and at the same time a theology of comfort that proclaims that suffering is redeemed through God's own suffering.

In a more recent book, *Mount Fuji and Mount Sinai: A Critique of Idols* (1985), Koyama goes a step further. He compares Mount Fuji, the cosmological center of the world in Japanese imperialistic ideology, with Mount Sinai, the place of God's epiphany. The image of a mobile God did not allow Mount Sinai to become the cosmological center and place of worship. It is rather God who "symbolizes the center of salvation. This center symbolism travels with the people."[98] Center symbolism, Koyama contends, whether of an individual person, a community, an ethnic group, a nation, or an empire, is always open to misuse and can be exploited by a destructive ideology.

When we talk about Christ as the center of the biblical message and of theology, then Christ is broken, because "he was bruised for our iniquities; upon him was the chastisement that made us whole" (Isa. 53:5). Koyama connects the image of the broken Christ with the Lord's Supper. Christ gives himself in the sacrament as the person of utter self-denial and at the same time he is the center of all things, as the New Testament asserts. This center person not only lived on the periphery by being born in a stable and as someone who had nowhere to lay his head (Luke 9:58), but "he established his centrality by going to the periphery."[99] This means that he was a friend of tax collectors and sinners (Luke 7:34) and cared for those for whom nobody else cared. Koyama considers the whole life of Jesus sacramental. "When holiness and brokenness come together for the sake of the salvation of others, we have Christian sacrament. Christian theology then is fundamentally sacramental theology since Jesus Christ is the central sacrament of our faith. In him the holiness of God is expressed through the brokenness of Jesus Christ." Since Jesus, however, went to the periphery, we too cannot just focus on the center, the altar, but must take the side trip to our brothers and sisters and first be reconciled with them.

It is no surprise that Koyama refers to Luther's theology of the cross. Even

---

98. Kosuke Koyama, *Mount Fuji and Mount Sinai: A Critique of Idols* (Maryknoll, N.Y.: Orbis, 1985), 88.

99. See Koyama, *Mount Fuji*, 243, for this and the following quote.

if the cross is at the periphery of humanity, it is still the center of all faith and of the world, because wherever Christ is, there is the center. But it is a different center from that of ideology, because it is the point of denial of self-centeredness. "The message of the cross is that . . . God in Christ embraces the self-centered humanity, and out of this divine embrace, through the mystery of grace, healing will flow into human history."[100] Even when God has the last word about the world and humanity, he is not a totalitarian God, in contrast to totalitarian regimes that pretend to have the last word. A God who revealed himself in Jesus Christ who is crucified, who walks toward the periphery, and who is passionately concerned about the welfare of people — a Christ who saves others and does not save himself — such a God cannot be totalitarian. Koyama's christocentric theology, through his own firsthand experience, is in tune with the need for contextualization yet weaves together the richness of his own tradition with the concrete situations of life.

A Story Theology: C. S. Song

Choan-Seng Song (b. 1929) was born in Taiwan and received his undergraduate degree in philosophy from National Taiwan University and his degree in theology from the New College, University of Edinburgh, Scotland. In 1965 he received his Ph.D. from Union Theological Seminary in New York, then taught Old Testament and systematic theology at Tainan Theological College, Taiwan, where he was principal from 1965 to 1970. He was associate director of the Faith and Order Commission of the WCC (1973-82) and director of studies of the World Alliance of Reformed Churches (1983-86). Since 1986 he has been professor of theology and Asian cultures at Pacific School of Religion in San Francisco and professor at the regional South East Asia Graduate School of Theology.

In his *Third-Eye Theology: Theology in Formation in Asian Settings* (1979), he first put forth his contextual theology that is "open to the mysterious ways of God who in Christ becomes human flesh in Asia."[101] In *Theology from the Womb of Asia* (1986), Song explains that theology must have four ingredients: "(1) It is the power of *imagination* given to us by God who created us human beings in the divine *image*; (2) it is the *passion* that enables us to feel the *com-*

---

100. Koyama, *Mount Fuji,* 252.

101. Choan-Seng Song, *Third-Eye Theology: Theology in Formation in Asian Settings,* rev. ed. (Maryknoll, N.Y.: Orbis, 1990), 37. For a succinct summary of his theology see Limuel Equina, "Faith and Culture in the Theology of C. S. Song," in *Theology at the Beginning of the 3rd Millennium in a Global Context — Retrospect and Perspectives,* ed. David C. Ratke (Frankfurt am Main: Peter Lang, 1999), 279-92.

passion of God in us and in others; (3) it is the experience of *communion* that makes us realize we are *responsible* for one another and for God; and (4) it is the *vision* of God's redeeming presence in the world, enabling us to *envision* a new course for theology."[102] In a narrative and often poetic way, Song unfolds his theology according to these four components. Throughout his theology it is important for Song not to conceptualize too quickly and to arrive at a theological compendium, but to image theology with many examples, stories, and even poems from the Asian context, so that God can be imaged in the heart of the Asian peoples (cf. 64).

Theology from the womb means that birth is given to theology as we hear, for instance, in Mary's Magnificat (cf. 119). It is again interesting how important a theology of the cross is for Song, because of the affinity between broken humanity and the broken body of Jesus. "But the broken body of Jesus is different from ours. It is the body of the compassionate God. It is broken to release the redemptive power of God. Its blood is shed to give rise to a community of wholeness. It is the reign of God that breaks out of the broken body of Jesus" (174). Beyond these analogies, there is the uniqueness of the body of Christ that instills hope amidst all brokenness, because theology is a testimony to the faith and love of God who makes new life and the world.

Song spelled out his theology in more detail in a three-volume Christology. In volume 1, *Jesus, the Crucified People* (1989), as we can glean from the title, the theology of the cross occupies center stage. What occurs on the cross is not something that occurs within the Trinity, Song asserts, because "such 'trinitarian' language makes little sense of the cross on which Jesus died. . . . The cross means human beings rejecting human beings. . . . This is what the cross of Jesus means and symbolizes. It was not planned by his Abba-God, but by human beings."[103] Similarly the real Jesus is not the Jesus enshrined in a cathedral or dictated by church traditions. "The real Jesus is the love of God that creates miracles of life in the world. He is the pain of God mingled with the pain of humanity. He is the hope of God that people manifest in the midst of despair."[104] We notice here a continual shifting between the history of Jesus and the history of humanity, one pointing to the other, while human history lives out of and gains hope from the divine history. The same method is employed in volume 2, *Jesus and the Reign of God* (1993), which focuses on the reign of God and on the kingdom.

---

102. C. S. Song, *Theology from the Womb of Asia* (Maryknoll, N.Y.: Orbis, 1986), 3. Page references for this work are placed in the following text.

103. C. S. Song, *Jesus, the Crucified People* (Minneapolis: Fortress, 1996 [1989]), 99.

104. Song, *Jesus, the Crucified People*, 14.

Song does not want to follow a philosophical approach, constructing a Christology detached from its historical roots, nor does he want to engage in a biographical approach, which often leads to a faulty reconstruction of Christology. He prefers to move "from the message of Jesus to his life and ministry" because the message communicates.[105] There is a dynamic relationship between the message and the bearer of the message. Central to Jesus' message is the reign of God, which Song wants to make relevant to the present-day world. The vision of God's reign, of a new heaven and a new earth, must have a close relationship to reality, because if it is not anchored in the reality of this world, it becomes an illusion. While "the reign of God is that dynamic at work inside history through men, women, and children, that power of redemption that mends, heals, and re-creates the entire creation for the day of a new heaven and a new earth," this reign is not completely outstanding.[106] It is already present, in "stories of hope grown out of a life of despair, poems of joy risen out of deep sorrow, hymns of praise sung from a heart beset by pain."[107]

In the third volume, *Jesus in the Power of the Spirit* (1994), Song moves beyond the dialectic of hope and despair, joy and sorrow. While Easter is neither in the past nor in the future, "for us human beings our history must be a history of Easter experiences. It consists of stories of human beings, as individuals and as communities, brought back to life from death again, and again in anticipation of fulfillment in the life and history of God."[108] It is clear for Song that if there is no final fulfillment at the end, we are at the most treading water. "So human history, Christian or not, is merely an endless tale of miseries and tragedies, if it is not at the same time the history of Easter experiences." There is a final release of the tension between already and not-yet, between anticipating and then again being disappointed. The resurrection of Jesus shows us the direction in which history is moving. In a recent publication, *The Believing Heart: An Invitation to Story Theology* (1999), Song again emphasizes how important it is for people in Asia, and perhaps everywhere, to practice story theology, which focuses on Jesus who came "to resurrect love in the world so that there will be life in the world."[109] Song's compassionate theology is different, because it is a theology out of life for life, illustrated and mediated through countless life stories.

105. Cf. C. S. Song, *Jesus and the Reign of God* (Minneapolis: Fortress, 1993), xi.

106. Song, *Reign of God*, 79.

107. Song, *Reign of God*, 150.

108. See C. S. Song, *Jesus in the Power of the Spirit* (Minneapolis: Fortress, 1994), 310, for this and the following quote.

109. C. S. Song, *The Believing Heart: An Invitation to Story Theology* (Minneapolis: Fortress, 1999), 315.

Minjung Theology: Byung-Mu Ahn

In reference to Asia we should at least mention Minjung theology, with its most significant representative being **Byung-Mu Ahn** (1922-96), who was born in what is now North Korea and obtained his doctorate in New Testament from the University of Heidelberg in 1965. Minjung originated in the 1970s as a theology of the marginalized, the oppressed, the exploited, and the politically and socioeconomically deprived through the Korean military regime. *Min* means people and *jung* means crowd, masses, or multitude. The task of theology according to Minjung theologians is for society to address and correct these problems of marginalization. Because society has rapidly changed in South Korea since the 1970s, first with the immense economic upswing and then most recently through a more democratic representation, Minjung theology in Korea has lost its urgency.

The Indian Tradition and Dalit Theology

In the vast Indian subcontinent, there have been repeated attempts by Hindus to adopt Christ and to adapt Christianity within the Hindu system. These have been facilitated by the numerous salvation historical incarnations of the godhead *(avatara)*, resulting in a multitude of gods, of whom Jesus Christ could easily be considered a divine manifestation.

The Approach to Christianity from the Hindu Side: Swami Vivekananda, S. Radhakrishnan, Mahatma Gandhi, and B. Upadhayaya

Swami Vivekananda (1863-1902), the founder of the Rama Krishna Mission and one of the leading participants in the World Parliament of Religions in Chicago in 1893, proposed a mutual assimilation of religions. "The Christian is not to become a Hindu or a Buddhist, nor a Hindu or a Buddhist to become a Christian. But each must assimilate the spirit of the others and yet preserve his individuality and grow according to his own law of growth."[110] For Vivekananda, Jesus is a Yogi who through renouncing everything, including ego-consciousness, realized himself as God in his spirit and showed others the path for the same spiritual realization. The work of Jesus and of all the great Ones

---

110. *The Complete Works of Swami Vivekananda* (Calcutta: Advaita Ashrama, 1998), 1:24, from his address at the final session of the Parliament of Religions (Sept. 27, 1893).

who preceded him and came after him continues. Therefore, Vivekananda concludes: "Our salutations go to all those Godlike men and women who are working to help humanity, whatever be their birth, colour, or race!"[111]

Sarvepalli Radhakrishnan (1888-1975), born of Brahmin parents and educated at Madras Christian College, was professor of Eastern religions and ethics at Oxford, England (1936-52), and president of India (1962-67), among many other distinguished appointments. Being educated at a Christian college, he had a good grasp of the Christian faith. Yet his appreciation for both his teachers and the Christian faith notwithstanding, he remained committed to his Hindu faith. He understood Jesus to be one among the many incarnations of God who showed perfect spiritual oneness with God. He wrote: "To an educated Hindu, Jesus is a supreme illustration of the growth from human origins to divine destiny."[112] Jesus "breaks away from the Jewish tradition and approximates Hindu and Buddhist thought."[113] Nevertheless, Jewish and mystic tendencies can be discerned in Jesus and in the later development of the church. **Mahatma Gandhi** (1869-1948), too, the father of modern India, appreciated Jesus. In his addresses he made frequent use of the Sermon on the Mount. But important for Gandhi was not the historical Jesus, but his principles and their realization today.[114]

Generally speaking, there has been considerable appreciation of Christianity and Christian principles by Hindus. But especially the theory of karma, meaning the notion that the sum total of your previous existence follows you into your present one, as expressed in the caste system and the strong integration of the individual into that system, makes it exceedingly difficult to accept fully the Christian message and to break with one's Hindu past. Usually there is only a more or less open recognition of the merits of Christianity.[115] If one makes the break, it may not always be a happy situation, as **B. Upadhayaya** (1861-1907) discovered, who was one of the first Indian Christian theologians in the modern period. Upadhayaya, a Hindu Brahmin from Bengal, joined the Church of England in 1891 and later became a Roman Catholic and an ascetic.

---

111. *The Complete Works of Swami Vivekananda* (1995), 4:153, in a presentation of 1900 entitled "Christ, the Messenger."

112. S. Radhakrishnan, "Reply to Critics," in *The Philosophy of Sarvepalli Radhakrishnan*, ed. Paul A. Schilpp (New York: Tudor, 1952), 807.

113. S. Radhakrishnan, *Eastern Religions and Western Thought* (Oxford: Oxford University Press, 1969 [1939]), 176.

114. Cf. Mohandas Gandhi, *Essential Writings*, selected with an introduction by John Dear (Maryknoll, N.Y.: Orbis, 2002), 78-81.

115. Cf. the study by Herbert E. Hoefer, *Churchless Christianity* (Madras: Gurukul Lutheran Theological College and Research Institute, 1991).

He proposed an indigenous model of theology and advocated monastic life. But because he lacked encouragement for his thoughts, he returned to Hinduism toward the end of his life. He had proposed a Christology within the framework of Advaita (nondualistic) philosophy (i.e., God and the world are not two distinct realities). Christ is the image of Brahman, in whom the fullness of the Godhead dwells.

An Uncompromising Use of the Indian Religious Idiom: A. J. Appasamy, P. Chenchiah, and V. Chakkarai

When we come to the twentieth century, there is first **Aiyadurai Jesudasen Appasamy** (1891-1975), a theologian and bishop who identified himself with the bhakti tradition and its exposition by Ramanuja (d. 1137), an Indian philosopher who developed a philosophical system of modified nondualism. Appasamy was born into a Christian family and had the opportunity to study theology in the West, at Hartford Seminary, Harvard, and Oxford. He received his doctor of philosophy degree from Oxford in 1922 with a thesis entitled "The Mysticism of Hindu Bhakti Literature Especially in Its Relation to the Mysticism of the Fourth Gospel." This was then published in expanded form as *Christianity as Bhakti Marga: A Study in the Mysticism of the Johannine Writings.* Later he became bishop of a diocese of the Church of South India and promoted evangelical piety.

Since God is immanent in the world, Appasamy contends, all people have seen the light, but the fullest light is found in Jesus, since in him the Logos dwells fully.[116] Jesus is the *avatara* (i.e., descent of God) of this Logos, not in the Hindu understanding as a theophany, but as incarnation. Important is that Jesus is the one and only *avatara*, the exclusive embodiment of God. "We believe that Jesus was the *Avatara*. God lived on the earth as a man only once and that was as Jesus. . . . Jesus was the one and the only *Avatara*, . . . among all the great religious figures in the world there is no one except Jesus who could be regarded as an Incarnation of God."[117]

For Appasamy the way of bhakti (i.e., loving devotion to a personal God) was the closest approach for the Indian to the Christian faith, and therefore the best vehicle for an Indian theology. The other concept that is important is *moksa* (i.e., release or salvation), which described for him the life in Christ ac-

---

116. Cf. A. J. Appasamy, *Christianity as Bhakti Marga: A Study in the Mysticism of the Johannine Writings* (London: Macmillan, 1927), 38-40.

117. A. J. Appasamy, *The Gospel and India's Heritage* (Madras: SPCK, 1942), 259.

cording to Paul. "Through faith and loving self-surrender we are united with Christ, yet it is a union in which we are not absorbed; the believer and his Lord retain their distinct personalities."[118] It is not an identity but a loving communion. While according to Hindu tradition the world often has no reality, Appasamy emphasized that God is not identical with the world, nor is the world a mere illusion. For him God is present and active in the world as Logos, using the world as his instrument. "The Logos, whose silent and mysterious work is as wide as the universe and as long as eternity, is none other than the Jesus whose words and deeds during His Incarnation have become the source of endless inspiration to men."[119] In Christ this world-creating power of the Logos became incarnate in the human body of Jesus so that people could interact with him in word and deed.

Pandipeddi Chenchiah (1886-1959) came from a Brahmin family and converted from Hinduism while studying at Madras Christian College. He was a lawyer by profession, a chief judge of the Pudukkottah princely state in South India, and a lay theologian. He developed his theology from his own experience according to 2 Corinthians 5:17, "If anyone is in Christ, there is a new creation." The church, its dogmas, sacraments, and rituals present Christ only indirectly. There must be a direct encounter with Christ through which one receives a divine and transforming power, and in turn one can help transform the world. Since Christ is the first fruit of the new creation, those who are in him participate in a totally new kind of humanity. "Jesus is the *adi-purusha* (original man) of a new creation. . . . In Jesus, creation mounts a step higher. . . . Jesus is the origin of the species of the sons of God. . . . I feel the two great urges of Indian Christians are a desire for direct contact with Jesus *(Pratyaksa)* and an aspiration for re-birth — to be born a son of God in the image of Jesus. . . . True evangelism consists in reproducing Jesus. The Indian Christian should harness the Holy Spirit to the creation of new life."[120] This direct experience of Christ is based on the figure of the historical Jesus, lest our interpretation of Christ come out of our own aspirations and projections. This is what he called the raw fact of Christ, the historical reality of Jesus of Nazareth and the concept of the new being.

For Chenchiah, Christ is different from God and from human beings. He is a new creation, not the perfect human being, the new human being that transcends perfection. In demarking Christianity from Hinduism, he said: "Hindu-

---

118. According to R. H. S. Boyd, *India and the Latin Captivity of the Church: The Cultural Context of the Gospel* (London: Cambridge University Press, 1974), 27.

119. Appasamy, *Christianity as Bhakti Marga*, 44.

120. P. Chenchiah, as quoted in Boyd, *India*, 31.

ism makes the perfect man, Christianity the new Man. Hinduism harnesses the *Mahasakti* [great power] of nature and man, Christianity brings into evolution the new *Sakti* [power] of the Holy Spirit. Jesus is the first fruits of a new creation. Hinduism [is] the final fruits of the old creation."[121] Again we see here the attempt to translate the Christian message into the Indian religious idiom without compromising that which Chenchiah considered essential to this message.

Vengal Chakkarai (1880-1958) was a Hindu convert, his father belonging to the Vedanta school (i.e., one of the six Indian philosophical systems) and his mother to the bhakti tradition. He was baptized in 1903 and worked for the Danish Missionary Society as an evangelist and educator. In 1941 he was elected mayor of Madras. His theology is christocentric, because Christology is for him the starting point of theology. "Our knowledge of God must be founded on the experience and consciousness of Jesus and not on *a priori* speculations like those of Anselm in Europe and Sankara in India. . . . If there is a God or if there are elements in Him unrelated to Jesus and existing outside Him, they are simply non-existent to us."[122] This means the Christhood of God is the manifestation of God in the face of Jesus, since God is the unmanifested and Jesus is the manifested. Only through the experience of Christ can we have knowledge of God, and this means through bhakti, through the mystical experience in our heart. Through Christ's incarnation God assumes human immanence, and in Christ's historicity transcendence and immanence are united, which can only be understood properly if directly experienced.

God's incarnation does not end with Jesus, but continues through the work of the Holy Spirit as a dynamic and continuing presence of God. God can be known only through the experience of the living Christ, the permanent *avatara* of God, and the living Christ can be known only through the experience of the Spirit, because *"Jesus Christ is the Incarnation or Avatar of God; the Holy Spirit in human experience is the Incarnation of Jesus Christ."*[123] This Christian mysticism is not without the cross, because the cross is where sinful humanity meets God, and in some mysterious way the cross opens a channel in the human heart by which the divine *sakti* (i.e., power) flows as a mighty stream into the history of humanity and thereby becomes the active energy of a new world order. Again we notice here the use of Indian religious concepts to express the tenets of the Christian faith in an uncompromising way without

121. P. Chenchiah, "Christian Message in a Non-Christian World: An Indian View of Dr. Kraemer's Exposition," in *Rethinking Christianity,* ed. D. M. Devasahayam and A. N. Sudarisanam (Madras: Hogarth Press, 1938), appendix, 43.

122. V. Chakkarai, *Jesus the Avatar* (Madras: CLS, 1926), 212-13.

123. Chakkarai, *Jesus the Avatar,* 121.

sacrificing a point of contact between the Indian religious context and the Christian faith.

A Christ-Centered Ecumenical Theology: M. M. Thomas

M. M. Thomas (1916-96) has been perhaps the most prominent ecumenical theologian of India, though a layperson. He belonged to the Mar Thoma Church and was its first full-time secretary in the youth department, beginning in 1945. From 1947 to 1953 he was on the staff of the World Student Christian Federation in Geneva, and after that was involved in ecumenical ventures in Geneva, serving from 1968 to 1975 as the chairperson of the Central Committee of the WCC. He was also active on the Indian scene, having moved from an associate director to the director of the Christian Institute for the Study of Religion and Society (CISRS). From 1989 to 1994 he was governor of Nagaland, a state in northeast India.[124] As with all Indian theologians, it is clear for Thomas that "the context of Indian Christian theology is the dialogue between Christ and India."[125] But in delineating the criteria for an Indian Christian theology, he uses no Indian religious concepts, but rather envisions a "Christ-centered syncretic process" in which the beliefs and expressions of the peoples of the world contain elements that can serve as a starting point for unveiling Christ and his significance.[126] This means that the world religions, including the religions of India, can serve as a point of contact for the Christian message. (We remember that African theologians argued along similar lines about the religious heritage of Africa.) The reason for this is that "every man, whether he acknowledges God mentally or not, has a dimension of self-awareness of the presence of the ultimate and of ultimate responsibility."[127] There is already a point of contact within each human being. Since Christ transcends the culture of Western Christendom and is able to relate himself creatively to other cultures, there is also the possibility of "Christ reforming all religions and in-forming Himself in them."[128]

About India, Thomas is primarily concerned that Christian theology does its homework, meaning first of all that it recognizes that a living theology is al-

---

124. For his ecumenical activities see M. M. Thomas, *My Ecumenical Journey, 1947-1975* (Trivandrum, India: P. M. Oommen of Ecumenical Publishing Centre, 1990).

125. M. M. Thomas, *The Acknowledged Christ of the Indian Renaissance* (London: SCM, 1969), 316.

126. M. M. Thomas, *Man and the Universe of Faiths* (Madras: CSL, 1975), 157.

127. Thomas, *The Acknowledged Christ*, 285.

128. Thomas, *Man*, 151.

ways situational or contextual. Indian theology must reevaluate the classical and confessional theological traditions it has inherited from the West, even to the point of understanding anew the meaning of orthodoxy and heresy, because even "the best theological definitions of the faith are necessarily fragmentary, one-sided, situation-bound and inadequate to express the plenitude of God in Jesus Christ."[129] A heretic, then, is someone who considers his or her own theology to be absolute and who therefore separates from the continuity of the great vision and the unity of the church, whereas orthodoxy endeavors to stand within the historical community of the great tradition and to affirm the unity with the universal community of the faithful.

Theology, according to Thomas, is a rational understanding of the truth and the meaning of its commitment. "The divine-human encounter of faith at spiritual depth comes to consciousness in theology, and makes possible its own critical evaluation so that a renewed commitment of faith and a correction of its expressions are continually made possible."[130] Theology is not an intellectual enterprise, but is rooted in faith and seeks to understand this faith in the Anselmian tradition. Theology is also not isolated, but it is the servant of the community of faith. It helps the church to understand, evaluate, and renew its nature and functions. This means that theology is not only embedded in the community, but also relates to the community because knowing and doing belong together for Thomas. While there are certainly many influences discernible in Thomas's theology, such as Karl Barth, but also Emil Brunner, his Christ-centered theology at the same time reacts against some currents in Indian reflection, such as that of Raimon Panikkar, for whom Christ, as we will see later, in an implicit way emerges from the Hindu religious context. For Thomas, however, Christ can emerge only when he is named, however partial and inadequate such naming may be.[131]

Christ among the Religions of India: Stanley Samartha and Raimon Panikkar

Before we turn to Panikkar, we will briefly focus our attention on **Stanley J. Samartha** (1920-2000). He was born in a small village in Karnataka, one of the four states in South India. His high school and college studies were done in

---

129. Thomas, *The Acknowledged Christ*, 310.

130. Thomas, *The Acknowledged Christ*, 289-90.

131. Cf. Thomas, introduction to *The Acknowledged Christ*, x, where he states that he chose the title of his book in direct opposition to Panikkar's book.

Mangalore, in Roman Catholic institutions, where he concentrated on economics and history. Immediately after college he decided to study for the ministry. Samartha began his theological studies at United Theological College (UTC) in Bangalore in 1941 and completed them four years later, after which he became assistant pastor and lecturer in theology and religions at the Basel Evangelical Mission Theological Seminary in Mangalore. A few years later he undertook graduate studies, first at Union Theological Seminary in New York and later at the Hartford Seminary Foundation in Hartford, Connecticut. At Union he did a master's thesis entitled "The Hindu View of History according to Radhakrishnan," which he developed into the doctoral dissertation "The Hindu View of History according to Representative Thinkers." Having spent a semester in Basel, where he appreciated Barth and the missiologist Hendrik Kraemer (1888-1965), who served as the first director of the Ecumenical Institute in Bossey, near Geneva, he returned to India in 1952 and was appointed the first Indian principal of his alma mater, now Karnataka Theological College in Mangalore. From 1960 to 1966 he served as professor of history and philosophy of religions at the UTC in Bangalore, and then for two years as principal of Serampore College near Calcutta. From 1968 to 1970 he was secretary in the Department of Studies in Mission and Evangelism at the WCC in Geneva, and from 1971 to 1980 director of the newly founded subunit on Dialog with People of Living Faiths and Ideologies. Upon his return to India, he was for five years a consultant to CISRS and visiting professor at UTC. After 1989 he was a member of the committee supervising doctoral studies in theology and religions of the South Asia Theological Research Institute.

He was involved in the dialogue with other religions apart from his academic pursuits. Even his seminary teaching was geared in this direction. This dialogue was also his main interest, guided by the fundamental principle "that God is an Absolute that can never have a full, final expression in any religion or revealer."[132] Samartha claimed that the name "Christ" cannot biblically or theologically be restricted to the historical figure of Jesus of Nazareth, because he was before Abraham (John 8:58) and is the same yesterday, today, and tomorrow (Heb. 13:8), and "he is also the One who makes all things new and calls us to participate in his work everywhere."[133] This means that Christ is larger than the historical figure of Jesus of Nazareth.

In a more recent publication, Samartha went beyond the universal Christ

132. Stanley J. Samartha, *Between Two Cultures: Ecumenical Ministry in a Pluralist World* (Geneva: WCC, 1996), 155, in a remark by Paul Knitter, to whom Samartha was very close.

133. Cf. Stanley J. Samartha, "Mission and Movements of Innovation," in *Mission Trends No. 3: Third World Theologies*, ed. Gerald H. Anderson and Thomas F. Stranksy (Grand Rapids: Eerdmans, 1976), 242.

in opting for a "theocentric christology." Again he wanted to back up his claim with the New Testament, saying the belief "in the ontological priority of God is also taken for granted by Jesus Christ and his hearers in the New Testament."[134] Samartha concluded that God is prior to Christ, since God gave his only begotten son (John 3:16) and was in Christ, reconciling the world to himself (2 Cor. 5:19). While he noted that a Christomonism does not do full justice to the New Testament, he claimed that a theocentric theology provides more theological space for Christians to live together with neighbors of other faiths. Yet for Samartha a theocentric Christology does not abandon the distinctiveness of Jesus Christ, but "it makes commitment to God in Jesus Christ possible without taking a negative attitude toward neighbors of other faiths, and at the same time it offers a more comprehensive conceptional framework for dialog with these neighbors" (88). The theocentric includes the christocentric, and it recognizes the theological significance of other revelations and other experiences of salvation without giving up the distinctive experience of Jesus Christ.

While Christology always has to do with Jesus Christ, christological reflection, Samartha asserted, cannot be concerned only with the question of Jesus Christ, but also must deal with the meaning of God, or ultimate reality, for human existence. "There can be no christology without theology," and "no *Christian* theology apart from Jesus Christ," but "there can be and are theologies without reference to Jesus Christ," namely, in other religions. "To ignore or deny this fact," Samartha claimed, "is to be insensitive to the faiths of our neighbors" (92). With this assertion, of course, he rejected the notion that God has been revealed *only* in Jesus of Nazareth in order to redeem humanity, or, to put it differently, that this revealing and redemptive activity took place once and for all in Jesus of Nazareth. Samartha said: "The way to a revised christology, however, is not through diminishing the centrality of Jesus Christ to Christian life or diluting the christological substance in theology" (95). Christ still remains central for Christians, but not necessarily so for others, though many others also have great respect for Jesus Christ, his teachings, his life, cross, and resurrection.

The revised Christology led Samartha to a different understanding of incarnation: "The Incarnation, I wish to suggest, is best understood not solely in terms of 'deity,' but in terms of 'divinity.' It is one thing to say that Jesus of Nazareth is divine, and quite another thing to say that Jesus of Nazareth is God. That Jesus is divine is the testimony of the gospels" (118). Though Samartha did not say this outright, what seems to underlie his assertion here

---

134. Stanley J. Samartha, *One Christ — Many Religions: Toward a Revised Christology* (Maryknoll, N.Y.: Orbis, 1991), 88. Page references for this work are placed in the following text.

is that in the Indian tradition, which knows of many divinities, a divine Jesus can easily be accommodated, but not a Jesus being *the* deity, because that is too exclusive. That Samartha also departed from the early christological decisions such as the Council of Nicea (A.D. 325) was of little concern to him. It was much more important for him to be in conversation with other religious traditions.

When he outlined the marks of a revised Christology, he noted that "the kingdom of God is the central message of Jesus." The three characteristics of the kingdom are its comprehensiveness, its corporate character, and the "question of *power* and power relationships within the Kingdom" (134). What is missing here is the eschatological aspect of the kingdom. This goes together with him bringing cross and resurrection so close together that "one has therefore to speak of the 'cross-resurrection' event, rather than of two separate incidents, and of Jesus as 'the crucified-and-risen One'" (137). Since the resurrection would have an eschatological component, it is seen together with the cross where the eschatological component can be more easily omitted. If Jesus is not seen as the eschatological event, then it is easy to consider him as one event among others. That is exactly what Samartha was doing in order to facilitate the dialogue with other religious traditions.

Raimon Panikkar (b. 1918), too, was very much interested in the dialogue with Indian religions. He was born in Barcelona, Spain, to a Hindu Indian father and a Roman Catholic Spanish mother and was brought up in strictest Roman Catholic orthodoxy. His scholarship spans half a century and he has written several dozen books. He received a doctorate in philosophy (1946), and another one in chemistry (1958), both from the University of Madrid, and additionally a doctorate in theology (1961) from the Lateran University in Rome with a thesis that was subsequently published as *The Unknown Christ of Hinduism* (1964; rev. ed. 1981). Panikkar is a Roman Catholic priest, ordained (1946) in the diocese of Varanasi, India. He has taught in Madrid (1945-51), in India (1947-73), at the Center for the Study of World Religions at Harvard University (1967-71), and at the University of California in Santa Barbara (1971 until retirement).

Very much in the vein of Vatican II, he claimed in *The Unknown Christ of Hinduism* that God's salvific work is present and active in all religions through the salvation provided for by Christ. "Christ is the universal redeemer. There is no redemption apart from him. Where there is no redemption there is no salvation. Therefore, any human person that is saved — and we know by reason and by faith that God provides everybody with the necessary means of salvation — is saved by Christ, the only redeemer. This amounts to saying that Christ is present in one form or another in every human being in his religious way to

God."[135] Through God the Father and the power of the Holy Spirit, Jesus, the historical person, can be universalized in his salvific presence.

Later, Panikkar abandoned this christocentric position, saying: "Each culture and religion, like each individual being, is unique."[136] This means that the Christian faith is unique as the Christian faith in the same way that Hinduism is unique as Hinduism. Each religion can also be translated into other cultures, but by adopting the corresponding references the original tradition is modified. "For example, if we were to translate *agape* with *karuna, psyche* with *atman, Christos* with *abhisheka, logos* with *tao, theos* with *allah,* Christian theology would itself undergo a transformation. Each new term or image not only connotes a different universe of discourse; it also opens up the sluices for the living waters of the other culture."[137] Christian theology therefore not only transforms the culture it enters, but is also transformed by that culture by picking up connotations it formerly did not possess. Panikkar is not worried by this transformation; to the contrary, he is convinced that "each religious tradition has a claim to a potential fullness. . . . Religions are projects of *salvation* — using this word as standing for the goal of Man's life in whatever sense. Each religion is a project to help, enlighten, transform . . . the concrete person for the fulfillment of human life."[138]

Panikkar continues: "At the same time, I am fully convinced that neither my ego, nor all christians, nor even all my fellow human beings are ever going to exhaust the knowledge of such a Mystery. I discover at the same time that there are other people, other world views, other religions (other windows)."[139] This means that the ultimate mystery to which all religions point and from where they come can never be exhausted. Each religion contributes its own perspective to elucidating this mystery. There is then no longer one universal truth but a context in which a believing member of a religion, in one way or another, holds his or her religion to be true.

One's religious truth cannot be absolutized and universalized. Rather one will discover that "no religion, ideology, culture, or tradition can reasonably claim to exhaust the universal range of human experience or even the total

135. Raimon Panikkar, *The Unknown Christ of Hinduism* (London: Darton, Longman and Todd, 1968), 33-34.

136. Raimon Panikkar, "Can Theology Be Transcultural?" in *Pluralism and Oppression: Theology in World Perspective,* ed. Paul F. Knitter (Lanham, Md.: University Press of America, 1991), 18.

137. Panikkar, "Can Theology Be Transcultural?" 17.

138. Raimon Panikkar, "A Self-Critical Dialogue," in *The Intercultural Challenge of Raimon Panikkar,* ed. Joseph Prabhu (Maryknoll, N.Y.: Orbis, 1996), 268.

139. Panikkar, "A Self-Critical Dialogue," 269.

manifestation of the sacred."[140] This does not mean that all religions say the same thing or should merge, but one will discern and appreciate the respective contributions of each religion. Panikkar calls for an "ecumenical ecumenism" in which each religion can contribute toward the development of the full humanness of humanity. When Panikkar returned to his native Spain, after an absence of fifteen years, he could therefore say: "I 'left' as a christian, I 'found' myself a hindu, and I 'return' a buddhist, without having ceased to be a christian."[141] He could enter into the other traditions, appreciating their "fruits" without abandoning his own Christian persuasion.

But Panikkar goes even one step further toward an all-embracing synthesis in a cosmotheandric experience. With this term he does not want to reduce everything to a single universal principle. To the contrary, he assures us that the divine, the human, and the cosmic (freedom, consciousness, and matter) are one, but "cannot be reduced to a single principle."[142] While prehistoric humanity divinized the cosmos and, being mainly turned toward the past, worshiped the ancestors, and historical humanity is mainly turned toward the future and worships the God who shall be, modern or postmodern humanity, what Panikkar calls the "transhistorical Man," assumes a more or less conscious theanthropocosmic vision of the universe. "He finds himself, in varying degrees of harmony and tension, within a cosmotheandric *reality* in which all the forces of the universe — from electromagnetic to divine, from angelic to human — are intertwined. He lives mainly in the present. He is very cautious in worshipping. If at all, he would reverence the intersection of past and future, of the divine and the human."[143] Panikkar finds this interest in the present especially in the new religions and in many religious facets that one usually associates with the so-called New Age movement.

Panikkar has moved from a christocentric to a pluriform and then a cosmotheandric religiosity, which also shows his deep mystic inclinations. The issues raised by Panikkar and Samartha concerning the relationship between the Christian faith and other religions has to be picked up in the following chapter, since this is one of the most pervasive and enduring themes in current theological discourse. But before we leave the Indian scene, we will discuss Dalit theology, a peculiarly Indian phenomenon.

140. Raimon Panikkar, *The Intrareligious Dialogue*, rev. ed. (Mahwah, N.J.: Paulist, 1999 [1978]), 106.
141. Panikkar, *The Intrareligious Dialogue*, 42.
142. Raimon Panikkar, *The Cosmotheandric Principle: Emerging Religious Consciousness*, edited with an introduction by Scott Eastham (Maryknoll, N.Y.: Orbis, 1993), 121.
143. Panikkar, *The Cosmotheandric Principle*, 127.

Dalit Theology: Arvind Nirmal and V. Devasahayam

While India today has a middle class that is larger in number than that of western Europe, one must not forget that at least 40 percent of the population in India still lives below the poverty line. Among these are the so-called untouchables who belong to no caste and therefore lack the communal support a caste gives to individuals. Many of these, perhaps out of despair, joined Christian churches, so that in many churches these Harijans or Dalits form the largest group. Due to the advocacy of B. R. Ambedkar (1891-1956) and his devoted disciple Shyam Sunder (1908-75), the government inaugurated many programs for the so-called *scheduled castes and tribes,* i.e., underprivileged castes and groups that need special governmental support. Since Christians supposedly receive overseas help, they are excluded from these government measures.

Among the Christians a special theology, Dalit theology, developed as an advocacy theology for all the Dalits. Its main proponent was **Arvind P. Nirmal** (1936-95), who belonged to the Church of North India, himself being a Dalit Christian, and who taught at Gurukul Lutheran Theological College and Research Institute in Madras, and before that at UTC in Bangalore. At Gurukul he also was dean of the Department of Dalit Theology.

Dalit theology is a theology by the Dalits for the Dalits. As Nirmal observed: "Most of the contributions to the Indian Christian Theology in the past came from caste converts to Christianity. The result has been that Indian Christian Theology has perpetuated within itself what I prefer to call the *'Brahminic'* tradition."[144] Indian theology has largely remained elitist, by following the Brahminic tradition. It was only in the 1970s, due to the influence of liberation theology, that the Indian theological scene changed considerably and a third-world theology emerged. But this third-world theology "failed to see in the struggle of Indian dalits for liberation a subject matter appropriate for doing theology in India." But the struggle of Indian Dalits is a story that provides Indian Dalit theology with a liberation motif that is authentically Indian. "This story needs to be analyzed and interpreted theologically" (57).

Since Nirmal himself was a Dalit, he was not talking of a theology *about* the Dalits, or theological reflection upon the Christian responsibility to the depressed classes. He was also not talking about a theology *for* the depressed classes, but one that comes *from* these depressed classes, a theology the Dalits themselves would like to expound. According to Nirmal, a Christian Dalit the-

---

144. Arvind P. Nirmal, "Towards a Christian Dalit Theology," in *A Reader in Dalit Theology,* ed. Arvind P. Nirmal (Madras: Gurukul Lutheran Theological College and Research Institute, 1991), 54. Page references in the following text are to this essay.

ology "will be based on their own dalit experiences, their own sufferings, their own aspirations, and their own hope. It will narrate the story of their *pathos* and their protest against the socio-economic injustices they have been subjected to throughout history. It will anticipate liberation which is meaningful to them. It will represent a radical discontinuity with the classical Indian Christian Theology of the Brahminic tradition" (58-59).

Dalit theology also has to do with roots, identity, and consciousness, and it picks up Ambedkar's slogan for the Dalits: "unite, educate, and agitate" (61). Since the Dalits were treated as "no people," the goal is the realization of the full humanness being created in the image of God. Since the dominant religious tradition denied to the Dalits the right to pray in the temples, they come to Jesus and his Father and recognize his Dalitness, since he is a God who serves the customary role of Dalits. Nirmal sees noteworthy features of Jesus' life in "his total identification with the dalits of his day. Again and again Jesus is accused of eating and drinking with publicans, tax collectors and 'sinners' of his day (Mk 2:15-16)" (67). What Dalit theology does, according to Nirmal, is to find points of identification in the biblical story, both in the Old Testament and the New, with the experience and the aspirations of the Dalits.

V. Devasahayam (b. 1949) is a theologian from the Church of South India who followed Nirmal as professor of systematic theology and head of the Department of Dalit Theology at the Gurukul Lutheran Theological College and Research Institute (1990-99), and is presently bishop of the diocese of Madras of the Church of South India. He remarked that the "Dalit church with upper caste leadership and upper caste theology forgot the social base of the Indian church."[145] Yet the Dalits challenge the accommodation to the caste system and the resultant division, discrimination, and domination. Dalit theology cannot be contextual in the sense of advocating the status quo, but it is taking note of the fact that both in India and among Christians worldwide the vast majority of the people are Dalits.

Since the caste system in India is not just based on economic foundations, but on religious ones, especially through the karma theory, Dalit theology must challenge these religious assumptions. Since the Bible "witnesses to God's being in the world as characterized by liberating activity, struggling against forces of oppression, . . . theology, then, becomes the story of God's struggle over oppressive forces of sin and Satan and God's victory in obtaining for us salvation and liberation."[146] For Dalit theologians the caste system is an idolatry that enslaves

---

145. V. Devasahayam, "Doing Dalit Theology: Basic Assumptions," in *Frontiers of Dalit Theology,* ed. V. Devasahayam (Gurukul: ISPCK, 1997), 270.

146. Devasahayam, "Doing Dalit Theology," 276.

and destroys the Dalits. Such a system must be identified and exposed, and attempts must be made to dismantle it. Dalit theology therefore is the Indian variety of liberation theology. It does not simply attack unjust economic structures as does liberation theology, but it exposes the underlying socioreligious problems and challenges them by proclaiming a God who has no favorites and for whom all humans are God's children.

FOR FURTHER READING

James H. Cone (b. 1938)

Burrow, Rufus. *James H. Cone and Black Liberation Theology.* Jefferson, N.C.: McFarland & Co., 1994.

Cone, James H. *Black Theology and Black Power.* Maryknoll, N.Y.: Orbis, 1999 [1969].

———. *A Black Theology of Liberation.* Maryknoll, N.Y.: Orbis, 1995 [1970].

———. *My Soul Looks Back.* Maryknoll, N.Y.: Orbis, 1986.

Cone, James H., and Gayraud S. Wilmore, eds. *Black Theology: A Documentary History.* Vol. 1, *1966-1979.* 2nd rev. ed. Maryknoll, N.Y.: Orbis, 1993.

———. *Black Theology: A Documentary History.* Vol. 2, *1980-1992.* Maryknoll, N.Y.: Orbis, 1993.

Hopkins, Dwight N., ed. *Black Faith and Public Talk: Critical Essays on James H. Cone's Black Theology and Black Power.* Maryknoll, N.Y.: Orbis, 1999.

Singleton, Harry H. *Black Theology and Ideology: Deideological Dimensions in the Theology of James H. Cone.* Collegeville, Minn.: Liturgical Press, 2002.

Stewart, Carlyle Fielding. *God, Being, and Liberation: A Comparative Analysis of the Theologies of James H. Cone and Howard Thurman.* Lanham, Md.: University Press of America, 1989.

J. Deotis Roberts (b. 1927)

Cone, Cecil W. *The Identity Crisis in Black Theology.* Nashville: Henry Belin, 1975.

Gardiner, James, and J. Deotis Roberts, eds. *Quest for a Black Theology.* Philadelphia: Pilgrim Press, 1971.

Roberts, J. Deotis. *A Black Political Theology.* Philadelphia: Westminster, 1974.

———. *Black Theology in Dialogue.* Philadelphia: Westminster, 1987.

———. *Liberation and Reconciliation: A Black Theology.* Rev. ed. Maryknoll, N.Y.: Orbis, 1994.

Thomas, Gerald. "James Deotis Roberts." In *Baptist Theologians,* edited by Timothy George and David S. Dockery, 627-39. Nashville: Broadman, 1990.

Cornel West (b. 1953)

West, Cornel. *The Cornel West Reader.* New York: Basic Civitas Books, 1999.

———. *Prophesy Deliverance! An Afro-American Revolutionary Christianity.* Louisville: Westminster John Knox, 2002 [1982].

Wood, Mark David. *Cornel West and the Politics of Prophetic Pragmatism*. Urbana: University of Illinois Press, 2000.

Yancy, George. *Cornel West: A Critical Reader*. Malden, Mass.: Blackwell, 2001.

Vine Deloria (b. 1933)

Deloria, Vine. *Behind the Trail of Broken Treatises: An Indian Declaration of Independence*. New York: Dell, 1974.

———. *Custer Died for Your Sins: An Indian Manifesto*. Norman: University of Oklahoma Press, 1988 [1969].

———. *For This Land: Writings on Religion in America*. Edited with an introduction by James Treat. New York: Routledge, 1999.

———. *God Is Red: A Native View of Religion*. 2nd ed. Golden, Colo.: Fulcrum, 1994.

———. *We Talk; You Listen, New Turf*. New York: Macmillan, 1970.

Clodovis Boff (b. 1944)

Boff, Clodovis. "Clodovis Boff." Interview by M. Puleo. In *The Struggle Is One,* edited and translated by M. Puleo, 144-61. Albany: State University of New York Press, 1994.

———. *Feet-on-the-Ground Theology: A Brazilian Journal*. Translated by Philip Berryman. Maryknoll, N.Y.: Orbis, 1987.

Cunningham, David S. "Clodovis Boff on the Discipline of Theology." *Modern Theology* 6 (Jan. 1990): 137-58.

Leonardo Boff (b. 1938)

Boff, Leonardo. *Church: Charism and Power; Liberation Theology and the Institutional Church*. Translated by John W. Diercksmeier. New York: Crossroad, 1985.

———. *Liberating Grace*. Translated by John Drury. Maryknoll, N.Y.: Orbis, 1979.

———. *The Path to Hope: Fragments from a Theologian's Journey*. Translated by Philip Berryman. Maryknoll, N.Y.: Orbis, 1993.

Boff, Leonardo, and Clodovis Boff. *Liberation Theology: From Dialogue to Confrontation*. Translated by Robert R. Barr. San Francisco: Harper and Row, 1986.

Cox, Harvey. *The Silencing of Leonardo Boff: The Vatican and the Future of World Christianity*. Bloomington, Ind.: Meyer-Stone, 1988.

Ferm, Deane William. *Profiles in Liberation: 36 Portraits of Third World Theologians*. Mystic, Conn.: Twenty-Third Publications, 1988.

Waltermire, Donald. *The Liberation Christologies of Leonardo Boff and Jon Sobrino: Latin American Contributions to Contemporary Christology*. Lanham, Md.: University Press of America, 1994.

Gustavo Gutiérrez (b. 1928)

Brown, Robert McAfee. *Gustavo Gutiérrez: An Introduction to Liberation Theology*. Maryknoll, N.Y.: Orbis, 1990.

Ellis, Marc H., and Otto Maduro, eds. *Expanding the View: Gustavo Gutiérrez and the Future of Liberation Theology.* Maryknoll, N.Y.: Orbis, 1990.

———. *The Future of Liberation Theology: Essays in Honor of Gustavo Gutiérrez.* Maryknoll, N.Y.: Orbis, 1989.

Gutiérrez, Gustavo. *Gustavo Gutiérrez: Essential Writings.* Edited by James B. Nickoloff. Minneapolis: Fortress, 1996.

———. *A Theology of Liberation: History, Politics, and Salvation.* Translated and edited by C. Inda and J. Eagleson. 15th anniversary edition with a new introduction by the author. Maryknoll, N.Y.: Orbis, 1988.

Sallie McFague (b. 1933)

Carroll, B. Jill. "Models of God or Models of Us? On the Theology of Sallie McFague." *Encounter* 52 (Spring 1991): 183-96.

Finger, Thomas. "Trinity, Ecology, and Panentheism." *Christian Scholar's Review* 27, no. 1 (1997): 74-98.

McFague, Sallie. *Body of God: An Ecological Theology.* Minneapolis: Fortress, 1993.

———. *Life Abundant: Rethinking Theology and Economy for a Planet in Peril.* Minneapolis: Fortress, 2000.

———. *Metaphysical Theology: Models of God in Religious Language.* Philadelphia: Fortress, 1982.

———. *Models of God: Theology for an Ecological, Nuclear Age.* Philadelphia: Fortress, 1987.

Schrein, Shannon. *Quilting and Braiding: The Feminist Christologies of Sallie McFague and Elizabeth A. Johnson in Conversation.* Collegeville, Minn.: Liturgical Press, 1998.

Elisabeth Schüssler Fiorenza (b. 1938)

Fiorenza, Elisabeth Schüssler. *Bread Not Stone: The Challenge of Feminist Biblical Interpretation.* Boston: Beacon Press, 1995 [1984].

———. *But She Said: Feminist Practices of Biblical Interpretation.* Boston: Beacon Press, 1992.

———. *Discipleship of Equals: A Critical Feminist Ekklesia-logy of Liberation.* New York: Crossroad, 1993.

———. *In Memory of Her: A Feminist Theological Reconstruction of Christian Origins.* New York: Crossroad, 1994 [1988].

———, ed. *The Power of Naming: A Concilium Reader in Feminist Liberation Theology.* Maryknoll, N.Y.: Orbis, 1996.

Leonhard, Richard. *Beloved Daughters: 100 Years of Papal Teaching in Women.* Foreword by Elizabeth Johnson. Melbourne, Australia: David Lovell, 1995.

Minor, Mitzi L. "Schüssler Fiorenza, Elisabeth (b. 1939)." In *Historical Handbook of Major Interpreters,* 606-10. Downers Grove, Ill.: InterVarsity, 1998.

Pears, Angela. "Women's Experience and Authority in the Work of Elisabeth Schüssler Fiorenza." *Modern Believing,* n.s., 36 (July 1995): 16-21.

Rosemary Radford Ruether (b. 1936)

Ramsay, William. *Four Modern Prophets: Walter Rauschenbusch, Martin Luther King, Jr., Gustavo Gutiérrez, Rosemary Radford Ruether.* Atlanta: John Knox, 1986.

Ruether, Rosemary Radford. *Disputed Questions: On Being a Christian.* Maryknoll, N.Y.: Orbis, 1989.

―――. *Gaia and God: An Ecofeminist Theology of Earth Healing.* San Francisco: HarperSanFrancisco, 1992.

―――. *New Woman, New Earth: Sexist Ideologies and Human Liberation.* New York: Seabury Press, 1975.

―――. *Sexism and God-Talk: Toward a Feminist Theology.* Boston: Beacon Press, 1983.

Tatman, Lucy. *Knowledge That Matters: A Feminist Theological Paradigm and Epistemology.* New York: Sheffield Academic Press, 2001.

Mary Daly (b. 1928)

Daly, Mary. *Beyond God the Father: Toward a Philosophy of Women's Liberation.* Boston: Beacon Press, 1985 [1973].

―――. *Outercourse: The Be-dazzling Voyage; Containing Recollections from My Logbook of a Radical Feminist Philosopher (Be-ing an Account of My Time/Space Travels and Ideas — Then, Again, Now, and Now).* San Francisco: HarperSanFrancisco, 1992.

―――. *Pure Lust: Elemental Feminist Philosophy.* Boston: Beacon Press, 2001 [1984].

Hoagland, Sarah Lucia, and Marilyn Frye, eds. *Feminist Interpretations of Mary Daly.* University Park: Pennsylvania State University Press, 2000.

Madsen, Catherine. "The Thin Thread of Conversation: An Interview with Mary Daly." *Cross Currents* 50, no. 3 (Fall 2000): 332-48.

Delores S. Williams

Burrow, Rufus, Jr. "Toward a Womanist Theology and Ethics." *Journal of Feminist Studies in Religion* 15 (Spring 1999): 77-95.

Roberson, Rachel. "Seeking 'A Way out of No Way.'" *Witness* 83, no. 4 (Apr. 2000): 30-31.

Williams, Delores S. *Sisters in the Wilderness: The Challenge of Womanist God-Talk.* Maryknoll, N.Y.: Orbis, 1993.

Desmond Tutu (b. 1931)

Du Boulay, Shirley. *Tutu: Voice of the Voiceless.* Grand Rapids: Eerdmans, 1988.

Hulley, Leonard, Louise Kretzschmar, and Luke Lungile Pato, eds. *Archbishop Tutu: Prophetic Witness in South Africa.* Cape Town: Human and Rousseau, 1996.

Tutu, Desmond. *Crying in the Wilderness: The Struggle for Justice in South Africa.* Edited and introduction by John Webster. Foreword by Trevor Huddleston. Grand Rapids: Eerdmans, 1990.

―――. *No Future without Forgiveness.* New York: Doubleday Image, 1999.

———. *The Personal Papers of Archbishop Desmond Tutu.* Edited by Leatlhaba Phayane. Bellville: University of the Western Cape Press, 1999.

John S. Mbiti (b. 1931)

Burleson, Blake Wiley. "John Mbiti's Theology as a Reflection of the Archaic Notion of Corporate Personality." *Africa Theological Journal* 21, no. 2 (1992): 164-87.
Mbiti, John. *Concepts of God in Africa.* London: SPCK, 1970.
———. *New Testament Eschatology in an African Background: A Study of the Encounter between New Testament Theology and African Traditional Concepts.* London: SPCK, 1978 [1971].
Nelson, F. Burton. "New Frontiers in African Theology." *Evangelical Review of Theology* 14 (July 1990): 209-24.
Olupona, Jacob K., and Sulayman S. Nyang, eds. *Religious Plurality in Africa: Essays in Honour of John S. Mbiti.* New York: Mouton de Gruyter, 1993.

Kwesi A. Dickson (b. 1929)

Anum, Eric. "Comparative Readings of the Bible in Africa: Some Concerns." In *The Bible in Africa: Transactions, Trajectories, and Trends,* edited by Gerald West and Musa W. Dube, 457-73. Leiden: Brill, 2000.
Dickson, Kwesi A. *Theology in Africa.* Maryknoll, N.Y.: Orbis, 1984.

Mercy A. Oduyoye (b. 1934)

Gibellini, Rosino, ed. *Paths of African Theology.* Maryknoll, N.Y.: Orbis, 1994.
Nelson, F. Burton. "New Frontiers in African Theology." *Evangelical Review of Theology* 14 (July 1990): 209-24.
Oduyoye, Mercy A. *Hearing and Knowing: Theological Reflections on Christianity in Africa.* Maryknoll, N.Y.: Orbis, 1986.
Pemberton, Carie. "Harmony in Africa: Healing the Divided Continental Self — Mercy Amba Oduyoye, Feminist and Theologian." In *Challenging Women's Orthodoxies in the Context of Faith,* edited by Susan Frank Parsons, 89-108. Aldershot: Ashgate, 2000.

Kazoh Kitamori (1916-98)

Kitamori, Kazoh. *Theology of the Pain of God.* English translation from the 5th ed. Richmond: John Knox, 1958.
McWilliams, Warren. "Divine Suffering in Contemporary Theology." *Scottish Journal of Theology* 33 (Feb. 1980): 35-53.
Michalson, Carl. *Japanese Contributions to Christian Theology.* Philadelphia: Westminster, 1960.
Surin, Kenneth. "The Impassibility of God and the Problem of Evil." *Scottish Journal of Theology* 35 (Apr. 1982): 97-115.

Kosuke Koyama (b. 1929)

Fleming, Kenneth. *Asian Christian Theologians in Dialogue with Buddhism.* New York: Peter Lang, 2002.

Irvin, Dale T., and Akintunde E. Akinade, eds. *The Agitated Mind of God: The Theology of Kosuke Koyama.* Maryknoll, N.Y.: Orbis, 1996.

Koyama, Kosuke. *Mount Fuji and Mount Sinai: A Critique of Idols.* Maryknoll, N.Y.: Orbis, 1985.

———. *Waterbuffalo Theology.* Maryknoll, N.Y.: Orbis, 1974.

Morse, Merrill. *Kosuke Koyama: A Model for Intercultural Theology.* New York: Peter Lang, 1991.

Choan-Seng Song (b. 1929)

Chan, Stephan T. "Narrative, Story and Storytelling: A Study of C. S. Song's Theology of Story." *Asia Journal of Theology* 12, no. 1 (Apr. 1998): 14-45.

Fleming, Kenneth. *Asian Christian Theologians in Dialogue with Buddhism.* New York: Peter Lang, 2002.

Sala, Ulisese. "An Attempt to Do Pacific Theology." *Pacific Journal of Theology,* n.s., 16 (1996): 7-13.

Song, C. S. *The Believing Heart: An Invitation to Story Theology.* Minneapolis: Fortress, 1999.

———. *Jesus and the Reign of God.* Minneapolis: Fortress, 1993.

———. *Jesus in the Power of the Spirit.* Minneapolis: Fortress, 1994.

———. *Jesus, the Crucified People.* Minneapolis: Fortress, 1996 [1989].

———. *Third-Eye Theology: Theology in Formation in Asian Settings.* Rev. ed. Maryknoll, N.Y.: Orbis, 1990.

Swami Vivekananda (1863-1902)

Radice, William, ed. *Swami Vivekananda and the Modernisation of Hinduism.* Oxford: Oxford University Press, 1999.

Reminiscences of Swami Vivekananda, by His Eastern and Western Admirers. Calcutta: Advaita Ashrama, 1964.

Rolland, Romain. *The Life of Vivekananda and the Universal Gospel.* Calcutta: Advaita Ashrama, 1960.

Vivekananda, Swami. *The Complete Works of Swami Vivekananda.* 8 vols. Calcutta: Advaita Ashrama, 1970-73.

Sarvepalli Radhakrishnan (1888-1975)

Minor, Robert. *Radhakrishnan: A Religious Biography.* Albany: State University of New York Press, 1987.

Radhakrishnan, S. *Eastern Religions and Western Thought.* Oxford: Oxford University Press, 1969 [1939].

Samartha, S. J. *Introduction to Radhakrishnan: The Man and His Thought.* New York: Association Press, 1964.

Schilpp, Paul Arthur, ed. *The Philosophy of Sarvepalli Radhakrishnan.* New York: Tudor, 1952.

Mahatma Gandhi (1869-1948)

Gandhi, Mohandas. *Essential Writings.* Selected with an introduction by John Dear. Maryknoll, N.Y.: Orbis, 2002.

———. *The Essential Writings of Mahatma Gandhi.* Edited by Raghavan Iyer. New York: Oxford University Press, 1993 [1991].

Radhakrishnan, S., ed. *Mahatma Gandhi: Essays and Reflections on His Life and Work.* Bombay: Jaico Publishing House, 1964.

Wadhwa, Madhuri. *Gandhi between Tradition and Modernity.* New Delhi: Deep and Deep Publications, 1991.

B. Upadhayaya (1861-1907)

Lipner, Julius. *Brahmabandhab Upadhyay: The Life and Thought of a Revolutionary.* Oxford: Oxford University Press, 1999.

Tennant, Timothy. *Building Christianity on Indian Foundations: The Legacy of Brahmabandhav Upadhyay.* Delhi: ISPCK, 2000.

Aiyadurai Jesudasen Appasamy (1891-1975)

Appasamy, A. J. *A Bishop's Story.* Madras: Christian Literature Society, 1969.

———. *Christianity as Bhakti Marga: A Study in the Mysticism of the Johannine Writings.* London: Macmillan, 1927.

———. *The Gospel and India's Heritage.* Madras: SPCK, 1942.

Francis, T. Dayanandan. "A. J. Appasamy: A Christian Forerunner of Inter-religious Dialogue in India." In *Keeping Hope Alive: Theological Insights from the Past for Today,* edited by J. Athyal, 113-32. Madras: Academy of Ecumenical Indian Theology and Church Administration, 1993.

Thangasamy, D. A. "Views of Some Christian Thinkers on Indian Conversion and Baptism." In *Religion and Society: The First Twenty-five Years, 1953-1978,* edited by Richard W. Taylor, 265-81. Bangalore: Christian Literature Society, 1982.

Pandipeddi Chenchiah (1886-1959)

John, Mathew P. "The Use of the Bible by Indian Christian Theologians." *Indian Journal of Theology* 14 (Apr.-June 1965): 43-51.

Thangasamy, D. A. "Significance of Chenchiah and His Thought." *Religion and Society* (Bangalore) 10 (Summer 1963): 27-35.

———. "Views of Some Christian Thinkers on Indian Conversion and Baptism." In *Religion and Society: The First Twenty-five Years, 1953-1978,* edited by Richard W. Taylor, 265-81. Bangalore: Christian Literature Society, 1982.

Vengal Chakkarai (1880-1958)

Chakkarai, V. *Jesus the Avatar.* Madras: CLS, 1926.

John, Mathew P. "The Use of the Bible by Indian Christian Theologians." *Indian Journal of Theology* 14 (Apr.-June 1965): 43-51.

Thangasamy, D. A. "Views of Some Christian Thinkers on Indian Conversion and Baptism." In *Religion and Society: The First Twenty-five Years, 1953-1978,* edited by Richard W. Taylor, 265-81. Bangalore: Christian Literature Society, 1982.

Thomas, P. T. *The Theology of Chakkarai: With Selections from His Writings.* Bangalore: Christian Institute for the Study of Religion and Society, 1968.

M. M. Thomas (1916-96)

Athyal, Jesudas M., ed. *M. M. Thomas: The Man and His Legacy.* Thiruvalla: Thiruvalla Ecumenical Charitable Trust, 1997.

Thomas, M. M. *The Acknowledged Christ of the Indian Renaissance.* London: SCM, 1969.

———. *Man and the Universe of Faiths.* Madras: CSL, 1975.

———. *My Ecumenical Journey, 1947-1975.* Trivandrum, India: P. M. Oommen of Ecumenical Publishing Centre, 1990.

Thomas, T. Jacob. *Ethics of a World Community: Contributions of Dr. M. M. Thomas Based on Indian Reality.* Calcutta: Punthi Pustak, 1993.

Stanley J. Samartha (1920-2000)

Aleaz, K. P. "Dialogical Theologies: A Search for an Indian Perspective." *Asia Journal of Theology* 6 (Oct. 1992): 274-91.

Anderson, Gerald H., and Thomas F. Stranksy, eds. *Mission Trends No. 3: Third World Theologies.* Grand Rapids: Eerdmans, 1976.

Jathanna, Constantine D., ed. *Dialogue in Community: Essays in Honour of Stanley J. Samartha.* Mangalore, India: Karnataka Theological Research Institute, 1982.

Klootwijk, Eeuwout. *Commitment and Openness: The Interreligious Dialogue and Theology of Religions in the Work of Stanley J. Samartha.* Zoetermeer: Uitgeverij Boekencentrum, 1992.

Samartha, Stanley J. *Between Two Cultures: Ecumenical Ministry in a Pluralist World.* Geneva: WCC, 1996.

———. *One Christ — Many Religions: Toward a Revised Christology.* Maryknoll, N.Y.: Orbis, 1991.

Raimon Panikkar (b. 1918)

Ahlstrand, Kajsa. *Fundamental Openness: An Enquiry into Raimundo Panikkar's Theological Vision and Its Presuppositions.* Uppsala: Swedish Institute for Missionary Research, 1993.

Panikkar, Raimon. *The Intrareligious Dialogue.* Rev. ed. Mahwah, N.J.: Paulist, 1999 [1978].

———. *The Cosmotheandric Principle: Emerging Religious Consciousness.* Edited with an introduction by Scott Eastham. Maryknoll, N.Y.: Orbis, 1993.

————. *The Unknown Christ of Hinduism.* London: Darton, Longman and Todd, 1968.

Prabhu, Joseph, ed. *The Intercultural Challenge of Raimon Panikkar.* Maryknoll, N.Y.: Orbis, 1996.

Thumma, Anthoniraj. *Breaking Barriers: Liberation of Dialogue and Dialogue of Liberation; The Quest of R. Panikkar and Beyond.* Delhi: ISPCK, 2000.

Arvind P. Nirmal (1936-95)

Balasundaram, Franklyn J. "The Contribution of A. P. Nirmal to Theology and Especially to Dalit Theology." *Religion and Society* (Bangalore) 45, no. 3 (Summer 1998): 84-100.

Devasahayam, V. "Doing Dalit Theology: Basic Assumptions." In *Frontiers of Dalit Theology,* edited by V. Devasahayam (Gurukul: ISPCK, 1997).

Jathanna, O. V. "Indian Christian Theology: Methodological Reflections." *Bangalore Theological Forum* 18 (Apr.-Summer 1986): 59-74.

Nirmal, Arvind P. "Towards a Christian Dalit Theology." In *A Reader in Dalit Theology,* edited by Arvind P. Nirmal. Madras: Gurukul Lutheran Theological College and Research Institute, 1991.

Sebastian, J. Jayakiran. "Creative Exploration: Arvind P. Nirmal's Ongoing Contribution to Christian Theology." *Bangalore Theological Forum* 31 (Dec. 1999): 44-52.

15   A Vigorous Dialogue

In some ways theology is questioning its own premises. This is evident in qualifying adjectives such as "postmodern," "nonfoundationalist," or "deconstructionist." They explicitly or implicitly admit that what was once seen as the unquestioned foundation of theology, such as revelation, dogma, or the word of God, can no longer be presupposed. These new theological nuances are but one sign of a vigorous dialogue in theology. Additionally, in other areas of scientific and intellectual pursuit, assumptions that were once considered certain have become shaky. Therefore members of these pursuits look for new dialogue partners to help them elucidate the way toward the future. We can see this most clearly in the notion of progress that once was unquestioned. But now we have noticed that it is no longer so clear what actual progress is, whether in societal restructuring or in the technological conquest. Then there is the astounding rejuvenation of other world religions. While barely fifty years ago some considered them hopelessly outdated and in continuous retreat, now other religions reassert themselves with increasing vigor, and pose a new challenge to Christian theology.

Yet this new situation also invites renewed dialogue. The most recent dramatic shift in Christian theology came in the late 1960s from the theology of hope, which expressed dissatisfaction with a dialectic thinking that seemed either static or to relegate theology to a ghetto experience. Wolfhart Pannenberg and Jürgen Moltmann have particularly taken the reins of this movement and emphasized the need for a new approach to theological discourse.

Theology of Hope: Jürgen Moltmann and Wolfhart Pannenberg

In 1967 **Jürgen Moltmann** (b. 1926) came out with a book that changed the theological landscape. In his *Theology of Hope: On the Ground and the Implications of a Christian Eschatology,* he emphasized that Christian theology is totally eschatological. At the same time, he showed his dissatisfaction with Karl Barth, for whom the eschatological moment, so to speak, comes vertically from above. Moltmann asserts that such an approach produces a static eschatology that threatens to relegate the eschatological moment to the so-called last things that some day will occur.

Moltmann writes with a passion. This is not unrelated to an experience in World War II. When he witnessed his hometown Hamburg in ruins, he cried out to God in anguish and despair. As a seventeen-year-old, he was drafted into the German armed forces toward the end of the war. Fortunately he survived and became a prisoner of war in Belgium and Scotland where he started his theological studies. These experiences thwarted his childhood dreams "to study physics and mathematics."[1] In 1948 he returned to Germany and began his theological studies at Göttingen. Here he did his doctorate on Christoph Pezel (1530-1604), a Reformed theologian from Bremen. He then served near Bremen as pastor until he became professor at the Theological Seminary (Theologische Hochschule) in Wuppertal in 1958. He joined the theological faculty in Bonn in 1963, and four years later went to the University of Tübingen, where he taught until his retirement in 1994.

Moltmann is one of the internationally best-known Reformed theologians. His books have been translated into many languages, and he has been amazingly productive far beyond retirement. While his writings cover nearly every facet of theology, he deliberately avoided writing a systematic theology. His emphasis is not on developing a system, but he addresses specific issues he believes are both timely and important with numerous treatises. Moltmann "has demonstrated an outstanding ability to appreciate and to integrate insights from the most varied sources, theological and otherwise."[2] This can be seen especially well from his largely autobiographical book *Experiences in Theology: Ways and Forms of Christian Theology* (1999; Eng. trans. 2000), where he admits in the preface that "the biographical dimension is an essential dimension of theological insight."[3] He

---

1. So in his enlightening autobiography "Lived Theology: An Intellectual Biography," *Asbury Theological Journal* 55 (Spring 2000): 9.

2. So rightly Richard Bauckham, *The Theology of Jürgen Moltmann* (Edinburgh: T. & T. Clark, 1995), x.

3. Jürgen Moltmann, *Experiences in Theology: Ways and Forms of Christian Theology,* trans. Margaret Kohl (Minneapolis: Fortress, 2000), xviii.

then indicates how his own theology has been shaped by his own person, by congregational and ecclesial life, by the university, and by all the other impacts, theological and otherwise, he has encountered in his life.

There are continuing themes in Moltmann's theology: first, the social concern for justice and then, not unrelated to it, the emphasis on hope. For Moltmann the doctrine of Christian hope "embraces both the object hoped for and also the hope inspired by it."[4] He no longer confines eschatology to discourse about the so-called last things that will happen in the end, but considers the whole cause that drives toward this end. Backed by the earlier thesis of Ernst Käsemann that "apocalyptic was the mother of all Christian theology,"[5] Moltmann claims that Christianity in its totality is eschatological, and nothing that pertains to it is exempt from this. With this he reiterates, of course, the famous dictum of Barth in his commentary on Romans: "If Christianity be not altogether thoroughgoing eschatology, there remains in it no relationship whatever with Christ."[6]

Moltmann distinguishes between the Israelite religion of promise and the static epiphanic religions in the environment of Israel. After the Israelites' conquest of Palestine, Yahweh still appeared as the promising God who pointed to a new future. This meant that the Old Testament promises were never superseded by historic events, but were constantly modified and expanded. Of course, some were realized in history. These "fulfilled" promises to which Israel owed its existence (the exodus, the Promised Land, David's kingship) proved, amid all the upheavals of history, to be a *continuum* in which Israel was able to recognize the faithfulness of its God. Yet, the promises were not completely resolved in any event, but there remained an overspill that pointed to the future. "The tension between promise and fulfillment was not left behind by the simple progression of Israel's history, but was much more strongly creative of Israel's historic progress."[7]

Moltmann sees the same feature in the New Testament, because the revelation in Christ is at the same time good news and promise. This revelation presupposes the law and promise of the Old Testament, since Yahweh (the God of Abraham, Isaac, and Jacob, the God of promise) resurrected Jesus, and Jesus was a Jew.

4. Jürgen Moltmann, *Theology of Hope: On the Ground and the Implications of a Christian Eschatology,* trans. J. W. Leitch (New York: Harper and Row, 1967), 16.

5. Ernst Käsemann, "The Beginnings of Christian Theology" (1960), in Ernst Käsemann, *New Testament Questions of Today,* trans. W. J. Montague (Philadelphia: Fortress, 1969), 102.

6. Karl Barth, *The Epistle to the Romans,* translated from the 6th edition by Edwyn C. Hoskyns (London: Oxford University Press, 1963), 314.

7. Moltmann, *Theology of Hope,* 112. References to this work are placed in the following text.

This means that Jesus is not to be understood as a particular case of humanity in general, but rather from the perspective of the Old Testament history of promise and in conflict with it. Jesus is not a *theos aner* (divine man) who descended from heaven and whose life on earth is only a temporary episode. On the contrary, Jesus' life, work, death, and resurrection have utmost significance and are described in the categories of expectation appropriate to the God of promise.

The Old Testament history of promise does not simply find its fulfillment in the gospel, but it finds its future in the gospel. Because the gospel is promise, it is a guarantee of the promised future (148). Here the centrality of Christ's resurrection for the Christian faith becomes evident. The resurrection of Christ is a "history-making event" from which all other history is enlightened, questioned, and transformed (180). The stories of the resurrection stand in the line of prophetic and apocalyptic expectations, hopes, and questions about what is bound to come according to the promises of God. Cross and resurrection point toward the future in promising the righteousness of God, the new life as a result of the resurrection from the dead, and the kingdom of God "in a new totality of being" (203).

Moltmann understands the Easter appearances as call appearances in which the recognition of Christ coincides with the recognition of his mission and his future. Again the forward thrust becomes noticeable. Moltmann concludes that for theology the reality of the world becomes historic in that theology's mission to the world is seen to be the field of the missionary charge and is examined in a search for real possibilities for the world-transforming missionary hope. "The call to obedient moulding of the world would have no object, if this world were immutable" (288). The world must be open toward the future for good or ill. Secularization has realized these Christian expectations in the field of world history and has outstripped the Christian hope in a chiliastic way. Thus we cannot reject the revolutionary progressiveness of the modern age; instead, we must incorporate the open horizons of modern history into the true eschatological horizon of the resurrection and thereby "disclose to modern history its true historic character" (303). The church cannot confine itself to serving individuals and acting as a conservative force, as society might expect it to. The task and mission of the church is determined by its own peculiar horizon — the eschatological expectation of the coming kingdom of God, the coming righteousness and the coming peace, and the coming freedom and dignity of all humanity. This means "the realization of the eschatological *hope of justice,* the *humanizing of* man, the *socializing* of humanity, *peace* for all creation" (329).

Moltmann's impressive approach makes eschatology meaningful for present-day life. He goes beyond Albert Schweitzer in pointing out that not only the proclamation of Jesus but all of biblical religion is totally eschatological in outlook. He rightly accuses the church of the past of leaving the earthly-eschatological anticipation of the kingdom of God too readily in the hands of "the fanatics and the sects" (329). In reacting against this evident neglect, however, Moltmann draws the future-directedness of eschatology so much into human reach that autonomous humanity will have trouble understanding that all its work is only of anticipatory character. That some accuse Moltmann of reintroducing a concept of the kingdom of God once advocated by liberal nineteenth-century German Protestantism is indicative of this evident danger.[8] This coincides with another observation. Moltmann moves so far away from a one-sided emphasis on the so-called last things to a total eschatological outlook that he almost forgets to mention these last things. And when he does, he describes them mostly as earthly, humanly engendered goals, such as peace for all creation and the socialization of all humanity.

In later writings Moltmann pursues the same topic from other angles. For instance, in *The Crucified God* (1972) he states at the outset: "The cross is not and cannot be loved. Yet only the crucified Christ can bring the freedom which changes the world because it is no longer afraid of death."[9] After developing a theology of the cross, Moltmann arrives at the conclusion that since the rejected Son of Man was raised up in the freedom of God, "faith in the resurrection becomes faith that raises up, wherever it transforms psychological and social systems, so that instead of being oriented on death they are oriented on life."[10] Even the theology of the cross therefore urges the psychological and political liberation of humanity.

Similarly, we read in his ecclesiology, *The Church in the Power of the Spirit* (1975): "Prayer for the Spirit makes people watchful and sensitive. It makes them vulnerable and stimulates all the powers of the imagination to perceive the coming of God in the liberation of man and to move into accord with it. This prayer therefore leads to political watchfulness, and political watchfulness leads to prayer."[11] Eschatology, for Moltmann, implies liberation in this world

---

8. Cf. Heinz Eduard Tödt, "Aus einem Brief an Jürgen Moltmann," in *Diskussion über die "Theologie der Hoffnung" von Jürgen Moltmann*, ed. Wolf-Dieter Marsch (Munich: Chr. Kaiser, 1967), 197. Yet Moltmann's own intentions are just the opposite. He wants to "restore the messianic character of hope of the Christian faith" to contradict and resist the tendency to turn the Christian faith into a civil religion. Cf. Jürgen Moltmann, *Politische Theologie — Politische Ethik* (Munich: Chr. Kaiser, 1984), 31.

9. Jürgen Moltmann, *The Crucified God: The Cross of Christ as the Foundation and Criticism of Christian Theology*, trans. R. A. Wilson and J. Bowden (New York: Harper, 1974), 1.

10. Moltmann, *The Crucified God*, 294.

11. Jürgen Moltmann, *The Church in the Power of the Spirit: A Contribution to Messianic Ecclesiology*, trans. M. Kohl (New York: Harper, 1977), 287.

in terms of political and economic liberation, human solidarity, solidarity with nature, and the struggle for hope. Moltmann rightly reminds us that eschatology leads to action instead of otherworldly passivity or resignation. But his almost exclusively sociopolitical emphasis reminds us too much of the vain human endeavors to establish a theocracy or an earthly utopia, so that we dare not assent to it without expressing a strong eschatological proviso to all such human pursuits.

In one of his most recent major writings, *The Coming of God*, while picking up on his emphasis in his previous *Theology of Hope*, he alleviates some of our fears. He still insists that Christian eschatology is not about apocalyptic final solutions, because its subject is not the end at all. "On the contrary, what it is about is the new creation of all things."[12] Eschatology does not focus on some kind of cataclysm, but again on hope: hope for eternal life, for the kingdom of God, for a new heaven and a new earth, and for the glory of God and what this hope effects. He wants to draw together the different horizons of hope into a single focus, "the cosmic Shekinah of God" (xiii). This cosmic dwelling of God in his creation is the eschatological goal. Therefore Moltmann puts forward "Advent as eschatological category, and the category Novum as its historical reverse side" (6). This means that the emphasis is not on what is going to happen somewhere out in the future, but the decisive facet is God's coming and his arrival. God's coming future enables a new human becoming. The arriving kingdom of God makes possible the conversion to this future. We notice here, again, as in all of his writings, the summons to action, yet a summons contingent on God's initiative. This becomes most evident in his extensive treatment of millenarian hopes.

While Moltmann rejects the secular millenarianism of the present that betrays a naive faith in progress, he also rejects a naive biblical apocalyptic millenarianism of a triumphalistic type. Yet he claims: "The 'Thousand Years' reign of Christ, 'the kingdom of peace,' is hope's positive counterpart to the Antichrist's destruction of the world in a storm of fire, and is indispensable for every alternative form of life and action which will withstand the ravages of the world here and now. Without millenarian hope, the Christian ethic of resistance and the consistent discipleship of Christ lose their most powerful motivation" (201). This means that without the hope that Christ will erect his kingdom and indeed does so in a visible way, we are in danger of losing our incentive to resist the forces of evil. Eschatology therefore provides, for Moltmann, the energizing power to form a contrast community to society. Similar to Barth's

---

12. Jürgen Moltmann, *The Coming of God: Christian Eschatology,* trans. Margaret Kohl (Minneapolis: Fortress, 1996), xi. References to this work are placed in the following text.

claim in his *Epistle to the Romans,* but this time carried through the different loci of the Christian faith, theology is thoroughly eschatological.

How far Moltmann distances himself from a traditional doctrine of the last things can be gleaned from his understanding of the last judgment. Judgment, he says, is the side of the eternal kingdom that is turned toward history. When he claims that in the last judgment all sins, every wickedness and every act of violence, the whole injustice of this murderous and suffering world, will be condemned and annihilated, one might still conclude that he espouses the twofold outcome in the traditional sense. Yet he means that only the negativity will be condemned and annihilated, and not those who committed acts of negativity. Therefore he states: "In the divine judgment all sinners, the wicked and the violent, the murderers and the children of Satan, the Devil and the fallen angels will be liberated and saved from their deadly perdition through transformation into their true, created being, because God remains true to himself, and does not give up what he has once created and affirmed, or allow it to be lost" (255). There will be a universal homecoming, which will include even the devil and the fallen angels. God's final victory therefore does not include any condemnation of what he has once created, but the condemnation and elimination of the negativity into which the created fell. God's judgment puts things right, and "in the truth of Christ it is the most wonderful thing that can be proclaimed to men and women" (255). Who could object to that kind of prospect? Whether that vision is not too optimistic remains to be seen. One thing, however, is certainly clear in Moltmann's view: the new creation will be universal and all-embracing. There are no dark spots left on the landscape.

It would be difficult to talk about Moltmann and not mention the neo-Marxist philosopher Ernst Bloch (1885-1977) and his three-volume work *The Principle of Hope* (1969; Eng. trans. 1986). Bloch showed that hope is a universal characteristic of humanity. From the first cry of a newborn baby to a tired old person waiting for eternal bliss, human existence is characterized by hope and a movement toward the future. Bloch's Jewish heritage and Marxist persuasion come together to allow him to advocate the human attainment of a new world. For Bloch, it is insignificant how one names this goal of human hope and human striving, be it eternal happiness, freedom, the golden age, a land of milk and honey, or union with Christ in the resurrection. All these symbols and pictures illuminate hope and lead it to the ultimate goal that no one has yet reached and that will be our actual "homeland." *"True genesis is not at the beginning but at the end."*[13]

---

13. Ernst Bloch, *The Principle of Hope,* trans. Nevil Plaice et al., 3 vols. (Cambridge: MIT Press, 1986), 3:1375.

Bloch goes beyond the primitive projection hypothesis of Feuerbach and claims that this projection (i.e., the future) is certainly our god.[14] God is the utopian hypostasis of unknown humanity, meaning a humanity that is still to be created. When complete identity between our true humanness and our present condition is reached, we will occupy the place of God and religion will cease to exist. Consequently, Bloch has no reason to be hostile toward religion, because it enlightens hope and gives it its direction. But the metaphysical dimension of religion is collapsed in the physical, since the future of the resurrected Christ and the future of God are the future of hidden humanity and the hidden world. Bloch thus offers a metareligion, *"transcending without any heavenly transcendence"* and conceiving the metaphysical as our ultimate goal in the physical.[15] Eschatology under these presuppositions becomes a fiction,[16] and we end up with a new earthly kingdom without God.[17]

Bloch is certainly right and realistic when he points to the discrepancy between our actual existence and our selfhood, between the individual and the society, and between humanity and nature, which has to be overcome if we want to attain the ultimate identity for which we are striving. But even if we concede to Bloch that achieving this identity is an attainable goal, we are still faced with the ultimate discrepancy between being and nothingness. Moltmann captures this deficiency very well: "All utopias of the kingdom of God or of man, all hopeful pictures of the happy life, all revolutions of the future, remain hanging in the air and bear within them the germ of boredom and decay — and for that reason also adopt a militant and extortionate attitude to life — as long as there is no certainty in face of death and no hope which carries love beyond death."[18] While Moltmann was inspired by this hopeful proposal and by the engagement Bloch showed, he discerned that without hope sanctioned and guaranteed by God, human striving will always come up short and end in failure or at least in having its things only half accomplished.

While Moltmann surprised the theological world with a book, it was only a small essay, "Dogmatic Theses on the Doctrine of Revelation" (1961), through which **Wolfhart Pannenberg** (b. 1928) received the immediate attention of the theological world. This was no surprise, since Pannenberg claimed: "In contra-

14. Cf. Jürgen Moltmann, "Hope and Confidence: A Conversation with Ernst Bloch," *Dialog* 7 (1968): 43.

15. Cf. Bloch, *The Principle of Hope*, 3:1288, in his discussion of Feuerbach.

16. So Gerhard Sauter, *Zukunft und Verheissung: Das Problem der Zukunft in der gegenwärtigen theologischen und philosophischen Diskussion* (Zürich: Zwingli Verlag, 1965), 354.

17. Cf. the striking title of Alfred Jäger's investigation into Bloch's eschatology: *Reich ohne Gott: Zur Eschatologie Ernst Blochs* (Zurich: EVZ-Verlag, 1969).

18. Moltmann, "Hope and Confidence," 49.

distinction to the special appearances of the Godhead, revelation in history is open to everyone. It has universal character."[19] With this claim Pannenberg wanted to direct our attention away from God's self-disclosure in the "ghetto" of a special salvation history toward God's self-disclosure in the open court of universal history. Pannenberg's shift was not just a rejection of Oscar Cullmann's emphasis on salvation history, because for him at least that kind of history provided the red thread by which one could make sense of history in general. Rather it was a rejection of the up-to-then prevailing existential history favored by Rudolf Bultmann, and Barth's abandoning the natural world in favor of God's total otherness. Pannenberg claims revelation can be maintained in the court of reason and by appealing to a universal history, and thus a Hegelian influence becomes discernible in his thinking.

There are other facets in Pannenberg's approach that associate him closely with Moltmann, namely, his claim in thesis 2: "Revelation is not comprehended completely in the beginning, but at the end of the revealing history."[20] History makes sense only when viewed from its end. For this perspective Jesus of Nazareth and his resurrection become crucial. As Pannenberg claimed: "The universal revelation of the deity of God is not yet realized in the history of Israel, but first in the destiny of Jesus of Nazareth, insofar as the end of all events is anticipated in his destiny."[21] The destiny of Jesus does not have a universal character just because the end of all history *was envisioned* in that destiny. This assertion taken by itself would only be a repetition of Schweitzer's claim that Jesus believed that with his life, or at least with his death, the end of the world would come, a belief Schweitzer said was never realized. Pannenberg, however, goes a decisive step further, stating that in Jesus the end of the world has indeed occurred in proleptic anticipation. What had been anticipated as the end and fulfillment of history, the resurrection of the dead, has in fact *happened* in a proleptic way in and with Jesus. Since the history came to its conclusion in the destiny of Jesus, this destiny is the key to our understanding of God's self-disclosure. The Christ event has truly eschatological character, since there is no further self-disclosure of God necessary beyond this event. At the end of the

19. Wolfhart Pannenberg, thesis 3 of "Dogmatic Theses on the Doctrine of Revelation," in *Revelation as History*, ed. Wolfhart Pannenberg, trans. D. Granskou (New York: Macmillan, 1968), 135. One should note, however, the sometimes inaccurate translation.

20. Pannenberg, "Dogmatic Theses" (thesis 2), 131.

21. Pannenberg, "Dogmatic Theses" (thesis 4), 139, translation mine. For the discussion of Pannenberg's concept of revelation in history, cf. also Wolfhart Pannenberg, "Insight and Faith," in *Basic Questions in Theology: Collected Essays*, trans. G. H. Kehm (Philadelphia: Fortress, 1970), 2:28-45, in his discussion with Paul Althaus; and "Redemptive Event and History," 1:15-80.

world there will only occur on a cosmic scale what happened in and with Jesus on an individual scale.

Jesus is the paradigm and the anticipation of our own future and at the same time the inspiration and possibility of living toward that future. In Jesus, God's love was announced to us before his kingdom had fully come. Thus the coming of the kingdom should not cause surprise or terror. Since Jesus announced it, we are able to open ourselves to God's future. We can find communion with him who decides the future of all things and can anticipate the final significance and essence of all things. Of course, the communion with God that is possible through Christ necessitates our active participation in his creative love that supports all creatures, grants them their limited duration, and brings them to fulfillment of life by relating them to one another. Immediately we notice the individual and social ethical implications of Pannenberg's approach to eschatology. Since we are able to participate proleptically in the promised future, we are encouraged to anticipate this future proleptically.

Yet Pannenberg cautions that Jesus was only the forerunner and herald of the still-imminent kingdom. Thus we should not destroy and disdain the values of past and present in the name of the future. Pannenberg reminds us: "The history of modern revolutions illustrates the fatal flaw in living so exclusively for the future that all cherishing and celebrating of the present are precluded."[22] Pannenberg cautions us not to pursue such unrealistic futurism, since the ultimate fulfillment of the coming kingdom is beyond our human power to effect. But he also reminds us that we are far from being relegated to inactivity. On the contrary, we are inspired to prepare the present for the future to come. Such preparation is the work of hope carried out by love and will make our present conditions more attuned to the promised future. Together with the world we live in, we must be open beyond ourselves to the future of God's kingdom.

Since Jesus is central to Pannenberg's understanding of history and also of God's self-disclosure, it comes as no surprise that his first major work was a Christology, *Jesus — God and Man* (1964; Eng. trans. 1968). Characteristic for him is the contextualization of Jesus. He demonstrates that Jesus' life and destiny can be appropriately understood only in the horizon of the Judeo-Christian tradition. From there he concludes that the resurrection indeed was and signified the end of history. He understands the resurrection of Jesus "as a historical event."[23] The reason for this claim is that the origin of early Chris-

22. Wolfhart Pannenberg, *Theology and the Kingdom of God,* ed. Richard J. Neuhaus (Philadelphia: Westminster, 1969), 126.

23. Wolfhart Pannenberg, *Jesus — God and Man,* trans. L. Wilkins and Duane A. Priebe (Philadelphia: Westminster, 1977), 98.

tianity can be properly explained only in the light of the eschatological hope in the resurrection from the dead based on the appearances of the resurrected one. For Pannenberg Christ's resurrection is no faith statement, but one based on historical research insofar as historical research can ascertain truthfulness of events like those entailing resurrection. Faith for Pannenberg is not believing something one could ascertain by reason, but trust in the faithfulness of God. To make Christology plausible for today, Pannenberg also traces the development of christological thinking from the decisions of the early church up to the present. It is one of the peculiarities of Pannenberg's thinking that he always argues from a traditio-historical context.

Since for Pannenberg theology has to assert itself within the context of the sciences, his next major work was *Theology and the Philosophy of Science* (1973; Eng. trans. 1976). For Pannenberg theology is the "science of God."[24] Since God is not an object matter among others, God can be approached only in an indirect way, and since "God is the all-determining reality, . . . everything which exists should be shown to be a trace of the divine reality. . . . Theology as the science of God would then mean the study of the totality of the real from the point of view of the reality which ultimately determines it both as whole and in its parts."[25] This means that God is essential for us so that we can recognize the whole of reality in its proper dimensions and context. Since our recognition of reality is always provisional, the secular sciences are not any more definitive than is theology. To the contrary, since theology considers all of reality and since it anticipates in the resurrection already the end of all history, it can even provide a deeper insight than do other sciences. Yet theology, too, has to wait till the end to see whether its projective anticipations are indeed true.

In his next major work, *Anthropology in Theological Perspective* (1983; Eng. trans. 1985), Pannenberg claims that the secular description of humanity must be deepened through another "theologically relevant dimension."[26] Secular knowledge therefore is only partial and incomplete unless it also considers a religious or theological dimension. Finally, Pannenberg summed up his whole enterprise in a three-volume *Systematic Theology* (1988-93; Eng. trans. 1991-98).

Who is this theologian who unashamedly claims both reason and revelation as proper domains of theology and challenges the secular sciences to take notice of an intrinsic religious dimension? Similar to Moltmann, Pannenberg

24. So Wolfhart Pannenberg, *Theology and the Philosophy of Science,* trans. Francis McDonagh (London: Darton, Longman and Todd, 1976), 297, where he entitles chap. 5 "Theology as the Science of God."

25. Pannenberg, *Philosophy of Science,* 302-3.

26. Wolfhart Pannenberg, *Anthropology in Theological Perspective,* trans. Matthew J. O'Connell (Edinburgh: T. & T. Clark, 1999 [1985]), 20.

encountered the cruel and tragic sides of World War II. Born in Stettin, in the heart of what once was Germany, less than two hours east of Berlin, now part of Poland, he and his family moved to Aachen, near the western border of Germany, and witnessed that city being engulfed by flames as a result of a British air raid. He even briefly served as a soldier in World War II at the age of sixteen, was taken prisoner by the British, and spent a few months in a prison camp. His father was a civil servant, and good schooling was a natural for him. Early he read Nietzsche and also Kant.

"On the sixth of January [1945], while I was walking back home from school (instead of using the train) — a somewhat lengthy walk of several hours — an extraordinary event occurred in which I found myself absorbed in the light of the setting sun and for one eternal moment dissolved in the light surrounding me. When I became aware again of my finite existence, I did not know what had happened but certainly knew that it was the most important event of my life."[27] This vision of his own finitude encountered by the infinite was so overwhelming that he even related this incident in an autobiographical sketch more than forty years later. It influenced him to enroll at Humboldt University in East Berlin in 1947, studying philosophy and theology, soon deciding "to be a theologian for the rest of my life."[28] He also seriously studied Marxism, but soon overcame his fascination with Marxist ideas. He has been allergic to them ever since, as is evidenced by his criticism of Latin American liberation theology. Then he continued his studies at Göttingen for a year, studying with Friedrich Gogarten and the Kantian philosopher Nicolai Hartmann (1882-1950). From there he went to Basel to study with Barth and also with the philosopher Karl Jaspers (1883-1969).

In 1950 he continued his studies at Heidelberg, where especially the Old Testament scholar Gerhard von Rad (1901-71) fascinated him. There he was also instrumental in forming the so-called Heidelberg Circle, a group of young theologians interested in the impact of Rad's exegetical vision on systematic theology. A good ten years later the group published *Revelation as History* (1961; Eng. trans. 1968), to which Pannenberg contributed his "Dogmatic Theses on the Doctrine of Revelation." Also the church historian Hans von Campenhausen (1903-89) and the Lutheran systematician Edmund Schlink (1903-84) were important for him. Under the latter he did his doctoral thesis, "Doctrine of Predestination of Duns Scotus in the Context of the Development of Scholasticism" (Die Prädestinationslehre des Duns Scotus im Zusammenhang der

---

27. Wolfhart Pannenberg, "An Autobiographical Sketch," in *The Theology of Wolfhart Pannenberg*, ed. Carl E. Braaten and Philip Clayton (Minneapolis: Augsburg, 1988), 12.

28. Pannenberg, "An Autobiographical Sketch," 13.

scholastischen Lehrentwicklung) (1954), at the early age of twenty-five, and only two years later his *Habilitation*, "Analogie und Offenbarung" (Analogy and Revelation). In 1958 he began his teaching career as professor of systematic theology at the Theological Seminary (Theologische Hochschule) at Wuppertal, where he, with Moltmann, taught for three years, at which point he was called to the University of Mainz. From 1967 to his retirement in 1994 he was at the University of Munich. He declined calls to Heidelberg and also to Harvard. Yet he had been a visiting professor at Harvard, Claremont, and Chicago, having his most attentive audience in America.

While Pannenberg claims that he "never became a Hegelian," he "decided that theology has to be developed on at least the same level of sophistication as Hegel's philosophy."[29] Indeed, the breadth of his undertakings has certainly a resemblance to Hegel, and also the unashamed wedding together of reason and revelation. Though sometimes he can be carried away, as when he compared the working of the Holy Spirit with the field theory in physics, he has been one of the most thought-provoking theologians of the latter part of the twentieth century, and by his astounding command of the history of thought and of theology also one of the most erudite. Nevertheless, he is not a highbrow intellectual but has a passion for ecumenical rapprochement, especially between Protestants and Roman Catholics. He has also served on the Faith and Order Commission of the World Council of Churches for many years.

Theocentric Theology: John Hick and Paul Knitter

Already in the 1960s Pannenberg reminded theology that it can no longer turn its back to the "urgent questions concerning Christianity as a religion amongst religions."[30] With reference to Paul Tillich's last public lecture in Chicago on "The Significance of the History of Religions for the Systematic Theologian" (1965), and to Ernst Troeltsch's history of religion approach to the Christian faith, Pannenberg asserts that we need a new theology of the history of religion. In the latter part of the twentieth century, the discussion about the place of Christianity among the world religions was forcefully placed on center stage through the writings of John Hick and Paul Knitter.

John Hick (b. 1922) was born in Scarborough, England, and first studied law at the University College in Hull. After being converted to evangelical

29. Pannenberg, "An Autobiographical Sketch," 16.

30. Wolfhart Pannenberg, "Toward a Theology of the History of Religions" (1962), in *Basic Questions in Theology*, 2:66-67.

Christianity, he enrolled at Edinburgh University to study philosophy, intending to become a Presbyterian minister. His education was interrupted by World War II, and in 1948 he graduated with an M.A. from Edinburgh; in 1950 he obtained a doctor of philosophy at Oxford University. His theological studies were done at Westminster Theological College at Cambridge (1950-53), after which he served as a Presbyterian minister in Northumberland. In 1956 he received a call as assistant professor of philosophy at Cornell University, Ithaca, New York. Only three years later he became professor of Christian philosophy at Princeton Theological Seminary, and in 1964 he returned to Cambridge University as a lecturer in divinity. Three years after that he was appointed professor of theology at the University of Birmingham in England, and finally from 1980 to 1992 he was professor of philosophy of religion at the Claremont School of Theology in Claremont, California.

While Hick has written on a variety of topics, from *Biology and the Soul* (Cambridge: University Press, 1972) to *The Ontological Argument for the Existence of God* (Macmillan, 1968), he concerned himself more than many others with the place of the Christian faith among the world's religions. He does not ignore the fact that "in many of our [British] cities now . . . Hindu and Sikh temples and Muslim mosques have been added to the Jewish synagogues which have long been there."[31] This presence of other religions on once exclusively Christian soil raises for him not just practical questions, but also fundamental theological ones regarding the Christian attitude toward the other world religions. For Hick, salvation is no longer contained in the notion that Christ had died for us on the cross and therefore God will forgive and accept us. According to Hick, "salvation consists in human beings becoming fully human, by fulfilling the God-given potentialities of their nature." This gradual growth is then "a slow and many-sided process" that is not just reserved for Christians, but open for everyone (79). Hick picks up here on Karl Rahner's notion of "anonymous Christians" and claims that "devout men and women of other faiths are in some hidden but saving sense Christians" (80). Hick calls for a "Copernican revolution" in our understanding of the religions. No longer is Christianity at the center of the universe of faith, while the other religions are judged according to their nearness or distance from it, but rather God is at the center, and we must see "both our own and the other great world religions as revolving around the same divine reality" (82).

Hick suggests that the differences between the variant forms of religious experience in thought should not be played down, but one should realize "that

---

31. John Hick, *The Second Christianity* (London: SCM, 1983 [1968]), 76. References to this work are placed in the following text.

the great world faiths embody different perceptions and conceptions of, and correspondingly different responses, to the Real or the Ultimate from within the major variant cultural ways of being human" (86). This means that fascinating differences but also a basic complementarity exist between the religious traditions.

Hick pointed out how such complementarity can be achieved in his book *Death and Eternal Life* (1976). He does not assume that once we die we will immediately reach our final destiny — being with God:

> The persisting self-conscious ego will continue to exist after bodily death. We shall not however, in most cases, attain immediately to the final "heavenly" state. Only those whom the religions call saints or buddhas or arhats or *jivanmuktas* have fulfilled the purpose of temporal existence, which is the gradual creation of perfected persons — their perfection consisting . . . in a self-transcending state beyond separate ego-existence. But those of us who die without having attained to our perfection continue further in time as distinct egos.[32]

If the human ego is immortal and still has to attain perfection, then Hick opts for "many lives in many worlds" (414). The problem of maintaining one's ego identity together with a growth through purposive life, according to Hick, seems "to be more easily accommodated by the theory of many lives in many worlds than by the idea of the immortal ego" (413). This could also include the possibility of repeated "re-becomings" in other spheres beyond this world. There could be a vertical rather than a horizontal reincarnation in which we develop to ever more perfected selves. For some it would mean reaching their perfection with one more life, for others with a few more, and for the worst, one should think in terms of tens or hundreds of lives. At the end the human individual becomes perfected by becoming more and more a person and less and less an ego. Hick then suggests this as our goal: "What Christians call the Mystical Body of Christ within the life of God, and Hindus the universal Atman which we all are, and mahayana Buddhists the self-transcending unity in the Dharma Body of the Buddha, consists of the wholeness of ultimately perfected humanity beyond existence of separate egos" (464). By weaving together different images of the major world religions, Hick provides a global religious eschatology.

Hick has reiterated over and over again his Copernican revolution in theology, away from the Christianity-centered universe of faith to a God-centered

---

32. John Hick, *Death and Eternal Life* (New York: Harper and Row, 1976), 399. References to this work are placed in the following text.

universe.[33] According to Hick, God is the sun from whom all light and life originate and whom all religions reflect in their own ways. Hick hypothesizes that God, the ultimate divine reality, revealed, in what Karl Jaspers called the axial period (ca. 800-500 B.C.), his presence and will to humanity through a number of especially sensitive and responsive persons, who in turn gave rise to different world religions, according to the history, culture, language, and climate of their particular time and place.[34]

Since Hick feels that it is unlikely "that Jesus thought of himself as God incarnate," it is no surprise that Hick was one of the editors of *The Myth of God Incarnate*.[35] The notion that a special human being is the "son of God," Hick claims, "is a metaphorical idea which belongs to the imaginative language of a number of ancient cultures."[36] The Christian tradition turned this metaphor into a metaphysical term pronouncing that Jesus is the second person of a divine Trinity. This resulted in the doctrine of the unique divine incarnation, which has led to a Christian imperialism and poisoned relationships with other religions. Today we see the Christian tradition as one of a plurality of contexts of salvation within which the transformation of human existence from self-centeredness to God-centeredness is occurring. It can no longer be claimed, since the empirical evidence stands against it, that "Christianity constitutes a more favorable setting for this transformation than other traditions."[37] We must be much more modest in our claims today. As Christians "we can revere Christ as the one through whom we had found salvation, without having to deny other points of reported saving contact between God and man. We can commend the way of Christian faith without having to discommend other ways of faith. We can say that there is salvation in Christ without having to say that there is no salvation other than in Christ."[38] Apparently Christ is just one voice among many.

How does Hick arrive at such a positive evaluation of the world religions? He believes each religion is a mixture of the influence of the divine

---

33. Cf. John Hick, *God and the Universe of Faiths* (London: Collins, Fount Paperbacks, 1977), 131.

34. Cf. John Hick, "Whatever Path Men Choose Is Mine," in *Christianity and Other Religions: Selected Readings*, ed. John Hick and Brian Hebblethwaite (Philadelphia: Fortress, 1980), 182-83.

35. Hick, "Whatever Path," 184.

36. For the quotation and the following see John Hick, *God Has Many Names* (Philadelphia: Westminster, 1982), 8.

37. John Hick, *Disputed Questions in Theology and the Philosophy of Religion* (London: Macmillan, 1993), 85.

38. Hick, "Whatever Path," 186.

spirit and of specific human traditions.[39] The divine spirit or the divine logos has been at work as long as there has been humanity and is still at work today as the various religious traditions increasingly interact with each other. Hick does not see himself as being unfaithful to the revelation of God's limitless love in Jesus when he conceives of this as only one particular disclosure of a universal reality. On the contrary, he feels he is taking "the universal reality of God's love seriously," since that love is extended to humanity in a multitude of ways.[40] Hick understands a Christian not as someone who conceives of Christ as the one in whom God disclosed himself in an unsurpassable way, but "as one who affirms one's religious identity within the continuing tradition that originated with Jesus."[41] There is no longer an ontological truth claim to be affirmed in terms of exclusivity, but a relational one in terms of affinity. There is no singular revelation, but a multivalent one, and the world's religions "are culturally-conditioned human responses to God's revelation."[42] Jesus is not *the* human face of God as if there were no others, but a human face alongside but not in competition with others.

For Hick the religions are "expressions of the diversities of human types and temperaments and thought forms."[43] For instance, Christian ideas have been formed within the intellectual framework provided by Greek philosophy, and the Christian church was molded as an institution by the Roman Empire and its systems of laws. "The Catholic mind reflects something of the Latin Mediterranean temperament and the Protestant mind something of the northern Germanic temperament."[44] Similar observations can be made about the other religions of the world. For Hick religion is not just a cultural phenomenon. It certainly is a way of life, but "we must insist that religion involves knowledge of God."[45] In the various forms of religious experience we have human encounters with the divine reality, and humans have developed theological doctrines or theories to conceptualize the meaning of those encounters.

While Hick is correct that each religious tradition "has constituted its own unique mixture of good and evil," he strongly asserts the nonabsoluteness

---

39. See for the following Hick, *The Second Christianity*, 88-89.

40. Hick, *The Second Christianity*, 92.

41. Hick, *Disputed Questions*, 55.

42. So correctly Gregory H. Carruthers, *The Uniqueness of Jesus Christ in the Theocentric Model of the Christian Theology of World Religions: An Elaboration and Evaluation of the Position of John Hick* (Lanham, Md.: University Press of America, 1990), 41.

43. John Hick, "The Outcome: Dialogue into Truth," in *Truth and Dialogue: The Relationship between World Religions*, ed. John Hick (London: Sheldon, 1974), 142.

44. Hick, "The Outcome," 141.

45. Hick, "The Outcome," 148.

of Christianity.[46] Yet with regard to a lively dialogue with other religions, he concedes: "We live amidst unfinished business; but we must trust that continuing dialogue will prove to be dialogue into truth, and that in a fuller grasp of truth our present conflicting doctrines will ultimately be transcended."[47] Hick can only advance hope and not much more except the assurance "that each of the great streams of faith within which human life is lived can learn from the others."[48] Indeed, by studying other religions one can always learn about one's own. Yet Hick must face the question why for such a gain one needs unilaterally to dismantle the Christian truth claim. Perhaps what is hidden behind his whole approach is that from the Judeo-Christian angle we have formed a historical consciousness, which makes us aware "of the historico-cultural limitation of all knowledge and religious beliefs, and the difficulty, if not impossibility, of judging the truth claims of another culture or religion on the basis of one's own."[49] While the Judeo-Christian tradition, at least in its Western form, has faced the Enlightenment, and consequently developed a historical consciousness that makes it critical of itself and of others, such historical consciousness is largely missing in other religions. There are no critical editions of the sacred writings of other traditions promulgated from within, and therefore the dialogue, though certainly needed, is usually offered from the Judeo-Christian side.

Many share Hick's sentiment that we must reconsider the claim of the uniqueness of the Christian faith. Historians of religions such as Wilfred Cantwell Smith (b. 1916) and Raimundo Panikkar could be cited here, as well as Stanley J. Samartha and Rosemary Radford Ruether. A most forceful and influential advocate of religious pluralism has been **Paul Knitter** (b. 1939), a Roman Catholic theologian who joined the Society of the Divine Word, a Roman Catholic missionary society, in 1958 with the intention of becoming a missionary. At the society's seminary in Illinois he received his B.A. degree in philosophy and was then sent to continue his studies at the Pontifical Gregorian University in Rome. He arrived there just at the beginning of Vatican II, and of course was fascinated by the new openness toward other religions, especially under the leadership of Karl Rahner. Knitter even experienced Rahner as visiting professor at the Gregorian University in 1965. Upon obtaining a B.A. in 1964 and two years later a licentiate in theology, he wanted to take up his doctoral studies with Rahner at

---

46. John Hick, "The Non-Absoluteness of Christianity," in *The Myth of Christian Uniqueness: Toward a Pluralistic Theology of Religions*, ed. John Hick and Paul Knitter (Maryknoll, N.Y.: Orbis, 1987), 30.

47. Hick, "The Outcome," 155.

48. So Hick, *God Has Many Names*, 136.

49. So correctly Paul Knitter, preface to *The Myth of Christian Uniqueness*, ix.

the University of Münster, but found out that somebody else had researched the topic on which he wanted to focus, namely, the Roman Catholic attitude toward other religions. He was then advised to treat the same topic with regard to Protestant theology. Therefore he moved to the Protestant Theological Faculty at the University of Marburg, and became the first Roman Catholic theologian to receive a doctorate from that institution. In his thesis he urged a more open dialogue and the study of other religions in order to overcome the negative attitude concerning the possibility of salvation in these religions.[50] Upon obtaining his doctorate, he started his teaching at the Catholic Theological Union in Chicago in 1972. Having left the Society of the Divine Word, he moved three years later to Cincinnati, to teach there as professor of theology in the religion department at Xavier University until his retirement in 2002.

It was about the time Knitter moved from Rahner to Panikkar and Hick that his book *No Other Name? A Critical Survey of Christian Attitudes toward the World Religions* (1985) appeared. In this publication Knitter contends that the name of Jesus Christ implies a language of personal commitment rather than ultimate truth. He proposes a theocentric model of Christology and asserts a relational uniqueness for Jesus in which Jesus is unique in his relationship with us, and therefore is not normative, but also not exclusive.[51] Knitter finds this theocentric Christology justified, since Jesus' original message was theocentric too. After Jesus' death and resurrection the focus shifted from a theocentric to a christocentric approach, since the proclaimer became the proclaimed. Yet "Jesus gave us no christology."[52] However, he seemed to feel and claim a special intimacy with God, a special sonship, and he had a deep awareness of God as his father that was in line with the Jewish tradition.

When the New Testament writers expressed their conviction that Jesus is exclusive or at least normative, saying there is "no other name" by which one can be saved (Acts 4:12) or that Jesus is the "only begotten Son of God" (John 1:14), one has to understand these claims, according to Knitter, in their historical and cultural context. In the classicist culture of that time, something had to have certain unchanging and normative qualities in order to be true and reliable.[53] Moreover, given the prevailing Jewish eschatological and apocalyptic thought patterns, it was natural that as a Christian one should interpret one's experience of God in Jesus as final and unsurpassable. Furthermore, we must

---

50. Cf. Paul Knitter, *Towards a Protestant Theology of Religions: A Case Study of Paul Althaus and Contemporary Attitudes* (Marburg: N. G. Elwert, 1974), 209.

51. Paul Knitter, *No Other Name? A Critical Survey of Christian Attitudes toward the World Religions* (Maryknoll, N.Y.: Orbis, 1985), 171-72.

52. Knitter, *No Other Name?* 174.

53. For the following see Knitter, *No Other Name?* 182-83.

consider the minority status of the Christians within the larger Jewish community and within the vast Roman Empire. To defend itself the community needed clear identity and total commitment. The doctrinal language that we encounter in the New Testament and that sets forth an exclusive and normative Christology should therefore be called "survival language"; it was necessary for the survival of the community. By defining Jesus Christ in absolute terms, by announcing him as the one and only savior, the early Christians cut out for themselves an identity different from that of all their opponents or competitors. Such language also evoked a total commitment that would seal them in the face of persecutional ridicule.[54] Since this context is not the same as our contemporary context, Knitter concludes, we can return to a theocentric Christology that is nonnormative and nonexclusive.

Knitter eventually moved beyond the nonnormative and nonexclusive to actual pluralism. As he claims, this shift was especially the experience of the "unbelievable and sometimes overwhelming religious richness . . . and a multitude of religions which since centuries had lived there and communicated with each other (on a practical level)."[55] For Knitter the starting point for dialogue is threefold: first, his experience with various religions living together in one and the same locality, then his deep empathy for the validity of other religious traditions, and finally his own Christian faith that he is not willing to abandon. Therefore he wants to foster a dialogue maintaining "the richness of pluralism without allowing it to disintegrate into the pap of relativism."[56] To attain such dialogue, Knitter claims that one must adopt a hermeneutics of suspicion, being hermeneutically suspicious of our given Christian positions concerning outsiders, because too often interpretations of Scripture and formulations of doctrine become ideology, "a means of promoting one's own interests at the expense of someone else's" (182).

Knitter suggests that we should give up the search or the claim of a "common ground" that different religions share. It may not even be true that we strive for the same in all religions or even have the same God. If we attempt to establish or distill a common essence or center, "we all too easily miss what is genuinely different, and therefore what is genuinely challenging or frightening, in other religions" (184). It may even be that there is not *one* ultimate behind all the world religions, but several ultimates. Against such radical pluralists as John

54. Knitter, *No Other Name?* 184.

55. So Paul Knitter in his enlightening autobiographical remarks in Paul F. Knitter, *Horizonte der Befreiung. Auf dem Weg zu einer pluralistischen Theologie der Religionen*, ed. Bernd Jaspert (Frankfurt am Main: Otto Lembeck, 1997), 22.

56. Paul Knitter, "Toward a Liberation Theology of Religions," in *The Myth of Christian Uniqueness*, 181. Page numbers of this essay have been placed in the text.

Cobb or Raimundo Panikkar, Knitter is not yet willing to give up completely a common starting point or a common ground. But he shifts the commonality from the *theos*, the divine, to the *soteria*, salvation. There he comes back again to his earlier publication, *No Other Name?* where he talked about a survival language. This survival language is actually an action language. According to Knitter, Jesus "was called 'one and only' or 'only begotten,' not *primarily* to give us definite theologico-philosophical statements, and not *primarily* to exclude others, but rather to urge the action or practice of total commitment to his vision and way" (196). This means the supposedly ontological language is actually a praxis-oriented language. Jesus wants to call us to action, and therefore in the center is not the issue of ontology but of activity.

This shift in emphasis goes together with Knitter's increasing concern with global responsibility, a notion that also shows the influence of Hans Küng and his global ethos.[57] While there is indeed a need for the world's religions to come together in a common search for peace and for assuming global responsibility, as Pope John Paul II showed by inviting leaders of various world religions to Assisi, Italy, for prayer, one wonders whether action is not also intrinsically related to being. The orthopraxis that Knitter advocates and he sees as possible for a pluralistic approach toward religions, cannot be engendered and maintained without an appropriate ontological foundation. Yet exactly the diversity in perceiving that foundation leads to all kinds of actions, from the medieval inquisition to the saintliness of Mother Teresa of Calcutta (1910-97), and from religiously motivated suicide bombings in Palestine to the brilliant Ottoman civilization under Suleiman the Magnificent (1494/95–1566). As in our perception the world is getting smaller and people are growing together, indeed Christian theology cannot escape the necessity of dialogue with other world religions to further the human good or at least human survival. To that extent we will see further attempts to foster dialogue with other religions.

Theology and Science: Ralph Wendell Burhoe, Ian Barbour, and Karl Heim

Toward the last part of the twentieth century, the dialogue between theology and science entered a new phase. While through the impact of scientific materi-

---

57. Cf. Paul Knitter, *One Earth Many Religions: Multifaith Dialogue and Global Responsibility*, preface by Hans Küng (Maryknoll, N.Y.: Orbis, 1995), but also his autobiographic remarks in *Horizonte der Befreiung*, 23, where he mentions his "friend and colleague Hans Küng" and his project "global ethos."

alism and exuberant evolutionary thinking nineteenth-century theology often found itself on the defensive, this sentiment changed drastically in the twentieth century. Especially through Karl Barth and his influence there was initially a clear demarcation between the scientific sphere and the religious one. One did not have much to do with the other. The consequence was that the dialogue between the two virtually ceased, at least on the European continent where Barth's influence was most clearly felt. Theology progressed in its own field and science conquered the world and often the minds of the people. Yet, since the 1960s there has been increasing disenchantment with science, as documented by the ecological movement. Far from guaranteeing human survival and well-being, the unimpeded expansion of scientific and technological progress seemed to threaten that very survival and well-being. Suddenly science was no longer perceived as the queen that presumably knew all the answers, but science itself was looking for answers, and that through more dialogue with other disciplines, such as theology and philosophy.

The person who fostered more than anyone else in the USA the dialogue between various scientific disciplines and theology was **Ralph Wendell Burhoe** (1911-97). He was born in Somerville, Massachusetts, into a "seriously pious family."[58] The Baptist tradition he inherited soon gave way to other influences, especially as he entered Harvard in 1928 and was confronted with Alfred North Whitehead and the legacy of William James. In 1932 Burhoe entered Andover Newton Theological School still intending to become a minister. But gradually his vocational desires changed and he found employment at the Blue Hill Meteorological Observatory of Harvard University, where he studied meteorology and climatology as an undergraduate. From 1947 to 1964 he was an executive officer of the American Academy of Arts and Sciences (AAAS).

It was during his time at the AAAS that Burhoe was instrumental in founding the Institute on Religion in an Age of Science (IRAS, 1955). This institute was intended to bring together the different departments of human understanding because "any doctrine of human salvation cannot successfully be separated from realities pictured by science."[59] Beyond that it sponsored the annual conference on "Religion in an Age of Science," or the Star Island Conferences held on Star Island off Portsmouth, New Hampshire. There were also other conferences and seminars, a publication program, lectures and seminars at colleges and theological schools, and the development of a center for re-

---

58. So David R. Breed, "Ralph Wendell Burhoe: His Life and His Thought I," *Zygon* 25 (1990): 323; hereafter "Ralph Wendell Burhoe I."

59. According to the "Statement of Purpose" as reprinted in Breed, "Ralph Wendell Burhoe I," 348.

search and advanced study at the Unitarian Meadville/Lombard Theological School in Chicago. This means that Burhoe's vision of a new natural theology based on science was most receptively welcomed by the Unitarian Universalist Association.

In 1966 *Zygon: Journal of Religion and Science* was founded by Burhoe at the Meadville/Lombard Theological School. That same year the Center for Advanced Study in Theology and the Sciences (CASTS) was also established, also at Meadville/Lombard. In 1972 the center was renamed the Center for Advanced Study in Religion and Science (CASIRAS). In 1972 Burhoe retired from Meadville, and in 1980 he received the Templeton Prize for progress in religion. In 1988 CASIRAS joined with the Lutheran School of Theology at Chicago (LSTC) to establish the Chicago Center for Religion and Science under the leadership of theologian Philip Hefner (b. 1932) and physicist Thomas Gilbert (b. 1922). LSTC is now also the home for *Zygon* and for the Annual Chicago Advanced Seminar in Religion and Science that Burhoe began at Meadville in 1966.

The Templeton Prize, established in 1972 by the American financier John M. Templeton (b. 1912), is the world's largest annually bestowed monetary award. It is designed "to stimulate the knowledge and love of God on the part of mankind everywhere."[60] Other recipients have been the theologians Thomas F. Torrance (1978), Stanley L. Jaki (1987), Ian Barbour (2000); the philosopher Carl Friedrich von Weizsäcker (1989; b. 1912); and the scientists Arthur Peacocke (2001; b. 1924), Paul Davies (1995; b. 1946), and John Polkinghorne (2002; b. 1930), among others.

Burhoe considered religion from a socioevolutionary perspective as "an evolving cultural art whose function is to orient us to the ultimate goals and conditions for life at the top of the hierarchy of values."[61] To attain that kind of orientation, Burhoe advocated a rational interpretation of religion in the light of the sciences. In so doing, we can mine the insights of the sciences to enlighten the human mind and to further the essential role of humanity for human welfare. The most important accomplishment of Burhoe was to facilitate dialogue among theologians and scientists of often quite different ideological religious and theological persuasions, albeit within the context of the Judeo-Christian tradition. His journal *Zygon* achieved a circulation far beyond the confines of theological journals.

---

60. According to the Templeton Foundation, as reprinted in David R. Breed, "Ralph Wendell Burhoe: His Life and Thought V," *Zygon* 26 (1991): 420; hereafter "Ralph Wendell Burhoe V."

61. So Breed, "Ralph Wendell Burhoe V," 411.

The actual grand seigneur of the dialogue between theology and science, in North America at least, is **Ian Barbour** (b. 1923). He combined theology and the sciences in his own training, similar to though more extensively than Burhoe. Barbour received a bachelor of science degree from Swarthmore College (1943), a master of science degree in physics from Duke University (1946), and a Ph.D. in physics from the University of Chicago (1950). His theological studies were done at Yale University, where he received a B.D. in 1956. He started out teaching in the department of physics at Kalamazoo College in Michigan (1949-53), then moved to Carleton College in Northfield, Minnesota, where he taught in the department of religion from 1955 to 1973 and became professor of religion and physics and director of the program in science, ethics, and public policy (1974-89). His most influential book was *Issues in Science and Religion* (1966), which was also translated into Spanish (1971) and Chinese (1993).

In this widely used textbook Barbour first traces the relationship between religion and science from the seventeenth century to the present, focusing in the seventeenth century on Galileo and Newton and in the eighteenth century on the Age of Reason, the romantic reaction and the responses by Hume and Kant. In the nineteenth century Darwin occupies center stage, while in the twentieth century Barbour moves from neoorthodoxy to process philosophy. In a second part, Barbour lays out the different methods employed by science and religion, concluding that both science and religion are selective as to their focus of interest. Then he shows the differences in the methods of the two fields. For instance, the degree of personal involvement is greater in religion than in science, because "revelation in historical events has no parallel in science" and "the intersubjective testability of religious beliefs is severely limited as compared to that of scientific theories or even scientific paradigms."[62]

Barbour also maintains that the contrast between science and religion is "*not as absolute as most recent theologians and philosophers have maintained*" (268). Yet he does not want to merge religion and science into a new kind of natural theology, but endeavors to present a theology of nature. Therefore he focuses in a third part on physics and indeterminacy, on humanity and nature, on evolution and creation, and finally on God and nature, concluding with the process views of Whitehead and Hartshorne. While Barbour shows an affinity to process theology in his own theology of nature, he "makes no attempt to set aside Christian beliefs" as he sees John Cobb doing in his Christian natural theology (453-54 n. 45). For Barbour "the context of theological discourse is always the worshipping community," and therefore "theology must start from historical

---

62. Ian Barbour, *Issues in Science and Religion* (Englewood Cliffs, N.J.: Prentice-Hall, 1966), 267. Page numbers from this work are in the text.

revelation and personal experience." Yet it must also include a theology of nature that does not disparage or neglect the natural order (453). Since the scientific laws are selective, abstract, and often statistical, Barbour sees no problem stating that God acts in history and nature. But he does not see this activity occurring in such a way that God's contribution can be separated from other causes. To the contrary, God acts in, with, and under other causes. This position, according to Barbour, seems to have been most convincingly advanced by Whitehead's vision of God's persuasive activity at various levels in the processes of this world.

While secular humanity trusts science and not God to fulfill its needs, Barbour feels this attitude is shortsighted. Though our mastery and control of nature has "considerable biblical support," Barbour points out that "without the concomitant biblical ideas of care and respect for nature," dominion can easily turn "into arrogance and ruthless subjugation."[63] Therefore, it is important to heed the biblical message that holds up "both an ideal of social justice and a model of man as a responsible self" lest our technological society become more and more unjust and also potentially self-destructive.[64] It is characteristic of Barbour that he considers both the dogmatic and the ethical aspect of the relationship between theology and science. He does not solely focus on how to relate God, creation, and humanity, but is also concerned with our ways of using science and of changing the world in which we live. Therefore it was not surprising that in his Gifford Lectures of 1989-91 Barbour spoke on both religion in an age of science and ethics in an age of technology.

The first part of the Gifford Lectures *(Religion in an Age of Science)* resembles his earlier book *Issues in Science and Religion*. This time he offers no historical introduction, but starts immediately by comparing religion and science and also indicating four ways of relating science and religion: conflict, independence, dialogue, and integration. Then he moves to specific issues in the discourse between the two fields, such as physics and metaphysics, astronomy and creation, evolution and continuing creation, human nature and God and nature. A special chapter is devoted to process thought because he still advocates the process model, believing that it "seems to have fewer weaknesses than the other models."[65] In the process model

> God is a creative participant in the cosmic community. God is like a
> teacher, leader, or parent. But God also provides the basic structures and

63. Ian Barbour, *Science and Secularity: The Ethics of Technology* (New York: Harper and Row, 1970), 7.

64. Barbour, *Science and Secularity*, 140.

65. Ian Barbour, *Religion in an Age of Science: The Gifford Lectures, 1989-1991* (San Francisco: HarperSanFrancisco, 1990), 1:270.

the novel possibilities for all other members of the community. God alone is omniscient and everlasting, perfect in wisdom and love, and thus very different from all other participants. Such an understanding of God, I have suggested, expresses many features of the religious experience and the biblical record, especially the life of Christ and the motif of the cross. Process thought is consonant with an ecological and evolutionary understanding of nature as a dynamic and open system, characterized by emergent levels of organization, activity, and experience.[66]

It is characteristic of Barbour that he does not give a wholehearted endorsement to process theology, but always argues carefully for the biblical basis of a theology of nature. Typical for process thought, however, Barbour rejects the notion of a creation out of nothingness, which means there was nothing prior to creation except God's own self. But much more important for him is that process thought avoids the dualisms of mind and body, of humanity and nature, and of history and nature.[67] Also, the ecological sensitivity of process theology is significant for Barbour. This becomes especially evident in the second part of his Gifford Lectures, which focuses on ethics.

The nineteenth century generally assumed that science-based technology would automatically lead to progress and improvement in human life. Indeed, we have witnessed that modern technology has increased food production, improved health, provided higher living standards and better communication. But at the same time, environmental and human costs have been increasingly evident. Therefore Barbour gives no unilateral endorsement nor a latent condemnation of technological progress. As he considers critical technologies with regard to agriculture, energy, computers, and at the same time looks at human and environmental values, it becomes clear for him that we must redirect technology so that humanity and the environment are not the victims but the beneficiaries of technological progress. Since the churches have usually supported the status quo but have also contributed to social change, Barbour is convinced that they "will have to change drastically if they are to facilitate the transition to a sustainable world."[68] More important for him, however, are certain biblical images still having significant power to evoke responses in humanity. There is first the prophet's commitment to justice stemming from a belief in the fundamental equality of all persons before God. Then there is the prophetic view that

---

66. Barbour, *Religion*, 1:269.

67. Cf. Barbour, *Religion*, 1:144-45 and 269.

68. Ian Barbour, *Ethics in an Age of Technology: The Gifford Lectures, 1989-1991* (San Francisco: HarperSanFrancisco, 1993), 2:261.

the whole of creation is part of God's purpose, and that we are accountable for the way we treat all forms of life.

Barbour looks for a new vision of the good life. He takes his cues from the biblical literature where good life is identified with personal existence in community and not with material possessions. The Bible recognized "the dangers of both poverty and affluence" and advocated the dignity of the individual and "the importance of interpersonal relationships." Here the Bible "offers a distinctive view of *persons in community* which avoids both collectivism and individualism"[69] and also asserts the ideal of simplicity. Again, Barbour looks for process theology, which asserts against a prevailing anthropocentrism "the interdependence of all beings and the intrinsic value of nonhuman life."[70] While Barbour sees that there are new opportunities for change toward a more just and sustainable world, there are also still enormous obstacles, such as individual and institutional greed, or the political power of corporations and bureaucracies with a vested interest in the status quo.

Barbour offers a balanced view both to the possibilities of dialogue between theology and science and also toward necessary changes we must make in our perception of both theology and applied science and technology. Barbour's lifelong engagement in the dialogue between theology and science earned him not only academic recognition in the English-speaking world, notably in North America, but also the monetary award and concomitant public recognition of the Templeton Prize for progress in religion.

The Templeton Foundation has been especially beneficial in fostering the dialogue between theology and science through its manifold programs, such as awards for courses in science and religion, or the Templeton Book Award for writings in theology and science. As generous as this program of the Templeton Foundation is, it also indicates that theological interests can be directed and fostered through financial rewards. Still, it must be said that the most creative minds in science, starting with Isaac Newton (1642-1727), Albert Einstein (1879-1955), and Stephen Hawking (b. 1942), in one way or other were always directed to ultimate issues beyond the physical world. This may indicate that the bifurcation between theology and science, which Barth advanced for theology's own self-protection, is no panacea, but only a temporary remedy. This has also been shown by one of Barth's German-speaking contemporaries, Karl Heim.

Karl Heim (1874-1958) is a rather solitary figure in German theology. He is one of the few who came out of a pietistic environment and basically remained a pietist throughout his life, something that did not endear him to his more criti-

69. Barbour, *Ethics,* 2:262.
70. Barbour, *Ethics,* 2:263.

cally minded colleagues. Nevertheless, he pursued the dialogue with the sciences with an intellectual rigor that was unparalleled during the first half of the twentieth century. Born in a parsonage in Württemberg, he studied theology at Tübingen (1892-96) and stayed at the Evangelische Stift as David Friedrich Strauss and Ferdinand Christian Baur had done. In 1899 he received his doctorate in philosophy at Tübingen with the thesis "The Theory of Knowledge and the Logic of Thomas Hobbes" (Die Grundzüge der Erkenntnistheorie und Logik von Hobbes). Then he served three years as traveling secretary of the evangelical student mission, and subsequently became tutor at a residence for theology students at Halle through the influence of Martin Kähler. In 1905 he got his licentiate in theology, again at Tübingen, with a thesis published as *The World View of the Future: A Discussion between Philosophy, Natural Science, and Theology* (*Das Weltbild der Zukunft. Eine Auseinandersetzung zwischen Philosophie, Naturwissenschaft und Theologie*, 1904). While most of his teachers did not think much of this book, it was greeted with enthusiasm by the students.[71] Here was a book by a theologian who sensed that with Einstein's work on relativity in 1905, the traditional causal mechanistic worldview of the nineteenth century had come to an end. He claimed: "We have lost our faith in matter."[72] Instead of a worldview based on the eternity of matter, Heim proposed an energetic worldview, which was dynamic and open toward the future.

In 1906 Heim did his *Habilitation* at the University of Halle with a thesis entitled "The Essence of Grace and Its Relationship to the Natural Functions of Humanity in Alexander of Hales" (Das Wesen der Gnade und ihr Verhältnis zu den natürlichen Funktionen des Menschen bei Alexander Halesius) (published in 1907). Since his first book, *The World View of the Future*, was such a success with the students and since they also flocked to his offerings at Halle, Heim wanted to enter academia. Yet his teachers were not impressed with him, especially since he was more popular with the students than some of them were. Yet a new faculty for Protestant theology was established at the University of Münster. The Prussian ministry of education in Berlin wanted to call professors who could attract students, and without the blessings of a professorial call committee, called Heim as professor of dogmatics in 1914.

In 1920 Heim received a call back to his alma mater, the University of Tübingen. Again it was not the theological faculty or even the senate of the university who called him, because both wanted Rudolf Otto, whose book *The Holy*

---

71. Karl Heim, *Ich gedenke der vorigen Zeiten. Erinnerungen aus acht Jahrzehnten*, 3rd ed. (Hamburg: Furche, 1960 [1957]), 103-4.

72. Karl Heim, *Das Weltbild der Zukunft. Eine Auseinandersetzung zwischen Philosophie, Naturwissenschaft und Theologie* (Berlin: C. A. Schwetschke, 1904), 144.

had just become popular. Again the secretary of education preferred Heim and gave the call to him, though he had only been in second place on the list submitted by the university.[73] During the twenty years he was active in Tübingen, his lectures were often given to overflowing classrooms and were often transmitted by loudspeaker into the neighboring classroom to accommodate the students. At the same time, he was preacher at the main church in Tübingen, the Tübinger Stiftskirche, and there again one needed to be there one hour ahead of time to obtain a seat in the large sanctuary. Heim was so attractive to students that when he took a sabbatical, many rooms that the townspeople of Tübingen rented out to students were left vacant, and he was asked not to take another sabbatical. Heim's reputation went beyond Germany. In 1937 the president of Princeton Theological Seminary, John Mackay (1889-1983), asked Heim to accept a call to the chair in theology that once Charles Hodge had occupied. Since Heim saw a major war threatening (World War II), he did not want to leave Germany, and similar to Dietrich Bonhoeffer, whom Union Theological Seminary in New York wanted to call, he declined with much regret.[74]

What made Heim so important for the dialogue between theology and science? We will at once notice this when we look at his six-volume main work, *The Evangelical Faith and Present-Day Thought* (*Der Evangelische Glaube und das Denken der Gegenwart*, 1931-52). While volumes 2 and 3 focus on Christology, volumes 4 and 5 are devoted to the dialogue between theology and science, as to a large extent is volume 6. The first volume focuses on whether transcendence is even thinkable. In it, *God Transcendent: Foundation for a Christian Metaphysic* (1931; rev. ed. 1934; Eng. trans. 1935), Heim introduces a dimensional view of the world and shows that transcendence is indeed a possibility in that worldview. God has not become homeless through the Copernican revolution, because God does not occupy a distinct space. Rather God must be associated with a certain dimension that is higher than the space-time configuration we occupy. While God's dimension includes all our possibilities, there are also possibilities available for God that transcend our own ways. Since a higher dimension always encloses a lower one, not the other way round, there is no way possible from us to God but only from God to us. Therefore God's self-disclosure becomes crucial if we want to know anything about God at all.

In volume 4, *Christian Faith and Natural Science* (1949; Eng. trans. 1953), Heim extensively discusses our present-day understanding of nature. Themes he took up in volume 1 are analyzed more extensively, for instance the fact that in this

---

73. According to Adolf Köberle, *Karl Heim. Denker und Verkündiger aus evangelischem Glauben* (Hamburg: Furche, 1973), 21, who was Heim's successor in Tübingen.

74. Cf. Heim, *Ich gedenke der vorigen Zeiten*, 292-98.

world we are always confronted with polarities, such as the either-ors of "I" and "it," of "I" and "you," of "yes" and "no," or of "here" and "there." These polarities often cause conflict and anxiety for us, but they cannot be solved within the dimensions we occupy. Yet God presents a superpolar dimension in which they are seen in an entirely new light and are brought to a resolution. But there are also new topics that find extensive treatment in this volume, for instance reincarnation and panpsychism, meaning everything in nature has some kind of soul, and also the issue of space in physics. Even the personhood of God, natural law, and orders of creation are touched on, topics dealing with behavioral science that have again gained attention. In volume 5, *The Transformation of the Scientific World View* (1951; Eng. trans. 1953), the dialogue with the sciences occupies center stage. Here we are confronted with the momentous changes introduced by the scientific discoveries at the beginning of the twentieth century, especially quantum mechanics and the theory of relativity. Also, the problem of causality gains special attention. In the light of present-day science, the issue of miracles and the enigmatic character of life are extensively discussed. While in the nineteenth century one either held that there was a causal nexus that determined everything without exception or simply believed that God can break through this causal nexus, such either-or is no longer necessary according to modern physics. In its innermost being nature is no longer strictly determined, but reminds us in its structure of the processes of life. Since "the process of nature in its deepest essence is not a dead mechanism whose course is laid down in fixed terms, but that is something which in some sense is alive; something which man can influence by the interposition of the will in the same way in which he can affect a human opponent," miraculous events can be understood as issuing forth from a will.[75]

The space with which we are confronted in our present reality is the space of objectivity. By objectively viewing this space, be it the huge dimensions of the cosmos or the minute dimensions of the human selves, we notice that the events in nature always occur according to certain laws. At the same time, we remember that the smallest building blocks of nature can no longer be completely and satisfactorily understood with the traditional concepts of causality. Heim concludes that therefore the macrocosmic order that is still binding for us is no arbitrary fate, but behind it is "always the one all-sovereign personality of the living God who guides all things."[76] So we can either stay with the order itself as an impersonal fate or look behind it and perceive God's personal guidance.

If we reject God, our existence and the world around us become totally ar-

75. Karl Heim, *The Transformation of the Scientific World View*, trans. W. A. Whitehouse (London: SCM, 1953), 174.
76. Heim, *Transformation*, 160.

bitrary. They make no sense whatsoever unless we endow them with some self-chosen meaning. This either-or can be seen most clearly in modern cosmology. Heim pointed this out in the last installment of his six-volume main work, *The World: Its Creation and Consummation; The End of the Present Age and the Future of the World in the Light of the Resurrection* (1952; Eng. trans. 1962). According to modern cosmology, the whole course of the universe "is merely an episode which appears out of nothingness and disappears again into nothingness, leaving no trace behind."[77] People shut out this depressing scenario generally by not reflecting upon it and in plunging into their obligations and joys in the present moment. According to Heim, we cannot escape this nihilistic sentiment on our own. A different and well-founded interpretation can only be offered to us as a gift, as the first Christian community experienced at Easter when its pessimism and anxiety were changed to optimism and confidence. Jesus Christ "emerged from the grave in complete bodily form. It is of essence of a transformation that the first body, which is the subject of the transformation, enters entirely into the new state and that nothing remains unchanged."[78] This new bodily form is immensely superior to the lethal form of the present world, and it commences with a totally new creation. This resurrection is the beginning of a new era that will change the whole universe in such a way that it will be totally transformed.

Heim, who had been influenced since his youth by Kant's distinction between the phenomenal and the noumenal, showed with convincing clarity that we cannot reach God on our own. Yet he also learned from Kant that God, immortality, and life eternal are essential for humans if they want to resolve the tension in which they find themselves in this life. Therefore Heim focused all his energy on pointing out that this religious dimension is not just a practical necessity, but something that indeed belongs intrinsically to our world as its presupposition, its undergirding, and as its goal. In this way the claim by Pannenberg that the scientific findings need a deepening and enlargement and Heim's insistence on the either-or of despair or Christian faith are quite similar in their intentions. Some of Heim's arguments seem even more modern than those of Pannenberg; for instance, his dimensional thinking borrowed from geometry provides more conceptual possibilities for a scientist to leave space for God than does Pannenberg's field theory.[79] It is not without significance that in a thorough review of Heim's works Barbour calls his dimensional thinking "a

77. Karl Heim, *The World: Its Creation and Consummation; The End of the Present Age and the Future of the World in the Light of the Resurrection*, trans. Robert Smith (Philadelphia: Muhlenberg, 1962), 149.

78. Heim, *The World*, 146.

79. Cf. John Polkinghorne's comments on Pannenberg's field theory in "Wolfhart Pannenberg's Engagement with the Natural Sciences," *Zygon* 34 (1999): 153-55.

valuable attempt to provide intellectual ground for the possibility of revelation."[80] Heim never was interested in founding a certain school of thought; however, he influenced a whole generation of pastors and many laypeople, among them many scientists. It is also noteworthy that in recent years doctoral theses have repeatedly focused on his work, since on the European continent, too, the dialogue between theology and the sciences gains renewed momentum.[81]

FOR FURTHER READING

Jürgen Moltmann (b. 1926)

Bauckham, Richard. *The Theology of Jürgen Moltmann.* Edinburgh: T. & T. Clark, 1995.

Moltmann, Jürgen. *The Church in the Power of the Spirit: A Contribution to Messianic Ecclesiology.* Translated by M. Kohl. New York: Harper, 1977.

―――. *The Coming of God: Christian Eschatology.* Translated by Margaret Kohl. Minneapolis: Fortress, 1996.

―――. *The Crucified God: The Cross of Christ as the Foundation and Criticism of Christian Theology.* Translated by R. A. Wilson and J. Bowden. New York: Harper, 1974.

―――. *Experiences in Theology: Ways and Forms of Christian Theology.* London: SCM, 2000.

―――. *Theology of Hope: On the Ground and the Implications of a Christian Eschatology.* Translated by J. W. Leitch. New York: Harper and Row, 1967.

Müller-Fahrenholz, Geiko. *The Kingdom and the Power: The Theology of Jürgen Moltmann.* Minneapolis: Fortress, 2001.

Wolfhart Pannenberg (b. 1928)

Albright, Carol Rausch, and Joel Haugen, eds. *Beginning with the End: God, Science, and Wolfhart Pannenberg.* Chicago: Open Court, 1997.

Braaten, Carl E., and Philip Clayton, eds. *The Theology of Wolfhart Pannenberg.* Minneapolis: Augsburg, 1988.

Pannenberg, Wolfhart. *Anthropology in Theological Perspective.* Translated by Matthew J. O'Connell. Edinburgh: T. & T. Clark, 1999 [1985].

---

80. Ian G. Barbour, "Karl Heim on Christian Faith and Natural Science," *Christian Scholar* 39 (Sept. 1956): 237.

81. Cf. Atso Eerikäinen, *Time and Polarity: The Dimensional Thinking of Karl Heim* (Helsinki, 2000), and Thomas Kothmann, *Apologetik und Mission. Die missionarische Theologie Karl Heims als Beitrag für eine Missionstheologie der Gegenwart* (Neuendettelsau: Erlanger Verlag für Mission, 2001). Verena Grüter, *Begegnung mit dem göttlichen Du — Karl Heims Christologie im theologiegeschichtlichen Kontext* (Hamburg: Dr. Kovac, 2000).

————. *Jesus — God and Man.* Translated by L. Wilkins and Duane A. Priebe. Philadelphia: Westminster, 1977.

————. *Theology and the Kingdom of God.* Edited by Richard J. Neuhaus. Philadelphia: Westminster, 1969.

————. *Theology and the Philosophy of Science.* Translated by Francis McDonagh. London: Darton, Longman and Todd, 1976.

————, ed. *Revelation as History.* Translated by D. Granskou. New York: Macmillan, 1968.

Polk, David P. *On the Way to God: An Exploration into the Theology of Wolfhart Pannenberg.* Lanham, Md.: University Press of America, 1989.

Walsh, Brian. *Futurity and Creation: Explorations in the Eschatological Theology of Wolfhart Pannenberg.* Toronto: Association for the Advancement of Christian Scholarship, 1979.

John Hick (b. 1922)

Carruthers, Gregory H. *The Uniqueness of Jesus Christ in the Theocentric Model of the Christian Theology of World Religions: An Elaboration and Evaluation of the Position of John Hick.* Lanham, Md.: University Press of America, 1990.

D'Costa, Gavin. *John Hick's Theology of Religions: A Critical Evaluation.* Lanham, Md.: University Press of America, 1987.

Hewitt, Harold, Jr., ed. *Problems in the Philosophy of Religion: Critical Studies of the Work of John Hick.* Houndsmills, England: Macmillan, 1991.

Hick, John. *Death and Eternal Life.* New York: Harper and Row, 1976.

————. *Disputed Questions in Theology and the Philosophy of Religion.* London: Macmillan, 1993.

————. *God and the Universe of Faiths.* London: Collins, Fount Paperbacks, 1977.

————. *God Has Many Names.* Philadelphia: Westminster, 1982.

————. *The Second Christianity.* London: SCM, 1983 [1968].

————, ed. *Truth and Dialogue: The Relationship between World Religions.* London: Sheldon, 1974.

Hick, John, and Paul Knitter, eds. *The Myth of Christian Uniqueness: Toward a Pluralistic Theology of Religions.* Maryknoll, N.Y.: Orbis, 1987.

Sharma, Arvind, ed. *God, Truth, and Reality: Essays in Honour of John Hick.* New York: St. Martin's Press, 1993.

Paul Knitter (b. 1939)

Gillis, Chester. "Radical Christologies? An Analysis of the Christologies of John Hick and Paul Knitter." In *The Myriad Christ: Plurality and the Quest for Unity in Contemporary Christology,* edited by Terrence Merrigan and Jacques Haers, 521-34. Leuven: University Press, 2000.

Heim, S. Mark. "Thinking about Theocentric Christology." *Journal of Ecumenical Studies* 24 (Winter 1987): 1-16.

Knitter, Paul. *No Other Name? A Critical Survey of Christian Attitudes toward the World Religions.* Maryknoll, N.Y.: Orbis, 1985.

————. *One Earth Many Religions: Multifaith Dialogue and Global Responsibility.* Preface by Hans Küng. Maryknoll, N.Y.: Orbis, 1995.

————. *Towards a Protestant Theology of Religions: A Case Study of Paul Althaus and Contemporary Attitudes.* Marburg: N. G. Elwert, 1974.

Swidler, Leonard, and Paul Mojzes, eds. *The Uniqueness of Jesus: A Dialogue with Paul F. Knitter.* Maryknoll, N.Y.: Orbis, 1997.

Ralph Wendell Burhoe (1911-97)

Breed, David R. *Yoking Science and Religion: The Life and Thought of Ralph Wendell Burhoe.* Chicago: Zygon, 1992.

Hefner, Philip. "Ralph Burhoe's Evolutionary Theory of Religion." *Zygon* 33 (Mar. 1998): 165-69.

Peters, Karl E. "The Open-Ended Legacy of Ralph Wendell Burhoe." *Zygon* 33 (June 1998): 313-21.

Ian Barbour (b. 1923)

Barbour, Ian. *Ethics in an Age of Technology: The Gifford Lectures, 1989-1991.* San Francisco: HarperSanFrancisco, 1993.

————. *Issues in Science and Religion.* Englewood Cliffs, N.J.: Prentice-Hall, 1966.

————. *Religion in an Age of Science: The Gifford Lectures, 1989-1991.* San Francisco: HarperSanFrancisco, 1990.

————. *Science and Secularity: The Ethics of Technology.* New York: Harper and Row, 1970.

Cantor, Geoffrey, and Chris Kenny. "Barbour's Fourfold Way: Problems with His Taxonomy of Science-Religion Relationships." *Zygon* 36 (Dec. 2001): 765-81.

Polkinghorne, J. C. *Scientists as Theologians: A Comparison of the Writings of Ian Barbour, Arthur Peacocke, and John Polkinghorne.* London: SPCK, 1996.

Russell, Robert John. "Does Creation Have a Beginning?" *Dialog* 36 (Summer 1997): 180-87.

Karl Heim (1874-1958)

Allen, Edgar Leonard. *A Guide to the Thought of Karl Heim: Jesus Our Leader.* London: Hodder and Stoughton, 1950.

Channing-Pearce, Melville. *The Terrible Crystal: Studies in Kierkegaard and Modern Christianity.* London: Kegan Paul, Trench, Trübner, 1940.

Heim, Karl. *Christian Faith and Natural Science.* Translated by N. Horton Smith. New York: Harper, Harper Torchbook, 1957.

————. *The Church and the Problems of the Day.* London: Nisbet, 1936.

————. *God Transcendent: Foundation for a Christian Metaphysic.* Translated from the 3rd German edition by Edgar Primrose Dickie. Introduction by Edwyn Bevan. New York: Scribner's, 1936.

————. *Jesus the Lord: The Sovereign Authority of Jesus and God's Revelation in Christ.* Translated by D. H. Van Daalen. Philadelphia: Muhlenberg, 1961.

————. *Jesus the World's Perfecter: The Atonement and the Renewal of the World.* Translated by D. H. Van Daalen. Philadelphia: Muhlenberg, 1961.

————. *The Transformation of the Scientific World View.* Translated by W. A. Whitehouse. London: SCM, 1953.

————. *The World: Its Creation and Consummation; The End of the Present Age and the Future of the World in the Light of the Resurrection.* Translated by Robert Smith. Philadelphia: Muhlenberg, 1962.

Holmstrand, Ingemar. *Karl Heim on Philosophy, Science, and the Transcendence of God.* Uppsala: Uppsala University Press, 1980.

Stanley L. Jaki (b. 1924)

Haffner, Paul. *Creation and Scientific Creativity: A Study in the Thought of S. L. Jaki.* Front Royal, Va.: Christendom Press, 1991.

Jaki, Stanley. *A Mind's Matter: An Intellectual Autobiography.* Grand Rapids: Eerdmans, 2002.

Sharpe, Kevin J. "Stanley L. Jaki's Critique of Physics." *Religious Studies* 18 (Mar. 1982): 55-75.

Conclusion

We have concluded our journey through two hundred years of theology. Is there anything significant at the end to which we should point? As we indicated with the title of chapter 15, "A Vigorous Dialogue," one thing is for sure: theology is by no means a dead horse. The prediction that religion is on the way out has not come true, neither for the Christian "religion" nor for other religions of the world. Today we notice that religion is more alive than ever, and the number of those who believe in God or some kind of deity has dramatically increased, especially since the demise of Communism.

Countries that had hardly any Christians just two hundred years ago, now have theological seminaries and departments of religion in which serious theological reflection is conducted. Theology has spread from Europe to America, and from there to the rest of the world. But this expansion must be carefully distinguished from any kind of neocolonialism that, unfortunately, also occurs in theology. Such kind of domination is usually and rightfully rejected. Instead, at best we encounter an amazing contextualization of theology. In the same way as someone cannot believe for someone else, theology cannot be done on behalf of others. Every believer, every tribe, every nation, and every region must own its theology, otherwise this theology is not authentic and does not collaborate with one's own experience. It is exactly this kind of regional contextualization that is the most exciting event in the twentieth century, alongside gender and ethnic contextualization. This also gives us the assurance that theology is not an alien intrusion, but owned by those Christians who conduct it, be it at Harvard, Massachusetts, or at Lae, Papua New Guinea.

We have also noticed that theological reflection is no longer restricted to the traditional venerable institutions, such as Oxford or Berlin. The spread of religion departments assured that theological reflection would proliferate in places that for generations were closed to theological pursuits. Since many of these institutions are secular institutions of higher learning, Christian theology usually does not enjoy a privileged position in them. It must assert itself alongside other religious traditions such as Buddhism, Hinduism, and Islam. This is also true on the global scene, where these other religions exhibit increased self-confidence. Christian theology can no longer conduct its business in isolation. The opening up of a multitude of departments of religious studies within the university context also means that Christian theology is no longer a tightly controlled ghetto experience reserved for ecclesial purposes. It must engage with other disciplines that also seek knowledge and understanding of humanity and the world around us. Christian insights need to be correlated with truth claims advanced by other disciplines.

While denominational affiliations are still significant, because they provide the historical context for theological reflection, theology has become ecumenical. This is true within the Protestant fold, but also beyond it. We remember that Vatican II signaled the entry of the Roman Catholic Church and its theologians into the ecumenical dialogue, a dialogue that since the fall of the Iron Curtain has had an increasing attraction also for the Orthodox communion. Though involuntarily Orthodox theologians already ventured to the West in the aftermath of the Soviet Revolution (1917), in recent years there have begun increased cooperation and mutual support among the three major Christian traditions and their theologians.

Another item should be highlighted: outsiders often get the idea that there is nothing new in theology. The content and the issues of theology remain the same, only the names of the theologians change. In one way this is indeed true. In theology, as in the other learned enterprises, one generation is replaced by another. Moreover, the content of the Christian faith, meaning its biblical rootage and its formation through tradition, is important for any serious theological reflection. It will always remain as a decisive starting point for theology, even for those who revolt against it. One could even say that the issues stay the same. We are still concerned about how to correlate faith and knowledge, about the relationship between the Christian faith and other religions, and how significant the Christian hope is for our life and faith. But if we were to conclude that therefore nothing new occurs in theology, we would be totally off the mark.

With one theologian after another, we have noticed how much the theologian's theological reflections were shaped by his or her respective context. Theologians are not only people of their time, but if they are worth their salt as theologians, they are attuned to the needs of their time. Theology is always contextual, stemming from its own time and speaking to it. Sometimes this is done more vigorously than at other occasions, but this context is never absent. Stemming the tide of scientific materialism was an important issue in the nineteenth century. Another one was the challenge of the Industrial Revolution and how to address the issues that came with it, such as the plight of the workers and the rapid urbanization of the masses. We could also think of neo-Reformation theology, which alerted us to the fact that the optimism of the nineteenth century had gone too far. If people become too self-confident, they will run into disaster, as World War I had shown. We could also point to similar contextualizations in the twentieth century, such as the unequal treatment of men and women and the underprivileged status of African Americans in the United States. But what did theology actually do with all these contexts? Did it just jump on the bandwagon, or was it a trailblazer, confronting the people with the gospel and the ethical consequences this gospel entails? It is difficult here to give a definite answer. As with Christians in general, theological reflection too is not without blemishes. But it also has something to offer to the world. How difficult it is to escape from being attracted to the current mood and to retain one's prophetic voice as can be seen with Dietrich Bonhoeffer.

In the spring of 1939, as World War II was imminent, Bonhoeffer decided to accept the invitation from Union Theological Seminary in New York to teach there. This way he could start his academic career. To stay in Germany and become a conscientious objector to Hitler's army would only add to the problems his friends had with Bonhoeffer's participation in the German "Confessing Church." A month later, however, Bonhoeffer returned to Germany. As he told Reinhold Niebuhr: "I have made a mistake in coming to America. I must live during this difficult period of our national history with the Christian people of Germany, I have no right to participate in the reconstruction of Christian life in Germany after the war if I do not share the trials of this time with my people. . . . Christians in Germany will face the terrible alternative of either willing the defeat of their nation in order that Christian civilization may survive, or willing the victory of their nation and thereby destroying our civilization."[1] Bonhoeffer returned to Germany and paid with his life for this decision. Through his sacrificial death he virtually became a saint and inspired countless others through his life and through his writings. It is difficult to guess whether his presumably successful teaching career at Union Seminary in New York would have had the same impact.

---

1. As reprinted in Eberhard Bethge, *Dietrich Bonhoeffer: Theologian-Christian-Contemporary*, trans. Eric Mosbacher et al. (London: Collins, 1970), 559. Cf. also Francis H. House, "Zwischenkirchliche Beziehungen in Kriegszeiten. Erwägungen eines Engländers," *Reformatio* 1 (1980): 511, for the context of this quote.

Christian theology during the last two hundred years certainly has not changed the face of this world as drastically and visibly as has science and technology. Yet without theological reflection, in these turbulent and exciting times, important words of encouragement and caution, inspiration and direction would have been missing. But most importantly theology has not lost sight that it is not a business conducted just for other people or for oneself. Christian theology is ultimately, as Bonhoeffer has shown, a witness to God in Christ, from whom and to whom we are and in whom we have our being.

Bibliography

Abraham, K. C., ed. *Third World Theologies: Commonalities and Divergences.* Maryknoll, N.Y.: Orbis, 1990.

Barth, Karl. *Protestant Theology in the Nineteenth Century: Its Background and History.* New ed. Grand Rapids: Eerdmans, 2002.

Blackwell Encyclopaedia of Modern Christian Thought. Edited by Alister E. McGrath. Cambridge, Mass.: Blackwell, 1993.

Blumhofer, Judith L., and Joel A. Carpenter. *Twentieth Century Evangelicalism: A Guide to the Sources.* New York: Garland, 1990.

Brown, Colin. *Jesus in European Thought, 1778-1860.* Durham, N.C.: Labyrinth, 1985.

Christ, Carol P., and Judith Plaskow, eds. *Womanspirit Rising: A Feminist Reader in Religion.* San Francisco: HarperSanFrancisco, 1992.

Clifford, Anne M. *Introducing Feminist Theology.* Maryknoll, N.Y.: Orbis, 2001.

Dictionary of Third World Theologies. Edited by Virginia Fabella and R. S. Sugirtharajah. Maryknoll, N.Y.: Orbis, 2000.

Dorrien, Gary. *The Making of American Liberal Theology: Idealism, Realism, and Modernity, 1900-1950.* Louisville: Westminster John Knox, 2003.

Ferm, Deane William. *Contemporary American Theologies: A Critical Survey.* Rev. ed. San Francisco: HarperSanFrancisco, 1990.

Ford, David F., ed. *The Modern Theologians.* Cambridge, Mass.: Blackwell, 1990.

Frei, Hans. *The Eclipse of Biblical Narrative: A Study in Eighteenth and Nineteenth Century Biblical Hermeneutics.* New Haven: Yale University Press, 1977.

Gay, Peter. *The Enlightenment: An Interpretation.* 2 vols. London: Wildwood House, 1973.

Grenz, Stanley J., and Roger E. Olson. *Twentieth-Century Theology: God and the World in a Transitional Age.* Downers Grove, Ill.: InterVarsity, 1992.

Knitter, Paul. *Introducing Theologies of Religion.* Maryknoll, N.Y.: Orbis, 2002.

Livingston, James C. *Modern Christian Thought.* 2nd ed. 2 vols. Upper Saddle River, N.J.: Prentice-Hall, 1997-2000.

Macquarrie, John. *Twentieth-Century Religious Thought.* 5th ed. London: SCM, 2001.

Marsden, George. *Fundamentalism and American Culture: The Shaping of Twentieth Century Evangelicalism, 1870-1925.* New York: Oxford University Press, 1980.

McGrath, Alister. *The Making of Modern German Christology.* 2nd ed. Grand Rapids: Zondervan, 1993.

Mitchem, Stephanie Y. *Introducing Womanist Theology.* Maryknoll, N.Y.: Orbis, 2002.

Musser, Donald W., and Joseph L. Price, eds. *A New Handbook of Christian Theologians.* Nashville: Abingdon, 1996.

Nehring, Andreas, ed. *Prejudice: Issues in Third World Theologies.* Madras: Gurukul Summer Institute, 1996.

Papers of the Nineteenth Century Theology Group. Presented at the Annual Meetings of the American Academy of Religion. Edited by Claude Welch et al. Vols. 1-16 duplicated at Berkeley, Calif.: Graduate Theological Union, 1974-1990; vols. 17-32 printed at Colorado Springs: Colorado College, 1991-2002; vols. 33- published at Eugene, Ore.: Wipf and Stock, 2003-.

Peerman, Dean G., and Martin E. Marty, eds. *A Handbook of Christian Theologians.* Nashville: Abingdon, 1965.

Pelikan, Jaroslav. *The Christian Tradition: A History of the Development of Doctrine.* Vol. 5, *Christian Doctrine and Modern Culture* (since 1700). Chicago: University of Chicago Press, 1989.

———, ed. *Twentieth-Century Theology in the Making.* Translated by R. A. Wilson. 3 vols. New York: Harper and Row, 1969-70.

Reardon, B. M. G. *Liberal Protestantism.* Stanford: Stanford University Press, 1968.

———. *Religion in the Age of Romanticism.* Cambridge: Cambridge University Press, 1985.

———. *Roman Catholic Modernism.* Stanford: Stanford University Press, 1970.

Smart, Ninian, John Clayton, Patrick Sherry, and Steven T. Katz, eds. *Nineteenth-Century Religious Thought in the West.* 3 vols. Cambridge: Cambridge University Press, 1985.

Stephenson, A. M. G. *The Rise and Decline of English Modernism.* London: SPCK, 1984.

Theologische Realenzyklopädie. 37 vols. Berlin: Walter de Gruyter, 1977ff.

Toulose, Mark G., and James O. Duke, eds. *Makers of Christian Theology in America.* Nashville: Abingdon, 1997.

Vidler, A. R. *The Modernist Movement in the Roman Church.* Cambridge: Cambridge University Press, 1934.

Welch, Claude. *Protestant Thought in the Nineteenth Century.* 2 vols. New Haven: Yale University Press, 1972-85.

Index of Names

Index of Subjects